Composing to Communicate

A Student's Guide to College Writing

ROBERT SABA

Florida International University

CENGAGE
Learning™

Australia · Brazil · Mexico · Singapore · United Kingdom · United States

Composing to Communicate: A Student's Guide to College Writing
Robert Saba

Product Director: Monica Eckman

Product Team Manager: Nicole Morinon

Product Manager: Laura Ross

Senior Content Developer: Leslie Taggart

Content Developer: Craig Leonard

Associate Content Developer: Rachel L. Smith

Product Assistant: Claire Branman

Senior Content Managing Developer: Cara Douglass-Graff

Marketing Director: Stacey Purviance

Senior Content Project Manager: Rosemary Winfield

Senior Art Director: Marissa Falco

Manufacturing Planner: Betsy Donaghey

IP Analyst: Ann Hoffman

IP Project Manager: Sarah Shainwald

Production Service: Andrea Archer, Angela Urquhart, Thistle Hill Publishing Services

Compositor: Cenveo® Publisher Services

Text Designer: Liz Harasymczuk Design

Cover Designer: Ink Design Inc.

© 2017 Cengage Learning

WCN: 01-100-101

ALL RIGHTS RESERVED. No part of this work covered by the copyright herein may be reproduced, transmitted, stored, or used in any form or by any means graphic, electronic, or mechanical, including but not limited to photocopying, recording, scanning, digitizing, taping, web distribution, information networks, or information storage and retrieval systems, except as permitted under Section 107 or 108 of the 1976 United States Copyright Act, without the prior written permission of the publisher.

For product information and technology assistance, contact us at **Cengage Learning Customer & Sales Support, 1-800-354-9706**.
For permission to use material from this text or product, submit all requests online at **www.cengage.com/permissions**. Further permissions questions can be emailed to **permissionrequest@cengage.com**.

Library of Congress Control Number: 2015953364

Student Edition:
ISBN: 978-1-285-18901-7

Loose-leaf Edition:
ISBN: 978-1-305-94443-5

Cengage Learning
20 Channel Center Street
Boston MA 02210
USA

Cengage Learning is a leading provider of customized learning solutions with employees residing in nearly 40 different countries and sales in more than 125 countries around the world. Find your local representative at **www.cengage.com**.

Cengage Learning products are represented in Canada by Nelson Education, Ltd.

To learn more about Cengage Learning Solutions, visit **www.cengage.com**.

Purchase any of our products at your local college store or at our preferred online store **www.cengagebrain.com**.

Printed in the United States of America

Print Number: 01   Print Year: 2015

To Caroline and George

BRIEF CONTENTS

CONTENTS

CHAPTER 10 ▶ Analyzing Stories   419

PART III

Clear Writing and Professional Presentations   501

FOR STUDENTS: ABOUT THE AUTHOR

When I graduated from college, I had no intention of becoming a teacher. I was interested in journalism, advertising, or some other line of business, but the economy was bad, and good jobs were hard to come by. I ended up processing claims for an insurance company in Los Angeles. In principle, it was a job I was lucky to have. It offered the possibility of a future. The problem was, the work seemed dull and repetitive to me. Even as I kept showing up and collecting decent paychecks, I knew I wanted to do something that I found more interesting with my life.

One day, I skipped work and drove across town to the University of Southern California to inquire about graduate school. I wasn't sure it was what I wanted to do, assuming I could even get in, but a few months later, I was a student again, attending a university rightfully known (in no *particular* order) for its excellent academics, athletics, beautiful campus, famous library, and attractive women. The classes were interesting. I read great books, listened to eloquent lectures, took copious notes, and now and then, made nervous contributions to the class discussions. There was nothing not to like until a few weeks into the semester, when I had to complete my first writing assignment.

I started four or five days before the deadline, which was smart, but even so, after several hours at my desk, I managed to produce only a few lame sentences. I gave up and tried again the next day, with similar results. Writing "papers" had never been a problem for me as an undergraduate. I wrote them, and usually earned good grades, but unfortunately, I had no awareness of how I did it. By the end of the second day, my frustration turned into panic. I had produced a half page of jumbled ideas. What had I gotten myself into? I didn't know how to write. I decided to take the next day off. I still had a few days left until the deadline. Desperation might inspire me. If not, maybe the insurance company would have me back.

I believe in the adage that we make our own luck, but now and then we are beneficiaries of sheer luck, too. On my self-appointed day off, I received a letter from my best friend, a writer and teacher from Albuquerque, who was then living abroad in Paris. His letters came about once a month, never less than four or five pages long, typed, single-spaced, and double-sided to save on postage, and they were like movies arriving in the mail (before anyone had heard of Netflix), full of humorous incidents, odd characters, rants, and vivid images of life in one of the world's great cities. I read his letter that day, savoring every word and marveling, as I always did, at how his words came alive on the page. When I finished reading, I wrote him back—no doubt, an anemic letter compared to his, but still, two or three pages, in his postage-saving format, about life in Los Angeles, a city that has its own share of quirks, charms, and odd characters to write about. As I was folding the letter into an envelope, I thought, "I can write this letter, but I can't write that paper. What's the difference?"

The next day I went to work on the paper again, writing it the only way I apparently knew how, the way I had written the letter, focusing on what interested me, why I was interested, and why I thought someone else might be, or should be, and saying all of that as clearly and directly as I could, not worrying about how it sounded or might be judged. The writing went much better. I submitted the paper on time, and the professor's judgment wasn't terrible—a "B," with a comment along the lines of, "Interesting but doesn't add up to much." Well, at least, I had proven I wasn't completely out of my depth.

As the semester progressed, my papers improved and were a little easier to write. By the end of the term, I had done well enough in my coursework to earn a fellowship to teach first-year composition. I was given a crash training course while I was already teaching my first class. What I mainly learned from the training course, as well as from teaching the class, was that I didn't know much. I was teaching a skill I was still learning myself, not a skill I had figured out or mastered. Yet I did know something: how difficult, humbling, and even scary writing could be, how easy it was to get stuck and fail, especially when writing a college "paper," which, stripped to its bones, is a test or exam, meant to expose you as capable or not. Fortunately for my students, I also had a few unfledged but viable ideas about how to address these problems, how to help students move past them, write with more confidence, and see better results.

Today, those formative experiences as a graduate student and student teacher are "long ago and far away." I have taught college writing for more than twenty-five years, and I know much more now than I did then, but not so much that I have forgotten what still matters and applies most: what it is like to be a student, how difficult writing can be, and above all, what writers can do to make writing easier, more effective, and enjoyable. Those basic goals, and my belief in the value that writing has for students and the value of what students have to say, remain the foundation of my teaching and go to the heart of why I have written this book.

—Robert Saba

FOR INSTRUCTORS: ABOUT THE BOOK

Composing to Communicate: A Student's Guide is a product of my observations and research about why so many students have trouble acquiring college writing skills and succeeding in college writing classes. The book's instructional content focuses on three problem areas: (1) students' motivation to write and acquire writing skills; (2) their confusion about writing as a result of dissonant instruction; and (3) their frustration with writing tasks and assignments that don't appear to have practical applications.

Composing to Communicate addresses these problems by initiating a "conversation" with students, validating issues they have with writing, and examining ways they can resolve them. The book takes the position that students have a more sophisticated grasp of rhetorical methods and strategies than they realize or are given credit for. Rhetoric isn't primarily extrinsic knowledge students need to *learn*; it consists of linguistic skills and cognitive abilities they already have and use, skills and abilities that need to be *elicited* more than *taught*.

The central concept developed in the book is that writing is, first and foremost, a communication skill. Communication, when classified as a "skill," is fundamentally about addressing issues and supporting views—in other words, trying to solve problems. Looking at writing from this perspective promotes writing as an active, goal-oriented process that is relevant to students' personal lives as well as careers.

The book also has an underlying goal of addressing institutional and technological realities that are having an impact on college writing classes today. Many writing classes are larger and more diverse than they used to be. As a result, a good textbook has to provide instruction that is interesting, accessible, and valuable to students who may come from very different backgrounds and have different skill levels, yet sit in the same classroom.

Today, online classes are another reality for students and teachers that textbooks need to address. In order to support online as well as face-to-face classes, a textbook has to be detailed and thorough without overwhelming students working on their own. *Composing to Communicate* can be used effectively by students taking first-year composition in any course format.

CORE FEATURES

Composing to Communicate demonstrates how communication principles shape, support, and facilitate the entire writing process, from invention and planning to organizing, drafting, and revising. The book includes many practical features that help students refine their writing skills and complete assignments effectively.

Students Learn to Communicate to Solve Problems

Communication and problem-solving framework. The book presents eight guided writing projects designed to stimulate students' interest in their writing and develop skills that "transfer" to the writing tasks students will do in their other college courses and professional lives. The projects are narratives, profiles, evaluations and reviews, arguments, research projects, literary analyses, writing beyond the page, and public writing and community engagement. Writing projects share a consistent framework of communication and problem-solving goals that reinforce the book's core pedagogy and help students write with clarity and confidence.

Practical transfer of writing methods and skills. The guided assignment chapters in Part II explain the role and relevance of each genre of writing and how the methods and skills students acquire transfer to writing in different college disciplines and professional life.

Case studies of people communicating and solving problems. The concept of writing as communication and problem solving is illustrated in Part I and Part III through short case studies that describe real people communicating and solving problems (listed inside the back cover). These case studies, as well as readings throughout the book, also illustrate how rhetorical principles and appeals associated with writing apply to other media and forms of communication.

Multimodal options. The last assignment chapter—Chapter 11, "Writing Beyond the Page: Shifting Genres and Using New Media"—can be assigned as a stand-alone project, or in conjunction with Chapter 9, "Public Writing and Community Engagement," to give students multimodal options for a public-writing project. In addition, Chapter 11 can be assigned as a follow-up ("genre shift") to any writing project students already have completed in the course. Creating a multimodal version of a project they already have completed allows students to focus on the rhetorical strategies and design features of a multimodal text without the burden of developing content from scratch. Chapters 7 and 8 ("Arguments That Matter" and "Navigating Research Projects") are projects that lend themselves especially well to a multimodal follow-up because students will have ample and cogent content to work with.

Students Communicate in Words and Images

Student proposals, essays, and interviews. Each guided assignment chapter in Part II features a student essay proposal, followed by an interview with the student writer in which the student discusses his or her writing process and the challenges the assignment presented. The student's final draft appears at the chapter's end, along with a postessay interview in which the student discusses what she or he has learned. See the front inside cover for details.

Student artwork in every chapter. Chapter-opening artwork created by student artists offers a reminder that problem-solving communication occurs in multiple media. Each piece is accompanied by the artist's statement about the communication problem he or she was trying to solve.

Students Stay on Track with Projects

A conversational tone. Without compromising the substance of the instruction or the rigor of the assignments, *Composing to Communicate* takes a conversational "how to" approach to writing and rhetoric, and expressly avoids or demystifies jargon that tends to impede students from seeing themselves as writers.

Heuristic classifications and lists. Chapters include heuristic classifications and lists that help students look beyond shopworn topics to come up with original and interesting ideas for their projects.

Templates for proposals, storyboards, and organization. Assignment chapters include a variety of templates that help students plan and draft their essays productively.

Checklists and timelines in each assignment chapter. Assignment chapters walk students through a realistic writing process and include checklists and timelines to help students gauge their progress and manage their time effectively.

Students Use Active Learning Strategies

Clear learning objectives. Chapters begin with a list of key learning objectives to help students focus on important ideas, and they end with exit questions that help students review and evaluate what they have learned.

Advice about common writing problems and mistakes. Assignment chapters offer advice about common writing problems and mistakes associated with a specific genre or project. This advice helps students address problems and mistakes in their drafts and submit more polished work.

Peer review questions. Each assignment chapter includes peer review questions that help students respond to each other's work and receive meaningful feedback.

Tech Tips. Chapters include "Tech Tips" about relevant digital resources—software, websites, and apps—that can help students improve their writing and complete projects. Tech Tips cover invention (MindMup, Bubbler, StoryCorps); reading (Spreeder); research (CQ Researcher, Techmeme); style, grammar, and diction (Lexipedia, COCA Corpus, Grammar Bytes, TagCrowd); as well as resources for multimodal projects (GoAnimate, Compfight, Glogster).

Active learning and group work exercises and activities. Every chapter contains on average five or six "Reflection" or "Working Together" activities designed to engage students with their coursework and learn from one another as writers. An icon �֎ quickly identifies opportunities for students to collaborate.

Students Read Widely

Composing to Communicate: A Student's Guide includes a diverse selection of fifty professional articles and essays, as well as song lyrics, stories, and poems. Shorter readings are presented within the chapters to illustrate writing methods and concepts. Relevant "additional readings" by professional writers, as well as by students, are included at the end of some chapters, and others are available in MindTap, the book's online component and course-resource portal.

ORGANIZATION

Composing to Communicate is organized in three parts. **Part I, *Writing to Communicate and Solve Problems*,** consists of three chapters designed to engage students in writing and to introduce the book's communication-based pedagogy:

► Chapter 1, "The Relevance of Writing," examines the value of a college writing course, taking the position that, above and beyond practical applications, writing encompasses a set of skills universally identified with professional success and distinction. Those skills are effective communication, critical thinking, and problem solving. Students need communication and critical thinking skills ("soft skills") as much as discipline-specific training ("hard skills") in order to excel in their future careers. Chapter 1 also covers misconceptions about writing, approaches to becoming a good writer, the value of essays as a form of writing, the basis of an effective style, and academic writing as "conversation" about solving problems.

▶ Chapter 2, "Planning Essays as Communication," presents the book's core communication pedagogy and explains how it applies to planning and organizing different kinds of essays and writing tasks.

▶ Chapter 3, "An Overview of the Writing Process," provides a "hands-on" discussion and examples of what it takes to produce effective (reader-relevant) writing.

Part II, *Writing Projects and Essays*, presents eight guided assignments designed to reinforce the core pedagogy and teach students how to adapt it to different genres, purposes, and tasks.

Six of the guided assignments are based on established, first-year-writing genres:

▶ "Narrative Essays" (Chapter 4)
▶ "Profiles" (Chapter 5)
▶ "Evaluations and Reviews" (Chapter 6)
▶ "Arguments That Matter" (Chapter 7)
▶ "Navigating Research Projects" (Chapter 8)
▶ "Analyzing Stories" (Chapter 10)

Two assignments are nontraditional, designed to give students the latitude to use their rhetorical knowledge and skills in realistic ways to reach audiences outside the classroom:

▶ "Public Writing and Community Engagement" (Chapter 9) engages students in advocating for change or progress using knowledge acquired from personal experience and research.

▶ "Writing Beyond the Page: Shifting Genres and Using New Media" (Chapter 11) teaches students to apply writing concepts and skills to multimodal "texts" or compositions (a slide show, podcast, web page, video, photo-essay, and so forth).

Part III, *Clear Writing and Professional Presentations*, consists of four chapters that provide practical instruction and information about important, writing-related subjects. These chapters are:

▶ "Developing an Effective Style" (Chapter 12)
▶ "Writing in the Workplace: How College Writing Skills Transfer" (Chapter 13)

▶ "Using and Documenting Sources" (Chapter 14)

▶ "Text to Speech: Advice about Oral Presentations and Public Speaking" (Chapter 15, presented only in the online MindTap)

MINDTAP

MindTap® English for Saba's *Composing to Communicate: A Student's Guide*, 1st Edition engages your students to become better thinkers, communicators, and writers by blending your course materials with content that supports every aspect of the writing process:

▶ Interactive activities on grammar and mechanics promote application in student writing.

▶ An easy-to-use paper management system helps prevent plagiarism and allows for electronic submission, grading, and peer review.

▶ A vast database of scholarly sources with video tutorials and examples supports every step of the research process.

▶ Professional tutoring guides students from rough drafts to polished writing.

▶ Visual analytics track student progress and engagement.

▶ Seamless integration into your campus learning management system keeps all your course materials in one place.

MindTap lets you compose your course, your way.

INSTRUCTOR RESOURCES

The instructor's manual, found through login.cengage.com, provides correlated learning objectives, teaching suggestions, suggested answers to exercises, and sample course syllabi to assist instructors in teaching the course.

ACKNOWLEDGMENTS

After this detailed description of the book and its features, I think it is important to acknowledge that writing classes are not mainly about textbooks; they are mainly about the interactions between teachers and students, as well as the interactions among students themselves. During my career as a teacher, I have had the privilege of observing dozens of excellent writing classes taught by my colleagues. What I've learned is that no two classes are alike. The unique energies and chemistry that different teachers and students bring to different classes are precisely what make the classes excellent. When all is said and done, a good textbook is more than the sum of perspectives, resources, and information it provides. A good textbook supports a stimulating, productive, and enjoyable learning environment for teachers and students. I hope *Composing to Communicate*, more than anything, is that kind of book, a book that cultivates the common ground where teachers' and students' goals intersect and flourish.

I could not have written this book without the help of many people. Among them are two contributing writers, my friends and colleagues Paul Feigenbaum at Florida International University and Ben Lauren, now at Michigan State University, who conceived, designed, and substantially wrote Chapters 9 and 11, respectively, and also gave me generous advice about other sections of the book.

I am deeply indebted to three other people, without whose help I could not have written the book at all. My dear friend and former colleague Sanford (Sandy) J. Smoller read all of the drafts and revisions of the manuscript; his invaluable advice and perceptive criticism imbue every page of the book. Two people on my Cengage development team, freelance editor Craig Leonard and senior content developer Leslie Taggart, worked with me on the project from the very first day, read every page, and helped design every chapter. Their creativity, insights, and expertise have profoundly shaped the book. Their contributions are, quite simply, inextricable from my own.

Among many other people at Cengage who have lent their talents to the production of the book, I owe special thanks to Laura Ross, English product manager, for her insight, energy, and leadership (and also, her refreshing sense of humor whenever things get too serious!). I also want to thank Marissa Falco, Rosemary Winfield, and Stacey Purviance for their hard work and essential contributions. I would be remiss not to acknowledge the role of former Cengage product manager Margaret Leslie in shaping the vision of the book and infusing the project with her expertise and insights. I also want to thank two fine Cengage authors, Harry Phillips and Mark Connelly, for their advice and encouragement.

Two of my cherished colleagues at Florida International University, Michael Sohan and Darrel Elmore, reviewed the book in manuscript and suggested many improvements. Michael, in addition, provided materials for a wryly amusing (what else is new?) "Reflection to Response" activity in Chapter 13. Nick Vagnoni generously shared ideas for activities in Chapter 5. My friend and mentor John Dufresne contributed a version of his cool invention activity on making lists, adapted from his guide to writing fiction, *The Lie That Tells a Truth*. My dear friend Kenneth Claus shared perceptive insights about the art of public speaking for Chapter 15 and also contributed a cogent reading about adversity. Other colleagues to whom I owe thanks for advice and support are Kimberly Harrison, Michael Creeden, Cindy Chinelly, Vernon Dickson, Jamie Sutton, Shelley Wick, Karl Klint, Jen Bartman, Vanessa Sohan, Wanda Raiford, Carmela Mcintire, and Maheba Pedroso. I also want to thank my former colleague and longtime friend Greg Bowe, who taught me that, no matter how long you have done something, there are always new things to learn and better ways to do it.

The contributions of many talented students have profoundly enriched this book. In particular, I want to thank Brian Lawrence, Eric Hunter, Kierstin Koppel, Karla Pereira-Silva, Steven Fernandez, Thais Torquez, Arlet Montes, Amanda McDole, Cristina Alonso, Abigail Dominguez-Trujillo, Carolina Souto, Michelle Saunders, Ashley Miller, Allison Kopp, Okeko Donaldson, Fangyu Xu, and Aaron Cervantes. I also want to thank Joseph Richardson from the Florida International University Alumni Office, who helped me reconnect with a number of former students who had graduated.

These acknowledgments would be incomplete if I failed to remember my dear friend Phillip Karrh, whose love of writing, reading, and languages has influenced every page of this book. My lifelong academic friends (and conference accomplices), Harry Rosser of Boston College, Bill Cloonan of Florida State University, and Alex Dunlop of Auburn University, have provided generous support, not just for this book, but for all of my career endeavors. My beloved wife, Caroline, and my son, George, both so accomplished in their own careers, yet giving to mine, have been a source of inexhaustible inspiration and sustenance.

Finally, a special thanks to all of the reviewers who provided helpful contributions throughout the writing and revising of this book:

Susan Achziger, Community College of Aurora

Kara Alexander, Baylor University

Victoria Appatova, University of Cincinnati

Ellen Barker, Nicholls State University

Airek Beauchamp, SUNY Binghamton

Lara Behr, Ivy Tech State College–Lafayette

Micheal Callaway, Mesa Community College

Peter Caster, University of South Carolina–Upstate

Sherry Cisler, Arizona State University West

Brenda Craven, Fort Hays State University

Darrel Elmore, Florida International University

Karen Feldman, Seminole State College

Jennifer Garcia, Ventura College

John Gides, California State University, Northridge

Patricia Golder, Victor Valley College

Sarah Gottschall, Prince George's Community College

Carey Goyette, Clinton Community College

Tami Haaland, Montana State University Billings

Candy Henry, Westmoreland County Community College

Shawn Houtsinger, University of Wisconsin–Parkside

Amelia Keel, Lone Star College (Kingwood College)

Henry Kim, Ventura College

Wendy King, Arizona State University

Lisa Klotz, University of Alabama

Elizabeth Langenfeld, San Bernardino Community College

Michael Lewis, Savannah State University

Yingqin Liu, Cameron University

Michael Lueker, Our Lady of the Lake University

Terry McCammon, Ivy Tech Community College

Carol McCarthy, Delgado Community College

Heather McFall, Ivy Tech Community College–Central Indiana

Catherine Moran, Bristol Community College

Sheryl Mylan, College of DuPage

William Nedrow, Triton College

Virginia Nugent, Miami Dade College–North

Kathleen O'Brien, Art Institute of Portland

Mary Grace Paden, John Tyler Community College–Chester

Kyle Page, Clinton Community College

Amy Ratto Parks, Helena College

Coretta Pittman, Baylor University

Andrew Preslar, Lamar State College at Orange

Jeff Provine, Oklahoma State University–Oklahoma City

Valerie Russell, Seminole State College of Florida

Beverly Slavens, Arkadelphia High School

Noel Sloboda, Penn State University–York Campus

Michael Sohan, Florida International University

Helen Szymanski, College of DuPage

Janice Taraborelli, Johnson & Wales University–Denver

Cynthia VanSickle, McHenry County College

Melanie Wagner, Lake-Sumter Community College

Raymond Watkins, Central Carolina Technical College

Joe Wilkins, Waldorf College

—Robert Saba

PART ONE

Writing to Communicate and Solve Problems

> **"** *Rhetoric is the art, practice and study of human communication.* **"**
> —Andrea Lunsford

Courtesy Keli O'Mara

KELI O'MARA

Video Game Diety

This piece was an attempt to be an intrusive lens into individuals' private moments. When creating the piece, I encountered problems representing hands in the foreground of each piece so I would be forced to overcome my shortcomings.

CHAPTER ONE

The Relevance of Writing

> *The essay's engine is curiosity; its territory is the open road.*
> —Cheryl Strayed, *Best American Essays 2013*, Editor

CHAPTER LEARNING OBJECTIVES

In this chapter, you will learn to:

- ▶ Approach your writing as a form of communication and problem solving.
- ▶ Appreciate the value and importance of writing as a professional skill.
- ▶ Understand the objectives of college writing and what professors want.
- ▶ Overcome aversions to writing.
- ▶ Understand what "essays" really are.
- ▶ Develop basic qualities of an effective style.

WRITING AS COMMUNICATION

A writing course is one of the most important courses you can take in college. Writing helps you develop skills that are universally identified with success and distinction. Those skills are: effective communication, critical thinking, and problem solving. Even if you would never voluntarily take a writing course, you know that good communication skills contribute to success in almost any field. Humanitarian leaders, great presidents, CEOs, entrepreneurs, media personalities, famous scientists, and coaches are "good communicators"—usually outstanding communicators.

When people think of communication skills, they usually think of speaking, but speaking and writing are companion skills. Effective speaking and writing share the same communication strategies. A good writer is a good communicator.

Writing and Communication as Problem Solving

Whether you are writing or speaking, communication skills are important because they allow you to reach out and connect to people for the purpose of solving problems. Martin Luther King, Jr. was an exceptional communicator because he inspired Americans to join him in solving the problem of racism in America. Presidents like John F. Kennedy, legendary coaches like Vince Lombardi, scientists like Robert Oppenheimer, and entrepreneurs like Steve Jobs all were exceptional communicators for similar reasons: they communicated to connect to people and solve problems they cared about.

Verbal skills—a large vocabulary and "a way with words"—have a role in communication but not a primary role. We all have heard speeches or read articles that are verbally sophisticated but dull.* Good communication is a product of thinking more than verbal mechanics. It means figuring out how to connect to your audience for the purpose of solving problems you care about. When all is said and done, problem solving is the most important professional skill there is, the skill people are recognized and rewarded for above all others. Every field, from sales to finance to engineering, architecture, and accounting, requires complex problem solving on a daily basis.

Writing a textbook like this one is all about communication to solve problems. The main problem for me, the writer, is how to help college students become better writers. To solve the problem, the book must be accessible. I have to remember that students come from different backgrounds, have different interests and career paths, and also are busy, are often "stressed," and

---

* The following passage is an example of sophisticated wording that "goes in one ear and out the other": "Perhaps some silly warnings are 'necessary' to fend off the Fourth Branch of government, a.k.a. trial lawyers. But this merely underscores the fact that all this noise is symptomatic of modern derangements. Solemn warnings about nonexistent risks, and information intended to spare us the slightest responsibility for passing through life with a modicum of attention and intelligence—these express, among other things, an entitlement mentality…" (from an article by George W. Will, titled "Inundated by a River of Words").

have other classes to take and demands on their time. The information in the book must be useful but also interesting. I have to pay attention to my style and try to avoid scholarly words like *kairos*, recursive, and metacognitive, unless they are important and I define them.

Ideally, I want the book to be friendly, like someone you enjoy spending time with and going to for advice, rather than a dry source of information.

COMMUNICATION SITUATIONS AND GOALS

Communication means sharing thoughts, ideas, and feelings. Most of the communicating we do is in response to situations that motivate or compel us to share. In these situations, we "reach out" to a person or people—that is, an *audience*—with a purpose or goal in mind.

A college student might routinely do the following:

- ▶ Text a friend to entice her to go to a movie instead of studying for an exam.
- ▶ Meet with a dormitory RA to request a change of roommates.
- ▶ Write a "letter to the editor" of the campus newspaper objecting to a mandatory athletic fee.
- ▶ E-mail a professor expressing disappointment or disagreement with a grade.
- ▶ Compose a personal statement or essay for a scholarship, or admission to a graduate program.

These different situations—sometimes called "rhetorical situations"—vary in importance. Generally, more important situations require more difficult responses. The personal statement you write for admission to a graduate program has a lot riding on it. It will be harder to plan and compose than the text message enticing a friend to go to the movies. What qualities is the scholarship committee looking for in your personal statement? What can you say about yourself that speaks to those qualities but comes across as authentic, not clichéd or predicable?

Depending on the circumstances, even the text message to entice a friend to go to the movies may test your communication skills, too. Suppose your friend is obsessed with earning high grades and studies all the time at the expense of her physical and mental well-being? What can you say that will entice her to break out of the pattern?

Successful communication requires an understanding of each situation or context—in particular, the audience, purpose, goal, motivation, and the medium or genre.

Audience

Effective communication requires an understanding of the audience and its "frame of reference," attributes like age, race, gender, level of education, values, beliefs, and personality. To be an effective communicator, you must figure out what the audience wants, expects, or needs from the communication process and how to get people interested in what you have to say, hold their attention, overcome indifference or resistance, and answer the questions people instinctively ask when demands are made on their time: So what? Why should I? What's in it for me?

Purpose, Goal, and Motivation

Effective communication must be compelling and focused. Good communicators tap into a source of motivation and understand their purpose or goal. Often, for both professional and personal reasons, people communicate on their own initiative, for their own purposes. Sometimes people communicate because they are obliged to (for example, when a professional or a student is assigned a writing or speaking task). Either way, effective communication starts with a person's engagement in the communication process. Good communicators understand the importance of being motivated (see Figure 1.1). If a task is required of them, whether in the workplace or college, they approach it as an opportunity for expression and connection. They find a way to buy into and "own" the task, a way to instill it with

FIGURE 1.1 Effective communication that moves from motivation to a goal starts with a person's engagement in the communication process.

their interests, passions, abilities, and views. At the same time, good communicators understand that personal expression and connection are just the means to an end. They stay focused on the larger purpose or goal—what they want people to be thinking or doing in response to the communication process.

Medium or Genre

Effective communication requires an understanding of the medium and/or genre being used. A medium is a means of delivering information or messages. TV, movies, radio, newspapers, magazines, and the Internet are common and popular media (the plural for *medium*). Most media have recognizable kinds of communication called *genres*. Within a print medium like newspapers, for example, some common genres are news stories, editorials, obituaries, exposés, and gossip columns. Newspaper writers must understand the medium as well as the specific genre they are using. Writing an obituary is much different from writing an editorial or a gossip column. Different genres require different styles of writing, come with different rules and guidelines, and target different audiences.

In professional life and college, you do not always have a choice of the medium and genre you use. However, when you do have a choice, the choice matters. For example, if you were having a problem at work and wanted to discuss it with your supervisor, you could choose to meet and talk face to face; talk over the telephone; or write an e-mail, letter, or memo. Each medium (talking face to face, phoning, or writing) and genre (e-mail, letter, memo) have advantages and disadvantages, have different conventions, and may require different strategies. You have to choose the medium and, when applicable, the genre that will most effectively communicate your message and help you achieve your communication goals. (You will learn more about genres of writing and their conventions in the next chapter.)

Communication is more complex than we tend to realize, but nothing about it is intimidating. We do it all the time, usually with pleasure, because it can enrich our lives and reward us.

Analyzing the communication process in different situations, as described above, is something we usually do more instinctively than consciously. But whether we are writing, speaking, or using visual forms, being *aware* of the complexities of the communication process helps keep us up to the task. We all have had frustrating experiences with communication when our goals were misunderstood, unappreciated, or rejected. Sometimes these experiences are the result of our not being mindful enough of a situation or attuned to its complexities. When we communicate with an awareness of what we are doing, we are more likely to receive positive results.

Writing and Communication in the Workplace and Professional Life

Anyone who is skeptical about the value of a college writing course should consider these findings:

▶ A College Board survey of 120 American corporations identifies writing specifically as a "'marker' of high-skill, high-wage professional work," particularly "in sectors of the economy that are expanding."

▶ Employers surveyed for the Accrediting Council for Independent Colleges and Schools (ACICS) rank "written communication skills" on virtually the same level of importance as "job-specific knowledge."

▶ Employers surveyed for the Association of American Colleges and Universities cite "written and oral communication" as the number-one area that colleges need to emphasize more.

These findings give us a window on the realities of professional life, and tell us that job-specific knowledge is not enough to ensure professional success. The pace of technical innovation is so dizzying today that businesses, jobs, and careers appear and disappear overnight. More than ever, being successful means being adaptable and having core communication and critical thinking skills that cross over to every field of endeavor.

COMMUNICATING TO SOLVE PROBLEMS

●●● Comedian Jon Stewart Demands Federal Health Care Funds for 9/11 First Responders

Jon Stewart is known for his political humor and satire, yet over the course of his career, he has usually avoided advocating for political causes. However, as a New Yorker, he was profoundly shaken by 9/11, and for a long time afterward he had trouble doing his popular *Daily Show*. He took the horror of 9/11 and the heroism of the first responders very personally.

In December 2010, when a bill to provide healthcare funds for first responders was being filibustered in the Senate and ignored by major news outlets, Stewart abandoned his

FEMA / Alamy

A firefighter searches for survivors amidst the ruins of the World Trade Center.

usual stance against political advocacy and delivered the commentary transcribed below (video clips of Stewart's commentary are available online).

> Before we go, I want to talk one last time about something called the Zadroga bill. [Zadroga] was an NYPD detective who died in 2006 from respiratory illness thought to be caused by the dust he inhaled while working at Ground Zero after 2001.

> This bill would provide $7 billion in medical and financial benefits for Ground Zero workers who get sick, and they're going to pay for it by closing a corporate tax loophole. It's a win, win, win, win. Just [bleep] do it!!! The House of Representatives passed it, and it would pass in the Senate, if it came to an up-or-down vote. They have more than the 50 votes they need. But [some senators] have filibustered it, won't allow the bill to come up for a vote…. What's more, none of the three broadcast networks have mentioned any of this on their evening newscasts for two and a half months….

> This is an outrageous abdication of responsibility to those who were most heroic on 9/11.

Stewart created his *Daily Show* to entertain, as well as inform, but for this particular show, he deviated from his usual format, to speak out about an issue that deeply concerned him. His motivation to use his show to advocate for a cause was rooted in his respect and admiration for the heroic first responders who sacrificed their lives on 9/11. The only thing "funny" about Stewart's commentary is that, in a rational and humane world, it should not have been necessary for a TV comedian to step up and advocate for brave, patriotic men and women.

Days after the show aired, Congress passed the Zadroga bill into law. John Feal, founder of a nonprofit organization created for 9/11 responders, said, "What Jon Stewart did was he literally shamed conventional media and the U.S. government into doing the right thing."

Very few people have the ability to use a TV show as a forum for speaking out about problems they consider important, but assuming you did, who would your audience be and what kinds of problems would you bring to your audience's attention? What other methods, means, or media could you use to speak out, be heard, and help to precipitate progress or change? ●●●

THE BASICS OF PROBLEM SOLVING

Since writing to solve problems is a key concept in this course, problem solving needs to be understood in the way professionals and college professors understand it—that is, as a process that *leads* to solutions, but not always complete or permanent solutions.

Many of the problems we address in writing and life elude permanent solutions: war, poverty, pollution, crime, and traffic are just a few examples. Even in the sciences, problem solving usually is a process. The invention of vaccines to inoculate against diseases has not wiped out diseases, but only moved us further in that direction.

Sometimes professionals address and solve problems by thinking them through on their own and applying their experience and expertise. Students do the same when they write analytical essays, reflections, and personal narratives. But in professional life, most of the problems that need to be solved are too complex for solitary solutions. They require research—finding the best available information, reading, talking to and collaborating with other people, conducting surveys, and analyzing statistics and studies.

Critical Thinking in Problem Solving

Behind the ability to solve problems and communicate effectively are habits of mind, a productive way of thinking about ourselves and the world called "critical thinking." Critical thinking means embracing complexity instead of easy answers. It means analyzing, making distinctions, seeing different perspectives, asking good questions, and examining "conventional wisdom" and our own beliefs and assumptions. Critical thinking at its best is creative and innovative—what scholars and educators call "divergent," rather than "convergent," thinking. Student Eric Hunter, in an essay on the subject, defines "divergent" and "convergent" as follows:

> In thinking, there are two common ways to learn and solve problems. One is "convergent thinking," which focuses on gathering information to get a *single* answer. The other one is "divergent thinking," which generates creative ideas by exploring *many* possible solutions to a problem you want to solve.

Eric argues later in his essay that standardized testing in education is an example of convergent thinking—a one-size-fits-all solution to a complex problem. Ironically and unfortunately, as Eric points out, standardized testing promotes convergent thinking (find *the* right answer) and, therefore, inadequately prepares many smart and capable high school students for college, because in college, critical thinking—which involves divergent thinking—is emphasized. Eric's point is that divergent thinking would supply more varied, creative, and workable solutions to the problems that concern us as a society, from the quality of education to bullying, obesity, violence, immigration, jobs, and so on.

Writing promotes divergent thinking, because to write effectively, we have to think critically on more than one level. As you already know from reading pages 5–7, analyzing the communication process requires critical thinking. We have to understand the audience and its frame of reference, consider our motives, define our goals, and adapt to the conventions of an appropriate medium or genre.

When we write to communicate and solve problems, we must think critically about the subject matter, too, and integrate an analysis of the communication process with our critical thinking about the problem itself. If the problem is obesity, a writer who is obese, or was, might choose to write a personal narrative about the problem and analyze it through his experiences. A nutritionist who cares about the problem, but has no personal experience with it, might compose a study or report. A nutritionist who has personal experience with the problem might compose a study or report that incorporates her personal experience. But to write meaningfully about obesity, all of these writers have to break the problem down, think critically about it, and try to answer the same essential questions:

- ▶ What is the source of the problem?
- ▶ What are the consequences of the problem for individuals and society in general?
- ▶ Why does the problem persist?
- ▶ What views and assumptions or misconceptions are held about it?
- ▶ What solutions are in place?
- ▶ How well are they working?
- ▶ Are there creative, feasible, or better alternatives to solving the problem?

When we write to communicate and address complex problems, the process of writing helps us sort out our thoughts, understand our values and biases, recognize gaps or flaws in our reasoning, and see where we need to do more research or analysis. Writing is emphasized in college and valued in professional life because, among other things, it stimulates clear thinking and serves as a tool for learning and discovery.

College Writing and What Professors Want

Communication to solve problems is the essence of college writing and involves students in the kind of writing or speaking that challenges communicators in professional life. College professors look for essays, reports, and research papers that are interesting, complex, and probing. Professors are writers and researchers themselves, not just teachers. Their writing is steeped in problem-solving goals. When you write a "paper" for a college class, you enter an intellectual community that includes your professor. If you plan your college writing assignments with problem-solving goals in mind, you will be doing what your professors want and you will always be on the right track for earning good grades.

The following is an opening draft of a student essay on video games as art. As you read the essay, note how the student takes a subject that many would consider superficial, and by raising issues, asking good questions, and thinking critically about it, turns it into a problem-solving exploration.

Brian Lawrence // **VIDEO GAMES AS ART?**

AP Images/2K Games/Irrational Games

Image from the video game Bioshock Infinite.

Discovering an underwater city, sneaking around as a covert agent and exploring a vast kingdom are just a few of the adventures waiting in the realm of video games. When immersed in a video game, one truly escapes reality and embarks on memorable experiences, much in the same way that one escapes and feels transported when immersed in art.

Nonetheless, even after decades of existence, everything about video games only stirs up controversy. Questions about whether or not they influence violent behavior and negatively impact people academically and socially come to mind. However, I find some video games to be as engaging, well-crafted and intricate as many forms of art. A question that has lingered in my mind since the early days of Pac-Man and Pong is whether or not video games should be considered an art form.

Art can be seen as any medium that appeals to the emotions and senses. People consider film, dance, sculpture, literature, painting, and architecture art. Various forms of art affect different people in different ways. To a great extent, art is subjective. No two individuals perceive it the same way (Bowers). Of course, if video games were considered to be an artistic medium, they would differ from other forms of art. For instance, they lack the permanence of some art forms. One can watch a movie over and over again, and it will always play the same. When one reads a novel over and over again, the words will never change. When playing a video game, however, a person can interact with the game environment in many different ways, and make decisions that shape the way a story or scenario unfolds (Schubert 46). Does this interactivity—a lack of permanence—disqualify video games as art, or just mean they are different from other art forms?

The case against video games as art has been made vocally and frequently, most famously by the movie critic Roger Ebert. Ebert bases his argument on the fact that games are interactive. By this he means that because games require input from a player in order to progress in the storyline, the player's actions subvert some sort of intent (McCallon). Therefore, the purity of an artist's vision is never clearly manifested. For example, would a movie like *The Dark Knight* be considered such a great movie if every person who watched could pick the ending that they wanted to see?

Roger Ebert is not alone in his stance. In a *Newsweek* editorial from March 2000, titled "'Emotion Engine?' I Don't Think So," Jack Kroll argues that although games are fun and rewarding, they are incapable of transmitting emotional complexity, which is the root of art. In addition, video games do not possess the narrative structure of most traditional works of fiction. When watching a movie, if you regret something that occurs to the protagonist, you are helpless to do anything about it. However, in a video game, scenarios are reversible. The death of the player-character in a video game most likely means that the game will reset to an earlier stage. This suggests that complex narrative may be impossible in video games.

But the 2007 video game Bioshock raises some interesting questions about the interactivity argument. Set in "Rapture," a fictional, dystopian, underwater city during the 1960s, Bioshock is a first-person shooter game where the players take control of a nameless protagonist trying to stay alive and find a way out of the city. In the game's climax, the most riveting moment of the game, the player comes face to face with Andrew Ryan, the industrialist who built the city in the first place.

What makes this scene so riveting is the fact that Ryan reveals some information about the character you control for the story . . . . ∎

As with most good essays, the writer here has a personal stake in the central issue and sees its broader significance. His inquiry into whether video games are an art form matters to him personally and is meaningful to readers because understanding art—what it is, what draws us to it, and what it does for us—tells us a lot about ourselves as human beings. Of course, some video games deal in "sketchy" themes, but so does "art." Shakespeare's famous tragedy *Macbeth* is about two borderline personalities and their shared psychosis.

From Reflection to Response   Your Journal File and Personal Introduction

Writing and thinking about writing will be the main activities in this course. With that in mind, create a journal file on your computer that you will use exclusively for this course. You can call it anything you want—for example, "College Writing Journal" or "My Writing Notes."

In your file, type *Personal Bio and Introduction* (and a date for the activity).

The goal of this writing exercise is to introduce yourself to your classmates and instructor in more depth than traditional oral introductions do.

Compose the introduction in two parts. Make the first part informational, a short "bio" or "fact sheet" about yourself. Include a photograph if you want, and whatever basic information you would like to share. For example:

Name:

Place of birth:

Schools attended:

Achievements:

Anticipated college major:

Hobbies and interests:

Favorite movies, songs (etc.):

For the second part of your introduction, tell one story about your life that says something significant about who you are. Don't try to tell your complete life story. Instead, think of an incident, experience, or situation from any period of your life that illustrates something about your identity, values, or aspirations. Make the story interesting, but keep it relatively short and focus on expressing how and why the story says something significant.

After you compose your introduction, consider posting it on your course website, if you have one. This kind of introduction is especially useful in a writing course because you will be working closely with your classmates and instructor over the next few months.

> ### Tech Tip
>
> If you use Facebook, look over the "Info" and "Likes" sections on your profile page for ideas about information to include in your bio. To come up with an idea for a story to tell, try clicking through the "Life Event" section of your Facebook page. For example, under "Health and Wellness," Facebook prompts you to comment on overcoming an illness, quitting a habit, and losing weight. For some people, there can be a significant story related to dealing with those issues.

BECOMING A GOOD WRITER

> *" There is nothing to writing. All you do is sit down at a typewriter and open a vein. "*
>
> —RED SMITH, FAMOUS AMERICAN SPORTSWRITER

All of us have the same aptitude for writing that we have for speaking. If anything, effective writing is a more accessible skill than effective speaking. Writing ability requires no physical attributes like a strong voice, good enunciation, or a smooth delivery. A writer's "voice" is created out of words. Everyone who writes can have a great voice. In addition, practicing the craft of writing—using words and applying rhetorical principles effectively—can only benefit the spoken communication skills that everyone values and enjoys.

But writing takes effort and an attention to detail. In this respect, writing is a lot like cooking. Those of us who are not skilled cooks may see a recipe that looks easy enough to make—ten ingredients and six steps ("approximate preparation time, fifteen minutes")—and decide to whip it up for some friends, but once we get started, we realize the process is messier and more complicated than we thought. We have to dig out the right pots and pans, find the right seasonings, then wash, rinse, peel, chop, heat, stir, simmer, sprinkle, scrape, and "serve promptly." If we're lucky, we're sitting down to eat forty-five minutes after we started (and we still have dishes to wash), but in the end, if the food is tasty and dinner is enjoyable, we don't mind all the effort so much.

Time and Effort

As any journalist, screenwriter, songwriter, poet, or scholar will tell you, writing something often takes longer than we expect. We think we know what to say but once we actually start writing, we struggle with details, new ideas, organization, and wording. The truth is, most skills we practice require more time and effort than we would like to invest, but if we care, we have to make the investment to get results. A pianist spends weeks or months preparing for a performance. The same applies to actors, dancers, singers, and athletes. Behind the final product is a lot of time and effort.

Grammar and Mechanics

You can be willing to invest time and effort yet still feel frustrated or insecure about writing because you think you don't know enough about grammar to ever satisfy teachers and other professionals. But thinking you can't write because you don't know enough grammar is a wrong assumption. A person must "know" grammar in order to speak a language. Grammar is a mechanism for putting words together in coherent patterns that people can understand.

When some students say they don't know grammar, or their grammar is terrible, they mean they are unaware of how grammar works and have trouble analyzing it. The same is true of many professional writers. They have a limited ability to analyze grammar. What they do know, and what any good writer needs to know, are common rules and conventions of usage and punctuation. Unlike structural grammar, these rules are simple and straightforward—most students know *most* of them already.

For example, making an error like "Him and me went to the movies," or "between you and I" (rather than "between you and me"), or occasionally separating sentences with commas rather than a period, does not seriously affect a writer's ability to be understood. However, when the errors add up, they become a distraction, like a bad phone connection, full of ambient noise and static, that can make a call impossible to go on with.

Learning rules and conventions to eliminate this kind of static is relatively easy. Writing handbooks reduce the main sources of "static" to a few common mistakes—run-on sentences, fragments, vague pronoun references, dangling modifiers, and so on.* Even students without a lot of background in grammar can overcome these mistakes by learning one or two simple rules a week over a semester of writing instruction.

---

* Ten of the most common mistakes—all easy to correct—are covered in Chapter 12, "Developing an Effective Style."

A Very Short Grammar Lesson

You *know* that "Him and me went to the movies" is incorrect because if you were to write "Him went to the movies" or "Me went to the movies," you would hear the mistake and know to use subjective pronouns instead ("He" and "I"). But "him and me" has gained some currency in everyday speech, so even though it is ungrammatical, it sounds less jarring than "him went…"

You also *know* that "between you and I" is ungrammatical because, if you were to say or write something like "Would you buy a book for I?" you would hear the mistake. "Between you and I" is incorrect because "between" is a preposition and prepositions take "objective" pronouns ("me" is objective; "I" is subjective), but "between you and I" sounds correct because it is a common error that people make, including commentators on radio and TV.

In both cases, you know the rules, because you know "Him went to the movies" and "…buy a book for I" are ungrammatical.

Tech Tip

A number of websites provide quick and easy reference guides to common grammatical errors. Purdue University's Online Writing Lab (https://owl.english.purdue.edu/owl/section/1/5/) provides a list of topics that you can refer to if you are unsure about some aspect of grammar. If you need more in-depth information on the rules of grammar as well as punctuation, the website www.grammarbook.com gives detailed information on grammar rules like subject-verb agreement, who versus whom, and prepositions.

You Use Rhetoric—the Art of Communication—Every Day

Just as you enter this course knowing grammar, you also know most of the rhetorical strategies and methods that writing courses "teach"—methods of argumentation (rhetorical appeals) and developing ideas ("modes of discourse" such as comparison and contrast, or cause and effect). These strategies and methods are internalized during the early phases of language acquisition and cognitive development.

A small child in the checkout line of a grocery store, trying to persuade her mother to buy her a candy bar, can use a sophisticated range of rhetorical appeals and methods: "Jason's mom buys them for Jason…" (comparison and contrast); "I'll go to bed on time if you..." (cause and effect); "It's not a *candy* bar, it's a *health* bar..." (definition/classification); "Remember the time we were in Orlando and..." (narration/description), and so on.

This argumentative child also demonstrates that the communication goal (persuading Mom to buy the candy bar) invokes the appeals and methods, not the other way around. Every college student routinely uses rhetorical appeals and methods to talk a parent into something, ask a coach for more playing time, or explain to a significant other that the spark has gone out of a relationship.

The point is, you know more about writing and have more of an aptitude for writing than you might think, but if you are like most students, you have another major issue with writing that needs to be addressed.

Writing for "School"

> " *Nothing could have been worse for the development of my mind than Dr. Butler's school... The school as a means of education to me was simply a blank.* "
>
> —CHARLES DARWIN, *AUTOBIOGRAPHY*

Outside of school, most college students do a fair amount of writing and enjoy it—writing in the form of e-mails, text messages, tweets, and comments posted to social networks and discussion boards. Some students have personal websites or write blogs, poetry, song lyrics, and stories.

The biggest writing problem most students have is writing for school. For first-year college students, "school" specifically means secondary school. In the K through 12 curriculum, writing assignments tend to have little to do with communication, let alone problem solving. Essays often are stuffed into five-paragraph formats, and they mainly are written for assessment: Do they follow the format? Is the grammar correct?

Although college essays are "assessed," too, professors assess them for saying something and for perceptiveness, originality, critical thinking, and problem solving. As such, college essays mirror the forms and goals of professional writing, the kinds of writing people do in the workplace every day. Anyone writing a market analysis for a corporation, or writing advertising copy, a business plan, a grant, or a mission statement is essentially writing an essay. A case study of a gang member or teenage mother is an essay. Outside the context of work, the lyrics to a song, a long post to a discussion board, or even a video for YouTube to make a point—all of these are essays as defined here. They are attempts to communicate and solve problems.

The short essay that follows is a good example of a writer writing to communicate and solve a problem that concerns many people.

Leon Botstein

{ **HIGH SCHOOL, AN INSTITUTION WHOSE TIME HAS PASSED: LET TEEN-AGERS TRY ADULTHOOD**

Leon Botstein is a prolific author, an accomplished symphony conductor, and a distinguished educator, who was appointed president of Bard College in 1975. "High School, an Institution Whose Time Has Passed" appeared as an op-ed column in the *New York Times* in 1999.

Jemal Countess/Getty Image

THE NATIONAL OUTPOURING AFTER the Littleton shootings [Columbine] has forced us to confront something we have suspected for a long time: the American high school is obsolete and should be abolished. In the last month, high school students present and past have come forward with stories about cliques and the artificial intensity of a world defined by insiders and outsiders, in which the insiders hold sway because of superficial definitions of good looks and attractiveness, popularity and sports prowess.

The team sports of high school dominate more than student culture. A community's loyalty to the high school system is often based on the extent to which varsity teams succeed. High school administrators and faculty members are often former coaches, and the coaches themselves are placed in a separate, untouchable category. The result is that the culture of the inside elite is not contested by the adults in the school. Individuality and dissent are discouraged.

But the rules of high school turn out not to be the rules of life. Often the high school outsider becomes the more successful and admired adult. The definitions of masculinity and femininity go through sufficient transformation to make the game of popularity in high school an embarrassment. No other group of adults young or old is confined to an age-segregated environment, much like a gang in which individuals of the same age group define each other's world. In no workplace, not even in colleges or universities, is there such a narrow segmentation by chronology.

Given the poor quality of recruitment and training for high school teachers, it is no wonder that the curriculum and the enterprise of learning hold so little sway over young people. When puberty meets education and learning in modern America, the victory of puberty masquerading as popular culture and the tyranny of peer groups based on ludicrous values meet little resistance.

By the time those who graduate from high school go on to college and realize what really is at stake in becoming an adult, too many opportunities have been lost and too much time has been wasted. Most thoughtful young people suffer the high school environment in silence and in their junior and senior years mark time waiting for college to begin. The Littleton killers, above and beyond the psychological demons that drove them to violence, felt trapped in the artificiality of the high school world and believed it to be real. They engineered their moment of undivided attention and importance in the absence of any confidence that life after high school could have a different meaning.

Adults should face the fact that they don't like adolescents and that they have used high school to isolate the pubescent and hormonally active adolescent away from both the picture-book idealized innocence of childhood and the more accountable world of adulthood. But the primary reason high school doesn't work anymore, if it ever did, is that young people mature substantially earlier in the late 20th century than they did when the high school was invented. For example, the age of first menstruation has dropped at least two years since the beginning of this century, and not surprisingly, the onset of sexual activity has dropped in proportion. An institution intended for children in transition now holds young adults back well beyond the developmental point for which high school was originally designed.

Furthermore, whatever constraints to the presumption of adulthood among young people may have existed decades ago have now fallen away. Information and images, as well as the real and virtual freedom of movement we associate with adulthood, are now accessible to every 15- and 16-year-old.

Secondary education must be rethought. Elementary school should begin at age 4 or 5 and end with the sixth grade. We should entirely abandon the concept of the middle school and junior high school. Beginning with the seventh grade, there should be four years of secondary education that we may call high school. Young people should graduate at 16 rather than 18.

They could then enter the real world, the world of work or national service, in which they would take a place of responsibility alongside older adults in mixed company. They could stay at home and attend junior college, or they could go away to college. For all the faults of college, at least the adults who dominate the world of colleges, the faculty, were selected precisely because they were exceptional and different, not because they were popular. Despite the often cavalier attitude toward teaching in college, at least physicists know their physics, mathematicians know and love their mathematics, and music is taught by musicians, not by graduates of education schools, where the disciplines are subordinated to the study of classroom management.

For those 16-year-olds who do not want to do any of the above, we might construct new kinds of institutions, each dedicated to one activity, from science to dance, to which adolescents could devote their energies while working together with professionals in those fields.

At 16, young Americans are prepared to be taken seriously and to develop the motivations and interests that will serve them well in adult life. They need to enter a world where they are not in a lunchroom with only their peers, estranged from other age groups and cut off from the game of life as it is really played. There is nothing utopian about this idea; it is immensely practical and efficient, and its implementation is long overdue. We need to face biological and cultural facts and not prolong the life of a flawed institution that is out of date. ■

From Reflection to Response

Responding to "High School, an Institution Whose Time Has Passed"

Think about how the essay relates to some of the points made in this chapter—in particular, writing as a form of communication and problem solving. Working with two or three of your classmates, evaluate Botstein's "attempt" to reconsider the value of high school. Make a list of his key arguments. Are there counterarguments or opposing views that Botstein overlooks? How realistic are his ideas overall? What are the key obstacles to enacting the changes he advocates?

In *Holler If You Hear Me*, a book about the rapper Tupac Shakur, professor Michael Eric Dyson describes a videotaped interview that Tupac gave when he was seventeen and about to graduate from high school. In the interview, Tupac says this about education and school:

> I think we got so caught up in school being a tradition that we stopped using it as a learning tool.... I'm learning about the basics but... to get us ready for today's world, [the present curriculum] is not helping. They tend... to teach you to read, write, and [do] arithmetic, then teach you reading, writing and arithmetic again, then again, then again.... There should be a class on drugs. There should be a class on sex education, real sex education.... There should be a class on scams. There should be a class on religious cults. There should be a class on police brutality. There should be a class on apartheid. There should be a class on racism in America. There should be a class on why people are hungry.

Professor Dyson admires the "thoughtful engagement" that Tupac displays in the interview and adds: "It is clear that Tupac believes schools should be addressing the pressing social issues of the day . . . issues that are rarely explored in rich detail in our nation's educational institutions, especially in high school."

From Reflection to Response
Responding to Tupac Shakur's Comments on High School

Thinking about Tupac's comments, spend ten minutes writing down reasons you agree or disagree with him (or both). Then, working with two or three of your classmates, or on your own, develop your response in more detail by addressing the questions below.

- Does Tupac underestimate the value of reading, writing, and math? Are his suggestions less realistic than what Leon Botstein proposes in "High School, an Institution Whose Time Has Passed"? To what extent do Botstein and Tupac agree?

- Would teaching students about sex, drugs, scams, cults, or hunger have any real long-term value? Would teaching students about issues that might not directly apply to them or concern them—for instance, racism—be a waste of time, or a form of indoctrination?

- Looking back on your own education, can you see how some of Tupac's subjects could be taught in a meaningful way?

- Finally, based on your responses to Botstein's article and Tupac's statement, create a list of changes that you would make to improve high school education and the high school experience for future students.

JOINING THE CONVERSATION

> **❝** *Even on the highest throne, you're still sitting on your own butt.* **❞**
> —MICHEL DE MONTAIGNE

College writing assignments cover different genres, or kinds of writing, and go by different names—research papers, critiques, reports, and so on—but the word "essay" remains a popular umbrella term. Professors call their writing assignments essays because they appreciate the value of the essay as a form of writing and communication. Unfortunately, as noted earlier, most students think of essays as assessment instruments. In fact, essays, like different genres of music people listen to and enjoy, have a compelling tradition behind them in the "real world" of communication. The best musicians know and appreciate the origins of the music they create. Through their music, they consciously honor their musical heritage: there would be no Tupac Shakur, no Public Enemy, no Lady Gaga, Beyoncé, Foo Fighters, Dead Kennedys, or Slayer without the legendary blues artists of generations past like "Leadbelly," Bessie Smith, John Lee Hooker, Howlin' Wolf, and "Memphis Minnie" Douglas.

Like the music we listen to today, the essays people write as articles in newspapers and magazines, blogs on the Internet, or "papers" in college have a rich and compelling tradition behind them.

Connecting and "Talking" to Readers

Essays come from a specific place on earth, a region in the south of France that was once embroiled in wars, religious violence, and deadly Ebola-like plagues. This place is also known for its blue skies, sunshine, abundant produce, iconic wines, and beautiful scenery that, a thousand years ago, inspired poet-musicians called troubadours to compose songs that perfectly blend the physical and spiritual aspects of love.

As author Sarah Bakewell writes in *How to Live: Or a Life of Montaigne*, "Today, the word essay falls with a dull thud. It reminds many people of…school." And indeed, soon, for this course, you will sit down to write an essay of one kind or another, and no one can blame you if you associate the task with an assessment essay you wrote for school or an essay you dashed off under pressure for the SAT exam, but when you sit down to write your first college essay, wherever you are and whenever that is, if you start out thinking in another direction, about the random circumstances, difficulties, and beauty of human life, about blue skies, sunshine, vivid pigments, and troubadours, you'll be more realistically connected to the source and spirit of the task in front of you.

The word *essay* in French ("*essai*") means to attempt, or to try. A French writer named Michel de Montaigne (1533–1592), who was not a writer by vocation, coined the term to describe mostly short, thoughtful pieces he wrote about life and living. His essays are *attempts* to reach out to readers by writing honestly (sometimes honestly "to a fault") about himself, his observations, and the problems that life presents to all of us. Although he wrote many essays on many subjects, from cannibalism to sex, his overriding subject, reflected in the title of Sarah Bakewell's book about him, is about living, or specifically, "how to live?" In his characteristic way, Montaigne does not provide easy or definitive answers, but Bakewell identifies a few core suggestions that can be extrapolated from the sum of his essays:

How to Live?

▶ Don't worry about death.

▶ Pay attention.

▶ Survive love and loss.

▶ Question everything.

▶ Be convivial: live with others.

▶ Wake from the sleep of habit.

▶ Do something no one has done before.

▶ See the world.

▶ Reflect on everything; regret nothing.

▶ Give up control.

▶ Be ordinary and imperfect.

Although Montaigne's essays are thought-provoking, his ideas are not the deepest source of their appeal. It is the bond, or sense of connection, he creates with his readers. He writes in a conversational style that suggests someone talking to a reader, or thinking out loud, a voice in the room. His approach is all about being real, "up-close and personal," though not out of egotism or conceit: he puts himself at the center of his writing, in Bakewell's words, "to create a mirror in which other people recognize their own humanity."

The way Montaigne reaches out to readers and "speaks" to them in his essays remains a basic quality of essays today. The writer's presence and "voice" are not just accepted; they are expected and valued. Today, writing that is devoid of a writer's presence and voice, that is too disembodied and formalized, does not appeal to most readers.

Addressing Issues

The titles of most of Montaigne's essays show how rooted in addressing problems they are. The problems that concerned him remain relevant to life and people today:

Montaigne's Titles	Examples of Contemporary Relevance
Of Evil Means Employed to Good Ends	Guantanamo Bay, torture and waterboarding; preemptive war and military reprisals; vigilante justice.
Of the Disadvantage of Greatness	The lives of celebrities like Robin Williams, Junior Seau, John Lennon, and Tupac Shakur, or statesmen like Anwar Sadat and Yitzhak Rabin.
Of Drunkenness	Amy Winehouse, Justin Bieber; college binge-drinking and date-rape scenarios.
Of Cruelty	Terrorist acts, video executions, kidnapping, prison rape, bullying, animal abuse and neglect.

Soon after Montaigne's essays were published, an Englishman, Sir Francis Bacon (1561–1626), who was a scientist and scholar, wrote a collection of essays modeled on Montaigne's. Bacon's essays, like Montaigne's, are "attempts" to get at problems, to address issues and support views, as the titles also suggest:

Bacon's Titles	Examples of Contemporary Relevance
Of Revenge	Gang violence, Columbine killings, antiabortion bombings, Ismaaiyl Abdullah Brinsley's murder of New York City police officers.
Of Marriage and Single Life	Clerical and secular celibacy, gay marriage, living- together arrangements, divorce.
Of Ambition	Wall Street greed, white-collar crimes, Ponzi schemes, political power and corruption.
Of Suspicion	Hate crimes, culture wars, and xenophobia.

Informal and Formal Essays

Although Montaigne and Bacon wrote to achieve the same goals, they originated two different kinds of essays that are still generally recognized: informal (Montaigne) and formal (Bacon). Montaigne's informal approach reflects practical and worldly habits of mind, a more personal, meandering, and inductive style that moves toward expressing a view or thesis rather than highlighting one. Bacon's formal approach reflects a scientific bent, a more detached, focused, and deductive style that emphasizes a central view or thesis, an approach we might call "academic" today. Though these distinctions are valid, they are hardly etched in stone. Montaigne's essays are full of comments on the ideas of other writers and direct quotations from their works, a characteristic of formal or academic writing. Bacon's essays, on the other hand, are sprinkled with first-person pronouncements that are moving and surprise us at times.

From Reflection to Response   **A Conversation about College Writing**

Students come to college from different backgrounds and often have different perceptions about writing. As a way of joining a conversation about college writing, review the statements below and write a brief response to each, and then have a discussion about your responses with a group of your classmates and your instructor.

- College essays follow a formal structure.
- A college essay must have a thesis that is presented in the opening paragraph.
- Essays should always end with a summary of what has been said.
- A college essay must say something original.
- You can use your own experiences to support a point in a college essay.
- You should not write anything your instructor might disagree with.
- The way to develop a good style of writing is to study grammar and build up your vocabulary.
- The grade you receive on an essay is mostly a teacher's subjective opinion.
- If you can't outline an essay before you start writing, you are not going to get anywhere.
- Being a good writer means you can write quickly and with ease.

The Conversational Style

> **❝***Writing when properly managed is but a different name for conversation.***❞**
>
> —LAURENCE STERNE, *TRISTRAM SHANDY*

Along with taking different approaches to writing, Montaigne and Bacon write in different styles. Their styles, like their approaches, reflect differences in who they are, their personalities and habits of mind. In their own ways, they both write in a natural voice and use a conversational style, but they have different styles of conversation. They are like two candidates in a presidential debate, one more direct and emotional (Montaigne), the other more diplomatic and reserved (Bacon), but both authentic, interesting, capable, and engaging in their own way.

A conversational style can serve your writing exactly as it did theirs. A style based on your own "voice" is a reliable foundation for all writers and any kind of writing. Besides a writer's own "voice," what other foundation for writing is realistic or sensible? If we don't base our writing on our own voice, what do we base it on? Who are we pretending to be, and more importantly, why would we want to pretend?

Writing in a conversational style does not mean "write like you talk." To do that would be bad writing—wordy, repetitive, disorganized. A conversational style is a default style, a drafting style, or point of departure that can serve as a consistent foundation for your writing. It is the style of a painter doing sketches for a painting, not the painting itself.

Think of style in writing as similar to how we dress. We are always the same person, but we wear different clothes for different occasions. We dress casually when we hang around the house or do chores; somewhat less casually when we go to school, to a party, or out on a date; and more formally, dressier, for a job interview, a wedding, or a prom.

As writers, we change or adjust our style in a similar way for different purposes and readers. Sometimes we want our writing to be up-close and personal, to convey and evoke emotions. At other times, we want it to be more dispassionate and detached. But either way, the style always reflects who we are, and it emanates from our own voice. Fabricating a style that is disconnected from the way we speak, for example, a style designed to impress readers with "big" words and long sentences, is more like wearing a costume than clothes, a formula for bad writing. The following is a true story about a professional who struggled mightily with his writing until he learned to make his own "voice" the foundation of his style.

As a young instructor out of graduate school, I taught a business-writing course, in which one of the students—I will call him Hal—was much older than I was. Hal was a college graduate who had majored in business and worked for an international company. He was taking my course because he had to write periodic reports for his job and had been getting "flak" about his writing style from his managers and co-workers on the job.

The first assignment he submitted for class was a two-page memo that was hard to understand. When we reviewed it together, he explained what he was "trying to say" clearly enough. I suggested he rewrite the memo the way he had explained it to me. He was skeptical about doing that because he thought "it wouldn't sound good," but he went ahead and tried anyway. The rewrite was a page shorter, clear, and more to the point. I thought it was a big improvement, but Hal was still skeptical, thinking his managers and co-workers would be unimpressed by such a plain style of writing.

A week or two later, he approached me after class with a smile on his face. He had written a report for work using the plainer style. His managers and co-workers were thrilled! Moreover, he had spent less time and effort writing the report than he was accustomed to. He thanked me warmly, and proceeded to drop the course (since he already had a college degree, he did not need the credits)!

The moral of the story: Writing that impresses people is the kind of writing people like to read. It is clear and as detailed as it needs to be, but not puffed-up and wordy. It achieves its purpose and communicates well.

One of the main objectives of this course is to help you develop a capable and engaging style of writing. Style is the effect that a writer's words and ideas has on readers. Readers can have a strong response to a writer's style. If they like it, they might call it lucid, friendly, or vivid; if they don't, they might call it dense, pretentious, or dull.

As noted earlier in this chapter, writers adapt and modify their style for different audiences and occasions. However, the essence of a capable style is that it achieves a consistent result: it serves the writer's communication goals and elicits a positive response from readers.

The writer George Orwell is known for his direct and accessible style. In a famous essay, "Politics and the English Language," Orwell wrote the sentence below to illustrate what he considered a puffed-up and evasive style of writing, a use of language that is lazy or manipulative, rather than expressive:

Objective considerations of contemporary phenomena compel the conclusion that success or failure in competitive activities exhibits no tendency to be commensurate with innate capacity, but that a considerable element of the unpredictable must invariably be taken into account.

Orwell based the pretentious example on a sentence from the Bible (Ecclesiastes), which he considered more direct and meaningful:

I returned and saw under the sun, that the race is not to the swift, nor the battle to the strong, neither yet bread to the wise, nor yet riches to men of understanding, nor yet favour to men of skill; but time and chance happeneth to them all.

From Reflection to Response   Style and Tone

Considering Style

Read the sentence, and then working with two or three of your classmates, discuss what it means. What is the main idea? Do you as a group understand the meaning of "commensurate" and "innate"? What is your interpretation of "contemporary phenomena," "competitive activities," and "element of the unpredictable"? As a group, try to rewrite the sentence in simpler terms without losing any meaning.

Go back and read the passage from Ecclesiastes. Despite archaic words and wording, are there any parts of the sentence that are unclear? Do you agree with Orwell that the sentence from the Bible is more direct and meaningful? What do you think Orwell specifically liked about the "style" of the biblical sentence?

Considering Tone

As you will learn in reading Chapter 12 ("Developing an Effective Style"), a writer's choice of words largely determines the writer's style and its effect on readers. The choice of words also conveys a "tone," a feature of style that readers can have a strong response to as well. Tone in writing is similar to tone in speech: hints or insinuations that express a writer's attitude toward the subject matter or audience.

In conversation, a person might say, "That's a beautiful rug" and mean it, but she could say the same thing in a "sarcastic tone," referring to a rug that is torn and ready for the garbage bin. In speech, tone is created mostly by intonation and context. In writing, tone is more subtle because it is created exclusively by words and context.

With that in mind, read the passage below about Native American religions, from an American history textbook. Decide if the passage projects a noticeable tone about the subject matter, and if so, how would you describe the tone?

These Native Americans [in the Southwest] believed that nature was filled with spirits. Each form of life, such as plants and animals, had a spirit. Earth and air held spirits, too. People were never alone. They shared their lives with the spirits of nature.

James W. Loewen quotes this passage in his book *Lies My Teacher Told Me*. Loewen thinks the passage is well-intended but condescending. He says it "treats Native religions as a unitary whole," like "make-believe," rather than "persuasive belief systems." To illustrate his point, Loewen composed a summary of Christian beliefs that, in his opinion, projects a similar, condescending tone:

> These Americans believed that one great male god ruled the world. Sometimes they divided him into three parts, which they called father, son, and holy ghost. They ate crackers and wine and grape juice, believing that they were eating the son's body and drinking his blood. If they believed strongly enough, they would live on forever after they died.

Loewen concedes that his depiction of Christian beliefs is simplistic and potentially offensive, but he maintains that it is no more simplistic or offensive than the textbook's depiction of Native American religions.

 Regardless of what you think about the two passages, read them over with a group of two or three classmates, and identify specific words and phrases in each passage that may contribute to the perception of a condescending tone. Try to rewrite or rephrase the offending passages so that they "sound" more factual and respectful.

ACADEMIC WRITING AND ACADEMIC STYLE

An indication of the importance of writing courses is that they elicit more debate among educators than almost any other course in the college curriculum. One much-debated issue is the approach to writing advocated in this book: writing in a conversational style that is an expression of the person behind the words. Some professors assume that students will misinterpret "conversational" to mean "write the way you talk." In addition, they argue that college students have to learn to write in a so-called "academic style" in order to earn their degrees.

Composition scholar David Bartholomae presents a version of that argument in "Writing with Teachers: A Conversation with Peter Elbow":

> It is also obvious that there are many classrooms where students are asked to *imagine* that they can clear out a space to write on their own, to express their own thoughts and ideas, not to *reproduce* those of others [italics are mine]. (Bartholomae)

The statement implies that college students cannot express meaningful ideas of their own; they can only "imagine" doing this. Realistically, the most they can do is "reproduce" the ideas of others. The statement also implies that some naïve writing teachers "ask" students to do something unrealistic or impossible—in other words, "clear out a space to write on their own."

This "reproduce-ideas" argument plays into the stereotype that a first-year college writing class is a dreary rite of passage ("bonehead English"). In fact, because the class is grounded in communication about life and living, it is among the most interesting and enriching classes a student can take.

In addition, the reproduce-ideas argument attacks a position that does not exist.* To ask students to develop and express their own ideas is not the same thing as asking them to "imagine that they can clear out a space to write on their own."

No writer, at any level of ability, produces ideas in a vacuum or ever literally "clears out a space to write" on his own. Nor does a *writer* worthy of the name merely reproduce the ideas of others. Stenographers and translators do that. To write, as Montaigne and Bacon knew, is to join a conversation. Their contemporary Shakespeare, the most creative of writers, was profoundly influenced by the writing and ideas of others. All meaningful writing is a product of engagement with other people and their ideas, a product of reading, listening, learning, modeling, and synthesizing. Writers like Montaigne, Bacon, and Shakespeare read widely, thought about what they read, and learned from other writers in order to invent themselves. They also observed, thought about life, imagined, and discovered. Most of all, they wrote a lot.

In this course, you will do the same, and along with your classmates, you will join a conversation, talk, read, listen, think, imagine, discover, and above all, communicate a lot in writing. And you will be a better writer—a more confident, effective, and efficient writer—a few months from now than you are today.

> **"***We're talking about practice, not a game.***"**
> —ALLEN IVERSON, FORMER NBA BASKETBALL STAR

From Reflection to Response   Thinking and Writing about Education

Thinking

A. Read the lyrics to the song "Unconditional Love" by Tupac Shakur. Working with two or three classmates, or writing on your own, analyze the song from an educational perspective. List the problems Tupac identifies. Describe what he learned from dealing with them. What does he mean by "unconditional love," and why does he make that the title of the song?

B. "Fifth Grade Was a Little Better" is an excerpt from Charles Bukowski's autobiographical *Ham on Rye*, about growing up in Los Angeles in the 1930s, the era of the Great Depression. Bukowski expresses quite a bit of negativity about school. Do Bukowski's fifth-grade remembrances support any of the

---

* This kind of attack is a logical fallacy called a "straw man." You will learn more about fallacies like this one in Chapter 7, "Arguments That Matter."

ideas presented earlier in this chapter by Leon Botstein or Tupac Shakur? Is school the problem? If not, what is? Is the teacher a good teacher, and if so, why? Does she have any shortcomings? What do you make of the thoughts Henry expresses at the end of the excerpt?

Writing

Think back on your education, K through 12, and various issues or problems you experienced. You can use Table 1.1 to help you remember issues and experiences.

TABLE 1.1 Educational issues and problems to think about

Schools	
Types of schools and programs	all-girl, religious, for the "gifted" and the ungifted
Administration	dress codes, rules, censorship
Learning and social environment	facilities, class sizes, crime, awards, ceremonies, cliques, pressures to conform, etc.
Teachers	
The best and worst	learning from, coping with, standing up to or for, sorting out different educational philosophies, teachers as friends
Out-of-class teachers	influential person(s), mentors, ministers, counselors, employers, friends as teachers
Self-teaching and learning	from books, movies, significant experiences
Family	
Level(s) of education and attitudes toward	history of education in the family
Learning environment at home	books, computers, TV, noise, privacy, treatment of kids by adults
Preschooling	bedtime readings; stories told by parents, relatives, siblings
Literacy and Aptitude	
Language(s)	spoken at home, spoken at school, relevance to identity, learning a second language, having an accent, writing ability
Reading	first book, favorite book, struggles with, love of, aversion to, good places for
Ways of learning and aptitudes	visual, aural, learning that is difficult or easy, overachievement, underachievement

Once you have an idea, write the essay in a style and tone that comes naturally to you, as though you were writing an e-mail to a friend or posting a "Life Event" on Facebook. Think of the essay as an "attempt" to get at something, an issue or problem that will interest your readers. The only guideline is that you write it for someone to read, and ideally, enjoy—a classmate, your instructor, a roommate, a social-network friend, or just a random student who might find it lying on a table in the library.

There are *no other guidelines* or organization requirements. In fact, write the essay as it comes to you, without worrying about an introduction, body, conclusion, or thesis. Focus on making the essay real and interesting for someone to read. Tell your readers what you think. Your instructor, in particular, really cares and wants to know.

After you have written the essay, give it to someone in your class and find out what your classmate got out of it and what you could have done, if anything, to make it a more interesting or meaningful essay.

EVALUATE YOUR LEARNING

1. Identify some skills you hope to learn or improve in this writing course.

2. Imagine yourself four or five years from now working in a field or career that appeals to you. How would writing and communication skills help you succeed?

3. Rate your skills in the areas below (use a scale of 1 to 5, from low to high), and explain how the skills you have in those areas might contribute to your writing abilities:

    a. Resolving conflicts with people you know (friends, teammates, family members).

    b. Listening to what others have to say.

    c. Using new media and technology to communicate—social networks and blog sites (Twitter, Tumblr, Facebook, WordPress, Pinterest); audio, video, and animation software (Audacity, GarageBand, iMovie, GoAnimate); desktop publishing and slide shows (Publisher, PowerPoint, Keynote, Prezi).

4. If you were asked to write something that would interest people you don't know, what would you write about, and why do you think it would be of interest to your readers?

5. Research shows that motivation to succeed at something, whether it is a communication task, losing weight, or learning to play guitar, is only half the battle.bh People who most often succeed come up with a plan of action. The next chapter of this book is titled "Planning Essays as Communication." In preparation for reading the chapter, list some things you do, or think you should do, to plan a writing assignment.

ADDITIONAL READINGS

2Pac Shakur { "UNCONDITIONAL LOVE" LYRICS

Tupac Shakur (1971–1996), known by his stage name 2Pac, was born in New York City, the son of Black Panther activists, Billy Garland and Afeni Shakur. A creative and academically gifted child, he grew up to become a renowned hip-hop artist, whose career sadly was blighted by violent incidents and time in prison. In 1996, while embroiled in a feud with rival rappers, he was murdered in Las Vegas.

(What y'all want?)
Unconditional Love (no doubt)
Talking bout the stuff that don't wear off
It don't fade
It'll last for all these crazy days
These crazy nights
Whether you wrong or you right
I'm a still love you
Still feel you
Still there for you
No matter what (hehe)
You will always be in my heart
With unconditional love

[Verse 1]

Come listen to my truest thoughts, my truest feelings
All my peers doing years beyond drug dealing
How many caskets can we witness
Before we see it's hard to live this life without God, so we must ask forgiveness
Ask mama why I got this urge to die
Witness the tears falling free from my eyes, before she could reply
Though we were born without a silver spoon
My broken down TV, show cartoons in my living room (hey)
One day I hope to make it, a player in this game
Mama don't cry, long as we try, maybe things change
Perhaps it's just a fantasy
A life where we don't need no welfare

Shit with our whole family
Maybe it's me that caused it, the fighting and the hurting
In my room crying cause I didn't want to be a burden
Watch mama open up her arms to hug me
And I ain't worried bout a damn thang, with unconditional love

[Hook: repeat 2X]

In this game the lesson's in your eyes to see
Though things change, the future's still inside of me
We must remember that tomorrow comes after the dark
So you will always be in my heart, with unconditional love

[Verse 2]

Just got the message you've been calling all week
Been out here hustling on these streets, ain't had a chance to speak
But you know, with you and me it's on G
We could never be enemies, cause you been such a good friend to me
Where would I be without my dogs
No wonder why when times get hard
Cause it ain't easy being who we are
Driven by my ambitions, desire higher positions
So I proceed to make Gs, eternally in my mission
Is to be more than just a rap musician
The elevation of today's generation
If could make 'em listen
Prison ain't what we need, no longer stuck in greed
Time to plan, strategize, my family's gotta eat
When we make somethin out of nothing
No pleasure in the suffering, neighborhood would be good
If they could cut out all the busting
The liquor and the weed the cussing
Sending love out to my block
The struggle never stops (unconditional love)

[Hook]

[Verse 3]

I'll probably never understand ya ways
With everyday I swear I hear ya
Trying to change your ways while gettin paid at the same time
Just had a baby with the same eyes

Something inside, please let me die these are strange times
How come I never made it
Maybe it's the way I played it in my heart
I knew one day I gotta be a star
My hopes and all my wishes
So many vivid pictures, and all the currency
I'll never even get to see
This fast life soon shatters
Cause after all the lights and screams
Nothing but my dreams matter
Hoping for better days
Maybe a peaceful night, baby don't cry
Cause everythang gonna be alright
Just lay your head on my shoulder
Don't worry bout a thang baby
Girl I'm a soldier (huh)
Never treated me bad, no matter who I was
You still came with that, unconditional love
[Hook] - repeat to fade ■

Charles Bukowski { FIFTH GRADE WAS A LITTLE BETTER, FROM *HAM ON RYE*

Charles Bukowski (1920–1994) was born in Germany and came to
the United Sates with his parents as a small child. After dropping out of
Los Angeles City College in 1941, he tried his hand at many jobs including
dishwasher, parking lot attendant, truck driver, and mail carrier, until he began
his professional writing career at the age of thirty-five. Known for his honest,
unadorned poems and stories about life and people on the fringes of society,
he published more than forty books that attracted an international audience of
devoted readers.

THE 5TH GRADE WAS a little better. The other students seemed less hostile
and I was growing larger physically. I still wasn't chosen for the homeroom
teams but I was threatened less. David and his violin had gone away. The family had moved. I walked home alone. I was often trailed by one or two guys, of
whom Juan was the worst, but they didn't start anything. Juan smoked cigarettes. He'd walk behind me smoking a cigarette and he always had a different
buddy with him. He never followed me alone. It scared me.

I wished they'd go away. Yet, in another way, I didn't care. I didn't like Juan. I didn't like anybody in that school. I think they knew that. I think that's why they disliked me. I didn't like the way they walked or looked or talked, but I didn't like my father or mother either.

I still had the feeling of being surrounded by white empty space. There was always a slight nausea in my stomach. Juan was dark-skinned and he wore a brass chain instead of a belt. The girls were afraid of him, and the boys too. He and one of his buddies followed me home almost every day. I'd walk into the house and they'd stand outside. Juan would smoke his cigarette, looking tough, and his buddy would stand there. I'd watch them through the curtain. Finally, they would walk off.

Mrs. Fretag was our English teacher. The first day in class she asked us each our names.

"I want to get to know all of you," she said. She smiled.

"Now, each of you has a father, I'm sure. I think it would be interesting if we found out what each of your fathers does for a living. We'll start with seat number one and we will go around the class. Now, Marie, what does your father do for a living?"

"He's a gardener."

"Ah, that's nice! Seat number two... Andrew, what does your father do?"

It was terrible. All the fathers in my immediate neighborhood had lost their jobs. My father had lost his job. Gene's father sat on his front porch all day. All the fathers were without jobs except Chuck's who worked in a meat plant. He drove a red car with the meat company's name on the side.

"My father is a fireman," said seat number two.

"Ah, that's interesting," said Mrs. Fretag. "Seat number three."

"My father is a lawyer."

"Seat number four."

"My father is a... policeman..."

What was I going to say? Maybe only the fathers in my neighborhood were without jobs. I'd heard of the stock market crash. It meant something bad. Maybe the stock market had only crashed in our neighborhood.

"Seat number eighteen."

"My father is a movie actor..."

"Nineteen..."

"My father is a concert violinist..."

"Twenty..."

"My father works in the circus..."

"Twenty-one..."

"My father is a bus driver..."

"Twenty-two..."

"My father sings in the opera…"

"Twenty-three…"

Twenty-three. That was me.

"My father is a dentist," I said.

Mrs. Fretag went right on through the class until she reached number thirty-three.

"My father doesn't have a job," said number thirty-three. Shit, I thought, I wish I had thought of that.

One day Mrs. Fretag gave us an assignment.

"Our distinguished President, President Herbert Hoover, is going to visit Los Angeles this Saturday to speak. I want all of you to go hear our President. And I want you to write an essay about the experience and about what you think of President Hoover's speech."

Saturday? There was no way I could go. I had to mow the lawn. I had to get the hairs.

(I could never get all the hairs.) Almost every Saturday I got a beating with the razor strop because my father found a hair. (I also got stropped during the week, once or twice, for other things I failed to do or didn't do right.) There was no way I could tell my father that I had to go see President Hoover.

So, I didn't go. That Sunday I took some paper and sat down to write about how I had seen the President. His open car, trailing flowing streamers, had entered the football stadium. One car, full of secret service agents went ahead and two cars followed close behind. The agents were brave men with guns to protect our President. The crowd rose as the President's car entered the arena. There had never been anything like it before. It was the President. It was him. He waved. We cheered. A band played. Seagulls circled overhead as if they too knew it was the President. And there were skywriting airplanes too. They wrote words in the sky like "Prosperity is just around the corner." The President stood up in his car, and just as he did the clouds parted and the light from the sun fell across his face. It was almost as if God knew too. Then the cars stopped and our great President, surrounded by secret service agents, walked to the speaker's platform. As he stood behind the microphone a bird flew down from the sky and landed on the speaker's platform near him. The President waved to the bird and laughed and we all laughed with him. Then he began to speak and the people listened. I couldn't quite hear the speech because I was sitting too near a popcorn machine which made a lot of noise popping the kernels, but I think I heard him say that the problems in Manchuria were not serious, and that at home everything was going to be all right, we shouldn't worry, all we had to do was to believe in America. There would be enough jobs for everybody. There would be enough dentists with enough teeth to pull, enough fires and enough firemen to put them out. Mills and factories would open again. Our friends in South America would pay their debts. Soon we would all sleep peacefully, our stomachs and our hearts full. God and our great country would surround us with love and protect us from evil, from the socialists, awaken us from our national nightmare, forever...

The President listened to the applause, waved, then went back to his car, got in, and was driven off followed by carloads of secret service agents as the sun began to sink, the afternoon turning into evening, red and gold and wonderful. We had seen and heard President Herbert Hoover.

I turned in my essay on Monday. On Tuesday Mrs. Fretag faced the class.

"I've read all your essays about our distinguished President's visit to Los Angeles. I was there. Some of you, I noticed, could not attend for one reason or another. For those of you who could not attend, I would like to read this essay by Henry Chinaski."

The class was terribly silent. I was the most unpopular member of the class by far. It was like a knife slicing through all their hearts.

"This is very creative," said Mrs. Fretag, and she began to read my essay. The words sounded good to me. Everybody was listening. My words filled the room, from blackboard to blackboard, they hit the ceiling and bounced off, they covered Mrs. Fretag's shoes and piled up on the floor. Some of the prettiest girls in the class began to sneak glances at me. All the tough guys were pissed. Their essays hadn't been worth shit.

I drank in my words like a thirsty man. I even began to believe them. I saw Juan sitting there like I'd punched him in the face. I stretched out my legs and leaned back. All too soon it was over.

"Upon this grand note," said Mrs. Fretag, "I hereby dismiss the class..."

They got up and began packing out.

"Not you, Henry," said Mrs. Fretag. I sat in my chair and Mrs. Fretag stood there looking at me. Then she said, "Henry, were you there?"

I sat there trying to think of an answer. I couldn't. I said, "No, I wasn't there."

She smiled. "That makes it all the more remarkable."

"Yes, ma'am..."

"You can leave, Henry."

I got up and walked out. I began my walk home. So, that's what they wanted: lies.

Beautiful lies. That's what they needed. People were fools. It was going to be easy for me. I looked around. Juan and his buddy were not following me. Things were looking up. ■

Courtesy of Caitlin Ng.

CAITLIN NG

Learn About a Different Culture

In this piece, I was trying to illustrate an alternative view on what it means to learn about another person. Often times we see things with a limited perspective. But if we open up our field of vision to the variety of cultures surrounding us, our world opens itself up to peace.

CHAPTER TWO

Planning Essays as Communication

 I hate starting an essay. I dread the minute that I have to sit down and write a draft.

—A college writing student

CHAPTER LEARNING OBJECTIVES

In this chapter, you will learn to:

- ▶ Make communication goals the focus of your writing.
- ▶ Distinguish between two kinds of communication— communication to inform and communication to solve problems.
- ▶ Recognize how communication concepts cross over to different genres of writing, different art forms, and different media.
- ▶ Plan essays to present issues and support views.
- ▶ Organize essays using formal and informal patterns of development.

UNDERSTANDING COMMUNICATION GOALS

Planning implies having a goal. Writers at all levels share two subjective goals when they have something to write: they want to finish the task and do it well. For a college student, doing it well usually means getting an "A."

41

For Shakespeare it meant writing a hit play. These goals are real but don't help a writer plan.

Effective planning starts with seeing beyond subjective goals and including readers in your thinking process—in other words, understanding why you are writing and what you are trying to accomplish. Most of us read much more than we write, yet when we have a writing task in front of us, we focus on being a writer and forget what we know about being readers. When we do that, we short-circuit the planning process.

Connecting to Readers

A writer's most fundamental goal is to connect to readers in a meaningful and satisfying way. Doing that is difficult, though. Readers are real people of different ages, with different backgrounds, interests, and personalities. Like you, they are picky about what they read. They look for reasons not to read an article, essay, story, or whatever. A writer's job is to grab readers' attention and keep them interested. Of course, no article, essay, or story will appeal to everyone, just as no movie does, but good movies have a wide appeal, as do good essays. The way to ensure that you connect to most of your readers is to remember that writing is a form of communication: Base your writing on what readers are looking for.

COMMUNICATION TO INFORM

Communication can be described in different ways, but to plan an essay you only need to distinguish between two basic kinds—(1) *communication to inform* (to provide information) and (2) *communication to solve problems* (to address issues and support views).

The first kind—communication to inform—is the kind we do most often in our day-to-day lives. We call a friend to chat about a movie or a ballgame we saw, a new gadget or outfit we bought, a road trip we took, or the latest gossip about an acquaintance. Sharing this kind of information is useful and enjoyable. Most of us do it with ease.

COMMUNICATION TO SOLVE PROBLEMS

The second kind of communication—communication to solve problems—is trickier. You call your friend not because you want to chat but because you have a problem that you need to get off your chest and hope to resolve. Your friend has been dating someone you dislike. You have refrained from saying anything, but over time you have observed your friend changing to please this other person, and not for the better—behaving in self-centered or self-destructive ways. This behavior is affecting your friendship. You feel you have to say something about it: address the issue as you see it and express your point of view.

Now, you are involved in problem-solving communication and face a conversation in which the outcome matters and must be handled thoughtfully. Most of us are not especially good at this kind of communicating and don't do it with ease or pleasure, but it does command our attention because we recognize its importance. This is the kind of communication we have in mind when we refer to "communication skills" and people being "good communicators."

COMMUNICATING TO SOLVE PROBLEMS

●●● The Speed Sisters: Challenging Gender Stereotypes and Tradition

Their names are Marah, Mona, Betty, Rhana, and Noor. They are Palestinian women who love fast cars and motorsports. Until a few years ago, in the culturally conservative Palestinian Territories where they live, all of the race drivers were men. Most of the spectators were, too, but when a family friend took Marah Zahalka to a local autocross race, she immediately was hooked, and soon after, made friends with four women who shared her passion for motorsports. Defying gender stereotypes and cultural tradition, they formed a racing team called the Speed Sisters. Marah's relatives were so upset that they stopped talking to her. Male race drivers laughed at them. Noor Daoud remembers getting out of her racecar and hearing people tell her she should "get a husband" or "be cleaning house." Rather than give in to pressure, the women kept racing and started winning. Their goal was not just to pursue their passion but to change people's hearts and minds and, through their actions, be an inspiration to their fellow citizens. Today, they

Ian Gavan/Getty Images

The Speed Sisters, from left: Mona, Maysoon, Jayyusi, Amber (director), Noor, Betty, and Marah

are internationally known, cheered by fans at home, and the subject of the documentary film *Speed Sisters*, developed with support of the Sundance Institute.

The director of *Speed Sisters*, Amber Fares, is a Canadian-born filmmaker of Lebanese ancestry who grew up "eating a lot of hummus and playing a lot of hockey," but the terrorist attacks

continued

on "9/11" (September 11, 2001) disrupted her comfortable life and sense of identity. Suddenly, her parents, as Canadians of Middle-Eastern descent, were getting anonymous phone calls telling them to go back to where they came from. For the first time in her life, Fares felt like a stranger in her own country. In response, she packed a bag and her camera and traveled to Lebanon to learn about her roots.

Some years later she found herself on a backstreet of a town in the Palestinian Territories around midnight, watching a woman in a fast car ripping up the tarmac doing doughnuts, while thirty men cheered her on. That was Fares's introduction to the Speed Sisters. She realized there was a story to tell, not only about Arab women breaking stereotypes, but also about Arab men of character who support women and treat them as equals.

If you wanted to pursue an unconventional dream like the Speed Sisters did, how would you communicate your passion and get people on your side? Or if, like Amber Fares, you ever felt out of place in your own country because of xenophobia, bigotry, chauvinism, or some other form of mass ignorance, what would you do to open people's eyes and bring about change? ●●●

The Prevalence of Problems

Communicating to solve problems always commands our attention because it arises from a need that is more significant than providing or receiving information. Whether we like it or not, trying to solve problems is almost the definition of life. Our lives are an endless succession of problems, big and small, problems at home, at work, at school—financial problems, social problems, transportation problems, romantic problems, spiritual problems, image problems, and on and on. Even in pursuit of hobbies and fun—anything from sailing to golf to paintball to dancing to Internet role-playing games—we are faced with problems and challenged to find solutions.

Information is interesting and important when we need it, but problems engage us on a deeper level. We care about problems and connect to them even when they are not *our* immediate problems because we recognize that they might be someday, or at the very least, that they have an indirect relevance to our lives through people we know and care about.

From Reflection to Response   Communicating to Solve Problems

Like many of the concepts in this book, communicating to solve problems is not just a facet of college writing; it is something all of us do in our lives. With that in mind, open the journal file you have created for the course (see Chapter 1, page 14), type

"Communicating to Solve Problems," and then look at the table and think of one or more issues in your life that you tried to address and resolve through communication. Go back as far as you can remember. The issues can be in the distant past, the recent past, or current and ongoing. Most college students have had a variety of issues they tried to work out with their parents—for example, the choice of a school, permission to attend an event, use the family car, or go on a trip.

Categories	Issue/Problem	Person(s)	View
Close Relationships (parents, other family members, friends, significant others)	Curfew	Your mother or father	Mature enough to stay out late
Social Relationships (roommates, teammates, members of a club, band, religious group, or other organization)			
School (teachers, classmates, administrators, coaches)			
Work (supervisors, coworkers, customers)			

Communication problems also can extend to school, work, and your social life—problems with teachers, coaches, and classmates; with a supervisor or a coworker; or with your friends and significant others.

Along with the issue or problem you remember, identify the person or persons that you needed to speak to and the main point you tried to get across. If you think of problems you wanted to address but did not, try to remember why you held back and what you could or should have said.

Compose your journal entry by writing a paragraph or two, elaborating on one of the situations you remember and addressing some of the questions below.

- Why was the issue or problem important?
- How hard was it for you to talk about it?
- What strategies did you use to carry your points (for example, saying positive things first, or picking a specific time or place)?
- What view or message did you try to convey, to resolve the issue?
- Were you able to resolve it?
- Do you wish you had done or said anything differently?

HOW TO PLAN

If you have ever watched an old Hollywood movie about a writer or journalist, you may recall a scene that goes like this: the hero or heroine sits in front of a typewriter with a burning idea for a story, but instead of dashing it off, ends up ripping pages out of the typewriter and tossing them into the wastebasket. The problem the writer is having comes from a lack of planning. Yes, he or she has a good idea and feels inspired, but something isn't clicking; the idea and inspiration aren't enough.

Usually the writer in the movie will get the story on track. In real life, if a writer is persistent enough, he will do the same. But the hit-and-miss approach can be time-consuming and stressful. It is like straying from a path in the woods, getting lost, and trying to find your way out. You are happy when you finally do, but until then, it is no fun thrashing around wondering where you are, what direction you are going, or whether you will find your way out before dark. You could kick yourself for straying from the path and swear you will never make that mistake again.

The equivalent of the path for a writer is having an effective plan. But how do you devise a plan?

Addressing an Issue and Supporting a View

The first step in planning an essay (or any compelling communication task) is to identify the *issue* or problem you intend to address and resolve. If a writer can't identify an issue, it is unlikely that she will be able to write a meaningful essay, let alone plan one. But addressing an issue or problem is insufficient without the second part of the problem-solving process: supporting a view about the issue (a view usually is called an *argument* or a *thesis* in academic writing). Readers identify with issues but also are looking for a view or viewpoint—answers or solutions—to complete the communication process.

Let's examine this idea in a nonacademic context. Say you work for a company and are asked to write a report about sagging sales or the cost-benefits of a potential acquisition. Your report would not be complete or satisfying if it simply presented the problem. Readers would expect a view or solution: how to turn sales around, or whether or not the potential acquisition is a good idea.

Artistic communication works the same way. Movies and songs almost always are based on problems, launched by issues, but the audience also needs and expects a view or solution to provide closure and meaning. The movie *The Wrestler* portrays a washed-up icon of professional wrestling performing in grubby venues for small crowds, but the movie ultimately tells us that, even in a spiral of grotesque decline, a man can be a hero and an inspiration.

Movies as Communication

Good movies resonate with audiences because they are more than entertainment; they express meaningful views about life and living. The action/adventure movies about the English spy James Bond have appealed to audiences for five decades, in part because they are exciting, but also because they express meaningful views that resonate with audiences. Every Bond movie is a new adventure (another word for trouble) that starts with a dangerous assignment. The danger and difficulty of the assignment present an *issue* to which the audience connects. The way Bond deals with danger and difficulties translates to meaningful *views* that audiences consciously or unconsciously grasp. Early on, a Bond movie tells us that Bond is human, not invincible. He makes mistakes and often pays a price for them, but he remains determined, always thinking, observing, learning, and adapting. Determination contributes more to his success than physical strength, "tradecraft," or courage. But, of course, audiences expect that from an action hero. A more beguiling *view* that the movies express is that Bond, through all the danger and difficulties, in the face of treachery, self-doubt, and death, never loses his love of life, that quintessential human trait that makes him one of us. He lives in the moment and enjoys life as best as he can—the well-made martini, the gourmet dinner, the high-stakes action at the baccarat table, the beautiful woman with the mysterious smile, the sunrise over a tropical beach. In the absence of these views, audiences would be left indifferent and disappointed.

Songs as Communication

Music is a form of communication that influences people as much as movies do. Music speaks uniquely to our emotions. Songs that combine lyrics with music add a dimension of explicit meaning to the emotions they evoke. Like movies, songs communicate by addressing issues and presenting views. The song "Unconditional Love" by Tupac Shakur takes us through a life full of struggles, but it also presents the rapper's view of love as a means of coping and overcoming. The song "Poem to a Horse" by Shakira addresses a relationship issue or problem, but it completes the communication process by expressing a view about coping that provides meaning and closure.

Expressing a meaningful view completes the communication process. Essays also need to include both parts of the process to be effective: they need an issue to get the reader invested, and they need a meaningful view that moves the issue in a problem-solving direction. An essay that explores a relevant issue—let's say the melting of polar ice caps—and does not express some kind of view, for example, that the melting has harmful geoclimatic consequences or not, will perplex or disappoint readers.

An essay that deals with a toxic relationship between a stepchild and a stepparent and vividly describes painful incidents and bitter arguments but does not express a view, an approach to healing or moving on, will again perplex or disappoint readers.

To complete an effective communication process, a writer needs to present an issue and a viewpoint. It is accurate to say *no issue, no essay*. Without an issue, the reader will be hard put to grasp a reason for reading. It is also accurate to say *no viewpoint, no essay*. Without a view, the reader will feel mystified or shortchanged.

From Reflection to Response   Analyzing Movies as Communication

Option for Class

In class, tell your instructor and classmates about a good movie that you recently have seen in the theaters, or a movie that is a personal favorite of yours (for example, *Moneyball, War Horse, Black Swan, Fight Club, Gladiator, The Dark Knight Rises, The Lion King, and so on*).

Your instructor or a classmate will keep a list of titles on the board. As the list is being created, your instructor will put you into discussion groups of three or more students who have seen and enjoyed the same movie. In your group, summarize the movie's plot (or write a brief synopsis). Then collaborate on an analysis of the movie as communication by doing the following:

1. Identify the central issue driving the story. The central issue is almost always a significant dilemma, predicament, or frustration that with which the main character is grappling.

2. Explain the view, or message, that the movie communicates about the central issue. The view or message is inevitably linked to the ending, that is, how the story turns out.

After your group has finished the analysis, share with the class your insights about the movie as communication. Keep in mind that your goal is not to do an in-depth analysis or critique, just to briefly analyze how the movie communicates through a central issue (or set of related issues) and a view or message. Avoid a drawn-out synopsis or plot summary. Keep the synopsis as short as possible, and focus on the issue-and-view analysis.

Option for Home

Complete the activity above at home, in your writing journal. Divide the analysis into two parts: (1) a brief plot summary, and (2), an analysis of the movie as communication—in other words, the issues and views that emerge from the story.

Keep the plot summary as short as possible (a paragraph or two). Focus on the issue-and-view analysis—how and why does the movie connect to audiences? What are the messages it delivers?

Analyzing Songs as Communication

Go online and find the lyrics to a song whose meaning resonates for you. (If you can't think of a song offhand, consider Shakira's "Poem to a Horse," mentioned on page 47.) In your journal, write a short interpretation or analysis of the song, specifically making a case for what you think is the central *issue* the song addresses, and the *view* or message the songwriter wants to express. Quote specific lines to support your points.

Based on the central issue and view that you identified, explain why you think the song is relevant to a general audience. Share your analysis of the song with a classmate and see if she agrees with your conclusions or sees a different meaning.

Tech Tip

You can probably find the lyrics to your favorite song using a lyrics database like www.mldb.org, or lyricsfly.com. Song lyrics are very topical and can serve as a source of inspiration for essay topics.

Know Your Issue but Discover Your View

To plan an essay, you need to know the main issue before you begin writing. However, the view your essay will support—the main argument, message, or thesis—is different. When you plan certain kinds of essays, an academic argument, for example, you usually know your view in advance. If you think the interest rates on college loans are way too high and want to argue that they should be lowered, you know the view you plan to support.

Other kinds of essays—personal narratives, for example—can be planned without an initial view. You have to know the issue you are addressing and be aware that the essay needs to express a view in order to satisfy readers, but you can discover or clarify the view in the process of writing the essay.

Some college writing assignments are designed strictly for learning purposes or practice. The planning concepts described here do not apply to those kinds of assignments. For example, your writing instructor might ask you to "describe a memorable event that you attended." An assignment like that allows you to practice your writing in the same way that a soccer player might practice corner kicks to prepare for a game. But describing a memorable event for the sake of providing information about it is not a communication task in the problem-solving sense: it lacks a central issue and view.

However, if you planned the assignment to be more than a description, that is, with an issue and view in mind, then it would become an essay. Say the memorable event was controversial, a thrash metal or hip-hop concert. You planned your description not just to describe the concert but to show that the genre of music is misunderstood or underappreciated (an issue) and that it has artistic or cultural value (a view). Then you would be planning an essay. If the concert involved a brawl or rampant drug use (issues) that you wanted to describe *and* express a view about, again you would be planning an essay rather than just an exercise.

PLANNING DIFFERENT KINDS OF ESSAYS

The planning strategy described here reduces all essays to the same simple structure: issue + view. Yet, when we read good essays, the structure is hard to notice. Good essays seem more different than alike. The differences make essays interesting. But for a student trying to get a handle on how to write good essays, the differences also can be confusing.

Analyzing a Text

Let's assume you recently wrote a common kind of college essay, an essay that analyzes and evaluates a text. The text was a magazine or newspaper article about teaching "intelligent design" in high school biology classes.* The main issue you addressed in your essay was whether or not the article was convincing. Your view—in other words, your thesis—was that the article did not make a convincing case. You wrote that the writer was biased, used a false analogy, dismissed students' free-speech rights, and made several assumptions that lacked factual support.

When you turned in your essay, you thought it was excellent, but your instructor gave you a B. In his comments, he said your arguments were too one-sided and disorganized. You mentioned a false analogy but never explained why it was false. You ignored a couple of credible points that the author put forth. Your paragraphs needed better transitions, and you wrote some run-on sentences. Overall, your essay was pretty good but it could have been better.

---

*Intelligent design is the theory that science provides incorrect explanations for certain aspects of the universe or life (for example, evolution), and that the correct explanation is the existence of an "intelligent" cause or being.

Since you thought the essay was excellent, the grade probably disappointed you. But after reading your instructor's comments, you noticed the problems with the organization, the paragraph transitions, and run-ons. However, you still did not understand the comment about ignoring the author's credible arguments. Weren't you supposed to support *your* view?

Now, if your next assignment is to analyze another text, you have a good idea of what to do to improve the result. You realize that some readers, notably your instructor, expect you to acknowledge an author's credible points, even if you disagree with them.

However, your next essay assignment probably will be different from the one you just finished, especially in a writing class. One of the goals of the class is to give you experience writing in different genres, using different writing methods for different purposes and different audiences. Getting a new assignment may be refreshing, but it also presents a new set of challenges for you. Understanding the new challenges will help you transition smoothly from one assignment, or writing task, to another.

Understanding Different Genres, Methods, and Aims

Most writing courses and textbooks present assignments using one of three approaches to composing: (1) dominant modes or methods of writing (narration, comparison and contrast, extended definition, analysis, and so on); (2) aims or objectives of writing (describing, analyzing, explaining, persuading); and (3) genres or kinds of writing (narratives, profiles, reviews, arguments).

All three approaches to composing are *more or less* realistic, but to a great extent, they also are interconnected and interdependent. None of them gives a writer a complete handle on planning and composing a given task or assignment. In essence, the three approaches serve the same valid, but limited, purpose: They create a rationale for differentiating the writing tasks in a given course so that students can practice different writing methods and adapt their writing to different situations and challenges.

One virtue of the genre-based approach to assignments used in this course is that the concept of genres applies to most forms of communication, not just writing, and as such, is familiar to students. For example, if you visit an online music store like iTunes, you see the music classified by genres. Websites for movie reviews or on-demand streaming classify movies by genres, too. Different genres of writing that are either discussed in this course or selected for some of the guided assignments are included in the chart.

Different genres, whether they are kinds of songs, movies, or writing, have different characteristics that tell us something about what to expect from the communication process. In music, a blues song usually is about hardships

Music	Movies	Writing
Blues	Action	Blogs
Country	Adventure	Memos
Metal	Comedy	Newspaper columns
Pop	Drama	Profiles
Punk	Horror	Reports
Rap	Romance	Scholarly articles (research papers)
Rock	Science fiction	Evaluations and reviews

and suffering; the emotions expressed are likely to be sad. Punk is more likely to express anger or rage. Metal often is larger than life, geared toward grandiloquent statements. However, these distinctions only go so far. Anyone who cares about music will find generic descriptions lacking: some blues songs make grandiloquent statements, some punk is kind, and some metal is sad.

Genres of movies cross over in the same ways. The genres are based on noticeable distinctions, but the distinctions only tell us so much. Larger communication principles apply. The same is true for genres of writing. When you move from one writing task or assignment to another, you may need to adapt to different expectations or conventions, but larger communication principles still apply. You never have to start completely from scratch.

Assuming you wrote an essay analyzing a text for a previous assignment, two possibilities for a new assignment are as follows:

New assignment 1: Write an essay about an experience that defined you or changed your life in some way.

▶ **Also known as:** A narrative essay, or personal narrative.

▶ **Main learning goal:** Tell a story in order to make a point, express a view, deliver a message, or solve a problem.

▶ **Importance:** Narration or storytelling is an important way of communicating in all professional fields.

New assignment 2: Compose an argument that uses primary and secondary research to support a view about a problem you care deeply about.

▶ **Also known as:** A researched argument or research paper.

▶ **Main learning goal:** Support a view or solution using cogent reasoning and evidence drawn from field research (interviews, observations, surveys, and so forth) and secondary sources of quality (scholarly books, articles, and so on).

▶ **Importance:** Conducting research is an important method of gathering information and addressing problems in most academic disciplines and professional fields.

These two assignments are quite different from each other and from the response to a text that you wrote previously. The narrative essay will require a different style of writing (first person) and probably a different pattern of organization from the textual analysis. (Patterns of organization are covered on pages 61–64.) The researched argument is more similar in style and organization to a textual analysis but may be intended for a more specialized audience, and since the argument incorporates research, you will need to know something about rules and styles of documentation, and how to smoothly weave source material into your essay without quoting too much or too little, or losing your voice in a drone of summaries or paraphrases.

In short, you need to adapt to the conventions of the different genre, but the basic planning concept for new essays or writing tasks is the same: *issue + view*. To plan either of the new assignments—the narrative or researched essay—your starting point is to define the central issue or problem that the essay will address.

Narrative or Personal Essay

Let's take a brief look at how the planning principles apply to a narrative essay assignment. The first challenge the assignment presents is, what do you write about? You can make a case for almost any experience defining you or changing your life in some way—anything from adopting a dog to confronting a bully or hitting a home run in a baseball game. How do you evaluate those ideas and decide if they are "any good"?

The key is to remember that you are writing for your readers. Readers consciously or unconsciously expect an essay to address an issue and support a view. Unless your essay communicates in this way, you will have a hard time connecting to readers.

For example, say you recall an experience that was truly important to you—finding and adopting your dog and proverbial best friend, Emma.* You plan to describe how you were out riding your bike one day and came across a stray, unkempt, funny-looking mutt that you fell in love with at first sight. You brought the mutt home, named her, and cared for her. In your essay, you plan

---

* The name of my dog.

to describe how Emma changed your life, how caring for her made you feel needed and important, how she filled a vacuum, always happy to see you when you came home, always eager to interact and play.

Is the story of you and Emma good material for an essay? Dog lovers should be able to relate to your story, but in the absence of a clear issue, what is the point of the essay? What are your communication goals? Why should readers, even dog lovers, be interested in information about you and your dog?

Unless your essay answers these questions in the early going, most people won't read it. Nothing personal, but they already get it. There needs to be an issue that connects your experience to their lives in a meaningful way.

Identifying an Issue

If the experience unfolded a little differently, or as you planned your essay you remembered an issue that you initially forgot, the dynamics of the idea could change. Say while you were cleaning up Emma and feeding her in your garage, your dad came home from work. He glared at the stray dog, then at you: "No way! That mutt isn't staying. I'm calling Animal Services." Now you have an issue involving a battle of wills, family relations, parental authority, and so forth, an issue readers can identify with and connect to: you want to keep the dog. Your dad doesn't think you are mature or responsible enough to take care of her. Emma's fate—being adopted by you or "put to sleep"—hangs in the balance. Let's say there was a lot of discussion back and forth, a standoff, but you eventually prevailed. Readers will want to find out how you changed your father's mind. With an issue in focus, you can write a compelling essay.

Supporting a View

You also have the ability to make your narrative express and support a view. You had a major role in how the situation played out. In dealing with your dad, you know what you did right or wrong or could have done better or would do differently if you had to face a similar situation again. You learned something about yourself and other people, about disagreements and struggles. As a result, you have something to teach your readers.

The article that follows, by Ellen Goodman, a Pulitzer Prize-winning journalist, is an argument that addresses an issue about parenting and uses facts and reasoning to support a view. Good parents are supposed to be protective of their children, but at what point does *protective* become *overprotective* and problematic?

Ellen Goodman

{ **WHEN BIG FATHER/BIG MOTHER SPY ON THE CHILDREN**

Ellen Goodman is a writer, journalist, and syndicated columnist. In 1980, she won the Pulitzer Prize for Distinguished Commentary. She is credited with being one of the first women to introduce a woman's voice to the traditionally male-dominated op-ed pages.

PRETTY SOON, WE'RE GOING to have to amend the favorite mom and dad moniker of the moment. Those much vaunted helicopter parents are turning into black-helicopter parents. The image of parents hovering over their kids is morphing into the darker image of parents spying on their kids.

Here is the latest bit of high-tech surveillance equipment being marketed to parents. A company inauspiciously named Bladerunner has begun selling a jacket with a GPS device sewn into the lining. For a mere $500 plus $20 a month, a parent can track a child, or at least his jacket, all day long.

This is just a small addition to the family-friendly arsenal. We already have a full range of cellphones equipped with GPS. Indeed, the most common cellphone greeting is not "how are you?" but "where are you?" Parents are being sold the idea that they can trust but Wherify—the name of one among the many manufacturers offering services that beam your kids' whereabouts to your cellphone.

Want to monitor what your kids eat at school? MyNutriKids gives you the scoop from the lunchroom. Want an automatic alert if he got a B on the pop quiz? Go to GradeSpeed. Want to monitor her instant messages? There's IMSafer. And want to know if your 17-year-old is speeding? Alltrack not only tells you but lets you remotely flash the lights and honk the horn till she slows down.

There is also a "safety checks" service courtesy of Sprint to let you know if your kids showed up at soccer practice. And a "geofencing" service from Verizon that alerts parents if a child leaves the area circumscribed by her parents.

Next thing you know, there will be a chip implanted under your child's skin. No wait! Somebody's already invented that.

Once upon a time—that ever-popular era—a parent had two weapons for keeping kids out of danger: They kept their mouths open and their fingers crossed. Once upon that time, the second set of ears and eyes on children were those of neighbors.

Now we have a disharmonic convergence of anxieties, the dual fear that kids are endangered and/or dangerous, out of (our) control. There's the sense that we are raising children in a more treacherous culture. We teach preschoolers about stranger-danger, and only let them take candy from our friends if it's sealed. But even if kids aren't wandering in the neighborhood, they are wandering in the Internet with all of its unknown cul-de-sacs. What teenagers claim as MySpace, parents often see as an unmonitored public zone that leads predators to their doorstep.

At the same time, parents are expected to know and control everything their kids watch, eat, do—where they are, who they are texting, what channels and Websites they are viewing. So we have entered a technological arms race where even MySpace—whose space?—offers parents a way to track the changes posted by children.

"The culture of fear," according to Danah Boyd, a fellow at Harvard's Berkman Center for Internet and Society, "says that if you are not monitoring, you are a bad parent. Apparently, we're supposed to be stalking our kids." Having privatized child raising, we seem to be turning parents into private eyes.

I am by no means blasé about danger.

The implicit deal that comes with the cellphone is that kids get to roam and parents get to stay in touch. It's a mutual comfort society. But the downside to what MIT's Sherry Turkle calls "tethered adolescents" is real: "There's always a parent on speed dial." Teens are never really on their own. We may be protecting them right out of the ability to make their own decisions. Including their own mistakes.

It's not clear that a surveillance society actually provides more security. Consider the ubiquitous surveillance cameras at schools. What did they do for that Cleveland high school last month except to leave behind chilling, post-mortem pictures of the 14-year-old shooter? And how easy is it to drop the GPS jacket by the roadside?

Meanwhile, we may be raising a generation with low expectations of public privacy, trained by Big Mother to accept Big Brother. Did anyone notice how Lindsay Lohan and Paris Hilton made monitoring anklets into this year's fashion accessory?

As someone who has done my fair share of speed dialing, I am a believer in the text messaging and cellphoning that keeps parents and kids in contact. But there's a moment when the two-way tools of communication turn into the one-way tools of surveillance. Then the tether becomes a leash and parenting becomes stalking. We don't talk; we track. That's when it's time to say, Black Helicopter down. ■

From Reflection to Response

Responding to "When Big Father/Big Mother Spy on the Children"

Working with two or three of your classmates, plan a response to Goodman's essay. Identify the central issue and view that Goodman presents in her column, and then evaluate the case that she makes. The issue that will launch your response is the persuasiveness of Goodman's case. What will be your view? Has Goodman recognized a real problem or is it exaggerated? Has she adequately explained the significance or consequences of the problem she sees? Are there gaps or blind spots in her arguments? Has she adequately presented parents' legitimate concerns and motives? How will you support your view? What experiences or observations of your own will you include in your evaluation?

The short narrative that follows, "Impotent Demon" by LL Cool J, describes how the writer suffered a horrific experience as a child: his father shot his mother and his grandfather. "Impotent Demon" begins with his mother's recovery, when things appear to be getting better. As you read, make a note of the first *issue* that you see or sense during the mother's recovery. What are the words that raise the issue for you, and what do you think the issue is? Then make a note of each additional or related issue you notice as the story unfolds. Quote the exact words that express these issues.

LL Cool J { **IMPOTENT DEMON**

LL Cool J is an accomplished actor, writer, and hip-hop artist, who was born James Todd Smith in Bay Shore, Long Island, near New York City. "Impotent Demon" is an excerpt from his autobiography, *I Make My Own Rules*.

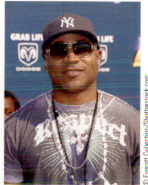

MY MOTHER ALMOST DIED. The shotgun pellets entered her lower back and fanned out. Several grazed her spinal column, and for a while she couldn't walk. She spent more than six months in the hospital recovering. During the first month, my grandmother took me to see her in the hospital every other day. I could only wave and smile at her through a glass partition, because they didn't allow little kids in intensive care.

After three months she was able to go from a wheelchair to a walker. From the walker she went to a cane, and then to a leg brace. At each transition, Roscoe was there. She met him a few months before the shooting at Northport VA Hospital, where she worked in the pharmacy. Roscoe was an assistant to a physical therapist. After the shooting he made it his mission in life to help my mother recover.

All the doctors told her she would never walk again, but Roscoe made her believe she could. And she did, which is a testament to her determination. Another trait I inherited from her. But from that point on, he had her head. With her gratitude, he wormed his way into her life. And my mother, feeling empty and vulnerable, just let him. She fell in love with the man she thought gave her the ability to walk again. I ain't mad at her, though, 'cause I know how that is. If you thought someone saved your life, you might fall for them too.

Roscoe was totally different from my father. He was always joking and playing around and laughing with my mother. Roscoe was one of those pretty boys. He had hazel eyes, a curly Afro, and a thick mustache. My father was big and tall, with big muscles and a thick waist. Roscoe was little, about five seven, the same height as my mother, and he wore platform shoes. I don't remember when I first laid eyes on him. It was like he was always there after my mother got out of the hospital. But I knew from jump he didn't like me, and I was definitely not fooling him. I must have been a threat to him.

Maybe because I was even smaller, he thought he could take out his frustrations on me. Maybe he just had a Napoleon complex because he was short. (All he ever talked about was this cousin of his who was "six feet four and two seventy-five" as if to show that somewhere in his genes was a big person. But that gene definitely missed him.)

Maybe he was jealous of the relationship I had with my mother and her family. Maybe I was an obstacle, getting in the way of his freedom with my mother. Or maybe I was just someone easy to take out his frustrations on. Easy target—little Napoleon's punching bag. Whatever the motivation, though, there's no real explanation for how he treated me.

When my moms got completely healthy she started working two jobs— the Suffolk County Developmental Center in Melville, Long Island, from 3:20 P.M. until 11 P.M., and the St. Alban's VA Hospital from midnight to 8 A.M. She had an hour to get from Suffolk County to Queens. Some nights she had to depend on Roscoe to drop her off and pick her up because he was using her car. Some nights he was late. Sometimes he made her wait for hours. He was too busy getting high, cheating on her, and beating on me.

My mother had a small, brick-and-tan house built for us in North Babylon. She had to work the two jobs just to pay the mortgage, and was carrying most of the weight. That left him at home with me the majority of the time and it was on—playtime for him. His idea of big fun was beating on me.

Roscoe beat me for just about anything. He would beat me for watching television, for lookin' at him funny, for looking out of the window watching other kids play. He didn't need a good reason. It was just a power trip. While my mother worked, Roscoe was home abusing her son. He was usually home when I came in from school, and it was like, "Let the games begin!"

He'd make me take off all my clothes and put my arms up on my bunk bed with the *Star Wars* sheets while he beat me. It was like the scene in *Glory* when Denzel Washington was getting beat down like a slave, except I was like eight years old. He'd even pull me out of the shower to get a beating. He didn't care how he beat me or with what.

He would rotate beating me with extension cords, vacuum cleaner attachments, and fists. He would punch me in the chest and knock the wind out of me—and then tell me to "raise up," get up for another punch. One time he threw me down a flight of stairs in our house. He even beat me for looking in the refrigerator. There's nothing worse than being hungry and staring into an empty refrigerator because your mother's man ate all the food after smoking a pound of weed—and then getting a beating for being hungry. Yo, it could freak you out.

It's around this time that I started wearing hats all the time. ■

From Reflection to Response   **Communicating Through Issues**

"Impotent Demon" is an excerpt from a book, not an essay, and as such, it presents a "slice of life." It does not express an explicit view or message at the end. All the same, do you think it contains an unexpressed, or *implicit*, view or message, and if so, what is it? Is there anything significant about LL Cool J starting to wear hats all the time? As you consider that question, ask yourself why LL Cool J chose to relate such painful details about his life. What do you think he learned, if anything, from what he went through, and what do you think readers can learn? Is LL Cool J's story relevant to an audience of general readers?

Discuss your observations with two or three of your classmates.

ORGANIZATION

> ❝ *A solution is useless without a good implementation plan.* ❞
> —CRAIG WORTMANN, *WHAT'S YOUR STORY?*

Once your plan for an essay is clear, the next step is to put the plan into effect. That means outlining, organizing, drafting, or some combination thereof. Organizing essays can frustrate writers at all levels. Students who have been taught to organize from an outline often try to make the essay fit a format—some tired template (introduction, body, and conclusion) or variation of the five-paragraph theme. This kind of mechanical organizing puts an essay into a straitjacket that limits its vitality. The one-paragraph introduction, three ideas, and mechanical conclusion of the five-paragraph essay is like a bicycle with training wheels, not a realistic way of going anywhere. The format makes organization easy, but at the cost of limiting your ability to develop ideas and communicate meaningfully. Readers don't want to read a training-wheel essay, and you are unlikely to ever see one in a real publication. To be a good writer, you have to move beyond the one-size-fits-all format, but what do you replace it with?

Compelling essays, whether they are written by students or professional writers, always have a fresh, organic feel and flow to them. At the same time, good essays strike us as focused and well-organized. What keeps them focused and organized, in spite of their organic feel, is the conceptual framework of issue and view that defines the direction, goals, and boundaries of the essay. Within this framework, a writer can compose with the freedom to be fresh, creative, and probing without getting lost or losing focus.

The Puzzle

We organize essays using principles of time (chronology), space, and logic in much the same way that we use grammar to make our words comprehensible. Most of us use these principles unconsciously. As a result, even experienced writers don't have easy answers for how they organize their writing, certainly no formulas. Most writers seem to rely on intuition, trial-and-error, and a little guesswork. They have a feel for organization, the way an experienced hunter has a feel for tracking game. As William Zinsser remarks in *On Writing Well*, organization is "like solving a puzzle."

For the experienced writer who has done it many times, solving the puzzle is interesting. For inexperienced writers, the puzzle can be exasperating. How can a college writer develop the kind of feel for organization that experienced writers have? The rest of this chapter will answer that question.

Solving the Puzzle

Where you express your view in an essay, early, late or in between, is the key to organization. Presenting the main issue to your reader is what starts the organizing process, but the process is incomplete until a central view (a message, argument, or thesis) is expressed and supported. The view can be expressed *anywhere* in an essay, from the first sentence (in tandem with the issue) to the last, or somewhere in between. This variable positioning of the view is the main reason that organization can seem so confusing.

The following is an example of a view expressed at the very beginning of an essay (in tandem with the issue):

> It is possible to stop most drug addiction in the United States within a very short time. Simply make all drugs available and sell them at cost. (Vidal)

The words "possible to stop...drug addiction" in the first sentence express the main issue (stopping drug addiction) *and* the view (that it is "possible" to do it). The next sentence elaborates on the view by explaining how to do it. The conceptual foundation of this essay is already complete. All the writer has to do now is explain and support this view.

Most essays begin by developing the main issue more extensively—for at least a paragraph or two—before expressing the view. Many essays delay expressing the view for longer than that, until the issue has been developed in considerable depth. Many other essays withhold the view until the end. In these essays, a detailed exploration of the issue, in effect, functions as support for the writer's view.

You can visualize and measure organization by two values, formal and informal, at opposite ends of a linear scale, as shown in Figure 2.1.

Formal Organization ——————— **Informal Organization**

Early View or Thesis   Late or Delayed View or Thesis

Academic Arguments   Narratives

FIGURE 2.1   **Formal and informal organization**

The Formal Organizational Pattern

An essay that expresses the view early follows a formal pattern of organization. This pattern parallels a method of logic or reasoning called *deduction*. *Deduction* means to proceed from a general principle or argument (a thesis) to specific facts and evidence, as illustrated in Figure 2.2.

Formal organization is the most common and traditional pattern for academic and scholarly writing. The view is presented early, after a relatively concise presentation of the issue. Most of the essay is devoted to supporting the central view or thesis. This approach usually is expected when you write a research paper or academic argument.

Opening/General Issue + View / Thesis	Middle/Specific Supporting details, reasons, and evidence	End/Specific To illuminate
• A presentation of the main issue that sets up a statement of the central view, argument, or thesis that the rest of the essay will support. • The presentation of the main issue should be as detailed as necessary to engage readers in the essay. However, a *general* premise, or thesis, sets the goal and direction of the essay. • No prescribed length for a formal opening exists. It can be as brief as a sentence or single paragraph, or as long as many pages, depending on the complexity and length of the essay.	• Develops effective support of the main view or thesis in a deductive pattern—in other words, factual evidence, specific information, and specific reasons. • Good support usually includes an honest examination of opposing views and counterarguments, and it should build toward a strong conclusion—in other words, from weaker evidence and reasons to the strongest.	• The strongest supporting point, evidence, or reason are the foundation of a good ending. Sometimes nothing more needs to be said. • However, writers sometimes amplify on the relevance and implications of their views, or they comment on unresolved issues or the need for further inquiry. • Good writers avoid mechanically repeating the main points of the essay, unless the essay is very long and complex.

FIGURE 2.2 **Essays at the formal end of the scale**

Below, the opening of an essay titled "Virtual Living" by Quentin Deakin follows a formal, or deductive, pattern of development.

> It's a fine but breezy late autumn day on a Channel ferry. I'm on deck watching the gulls trying to keep up. They sustain their flights into the headwind, only gradually falling away, a rare opportunity to see birds close up in flight. For every child up here enjoying nature, there are ten below deck either in the play area watching television or at the games consoles. For me they are living a virtual life. We are allowing this generation to grow up without an appreciation of what it is to be truly alive.

The brief, descriptive scene on the deck of the boat expresses the main issue: it is a fine day but most of the children are below deck watching TV or playing video games instead of "enjoying nature." The writer goes on to express a view, the thesis of the essay: "For me they are living a virtual life. We are allowing this generation to grow up without an appreciation of what it is to be truly alive." The rest of the essay focuses on developing and supporting that view or thesis.

Note that though the essay uses a formal pattern, the writer writes in the first person. The style of writing is casual or informal. After the opening, the writer shifts from narrative mode to argumentation, but he continues to write in the first person. A formal pattern, in other words, has no inherent bearing on the style of writing. (See pages 65–66 for more about organization and style.)

The scholarly article below, "How Trade Saved Humanity from Biological Exclusion," by R. D. Horan, E. H. Bulte, and J. F. Shogren, examines the extinction of our human relative, the Neanderthals. The article uses the formal pattern but a more impersonal, academic style.

> One of the great scientific puzzles is the cause of Neanderthal (Homo neanderthalensis) extinction around 30,000–40,000 B.P., when early modern humans (Homo sapiens) started spreading across the world. European Neanderthals are believed to have diverged more than half a million years ago from the lineage giving rise to humans (Mellars 1998), and the first Neanderthal-like creatures appeared around 300,000 B.P. (Gee 1996). Scientists have long asked what explains the species' sudden demise after such a long existence. Many anthropologists and paleontologists think it was not a coincidence that the fall of Neanderthals occurred at the same time when early humans rose to power. Homo sapiens are the suspected culprits, but exactly how early humans triggered Neanderthal extinction remains unsolved....

The authors are presenting the main issue here—what caused Neanderthal extinction? Since the issue is complex, the authors spend several pages discussing it, before they express the view or thesis that the rest of their article will support:

> Although no single theory is likely to explain all aspects of Neanderthal extinction...we find that the development of rudimentary economic exchange institutions—trade and division of labor—could have enabled humans to seal the fate of Neanderthals....

The Informal Organizational Pattern

An essay that delays the view, or expresses it toward the end, follows an informal pattern of organization. This informal pattern parallels a method of logic or reasoning called *induction*. Induction means to proceed from specific details and evidence to a general principle or argument, as illustrated in Figure 2.3.

Informal organization is the most common pattern for narrative and reflective writing. The view is delayed or expressed toward the end. Most of the essay is devoted to presenting and exploring the main issue in detail. The exploration of the issue functions as support for the view or thesis when it emerges.

Opening/Specific Issue presented in detail	Middle/Specific Development and exploration of the issue to support	End/General A View/Thesis to illuminate
• Begin with a specific and detailed presentation of the main issue.	• Develop and explore the details of the main issue in an inductive pattern, to seek and support a general view or message.	• Express a view or message ("thesis")—in other words, a lesson or general principle drawn from and supported by the specific details of the issue.

FIGURE 2.3   **Essays at the informal end of the scale**

Below is the opening of "He and I," an essay by Natalia Ginzburg, that follows an informal, or inductive, pattern:

> He always feels hot. I always feel cold. In the summer when it really is hot he does nothing but complain about how hot he feels. He is irritated if he sees me put a jumper on in the evening.
>
> He speaks several languages well; I do not speak any well. He manages—in his own way—to speak even the languages that he doesn't know.
>
> He has an excellent sense of direction. I have none at all. After one day in a foreign city he can move about in it as thoughtlessly as a butterfly. I get lost in my own city; I have to ask directions so that I can get back home again. He hates asking directions; when we go by car to a town we don't know he doesn't want to ask directions and tells me to look at the map. I don't know how to read maps and I get confused by all the little red circles and he loses his temper.

In this opening, the writer immerses the reader in the details of the issue, stark differences in personality between her and her husband. The essay explores their differences for several pages, and then near the end, she flashes back to when they first met and expresses a view about the nature of relationships, how they change who we are:

> I sometimes ask myself if it was us, these two people, almost twenty years ago...two people who conversed so politely, so urbanely, as the sun was setting; who chatted a little about everything perhaps and about nothing; two friends talking, two young intellectuals out for a walk; so young, so educated, so uninvolved, so ready to judge one another with kind impartiality; so ready to say goodbye to one another forever, as the sun set, at the corner of the street.

| From Reflection to Response | The Middle of the Formality Scale |

The discussion in this chapter centers on essays at the extreme ends of the formality scale, in other words, (1) essays that express the view or thesis in the opening (formal) or (2) essays that delay the view or thesis until the end (informal). These extremes are realistic and common, but they are not the only patterns writers use. Many essays develop a view or thesis somewhere between the beginning and end.

For an example, read the essay at the end of the chapter titled "Humans Ought to Use Nature to Serve Their Own Needs" by Tibor R. Machan. As you read, make notes about the organization. How many paragraphs are devoted to presenting the issue? In which paragraph does the writer express the central view or thesis? How would you summarize his main view, thesis, or argument? Which paragraphs, and how many, are devoted to developing and supporting the view?

Organization and Style

As suggested earlier, organization and style are distinct concepts. One does not determine the other. Decisions about organization and style are based on similar considerations—genre, purpose, subject matter, and audience—but the decisions are separate.

For example, an academic research paper almost always follows a formal pattern of organization, but depending on the subject matter and audience, the style can vary from formal—that is, specialized, objective, impersonal—to personalized and conversational. As the authors of *They Say / I Say* point out: "Academic writing doesn't mean setting aside your own voice....To succeed as a writer in college, you need not limit your language to the strictly formal."

Below is an example of an informal style in a formally organized essay by Gerald Graff, a professor at the University of Illinois and one of the authors of *They Say / I Say*. Graff begins his essay—"Hidden Intellectualism"—by expressing the view that colleges should do more to reach out to young people who are intelligent but not academically inclined. In support of the view, he writes:

> I offer my own adolescent experience as a case in point. Until I entered college, I hated books and cared only for sports. The only reading I cared to do or could do was sports magazines, on which I became hooked....In short, I was your typical, teenage anti-intellectual—or so I believed for a long time. I have recently come to think, however, that my preference for sports was not anti-intellectualism so much as intellectualism by other means.

The divergence between organization and style also can be seen in essays that follow an informal pattern but engage in complex thinking. The following is an example of an intricate, painstaking style in a personal essay titled "Leaving the Movies" by French cultural critic Roland Barthes:

> The film image (including the sound) is what? A *lure*. I am confined with the image as if I were held in that famous dual relation which establishes the image-repertoire. The image is there, in front of me, for me: coalescent (its signified and its signifier melted together), analogical, total, pregnant; it is a perfect lure: I fling myself upon it like an animal upon the scrap of "lifelike" rag held out to him...

Where to Express Your View

How do writers decide whether to express the view early, late, or somewhere in between—in other words, decide how to organize an essay? The genre, or kind of writing, and the expectations of your readers play a large role in the decision.

Readers of some academic genres—a classical argument or research paper—expect a view (or thesis) to be expressed early. They might feel confused or dissatisfied if it is not. Academic readers usually want to know what they are going to get out of an essay before they invest their time in it. The same applies to most business-writing genres—business letters, memos, and reports: the readers are busy and expect a view—what you are arguing or proposing—up front. On the other hand, readers of narrative (or story-based) genres are comfortable letting the story play out and discovering the view gradually or at the end. The tension and anticipation that the delayed view or thesis creates is part of the enjoyment. But there are *always* exceptions.

Now that you have tools for analyzing essays and communication in general, you will notice both patterns of organization, formal and informal, being used in every area of writing—in academic writing, business writing, journalism, and popular forms like blogs and songs.

Even movies, which are a narrative or story-based form (excluding *certain* "avant-garde" movies), sometimes follow a formal pattern—that is, they begin with the ending or resolution. A classic example is *Lawrence of Arabia*, which opens with the hero dying in a meaningless motorcycle accident. The rest of the movie supports the view that his life meant much more than his inglorious death.

To enhance your awareness of organization patterns, read the following three openings and try to determine if they are organized formally (in other words, include an early viewpoint, thesis, or central argument) or informally (in other words, delay the viewpoint, thesis, or central argument). As you read, if and when you identify a central view (the writer's view), highlight or write down the specific words that express it.

Naomi Wolf { THE PORN MYTH

AT A BENEFIT THE other night, I saw Andrea Dworkin, the anti-porn activist most famous in the eighties for her conviction that opening the floodgates of pornography would lead men to see real women in sexually debased ways. If we did not limit pornography, she argued—before Internet technology made that prospect a technical impossibility—most men would come to objectify women as they objectified porn stars, and treat them accordingly. In a kind of domino theory, she predicted, rape and other kinds of sexual mayhem would surely follow.

The feminist warrior looked gentle and almost frail. The world she had, Cassandra-like, warned us about so passionately was truly here: Porn is, as David Amsden says, the "wallpaper" of our lives now. So was she right or wrong?

She was right about the warning, wrong about the outcome. As she foretold, pornography did breach the dike that separated a marginal, adult, private pursuit from the mainstream public arena. The whole world, post-Internet, did become pornographized. Young men and women are indeed being taught what sex is, how it looks, what its etiquette and expectations are, by pornographic training—and this is having a huge effect on how they interact.

But the effect is not making men into raving beasts. On the contrary: The onslaught of porn is responsible for deadening male libido in relation to real women, and leading men to see fewer and fewer women as "porn-worthy." Far from having to fend off porn-crazed young men, young women are worrying that as mere flesh and blood, they can scarcely get, let alone hold, their attention. ■

Jon Kerstetter { TRIAGE

OCTOBER 2003, BAGHDAD, IRAQ. Major General Jon Gallinetti, U.S. Marine Corps, chief of staff of CJTF7, the operational command unit of coalition forces in Iraq, accompanied me on late-night clinical rounds in a combat surgical hospital. We visited soldiers who were injured in multiple IED attacks throughout Baghdad just hours earlier. I made this mental note: *Soldier died tonight. IED explosion. Held him. Prayed. Told his commander to stay focused.*

In the hospital, the numbers of wounded that survived the attacks created a backlog of patients who required immediate surgery. Surgeons, nurses, medics, and hospital staff moved from patient to patient at an exhausting pace. When one surgery was finished, another began immediately. Several operating rooms were used simultaneously. Medical techs shuttled post-op patients from surgery to the second-floor ICU, where the numbers of beds quickly became inadequate. Nurses adjusted their care plans to accommodate the rapid influx. A few less critical patient beds lined the halls just outside the ICU.

The general wanted to visit the hospital to encourage the patients and the medical staff. We made a one-mile trip to the hospital compound late at night, unannounced, with none of the fanfare that usually accompanies a visit by a general officer in the military. After visiting the patients in the ICU, we walked down the hallway to the triage room.

One patient occupied the triage room: a young soldier, private first class. He had a ballistic head injury. His elbows flexed tightly in spastic tension, drawing his forearms to his chest; his hands made stonelike fists; his fingers coiled together as if grabbing an imaginary rope attached to his sternum. His breathing was slow and sporadic. He had no oxygen mask. An intravenous line fed a slow drip of saline and painkiller. He was what is known in military medicine as *expectant*. ■

Gerald W. Lynch and Roberta Blotner { LEGALIZING DRUGS WOULD NOT LEAD TO A REDUCTION IN CRIME

In "The Challenge of Legalizing Drugs," Joseph P. Kane, S.J., presents a compelling description of the devastation wreaked on our society by drug abuse, but draws some troubling conclusions supporting the legalization of drugs. Father Kane argues that illegal drugs promote the proliferation of crime because of the huge profits associated with their import and sales. Violence and murder have increased dramatically as dealers and gangs compete for turf and drug profits. Youngsters are attracted to selling drugs in order to earn more money than they could ever hope to earn in legitimate jobs. Addicts steal to pay for their drugs. The criminal justice system is overwhelmed by the increasing number of drug arrests.

He further argues that because drugs are illegal, addicts are treated as criminals rather than as sick people in need of help. Addicts are often arrested and processed through the criminal justice system rather than offered legitimate rehabilitation or treatment. Finally, he states that illegal drugs exploit the poor, whose struggle to survive makes drug dealing a sometimes necessary alternative.

The solution to the problem, he concludes, is to legalize drugs while at the same time 1) changing attitudes within our society about drugs, 2) changing laws and public policy, and 3) providing drug education and treatment to all those who want it. While Father Kane's description of the toll drugs are taking on our society and our citizens is poignant, the solution to this problem is not legalization.

Legalizing drugs will almost certainly increase their use. This has been well documented in a number of studies. J. F. Mosher points out that alcohol usage and rates of liver disease declined significantly during Prohibition. Moreover, following repeal of the 18th Amendment, the number of drinkers in the United States increased by 60 percent. ∎

From Reflection to Response   Formal or Informal Openings

After analyzing the three openings on your own and deciding whether or not the central view is presented, form a group with two or three of your classmates and see if your conclusions and theirs are the same. In the openings that present a view or thesis, did you identify or highlight the same specific words?

From Reflection to Response   Planning an Essay and Drafting an Opening

Make a list of college-related issues that concern you, especially issues with which you have direct experience. (If you have a problem coming up with ideas, see pages 81–85 for information about useful invention techniques.) The following are examples of issues that concern many college students:

- Tuition costs
- Student loans and financial aid
- Dorm rooms and roommates
- Choosing an academic major
- Required (core, curriculum) courses
- Large classes
- Inadequate facilities or resources
- Cafeteria food
- Time management and workload
- Balancing studies and social life

- Textbook costs
- Joining a fraternity or sorority
- Alcohol and drug use
- Dating
- Homesickness and loneliness

After you identify an issue of significance to you, assume that you are going to write an essay about it. Apply the planning strategies you have learned: Who are you writing the essay for? Do you know the view you want to develop and support? How are you going to develop and support it?

Then consider how you will begin the essay—that is, how you will present the main issue in order to make it relevant and compelling to your readers. Will you organize the essay informally from that point, in other words, continue developing the issue and delay expressing your view or thesis, or will you take a formal approach and present the view or thesis early?

Draft your opening (one page, more or less). When you are finished, exchange drafts with a classmate and give each other feedback. Does the draft present the issue clearly? Is the reader drawn in? Does the organization—informal or formal—seem right for the essay, making it easy and interesting for a reader to follow?

EVALUATE YOUR LEARNING

1. What is your favorite genre of music? What are the key characteristics of the genre? Are there certain ideas or emotions that this genre manages to communicate better than other genres do?

2. Think of one of your favorite movies. What would you say is the main issue it deals with and the view it presents? How are the issue and view relevant to your life?

3. This chapter touched on several different kinds of college writing assignments—an analysis of a "text," a narrative essay, and an argument that supports a view with research, facts, and reasoning. Of the three kinds of assignments, which one would you feel most confident doing right now, and why? Which one would you feel least confident doing, and why?

4. If you were trying to help friends or siblings improve their writing, what are some concepts covered in this chapter that you think might help them?

5. What kinds of writing do you read for your own interest and pleasure? What qualities of this kind of writing appeal to you as a reader? Can you apply these qualities to your own writing?

6. Describe an effective piece of writing that you wrote for school or your own purposes. What motivated you to write the piece, and what is memorable about it to you?

ADDITIONAL READINGS

Tibor R. Machan { HUMANS OUGHT TO USE NATURE TO SERVE THEIR OWN NEEDS

Tibor R. Machan is a widely published, Hungarian-born American writer and libertarian philosopher. He is a professor emeritus of philosophy at Auburn University and a research fellow at the Hoover Institution.

NOT LONG AGO, A television talk show featured several animal rights advocates who enjoyed considerable airtime to defend their position both analytically and emotionally.

The program exhibited little of that famous media virtue: "balance." Almost everyone, including the host, championed the animal rights position. A law professor was on hand to raise a few skeptical questions, yet even this guest provided no clear-cut argument against the idea that animals enjoy rights akin to those of human beings.

One legal specialist claimed that animals must be regarded as possessing the exact same right to freedom that we assign to individual human beings. We heard how this guest had offered shelter to six dogs and were then told that this is a model that ought to be emulated throughout the world. The act was characterized as constituting a grant of asylum to the dogs—just as one might grant asylum to a political refugee from a totalitarian society.

This is also the position held by Harvard law professor Steve Wise, who has been making the rounds advocating full legal protection for at least "higher" animals like the great apes. Wise even claims to believe that these animals possess a moral nature—which, if true, would certainly give his case a fairly solid foundation inasmuch as rights are the political-legal instruments by which the moral nature of human beings is afforded scope and protection.

The Real Animal Kingdom

When the show was over, I merely filed away the experience, having already dealt with the issue of animal rights in many and various places. But then along came a National Geographic Explorer program on CNBC that in great detail depicted a polar bear's hunt for baby seals. First, we saw how the bear managed to capture and kill a baby seal. Next, we saw a mature polar bear fending off a young polar bear intent on the same seal carcass.

And then the narrator said something that was very interesting: "The older males are known to kill younger ones when fighting over carcasses."

The observation brought to mind the animal rights program of the night before and all its pat assumptions. How inconvenient that wild animals do not always behave with scrupulous decorum! No, the older bears do not share even a bit of the scavenged pickings but rather chase the young ones away or kill them outright, the better to keep everything for themselves. These greedy, violent animals seemed oblivious to the legal-moral status that had been conferred on them by the animal rights panelists just a few nights before. (Well, perhaps they don't get cable.)

Human Values

Of course, human beings have slugged it out over scarce resources through-out history (although in more recent times, as the values of civilization have taken stronger root, the win-win approach of the humane economy has tended to displace the dog-eat-dog approach of violence and warfare). But in most eras and in most places, it has always been a crime to kill a young person even in defense of one's property, let alone over wild prey. And where it isn't a crime, the bulk of world opinion regards such societies as barbaric and brutal, even in this age of multiculturalism.

So, given the evident lack of moral sense of even the highest rungs in the animal world, how can we seriously entertain the idea that animals have rights like human beings do? If such rights and such moral sensibility could be imputed to them, all the brutality in the animal world would have to be construed as criminal. But, quite sensibly, it is not. Why not?

Animals and Instinct

The reason is that animals, as a rule, behave as instinct dictates. In many cases, instincts dictate that the animals kill their own kind. Fish often eat their young, as do lions when impelled to do so by their genetic disposition, presumably to rid their pride of bastard offspring. Animals have no choice about how they conduct themselves, so no one can reasonably issue indict-ments against them, moral or legal (a practice once in force throughout Christian Europe, however). Inborn, hardwired prompters govern their lives.

On an intuitive level, everyone understands this, even the advocates of animal rights. Yes, some scientists argue that perhaps some of the higher animals, such as great apes or orangutans, have actually developed "culture," but this conclusion is based more on wishful—anthropomorphic—interpretation than any real evidence of culture and thought.

On the other hand, when people act brutally, we do feel justified in condemning them. Why? Why is it regarded as barbaric—and why should it be criminal—to kill children for fun, profit, or even survival if the lower animals can't rightly be blamed for violent behavior? Why indeed implore us to treat animals more humanely than some of us do?

I argue that what warrants such evaluation of human beings is that we are in fact fundamentally different from our animal kin in the wild.

Human Morality

The issues at stake are neither trivial nor academic, for they speak directly to the moral standing of human beings on this earth and how we should live our lives during the brief time we're here—whether we should be enjoying ourselves as best we can, or lashing ourselves continuously with a cat-o'-nine-tails in penitence for all the ants we stepped on today.

Sadly, environmentalists—not all of them, but all too many—seem to despise human beings and what we have wrought on this earth. They loathe all the invented, artificial, "unnatural" joys that spring from human imagination and human industry. From bridges to trains and planes to coal mines and soot-producing factories, it's all a dastardly affront, a rape of nature, in their eyes. A few—a very few, we must hope—would just as soon see humans out of the picture. The . . . sentiment of environmentalist David Graber, who hopes for the "right virus" to come along and decimate humanity, suggests that at least some radical environmentalists must be unhappy that medical researchers have killed a few monkeys in their search for the cause of the enigmatic SARS (severe acute respiratory syndrome) virus. Here we have a potentially dual affront: Animals have been killed, and humans might be saved.

It is indisputable that human activity sometimes causes environmental and other problems that must be dealt with. But it is one thing to argue for viable solutions to these problems. It is quite another to argue that humankind must leave the earth untouched altogether! I, for one, am grateful for all the despoiling. I don't want to do without air travel, word processing, or the Internet. I would have no fun—indeed, hardly any life—at all in a state of nature living off nuts and berries.

It is right for human beings to indulge in distinctively human activities. It is right to exploit nature to promote our own lives and happiness. There is no reason to feel guilt or shame about it. We are very much a part of nature—and nature is very much a part of us, too. [I argue] that no animals possess rights unless they also possess a moral nature—a capacity for discerning between right and wrong and choosing between alternatives. It is this moral capacity that establishes a basis for rights, not the fact that animals, like us, have interests or can feel pain.

This [essay] does not make a pitch for specific public policy changes but instead explores the standards of environmental philosophy on which public policy about the environment must rest. Central to this philosophy is the view that human beings are of paramount importance when public policies and, indeed, standards of personal conduct vis-à-vis the environment are being established. Whether it is possible to direct public policy toward an environmentalism that accepts humans as first in the hierarchy of nature depends on many factors, including what people believe about the place of human beings in the natural world. It also depends on whether a sound environmentalism can be crafted when humans are indeed put first. [I propose] that the answer is yes—indeed, that a human-first environmentalism is the only kind of environmentalism worth having.

Books

William M. Adams, *Against Extinction: The Story of Conservation.* London: Earthscan, 2004.

Priscilla Cohn, *Ethics and Wildlife.* Lewiston, NY: Edwin Mellen, 1999.

David Degrazia, *Animal Rights: A Very Short Introduction.* Oxford: Oxford University Press, 2002.

Jan Dizard, *Mortal Stakes: Hunters and Hunting in Contemporary America.* Amherst: University of Massachusetts Press, 2003.

Randall Eaton, *The Sacred Hunt.* Ashland, OR: Sacred Press, 1999.

Terry Grosz, *No Safe Refuge: Man as Predator in the World of Wildlife.* Boulder, CO: Johnson, 2003.

Arthur Jaggard, *The Ethics of Bow Hunting for Deer.* Bloomington, IN: Authorhouse, 2004.

David Petersen, *Heartsblood: Hunting, Spirituality, and Wildness in America.* Boulder, CO: Johnson, 2003.

Jim Posewitz, *Inherit the Hunt.* Guilford, CT: Globe Pequot, 2001.

Tom Regan, *The Case for Animal Rights.* Berkeley: University of California Press, 2004.

Philip Rowter, *The Hunting Instinct: Safari Chronicles on Hunting Game, Conservation, and Management in the Republic of South Africa and Namibia 1990–1998.* Huntington Beach, CA: Safari, 2006.

David E. Samuel, *Know Hunting: Truth, Lies, and Myths.* Cheat Lake, WV: Know Hunting, 1999.

Peter Singer and Jim Mason, *The Ethics of What We Eat: Why Our Food Choices Matter*. New York: Rodale, 2007.

Cass Sunstein, *Animal Rights: Current Debates and New Directions*. New York: Oxford University Press, 2005.

James A. Swan, *The Sacred Art of Hunting: Myths, Legends, and the Modern Mythos*. Minocqua, WI: Willow Creek, 2000.

Angus Taylor, *Animals and Ethics*. Peterborough, ON: Broadview, 2003.

The Animal Studies Group, *Killing Animals*. Urbana: University of Illinois Press, 2006.

Gary E. Varner, *In Nature's Interests?: Interests, Animal Rights, and Environmental Ethics*. New York: Oxford University Press, 2002.

Steven M. Wise, *Rattling the Cage: Toward Legal Rights for Animals*. Cambridge, MA: Perseus, 2000.

Periodicals

Jim Amrhein. "No Inherent Animal Rights: 'Righting' a Wrong." *Whiskey and Gunpowder*, 28 Mar. 2005. <www.whiskeyandgunpowder.com.>

Richard Brookhiser, "Straight Shooting." *National Review,* 20 Nov. 2006.

Tom Dickson, "Hunting Myths: Dispelling Some Myths About Hunting." Minnesota Department of Natural Resources, 2007. <www.dnr.state.mn.us/hunting/tips/myths.html.>

Kathy Etling, "Animal Activists Want Your Children." *The American Hunter*, Feb. 2007.

Camilla Fox, "The Case Against Sport Hunting." *Animal Issues*, Summer 2002.

Gary L. Francione, "Our Hypocrisy." *New Scientists*, 4 June 2005.

Graham Harvey, "Hunting Animals Is Wrong." *Open Democracy.net,* 13 Dec. 2002. <www.openDemocracy.net.>

Edwin Locke, "Animal 'Rights' Versus Human Rights." *Intellectual Conservatives.com*, 2 June 2005, <www.intellectualconservative.com.>

Dean Peerman, "Unsportsmanlike Conduct." *The Christian Century,* 6 Mar. 2007.

Michael Tichelar, "Putting Animals into Politics." *Rural History,* 6 Oct. 2006.

Steve Tuttle, "The Elusive Hunter." *Newsweek,* 12 Apr. 2006. ∎

Courtesy of Rob Rey

ROB REY

Ukulele Singer

In this painting, I was trying to capture the mood of an idle afternoon. The light spilling in through the window and cascading over this musician as she strummed her ukulele and became lost in its song presented the perfect scene to portray the strong emotional connection that we all have to music.

CHAPTER THREE

An Overview of the Writing Process

 I think good thoughts, whilst others write good words.
—William Shakespeare, Sonnet 85

CHAPTER LEARNING OBJECTIVES

In this chapter, you will learn to:

- ▶ View writing as a tool for learning and discovery, as well as communication.
- ▶ Generate ideas using invention activities like freewriting.
- ▶ Write good openings that serve as "hooks."
- ▶ Compose effective thesis statements.
- ▶ Draft and revise efficiently.
- ▶ Create a revision outline and incorporate feedback.
- ▶ Edit for quality control.

A PROCESS OF DISCOVERY

The concepts covered in the last chapter help you plan a writing task with communication goals in mind. This chapter focuses on the nuts and bolts of writing: what it takes to get it done and get it right. Like any skill, writing can be learned through practice. However, any kind of writing, whether it is an essay, a business report, a poem, or just an e-mail to a friend, involves a certain amount of creativity in the sense of making *something* out of *nothing*. In the words of Sidney Dobrin, an esteemed teacher and scholar, writing means "making stuff," turning something intangible— thoughts and feelings—into something tangible: meaningful words on a page or a screen.

The creative act adds an element of mystery to writing. Students often believe the mysterious part is the biggest part, that good writing requires special ability or talent. Though it is true that, at one time or another, most experienced writers will write something that materializes in a flash of inspiration, the flash of inspiration is an exception rather than the rule. To paraphrase the famous inventor Thomas Edison, for most of us most of the time, good writing is "one percent inspiration and ninety-nine percent perspiration"—a product of effort and hard work, not talent.

What students mistake for talent is really a mind-set. Good writers care about what they have to say, and they want to get it right. Writing is as hard for them as it is for anyone else, but they like to write, or love to write, because they consider writing an essential part of their life. They will do what it takes to make their writing express their ideas and feelings and connect to readers.

People who love writing include journalists, poets, screenwriters, novelists, playwrights, songwriters, and scholars. Lovers of writing are not necessarily highly educated or privileged. Tupac Shakur, who grew up poor, wrote plays and poetry as a child. He found writing to be a lifeline, a means of expression that did not require money, special equipment, or training—just the language he owned, something no one could take away from him. Many people, even those who are educated and well-off, find writing to be the same kind of lifeline.

The primary function of writing is communication, but writing is a means of learning and discovery as well. The focused thinking that good writing requires, the process of putting words on a page and shaping our thoughts, rewards us with discoveries about our feelings, ideas, values, and the world in which we live. When we finish writing something, we usually know and understand much more about the subject than we did when we started.

That sense of having learned and discovered is gratifying. It exhilarates us much like other achievements that come after hard work, such as winning a sporting event or delivering a fine performance.

COMMUNICATING TO SOLVE PROBLEMS

●●● **The Man Who Didn't Shower for a Year**

Rob Greenfield, a passionate outdoorsman and environmental activist, set out to change people's attitudes about the amount of water they use by taking a hundred-day bike ride across America and observing a strict set of eco-friendly rules that included bathing only with water "from natural sources such as lakes, rivers, and rain, or from wasted sources such as leaky faucets." Over the course of the bike ride, he consumed less than two gallons a day. After a hundred days without taking a shower, he decided to extend his goal to six months, then to a full year. At the end of the year, he posted a story about the experience on his website, RobGreenfield.TV.

Here is one of the photographs that Rob Greenfield posted with his story about his hundred-day bike ride across America.

"I might as well bring this up right away," Greenfield says at the beginning of the story. "You think I'm really stinky right? You think I smell like some sort of Swamp Monster? .... Actually, nope. When I say that I haven't showered, that doesn't mean that I wasn't bathing...."

Rob Greenfield's year without conventional bathing seems like an eccentric idea, but behind the idea is Greenfield's passion for preserving the earth's resources and encouraging others to conserve. As an activist, he works at getting his message out by blogging, maintaining a vibrant website, and using social media (he has thirty thousand followers on Twitter and nine thousand on Facebook). He and his campaigns have been featured on major media outlets including *USA Today*, *The Huffington Post*, *Fox News*, *BBC*, the Discovery Channel, and dozens of others. "Even if people start with little things," Greenfield told an interviewer, "it creates a ripple effect. I want people to feel inspired."

Changing people's attitudes about anything, whether it is the environment, race relations, women in combat, marijuana laws, or gay marriage, is seldom easy or done overnight. Achieving the goal requires a process. A successful process usually starts with believing in what you are doing, and applying yourself with the kind of passion, grit, and conviction that Rob Greenfield clearly has. If you had the time and resources to set off on a journey to inspire people to solve a problem, what would the problem be? What kind of journey would you take? What would you do to get the message out and create a "ripple effect"? ●●●

DEVELOPING A REVISION PROCESS

To write well, a work ethic is important. Most students enter college expecting to write the way they did in high school, but high school writing habits—dashing off an essay in one sitting and spell-checking it—are inadequate for most college and professional writing tasks. College writing, like any kind of writing that illuminates and engages readers, requires a composing process that will get it right. This process often is described as a series of steps or stages:

- ▶ Planning and invention (clarifying communication goals and coming up with ideas)
- ▶ Drafting
- ▶ Revising and incorporating feedback
- ▶ Editing

Writers go through this process to finish a task of any complexity, but they don't perform the steps in checklist fashion. Different writers have different work habits, and every writing task tends to get done differently. The steps or stages may recur or overlap. As you revise, you might need to adjust your initial plan, come up with new ideas, or redo an outline because the essay is losing focus or going in a different direction than you anticipated. As you edit, thinking your essay is finished, you might see a need to completely rewrite a paragraph, cut something out, or add new material to strengthen or replace a fuzzy idea or argument.

When all is said and done, the writing process boils down to a revision process: everything is up for revision. Good writing is a product of reviewing, reconsidering, changing, and improving at every stage from planning to editing.

PLANNING AND INVENTION

In the classic comedy *National Lampoon's Vacation*, a father, Clark Griswold, takes his family on a crazed, cross-country pilgrimage to a theme park called Walley World, only to learn upon arriving at the park that it is closed for maintenance. At that point, the father goes berserk.

The difference between Griswold's flawed vacation plan in the movie and a poorly planned essay is that the movie is funny.

Enough said about planning, which is covered in Chapter 2.

Invention, like planning, is mainly done before a writer starts a first draft. Invention means coming up with ideas—ideas for a subject to write about or for developing an essay you already have planned. Along with planning, invention helps a writer transition from thinking to actually writing. Invention is similar to practicing or warming up before an athletic event. Invention activities give a writer a head start and make drafting easier and productive. Some common invention activities include freewriting, brainstorming, clustering, taking notes, making lists, and outlining.

Freewriting

Freewriting, also called "automatic writing," is popular with song writers, poets, and fiction writers, because it taps into the subconscious and gets ideas flowing. Freewriting involves writing down all the thoughts that pass through your mind for a brief period of time, usually five minutes or so. The keys are (1) *write without stopping*, (2) don't think, and (3) don't censor or judge anything you write down. Just capture and record your thoughts even if they are garbled, trite, repetitive, embarrassing, and so forth.

Freewriting is an enjoyable way to generate ideas and retrieve thoughts and memories that are buried in your subconscious. Just a few minutes of freewriting can yield surprising results. The song "Nutmeg" by the Brooklyn-based rap group Das Racist reads very much like a product of freewriting:

> Queens Boulevard, Kierkegaard, hustle hard,
> hustle bustle OMG, on my guard, oh my god,
> Vic came back with three pizzas, give one to
> Dap, his stomach under-crowded, proud kid, young
> Samaritan, f___ a George Harrison, embarrassing,
> sitars no comparison, looking garish, hit it
> out the park, Roger Maris, plus Shea Stadium,
> Flushing, Corona, chop shop pop rocks,
> My Sharona, kid coboloba (?),
> hold up, slow up, blow up, pull-o, ver, get
> smart again, it's a cardigan, play the race card
> again, and again, and again, drinks at Bennigan's,
> where's Ralph Waldo, Ellison, person of
> color, yall can't see me? Shoot at you actors like a
> DP, Erna Anastos, aspestos
> apartments, smarter in a starter jacket, custom
> compartments, illuminati, in my mind soul and
> my body, pause, young Bobby, Digital
> hobby, physical, that's amazing, that's amazing
> that's amazing...

Brainstorming

Brainstorming is the same as freewriting except that instead of starting with a completely blank page, the writer directs her thoughts toward an idea, usually jotted down at the top of the page. For example, you might jot down a word or phrase that is central to your writing task: "Pressures of Being a Student-Athlete." However, the principles of writing without stopping and of recording all your thoughts, whether relevant or not, still apply.

Here is an example of brainstorming by a writer thinking about his relationship with his brother:

Brother

Leaving school in the Alps on the way to a long way from home with your habits and barber shop friends way too young for such leisure and attitude yet you were kind to spread the life around with anyone who loved to have fun and it was hard not to like the no responsibility of no hard work and entitlement of a generation being bashed by the greatest generation but then what did we really have to do with it all except live the tunes of anger and entitlement and the right to joy and the seeds of politically correct judgment songs, which is what they were and were not but who knows and who cares I mean I see that barber shop candy stripe whatever you call it definitely not unisex shave cream hot with towel and leather strap to sharpen the razor on and we were listening to Country Roads when the going was good...

Clustering

Clustering (sometimes called "mapping") is a more visual version of brainstorming. You write the main idea or keyword in the middle of a blank page. Then you generate associations that you circle and connect with straight lines, to create a grid of ideas. Figure 3.1 is an example of clustering about "expectations," created by writing consultants at the University of Richmond's Writing Center.

Tech Tip

If you like the concept of clustering to develop and visualize ideas, consider visiting websites such as bubbl.us, mindmup, and many others, which offer intriguing and advanced mind mapping tools.

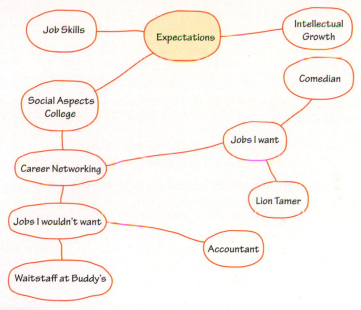

FIGURE 3.1 **Clustering example**

Notes, Lists, and Outlines

Note taking, list making, and outlining are traditional invention activities that also help develop ideas. The value of all these activities is that they give you a head start, so that when you sit down to write you already have ideas and material to work with. Planning, along with invention, helps you avoid the unpleasant experience of staring at a computer screen or blank piece of paper and feeling "blocked," not knowing what to say.

Below is an example of an informal outline for a research paper about children raised by same-sex parents. You can see how the outline will serve as a map or blueprint for a first draft, and it will give the writer a head start on the drafting process.

Example of an Informal Outline for a Researched Essay:*

Children Raised by Same-Sex Parents: Love *Is* Enough

1. **Introduction—issue + thesis:**

   Issue: Same-sex couples/parents with a child or children. I was raised by lesbian parents and consider myself well-adjusted and normal. But such a

---

*The sources referenced are just examples, not real sources.

family is outside the accepted "norm" and may be viewed as dysfunctional and harmful to the development of a child.

Thesis question: What is the effect, if any, on the well-being and social adjustment of a child raised by a same-sex couple?

Provisional/projected thesis: A child's well-being and social adjustment is not significantly affected by the nontraditional family and the parents' sexual orientation.

2. **Background information and opposing arguments:**

Background information: What defines "family" and "family values"?

Opposing views—i.e., some legitimate reasons why a child would be adversely affected (briefly summarize): (1) The child might be influenced to become homosexual (Tuckmann & *L.A. Sentinel* series, myself? or Prof. Silva). (2) Child would be deprived of healthy gender-identification—i.e., role models for both sexes (Parks & Rodriguez). (3) Family would lack legitimacy and consequently stability (esp. Parks & *L.A. Sentinel* series). (4) Child would experience inevitable stress due to social disapproval and, as a result, become alienated, isolated, and depressed (Parks & Rodriguez).

3. **Thesis support/body:**

Try to build from the least important to the most important points, so as to end with your strongest point or argument:

► No evidence that parents' sexual orientation influences child's. Same situation as heterosexual parents with child who turns out gay. Sexual orientation not a lifestyle choice. Gay parents actually more open, understanding, and accepting re: sexual orientation (Tuckmann & *L.A. Sentinel* series, myself &/or Prof. Silva).

► No evidence of a pattern of gender-role behavior that differs from other kids (as regards toys, types of games, TV programs, hobbies, social activities, kinds of friends, etc.)....(Parks & Rodriguez)....

► Misconception that homosexual parents are less committed to each other than heterosexuals. Stats show same level of commitment and family responsibility (myself? or Prof. Silva; Parks & *L.A. Sentinel* series).

► (Maybe?) In reality, no perfect "Leave It to Beaver" families truly exist....Show range of dysfunctions across the board (APA, Parks & Rodriguez)....

► No significant evidence of emotional damage or alienation from social disapproval, etc. (Parks & Rodriguez, and me).

4. Ending:

Quote from APA study or Prof. Silva interview (?).... Concede imperfect family for a child, yet perfection doesn't exist (?)....

From Reflection to Response   **Coming up with Ideas**

Sometimes the sum and substance of planning and invention is nothing fancy—just a matter of jotting down relevant thoughts. For many writers, like novelist John Dufresne, simply making a list is a useful invention activity. In his guidebook for creative writers, *The Lie That Tells a Truth*, Dufresne says, "Lists can be helpful for getting in touch with your useable past and your obsessions."

With this in mind, spend five to ten minutes creating a list in *one* of the categories below (suggested by Dufresne). After you have created your list, pair up with a classmate—preferably someone who has made a list on the same subject—and discuss whether your lists generate any interesting and usable ideas or issues for an essay.

1. List all of the friends you've ever had. Put an X beside those you've lost contact with.

2. List all of the moments you'd live over again for whatever reason. (Examples: To get them right this time. To enjoy them afresh.)

3. List everything you've ever done that you are ashamed of.

4. List your favorite songs.

5. List your goals for the next five years. Prioritize them.

THE ROUGH DRAFT

The first draft of any essay or written document is called a "rough draft" because it is supposed to be messy and deficient, "not for prime time," just material for you, the writer, to work with and improve. All the same, a rough draft can be hard to write because it involves a big first step in the writing process—going from ideas and notes to a tangible product you hope will evolve into a good finished essay.

First drafts usually fall *far* short of what we want to accomplish. To avoid discouragement, keep the purpose of the draft in perspective: it is just a starting point, something to work with. Getting the draft done is your mission and an accomplishment in itself. The following are some general tips for getting a draft done:

▶ **Write freely:** Write freely and uncritically. Don't worry about grammar, wording, transitions, and so on. You will address and improve those problems later. Stay focused on your goal, which is getting material down.

▶ **Be comfortable:** Write in your comfort zone. Writing is work. You want to be productive, but make it as easy on yourself as you can. If you need peace and quiet, find a quiet time and place. If tranquility makes you nervous, play music, go to a coffee shop, or write by a swimming pool or on a park bench. If you are a morning person, write when you wake up; if not, write at night. If you freeze up in front of a computer screen, compose in longhand on a writing pad; type it up and revise on the computer later. If writing on the computer works best for you, do that. The only rule is that you need to be productive.

▶ **Set a time limit:** Some writers can write for hours and stay focused. If you can do that, good, but most students cannot, and they end up wasting time or agonizing unproductively. Setting a realistic time limit before you start can make a writing task less intimidating. If an hour is realistic for you, write productively for an hour, then do something else, and write for another hour later in the day or the next day. You can produce a lot in an hour if you prepare and stay focused. Few college writing assignments can be drafted in one sitting anyway.

▶ **Talk about your draft:** Talking about a writing task usually makes it easier. The verbalizing process helps dissipate tension, clarify goals, and overcome problems. You don't need to talk to an expert. Running ideas by a classmate or friend can be helpful.

▶ **Start well before the deadline:** Start and finish your first draft *early* in the composing process. The point of a rough draft is to get material down so that you can improve it later. If you write your draft just before a deadline, you won't have time to improve it, which means you will end up turning in a rough piece of writing, not the finished product that college professors expect.

▶ **Reward yourself for writing the draft early:** Reward yourself for writing the draft and, especially, for finishing the draft early.

Procrastination is the main reason students get behind on writing assignments and end up doing poorly. Students who procrastinate usually prioritize fun before work. They put off the writing assignment and go to the movies, concerts, sporting events, and clubs, or they play video games, hang out at the rec center, drink beer, and so on.

Ironically, students who don't procrastinate, who manage their time well and do what it takes to get good grades, also go to the movies, concerts, sporting events, or play video games, and may even drink beer. They just do those things in a different sequence—*after* they finish their work, instead of before or while they should be working.

If you have problems with procrastination, try sequencing fun and work differently. Unless you intend to drop out of college, you will end up doing the work anyway; so why not do it in a way that yields better results? Get the draft done early instead of playing a video game, but reward yourself after you write the draft by playing the game, or going to the movies, or to a club, or doing something else that's fun for you. Whatever you enjoy doing, you will enjoy it more after accomplishing something.

WRITING THE OPENING

Writing the opening sentences and paragraphs of an essay often is the hardest part. According to conventional wisdom, a good opening is supposed to hook readers into an essay. A hook is an inspired or creative way to captivate readers. Unfortunately, inspiration and creativity are fair-weather friends: they will fail you at inconvenient times. Some writing guides come to the rescue with a handy list of "opening gambits" for students to try:

▶ Surprising facts

▶ A vivid scene

▶ An intriguing hypothetical situation

▶ Historical information

▶ A provocative quotation

▶ A "you-are-there" scenario ("You are thirty years old. For the past seven years, you have had a secure job with a major insurance company . . .")

The problem for a writer is which gambit to use, and why one and not another? In fact, lists like these have little value for most of us. Good ideas and writing strategies are not gambits that we pluck from a list. They come from having something to say and caring about your subject. The need to consciously manufacture a strategy suggests a lack of conviction on the writer's part and brings to mind gambits that launch trite assessment essays. For example, the unnecessary definition:

> According to Webster's dictionary, friendship is defined as... (Everyone knows what friendship means.)

Or the pseudo-controversial question:

> Do you think it is right to murder innocent children? (Everyone knows it is wrong to murder *innocent* children.)

Or the pointless generalization:

> In today's society, people like to enjoy themselves. (As opposed to when people liked to suffer?)

The truth is, the basis of a good opening *and* a hook is always at your fingertips: it is the *issue* driving the essay. No matter how inspired or creative a hook is, it has to present the main issue, or it will be irrelevant. A hook expresses what deeply concerns or captivates a writer about the issue she is writing about. If inspiration or creativity helps you convey that, great! If not, no worries. You can do fine without a creative hook. An honest statement of the main issue and why you consider it important will do the job.

If we look at compelling essays, we see again and again that they open with a presentation of the main issue. Here is the first sentence of George Orwell's narrative essay "Shooting an Elephant":

> In Moulmein, in Lower Burma, I was hated by a large number of people— the only time in my life that I have been important enough for this to happen to me.

Readers grasp the issue of Orwell being hated, and they connect to what they are reading. Being hated is not the whole issue. We see a related issue lurking, the fact that Orwell somehow is important, and his importance is linked to the hatred he inspires, perhaps even the source of it. But hatred is a core issue in the essay. By expressing it in the first sentence, Orwell is already bringing the essay into focus, signaling its purpose and hooking the reader. No one likes to be hated. Why is the writer hated? We want to find out.

Here is the opening of an essay titled "Under the Influence" by Scott Russell Sanders:

> My father drank. He drank as a gut-punched boxer gasps for breath, as a starving dog gobbles food—compulsively, secretly, in pain and trembling.

The opening tells us that the issue of a father's alcoholism is close to the writer's heart. Candid words and powerful images hook us into the essay.

Here is the opening of *Doublespeak* by William Lutz:

> There are no potholes in the streets of Tucson, Arizona, just "pavement deficiencies." The Reagan Administration didn't propose any new taxes, just "revenue enhancement" through new "user's fees." Those aren't bums on the streets, just "non-goal oriented members of society." There are no more poor people, just "fiscal underachievers." There was no robbery of an automatic teller machine, just an "unauthorized withdrawal".... The US [sic] Army doesn't kill the enemy anymore, it just "services the target." And the doublespeak goes on.

We understand that the issue here is language being manipulated to warp reality, an issue that affects all of us when we find out that words like "natural," "lite," and "nutritional" often don't mean what we expect.

From Reflection to Response — Starting from the First Sentence

This exercise will help you review some of the concepts for a good opening that are covered in this chapter.

According to journalist William Zinsser, "The most important sentence in any article is the first one. If it doesn't induce the reader to proceed to your second sentence, your article is dead." Effective writers say something meaningful, interesting, and relevant in the first sentence—usually by projecting the issue they are writing about.

On the next page are six opening sentences.* Read them and rank them on a scale from 1 to 5 based on the interest they generate (1 being the least interesting, 5 being the most). After ranking them, write down what you find interesting (or not so interesting) about each sentence. Note whether the sentence conveys an issue or not, and what you think the issue is.

---

*In order, these openings are from: "Breast Cancer and (Lack of) Social Graces," by Hollye Harrington Jacobs; "Guns on Campus: Ask the Virginia Tech Survivors, Not the Armchair Quarterbacks," by John Woods; "Let's Put Pornography Back in the Closet," by Susan Brownmiller; *Neither Here Nor There: Travels in Europe*, by Bill Bryson; "Black Men and Public Space," by Brent Staples; and "My Life As a Dog," by Chuck Palahniuk.

After you finish, form a group with two or three of your classmates and see if your rankings and assessments match. Do you and your classmates agree about the issue that the opening sentences project?

1. Socializing sure has changed since my breast cancer diagnosis.

2. At the Texas Capitol this Wednesday…there will be a public hearing on four bills that would force colleges and universities to allow handguns in classrooms.

3. Free speech is one of the great foundations on which our democracy rests.

4. I brought with me a yellow backpack so enormous that when I went through customs I half expected to be asked, "Anything to declare? Cigarettes, Alcohol? Dead horse?"

5. My first victim was a woman—white, well-dressed, probably in her early twenties.

6. The faces that make eye contact, they're twisted into sneers.

THESIS STATEMENTS

Along with hooks, students associate openings with thesis statements, and sometimes they are confused about what a thesis is and how to compose a good one. As you already know from reading Chapter 2, a thesis is nothing more than the main view, message, or argument that an essay supports. The thesis does not always have to appear in the opening part of an essay, but every essay needs a view, or thesis, in order to complete the communication process. In fact, a thesis is a feature of communication that we use every day when we express a view or opinion about any issue or problem.

If you tell a friend, "Buying a low-mileage used car is a better deal than buying a new car," that is a thesis statement: it expresses a view (buying a used car is more economical) about an issue (getting a good deal). The view, in effect, is a thesis because it could be right or it could be wrong, but it can be defended or supported. If you say, "Living with someone before getting married is the best way to ensure that you will be compatible partners," that is a thesis: it expresses a view (living together before marriage is a good idea) about an implicit issue (being compatible with a future spouse) but the view needs to be defended or supported with statistics, examples, reasons, and so forth, in order to be more than just a personal opinion.

The problem many college students have with thesis statements comes from previous instruction. Students often are taught in secondary school that a thesis is a single sentence with three supporting points that goes at the end of the opening paragraph. This definition is unrealistic. It makes a thesis statement more of a sterile formality than an expression of conviction or insight.

Professional articles and essays seldom have a single-sentence thesis with three supporting points at the end of the opening paragraph. Therefore, it should come as no surprise that, when students follow this formula, or feel obligated to do so, they often produce "thesis statements" that are bland, pointless, or predictable, and they set up uninteresting essays.

So what's the best way to write a thesis statement? The following guidelines will walk you through some of the common fallacies associated with thesis statements and what to do about them.

Placement of Thesis Statement

Always expressing the main view, or thesis, in a particular place (at the end of the first paragraph) is a bad idea. As noted earlier, where the thesis goes in an essay can vary, depending on the kind of essay you are writing and the strategies you want to use. The thesis can be in the very first sentence, or *before* the end of the first paragraph, or in the second or third paragraph, or later in the essay, or at the very end.

Although an essay has no set place for a thesis to go, many essays, especially academic essays, use the formal or deductive pattern of organization described in Chapter 2. In doing so, they present the central view or thesis *early* in the essay, that is, in the opening. Although *early* does not always mean in the first paragraph or at the end of the first paragraph, if the essay is relatively short—say, five pages or fewer—the first or second paragraph is a common location. Many of the writing projects in this course—for example, an academic argument or research paper—normally call for a formal pattern of organization. As such, when you are composing these projects, you should be thinking about an early presentation of your view or thesis, although not always or necessarily in the opening paragraph. On the other hand, some of the projects in this course— for example, the narrative essay (Chapter 4) and profile (Chapter 5)—often, or usually, follow an informal pattern of organization and, therefore, present the view or thesis later in the essay or at the end.

Length of Thesis Statement

The idea that a thesis statement has to consist of one sentence is an oversimplification. A statement by definition is an expression of something. It *can* be a single sentence, but it also can be more developed and complex—a paragraph, a page, or several pages: a policy statement or a declaration. A good thesis often is developed over several sentences or, sometimes, in long articles over several paragraphs or even pages. The number of supporting points depends on the complexity of the view or argument being presented.

Although composing a good thesis often takes more than a single sentence, when you distill or sum up your thesis in a sentence, you help your readers understand where the essay is going and what you are trying to accomplish. If you are writing in a formal pattern, which emphasizes argumentation, a succinct statement of the thesis as part of your opening is something for which to strive.

Number of Supporting Points in the Thesis Statement

As to mapping or previewing your supporting points in a thesis statement, having a mandatory three supporting points is illogical, but previewing the support you will develop later can help you focus and organize the essay and, again, help readers follow along. With that said, if your supporting points are numerous or complicated, including a preview in a one-sentence thesis statement can be cumbersome or impossible. Mapping or previewing is not a requirement of a good thesis statement, but when doable, it is worth considering. A common option is to include information that maps or previews your thesis support in the sentences that surround the central statement.

Composing an Effective Thesis Statement

Many handbooks and textbooks cover thesis statements in excruciating detail, implying that to write one takes technical proficiency. In fact, a good thesis statement merely expresses an insightful or stimulating view or argument and does not require any special skills to write. Composing a thesis statement is as simple as saying, "The worst way to promote 'green' polices is to spread exaggerated fears about natural disasters." No tricks or formulas are needed. When you are writing your thesis, use common sense and ask yourself some simple questions:

► Is the statement argumentative—that is, does it need to be defended, supported, or proven?

► Is it interesting? Does it present an idea that is fresh or surprising? Does it give an intelligent reader something to think about and a reason to continue to read?

► Is it clear?

► Is it specific enough to be supported in the essay?

If the answer to any of these questions is "not really," then you need to rethink your thesis or, perhaps, your whole essay. The following box contains some examples of thesis statements that need rethinking and revising:

Weak Thesis Statement		Improved Version	
Weak Thesis Statement	This essay will consider the effects of concussions on professional athletes. *("Considering effects" does not express a view or argument. Today, most readers know that concussions are dangerous. The thesis suggests that the essay will merely review information that readers may already know or can find on their own.)*	**Improved Version**	Much of the antisocial behavior that professional athletes are criticized for may be the result of concussions rather than character defects. *(This statement presents a plausible argument that the writer will have to support.)*
Weak Thesis Statement	There is no doubt that texting while driving can lead to fatal accidents. *(Not exactly an eye-opener. If little to no doubt exists, no compelling argument exists either. This thesis statement implies that the essay is targeting readers who are out of touch.)*	**Improved Version**	Raising awareness among young drivers about the dangers of distracted driving—especially texting—is the best approach to reducing the rate of fatal accidents. *(The statement puts forth a solution to the problem—"raising awareness"—and suggests that other approaches, such as laws and texting-while-driving "bans," are not as effective. Again, this statement presents a plausible argument that the writer will have to support.)*
Weak Thesis Statement	Marijuana should be legalized because we, as Americans, have a constitutional right to the "pursuit of happiness." *(The logic behind the statement suggests that Americans have the constitutional "right" to do anything that makes them happy. Even a "free country" cannot be that free.)*	**Improved Version**	Now that legal marijuana is available in some states, we have evidence that legalization does not lead to rampant and reckless use. *(The statement implies that the writer has factual and objective evidence to support the argument.)*
Weak Thesis Statement	If we all band together, world poverty can be eradicated. *(The statement makes a naive assumption—that people will band together for a good cause—and proposes to solve a problem that is more than likely too large and complex for an essay.)*	**Improved Version**	One approach to dealing with world poverty is to offer tax incentives to multinational companies that invest in the economic development of underdeveloped countries. *(This argument may or may not be realistic, but it is specific, reflects original thinking, and can be supported with reasoning and evidence.)*

Can a Question Be a Thesis Statement?

Students sometimes ask if a *question* can serve as a thesis statement. In fact, a good question, posed early in an essay, can function much like a thesis—that is, focus the essay and motivate readers to continue to read. But by definition, a question does not express a view or an argument. In that sense, a question cannot be a thesis, although the *answer* to the question—assuming the question raises an issue—can be, and often is, a thesis.

If, however, you are writing a scholarly essay that calls for an early presentation of a view or thesis—for example, an academic argument or research paper—you should avoid substituting a question for a clear view or thesis. Readers of scholarly essays expect a compelling thesis statement and are liable to see a question as lazy or inadequate.

On the other hand, many kinds of essays do not *require* a formal pattern or an early thesis to meet the readers' expectations. The writer decides. In writing informal essays, you can raise a question to serve as a thesis, but the actual thesis will be the answer to the question that your essay provides.

REVISION AND REWRITING

> ❝ *I have rewritten—often several times—every word I have ever published. My pencils outlast their erasers.* ❞
>
> —VLADIMIR NABOKOV

Revision literally means to "look again" or re-see. When we revise, we return to a draft, look for ways to improve it, and rewrite until we make it as good as we can. Revision is the reality behind good writing, but it is also the reality behind most forms of communication that have lasting value or relevance— movies, songs, photography.

Movies go through an extensive revision process called "postproduction" before they are ready for distribution. An axiom of filmmaking is that movies are made in the cutting room, rather than on location or the sets. Directors shoot many more hours of footage than the two hours of film we usually see. During postproduction, sound, music, and special effects are added, while the original footage is cut, moved around, and reassembled for optimum pacing and flow. Table 3.1 compares the steps taken in producing a movie to those taken in composing an essay.

Music is produced in a similar way. Recording sessions take time; musicians have to be patient and attentive to details. During a studio session, a song

TABLE 3.1 Movie production versus writing an essay

Movie Production		Essay Writing Process	
Preproduction	Writing a story synopsis and treatment; composing a screenplay and storyboards; setting up the production and shooting schedules.	**Invention and planning**	Coming up with ideas; evaluating ideas; conceptualizing issue and view; storyboarding or outlining.
Production	Filming all the scenes.	**Drafting**	Getting the rough version of the complete essay down.
Postproduction	Adding visual effects, sound effects, and music. Cutting and editing the film footage (a process called "montage"), to give the movie a good flow, pace, and clarity.	**Revising and editing**	Adding details, cutting unnecessary segments and words; polishing the essay, to give it a good flow, pace, and clarity.

almost never is recorded from beginning to end. Musicians play segments, hear something, stop, talk about it, reconsider, and start again. The music is mixed and remixed to produce the final product that people hear.

Professional photography requires the same kind of production process and revision. A photographer will take hundreds of photographs for an ad or magazine cover and then crop and meticulously photo-edit the best one for ideal exposure, color, and other effects.

Writers revise for the same reasons filmmakers, musicians, and photographers do. No rules exist for revising, but revision requires time and emotional distance from previous drafts, to enable the writer to "re-see" the material objectively. Right after drafting, we are too close to the material to see it the way a reader would. Waiting a day or so gives us a better perspective for judging and making improvements. The key is time. Revisions need spaces of time, to allow us to make effective changes.

Criticism, Feedback, and Help from Your Campus Writing Center

One of the best ways to get an objective perspective is to share a revision (a readable draft) with a friend, family member, or classmate. Your instructor may organize peer reviews in class or online for this purpose. Feedback from a variety of people, including people who are not in your class, can be very helpful. Sometimes your work will be criticized. Sometimes the feedback will be inconsistent and contradictory. You should process all of it but only apply what makes sense to you.

Another option is to get help with a draft at your campus writing center. Almost all colleges and universities have writing centers with trained tutors who are available to help you with your writing. Tutors can give you insightful feedback and help with all areas of your writing.

Revision Outlines

Outlines traditionally are written at the beginning of the writing process, but doing an outline while revising can be helpful, too, especially if you are having problems with organization and coherence. A revision outline is sometimes called a "reverse outline" (in other words, it is done after, instead of before, a draft). This kind of outline gives you an overview of what you have written and helps you see if your writing has missing, disconnected, or unnecessary parts.

The procedure for doing the outline is simple: go through the draft paragraph by paragraph and *briefly* (in a few words) summarize the content of each paragraph. Avoid being too detailed or specific. Your goal is to map the essay so that you can read it structurally and see how the parts fit together.

Doing a reverse outline is also a useful tool for analyzing someone else's writing, for example, a text you want to evaluate and respond to. The outline gives you a breakdown of the main ideas and how they are ordered.

From Reflection to Response | **Creating a Revision Outline of a Text**

To practice doing a "revision outline" of a text, read "Black Men and Public Space" at the end of the chapter (page 109) or "My Life As a Dog" (page 112). Jot down the main idea of each paragraph, and then use the outline to help you analyze the essay. Your goal is to identify the central issue the writer addresses in the essay and the main view (or thesis) the essay supports. As you do this activity, think about the following:

● "Black Men and Public Space" is a well-known essay that has appeared in many anthologies. It was first published in 1986. As you read and analyze it, ask yourself if it is still relevant today, and if so, why.

- "My Life As a Dog" presents an issue that could be seen as the exact opposite of "Black Men and Public Space." As you read and analyze "My Life As a Dog," ask yourself if it meets the criteria for an essay that you have learned in this course. Specifically, is a clear view expressed, and if so, what is it, and why is it relevant?

EDITING FOR A PROFESSIONAL PRESENTATION

Most writers edit as they revise, but editing is not the same thing as revising: it means correcting. As a distinct step in the writing process, editing comes last, when a writer has finished revising and generally is satisfied with the piece. Editing is like a product inspection in manufacturing, a final check for quality control before delivery.

Although diligent editing is essential, it does not translate to good writing. A perfectly edited essay can be dull and superficial. On the other hand, an interesting essay that is poorly edited can be like a defective DVD: readers may *want* to read the essay but the glitches and bugs are too annoying.

Good writers enjoy editing because they appreciate the craft of writing and find the fine points interesting, but one thing about editing that everyone likes is that the hard work is over. Once you finish editing an essay, you can feel like the great basketball coach Red Auerbach did when he knew his team (the Boston Celtics) had a game all but won: he would light a cigar, sit back on the bench, and enjoy the moment.

Some general tips for effective editing follow.

Don't Rely on Spelling and Grammar Checkers but Use Them

Effective editing requires reading over every word in your document. The spell-checker on your word processor is a useful starting point for editing but *not* a substitute for reading. A spell-checker won't catch missing words, or typos like "Go to my wed page" (since wed is a legitimate word, spell-check won't flag it). A spell-checker also won't flag sound-alike words that are misspelled, for example "Let's meet at you're house" or "Your a nice person." Nevertheless, a spell-checker does rid a document of many misspellings. Today, submitting a document littered with misspellings is not just unprofessional but inexcusable.

Grammar checking has even more limitations than spell checking, and a writer cannot rely on it to edit a document. A grammar check can flag perfectly fine sentences and constructions. Nevertheless, grammar checking sometimes calls attention to legitimate issues that need fixing.

Ask Someone to Read Your Final Draft for Typos and Other Problems

A reader who is not as familiar with a document as the writer often will catch mistakes, typos, missing words, and other kinds of problems that the writer misses through familiarity and fatigue. Ask someone to read over what you've written and help you identify mistakes and readability problems.

Read the Draft Out Loud or Try Text-to-Speech

Reading a document to yourself or someone else out loud can be an effective way to edit. When you pronounce and hear the words you wrote, you catch errors that the eye might skip over when you silently reread.

"Text-to-speech" software offers an appealing alternative to reading out loud: it lets your computer read the document to you. Using the text-to-speech feature on a computer may sound like a "geeky" way to edit, but it can be very helpful. By the time you reach the editing stage of the writing process, you are likely to be tired. Text-to-speech offers a change of pace. Instead of poring over the document again, you can listen to what you've written. The computerized voice is a bit slow and monotonous, but it gets the job done. If your writing has missing words, misspellings, awkward sentences, and so on, you will hear them, and, in fact, you are more likely to notice than you would through silent reading.

From Reflection to Response   **Activity One: Thinking about Editing**

Read the excerpt titled "Simplicity" (page 100), from William Zinsser's *On Writing Well*. Working with two or three classmates, review the editing changes Zinsser makes on page 102 (in the paragraph beginning with "The carelessness can take any number of forms").

Discuss why Zinsser made the changes that he did, and how you think they improve the readability of the paragraph. After you have finished discussing Zinsser's passage, read the paragraph below from the draft of a student essay. Working as a group, revise and edit the paragraph to improve the clarity and readability:

> Scientific proof has shown that women mature faster then men. If this is the case, why are there more and more cases where women are the older ones in the relationship? There is a noticeable trend that its has become popular for the women to be the dominant figure in the relationship. This has begun to take effect because of the shift in the rolls in society for

both men and women and the craving for a motherly figue for the man. After experiencing a failed attempt at this "new love", I believed this to be impossible, but I have come to realize that it is possible for these relationships to work.

Activity Two: Thinking about Your Own Writing Process

Read "The Maker's Eye," by Donald Murray (page 104). As you read, jot down the advice that seems most important and helpful to you. When you finish, write a brief description of your own writing process. Try to remember specific writing projects you have done, either on your own or for school. How do you come up with ideas? Where and when do you like to write? How much revising do you do? End your description by commenting on advice from "The Maker's Eye" that might help your writing.

EVALUATE YOUR LEARNING

1. What do you like most about writing, and what don't you like?

2. Of the "invention" activities covered in the chapter (for example, brainstorming, making lists, and so forth), which ones have you tried, or which ones do you consider the most appealing and useful?

3. Can you think of something you once wrote that helped you grow as a person—that is, understand yourself better, or better understand a problem you were writing about?

4. Can you think of something you wrote that did not come out the way you hoped it would? What was wrong with the final draft? Looking back, do you understand why it didn't come out better? Are there any approaches or activities covered in this chapter that might have helped you improve what you wrote?

5. Describe the ideal environment or conditions for your writing (for example, writing in the morning or at night; working in a quiet place or with music on in the background; writing in longhand or using a computer, and so on).

6. List three or four mistakes or problems you look for when you are editing a final draft (for example, grammar mistakes, punctuation problems, word choice, and so on).

7. If you were trying to help friends or siblings improve their writing, what are some concepts or approaches covered in this chapter that might help them most?

ADDITIONAL READINGS

William Zinsser   { **SIMPLICITY, FROM *ON WRITING WELL***

William Zinsser (1922–2015) is the author of more than a dozen books including *On Writing Well, Writing to Learn,* and *Writing about Your Life.* He began his career as a working journalist for the *New York Herald Tribune* and published freelance articles and columns in many distinguished magazines including *The New Yorker, The Atlantic, The American Scholar,* and *Smithsonian.*

CLUTTER IS THE DISEASE of American writing. We are a society strangling in unnecessary words, circular constructions, pompous frills and meaningless jargon.

Who can understand the viscous language of everyday American commerce: the memo, the corporation report, the business letter, the notice from the bank explaining its latest "simplified" statement? What member of an insurance or medical plan can decipher the brochure explaining his costs and benefits? What father or mother can put together a child's toy from the instructions on the box? Our national tendency is to inflate and thereby sound important. The airline pilot who announces that he is presently anticipating experiencing considerable precipitation wouldn't think of saying it may rain. The sentence is too simple—there must be something wrong with it.

But the secret of good writing is to strip every sentence to its cleanest components. Every word that serves no function, every long word that could be a short word, every adverb that carries the same meaning that's already in the verb, every passive construction that leaves the reader unsure of who is doing what—these are the thousand and one adulterants that weaken the strength of a sentence. And they usually occur in proportion to education and rank.

During the 1960s the president of my university wrote a letter to mollify the alumni after a spell of campus unrest. "You are probably aware," he began, "that we have been experiencing very considerable potentially explosive expressions of dissatisfaction on issues only partially related." He meant the students had been hassling them about different things. I was far more upset by the president's English than by the students' potentially explosive expressions of dissatisfaction. I would have preferred the presidential approach taken by Franklin D. Roosevelt when he tried to convert into English his own government's memos, such as this blackout order of 1942:

> Such preparations shall be made as will completely obscure all Federal buildings and non-Federal buildings occupied by the Federal government during an air raid for any period of time from visibility by reason of internal or external illumination.

"Tell them," Roosevelt said, "that in buildings where they have to keep the work going to put something across the windows."

Simplify, simplify. Thoreau said it, as we are so often reminded, and no American writer more consistently practiced what he preached. Open *Walden* to any page and you will find a man saying in a plain and orderly way what is on his mind:

> I went to the woods because I wished to live deliberately, to front only the essential facts of life, and see if I could not learn what it had to teach, and not, when I came to die, discover that I had not lived.

How can the rest of us achieve such enviable freedom from clutter? The answer is to clear our heads of clutter. Clear thinking becomes clear writing; one can't exist without the other. It's impossible for a muddy thinker to write good English. You may get away with it for a paragraph or two, but soon the reader will be lost, and there's no sin so grave, for the reader will not easily be lured back.

Who is this elusive creature, the reader? The reader is someone with an attention span of about 30 seconds—a person assailed by other forces competing for attention. At one time these forces weren't so numerous: newspapers, radio, spouse, home, children. Today they also include a "home entertainment center" (TV, VCR, tapes, CDs), pets, a fitness program, a yard and all the gadgets that have been bought to keep it spruce, and that most potent of competitors, sleep. The person snoozing in a chair with a magazine or a book is a person who was being given too much unnecessary trouble by the writer.

It won't do to say that the reader is too dumb or too lazy to keep pace with the train of thought. If the reader is lost, it's usually because the writer hasn't been careful enough. The carelessness can take any number of forms. Perhaps a sentence is so excessively cluttered that the reader, hacking through the verbiage, simply doesn't know what it means. Perhaps a sentence has been so shoddily constructed that the reader could read it in several ways. Perhaps the writer has switched pronouns in midsentence, or has switched tenses, so the reader loses track of who is talking or when the

5 --

is too dumb or too lazy to keep pace with the ~~writer's~~ train of thought. My sympathies are ~~entirely~~ with him.) ~~He's not so dumb.~~ (If the reader is lost, it is generally because the writer ~~of the article~~ has not been careful enough to keep him on the ~~proper~~ path.

This carelessness can take any number of ~~different~~ forms. Perhaps a sentence is so excessively ~~long and~~ cluttered that the reader, hacking his way through ~~all~~ the verbiage, simply doesn't know what [it] ~~the writer~~ means. Perhaps a sentence has been so shoddily constructed that the reader could read it in any of [several] ~~two or three different~~ ways. ~~He thinks he knows what the writer is trying to say, but he's not sure.~~ Perhaps the writer has switched pronouns in mid-sentence, or ~~perhaps he~~ has switched tenses, so the reader loses track of who is talking ~~to whom~~ or ~~exactly~~ when the action took place. Perhaps Sentence B is not a logical sequel to Sentence A -- the writer, in whose head the connection is ~~perfectly~~ clear, has not [bothered to provide] ~~given enough thought to providing~~ the missing link. Perhaps the writer has used an important word incorrectly by not taking the trouble to look it up ~~and make sure.~~ He may think that "sanguine" and "sanguinary" mean the same thing, but) ~~I can assure you that~~ (the difference is a bloody big one ~~to the reader.~~ [The reader] ~~He~~ can only ~~try to~~ infer ~~what~~ (speaking of big differences) what the writer is trying to imply.

Faced with [these] ~~such a variety of~~ obstacles, the reader is at first a remarkably tenacious bird. He ~~tends to~~ blame[s] himself~~.~~ ~~He~~ obviously missed something, ~~he thinks,~~ and he goes back over the mystifying sentence, or over the whole paragraph,

6 --

piecing it out like an ancient rune, making guesses and moving
on. But he won't do this for long. ~~He will soon run out of~~
~~patience.~~ (The writer is making him work too hard ──→harder
~~than he should have to work~~ ─ (and the reader will look for
~~a writer~~ who is better at his craft.
   one

      The writer must therefore constantly ask himself: What am
I trying to say? ~~in this sentence?~~ (Surprisingly often, he
doesn't know.) ~~And~~ Then he must look at what he has ~~just~~
written and ask: Have I said it? Is it clear to someone
encountering
~~who is coming upon~~ the subject for the first time? If it's
not, ~~clear,~~ it is because some fuzz has worked its way into the
machinery. The clear writer is a person ~~who is~~ clear-headed
enough to see this stuff for what it is: fuzz.

      I don't mean ~~to suggest~~ that some people are born
clear-headed and are therefore natural writers, whereas
others
~~other people~~ are naturally fuzzy and will ~~therefore~~ never write
well. Thinking clearly is ~~an entirely~~ conscious act that the
                          force
writer must ~~keep forcing~~ upon himself, just as if he were
embarking
~~starting~~ out on any other ~~kind of~~ project that requires ~~calls for~~ logic:
adding up a laundry list or doing an algebra problem ~~or playing~~
~~chess.~~ Good writing doesn't ~~just~~ come naturally, though most
                        it does.
people obviously think ~~it's as easy as walking.~~ The professional

Two pages of the final manuscript of this chapter from the First Edition of *On
Writing Well*. Although they look like a first draft, they had already been rewritten
and retyped—like almost every other page—four or five times. With each rewrite
I try to make what I have written tighter, stronger and more precise, eliminating
every element that is not doing useful work. Then I go over it once more, reading
it aloud, and am always amazed at how much clutter can still be cut. (In a later
edition of this book I eliminated the sexist pronoun "he" to denote "the writer"
and "the reader.")

action took place. Perhaps Sentence B is not a logical sequel to Sentence A—the writer, in whose head the connection is clear, hasn't bothered to provide the missing link. Perhaps the writer has used an important word incorrectly by not taking the trouble to look it up. The writer may think "sanguine" and "sanguinary" mean the same thing, but the difference is a bloody big one. The reader can only infer (speaking of big differences) what the writer is trying to imply.

Faced with such obstacles, readers are at first tenacious. They blame themselves—they obviously missed something, and they go back over the mystifying sentence, or over the whole paragraph, piecing it out like an ancient rune, making guesses and moving on. But they won't do this for long. The writer is making them work too hard, and they will look for one who is better at the craft.

Writers must therefore constantly ask: What am I trying to say? Surprisingly often they don't know. Then they must look at what they have written and ask: Have I said it? Is it clear to someone encountering the subject for the first time? If it's not, some fuzz has worked its way into the machinery. The clear writer is someone clearheaded enough to see this stuff for what it is: fuzz.

I don't mean that some people are born clearheaded and are therefore natural writers, whereas others are naturally fuzzy and will never write well. Thinking clearly is a conscious act that writers must force upon themselves, as if they were working on any other project that requires logic: adding up a laundry list or doing an algebra problem. Good writing doesn't come naturally, though most people obviously think it does. Professional writers are constantly being bearded by strangers who say they'd like to "try a little writing sometime"—meaning when they retire from their real profession, which is difficult, like insurance or real estate. Or they say, "I could write a book about that." I doubt it.

Writing is hard work. A clear sentence is no accident. Very few sentences come out right the first time, or even the third time. Remember this in moments of despair. If you find that writing is hard, it's because it is hard. It's one of the hardest things people do. ■

Donald M. Murray   { **THE MAKER'S EYE: REVISING YOUR OWN MANUSCRIPTS**

Donald Murray (1924–2006) was a Pulitzer Prize-winning journalist, author of several books on the art of writing, and a beloved teacher of writing and journalism at the University of New Hampshire. One of his former students,

Susan Ahearn-Pierce, who became a broadcast journalist, remembers Murray as a role model who "never approached writing as an expert," and "spoke about the fact that he was still learning to write, even after years as a teacher and published author."

WHEN STUDENTS COMPLETE A first draft, they consider the job of writing done—and their teachers too often agree. When professional writers complete a first draft, they usually feel that they are at the start of the writing process. When a draft is completed, the job of writing can begin.

That difference in attitude is the difference between amateur and professional, inexperience and experience, journeyman and craftsman. Peter F. Drucker, the prolific business writer, calls his first draft "the zero draft"— after that he can start counting. Most writers share the feeling that the first draft, and all of those which follow, are opportunities to discover what they have to say and how best they can say it.

To produce a progression of drafts, each of which says more and says it more clearly, the writer has to develop a special kind of reading skill. In school we are taught to decode what appears on the page as finished writing. Writers, however, face a different category of possibility and responsibility when they read their own drafts. To them the words on the page are never finished. Each can be changed and rearranged, can set off a chain reaction of confusion or clarified meaning. This is a different kind of reading which is possibly more difficult and certainly more exciting.

Writers must learn to be their own best enemy. They must accept the criticism of others and be suspicious of it; they must accept the praise of others and be even more suspicious of it. Writers cannot depend on others. They must detach themselves from their own pages so that they can apply both their caring and their craft to their own work.

Such detachment is not easy. Science-fiction writer Ray Bradbury supposedly puts each manuscript away for a year to the day and then rereads it as a stranger. Not many writers have the discipline or the time to do this. We must read when our judgment may be at its worst, when we are close to the euphoric moment of creation.

Then the writer, counsels novelist Nancy Hale, "should be critical of everything that seems to him most delightful in his style. He should excise what he most admires, because he wouldn't thus admire it if he weren't . . . in a sense protecting it from criticism." John Ciardi, the poet, adds, "The last act of the writing must be to become one's own reader. It is, I suppose, a schizophrenic process, to begin passionately and to end critically, to begin hot and to end cold; and, more important, to be passion-hot and critic-cold at the same time."

Most people think that the principal problem is that writers are too proud of what they have written. Actually, a greater problem for most professional writers is one shared by the majority of students. They are overly critical, think everything is dreadful, tear up page after page, never complete a draft, see the task as hopeless.

The writer must learn to read critically but constructively, to cut what is bad, to reveal what is good. Eleanor Estes, the children's book author, explains: "The writer must survey his work critically, coolly, as though he were a stranger to it. He must be willing to prune, expertly and hard-heartedly. At the end of each revision, a manuscript may look....worked over, torn apart, pinned together, added to, deleted from, words changed and words changed back. Yet the book must maintain its original freshness and spontaneity."

Most readers underestimate the amount of rewriting it usually takes to produce spontaneous reading. This is a great disadvantage to the student writer, who sees only a finished product and never watches the craftsman who takes the necessary step back, studies the work carefully, returns to the task, steps back, returns, steps back, again and again. Anthony Burgess, one of the most prolific writers in the English-speaking world, admits, "I might revise a page twenty times." Roald Dahl, the popular children's writer, states, "By the time I'm nearing the end of a story, the first part will have been reread and altered and corrected at least 150 times...Good writing is essentially rewriting. I am positive of this."

Rewriting isn't virtuous. It isn't something that ought to be done. It is simply something that most writers find they have to do to discover what they have to say and how to say it. It is a condition of the writer's life.

There are, however, a few writers who do little formal rewriting, primarily because they have the capacity and experience to create and review a large number of invisible drafts in their minds before they approach the page. And some writers slowly produce finished pages, performing all the tasks of revision simultaneously, page by page, rather than draft by draft. But it is still possible to see the sequence followed by most writers most of the time in rereading their own work.

Most writers scan their drafts first, reading as quickly as possible to catch the larger problems of subject and form, and then move in closer and closer as they read and write, reread and rewrite.

The first thing writers look for in their drafts is information. They know that a good piece of writing is built from specific, accurate, and interesting information. The writer must have an abundance of information from which to construct a readable piece of writing.

Next writers look for meaning in the information. The specifics must build to a pattern of significance. Each piece of specific information must carry the reader toward meaning.

Writers reading their own drafts are aware of audience. They put themselves in the reader's situation and make sure that they deliver information which a reader wants to know or needs to know in a manner which is easily digested. Writers try to be sure that they anticipate and answer the questions a critical reader will ask when reading the piece of writing.

Writers make sure that the form is appropriate to the subject and the audience. Form, or genre, is the vehicle which carries meaning to the reader, but form cannot be selected until the writer has adequate information to discover its significance and an audience which needs or wants that meaning.

Once writers are sure the form is appropriate, they must then look at the structure, the order of what they have written. Good writing is built on a solid framework of logic, argument, narrative, or motivation which runs through the entire piece of writing and holds it together. This is the time when many writers find it most effective to outline as a way of visualizing the hidden spine by which the piece of writing is supported.

The element on which writers spend a majority of their time is development. Each section of a piece of writing must be adequately developed. It must give readers enough information so that they are satisfied. How much information is enough? That's as difficult as asking how much garlic belongs in a salad. It must be done to taste, but most beginning writers underdevelop, underestimating the reader's hunger for more information.

As writers solve development problems, they often have to consider questions of dimension. There must be a pleasing and effective proportion among all the parts of the piece of writing. There is a continual process of subtracting and adding to keep the piece of writing in balance.

Finally, writers have to listen to their own voices. Voice is the force which drives a piece of writing forward. It is an expression of the writer's authority and concern. It is what is between the words on the page, what glues the piece of writing together. A good piece of writing is always marked by a consistent, individual voice.

As writers read and reread, write and rewrite, they move closer and closer to the page until they are doing line-by-line editing. Writers read their own pages with infinite care. Each sentence, each line, each clause, each phrase, each word, each mark of punctuation, each section of white space between the type has to contribute to the clarification of meaning.

Slowly the writer moves from word to word, looking through language to see the subject. As a word is changed, cut or added, as a construction is rearranged, all the words used before that moment and all those that follow that moment must be considered and reconsidered.

Writers often read aloud at this stage of the editing process, muttering or whispering to themselves, calling on the ear's experience with language. Does this sound right—or that? Writers edit, shifting back and forth from eye to page to ear to page. I find I must do this careful editing in short runs, no more than fifteen or twenty minutes at a stretch, or I become too kind with myself. I begin to see what I hope is on the page, not what actually is on the page.

This sounds tedious if you haven't done it, but actually it is fun. Making something right is immensely satisfying, for writers begin to learn what they are writing about by writing. Language leads them to meaning, and there is the joy of discovery, of understanding, of making meaning clear as the writer employs the technical skills of language.

Words have double meanings, even triple and quadruple meanings. Each word has its own potential of connotation and denotation. And when writers rub one word against the other, they are often rewarded with a sudden insight, an unexpected clarification.

The maker's eye moves back and forth from word to phrase to sentence to paragraph to sentence to phrase to word. The maker's eye sees the need for variety and balance, for a firmer structure, for a more appropriate form. It peers into the interior of the paragraph, looking for coherence, unity, and emphasis, which make meaning clear.

I learned something about this process when my first bifocals were prescribed. I had ordered a larger section of the reading portion of the glass because of my work, but even so, I could not contain my eyes within this new limit of vision. And I still find myself taking off my glasses and bending my nose toward the page, for my eyes unconsciously flick back and forth across the page, back to another page, forward to still another, as I try to see each evolving line in relation to every other line.

When does this process end? Most writers agree with the great Russian writer Tolstoy, who said, "I scarcely ever reread my published writings, if by chance I come across a page, it always strikes me: all this must be rewritten; this is how I should have written it."

The maker's eye is never satisfied, for each word has the potential to ignite new meaning. This article has been twice written all the way through the writing process [. . .]. Now it is to be republished in a book. The editors made a few small suggestions, and then I read it with my maker's eye. Now it has been re-edited, re-revised, re-read, and re-re-edited, for each piece of writing to the writer is full of potential and alternatives.

A piece of writing is never finished. It is delivered to a deadline, torn out of the typewriter on demand, sent off with a sense of accomplishment and shame and pride and frustration. If only there were a couple more days, time for just another run at it, perhaps then... ■

Brent Staples  BLACK MEN AND PUBLIC SPACE

Brent Staples earned a Ph.D. in psychology from the University of Chicago. After working for several years as a teacher, he began a distinguished career in journalism with the *Chicago Sun-Times* and later the *New York Times*. "Black Men and Public Space" originally appeared under another title in *Ms.* magazine.

My FIRST VICTIM WAS a woman—white, well dressed, probably in her early twenties. I came upon her late one evening on a deserted street in Hyde Park, a relatively affluent neighborhood in an otherwise mean, impoverished section of Chicago. As I swung onto the avenue behind her, there seemed to be a discreet, uninflammatory distance between us. Not so. She cast back a worried glance. To her, the youngish black man—a broad six feet two inches with a beard and billowing hair, both hands shoved into the pockets of a bulky military jacket—seemed menacingly close. After a few more quick glimpses, she picked up her pace and was soon running in earnest. Within seconds she disappeared into a cross street.

That was more than a decade ago. I was twenty-two years old, a graduate student newly arrived at the University of Chicago. It was in the echo of that terrified woman's footfalls that I first began to know the unwieldy inheritance I'd come into—the ability to alter public space in ugly ways. It was clear that she thought herself the quarry of a mugger, a rapist, or worse. Suffering a bout of insomnia, however, I was stalking sleep, not defenseless wayfarers. As a softy who is scarcely able to take a knife to a raw chicken—let alone hold it to a person's throat—I was surprised, embarrassed, and dismayed all at once. Her flight made me feel like an accomplice in tyranny. It also made it clear that I was indistinguishable from the muggers who occasionally seeped into the area from the surrounding ghetto. That first encounter, and those that followed, signified that a vast, unnerving gulf lay between nighttime pedestrians— particularly women—and me. And I soon gathered that being perceived as dangerous is a hazard in itself. I only needed to turn a corner into a dicey situation, or crowd some frightened, armed person in a foyer somewhere, or make an errant move after being pulled over by a policeman. Where fear and weapons meet—and they often do in urban America—there is always the possibility of death.

In that first year, my first away from my hometown, I was to become thoroughly familiar with the language of fear. At dark, shadowy intersections in Chicago, I could cross in front of a car stopped at a traffic light and elicit the thunk, thunk, thunk, thunk of the driver—black, white, male, or female—hammering down the door locks. On less traveled streets after dark, I grew accustomed to but never comfortable with people who crossed to the other side of the street rather than pass me. Then there were the standard unpleasantries with police, doormen, bouncers, cabdrivers, and others whose business is to screen out troublesome individuals before there is any nastiness.

I moved to New York nearly two years ago and I have remained an avid night walker. In central Manhattan, the near-constant crowd cover minimizes tense one-on-one street encounters. Elsewhere—visiting friends in SoHo, where sidewalks are narrow and tightly spaced buildings shut out the sky—things can get very taut indeed.

Black men have a firm place in New York mugging literature. Norman Podhoretz in his famed (or infamous) 1963 essay, "My Negro Problem—And Ours," recalls growing up in terror of black males; they "were tougher than we were, more ruthless," he writes—and as an adult on the Upper West Side of Manhattan, he continues, he cannot constrain his nervousness when he meets black men on certain streets. Similarly, a decade later, the essayist and novelist Edward Hoagland extols a New York where once "Negro bitterness bore down mainly on other Negroes." Where some see mere panhandlers, Hoagland sees "a mugger who is clearly screwing up his nerve to do more than just ask for money." But Hoagland has "the New Yorker's quick-hunch posture for broken-field maneuvering," and the bad guy swerves away.

I often witness that "hunch posture," from women after dark on the warrenlike streets of Brooklyn where I live. They seem to set their faces on neutral and, with their purse straps strung across their chests bandolier style, they forge ahead as though bracing themselves against being tackled. I understand, of course, that the danger they perceive is not a hallucination. Women are particularly vulnerable to street violence, and young black males are drastically overrepresented among the perpetrators of that violence. Yet these truths are no solace against the kind of alienation that comes of being ever the suspect, against being set apart, a fearsome entity with whom pedestrians avoid making eye contact.

It is not altogether clear to me how I reached the ripe old age of twenty-two without being conscious of the lethality nighttime pedestrians attributed to me. Perhaps it was because in Chester, Pennsylvania, the small, angry industrial town where I came of age in the 1960s, I was scarcely noticeable against a backdrop of gang warfare, street knifings, and murders. I grew up one of the good boys, had perhaps a half-dozen fistfights. In retrospect, my shyness of combat has clear sources.

Many things go into the making of a young thug. One of those things is the consummation of the male romance with the power to intimidate. An infant discovers that random flailings send the baby bottle flying out of the crib and crashing to the floor. Delighted, the joyful babe repeats those motions again and again, seeking to duplicate the feat. Just so, I recall the points at which some of my boyhood friends were finally seduced by the perception of themselves as tough guys. When a mark cowered and surrendered his money without resistance, myth and reality merged—and paid off. It is, after all, only manly to embrace the power to frighten and intimidate. We, as men, are not supposed to give an inch of our lane on the highway; we are to seize the fighter's edge in work and in play and even in love; we are to be valiant in the face of hostile forces.

Unfortunately, poor and powerless young men seem to take all this nonsense literally. As a boy, I saw countless tough guys locked away; I have since buried several, too. They were babies, really—a teenage cousin, a brother of twenty-two, a childhood friend in his midtwenties—all gone down in episodes of bravado played out in the streets. I came to doubt the virtues of intimidation early on. I chose, perhaps even unconsciously, to remain a shadow—timid, but a survivor.

The fearsomeness mistakenly attributed to me in public places often has a perilous flavor. The most frightening of these confusions occurred in the late 1970s and early 1980s when I worked as a journalist in Chicago. One day, rushing into the office of a magazine I was writing for with a deadline story in hand, I was mistaken for a burglar. The office manager called security and, with an ad hoc posse, pursued me through the labyrinthine halls, nearly to my editor's door. I had no way of proving who I was. I could only move briskly toward the company of someone who knew me.

Another time I was on assignment for a local paper and killing time before an interview. I entered a jewelry store on the city's affluent Near North Side. The proprietor excused herself and returned with an enormous red Doberman pinscher straining at the end of a leash. She stood, the dog extended toward me, silent to my questions, her eyes bulging nearly out of her head. I took a cursory look around, nodded, and bade her good night. Relatively speaking, however, I never fared as badly as another black male journalist. He went to nearby Waukegan, Illinois, a couple of summers ago to work on a story about a murderer who was born there. Mistaking the reporter for the killer, police hauled him from his car at gunpoint and but for his press credentials would probably have tried to book him. Such episodes are not uncommon. Black men trade tales like this all the time.

In "My Negro Problem—And Ours," Podhoretz writes that the hatred he feels for blacks makes itself known to him through a variety of avenues— one being his discomfort with that "special brand of paranoid touchiness" to which he says blacks are prone. No doubt he is speaking here of black men. In time, I learned to smother the rage I felt at so often being taken for a criminal. Not to do so would surely have led to madness—via that special "paranoid touchiness" that so annoyed Podhoretz at the time he wrote the essay.

I began to take precautions to make myself less threatening. I move about with care, particularly late in the evening. I give a wide berth to nervous people on subway platforms during the wee hours, particularly when I have exchanged business clothes for jeans. If I happen to be entering a building behind some people who appear skittish, I may walk by, letting them clear the lobby before I return, so as not to seem to be following them. I have been calm and extremely congenial on those rare occasions when I've been pulled over by the police.

And on late-evening constitutionals along streets less traveled by, I employ what has proved to be an excellent tension-reducing measure: I whistle melodies from Beethoven and Vivaldi and the more popular classical composers. Even steely New Yorkers hunching toward nighttime destinations seem to relax, and occasionally they even join in the tune. Virtually everybody seems to sense that a mugger wouldn't be warbling bright, sunny selections from Vivaldi's Four Seasons. It is my equivalent of the cowbell that hikers wear when they know they are in bear country. ■

Chuck Palahniuk { MY LIFE AS A DOG

Chuck Palahniuk is the acclaimed author of *Fight Club, Survivor, Choke,* and numerous other works of fiction. "My Life As a Dog" appeared in his collection of essays and articles titled *Stranger Than Fiction: True Stories.*

THE FACES THAT MAKE eye contact, they're twisted into sneers. The top lip pulled up to show teeth, the whole face bunched around the nose and eyes. One blond Huck Finn kid walks along after us, slapping our legs and shouting, "I can see your NECK! Hey, asshole! I can see your neck from behind …"

A man turns to a woman and says, "Christ, only in Seattle …"

Another middle-aged man says, loud, "This town has gotten way too liberal …"

A young man with a skateboard under one arm says, "You think you're cute? Well, you're not. You're just stupid. You look fucking stupid …"

This wasn't about looking good.

As a white man, you can live your whole life never not fitting in. You never walk into a jewelry store that sees only your black skin. You never walk into a bar that sees only your boobs. To be Whitie is to be wallpaper. You don't draw attention, good or bad. Still, what would it be like, to live with attention? To just let people stare. To let them fill in the blank, and assume what they will. To let people project some aspect of themselves on you for a whole day.

The worst part of writing fiction is the fear of wasting your life behind a keyboard. The idea that, dying, you'll realize you only ever lived on paper. Your only adventures were make-believe, and while the world fought and kissed, you sat in some dark room, masturbating and making money.

So the idea was, a friend and I would rent costumes. Me, a spotted, smiling Dalmatian. Her, a brown dancing bear. Costumes without gender clues. Just fun-fur suits that hid our hands and feet and big, heavy papier-mâché heads that kept anyone from seeing our faces. This gave people no visual clues, no facial expressions or gestures to decode—just a dog and a bear walking around, shopping, being tourists in downtown Seattle.

Some of this I knew to expect. Every December, the international Cacophony Society hosts a party called "Santa Rampage" where hundreds of people come into a city, all of them dressed as Santa Claus. No one is black or white. No one is young or old. Male or female. Together they become a sea of red velvet and white beards storming the downtown, drinking and singing and driving the police nuts.

At a recent Santa Rampage, police detectives met an arriving planeload of Santa Clauses at the Portland airport, corralling them with guns and hot pepper spray and announcing, "Whatever you're planning, the city of Portland, Oregon, will not look upon it kindly if you burn Santa Claus in effigy …"

Still, five hundred Santas has a power that a lonely bear and dog do not. In the lobby of the Seattle Art Museum they sell us tickets for fourteen bucks. They talk to us about the exhibits, the portraits of George Washington on loan from the nation's capital. They tell us where to find the elevators and give us museum maps, but the moment we push the elevator button—they throw us out. No refund for the tickets. No slack. Just a lot of sad head shaking and a brand-new security policy that bears and dogs may buy tickets but they may not look at the art.

A block away from the museum doors, the guards still follow us, until a new group of guards from the next building has us under surveillance. Another block down Third Avenue, a Seattle Police car cruises up, following us at a creep as we head north to the retail shopping center.

In the Pike Place Market, young men wait for the dog to walk past, then throw punches or karate kicks into the black-spotted fur. Right in the kidneys. Into the back of my elbows or knees, hard. Every time, every kick and fist. Then, these same men, they jump back, rolling their eyes at the ceiling and pretending to whistle as if nothing has happened.

These people behind mirrored sunglasses, dressed alike behind the stiff attitude of hip-hop and skateboards, being young downtown and looking to fit in. Outside the Bon Marche, along Pine Street, young men throw rocks, denting the papier-mâché heads and pounding the fur. Young women run up in groups of four or five, holding digital cameras the size of silver cigarette packs and clutching the dog and bear as photo props. Squeezed in, smiling with their breasts pressing warm and their arms around an animal neck.

The police still trailing us, we run inside the Westlake Center, running past Nine West on the first level of the shopping mall. Running past the Mill Stream store—"Gifts from the Pacific Northwest"—we're running past Talbots and Mont Blanc, past Marquis Leather. People ahead of us pull back, standing tight against Starbucks and LensCrafters, creating a constant vacuum of empty white floor for us to run into. Behind us, walkie-talkies crackle and male voices say, "…suspects are in sight. One appears to be a dancing bear. The second suspect is wearing a large dog head…"

Kids scream. People pour out of the stores for a better look. Clerks come forward to stare, their faces peering from behind sweaters and wristwatches in display windows. It's the same excitement we felt as kids when a dog got into our grade school. We're running past Sam Goody, past the Fossil store, the walkie-talkies right behind us, the voices saying, "…the bear and the dog are westbound, headed down the first-level access way to the Underground Eatery…" We're running past Wild Tiger Pizza and Subway Sandwiches. Past teenage girls sitting on the floor, yakking on the pay phones. "Affirmative," the walkie-talkie voice says. From behind us, it says, "…I'm about to apprehend both alleged animals…"

All this fuss, this chase. Young men stone us. Young women grope us. Middle-aged men look away, shaking their heads and ignoring the dog that waits in line with them at Tully's for a grande latte. A middle-aged Seattle guy, tall with a blond ponytail and his panes rolled to his knee, exposing bare calves, he walks past, saying, "You know, there's a leash law in this town."

An older woman with her beauty parlor hair silver-rinsed and sprayed into a pile, she tugs at one spotted dog arm, tugging the fur and asking, "What are you promoting?" She trails along, still tugging the fur, asking, "Who's paying you to do this?" Asking louder, "Can't you hear me"? Saying, "Answer me." Asking, "Who do you work for?" Saying, "Tell me..." She's clutching us for half a block, until her grip breaks.

Another middle-aged woman, pushing a stroller the size of a grocery cart, packed with disposable diapers, formula, toys and clothes and shopping bags, with one tiny baby lost somewhere in the mix, in the concrete middle of Pike Place Market, this woman shouts, "Everyone get back! Get back! For all we know they could be strapped with bombs inside those costumes..."

Everywhere, there's the brain scramble as security guards create public policy to deal with people dressed as animals.

A friend of mine, Monica, used to work as a clown for hire. While she twisted balloons into animals at corporate parties, men were always offering her money to fuck. Looking back, she says that any woman who'd dress as a fool, who'd refuse to look attractive, she was seen as loose, wanton, and willing to fuck for money. Another friend, Steve, wears a wolf costume to Burning Man each year and fucks his brains out because, he says, people see him as less than human. Something wild.

By now, the backs of my knees hurt from caking kicks. My kidneys ache from getting punched, and my shoulder blades from pitched rocks. My hands are running with sweat. My feet are sore from too much walking on concrete. On Pine Street young women drive past, waving from cars and screaming, "We love you..."

All these people behind their own masks: their sunglasses and cars and fashions and haircuts. Young men drive past, screaming, "Goddamn fucking FAGS..."

By now, I don't give a shit. This dog could walk around this way forever. Walking taller. Blind and deaf to people's shit. I don't need to wave, to pander and pose with kids for pictures. I'm just a dog smoking a cigarette outside Pottery Barn. I lean back, one leg lifted against the facade of Tiffany and Company.

I'm just the Dalmatian making a cell-phone call in front of Old Navy. It's the kind of cool, a feeling of being self-contained, that white guys can live a lifetime without.

By now it's sweating hot. It's late afternoon, and FAO Schwarz is almost deserted. Inside the big glass doors, a young guy is dressed as a toy soldier in a red tailcoat with a double row of brass buttons and a towering black helmet. The escalators are empty. The Barbie Shop is empty. The toy soldier plays with a radio-controlled race car, alone and trapped inside on the first sunny day Seattle has seen in months.

The toy soldier looks up from his job, at the dog and bear coming through the door, and he smiles. Ignoring his race car, letting it drive into a wall, the soldier says, "You guys rock!" He says, "You SO totally rule." ■

PART TWO

Writing Projects and Essays

> **" "** *I want my students to know what writers know—how to bring their life and their writing together.* **" "**
>
> —Nancy Sommers, "Between the Drafts"

In *Part 1*, we looked at writing as a form of communication to solve problems.

Think of *Part 2* as a journey through a selection of writing projects that are designed to help you develop your writing skills for college and professional life. As you work on these projects, consider reading Chapter 12, "Developing an Effective Style," for practical advice about style and mechanics.

Courtesy of Victoria Gedvillas

VICTORIA GEDVILLAS

Pinner

This piece was a response to an assignment to create a cohesive illustration featuring words from one randomly chosen page of the dictionary. The page I opened up had the words pin-up, pin oak, pinner, pinnacle, pinto, pinwheel, pinyon, and pinweeds. The problem I was trying to solve was making an illustration consisting of strange things seem not so strange.

CHAPTER FOUR

Narrative Essays

> " Narrative is about understanding what it is like to have the life of someone else, and it is enormously important because our moral intelligence is developed that way. "
>
> —Scott Turow, novelist and former U.S. Attorney

CHAPTER LEARNING OBJECTIVES

In this chapter, you will learn to:

- ► Understand the role and importance of narrative writing.
- ► Plan an essay with reader-relevant communication goals.
- ► Write from firsthand knowledge and experience.
- ► Use an informal, or inductive, pattern of organization.
- ► Begin an essay with a compelling presentation of the main issue.
- ► Write in a "conversational" style that projects an engaging and appropriate writer's "voice."

WRITING NARRATIVES TO COMMUNICATE AND SOLVE PROBLEMS

Narratives, whether spoken or written, essentially are stories. Stories are synonymous with communication. Throughout human history, they have been the most common, compelling, and effective way we share information, feelings, and ideas, the way we learn to understand and care about each other, and try to solve problems that affect the quality of our lives.

Most of what we know about history, human progress, our closest friends, and our own families comes to us through narratives. Whether they are delivered orally, or as books, essays, lyrics with music, or through the images of a film, narratives engage and instruct us by taking us out of our own lives and into the lives of other people.

Although it is easy to see narratives as a way of communicating and connecting, we don't routinely see them as a way of solving problems. Persuasive essays, for example, have obvious, problem-solving goals: Mr. X is doing a poor job as president, so we need to elect Mr., Ms., or Mrs. Y.

Narratives, on the surface, seem to be about sharing experiences. However, more often than not, when we use narratives to communicate, we do so to address problems and to try to find solutions. Narratives in the form of essays, correspondence, memoirs, testimonials, biographies, depositions, reports, and so on, always have played an important role in addressing scientific, philosophic, medical, legal, and cultural issues or problems.

Routinely, scientists write narratives to describe the process and significance of their methods, experiments, and discoveries. In the social sciences, anthropologists, sociologists, and psychologists write narrative-based cultural histories, field reports, and case studies to record their observations and findings. In business communications, narratives are valued as a way of illustrating methods, profiling successful people, and supporting solutions to problems. The importance of narratives in the humanities—history, philosophy, and literature—hardly bears mentioning.

Students, as well as professionals, who understand and can use narrative methods will benefit as writers and communicators.

BASIC ELEMENTS OF NARRATIVES

A narrative is the story of an event, or series of connected events, and the people involved. A narrative *essay*, like other kinds of essays, addresses a central issue and supports a view—in other words, it is written with readers and problem-solving goals in mind. With that said, not all narratives have obvious, problem-solving goals. Jokes or anecdotes are short narratives that present absurd, odd, or ironic events and behavior mainly to entertain or amuse. Some narratives mainly are written or spoken to serve as information about life in previous eras (a chronicle) or unfamiliar places (a travelogue), but regardless of their purpose, most narratives share basic elements that appeal to readers and listeners. The short narrative below, an anecdote from Clarence V. Price's *Memoirs of Flora*, provides a quaint record of life in the town of Flora, Illinois, during the late nineteenth century:

> We used to have revival meetings in tents on south Main Street. These were shouting affairs. I picked up a good story about a revival meeting. It seems that a little fellow with a squawky voice got religion. He got up and said, "I used to smoke and drink and do everything bad, but now I hope to be a better man." After he finished, a woman got up, cupped her ear, and said, "Louder." He turned toward her and in a very loud voice repeated his testimony. Then another person called for a repetition. Then another said, "What did you say?" By this time he was nettled and he turned in the direction of the last inquirer and said, "I said go to hell. That's what I said."

Price's anecdote has four basic elements readers expect from a narrative:

- ▶ An event
- ▶ A setting
- ▶ Descriptive details
- ▶ A point

The event the anecdote presents is the revival meeting, together with a sequence of related events (incidents or "scenes") within the larger event: people getting up, yelling, "Louder.... What did you say?" The anecdote also evokes a setting—"...tents on south Main Street..."—and uses descriptive details that bring the event to life ("These were shouting affairs.... a little fellow with a squawky voice.... a woman got up, cupped her ear..."). Finally, the anecdote also makes a point: it says, in a lighthearted way, that righteousness can be crabby. Narrative essays are longer and more detailed than jokes or anecdotes, but they use the same basic narrative elements to engage readers, address issues, and support views.

A STUDENT'S ESSAY PROPOSAL

As you begin thinking about your narrative-essay project, read a proposal that first-year student Kierstin Koppel wrote for a similar project, based on the following instructions:

Write a narrative essay that develops a meaningful viewpoint or message about an issue that you have firsthand experience dealing with.

Romantic Gamesmanship: A Narrative Essay Proposal

Kierstin Koppel

1. The Main Issue or Problem the Narrative Will Address

Women can become obsessed trying to pick apart the male brain when it comes to relationships. We look for advice, anything that can shed light on how to "play the game." Magazines, chick flicks, and most recently, popular books such as *He's Just Not That Into You* and *Why Men Love Bitches* find multi-million dollar markets that feed off female insecurities. These books explore why it seems that mean, lazy, or less deserving females are in happy relationships. "Bitches" get the good guy, and the good girls are left in the dust.

These books tell you how to play the game to get a guy to fall for you. The irony is that if you play according to the books, you may very well get a guy to fall for you, but he's falling for a "you" that you have created just to mask your own personality. The idea of playing the game creates a facade, a faux personality, and therefore a fake relationship. Playing the game just lands you in a catch-22, and in the meantime, you could be missing out on a great guy.

2. The Viewpoint, Message, or Solution the Narrative Will Support

Staying true to yourself is always best. Through experimenting in following a book's advice, I found out who I really was, and who I never want to be. The guys you attract when playing the game, are not the guys you ultimately want to be with.

3. Reason for Choosing the Issue and Communication Goals

After a series of bad relationships, I became curious about the male brain. I noticed mean or ditzy girls around me, most of whom had little to offer, including intelligence, were happily involved in relationships and taking all the cute guys "off the market." I wondered what drew these guys to mean or ditzy girls. Then I stumbled across a book called *Why Men Love Bitches* and read it out of curiosity, not really expecting to find anything of relevance.

The book makes some valid points and teaches you how to "play the game." So I thought I would give it a try. Within a month I found that the game definitely worked for attracting guys. I was batting them off left and right, but none were attracted to the real me. They were all attracted to this person I created, the role I was playing. I ended up unhappy, pretending to be someone I didn't really like. Ironically the book taught me, who I really was, what made me special and different from everyone else. I realized that girls who were "bitches," who attracted all the guys and seemed to have it all, were missing out on the true reason and benefits of a relationship.

4. The Reader-Relevance and Audience
I think my message is relevant to all readers because we are always searching for love. The secret is that there really is no secret. It is when we are honest with ourselves, learn to accept ourselves and remain true to ourselves that we are most happy. The message is: always be and accept yourself for who you are. Everyone has built up an image or has done something that is out of character. When we take down the wall we build around ourselves, this is when we can let love in. ■

Interview with the Student Writer

Courtesy of Kierstin Koppel

Kierstin Koppel was born in Miami, Florida, but grew up in Los Angeles, California. By the time she was thirteen, she was immersed in the entertainment industry in Los Angeles and did a lot of acting. Eventually, she moved back to Miami, was admitted to Florida International University, and decided she wanted to transition from acting to political journalism. She declared journalism as her major, but eventually changed to political science. She plans to pursue a career in public policy and politics.

In responding to the questions below about her proposal, Kierstin suggests that the idea for her essay came to her by accident. However, note that she mentions having read the assignment instructions earlier that day.

The mathematician Henri Poincaré once observed that when we come up with ideas that seem spontaneous, they often are a delayed result of conscious thinking. We start thinking about a problem, such as what to write an essay about, and then for one reason or another, we put it aside, but our minds continue to work on the problem unconsciously. If we come up with an idea later, when we are thinking about other things, we might feel as though we've experienced a "flash of inspiration," but the real source is the conscious thinking we did.

- **Kierstin, coming into college, how did you see yourself as a writer, and how much writing did you do?**

- Writing was always a passion of mine, in particular, poetry and free form. Growing up, I found that I was able to express myself through writing and paint a picture of how I viewed the world. I participated in creative writing contests and entered some of my writing in youth fairs and other kinds of competitions. However, when I entered college, I still was not very confident in my writing ability and knew that developing composition skills would be vital to my professional success in the workforce. My strength as a developing writer was my ability to be detailed and descriptive. My weakness was staying focused and organized. I was never good at narrative writing. The whole "beginning, middle, and end" thing was always a problem for me. So when I got this narrative assignment in my first-year writing class, it was a challenge for me.

- **How did you come up with the idea for the essay?**

- The day I read the assignment prompt, I was at home, and my mother was having the carpets cleaned. The Stanley Steamer man found the book [*Why Men Love Bitches*] while he was working, and gave it to me. A little embarrassing, but seeing the book brought back everything!

Working Together

INTERVIEW A CLASSMATE

Before reading the rest of this chapter and writing a proposal of your own, sit down with a classmate and take turns interviewing each other about issues or problems that you have had "firsthand experience" dealing with and that might serve as material for a meaningful narrative essay. Think of recent issues you have dealt with, but also think back to your early teens and childhood.

As you discuss various issues, ask each other some of the questions below; they will help you make a decision about a subject later on.

- How motivated would you be to write about the issue?
- Would you be comfortable writing candidly about it, or is it too sensitive or personal?

- Does the issue translate to an intriguing story? In other words, is there an event or series of events—things happening and happening next—that you could describe to bring the issue to life and keep readers interested?
- Is there a meaningful learning experience behind the issue that would translate to a relevant view or message—in other words, answer the "So what?" question ("Why should I care?") for your readers.

As you interview each other, take notes and then give those notes to the person you interviewed.

NARRATIVE ESSAYS AND COMMUNICATION GOALS

The challenge of this narrative assignment begins with planning an essay that has communication goals and a problem-solving purpose. If you see the purpose of the essay as providing information about yourself and your life, or something that happened to you, you won't be writing for a realistic audience.

Your essay, in fact, could resemble the "wild bore" that most of us have met at a social gathering, the egotistical person who maneuvers you into a corner and bombards you with information about himself and his family, friends, possessions, and accomplishments. If your essay is like that, all about you and for you, a close friend of yours might read it; however, general readers, people who don't know you and are not invested in your happiness, will only read your essay if you make it interesting and relevant to them from the beginning.

Making a narrative essay connect to readers is especially challenging because this kind of essay—sometimes called "a personal essay" or "personal narrative"—comes entirely from you, the writer, and from your life. As the writer, you are on your own, left to your own resources. You can't go to the library for help. You can't rely on other people's ideas. You can't ask your instructor for a topic. All you can do is think about your own life, analyze issues you have dealt with, and figure out how the story of coping and overcoming, or failing to cope and overcome, can connect you to your readers and enlighten them.

A good way to sum up the challenge of writing a narrative essay is that it is an essay *about you but for your readers*. If it is just about you and for you, then the "wild bore" factor comes into play. The purpose for writing is unclear. Your ability to write an essay that communicates and connects to readers will be haphazard at best.

With that said, to write an effective narrative essay, you, as the writer, have to be invested in the essay, too. You have to care about it and have a conviction that you have something meaningful to say. Thus, the first communication problem has to do with you. What can you write about? What do you want to write about? What will motivate you to write?

As you think about writing a narrative essay with communication goals, read the excerpt below from *Notes of a Native Son* by James Baldwin. *Native Son* describes Baldwin growing up in a climate of deeply entrenched racism that prevailed in America in the 1930s. Notice how Baldwin "speaks" to the reader in a conversational "voice," and how the details of his story—the issues, events, and emotions raised—generate insights and views about social class and family dynamics, as well as the central issue of race.

James Baldwin { **FROM *NOTES OF A NATIVE SON***

David Gahr/Getty Images

James Baldwin (1924–1987) is a celebrated writer, known for his evocative writing about personal identity and the racial divide in America. His essays are collected in *Notes of a Native Son*, *Nobody Knows My Name*, and *The Fire Next Time*. His works of fiction include *Go Tell It On the Mountain*, *Giovanni's Room*, and *Going to Meet the Man*.

THE ONLY WHITE PEOPLE who came to our house were welfare workers and bill collectors. It was almost always my mother who dealt with them, for my father's temper, which was at the mercy of his pride, was never to be trusted. It was clear that he felt their very presence in his home to be a violation: this was conveyed by his carriage, almost ludicrously stiff, and by his voice, harsh and vindictively polite. When I was around nine or ten I wrote a play which was directed by a young, white schoolteacher, a woman, who then took an interest in me, and gave me books to read, and, in order to corroborate my theatrical bent, decided to take me to see what she somewhat tactlessly referred to as "real" plays. Theater-going was forbidden in our house, but, with the really cruel intuitiveness of a child, I suspected that the color of this woman's skin would carry the day for me. When, at school, she suggested taking me to the theater, I did not, as I might have done if she had been a Negro, find a way of discouraging her, but she agreed that she should pick me up at my house one evening. I then, very cleverly, left all the rest to my mother, who suggested to my father, as I knew she would, that it would not be very nice to let such a kind woman make the trip for nothing. Also, since it was a schoolteacher, I imagine that my mother countered the idea of sin with the idea of "education," which word, even with my father, carried a kind of bitter weight.

Before the teacher came my father took me aside to ask why she was coming, what interest she could possibly have in our house, in a boy like me. I said I didn't know but I, too, suggested that it had something to do with education. And I understood that my father was waiting for me to say something—I didn't quite know what; perhaps that I wanted his protection against this teacher and her "education." I said none of these things and the teacher came and we went out. It was clear, during the brief interview in our living room, that my father was agreeing very much against his will and that he would have refused permission if he had dared. The fact that he did not dare caused me to despise him: I had no way of knowing that he was facing in that living room a wholly unprecedented and frightening situation.

Later, when my father had been laid off from his job, this woman became very important to us. She was really a very sweet and generous woman and went to a great deal of trouble to be of help to us, particularly during one awful winter. My mother called her by the highest name she knew: she said she was a "Christian." My father could scarcely disagree but during the four or five years of our relatively close association he never trusted her and was always trying to surprise in her open, Midwestern face the genuine, cunningly hidden, and hideous motivation. In later years, particularly when it began to be clear that this "education" of mine was going to lead me to perdition, he became more explicit and warned me that my white friends in high school were not really my friends and that I would see, when I was older, how white people would do anything to keep a Negro down. Some of them could be nice, he admitted, but none of them were to be trusted and most of them were not even nice. The best thing was to have as little to do with them as possible. I did not feel this way and I was certain, in my innocence, that I never would. ■

From Reflection to Response   Responding to *Notes of a Native Son*

1. Why do you think Baldwin was motivated to write this narrative?

2. Although Baldwin's narrative as presented here is an excerpt, not a complete essay, does it make a point at the end? If so, what is the point as you see it? Does the narrative reflect any change in the narrator's outlook on life from beginning to the end?

3. Compelling narratives are built on relevant details and pieces of information that allow readers to share in the writer's experiences and evaluate the events the narrative presents. Review the details and pieces of information from *Notes of a Native Son* listed below, and sum up the view that the narrative expresses about Baldwin's father. How does Baldwin feel about his father? What does he want the reader to learn or understand? Why is Baldwin's father such a prominent part of the narrative?

   • The only white people who came to our house were welfare workers and bill collectors.

- My father's temper, which was at the mercy of his pride, was never to be trusted.

- Theater-going was forbidden in our house, but, with the really cruel intuitiveness of a child, I suspected that the color of this woman's skin would carry the day for me.

- It was clear, during the brief interview in our living room, that my father was agreeing very much against his will and that he would have refused permission if he had dared. The fact that he did not dare caused me to despise him.

- In later years, particularly when it began to be clear that this "education" of mine was going to lead me to perdition, he became more explicit and warned me that my white friends in high school were not really my friends and that I would see, when I was older, how white people would do anything to keep a Negro down....I did not feel this way and I was certain, in my innocence, that I never would.

4. In a paragraph or so, describe the narrator of *Notes of a Native Son* as you would describe someone to a friend. Is he interesting, likeable? What are some of his personality traits?

5. Although Baldwin is writing about being nine or ten years old, here and there he uses sophisticated words (*ludicrously, corroborate, tactlessly, vindictively, intuitiveness, perdition*). What effect do these words have on your perception of the boy's character? Are there any details in the narrative to suggest that Baldwin, as a ten-year-old, realistically might have used words like this?

COMING UP WITH IDEAS

All of us have dealt with issues that we can write compelling narratives about, but identifying those issues can be hard. Our lives are complex. The issues we deal with are multifaceted and interconnected. Often we prefer to forget or repress issues to lighten the burden of moving on. We tend to focus on immediate, pressing, unresolved issues, which for a variety of reasons are not always the most interesting or feasible to write about.

Breaking down your life into categories of experience is a good way of getting a broad view of issues you can write about. Take a look at the categories in the box, and as you think about issues, ask yourself a simple but important question: does the issue lend itself to an interesting story?*

---

*Note that issues and categories can overlap. Don't worry about that. The goal is to come up with ideas. The classification is not important.

Categories of Experience	Examples
Literacy & Education	• Learning to read, write, speak, communicate • Good and bad teachers • Overachieving and underachieving • Private vs. public schools, or homeschooling • School censorship • Favoritism, social issues, cliques, etc. • Learning outside of school, from "role models," family members, friends
Relationships	• Parents and stepparents • Brothers and sisters • Friends • Teammates • Love interests, spouses, and dates
Work & Responsibilities	• Conflicts with coworkers or superiors • Ethics and harassment • Problems with customers • Working for your family • Chores and domestic responsibilities
Identity & Lifestyle	• Moving and adapting • Ethnicity • Sex and sexuality • Bad habits and addiction • Music, pastimes, recreation • Religion and faith

The sections that follow explore each of these categories of experience in more detail.

Literacy and Education

Since literacy is relevant to the content of this course, your instructor may ask you to write your narrative essay specifically about a literacy issue, that is, learning to read, write, speak, and communicate, or an issue related to using those skills. Literacy presents issues for many people, especially those who adopt a second language and culture.

Literacy issues fall under the broader category of education, in particular, issues related to schooling—overachieving, underachieving, teachers, fitting in socially, and adapting to certain kinds of schooling (public, private, religious, boarding, military, or home school). In Chapter 1, literacy and education were the subjects of a practice writing assignment. If you completed that assignment, you might consider building on it for this narrative essay.

Relationships

Relationships are a source of support and happiness in our lives, but they are also problems. Even good relationships are checkered with disagreements, misunderstandings, conflicts, and disappointments. Relationships force us to grow or change, and they enlighten us about ourselves and other people. Relationship issues tend to have universal appeal, and as such, can be powerful subjects for narrative essays.

Work and Responsibilities

Some people like their jobs, some don't, but even the best jobs come with problems involving workload, job security, unpleasant duties, unfair compensation, respect, rights, fellow-workers, and overbearing superiors. A few specific examples follow:

▶ A coworker takes credit for work you did or an initiative you took.

▶ Your employer or boss does something unethical or illegal, or is obnoxious, or too demanding.

▶ Customers are rude, verbally abusive, manipulative, dishonest, or stingy tippers.

▶ The job appears easy or glamorous from the outside—you're a "cast member" at Disney World, or a friendly bank teller—but the reality behind the scenes is different.

If you have never had a job, you almost certainly have had responsibilities. Some responsibilities create problems similar to the ones mentioned above: parents require you to work for them, take care of your siblings or grandparents, do the cooking and cleaning, and other chores. Work and responsibilities can weigh heavily on us and detract from the quality and enjoyment of our lives. As such, they are a source of issues for narrative essays.

Identity and Lifestyle

A person's identity is a combination of genes, fate, and free will. On the one hand, identity is determined by circumstances beyond our control—race, ethnicity, nationality, physical traits, and social class. On the other hand, we create an identity by the lifestyle choices we make—how we dress, the music we listen to, the values we embrace, the things we like to do, and the kinds of people we associate with.

These circumstances and choices help define who we are and give us an identity. Most of us have made regrettable lifestyle choices at some point in our lives—developed bad habits, picked the wrong friends, engaged in dangerous, illegal, or antisocial activities. A bad choice or decision can be a good issue to write about, if you are comfortable writing about it.

Even if you have managed your life pretty well, tried to be a good person, and followed the golden rule, you can be certain that your identity is an issue or a problem for somebody else, in some way: Some people will disapprove of something about you or something you do.

If you happen to be Black or Hispanic, you're a problem in the eyes of some people. If you're French or Polish, you're a problem for some. If you're Jewish or Muslim, or Amish, you're a problem. If you're gay, you're a problem. If you're sexually active, or celibate, or a virgin, you're a problem. If you're poor, if you believe in God or don't believe, or you're a Wiccan, or if you like to surf, skydive, fish, hunt, listen to hip-hop or country music, or customize your car; if you have tattoos, or blue hair, or you love nature, or bird watching; if you're a socialist or a young Republican, pro-war or pro-peace, or you belong to a sorority, or you're a football player, an artist, a thespian, or a jogger—if you're anything at all or do anything at all, whoever you are and whatever you do, then in some people's minds, you're one of the reasons why the world is a mess, why life is frustrating.

If you have a story to tell about an issue related to your identity or lifestyle, writing a narrative essay about it can be a powerful way to enlighten readers and connect to them.

From Reflection to Response   **Generating Ideas**

At home or in class, spend five minutes freewriting, brainstorming, clustering, or "mind mapping" about issues in your life. After you finish, review the categories of experience chart on page 129 and create a list of issues you have dealt with in each category.

After coming up with a list of issues, circle the issues you would most like to write an essay about and discuss them with a group of your classmates. Ask your classmates what their views are, which issues they are most interested in, and what they would like to learn from your experiences.

> *Tech Tip*
>
> If you are having trouble coming up with an idea for your essay, try the following:
>
> - Visit a social network site you belong to, and review some of the information you have posted about yourself. You might come across an incident or situation worth writing about.
>
> - Visit themoth.org online and listen to some stories or read some of the blogs that have been posted. Storycorps.org offers a compelling collection of interviews and testimonials, as well as resources that can help you generate ideas for your own stories.
>
> - Try a web-based mapping tool like bubbl.us or MindMup to help you generate ideas.
>
> - If you have an idea but aren't sure about it, post it to the discussion board on your course website (if you have one), or run it by some of your social-network friends and contacts.
>
> - Create a short podcast (sixty seconds or so) that describes an issue and experience on which you might base the essay. A short podcast can serve as an initial summary or outline of an essay, and it can help give you an objective sense of how readers might respond. You also can play or e-mail the podcast to classmates and see what they have to say about your idea.
>
> - To create a podcast, all you need is a cell phone that has a memo feature, but you also can use free software like Audacity, or an app like GarageBand.

While you consider different ideas for your essay, read the narrative titled "Crossing the Border" by Diane Thiel. Notice how Thiel puts the reader "in her shoes" by using relevant, descriptive details to launch and sustain her story—the perplexing delays, the miscommunications, and the sense of mounting, cultural estrangement.

Diane Thiel { CROSSING THE BORDER, FROM *THE WHITE HORSE: A COLOMBIAN JOURNEY*

Diane Thiel, a graduate of Brown University, is a poet, translator, Fulbright Scholar, and author of ten books including *Resistance Fantasies, The White Horse: A Colombian Journey*, and *Winding Roads: Exercises in Writing Creative Nonfiction*.

Alexander Thiel-Hadjilambrinos, 2013

She has received numerous awards for her writing, and is currently a Professor of English and Creative Writing at the University of New Mexico.

WE ASKED ABOUT THE boat at least ten times the next morning—at the Torres house, at Rosita's. We also asked some of the children who came to find us each morning, thinking they might be the most likely to know. But everyone had a different answer. Some said it would come in the afternoon. Some said no more boats until after Christmas. The boat had actually been there when we arrived a few days before, but for whatever reason, no one had told us about it. So we kept walking down to the dock to check.

It was a new feeling, this helplessness, a reliance on the whims of the tides and a single boat and its captain. I was still used to Miami time and the way in the States you can get everything you want when you want, provided you have the money. Ana Maria really wanted to be in Colombia for Christmas, and it was already the 23rd. Her friend Ricardo was planning to meet us at the port in Punta Ardita to take us down the coast to his piece of land to stay for a week on the ocean.

In one way, it was a good thing that we missed the boat the day we arrived in Jaqué because we ended up speaking to town officials about the environmental project in Punta Ardita, Colombia, and about how we would like to start a similar program in Jaqué—to improve the water conditions, to promote crafts for sale, to clean up the beaches, and other plans. We were told that the town council allots land and that we should write a request to set up an environmental station there. We wrote it immediately and were told we would find out the response in a few weeks, on our way back. So we saw our delay in Jaqué as a blessing, but we really didn't want to miss the next boat.

"Ardita es Colombia," said the older official.

To our relief, it finally arrived with the tide in the late morning, and we went to pay, reserve our places, and fill out the paperwork to leave the country. As the officials looked at our papers and heard where we were headed, they began discussing whether the tiny village of Punta Ardita was Panama or Colombia. They were in disagreement as to whether we were actually leaving the country. Jaqué and Jurado were the two border towns, but Punta Ardita and Ricardo's place sat somewhere between them.

"No, I think it's Panama." said the younger.

"Are you going anywhere else?" they asked.

"To visit an indigenous village up the river from Jurado," Ana Maria said.

"Now Jurado, that's Colombia," a third man piped in. "Terrible town. Dirty. Are you sure you want to go to Jurado?" "Well, we're not really going to Jurado," Ana Maria answered. "Just around it."

One official pulled out a map, and the three men leaned into it, noting where *la frontera* actually was. The older one ran a thick finger down a dotted line to the ocean, hesitated, and then made his decision: *"Ardita es Colombia,"* he proclaimed.

At first, I thought it strange that they did not know where one country ended and the other one began. But then I thought about the imaginary lines that make such demarcations and the fact that Panama was part of Colombia until the turn of the century, when the canal made Panama such valuable territory to foreign interests. This tiny checkpoint suddenly felt like a huge border, a significant frontier rich with history, the edge of the other continent.

They sent our passports into the back room, and after a few moments we were called in. A middle-aged, uniformed man with slicked-back hair sat behind a desk. An oscillating fan sat on a box in the corner, nearly blowing the one decoration, a calendar, off the wall. I noticed what looked like a bullet hole in the wall under the calendar. The hole reappeared each time the fan turned.

"And why are you two going to Colombia?" the slicked-back man asked.

"To spend Christmas with a friend," said Ana Maria. I just smiled.

He had Ana Maria's passport open, admired her picture, and asked flirtatiously if she was married: *"Casada o soltera?"*

"Prometida," she lied, saying that she was engaged.

He motioned at me: "Does she speak Spanish?"

"Si," I answered.

He smiled. *"Casada o soltera?"* he opened my passport.

"Prometida," I answered, following Ana Maria's lead.

"Too bad," he said. "But you must have crazy fiancés to send you out to the jungle alone. And at Christmas!" He shook his head gravely at the foolishness of our imaginary men. "When are you returning?"

Ana Maria explained that I would be coming back in a few weeks by myself, as she had to remain in Colombia a few weeks longer.

"Well," he said, winking at me, "if you have any problems when you return, just come and see me." He stamped my passport and, before closing it, leafed back to the first page and kissed my picture. "Just come and see me," he said again and showed us out.

The boat that would take us over the *frontera* was a tiny motorboat, almost a dinghy. The captain was a young Colombian boy who introduced himself as Archangel. I was surprised by the name, and when he walked away for a moment, Ana Maria whispered to me that his father, Momento, had named all of his sons for angels and saints. "Let's see," she said, "there's Santo, and Lazaro, and Archangel, and I forget the others right now." We were interrupted by Archangel's return. For some reason, he had seemed unsure that he could take us, but then agreed after a short discussion with some officials.

When the plane from Panama City arrived that afternoon, the children who had been our shadows suddenly disappeared, and a half hour later a party of ten or so arrived to board the boat. The mayor of Jurado, the Colombian village close to Punta Ardita, was in the party with his family and entourage and about fourteen huge bags of Panama City Christmas purchases. There was no way we would all fit in that boat.

We did. Somehow they loaded every bag into the boat and then everybody. We were tightly packed. Ana Maria sat me down next to a young man, whispering to me, "It's the mayor's son, Nigel. Talk to him." She wanted me to tell him about our plans for Punta Ardita, the plans we would be proposing as alternatives to cutting the rain forest for lumber.

The tide had come in, and it was finally high enough to leave Jaqué. The waves were huge, especially when we first headed out into the ocean. The boat climbed up each wave, reached a crest, and then slammed down into the water. My body rose completely off the seat and slammed down with it.

"We're lucky," Nigel yelled over the waves. "It's pretty calm today. It's usually much worse."

I nodded and tried to keep my lunch down. It happened about ten times before we were far enough out in the ocean to be beyond the breaking waves. It was much calmer out there as long as we kept moving, but the wind and the engine still made it hard to hear.

Nigel began asking me questions, which I answered in a rudimentary way, about where we were from, why we were headed to Colombia. I had to ask him to repeat everything three times and still only understood about half. Tired, I finally began resorting to the "*Si*" and smiling which Ana Maria had warned me about.

"You are a very beautiful woman," Nigel said.

I thanked him, becoming used to the Latin way.

"You know, I've been feeling that I'd like to settle down soon" was another sentence I caught completely.

"It's good to settle down," I agreed innocuously, or so I thought.

There were a few sentences I didn't catch in the wind, so I just smiled and nodded.

Finally, he said something and looked at me so intensely that I knew I had to get him to repeat it.

"I said," he moved close to my ear, "that I've been looking for the right woman to float by." He paused. "I'm so glad you'll be in Jurado tonight for the disco."

I instantly stopped smiling and nodding. I wondered what else I had agreed to.

It was one of several such conversations on the trip. I was speaking to Nigel in a frank, matter-of-fact way. I realized that in his culture my behavior, perhaps my very presence, might be viewed as flirtation or invitation. I quickly began undoing the web I had inadvertently woven on the ride.

I thought about the passport official's personal questions, his kissing my picture, and what my response might have been if such a thing had happened back home. But I wasn't back home. Here, I realized that just being an unescorted woman could cause a great deal of miscommunication. Over the loud engine and with salt spray in my eyes, I found myself declining, as politely as I could, both the disco and, more subtly, marriage. ■

From Reflection to Response   **Responding to "Crossing the Border"**

Working with a small group of classmates, or writing on your own in your journal, respond to the questions below.

1. Why do you think Thiel was motivated to write this narrative? What are her communication goals?

2. The opening of "Crossing the Border" seems to be about routine inconveniences and frustrations. What details or observations suggest that there may be a larger issue or problem under the surface?

3. Although "Crossing the Border" is an excerpt from a longer work, it conveys a view or message at the end. In narrative essays, the view or message (or solution to the problem) usually is a learning experience that the writer considers meaningful and shares with readers. In your own words, what is the learning experience that "Crossing the Border" shares?

4. As someone preparing to write a narrative essay of your own, comment on what you learned from Diane Thiel's narrative that you can apply to writing your own essay. Identify an incident or scene in the narrative that held your attention the most. List some of the descriptive details that bring the incident or scene to life. What does Thiel's use of dialogue contribute to the narrative?

EVALUATING IDEAS

If you spend time brainstorming and talking to classmates and your instructor about this writing project, you should come up with some interesting ideas. How do you decide which one to go with?

Consider this example: One summer your parents made you participate in an emergency rescue mission, or a ministry organized by your church. You traveled to a distant, rural community on a smelly school bus, to help the victims of a hurricane rebuild their homes. You went only because your parents forced you. You really wanted to spend the summer at home hanging out with your friends, going to movies and parties, and working part-time at the mall. You resented being forced to volunteer, hated your parents for interfering with your life. You had worked hard all year in school, and you deserved a rest. You had nothing in common with the do-gooders in your volunteer group.

Is this a good issue to write a narrative essay about? Would someone want to read about this? Maybe. First, you have to ask yourself whether there is a story to tell. Good narratives need movement. Things happen—incidents, situations, confrontations that you can describe and re-create. In addition, things change; you change. The story goes somewhere, takes readers somewhere. If the rescue mission changed you or your attitude in some way, opened your eyes, then you probably have an interesting essay to write. The story goes somewhere and means something. But if you don't have a destination beyond the starting point—your resentfulness and anger—where is the narrative going?

As you consider various ideas for this essay, you might remember a frightening, unusual, or dramatic experience that would be interesting to share with readers. Perhaps you witnessed a robbery in a convenience store or were on an airplane that had to make an emergency landing.

Even if the experience is interesting, it might not sustain a good essay. An essay has to develop meaning for readers, an illuminating view. A good narrative essay has to teach your readers something about life through your experience. There has to be a real learning experience embedded in the issue you write about.

As the writer, you don't have to have the learning experience worked out from the beginning, but you do need to have a conviction that by writing the essay—telling the story you have to tell—you can flesh out a meaningful learning experience and transfer it to your readers.

Some writers and writing teachers call this learning experience "answering the 'So what?' question." If a reader thinks "So what?" (or "Why should I care?") at the end of the essay, and the essay doesn't offer a good answer, then the essay will fall short of the reader's expectations.

Essays about incidents that are random or coincidental and do not have an intrinsic meaning or connection to the writer's life—for instance, the robbery you witnessed, or the emergency landing mentioned above—may not offer good answers to the "So what?" question, perhaps only clichés along the lines of "live every day to the fullest" or "always tell your mother you love her" (before you go to a convenience store). Your readers will feel disappointed and cheated if your message is that obvious or predictable.

As you evaluate ideas for your essay, consider some of the potential stumbling blocks covered in Table 4.1.

TABLE 4.1 Problems and possible solutions for evaluating ideas

Problem	Solution
Are you still in the process of dealing with the issue? Is it too immediate and unresolved for perspective and closure?	Issues you are in the process of dealing with can be compelling, but also hard to develop a view or message about, because they are unsettled. For instance, if you are just starting college and maintaining a long-distance relationship with your high school boyfriend or girlfriend, you have an issue to write about, but you don't know the outcome. You could write a more meaningful essay a year from now. You would know more about the issue, have more of a story to tell, and be in a better position to teach readers something about long-distance relationships.
Are you comfortable writing about the issue?	Effective narrative essays are honest, detailed, and factual; they tell the truth "warts and all." If an issue is too personal or sensitive for you to write about candidly, you should leave it alone.
Is the issue your issue, not someone else's?	The most illuminating narrative essays are about the writer, a subject the writer knows inside and out. If your essay is mainly about someone else, for example, a sibling who has a drug problem, it might be interesting, but your ability to tell the whole story, the inside story, will be limited. Your sibling could write a much better essay about his or her drug problem than you can, because he or she knows the issue inside out, how and when it started, why, and all the consequences. What you could write about is how the sibling's drug problem affected you—how it threw your life into disarray, how you tried to intervene, succeeded or failed, and learned from the experience. Dealing with the sibling's problem as your issue could make for a compelling narrative.
Is the issue too subjective or psychological for a narrative?	Some issues that affect us profoundly, like the death of a loved one, or dealing with an injury or illness, can be difficult to write narratives about. These issues evoke deep emotions but our experience of the issue is more internal than external. The events, incidents, situations, and confrontations that narratives need for movement may be limited or hard to flesh out. Conversely, issues that do not have such a profound effect on us, that are on the light or humorous side of life—for example, dealing with a parent's idiosyncrasies, or shopping with a boyfriend—can sustain compelling narratives if they conjure interesting incidents, events, situations. *Meaningful essays do not have to be based on earthshaking issues.*
Is the issue too large, enduring, and complex for the assignment?	Issues that cover many years or a lifetime—let's say a difficult relationship with a stepparent—can be hard to compress into an essay. The key to making issues like these manageable is careful planning and storyboarding. Rather than try to tell everything in summary fashion, identify a sequence of important scenes and incidents that will convey the story.

TABLE 4.1 (continued)

Problem	Solution
Is there a "learning experience" in your idea, or is it just something interesting or dramatic that happened—a "slice of life"?	Sometimes an experience such as the robbery previously mentioned can seem worth writing about but lack the meaning that a narrative essay needs in order to deliver a view or message.

WRITING A PROPOSAL

After you have decided on an issue for your essay, your instructor might ask you to write a short proposal. Writing a proposal can help you plan an essay—that is, define its key elements before you start drafting. In addition, the proposal gives prospective readers like your instructor and classmates an opportunity to make helpful suggestions.

In a business or professional context, proposals usually are written to secure authorization to perform a task or provide a service. For example, an engineering firm, or a construction company, might submit a proposal to a government agency for a public works project. Often the person or people reading the proposal are receiving many of them. They expect the proposal to be formatted and organized in a way that makes the essential information easy to find and read. Proposals that are poorly formatted and disorganized may never be read, even if the content is worthwhile.

Composing a proposal for a college writing project mirrors the professional situation. Your instructor, the primary reader, more than likely will be receiving dozens of proposals and reviewing them in order to authorize projects and give useful feedback. With that in mind, take a professional approach to the formatting and organization so that your instructor can access the key information efficiently.

Format the proposal in *business style*, rather than essay style, using the section headings below (numbered or bulleted), block paragraphs, and single-spacing. Business style prioritizes efficient reading and white space. At the same time, the block paragraphs and single-spacing generally reduce the number of pages.

1. **The Main Issue or Problem** your essay will evoke (approximate length: a few sentences or more).

2. **The Viewpoint, Message, or "Solution"** you intend to support (a few sentences or more). Your view or message often will not be completely worked out at this stage of the writing process. For now, envision a

viewpoint or message. As you compose your essay, the view or message will crystallize. Remember that the essence of a relevant view or message for a narrative essay is the learning experience you derived from dealing with the issue or problem you are writing about.

3. **Your Reasons for Choosing This Issue and Your Communication Goals.** Elaborate on why the issue or problem is important to you, your motivation for writing about it, and what you want to communicate (at least a paragraph or two).

4. **The Reader-Relevance and Audience.** Elaborate on who your readers might be and why you think readers will be interested in your essay—specifically, what you think the essay might be able to teach them (a paragraph or two).

WRITING A ROUGH DRAFT

> **❝***When asked about the most frightening thing he had ever encountered, novelist Ernest Hemingway said, "A blank sheet of paper." And none other than the Master of Terror himself, Stephen King, said that the "scariest moment is always just before you start [writing].*❞
>
> —RICHARD NORDQUIST, "WRITERS ON WRITING:
> OVERCOMING WRITER'S BLOCK"

Since we tell stories all the time, it might seem that this essay should flow naturally, almost write itself. In fact, narratives can easily stray off the point and lose focus. Informal essays in general are harder to keep focused than formal essays.

A formal essay—an academic argument or research paper, for example—lays out the communication goals in the opening. The writer tells the reader what the central issue is and presents a view (the thesis or main argument). The rest of the essay supports the view in a deductive pattern, going from the general view to specific evidence and reasons. Thus, a formal essay lays out a blueprint for the whole essay in the beginning. Both the writer and reader have a clear idea of where the essay needs to go and what the writer needs to do.

Most narrative essays, however, are organized informally. As you learned in Chapter 2, informal essays use an inductive pattern, going from the specifics of the issue in the opening to a general view or message in the end. The issue—the story—is what the essay is mostly about. The view emerges gradually, and it often only crystallizes at the very end. That means the ultimate goal of the essay—to present a view—is unstated and suspended through most of the essay.

The main issue, along with the time frame, or chronology, of events, is the only organizing principle keeping the essay in focus as it moves toward a conclusion.

As a result, in planning and drafting a narrative, it is crucial to define the central issue as specifically as possible and keep it in focus. If your essay is about a difficult relationship you had with your stepmother, you cannot write about every facet of the relationship. What is the *specific* issue? Maybe the stepmother was a hypocrite or two-faced. If so, her hypocrisy is the central issue, and your narrative should focus on that. Maybe you were a big part of the problem, so immature and petulant that you made a good relationship impossible. Then the essay would focus on your bratty behavior.

The Opening

The most reliable way to begin any essay is with a compelling presentation of the central issue. Narrative essays often present the central issue "in the moment." In other words, they begin with an incident, situation, event, or "scene" that immerses the reader in the issue and launches the essay dramatically—for example, the night you caught your stepmother rummaging through your purse, or the time you told your friends that a guy you just met at a party would drive you home.

Assuming you start with a relevant incident, one that projects the central issue, readers usually like an opening "in the moment." It involves them in the essay, and it gives them the sense of experiencing the issue for themselves.

Below, notice how Megan Daum's narrative essay, "On the Fringes of the Physical World," opens "in the moment":

It started in cold weather; fall was drifting away into an intolerable chill. I was on the tail end of twenty-six, living in New York City and taking part in the kind of urban life that might be construed as glamorous were it to appear in a memoir in the distant future. At the time, however, my days felt more like a grind than an adventure: hours of work strung between the motions of waking up, getting the mail, watching TV with my roommates, and going to bed. One morning I logged on to my America Online account to find a message under the heading "is this the real meghan daum?" It came from someone with the screen name PFSlider. The body of the message consisted of five sentences, entirely in lowercase letters, of perfectly turned flattery, something about PFSlider's admiration of some newspaper and magazine articles I had published over the last year and a half, something else about his resulting infatuation with me, and something about his being a sportswriter in California.

The opening immerses us in the central issue: the writer is leading an unglamorous life, more "like a grind than an adventure"—getting up, going to work, watching TV at night. Readers understand that she is bored. When she gets the message from PFSlider, she seems pleased and flattered. Should she be? Who is PFSlider? He could be anything from a psychopath to Prince Charming, but the writer seems focused on the charming part.

She has put us in her shoes, re-created the issue with details that we can grasp, evaluate, and connect to. Most readers will want to keep reading to find out what happens and what it means to them. Notice that no view, message, or thesis is presented or implied in this opening. Some narrative essays start with a view. Even great novels can. (For example, "It was the best of times, it was the worst of times"—the opening of Charles Dickens's *A Tales of Two Cities*.) But the most common narrative approach is to develop and support the view gradually, through the details of the story, and let the view crystallize at the end.

From Reflection to Response   Analyzing Narrative Openings

Below are opening sentences from two narrative essays, "Unfair Game" by author and journalist, Susan Jacoby, and "Roommates from Hell" by student writer, Karla Pereira. Both openings convey the central issue in the moment, through a scene or incident, rather than stating it. Read the two openings and, for each, see if you can determine what the central issue is. What details convey the issue? Does the opening make you want to continue reading?

Unfair Game

My friend and I, two women obviously engrossed in conversation, are sitting at a corner table in the crowded Oak Room of the Plaza at ten o'clock on a Tuesday night. A man materializes and interrupts us with the snappy opening line, "A good woman is hard to find."

Roommates from Hell

"Holy s——, is that my shirt?" I asked myself when I walked into my dorm room, and stared at my roommate in disbelief. She was posing in front of the mirror wearing not just my cutest shirt, but *the* shirt that I was going to wear to a party that night.

Working Together

Draft the opening of your narrative essay. Consider describing an incident, situation, or event that conveys the issue in the moment. Your goal is to make the central issue as clear and compelling as you can. After you finish writing the draft, discuss it with a small group of classmates. Is the central issue clear? Does the opening make them want to continue reading? Can it use more details?

> **"** *I remember standing on a street corner with the black painter Beauford Delaney . . . and he pointed down and said, 'Look.' I looked and all I saw was water. And he said, 'Look again,' which I did, and I saw oil on the water and the city reflected in the puddle. It was a great revelation to me.* **"**
>
> —James Baldwin, *The Paris Review*, interview by Jordan Elgrably

Using Description and Details

Good narrative essays re-create experiences through description and details. To some extent, narrative essays are like movies in words, and as such, follow the principle of "*show, don't tell.*" No narrative or movie shows everything. That would be tedious. But good narratives and movies *show* significant incidents and scenes; otherwise, they run the risk of disappointing the audience. The problem with showing is that it takes time and patience. Telling, which means generalizing or summarizing—reporting your feelings rather than evoking them—is a lot easier to do, but less interesting:

> It was a *terrible* concert, the worst concert I've ever been to! The music was awful. The band and their fans were degenerates.

That piece of information is impossible for a reader to evaluate. Was the concert really bad or is the writer just opinionated? If the concert is an important part of the essay, the writer has to develop details that show and support the negative perceptions. The generalized opinion has little value.

As you draft the essay, describe the significant incidents, scenes, and conversations that move the story forward and bring the central issue to life. Develop details that put readers in your shoes. Think visually, trust your memories and the images in your mind, and use dialogue to re-create important conversations (for more on dialogue see page 146–148).

Finally, remember that you are writing an essay, not just telling a story. That means you are writing to develop a view or make a point. Before all is said and done, you need to understand the meaning of your narrative and convey that to your readers. Good narrative essays require as much analytical thinking as any other kind of essay, perhaps even more; the difference is that you are analyzing your own experience and the meaning it has to you and others, not a public issue or problem. If your essay ends without delivering a meaningful message, explicitly or implicitly, you will leave readers dissatisfied. The ending needs to deliver what journalists call a "kicker"— essentially your reasons for recounting the story, and the learning experience embedded in it.

From Reflection to Response   Expressing a View in a Narrative Ending

Below are the endings to the two essays whose openings are presented in the activity on page 142. Reread the openings; then read the endings and summarize the view or message that the writer is conveying. What seems to have changed?

Unfair Game

Mistakes can easily be corrected by the kind of courtesy so many people have abandoned since the "sexual revolution." One summer evening, I was whiling away a half hour in the outdoor bar at the Stanhope Hotel. I was alone, dressed up, having a drink before going to meet someone in a restaurant. A man at the next table asked, "If you're not busy, would you like to have a drink with me?" I told him I was sorry but I would be leaving shortly. "Excuse me for disturbing you," he said, turning back to his own drink. Simple courtesy. No insults and no hurt feelings....

Roommates from Hell

All we needed to make this work was a little more respect and honesty. I never thought living with people I knew nothing about was going to be so difficult. I figured that all it required was being nice, sharing our life stories, and "kissing some butt" just so we'd get along. I never thought about having to set rules for them so that we wouldn't run into problems.

Today some guy said something to me that was incredibly rude and inappropriate. You know what? I told him to "f____ off!"

Storyboarding Your Narrative

Storyboarding is a method used in many art forms to organize the parts that will create the whole—usually a sequence of images or scenes. Since a narrative essay draws on scenes from the writer's life, creating a storyboard can help you visualize and organize your essay—give you a blueprint to follow.

If the issue spans a long period of time—for example, a conflict with a stepparent—you won't be able to show everything or include every significant incident in the essay. Instead, you should be selective and include enough key scenes and details to ensure that the reader can grasp and evaluate your experience. The scenes that you choose to describe should *build* toward a climax that supports the message you deliver.

If the issue spans a short time frame—for example, something that happened one night at a party—and therefore essentially involves just one isolated event, use the storyboard to identify incidents or scenes within the event that you are going to describe or re-create in detail.

You can create your storyboard in any format that is convenient for you. The format in the box uses some sample "captions" from an essay a student wrote about conflicts with her stepfather.

Storyboard for: (*Working Title*)

Scene # 1 Caption:	Scene # 2 Caption:
Example: I'm late, about to leave for dance practice…	Example: My boyfriend comes over to pick me up for a movie
Scene Description/Details:	**Scene Description/Details:**
My stepfather, watching TV in the living room, tells me I can't use the car. Why? Because he says so…	My stepfather disrespects him…
Scene # 3 Caption:	**Scene # 4 Caption:**
Example: I lose it with my mom	Etc.
Scene Description/Details:	**Scene Description/Details:**
She tells me I'm selfish and immature…	

From Reflection to Response   **Storyboarding a Narrative**

For practice, before you storyboard your own narrative, do a revision outline or storyboard of Diane Thiel's "Crossing the Border." (If you prefer, you also can outline or storyboard the narrative essay titled "Roommates from Hell" at the end of the chapter.) Then go ahead and storyboard your own essay.

Using Dialogue

Because narrative essays are based on real life experiences, they usually include significant conversations—in other words, dialogue, the words people say to each other at key points in the essay. When used selectively to illuminate key scenes and incidents, dialogue adds realism to an essay and can convey important insights. Readers want to "hear" what people say at these key moments. However, dialogue can be ponderous and counterproductive when it is included randomly, overused, or poorly written.

To write effective dialogue, you need to be aware of a few basic rules and conventions. Below is a passage of dialogue from G. Gordon Liddy's best-selling autobiography, *Will*. The speaker of the first line has caught the writer, Liddy, in the act of obeying a strange order:

> . . . "Just who are you and what the hell do you think you're doing?"
> "I'm Special Agent Liddy of the FBI and I'm letting the air out of your tires," I said, continuing to do so.
> "I don't believe this!"
> "Believe it," I said as the second tire went completely flat.
> "I demand to see your superior immediately!"
> "Yes, sir," I said, getting back to my feet, "if you'll just follow me, I'd be delighted to take you right to him."

Note how the dialogue is formatted: the writer begins a new paragraph each time the speaker changes. Now read the passage without paragraphing:

> "Just who are you and what the hell do you think you're doing?" "I'm Special Agent Liddy of the FBI and I'm letting the air out of your tires," I said, continuing to do so. "I don't believe this!" "Believe it," I said as the second tire went completely flat. "I demand to see your superior immediately!" "Yes, sir," I said, getting back to my feet, "if you'll just follow me, I'd be delighted to take you right to him."

Lumped into one paragraph, the dialogue is dense and hard to read. When you write dialogue, correct formatting—that is, beginning a new paragraph with each change of speaker—makes the dialogue easy to read and crisp.

Because dialogue reports what people actually say, writing dialogue in a narrative essay raises the issue of using slang, curse words, phonetic spelling, and bad grammar—let's call it colloquial or "street" language. In real life, some people say "bling" for jewelry, use the "F word," and speak ungrammatically ("Me and him went to the game...").

Should dialogue include the language of the "street"? The answer is yes, but be sensible about it. Good dialogue should be realistic, an accurate *representation* of what people say, although not a word-for-word *transcription* (which tends to come across as chatter).

As a general rule, dialogue should reflect how people talk, but you still need to be considerate of your audience, because the essay is for them. Vulgarity and swear words, in particular, can be offensive, and for a writer's communication purposes, counterproductive.

Suppose your narrative is about a feud you had with your next-door neighbor named John. You describe a confrontation with John in which you lose your temper and call him an "Ass____e!" Most adult readers, including college students, will accept the realism of that word, even if they find it crude. They will understand that you are using the word to accurately express what happened. But in a general audience, some people might be offended by the word, so it would be sensible for you to consider an alternative: "Lowlife!" or "Jerk!" are not as strong as "Ass____e!" but get the idea across.

Being considerate of your audience extends to writing phonetic dialogue. Phonetic spellings such as "wanna" for "want to" or "wimmen" for "women" may seem realistic, but they tend to be an unnecessary distraction and annoyance for readers. Most of us actually pronounce "want to" or "women" as "wanna" and "wimmen," which means that as we read we mentally use that pronunciation anyway.

The problem with the phonetic spelling is that it looks strange on the page. As we encounter these phonetic spellings, we are reading a different language than we are used to, and we have to translate as we read. Even worse, sometimes the phonetic spellings can be misleading. Writing "weeeel" for "well" to show that the speaker drawls out the word doesn't work, because the reader will read it as "wheel." Similarly, if a character says "Ah need a new paramore," meaning a new "power mower," the reader may think the character is saying "paramour"—that is, a new lover or mistress.

Outside of dialogue, you should avoid using "street language" in a narrative (or any essay) unless you have a clear and convincing reason for doing so, *and* you are sure your readers will understand the reason. Otherwise, readers are likely to think you are just a bad writer. Street language tends to be a lazy substitute for effective wording and thinking. A construction like "I was *damn* lonely that summer" means *nothing* more than "I was very lonely." A good writer delivers truth through factual details: "I spent that summer playing video games alone, doing crossword puzzles, surfing the Internet, and watching old movies and cartoons, until one day, I was so desperate for companionship, I walked into the Church of Scientology."

Verb Tenses

Narrative essays are about the past, an event or events that occurred before you sat down to write. Therefore, the past tense is the logical and realistic verb tense for narrative writing. A narrative essay whose opening we looked at earlier—"On the Fringes of the Physical World"—is written in the past tense:

> It *started* in cold weather; fall *was* drifting away into an intolerable chill. I *was* on the tail end of twenty-six, living in New York City…[my italics]

However, many professional writers—fiction writers and historians, as well as essayists—like to write narratives in the present tense, to create a sense of immediacy, as though the narrative—to borrow a computer term—is unfolding in real time.

Written in the present tense, the opening above would read like this:

> It *starts* in cold weather; fall *is* drifting away into an intolerable chill. I *am* on the tail end of twenty-six, living in New York City…[my italics]

Readers know the writer is remembering—writing about the past but using the present tense for effect. Readers get used to the effect and tend to forget about it as the narrative unfolds. The use of the present tense for effect is a stylistic choice that a writer makes. All things considered, it is not an important choice, but it can be a bad choice if the writer starts jumping back and forth from present tense to past tense for no reason. Arbitrary tense shifts create a distraction that is more annoying than stylish. Inexperienced writers can have trouble keeping verb tenses consistent. Writing your narrative essay in the present tense is a stylistic burden you probably don't need. The past tense is easier to manage and also more realistic.

A Title

Essays, like movies, need titles. Titles are a professional feature and aid to reading. An essay that has no title, or is titled something mindless like "Assignment # 2," sends a negative message, and more often than not, promises a dull reading experience.

Titles don't have to be intriguing or creative. A title that announces the subject of an essay is good enough, but if the title projects the issue that the essay is about, so much the better—for example, "Roommates from Hell," instead of just "My Roommates."

If the title is intriguing or creative, "Unfair Game" or "On the Fringes of the Physical World," that is a plus, too. A creative title tells readers the opposite of what "Assignment # 2" says—namely, that the writer is thoughtful and has something to say.

YOUR ESSAY CHECKLIST

The timeline for writing a narrative depends on how long and detailed it will be, but regardless of the length, in order to write a narrative that will do justice to your subject and theme, you need to go through a realistic process of invention, drafting, revision, and editing. Use the checklist in the box as a guide for developing your essay and managing your time effectively.

✔ Task	Description	Time Frame
☐ **Choose a subject**	• Develop ideas for the essay, and discuss them with your classmates, instructor, and others. • Remember that the essay is *about* you, but *for* your readers, people you don't necessarily know. • Your goal is to re-create your experience of the central issue—*significant* situations, incidents, scenes, and conversations that convey the reality of your experience and put readers "in your shoes."	At least a day or two.
☐ **Write a proposal**	• Start planning your essay by writing a proposal that defines the central issue, projects a view or message, and explains the essay's relevance to your readers.	A half hour or so.
☐ **Create a storyboard or informal outline**	• Storyboard the key incidents, scenes, or events in the essay.	A half hour or so.
☐ **Write a rough draft**	• Start drafting the essay. • Make sure the opening presents the main issue. • Try to begin the narrative "in the moment" or in "real time," by re-creating a significant incident or scene that conveys the main issue and puts readers in your shoes. • As you draft your key scenes, strive to "show" more than "tell." • Use descriptive details and dialogue to strengthen the key scenes. • The narrative essay should develop a closing view, message, or insight (sometimes called a "kicker") that conveys the learning experience you had and the relevance of the essay to your readers.	The time frame will vary. Compose the first draft in more than one sitting if necessary.

(continued)

✔ Task	Description	Time Frame
☐ **Revise**	• Revise the essay as many times as you need to, making improvements until you "get it right." • If you run into problems during the revision process, do a revision outline (as described in Chapter 3, page 96). The revision outline will help you see if the narrative has gaps—disconnected or underdeveloped parts.	Plan on doing at least several revisions over the course of a week.
☐ **Seek peer review**	• Ask for feedback from your friends, as well as your classmates, during the revision process (see peer review questions). • Post a readable draft of the essay to your course website or Facebook page if you have one. • Consider visiting your instructor during office hours for advice and help, or take a draft to your campus writing center for advice from a trained tutor.	Varies.
☐ **Edit your essay**	Before you submit the essay, make sure you edit it carefully. Consider using the text-to-speech feature on your computer to hear how the essay sounds and help you catch mistakes or typos. Check for the following: • Helpful paragraphing (see Chapter 12 for more about this and the other elements of grammar and mechanics listed here) • Effective wording and word choice (avoid arbitrary slang or colloquialisms) • Correctly formatted dialogue • Consistent verb tenses • Sentence punctuation (eliminate run-ons and comma splices) • General grammar and mechanics (subject-verb agreement, pronoun reference, placement of commas)	Varies.

PEER REVIEW

Chapter 3 (on the writing process) equates good writing with revising. Getting feedback from people can be a huge aid to revision. In college writing classes, "peer review"—giving and getting feedback from classmates—is a common practice and can be especially helpful, because your classmates are usually working on the same project that you are and understand its goals and challenges.

Most instructors try to organize peer reviews for students while an assignment is in progress. Although peer reviews can give you valuable perspectives on a draft, the feedback may not always be useful. People have different interests and tastes, which you need to take into account. The best approach to feedback is to be open-minded and grateful for it—think about the responses you get. If a response strikes you as valid, act on it. If not, leave it alone (but still respect the contribution).

Remember that feedback from people outside your class can be helpful, too. Consider showing a draft of your essay to a friend, roommate, sibling, parent, or relative. The essay is about a real issue in your life, and people are interested in real issues because they are always dealing with them.

Below are some peer-review questions to guide your classmates' feedback. Consider also adding questions of your own that focus on parts of a draft that you have doubts or concerns about.

1. Does the opening of the essay convey a clear and compelling issue that involves you in the writer's experience? If so, what is the issue? Is it presented in the moment (that is, through a scene or incident), or is it a generalized explanation? Offer any suggestions you can for making the opening more interesting and compelling.

2. After the opening, is the continuation of the narrative detailed enough, or is it too generalized, more like a report than a story? Point out details you find effective, as well as parts of the essay that could use more details, description, or development. Overall, how well does the narrative put you in the writer's shoes and allow you to experience and evaluate the writer's choices, reactions, mistakes, and feelings?

3. What is the view, message, or learning experience that the essay conveys at the end? Quote words from the essay that express it. In your opinion, does the message answer the "So what?" question? Or is it too obvious and predictable, like a Hallmark card?

4. Evaluate the readability of the essay. Does it have an effective title? Is the essay well-edited and "reader-friendly"—in other words, easy to read and follow? Do the different parts of the essay flow together, or are they choppy and disconnected? If dialogue is used, is it formatted correctly? Are the verb tenses correct and consistent (in other words, are there any arbitrary shifts from past tense to present and vice versa)? Point out any problems or distractions that you noticed with organization, wording, grammar, punctuation, or paragraphing, and offer suggestions for improvements.

STUDENT ESSAY: FINAL DRAFT

Below is the final version of the narrative essay that first-year student Kierstin Koppel wrote (see her proposal at the beginning of the chapter). After the essay, Kierstin discusses her writing process and offers some interesting advice.

Kierstin Koppel // **AN EXPERIMENT IN ROMANTIC GAMESMANSHIP**

"Your boyfriend has been cheating on you for over a year, with me."

My hands trembled and my mouth became suddenly parched when I heard the cold voice on the other side of the phone. Panicking, I hung up and sat there in shock. A million thoughts flooded my head. Everything began to make sense. The aloofness and constant excuses. I had been completely naive for over a year!

I took a deep breath, composed myself, and began brainstorming about all the evil ways to get even with him. I dabbled between egging his car, spreading a STD rumor around to all the girls, and even placing poison ivy in his bed. After some serious considerations, I realized I lacked the guts to do any of the horrific acts, so I decided to write a note.

"Things are not working out. Sorry."

I slipped it under his door, and walked away from the relationship. Even violated and humiliated, I was sickeningly polite. I didn't know what I had done wrong, but I still apologized. Pacing back and forth with the cell phone glued to my side, I waited for a phone call from him inquiring about my abrupt decision to end the relationship . . . But he never called. Whether he had known that she called me, or he just didn't care, I'll never know.

I sat curled up like a couch potato, sulking in self-pity and indulging in Ben and Jerry's Cherry Garcia ice cream for three days. I watched "Sex in the City" reruns on HBO, until I ran out of comfort food. Finally, I mustered up enough strength to peel myself off the couch with unbrushed teeth and hair and make my way to the grocery store.

I was dazed, but not enough to ignore the staring as I passed people by on the streets. I must have looked like a walking zombie because I caused a toddler to burst into tears, scream "Monster!" and run to her mommy's side for comfort. I couldn't care less. Not because I was so tragically in love with this guy, but because I felt so belittled. Am I not good enough? Am I too passive? Or nerdy? What did this girl look like? What did she have over me? Was her appearance as icy as her voice? Was she as confident and fierce as her attitude? All these thoughts rushed through my head as I stood staring at ice cream.

I spent 20 minutes in the frozen food aisle debating between Chocolate Mint or Vanilla Bean, as if it was a life or death situation. Finally, I settled on Rocky Road. I thought the symbolism was appropriate for the occasion. Then as my luck would have it, I was stuck waiting in the checkout line looking like crap in my lounge pants and cozy boots behind a gorgeous girl. My complete opposite. As if I needed something else to make me feel inferior at the moment: black leather, knee-high stiletto boots ran up her toned calves ending fiercely above the knee. Her mini skirt banded perfectly around the curves of her hips, and her cinnamon hair draped along her shoulders meticulously styled. A Louis Vuitton purse swung from one hand, and the other arm was wrapped around the bulging arm of a statuesque man. A Greek god.

Then, it hit me. Greek God was my boyfriend! Shocked by his pristine appearance, and even more mortified by his strikingly gorgeous new "catch," I quickly hid my face behind my ice cream carton in shame. While spying and attempting to disguise myself as much as possible in the effort to avoid a confrontation, I noticed his change in behavior. He purchased a bottle of fine wine. Then he rushed ahead to hold open the door of his car for her. Ironic how he was "Mr. Cheapo" in our relationship, and had failed to show this gentleman side. In his eyes she was a "Royal Highness," too good to open doors for herself, and she knew it. I waited to see her smile of appreciation, but instead, her attitude-ridden face remained stiff, her nose turned up, and her ruby red lips were sealed. She was clearly spoiled and expected nothing less from her perfect guy, who bowed in her presence. Any half intelligent bystander would conclude he was officially "whooped" and the woman was officially a "bitch." Too bad her personality was like acid and quickly would disintegrate her good looks. Rocky Road and I stood there, baffled, as I tried to grasp why perfectly good, deserving women remain single while the "bitches" get the guys. I was determined to find out why.

There had to be something I was seriously doing wrong, or perhaps a secret I had yet to find out. By the time I left the store, the cold air had settled into the valley and darkness was beginning to blanket the sky. My new mission trumped my ravenous appetite, so I tossed the ice cream in the trash can and wandered into my favorite book store. I was drawn like a magnet to the self-help/relationship aisle. I ran my fingers along the spine of each newly imprinted tome of wisdom, searching for something to pop out at me. The books were all cynically titled along the lines of *He's Just Not That Into You*, or *It's Called a Break Up Because It's Broken*. I found it astonishing that a lucrative market is based on the insecurities of women, and now I was one of them. Women search desperately for relationship answers attempting to gain insight by dissecting the male brain as if men are some alien species. I guess men really are from Mars.

I reached the end of the aisle and landed on a little white book with bold writing creatively illustrated in a woman's red lipstick: *Why Men Love Bitches* by Sherry Argov. The title, along with the ruby-colored lipstick, instantly conjured the image of my former boyfriend's cinnamon-haired "Royal Highness." Aha! Her secret. I plucked the book off the shelf, and a few minutes later, curled up with it and a vanilla latte in the corner of the store. I became engulfed in each word. One chapter was more clever than the next. The book was a clear game plan for catching guys and included a detailed description of all the rules to go about it.

Reading, I discovered I was a "repeat offender." I was guilty of being the "nice girl" time and time again. Even when having been cheated on, I apologized. I found out that I was too simple, uncompetitive, easy-going, shy, and certainly *not* high maintenance. Right there and then I decided, gone were the days of being accommodating, easily accessible, and a pushover. I was ready to give the "bitch" a try!

By the time I was able to tear my head out of the pages of the book, the store was getting ready to close and had vacated out. I quickly purchased the book and scrambled out the doors. The city was in full party mode by now, and I was in sweat pants. As I passed a local bar a group of good-looking college guys whistled and stared. What they saw through my disastrous appearance is a mystery to me, but guys will be guys. Normally I would have just kept my head down and avoided eye contact; however, this time something compelled me to turn around and flick the guys off. They were victims of my bottled up emotions, but to my surprise, became oddly intrigued by my out-of-character actions. "Oh man, she's hot!" one howled. I secretly felt empowered. I could feel it in my bones. This was the beginning of something new.

By the time I reached my apartment, I had revisited almost every moment of my last relationship realizing that I had been completely myself the whole time, and maybe that was never going to be good enough for anyone. So then it was settled. I would change. The next morning I woke up with a new spirit, grabbed my credit card and went shopping. I stocked up on stilettos, mini skirts, red lipstick and nails to go with it. I had a new attitude and a new look.

I started "hitting the town" full force. Nightlife was the good life. Soon I was known by my first name at all the hotspots, and morphed into a master manipulator. My cell phone contacts grew from 50 to 150 numbers in a month, and they were all very eligible bachelors. I had men eating out of the palm of my hand, and took advantage of one guy in particular financially, indulging in a lavish lifestyle with him that I had been deprived of in my previous relationship. Finally, I breathed a sigh of relief at the power of knowledge. I was no longer on the outside of the game, but instead held the secret to the male brain and had risen to the top of the food chain.

Someone once told me, when you rise fast, you fall fast. I woke up one morning and realized, I had no clue who the person looking back in the mirror was. Where had my values gone? My moral compass was so off kilter; I had abandoned myself. What was worse, I realized that not one guy knew anything about the "real" me. They had fallen for some person I created. They were attracted to this facade, but in reality, that person was so far from who I am, and who I would ever want to be. Certainly, I wasn't happy, and I was pretty sure I wasn't making guys happy either, just driving them crazy. Even though we "bitches" look like we have it all, we have nothing because we're too busy pleasing ourselves and playing games. We never find true love. I didn't know how to get myself out of it, though. I felt stuck in someone else's body. I couldn't just disappear off the face of the earth, or show up at the clubs in my old clothes. I was programmed to work this way now, be a "bitch." The secret had been revealed and I could never go back.

On the way to work one morning I stopped into the bookstore for a coffee but before I could reach in my bag to pay, a guy behind me reached over and took care of it. I turned to look up and was instantly smitten by the romantic eyes and warm smile of this guy.

"The coffee is on me. I'm Ben." He held out his hand, but I was still transfixed on his deep blue eyes.

"Ma'am your coffee."

The employee snapped me out of my trance, causing me to spill the boiling drink all over myself. I was in extreme pain. I didn't know why I was nervous. I knew the game plan better than I knew my own phone number.

"Just play by the rules," I thought. We talked casually for a while. It ended with him asking me out on a date. I agreed without hesitation. Something about this guy was different. Very different.

Two months went by. One night we were going out for a romantic dinner. He arrived at my apartment a little too early because he always was sickeningly punctual. While I finished unrolling the curlers from my hair, he snooped around my apartment looking at old embarrassing pictures. Suddenly, he opened my bathroom and stood in the doorway with my *Why Men Love Bitches* book clutched in his hand.

"NO!"

My worst nightmare had just come true. I was speechless. Everything from my toes to my cheeks became numb as he began waving the book in the air. He stood there shocked and then tossed the book in the garbage.

"This is not always true you know? I would have never pegged you for the type of girl who would read this junk." His words hit me like bullets. My face turned bright red and my body was warm as a furnace from embarrassment. My little secret had just been aired out to dry.

Over dinner he explained the reason he liked me. "You are different, simple, bashful, and easy to get along with. More than that, I love you in your lounge pants and cozy boots, and how you watch the history channel and read books for fun. I like you because you're klutzy and not afraid to be yourself. You are not one of those girls at the clubs in mini skirts looking to play games. You are you," he recited.

Oh the irony...At that moment I realized he knew exactly who I was, and that was enough for him. I didn't have to be the "bitch," and subconsciously had forgotten to play by the rules from the moment we met. The game didn't apply to him, yet he had fallen, and I had fallen back. Although I temporarily deviated from who I was, I decided to turn in my trashy stilettos forever and embrace my cozy boots. Gone were the days of the "bitch." I was ready to be myself. ∎

Interview with the Student Writer

● **Kierstin, how did you go about composing this essay?**

● I like to write my first drafts in longhand, then I'll type up the draft, making changes and improvements. After that, I keep revising until I'm satisfied with what I have. I usually need to write at least three drafts before I'm satisfied.

● **Did anyone read your drafts while you were composing the essay?**

● I may have gotten peer reviews, but in general, I don't like showing my first drafts to people until I'm fairly satisfied with what I've written. Getting feedback too early can be confusing for me. I learned that from acting. I prefer to get feedback after my own ideas are fully developed.

● **Was there anything difficult about writing the essay?**

● Once I came up with the idea, writing the essay was pretty easy, because I was passionate about the topic. When I'm *not* interested in a topic, then writing tends to be a lot more difficult.

- **What did you learn from writing the essay?**

- Mainly, it got me past my difficulties with narrative writing, the concepts for the beginning, middle, and end. It's like learning to ride a bike: after you do it the first time, it comes naturally.

- **What advice would you give to other students about writing this kind of essay?**

- I'm a very conservative person, so I would say don't "filter." If you have an idea you're passionate about, go for it. Don't overthink. And pay attention to the details!

EVALUATE YOUR LEARNING

1. What motivated you to write about the issue you chose for this writing project?
2. What are some other issues or areas of your life that you could write a meaningful narrative essay about?
3. If you had time to revise your essay some more, what changes or improvements would you make?
4. Did writing the essay give you any insights about yourself or your experiences that you were not conscious of before?
5. What advice would you give to a sibling or another student about writing a narrative essay?

ADDITIONAL READINGS

Karla Pereira // **ROOMMATES FROM HELL**

Karla Pereira graduated from the University of South Florida with a BA in Communications. She has worked in banking for several years, but is now considering going back to school to earn a degree in nursing. She is happily married and the mother of a beautiful baby boy. (In case anyone wants to know, she did NOT remain in touch with the two roommates who are the subject of her essay!)

"Holy s_____, is that my shirt?" I asked myself when I walked into my dorm room, and stared at my roommate in disbelief. She was posing in front of the mirror wearing not just my cutest shirt, but *the* shirt that I was going to wear to a party that night. That's when I imagined both of my roommates going through my drawers, giggling as they tried on all my shirts, pants and even my underwear. It made me cringe and it made me hate them both.

I had started to hate them within a few days after we met. I had just gotten back to the dorm room one night when Farrah was braiding Jenna's hair and out of the blue they told me that they thought that I acted airheaded and dumb. "It's just the way that you talk to people," said Jenna, "They're going to think that you're dumb and easy." My mouth dropped open. Yes, I felt hurt. I knew that was not true but nothing inside me gave me the strength to defend myself. So I brushed it off and silently jumped into bed.

I felt so horrible hearing them call me those names. I had to do something. I had to punish them in some way. I needed the guts to come out and tell them that they made me mad. But instead of that I said, "Um…hey guys. I just want to tell you that if you want to use my computer then ask me first…please." Yes, the words came out. Nervous and unsure, but I managed to say them. I finally stuck up for myself, even though it had nothing to do with the air-headedness comment that they had made. Unfortunately, nothing changed, though. The next day I walked into my room to see Farrah playing solitaire on my computer while talking on my cell phone to Jenna. The only thing that ran through my head was, "It's okay. I'll let this slide for now."

One day, my friend Courtney decided to stop by my room, so we could hang out. I nervously let her in hoping that she would be treated well by my roommates, especially by Jenna, the rude, the "I'll say whatever the hell I want to say to anybody" kind of person, with her tough girl walk and vulgar approach to people. I was actually surprised at how polite Jenna was to Courtney…that is, right up until the time Courtney left and Jenna turned to me and said, "Now *that* was definitely an airhead," and walked to her room. I followed her into the room and stood there, ready to scream, punch, kick, turn her desk upside down, basically defend my friend in any way possible. Jenna was shuffling papers on her desk, about to engage in a session of studying when she finally noticed my presence in her room. My lips quivered, as I got ready to say something.

"What is it?" she asked me, placing her pen on the desk and waiting for my response. "Uh, it's nothing," I said stupidly as I walked out of her room. Oh, but I did make a promise to myself. Next time I would stick up for my friends instead of being a coward. But I didn't, and the story repeated itself. Jenna and Farrah did the same thing to Susie, Jillian, Mike, Gus, Alex, Roberta…

There would be days where I would find my hair dryer and my brush missing from my dresser, and of course, I would find them in the hands of Farrah, the queen of "borrowing without asking," as she ran the brush through her and Jenna's greasy hair, thinking that the two of them looked marvelous. My water bottles also turned up missing, the ones that my mom had bought me to put in my closet for my convenience. There would be times when they would both borrow my cute tops and then throw them on my bed smelling of cigarettes and body odor. It made me want to throw up.

But did I say anything to them? Nope. I just took a deep breath every time and decided I would isolate myself from them both, until things got better. They stepped all over me and treated me as an inferior, which is not what I was used to or good at dealing with. As my passive attitude continued, things just got worse, and the dorm room became a hellhole that I dreaded setting foot in. Every day when it was time to go back, I would hope they wouldn't be there, either because housing had messed up the room assignments, or a huge comet had smashed into the room while they were in there going through my things. Either one would have been great! Of course, neither happened, so I would just continue to come "home" and sit in my corner feeling sorry for myself and telling myself how badly I needed to move out and get new roommates who weren't so rude and obnoxious.

One day I somehow got the guts to tell them they should move into the same dorm room together, since they had gotten so close. I thought that I was doing them a favor, being helpful to them because their little minds couldn't think of such a simple concept as moving in together, but I knew they would say no if only so that they could continue to raid my belongings. That same day, just as I was leaving for class, I heard Farrah call my name:

"Karla, come back right after class because Jenna and I want to have a talk with you," she said calmly, almost so calmly that it sounded like a mother trying patiently to discipline her child.

I just nodded. I didn't want to come back after class. I never wanted to come back at all, but I did it anyway because I was so used to being stepped on by them. When I returned, they were seated in the room, patting the chair in front of them for me to sit in. I put my things down, sat, and waited. Jenna's eyes burned into mine when she started talking, as if I had hurt her in some way.

"Karla, we need to work things out about our housing situation. When you asked us why we don't move in together, we took that as you telling us you don't like us at all. You don't even try to make this work. All you do is isolate yourself from us, and..."

Farrah stepped in and continued Jenna's sentence. "...And that makes it hard for us to get to know you. We know nothing about you. Oh, and also, it really hurt me when you put that password on your computer so I couldn't use it." Farrah frowned the whole time she talked which made me stare more at her forehead creases than listen to what she was saying.

As they continued with their arguments, I felt my blood boil and my fists clench. My throat was dry. My stomach was turning. I had to say something to shut them up. Suddenly, my mouth opened. I started off by telling them I have a problem telling people what really bothers me, and standing up for myself. Then I said, "Please disregard what I just said." That's when I exploded and let them know about each and every little thing they said or did that made me want to push them out the window. The insulting of my friends, the dirty shirts, the water bottles, the hair dryer and brush, the borrowing of my clothes, the rudeness, the mean way they treated me. Everything came out that had been bottled up for so long.

"I don't appreciate at all having you guys go through my stuff when I'm not here. Wait, even when I'm here, just don't do it!" I was feeling so good I probably exaggerated some offences so they would get my point. They stared at me in amazement. I expected them to get up and argue with me, deny everything I had accused them of. I closed my eyes after I was done and squeezed the sides of the chair, as if I was on a rollercoaster that was about to go through the loop.

To my surprise, Farrah said, "Wow, I had no idea you felt this way about everything that has been going on. You're finally being honest with us. We have been living really uncomfortably since the beginning. Let's do something about it." Farrah sounded almost friendly, accepting me into her "Jenna and Farrah club." Later that afternoon, we constructed a plan together about how to make our dorm room a "home away from home," by actually talking and getting to know one another. And you know what? Now, our plan is working just fine. Today I yelled at them because they printed some photos from their camera and a few of the pictures showed them wearing my clothes again. It felt good to scold them and good to hear them apologize to me.

All we needed to make this work was a little more respect and honesty. I never thought living with people I knew nothing about was going to be so difficult. I figured that all it required was being nice, sharing our life stories, and "kissing some butt" just so we'd get along. I never thought about having to set rules for them so that we wouldn't run into problems.

Today some guy said something to me that was incredibly rude and inappropriate. You know what? I told him to "f___ off!" ■

From Reflection to Response   Responding to "Roommates from Hell"

1. As you learned from reading this chapter, most narrative essays are built on a few key incidents or scenes that move the narrative forward and help support the view or message the writer wants to deliver. What key incidents or scenes move the narrative forward in "Roommates from Hell"?

2. Good narrative essays contain descriptive details that put readers in the writer's shoes and allow them, as much as possible, to experience and evaluate the main issue or problem for themselves. Point out some descriptive details in "Roommates from Hell" that allow readers to experience and evaluate the writer's frustration with her two roommates.

3. The meaning and relevance of most narrative essays are linked to some kind of change that the writer undergoes—a better understanding of herself and the issue with which she is grappling. How does the writer change in "Roommates from Hell," and how is the change connected to the message or "solution" to the writer's problem?

Courtesy of Amanda Laurel Atkins

AMANDA LAUREL ATKINS

Adapting to You

In this piece, I was trying to capture the sometimes foreign feeling of a new relationship. No matter what kind of relationship it is, getting newly close to some-one can often feel like exploring a new territory.

CHAPTER FIVE

Profiles

> " We were all in the car on the way to the beach. Nathalie was talking to Eric on her cell phone. When she told him where we were going, he ordered her to get out of the car right there and wait for him on the corner. To our surprise, she did just that. "
>
> —From a student's profile of a closely watched girlfriend

CHAPTER LEARNING OBJECTIVES

In this chapter, you will learn to:

- ▶ Choose a compelling subject for a profile.
- ▶ Understand the concept of a theme, and write a profile that supports a central theme.
- ▶ Create a storyboard that highlights thematic events and details.
- ▶ Conduct preliminary research and field research to gather information about your subject.
- ▶ Use selective description and details to illuminate your subject and theme.
- ▶ Include images in your essay to enhance a reader's understanding of the subject and theme.

PORTRAITS IN WORDS

Profiles are portraits in words, primarily portraits of people, but also portraits of places and events, or virtually anything that can be "portrayed" in writing—a company, a small business, an occupation. Of the different genres of writing, profiles may be the most popular. Many articles in newspapers and popular magazines are profiles. Magazines like *Vanity Fair* are almost entirely devoted to profiles. Many others—*Rolling Stone, Forbes, Vogue,* and *The New Yorker*—extensively feature profiles. Many television documentaries or segments of news shows like *60 Minutes* are profiles. The social media pages that many of us create online are a form of self-portraiture, in other words, profiles of ourselves.

PROFILES THAT COMMUNICATE AND SOLVE PROBLEMS

At their best, profiles inspire and instruct, and in doing so, help us solve problems. In the social sciences, case studies and case histories—profiles of individuals or groups of people—are an established form of research and analysis. Respected journals in every field profile successful people—surgeons, pilots, fund managers, teachers, attorneys, and scientists—to instruct us about achievement. The business profile below, written for *Entrepreneur* magazine, demonstrates how Kris Wittenberg, founder of SayNoMore! Promotions and Be Good to People, used astute business instincts and a persistent mind-set to create a promising company.

Sarah Max { **A RUDE EXPERIENCE INSPIRES A "GOOD" BRAND**

Courtesy of Sarah Max

IN THE SPRING OF 2008 Kris Wittenberg was out at lunch in her small town of Eagle, Colo., when a woman was rude to her. Looking back, she can't remember the exact details. "I just remember coming back to my office and wondering why people can't just be good to people," she says.

The proverbial light bulb went off. Wittenberg, who runs a successful promotional products company, SayNoMore! Promotions, vowed to put "Be Good to People" on a T-shirt. In a moment of inspiration she went to GoDaddy.com to see if the website was available; much to her surprise, it was. "I bought it that moment," says Wittenberg, who also began the process of trademarking the slogan.

Despite her initial flurry of inspiration, it took Wittenberg nearly a year to finally make that T-shirt. At the time, her promotions company, which she runs with her husband, August, was generating more than $1 million in annual revenue and on track to double sales from the previous year. "I just didn't have time for another business," she recalls.

That changed later that year when the pharmaceutical industry—a major chunk of their business at the time—agreed to stop giving out logoed pens, pads and other goodies. "Seventy-percent of our business was gone," says Wittenberg. The recession, meanwhile, didn't help matters.

To add to their string of bad news, the Wittenbergs were sued by their homeowners association for a parking area related to a home addition (the suit was settled out of court and they were cleared of wrongdoing). The night before a meeting with the HOA, Wittenberg made a homemade Be Good to People T-shirt out of iron-on letters. "The meeting went horribly," she says, "but I had three people ask me where I got that T-shirt."

That's when Wittenberg began working on Be Good to People in earnest, ordering dozens of different products, from T-shirts and tumblers to blankets and satchels, all printed with the same mantra. Everything is in black and white, says Wittenberg, because the message is a fundamentally simple one.

When Wittenberg began selling the goods at weekend markets in nearby Minturn and Vail, sales were brisk. "People would buy four or five things and then come back and buy more," she says. Wittenberg also signed up a couple dozen independent retailers around the country. It wasn't enough to carry them through financially—but Wittenberg says it reignited her passion as an entrepreneur, which she credits for helping SayNoMore recover more quickly. "In 2010 we were back to where we were and have grown ever since," she says.

These days Wittenberg is working on handing over more of her day-to-day duties at SayNoMore to her husband and half a dozen employees. "Ideally, I'd like to focus more of my attention on building out BGTP," she says. Online sales are currently a small chunk of Be Good's business, though it has nearly 19,000 followers on Facebook. When bad things happen in the world, she adds, activity typically picks up, though it doesn't necessarily translate to sales.

Wittenberg is now speaking with investors and exploring alternative funding options. She'd like to build up her inventory, revamp the website and eventually take the concept global. "My vision is wherever you are in the world you'll see Be Good to People," she says, adding that her goal is to make it as ubiquitous as the smiley face was in the 1970s.

In the meantime, Wittenberg says that wearing Be Good to People garb has been an interesting social experiment. "I always wear BGTP when I travel, and I've met people because of it and even gotten upgrades I don't think I would have gotten otherwise," she says.

At the same time, having the slogan in front of her all day, she adds, has helped calm her usually intense personality. "We call them magic shirts because you put on a shirt and you're nicer," she says. "You can't wear your Be Good to People shirt and be a jerk." ∎

Notice how Sarah Max's profile of Kris Wittenberg, like most essays, is launched by an issue or problem readers can grasp and relate to: Wittenberg feels upset about someone being rude to her. Instead of forgetting about the incident, she has a productive response. She vows "to put 'Be Good to People' on a T-shirt," and then lays the groundwork for a business by registering a domain name on GoDaddy.com and "trademarking the slogan." Nevertheless, a year goes by before she actually creates a T-shirt. Wittenberg starts the business in response to financial setbacks she and her husband experience. "Be Good's" success helps them overcome a period of adversity.

A STUDENT'S ESSAY PROPOSAL

As you begin this project, read the proposal that first-year student Kierstin Koppel wrote for a profile about a mortician named Janet Teller and her job. Kierstin's first project for her course, a narrative essay, is presented in Chapter 4; this is her second project. Kierstin's proposal for this project was based on the following assignment instructions:

Write a profile that supports an illuminating theme about a person, place, or event that you consider interesting and noteworthy.

Profile Essay Proposal: Humanizing a Mortician
Kierstin Koppel

1. Subject of the Profile

The subject of my profile will be a mortician, Janet Teller, or possibly someone she works with. The profile will focus on the profession. When people hear the word "mortician," they are likely to think of a drab man in a lab coat who has odd, "Edward Scissorhands" characteristics. People think being a mortician is a morbid job that requires an iron stomach and a quirky personality. Most people think this is a job that is not suited for a "normal" individual.

2. Source of Interest

I personally have no interest in becoming a mortician but I'm interested in learning more about how and why a person would become one, considering the prejudices most people have.

When we go to a funeral service, we see the whole event, the obituaries, the coffin, the flowers, and often a perfectly prepped, dressed, and embalmed corpse that we are remembering as a living person. This prepped corpse is our last vision of the person whose life we are honoring but we don't think about the work that goes on behind the scenes to provide us with this vision. A mortician's job is kept in the dark. This writing project gives me an opportunity to shed some light on it.

3. The Central Theme

There are many preconceptions and stereotypes associated with being a mortician. Through field research—specifically an interview, and if possible, observations at a funeral home—I will try to provide an insider's view about the job. The theme I am expecting to develop is that morticians do not find their job odd at all; in fact, they probably are "realists." After all, death is a natural stage of life. I am sure morticians are aware of the preconceptions people have. I hope to find and support the theme that morticians are much different from their stereotypes.

4. Research Methods and Visual Materials

I plan to conduct an interview in person (or, if necessary, by phone). My hope is that the person I interview will give me a great perspective on the job, and expose some of the misconceptions people have. Ideally, I plan to visit a funeral home, and if possible, perhaps talk to more than one mortician.

5. Audience and Relevance

My classmates and instructor are my primary audience, but I think this subject will appeal to a wide variety of readers of different ages and backgrounds. Very few people know what it's like to be a mortician or why someone would become one. I also think the profile will shed some light on our attitudes about death, and maybe change the way some people think about funeral services and their meaning. ■

You will find the final version of Kierstin Koppel's profile at the end of this chapter. For background information about Kierstin and her writing, see Chapter 4, pages 123.

Working Together

CONSIDERING IDEAS

Spend five or ten minutes brainstorming or creating a preliminary list of people, places, and events you consider noteworthy and might be interested in writing a profile about. Focus on people and places you know well, and events you have attended, but you also can include subjects you don't know as well but have realistic access to and could research for the profile (in other words, a person you could meet and interview, a place you could visit and observe, or an event you could attend and experience).

After you finish compiling ideas, post them on your course website and ask for feedback, or form a group in class with three or four of your classmates and ask them which of your subjects they would most like to read about and what they would like to learn.

PROFILES AND COMMUNICATION GOALS: TRACING A THEME

> **❝** *A writer must regard his story through theme-colored glasses.* **❞**
> —FRANCIS FLAHERTY, *THE ELEMENTS OF STORY*

To write a good profile, you need to start with an interesting subject, a subject that intrigues you as the writer. Your challenge is to make the subject meaningful to readers. A meaningful profile is more than a collection of facts and information. It says something readers perceive as useful and relevant to their lives. Profiles accomplish this by supporting a central theme, a view about the subject that gives meaning to the facts, information, and descriptions that the profile presents.

The view a profile conveys is usually in response to a question, issue, or problem that the subject raises for the writer. For example, a profile of a "daredevil"—let's say someone who walks on a tightrope between skyscrapers—might raise the question: "Is this person foolish and irresponsible, or incredibly brave?" (Answers, of course, can vary.)

When you write a profile, sometimes you know your theme from the beginning. If the profile is about someone close to you, the theme—your main view of the person—may be the reason you are writing. When you don't know your subject personally or well, your theme usually develops as part of your research and writing process.

Sometimes deciding on a central theme is not an obvious or easy choice. Most subjects present more than one theme on which a writer could focus. In his book, *The Elements of Story*, newspaper editor Francis Flaherty addresses this problem as it pertains to a news story about a murder victim:

> A New York baker, a Mexican immigrant, has been robbed and murdered. This crime, unsolved, offers a writer many possible themes: the man's life; the ongoing investigation; his grieving wife and children back in Mexico; his forlorn co-workers; and the failure of a teeming city even to notice his horrible death.
>
> Tempting subjects, and in a book there may well be enough room to explore them all. But for an article of modest size, the disciplined writer will force herself to spotlight just one. Sarah Wyatt, the writer of a...story about just such a murder, chose the man's mourning co-workers as her topic. The title of her article reflected her choice: "An Empty Spot at the Counter."

Flaherty points out that Wyatt's story "did not ignore the unchosen themes." It mentioned the lack of witnesses and the baker's family back in Mexico, but Wyatt devoted most of the story to "her big focus," what the baker meant to his coworkers, their respect for his work ethic and skills, the warm memories they had of him, and their sense of loss.

To write an engaging profile, you need to make the same kind of thematic decision. If your subject is a politician, what is the theme you will highlight? It could be the hard work of politics that often goes unnoticed—the hectic schedule, speechmaking, traveling, and campaigning. It could be the politician's frustrations with the way the "system" works—lobbying, gerrymandering, "pork-barrel" projects, special interest groups, and campaign financing. Then again, it might be the rewards of public service, of being able to help the poor and sick, create tax incentives for businesses, improve education, and clean up the environment.

Francis Flaherty uses the expression "disciplined writer" in his comments about thematic choices, because he knows that if a writer tries to address multiple themes with equal emphasis, the likely result will be a disorganized and watered-down story.

Take a look at the opening of the case study below, from *The Meaning of Anxiety* by clinical psychologist Rollo May. Notice how the author establishes his central theme about the patient before delving into any biographical facts and background information:

Helen: Intellectualizing as a Defense Against Anxiety

On arrival at Walnut House, Helen walked into the office smoking a cigarette, appearing poised and nonchalant. Somewhat attractive, she exuded the vitality of a person who cultivates her spontaneity. The impression she created in the first interview was a snapshot of aspects of her behavior which later proved to be of considerable significance.

On her own initiative she stated immediately that she had no guilt feeling whatever about her pregnancy. She volunteered the information that she had lived with two different men since arriving in New York, asserting in the same breath that "only priggish people have any feelings about such matters." But there were indications of anxiety and tension beneath her ostensibly friendly and free manner of talking—during her frequent, breezy laughter, her eyes remained dilated, giving the appearance of some fright even while she laughed. Helen created the immediate impression both to the social worker and to me that she was employing her evasive, laugh-it-off techniques in order to cover over some anxiety, the nature of which was not yet apparent.

She was the twenty-two-year-old daughter of middle-class, Catholic parents....

The theme of Helen's "breezy" attitude covering up anxiety draws the reader into this study and defines its purpose. The psychologist presents the totality of his theme early in the profile—that is, his view that Helen is posturing to cover up her anxieties.

Profiles often move more gradually toward the view—the totality of the theme—but in order to have a focus and direction, a profile needs to put readers on the trail of the central theme from the very beginning. In other words, the profile needs to present or suggest a question, issue, or problem (Helen's posturing or "breezy" attitude) that anticipates the final view of the subject, the totality of the writer's theme.

The profile below, about a New England lobsterman, opens with an issue of routine, hard work that many readers can relate to, but the totality of the theme—the writer's final view of his subject—only emerges at the end.

E. B. White { OLD DAMERON, FROM "SECOND WORLD WAR" IN *ONE MAN'S MEAT*

Bachrach/Getty Images

E. B. White (1899–1985) is a much-beloved American essayist and author of the children's classic *Charlotte's Web*. "Old Dameron" is a profile included in *One Man's Meat*, a collection of essays and sketches that White wrote while living a dual existence as a farmer and writer on the coast of Maine during World War II.

SIX DAYS A WEEK, eight months of the year, in war or in peace, Dameron goes down the bay in the morning and hauls his traps. He gets back about noon, his white riding-sail showing up first around the point, then the hull, then the sound of the engine idling and picking up again as he pulls his last two traps. Sometimes, if the sun is right, we can see pinwheels of light as he hurls crabs back into the sea, spinning them high in air. And sometimes, if he has had a good catch of lobsters, we can hear him singing as he picks up his mooring. It is a song of victory, the words of which I've never made out; but from this distance it sounds like a hymn being clowned.

He is as regular as a milk train, and his comings and goings give the day a positive quality that is steadying in a rattle-brained world. In fog we can't see him but we can hear his motor, homebound in the white jungle; and then the creak of oar in lock, tracing the final leg of his journey, from mooring to wharf. He has no watch, yet we set ours by his return. (We could set it by his departure too if we were up—but he leaves at six o'clock.)

I went with him in his boat the other day, to see what it was like, tending seventy traps. He told me he's been lobstering twenty-five or six years. Before that he worked in yachts—in the days when there were yachts—and before that in coasting schooners. "I liked coasting fine," he said, "but I had to get out of yachting." A look of honest reminiscent fright came into his face. "Yachting didn't agree with me. Hell, I was mad the whole time."

"You know," he explained, pushing a wooden plug into a lobster's claw, "there's a lot o' them yacht owners who haven't much use for the common man. That's one thing about lobstering—it gives you a hell of an independent feeling."

I nodded. Dameron's whole boat smelled of independence—a rich blend of independence and herring bait. When you have your own boat you have your own world, and the sea is anybody's front yard. Old Dameron, pulling his living out of the bay at the end of twelve fathoms of rope, was a crusty symbol of self-sufficiency. He cared for nobody, no not he, and nobody cared for him. Later in the fall he would haul his boat out on his own beach, with his own tackle. He would pull the engine out, take it up through the field to his woodshed, smear it with oil, and put it to bed in a carton from the grocer's. On winter evenings he would catch up on his reading, knit his bait pockets, and mend his traps. On a nasty raw day in spring he would get the tar bucket out and tar his gear and hang it all over the place on bushes, like the Monday wash. Then he would pay the State a dollar for a license and seventy-five cents for an official measuring stick and be ready for another season of fishing, another cycle of days of fog, wind, rain, calm, and storm.

Freedom is a household word now, but it's only once in a while that you see a man who is actively, almost belligerently free. It struck me as we worked our way homeward up the rough bay with our catch of lobsters and a fresh breeze in our teeth that this was what the fight was all about. This was it. Either we would continue to have it or we wouldn't, this right to speak our own minds, haul our own traps, mind our own business, and wallow in the wide, wide sea. ■

From Reflection to Response   Analyzing "Old Dameron"

E. B. White's portrait of the lobsterman is framed by two observations that appear somewhat contradictory on the surface: the lobsterman follows a rigid routine, and yet the writer views him as "belligerently free." Working with two or three of your classmates, or in your writing journal, decide if these perceptions are compatible, and if they are, why. What do you respect or admire about the man's routine? What makes him "actively, almost belligerently free"? Do you think the author romanticizes him or exaggerates his symbolic importance? Explain why or why not.

As part of your response, consider the relevance of the passages below.

- Sometimes, if the sun is right, we can see pinwheels of light as he hurls crabs back into the sea, spinning them high in the air.

- He is as regular as a milk train, and his comings and goings give the day a positive quality that is steadying in a rattle-brained world.

- A look of honest reminiscent fright came into his face. "Yachting didn't agree with me. Hell, I was mad the whole time."

- He cared for nobody, no not he, and nobody cared for him.

- Then he would pay the State a dollar for a license and seventy-five cents for an official measuring stick and be ready for another season of fishing, another cycle of days of fog, wind, rain, calm, and storm.

Themes in Portraits

We think of painted and photographic portraits as physical representations, but when portraits are memorable, they express something meaningful about the subject's character or life. Figures 5.1 and 5.2 show two portraits that appear "true to life" but are not just representations. They are *products* of decisions the artist and photographer made about compositional elements—the setting, light, clothes, colors, postures, props, facial expressions, and so on. All these details create a unique perspective, an interpretation of the subject by the artist that translates to a dominant impression or theme. If the artists had made different choices—for example, if Ingres had painted Mademoiselle Riviere indoors instead of outside (see Figure 5.1), or if Mary Ellen Mark had photographed Tiny in color (see Figure 5.2), with more depth of focus, standing in her bedroom—the impression and meaning would change.

De Agostini/G. Dagli Orti/Getty Images

FIGURE 5.1 *Mademoiselle Caroline Riviere*, 1806, by Jean Auguste Dominique Ingres

Mary Ellen Mark

FIGURE 5.2 *"Tiny" in Her Halloween Costume*, Seattle, Washington, USA 1983, by Mary Ellen Mark

| **From Reflection to Response** | **Analyzing Themes in Portraits** |

Analyze one of the two portraits for thematic relevance. Resist the temptation to go online and find out what an "expert" has to say about either one. Just go by what you see. First, write a paragraph or two that describes what catches your eye and interests you most. Then, based on your observations, make a case for a meaning—a theme—you think the portrait conveys.

To guide your analysis, ask yourself some of the following questions:

- What is the first thing you notice when you look at the portrait—what draws your eye?
- How old is the subject?
- How would you describe the subject's "body language" and mood?
- What is the subject wearing?
- What is the setting?
- What is the occasion, if any?
- What objects or details are highlighted in the portrait, and how do they relate to the subject?
- What is in the foreground and background—in other words, what is prioritized or put at a distance, respectively?

PROFILING A PERSON: THE HUMAN FACTOR

A good profile of a person appeals to human interest—it takes us outside of our own lives, into the heart, mind, and life of another person. Our interest in other people can evoke empathy and promote what a sociologist calls "the reality of human interdependence." However, not every profile is positive, ennobling, or inspiring. To enlighten and instruct us about people, profiles "cover all the bases"—that is, cover the good, the bad, and the ugly about human life and behavior, just as great artists always have done. Cheesy tabloid profiles of famous people dealing with personal disasters ennoble by default ("at least, I am not that bad or miserable") and teach "lessons" that are too gross and obvious to mean much (don't murder your estranged wife, don't mix drugs and alcohol, don't make a sex tape and post it on the Internet). However, even these cheesy profiles illustrate something relevant about profiles as a genre: readers are drawn to other people's mishaps and flaws, because readers themselves suffer mishaps and have flaws.

> **"**_Where you stumble and fall, there you will find gold._**"**
> —JOSEPH CAMPBELL, AMERICAN WRITER AND SCHOLAR

Choosing a Subject

You might be tempted to write a profile about a famous person or public personality that you admire or idolize—a musician, star athlete, or actor—but if you have no direct access to this person, your profile will be based on second-hand information and lack the unique perspective that makes profiles interesting. Even if you have access to a famous person—let's say you babysit for a star athlete in your neighborhood—you should ask yourself what your profile will accomplish. What can you say that is not already known?

It is possible that the famous person you "know" is not a great subject. Public figures are constantly scrutinized. They value their privacy and are concerned about their "image." Your ability to develop a meaningful theme about someone like this might be limited. Indeed, if you want to go in the direction of a famous person and use access you have, a spouse of the person might be a more interesting subject.

"Ordinary people," like E. B. White's Dameron, can be more intriguing than those who are famous and successful. Ordinary people can provide the instruction, inspiration, and human interest for which readers look. Ordinary people also are original material. Many people you interact with every day have special talents, qualities, and character traits that can instruct and inspire, or if you want to go in a different direction, they have flaws. They have overcome or succumbed to patterns of behavior that are self-destructive or misguided.

If you write about someone you know _very_ well, ask yourself if you are too close or emotionally attached to write about the person objectively. Scott Sanders's "Under the Influence" (see MindTap online) is a powerful profile of the writer's father and his lifelong struggle with alcoholism. The profile is illuminating because it is objective and unsentimental, but very few writers, even professionals, have the desire or emotional fortitude to portray a flawed or dysfunctional parent for the world to see. If you can't be objective, you can end up writing a profile that is transparently sanitized, the "saint" or "hero" profile that portrays someone, usually a family member or parent, in an idealized and unrealistic light. A profile like that can be heartwarming to write but painful to read. Even if your mother or father is a "saint" or a "hero," you need to figure out why that is relevant to a reader. If you don't have a good answer (how lucky you are is not a good answer), you probably will be better off finding another subject. For most of us, parents are a subject to avoid. Writing about your boyfriend or girlfriend might be a bad idea for similar reasons.

From Reflection to Response   **A Sketch of a Friend (or "Frenemy")**

Compose a one- or two-page sketch of a friend of yours. Your goal is to bring out the qualities in this person that make him or her your friend, but to do this as *objectively* as possible, *without writing about yourself or your relationship with the person.*

If you prefer, compose a sketch of someone you have ambivalent feelings about (a "frenemy"). Follow the same guidelines: make the sketch objective.

After you finish the sketch, exchange yours with a classmate's and give each other feedback. Does a dominant theme come through? Is the depiction sufficient and meaningful? What would be required to enlarge the sketch to a full-scale portrait?

Along with people you already know, people who are part of your local or campus community can be excellent subjects. First, they are accessible, and second, they are likely to interest your most common audience, your classmates and instructor. Campuses have many people who could be good subjects. In your community, the possibilities are even greater.

You can use the table to help you develop ideas.

Categories of People	Examples
Family and friends	• Nuclear family (siblings) • Extended family (uncles, aunts, cousins) • In-laws, stepparents, guardians • Current "best" friend (or best friends), past or childhood friends, social media friends
Acquaintances	• Teammates and other people you know as part of a group or organization (members of a class, band, choir, social club, dance ensemble, support group, sorority, etc.) • Mentors and "role models" (coaches, teachers, counselors, etc.) • People you work with—coworkers, a supervisor

Campus community	• A faculty member, administrator, trustee, or board member (e.g., a professor who has unorthodox views and approaches, or a dean of student affairs)
	• A student who has an interesting campus job, function, or internship—a dorm RA, writing-center tutor, student-athlete, technician for computer services, writer or editor for the student paper, or broadcaster on the student radio station
	• An upper-division student in your major; a graduate student, or alumnus
Local community	• A community organizer, civic leader, politician, or public-sector employee
	• People in "high-profile" professions—a doctor, surgeon, psychologist, lawyer, prosecutor, police officer, business leader, journalist, radio or TV newsperson
	• People in "low-profile" professions—a bartender, dance instructor, DJ, flight attendant, bus or cab driver, local archivist, historical-society director, lifeguard, park ranger, or auto mechanic
	• People in unusual or odd professions or businesses—a mortician, psychic, astrologer, "carny," jockey, drug dealer, tennis pro, or auctioneer

From Reflection to Response   **Evaluating Ideas for a Profile of a Person**

Once you have an intriguing possibility for a subject, evaluate your idea using the form, and then discuss your idea and evaluation with a small group of your class-mates, to gauge their interest.

Subject # 1	
How well do you know the subject? Can you and will you interview the person? (List pros and cons about the choice.)	
What is your source of interest?	
What is the central theme that you'd like to develop?	
What details and information will you use to support your theme?	
What is the relevance for readers?	

> ## Tech Tip
>
> If you are having trouble coming up with a subject for your profile, go online and check interesting people you follow on social media sites (for example, Twitter or Tumblr), or people you are connected to on a professional network (for example, LinkedIn).

Conducting Research

If you write a profile about someone you don't know well or at all, you need to do research to gather information about the person. Research usually is broken down into two categories: *primary* (often called "field research") and *secondary*.

Primary research means that you develop your information and insights firsthand from "raw materials"—for example, by conducting interviews or surveys or analyzing documents written by a person you are researching (letters, published articles, a personal memoir, and so on).

Secondary research means drawing on work other people have done— often professional writers, specialists, or scholars—based on their examination of primary sources, as well as other secondary sources. (Examples include journal and magazine articles and books.)*

Profiles rely mainly on primary or field research—in particular, an interview of the subject and your firsthand observations. Sometimes secondary research on the subject can be useful, too. If you are writing about a local politician, you want might to read newspaper or magazine articles about the person. However, if you overrely on secondary research, you run the risk of writing a dull profile. As suggested earlier, profiles draw their vitality from a writer's firsthand perceptions and interactions with the subject.

Conducting Interviews

Asking someone you don't know for an interview might make you nervous, but if you reach out in a professional way and explain what you want to accomplish, most people will appreciate your interest in them.

---

*See Chapters 8 and 14 for detailed information about research methods.

Below are some tips to help you make an interview productive.

Scheduling an Interview

▶ Be flexible about when the interview takes place. Let the person propose a convenient time.

▶ Be flexible about how you conduct the interview. A traditional face-to-face interview is not always necessary. Journalists conduct many of their interviews over the phone. E-mailing questions is another option.

▶ If you schedule a face-to-face interview, try to conduct it in a place that is relevant to your profile. For example, if you are interviewing a dancer, do the interview at a dance studio instead of Starbucks. Observing a relevant location will give you insights and material for your profile.

Preparing for the Interview

▶ Read something the person has written or something that has been written about the person. Look at photographs. Talk to people who know the person.

▶ Write down questions in advance. Make sure the questions focus on your source of interest in the person and what you are trying to learn. Don't overprepare or write down too many questions. Sequence your questions so that you start with casual, conversational questions, and move to more probing or difficult questions later. Don't obsess over your prepared questions or be afraid to deviate from them. Listen to what the person has to say. Good interviewers are above all good *listeners*.

Conducting the Interview

▶ Arrive early. Being late can frazzle you and annoy the person you are interviewing.

▶ Dress appropriately. Overdressing or underdressing might raise questions about your character or judgment in a stranger's mind.

▶ Let the interview proceed like a conversation. As suggested above, don't feel you have to ask all the questions you prepared, but make sure you get the information you need. An old newspaper dictum is that you only get one chance for an interview. If you try to come back for more information, the person may not be willing or able to accommodate you, so make the first interview count. The way to do that is to be prepared and have clear goals.

Taking Notes

▶ In theory, you should take detailed notes when you conduct an interview, but in practice, detailed note-taking can create problems. Sometimes it disrupts the flow of the conversation or makes the person you are interviewing uncomfortable.

Consider taking only brief notes during the interview, but then devote time *immediately* afterwards to writing a detailed summary. Again, careful listening is the key.

Recording an Interview

▶ Recording an interview may seem like a great idea but can be more trouble than it is worth. Recording people without obtaining their permission is illegal in some states and unethical in any case. You should always ask for permission to record someone. If the person agrees, keep in mind that he or she still might feel uneasy about being recorded, which can diminish the value of the interview.

From your perspective as the writer, replaying and transcribing a recording later can be a tedious process. Maybe you will find a "pearl" that escaped your notice during the interview, but chances are, unless the interview is long and involved, if you take conventional notes, you will end up with the same information and less work to do.

PROFILING A PLACE

Profiles of places intrigue us for the same reasons that profiles of people do—they take us outside of our own lives and instruct us about the world in which we live. Like profiles of people, they convey a theme, that is, a view about the subject that answers a question or solves a problem and says something illuminating to readers.

Figure 5.3 shows Georges Seurat's famous painting titled *A Sunday on La Grande Jatte*, which is a large canvas (seven by ten feet) that depicts an array of people in a park on the river Seine in France. Seurat's painting is best known for its colorful rendition of the scene and Seurat's distinctive style, known as "pointillism" or painting in dots. (Today we might say that Seurat paints the "pixels" that create the whole image.) But the painting also projects a theme about the separation and isolation of the people gathered in the park.

Figure 5.4 is a photograph by George J. Price of Guatemala City in the early 1950s. Price's photograph evokes the mood of tension and intrigue that prevailed there at the time. The elected president of Guatemala, Jacobo

Artepics/Alamy

FIGURE 5.3 *A Sunday on La Grande Jatte* **by Georges Seurat, circa 1890**

Arbenz, who is pictured on a hanging placard, instituted reforms that threatened the holdings of American corporations like the United Fruit Company. These corporations, in turn, portrayed Arbenz as a Communist, lobbied for U.S. government intervention, and eventually got their wish when the CIA sponsored a coup that removed Arbenz from power in 1954.

Courtesy of Robert Saba

FIGURE 5.4 **Guatemala City by George J. Price, circa 1953**

In a subtle way, Price's photograph portrays the conflicting perspectives that were coming to a head at the time. The large picture of Arbenz on the placard suggests a Latin American "strongman" or "*jefe*," culturally repellant to many North Americans, while the shadowy figure in the foreground on the left suggests the clandestine, U.S. intervention that was already afoot and culturally repellant to many Latin Americans.

Below are two short, online postings that profile Venice Beach, California, at different stages in its history. Both could be called snapshots, rather than portraits, yet the details are unified by a central theme, or view, that the writers want to communicate.

One Man's View

Family Man { **BIZARRO WORLD**

© Tupungato/Shutterstock.com

Venice Beach, California

WELCOME TO VENICE BEACH. If you like to mingle with druggies, prostitutes, pimps, thugs, and thieves, you came to the right place. Maybe Venice was a nice place to visit years ago, a place for an afternoon of relaxation and entertainment, but no more—especially if you have a family and kids, and don't want to expose them to the dregs of society.

If you happen to go by mistake, you better leave before it gets dark or you may be robbed or worse. People high on drugs are everywhere you turn, staring into space on park benches, staggering up and down the boardwalk, or slipping in and out of medical marijuana stores to replenish their stash of weed. What were once quaint souvenir shops have turned into tattoo parlors. Mexican gangbangers are on the prowl. The beach is strewn with litter. The public restrooms reek of barf, urine, and stale marijuana smoke.

Whether you're a native of Southern California and have a family like me, or you're a tourist who's here to see the sights, stay away from this godforsaken place. My advice to you? Check out the Huntington Gardens, Griffith Park, Hollywood Boulevard, and Rodeo Drive in Beverly Hills, or go to a ball game. Or if you want to go to the beach, take a drive down the coast to Redondo for a real Southern California experience. But whatever you do, stay away from this pseudo-hip freak show. ■

The Way It Was

R. L. Huffstutter

{ **SOME THOUGHTS ABOUT THE VENICE BEACH OF FIFTY YEARS AGO AND WRITING "THE GREAT AMERICAN NOVEL"**

LET ME SIMPLY SAY that when I got off the bus and walked down to Venice West more than 50 years ago, it was a different scene.

I will never forget the thrill of smelling the variety of different foods drifting out of the small delis and cafes. I was fascinated by the elderly, bundled up on the bench, speaking the language of Eastern Europe. I was fascinated by the women and men in their mid-20s who smiled at me as though they had secrets I knew nothing about but would discover if I remained. They were artists, lovers, musicians, poets, writers, employees of the city, unemployed men and women, fry-cooks, donut bakers, street sweepers, alcoholics who had been hiding out since the Korean War, people with clothing that looked like it was from the 40s, youth like myself who had come to Venice to be cool and get drunk and party all night at the St Marks Hotel and then write poetry about being "beat" and send postcards back to our friends and tell them to come out and get drunk with us, sun and fun lovers, chicks with bodies that slipped out of the covers of the latest Playboy, guys showing off their abs at Muscle Beach, old people who smiled at everyone and called most everyone their own age by first names.

That was the Venice I arrived in fifty years ago—before they tore the cool buildings down, before they poured concrete where bungalows had been, before they razed the old International Village with all the cool but closed restaurants.

Oh, the liquor stores. There were lots of liquor stores. There was one on every corner and they were always running out of muscatel and paper bags. But that is all history now.

Right, it is gone now. And nobody had a lot of time back then for painting names on stuff because people were writing poetry and trying to write the "great American novel" all over again. There were lots of writers who were writers and lots of people who talked about writing. And there was the old Venice West Cafe where there really were poetry readings by candlelight every night. That was so cool—we could hardly wait to read our own stuff.

The old chairs and tables, the espresso machine, that strong, magic smell of espresso that I have never come across again in fifty years. I can still hear the steam valve hissing and smell the aroma of espresso filling up the entire place. Yes, that was Venice Beach, Venice West by the long-time, old-time beats.

I lived on Paloma Street and I am glad I caught a corner of the beat scene before it was gone forever.

I'm not done with this yet. I will always be writing this novel. ■

From Reflection to Response   Analyzing Different Views of Venice Beach

After reading the two web postings about Venice Beach, California, write a response that (1) describes the central theme that each writer wants to convey and (2) identifies the key details that the writer presents in order to express and support the theme.

Choosing a Subject

The place you choose to profile does not have to be extraordinary or impressive. Unassuming places—a beach or a bowling alley—can be good subjects if they have meaning for you and your readers. Consider locations noted in the list that follows:

- ▶ Your neighborhood, hometown, or a part of town (see Okeko Donaldson's photo essay on pages 466–467)
- ▶ Your campus
- ▶ Any place you go to relax and rejuvenate—a park, wildlife refuge, hiking trail, mall, bar, diner, coffee shop, rec center, gym, hairdresser, and so forth
- ▶ A foreign city or destination you know
- ▶ A memorial, shrine, place of worship, or historical landmark

To evaluate your ideas, ask yourself the questions below.

▶ What interests me, the writer, about this place?

▶ What might my readers not know and possibly find interesting or surprising?

▶ What common (and possibly incorrect) views do people hold about this place?

▶ How does this place communicate with the people who are part of it?

▶ What meaningful or surprising view (theme) can I develop about this place?

PROFILING AN EVENT

Profiling a memorable or unique event can enlighten readers about the world we live in and problems we share. Profiles like these sometimes are called exposés, because they are written to "expose" the reality of an event and give readers an "insider's view."

Consider the event depicted in Figure 5.5, which shows Théodore Géricault's *The Raft of the Medusa*. This painting was inspired by the wreck of a French Royal Navy frigate that ran aground in 1816. There were not enough life-boats for all of the men, so some of the survivors had to build a raft. Géricault's

PAINTING/Alamy

FIGURE 5.5   *The Raft of the Medusa* by Théodore Géricault, 1818–1819

Alfred Eisenstaedt/Getty Images

FIGURE 5.6 *V-J Day in Times Square*
by Alfred Eisenstaedt, 1945

painting depicts the survivors on the raft at a desperate point in their journey, when a rescue ship appears on the horizon but sails away without noticing them.

The painting conveys a theme of men responding in different ways to a horrific situation and elicits the emotions of "terror and pity" that lie at the heart of human tragedy.

Figure 5.6 is a photograph by Alfred Eisenstaedt titled *V-J Day in Times Square*. It was taken on August 14, 1945, and is an iconic depiction of the joy that followed President Truman's announcement that World War II had been won. ("V-J" is short for "Victory over Japan.") Over the years, however, the theme of joy and exuberance has given way to questions about whether "the kiss" was consensual and appropriate, regardless of the historic occasion.

The newspaper profile that follows is an example of an exposé that uses meaningful, descriptive details to transport readers to an urban music festival and give them an insider's view of the event.

Associated Press   { ULTRA MUSIC FESTIVAL BRINGS REVELING MASSES TO MIAMI

STRINGER/Reuters/Landov

Ezra Hrycyk dances with a hoola hoop
at the Ultra Music Festival

IT'S THE FIRST NIGHT of the Ultra Music Festival and Miami Fire-Rescue Lt. Robert Jorge is trying to help a man with a gash above his left eyebrow. He's been charged with assaulting a police officer and he lies on the pavement, hands tied behind his back, rambling to no end, his eyes staring off into oblivion.

"I believe in Jesus, Jesus Christ!" he screams. "I love Christ!"

"So do I," Jorge says. "From one Christian to another, I'm trying to help you out."

"You're a liar," the man cries.

In the distance, thousands are jumping and dancing below flashing neon lights. It is 10 p.m., and for the opening night of one of the world's largest electronic dance festivals, it's been relatively quiet. Miami Fire-Rescue officers have responded to 35 calls, everything from drunken teens to an ankle injury.

Jorge cleans the blood off the man's forehand and places a Band-Aid. The police suspect he's on "molly," a drug similar to ecstasy but often with a higher purity that's become popular in the electronic dance scene. Officers will wait until the drug starts to wear off before putting him in a police bus and taking him to jail.

Jorge puts the headphones connecting him to dispatch back on and heads again into the crowd. Incidents like this are certainly the exception; most of the partygoers are enjoying themselves and not getting into trouble. For those that do, police and rescuers have mobile command centers set up nearby. They watch the crowd from security cameras and have officers stationed around the festival, on foot and in small flatbed trucks with stretchers on top.

"The way they do this is like a mass casualty incident," Jorge says, explaining how they are ready to go into a crowd of thousands and find the person they need to treat. "We train for that."

Ultra is now in its 15th year and this year is taking place over two weekends. That raised some objections from Miami city commissioners, who came close to canceling the second weekend but agreed to let it go on after coming to an agreement with festival organizers to add more security. The event attracts the world's top DJs and producers, along with an expected 330,000 fans, mostly young people looking for a brief respite, others heavily into rave culture.

The festival is set up at Bayfront Park in the middle of downtown. Festival goers can go from one stage to another, the lights of the city beaming nearby. It's visually spectacular, and the crowd is a spectacle. Girls dress in tutus, bikinis and furry knee-length leg warmers. Guys go in shorts, T-shirt optional.

Jeremy and Tent Kloter, brothers from Tampa, wore American flag shorts and nothing else. They carried small beverage dispensing backpacks, first filled with cranberry vodka, then water. Both are tanned and well-toned and girls continually stop them to pose for photographs as the brothers make their way to the main stage.

For Jeremy Kloter, 22, the draw of the festival is simple: "I can be myself more."

The brothers disappear into the mass of partygoers.

"What's about to happen on this stage is insanity, pure insanity!" the DJ yells.

Melisa Jonson, 25, is being pushed in a wheelchair through the crowd. She was in a car accident when she was 5 years old and left paralyzed from the waist down. She's a culinary student in Miami and she and her friends have seen the festival from afar but never attended. They decided to go this year to see what it was all about.

A friend helps wheel Jonson through the dirt ground. Revelers walk and dance around her and she enjoys the music.

"My parents always told me whatever you want to do, just do it," she said.

Nearby one stage is The Heineken House, a beer lounge with LED lighting, fog machines and live feeds from the show so that people don't miss a minute, even while waiting in line for a drink.

Diego Allmaral is jumping up and down as he waits for a beer. Green colored lights cast a tint over him and his friend. He's from Venezuela and says his family left everything behind. He comes to Ultra every year and this year, he has a lot to celebrate. He's been accepted into Columbia University after studying at a community college.

"This is the best dance festival in the world!" he says.

Outside, a blonde woman in a black bikini and elaborate red, white and yellow Indian headdress, gives away the dozens of brightly colored, plastic bead bracelets stacked up her wrists. Her rave name is Molly Casa and she is a "PLUR mama," PLUR standing for peace, love, unity and respect. To get one of the 500 bracelets she spent days making people have to do a special hand signal along with her that symbolizes the mantra. She believes it is an exchange of energy.

"I feel my soul's purpose is to lead the youth in the rave scene to that spiritual fire in all of us," the 24-year-old says.

She started going to Ultra when she was 13 with an older boyfriend, and has come every year since.

"The sound of electronic music is evolving mankind," she says.

Fans who have seen her on the Internet come up gushing and make the hand signal with her.

Meanwhile, Jorge is on one of the small trucks responding to a call. The driver is honking the horn, the sound blurring into the music, as he tries to get people to move out of the way. They come to a young man who is sitting next to his brother. He can't tell officers his date of birth or his age. He can barely stand.

The boy's brother says he is 17. The officers call their mother to meet them at the hospital.

The officers don't know if he's been drinking or what.

"Too much of whatever," one says.

They strap the teen to stretcher and he's lifted onto the flatbed truck. Now they must make their way through the crowd in front of the main stage, where Afrojack has the crowd moving.

Jorge and another officer walk in front of the truck, clearing the way. The wheels of the truck crumple dozens of plastic water bottles and drink cups on the ground. Halfway through, several people come holding a young girl to the truck. She's almost passed out.

That is how Jorge will spend the night, going from one incident to another. When it's over, the crowds stream into the city and vendors hawk offers for after-parties and van rides to Miami Beach.

It's one night of the festival down. Five more to go. ∎

From Reflection to Response

Synthesizing Perspectives on an Urban Music Festival

The profile of the Urban Music Festival presents vivid details that give readers a feeling of being there. However, what exactly is the view of the festival that the writer conveys—in other words, the central theme of the profile?

Working with one or two of your classmates, or on your own, write a short response that identifies the main view, or theme, that you take away from the piece. As part of your response, consider why the profile begins and ends from the perspective of Robert Jorge, a Fire-Rescue lieutenant, treating a "casualty" of the festival.

Are casualties and their substance abuse the main themes of the profile, or are they outlying details that frame a larger picture? If the causalities and substance abuse are not the main theme, what is? How do the incidents described at the beginning and end of the profile relate to the details in the middle of the piece, and the main theme that you take away?

Choosing a Subject

The event you choose to profile does not have to be extraordinary or impressive, like a presidential inauguration or a protest. Unassuming events—a garage sale or a dance class—can be good subjects if they have meaning for you and your readers. Consider the events in the list that follows:

▶ A concert or sporting event (for example, NASCAR race, Oakland Raiders game, regatta)

▶ A political rally, march, or demonstration

▶ A visit by a dignitary

▶ A festival like Mardi Gras, Carnival (Brazil), or the "running of the bulls" in Pamplona

▶ A conference, convention, tournament, fair, forum, or exhibit of any kind (for example, a prayer meeting, county fair, farmer's market, gun show, fishing tournament, Civil War reenactment)

To evaluate your ideas, ask yourself the questions below.

▶ What interests me, the writer, about this event?

▶ What might my readers not know and possibly find interesting or surprising?

▶ What common (and possibly incorrect) views do people hold about this event?

▶ How does this event communicate with the people who are part of it?

▶ What meaningful or surprising view (theme) can I develop about this event?

WRITING A PROPOSAL

Once you have decided on a subject for your profile—a person, place, or event—write a proposal that lays out the key elements for your classmates and instructor to comment on.

In keeping with proposals you write for other projects, format this proposal in *business style*, to make it concise and accessible. Use the section headings below (numbered or bulleted), block paragraphs, and single-spacing.

Proposal for a Profile of a Person, Place, or Event

1. **Subject of the Profile**.

2. **Source of Interest**. Elaborate on why this subject is of interest or importance to you, and what your connection to the subject is.

3. **The Central Theme** (the issue and view) that you intend to develop about the subject, and why you think this theme is meaningful.

4. **Research Methods** (if applicable) **and Visual Materials** (for example, photographs). If you know the subject well, you may not need to do any research for the profile. Otherwise, discuss the research you will do. Conducting an *interview* is the most common kind of research for profiling a person, but you also might consider gathering secondhand information from print or online sources (for example, social network pages and websites) and talking to people who know the subject.

Observation of the person's environment and work is another form of research (for example, to write "Old Dameron," E. B. White spent a day with the lobsterman on his boat). If you are profiling a place, you might go there to refresh your memories.

Finally, consider using photographs or other *visual materials* (for example, a screenshot of a person's web page) to enhance the meaning and appeal of your profile. Inserting visuals into printed documents is easy to do with today's technology.

5. **Audience and Relevance**. Describe the primary audience you have in mind for the profile and the relevance your profile will have for people who read it. Will it inspire, instruct, or both, and why will the subject be relevant to readers? In considering your audience, your classmates and instructor always are realistic readers, but if you write a compelling profile, other readers and ways of reaching them through print or online media are realistic, too.

For example, if your profile is about someone who works for or attends your college, the profile would be relevant to a general campus audience of students, teachers, and administrators. An engaging profile of this kind could be published in a campus newspaper, newsletter, alumni magazine, or on the official college website. If your profile is about a community figure, it would be relevant to a community audience that reads the local newspapers. A profile of a friend of yours who has an indie rock band and a small, but loyal fan base, could be interesting to an online audience on Facebook, MySpace, or Tumblr.

WRITING A ROUGH DRAFT

To begin your profile effectively, focus on the central theme. The theme is a question, issue, or problem that the subject raises and the view your profile will support. Your opening, at minimum, needs to put your readers on the trail of the theme, that is, pose a relevant question or present an issue or problem. The totality of the theme, your view of the subject, can develop later, in an informal, inductive pattern, as it usually does in a narrative essay.

In simple terms, your opening needs to tell readers, "This profile is relevant to you and your life." Putting readers on the trail of a theme will give your profile a purpose and direction.

If you write about an "ordinary person," someone like E. B. White's "Old Dameron," you will expect readers to wonder about the relevance of the profile to them, and thus, the importance of having a theme should occur to you. In writing "Old Dameron," White knew that most readers have no great interest in lobstering and the people who do it. He knew it was his job as a writer to make the subject of his profile relevant by raising the issue of the lobsterman's rigid routine.

If your subject is someone special, however—someone like the daredevil who walks between skyscrapers—you might assume information about the "special" person is enough to carry the profile and hold your readers' interest, but in fact, without a theme, the profile won't have a direction and goal. Even if it gets off to an interesting start, say, a vivid description of a high-wire feat in Beijing, the "So what?" question will occur to the reader sooner or later. Maybe the daredevil sneaked past tight security to accomplish the feat. Maybe he trained with *Cirque du Soliel*. Maybe he is diabetic or married his high school sweetheart. Okay, but "So what?" *The opening needs to raise an issue or question* that puts readers on the trail of the theme.

The theme you present—the issue or question you raise and the view or answer your profile provides—takes care of the "So what?" question: Is this daredevil a social menace or a modern hero? Readers will want to know. An effective profile will provide an answer.

The opening of the profile below introduces a man who has an extraordinary life story: Pete O'Neal, a fugitive from justice and former member of the radical Black Panthers, living in exile in Tanzania. The author of the piece, journalist Christopher Goffard, understands that O'Neal's life story, unusual as it is, is not enough to answer the "So what?" question. O'Neal's story may appeal to some readers who are interested in history and politics, but for a broader audience, the profile has to say, "This man's story is relevant to you." Goffard manages to say that by conveying an issue (the man's assessment of his life as "a wild and wicked ride") that puts the reader on the trail of a theme:

Former Black Panther Patches Together Purpose in Africa Exile

Reporting from Imbaseni, Tanzania—The fugitive shuffles to his computer and begins typing out his will. He is about to turn 71, and it is time. "My life," he writes, "has been a wild and wicked ride...."

All Pete O'Neal has amassed fits on two pages: A small brick home with a sheet-metal roof. A few road-beaten vehicles. A cluster of bunkhouses and classrooms he spent decades building, brick by scavenged brick, near the slopes of Mt. Meru's volcanic cone. Everything will go to his wife of 42 years, Charlotte, and to a few trusted workers.

He prints out the will late one Saturday morning and settles into his reclining chair to check the spelling. He signs his name. Then, to guarantee its authenticity, he finds an ink pad, rolls his thumb across it, and affixes his thumbprint to the bottom of the page.

"I think that'll do it," he says.
When last he walked America's streets, O'Neal was a magnetic young man possessed of bottomless anger....

Of course, the story of O'Neal's past and how he came to be a fugitive and an exile from his country will be told in the profile, but Goffard's first task is to give readers a reason to read. Goffard does that by describing what he sees as significant about the man, not just the details of the man's life, but an assessment of his life, the "wild and wicked ride," in the context of a defining moment, "typing out his will." Like the portraits by Ingres and Mary Ellen Mark (pages 173), Goffard's profile comes across as "natural" but is designed to raise thematic questions about the meaning of O'Neal's life. The opening invites us to read further to find out the "verdict," or view, that the profile will support.

SPECIAL CONSIDERATIONS OF THE ESSAY

The sections that follow cover stylistic features of profiles that are important to consider as you draft and revise.

Using First or Third Person

Profiles are similar to narrative essays in their descriptive focus on people's lives and experiences, but instead of being primarily about the writer, profiles are about someone (or something) else, the subject of the profile. In many profiles, however, the writer's interactions with the subject are relevant to the meaning and theme. These kinds of profiles use a combination of the first and third person ("Old Dameron" is an example), rather than the third person only.

However, many intriguing profiles stick to the third person and keep the writer in the background, or "out of view," so to speak. These kinds of profiles have the virtue of putting the subject in sharper focus (Sarah Max's profile of entrepreneur Kris Wittenberg, and Christopher Goffard's profile of Pete O'Neal are examples).

As a rule of thumb, when the subject is someone you know and your interactions with the subject are relevant, a combination of first and third person makes sense. When the subject is someone you don't know, sticking to the third person usually has a more focused and professional effect.

Descriptive Writing

As portraits in words, profiles should be descriptive. Readers expect a *sense* of a subject's physical appearance along with a sense of place, the world the subject inhabits, but written descriptions should provide more than a visual representation of a person. (You can insert photographs in your document for that.) Good descriptions are purposeful. They contribute to the *meaning* of the profile and support the central theme.

The opening of Goffard's profile of Pete O'Neal mentions that O'Neal is about to turn seventy-one but provides no physical descriptions of him. Instead, Goffard focuses on details that are more important. O'Neal uses a "thumbprint" to sign his will, a precaution that might occur more readily to a fugitive from justice than the average person.

In his profile of "Old Dameron," E. B. White barely describes the lobsterman at all, but White's profile, like Goffard's, is full of "telling" details that support the theme of self-sufficiency, immersion in work, and a man's love for his trade.

The passage below from Phillip Lopate's personal essay titled "Against Joie de Vivre"* uses telling details to depict a self-satisfied, second-rate artist that the writer finds seriously annoying:

> Greeting us on the gangplank was an old man with thick, lush white hair and snowy eyebrows, his face reddened from the sun. As he took us into the houseboat cabin he told me proudly that he was seventy-seven years old, and gestured toward the paintings that were spaced a few feet apart, leaning on the floor against the wall. They were celebrations of the blue Aegean, boats moored in ports, whitewashed houses on a hill, painted in primary colors and decorated with collaged materials: mirrors, burlap, life-saver candies. These sunny little canvases with their talented innocence…bore testimony to a love of life so unbending as to leave an impression of rigid narrow-mindedness as extreme as any Savonarola. Their rejection of sorrow was total. They were the sort of festive paintings that sell at high-rent Madison Avenue galleries specializing in European schlock.

Settings and Locations

Making description purposeful also applies to settings and locations. Brief details here and there that create a sense of place and "atmosphere" are welcomed, but elaborate descriptions will bore readers unless the details contribute to meaning and theme. If your subject's house is painted blue or white or green, if the floors are wooden or tiled or carpeted, if the building is encircled

---

*The title literally means "against the joy of living."

by elms, palms, security cameras, or a wind farm—are these details thematically revealing or important? If not, you probably should leave them out and
move on to more important things.

Storyboarding the Profile

Since profiles often take the form of a narrative, or story, and use description,
creating a storyboard—a visual outline of scenes and key details—can help you
plan and organize your first draft. The sample storyboard uses details from
E. B. White's "Old Dameron."

Storyboard for: (*Working Title*)

Opening Scene, Description, or Exposition:	Scene, Description, or Exposition # 2:
Dameron's routine when he goes out to sea. Descriptions of what he does, what it is like....	I go out on the boat with him to see what it's like....
Details:	**Details:**
He does this six days a week, eight months out of the year....	He tells me about his past, esp. working on yachts ("mad the whole time")....
Scene, Description, or Exposition # 3:	**Scene, Description, or Exposition # 4:**
Observations about his "independence."	As we return with our catch, my thoughts about "freedom."
Details:	**Details:**
"Nobody cares for him" and vice versa...His off-season regimen and focus....	Dameron embodies or symbolizes everything we are fighting [the war] for....

YOUR ESSAY CHECKLIST

The timeline for writing a profile depends on how long and detailed the profile will be, and whether or not you will need to conduct an interview, or do
other kinds of research. Regardless, you need to go through a realistic process of drafting and revision in order to write a profile that will do justice to
your subject and theme. Use the checklist to guide your steps in developing
your essay and as a final check to make sure you have completed all of the
necessary steps. This checklist can also be used to help you plan your time
effectively.

✔ Task	Description	Time Frame
☐ **Choose a subject**	• Choose a subject that intrigues you. • Consider how much you know about the subject and your access to the firsthand information you will need. • To come up with the best subject, consider several people you know well, along with people you don't know well, or only "know of" but have the ability to meet for an interview. • Consider memorable or unique places and events. • As you consider subjects, discuss them with classmates, your instructor, and other people. • Think about your source of interest in the subject, and how this translates to a theme, or puts you on the path to finding a theme.	A day or so.
☐ **Schedule and conduct an interview, if applicable**	• If you intend to interview the subject of your profile, schedule the interview as soon as possible, so that if you run into a problem, you will have time to change to a different subject. If the interview is face to face, try to conduct it at a relevant location.	Varies.
☐ **Visit a site or refresh your memory, if applicable**	• If you plan to profile a place, make a "site visit," if possible, to refresh your memory and observations. • Take notes and photographs during your visit. • If you plan to profile an event—for example, a memorable concert or march you attended—consider looking for sources online, news stories, blogs, testimonials, magazine articles, and photographs that will refresh your memory and expand your perspective. (Remember to identify and cite any sources you use in your profile.)	Varies.
☐ **Write a proposal**	• Write a proposal that describes your subject, defines the theme you plan to develop, and identifies your audience.	A half hour or so.
☐ **Create a storyboard or informal outline**	• Create a storyboard or informal outline of scenes, descriptive details, and information you plan to include in your profile.	A half hour to an hour.

(continued)

✔ Task	Description	Time Frame
☐ **Write a rough draft**	• Start drafting the profile. Make sure the opening raises an issue, question, or problem that puts the reader on the trail of a central theme—in other words, the main view you intend to convey about your subject. • Include relevant descriptive details to make your subject real and compelling. • Think about whether you will use a combination of a first and third person point of view, or strictly the third person. • As you develop the draft, keep the central theme in focus, and support it with pertinent details and information.	Compose the first draft in more than one sitting if necessary, and aim to finish the draft at least a week before the final version is due.
☐ **Revise**	• Revise the profile as many times as necessary to make it coherent, vivid, and impacting. • If you run into problems with the organization, do a revision outline (as described in Chapter 3, page 96). The revision outline will help you see if the profile has gaps or disconnected parts.	Plan on doing at least several revisions over the course of a week.
☐ **Get peer review**	• Ask for feedback from classmates during the drafting process (see peer-review questions in regular text outside this table). • Visit your instructor during office hours for advice and help, or take a draft of the profile to your campus writing center. • Show your essay to your friends, or post a readable draft to your Facebook page if you have one.	Varies.
☐ **Edit your essay**	Before you submit the essay, make sure you edit it. Consider using the text-to-speech feature on your computer to hear how the essay sounds and help you catch mistakes or typos. Check for the following: • Helpful paragraphing (see Chapter 12 for more about this and the other elements of grammar and mechanics listed here) • Effective wording and word choice (avoid arbitrary slang or colloquialisms) • Correctly formatted dialogue • Consistent verb tenses • Sentence punctuation (fix run-ons and comma splices) • General grammar and mechanics (subject-verb agreement, pronoun reference, placement of commas)	Careful editing may involve a certain amount of revising, so the time frame can vary, but always plan on going over what you have written. Running a spell-check is not enough.

PEER REVIEW

As always, your classmates are an excellent source of feedback for this project, because they understand the writing and communication goals.

Below are some peer-review questions to guide your classmates' feedback. You also can ask questions of your own that focus on parts of a draft that you have doubts or concerns about.

1. What issue, question, or problem does the opening convey, to put readers on the trail of a theme? Is the opening detailed and compelling enough to draw you into the profile and keep you interested? Offer any suggestions you can for improving the opening.

2. What is the writer's central view of the subject—in other words, the central theme? Point out some descriptive details the writer presents to support this view or theme. Can you think of any additional details or information that would make the theme more compelling, relevant, or clear?

3. What do you consider to be the strongest part of the profile, and why? Point out any parts you consider unnecessary or uninteresting, and offer suggestions for improvements.

4. Are there aspects of the subject that you would like to know more about? Are there any details, or is there any information, that would help fill out the profile and support the writer's theme?

5. Comment on the readability of the profile. Is the paragraphing helpful? Is dialogue presented and used effectively (or overused)? Are there problems with wording, grammar, or mechanics that interfere with the clarity or "flow" of the profile? Offer suggestions for improvements.

STUDENT ESSAY: FINAL DRAFT

Below is the profile about a mortician that Kierstin Koppel composed for this project.

Kierstin Koppel // **HUMANIZING MORTICIANS**

The corpse lies bare under a white sheet waiting to be dissected and reconstructed through a series of surgical procedures. Corpses are not your typical customer, and embalming is not a typical job description, but for morticians, working on a corpse is an average "day at the office."

An hour earlier, as I crossed the gloomy cemetery grounds, then made my way along the corridors of the funeral home, I conjured up the image I had in my mind of what a mortician must look like: a peculiarly pale, introverted man in an old suit, most likely a man with a stale personality, who drives around in an eerie hearse and looms over the deceased. I figured I could pick this ghoulish figure out of a crowd, the horror-movie character who relishes the task of dismembering dead bodies, so unhappy with his morbid life that he becomes deeply attached to the deceased and cynical about the living, price-gouging the surviving family members by convincing them that the body must be showcased in a mahogany casket and made the centerpiece of an extravagant, $12,000 floral pageant, before it can be allowed to rot six feet under the earth.

Trying to relate to a mortician's job challenged and perplexed me. It's not a job that is ranked high on the list of what kids want to do when they grow up. Most of us are not blessed with cast iron stomachs. Personally, the very thought of blood makes my stomach turn. You would think that nobody would opt for a profession that concerns itself with dead bodies and the gloomy details of funerals, but for Janet Teller, the mortician I actually spoke to and got to know that day, nothing could be more fulfilling. The preconceived idea we have about morticians ignores their indispensable role in society. Because we fear death, we just don't want to contemplate what morticians do.

I never would have envisioned Janet as a mortician. She is a "blonde bombshell" who wears Converse sneakers and studied Mortuary Science at St. Petersburg College. No dusty suit, pallid complexion, or hearse. Instead, when we met, she wore jeans and had a healthy tan. Behind a tress of her golden locks, I caught a glimpse of a small tattoo on the slope of her collarbone, which only added to the mystery. Intrigued and stunned by a woman who contradicted all my preconceptions of what a mortician should look like, I asked her if people are surprised when she tells them about her job. She chuckled, and shyly confessed how, to help counter the stereotypes, she was asked to pose for a Calendar in 2006 featuring sexy morticians, funeral directors, and embalmers!

Janet has been working in a funeral home since the age of sixteen. As a teenager, her dream was to attend medical school to become a forensic pathologist and perform autopsies, but her father wanted to ensure that she could "stomach it." So before sending her off to med school, he secured her a job as an intern at a local funeral home. Janet was determined to disprove the stereotype that females are not "tough enough" for the job. She was confident she could outperform any male apprentice. Through the most horrific sights and repulsive smells, Janet kept her poker face.

While assisting her first preparation, she began "breaking up" the body of a deceased woman undergoing rigor mortis. Rigor mortis is the process in which the body begins to stiffen as a stage of decomposition. While Janet was adjusting the women's arm, the shoulder blade broke off and dislodged itself from the body. Then, without reason, the women's eye sockets sank back into her skull. Janet was mortified that she was destroying the body, but refused to panic for fear of appearing weak. "I quickly learned that these were all normal and common occurrences," she told me. The irony is that, in the effort to prove to her father that she was cut out for surgical work, she discovered that the "helping" aspect of the funeral business appealed to her more than forensic pathology.

Part of her job as a mortician is reconstructing a person's physical appearance. She refers to herself as a "de-glorified Hollywood makeup artist," equipped with all kinds of aesthetic wares such as eyelid glue, facial wax, filling putty, eye caps, and "forever young" embalming fluid for lasting, glowing skin. "Being a mortician is like wearing many different career caps," Janet noted. "Psychologist, surgeon, business administrator, makeup designer, even an event planner, all in one very intriguing package." Clearly, Janet has a healthy sense of humor as part of her skill set.

On a deeper level, Janet explained that death is simply a stage of life. "It is a normal process we all eventually go through." Her mortician's role covers the time of death to the final resting place. "One of the biggest downsides of this business is that you are always on call. Twenty-four hours a day, seven days a week, even holidays. In fact, holidays are very busy. Be it from the drinking and driving, the fattening food, or from the stress of too much family time, holidays are a very popular time to die."

Morticians must begin their work without delay, in a race against a body's natural decomposition process. Janet's elaborate description of the process made me queasy, so I will skip the details. In essence, though, the process starts when the deceased is moved to the morgue and the mortician prepares the remains. The mortician then proceeds to plan the ceremony according to the religious and cultural needs of the family, and finishes by disposing of the remains. Janet takes great care in presenting the deceased as pleasantly as possible. Her challenge is to give the family one last peaceful image of the person.

The reconstructive process in preparation for a "viewing" requires a very skilled and talented embalmer who has received extensive training. Embalming is a sanitary, cosmetic, and preservative process through which the body is prepared for viewing. When embalming a body, embalmers wash the body with a strong soap and replace the blood with embalming fluid to preserve the tissues. Then the "magician" comes into play when morticians reshape and reconstruct disfigured physical features by aesthetic feature setting. Lastly, they dress the body in clothing chosen by the family. The overall outcome is to achieve a rested and contented look. Morticians take on a very important task that must be done with reverence and respect.

Janet explained to me that morticians are often scapegoats for a family's grief. Morticians must be able to counsel the survivors with sensitivity, and understand their needs and concerns. For Janet, what appeals to her most about the job, apart from being able to use her surgical skills, is that it allows her to help a family in a time of desperation. Morticians must have composure, tact, and the ability to communicate with compassion. Contrary to the misconception that morticians do not like dealing with living people, Janet thoroughly enjoys helping the living cope with the loss of their loved ones.

"We all die," Janet said with a contorted smile. "Death is a normal part of life, and it will happen to every one of us."

Although I am very aware that this unfortunate event will occur to me, Janet's remark still hit me "like a ton of bricks." Here I was, standing in the actual location where I would wind up at the end of my life, and conversing with a person who could very well "prepare" me for viewing. The reality of death highlights the importance of morticians. They are so relevant to every person because everyone dies. Janet's words reminded me that a dead body is more than just a body. That body was a person, with a life, a family, and a purpose. Everyone deserves a proper goodbye and morticians assist in giving that gift. "A funeral is not only a service for the dead, but more importantly for the living left behind." It is the closure of a person's life, and the beginning of a long healing process for the mourning. Instead of the ceremony being about the death of a person, it is a mortician's job to help celebrate the life of the individual.

Janet finds fulfillment in her job and has learned to appreciate each and every day. Life is short, so it is important to seize the moment, take chances, and never put off what you can do or say today, for tomorrow. "Carpe Diem" is her mantra. Having seen it all, death by heart attacks, freak accidents, and electrocutions, just to name a few, Janet understands that life is fragile. Although she does not fear her own death, she has pictured members of her family on an embalming table and in a casket, which saddens her. "Contrary to stereotypes that morticians are detached emotionally, we experience normal feelings," Janet reflected. "We're humans, too."

Interview with the Student Writer

● **How did you come up with your idea for your profile?**

● I wanted to write a profile that would be a little risqué and engaging. Before writing anything, I always put myself in the readers' shoes. What would they want to read? What's interesting to them? What hasn't been done before? I came up with the idea of writing about a mortician during a conversation I had with my roommate at the time. Her mother worked for a funeral home, and possibly could arrange to give me permission to visit. As it turned out, she was the mortician I ended up interviewing and writing about. I learned about the "human" part of her, which allowed me to see past the stereotypes about the profession. The interview was rather informal, and I preferred it that way. It was easy to do and fascinating.

● **How did you go about composing the essay?**

● After I did the interview, I reviewed my notes, drafted the essay, and then revised it a few times.

● **Who read your drafts, and what reactions did you get?**

● I always read my drafts to my family and friends to see what their reaction is. This piece was very well received. It was clear that people were very curious about this profession!

● **What parts of the writing process were difficult for you?**

● Final revisions can be a little daunting, especially when you have a deadline to meet, but overall, I enjoyed the writing process for this project. When you love what you write about, the rest usually falls into place.

● **What parts were easy or enjoyable?**

● Once I came up with the idea, the whole project was enjoyable. Actually, I had a blast!

- **Thinking back, what did you learn from the project?**

- I learned that there is always a subject or an angle that has yet to be explored. Find it, and tell it. However boring an assignment may seem, try to think outside the box!

- **What advice would you give to other students about this kind of writing project or writing in general?**

- When you approach a writing project, do your best not to think in black and white, in other words, about just getting it done and turning *something* in. The world is full of colors, cultures, professions, and different perspectives. If you challenge yourself to see and go outside your comfort zone, you might be pleasantly surprised at what you find and can do.

EVALUATE YOUR LEARNING

1. How would you explain the concept of a theme to an inexperienced writer?
2. What are some subjects you considered for your profile? Why did you choose the subject you ended up writing about?
3. Did you create a storyboard before composing your profile, and if so, how closely does the profile follow your storyboard?
4. What are some things you learned about writing from doing this project?

ADDITIONAL READINGS

Steven M. Fernandez // **A CUBAN CHRISTMAS**

Steven Fernandez was born in Cleveland, Ohio, to Cuban parents and grew up in South Florida. He draws inspiration from his family and uses his writing to commemorate his Cuban–American culture and upbringing. Fernandez wrote "A Cuban Christmas" for a profile project in a first-year writing course at Florida International University. He is currently pursuing a law degree at Nova Southeastern College of Law.

THE YEAR IS 1998. My family had just moved to Weston, a small, conservative neighborhood in Broward County, Florida, which was about to get its first taste of "El Cubaneo" (Cubanism). Growing up in a predominantly Cuban neighborhood in South Miami until age eleven, I had assumed our way of life to be that of any other family and never thought we were anything out of the ordinary. Christmas time was rolling in, and thus, preparation for the big event would begin. Little did we know this would be the precursor to my realization that we were not like everyone else. Christmas was my favorite time of the year, and the one time when I could see all my extended relatives outside of the usual eighteen that I saw every weekend. The week of preparation for Christmas Eve was always a crazy time for my family, but one in which we all loved to take part. The events of the week beginning on December 20th and ending December 24th would open up my eyes to a much larger world for the very first time.

Since this was our first Christmas in a new house, my grandmother had decided the family should get together at our house instead of at hers, which was the tradition. The morning of the 20th, my grandfather, dad, two uncles Carlos and Jose and myself rode off in my dad's new red Land Rover Discovery to a farm in Pahokee, a small city in Central Florida. The men were entrusted with the solemn duty of driving to this faraway farm and selecting a suitable pig for our Christmas Eve dinner, as was the tradition.

After a few hours at the farm, we chose a pig. Normally, it would have been shot on sight but my father wanted to take it home alive and show me how his father had taught him to prepare a pig. Needless to say, as a young boy, I was excited to take home a live pig, but not as excited about the killing part. As we drove home, live pig in the trunk, my dad explained the process which we would use to kill the pig and prepare it for the big dinner, knocking the pig out, injecting something or other into the heart with a long needle, then gutting and bleeding it, and cracking the pig's spine with a machete. The rest of the job belonged to the women of the family.

The next day, I was excited to be able to play with the pig (the pig was not to be killed until tomorrow) and see my extended relatives who were arriving that day. The house already had eighteen people sleeping in it. That was only my immediate family. Soon I would realize we had a larger immediate family than some people have extended families. Today was the first party of several during this Christmas week. Every day was a celebration with tons of food, music, dancing, drinking, and cigar smoking. There was not much work to be done, aside from setting up some tables in the backyard. This was a day to be with all the relatives who were arriving every hour, and eat and drink in the yard in a big group as we always did. I spent the day playing around with my cousins until it was time for dinner. My grandmother turned on the Cuban music and we all ate, socialized, yelled across the many tables in the backyard at each other and made considerable amounts of noise. To me, it was a typical family gathering, and I thought nothing of it.

The next day, the 22nd, was the day the pig was to be killed. As I said, I was not particularly excited about this part but it was tradition. The men went to the garage. There were now ten or eleven men as opposed to four the day we chose the pig. My grandfather has always been in charge of the pig and usually did all the work as he was the most experienced, but today my dad wanted to do the work since it was his house. I remember my grandfather whacking the pig on the head, knocking it unconscious and then my dad sticking a long needle into its heart to kill it "peacefully" as I remember him pointing out. As he pulled the needle out, the pig came to, and in an attempt to escape this "garage of death," the pig took off running out of the garage. If you find yourself wondering why in the world the garage door was open, my uncle had opened it to let some cool air in, not the brightest idea ever. My grandfather ran off chasing the pig with a baseball bat; my dad did the same with a machete as it was the first thing he found, and a few of my uncles took off in one of their cars and another few in another car to chase the pig. I jumped in the car with Carlos, Jose and my other uncle Tony. Just a block from my house, my grandfather and dad caught the pig. My grandfather beat it with the bat as my dad held it down. Across the street, an elderly couple watched. The old lady screamed; the man yelled some insults at my family as we dragged the pig back to our garage. What a beginning to our day.

A little later the police arrived at our house saying they had received a call regarding animal abuse. My parents explained the situation and the police understood what had taken place and realized that our neighbors did not understand that this was a family event. The rest of the day was spent preparing the pig and setting up the backyard while my grandfather built his yearly grill for roasting the pig which was made from the gas tank of an eighteen wheeler, some iron construction bars and wood.

That night we received a call from our Neighborhood Association, saying a complaint had been filed for illegal construction taking place at our house. This illegal construction was only my grandfather building his grill with power tools but it was enough for our neighbor to report us. I will never forget my grandmother saying to my mom, "These bunch of stiffs don't know how to live life. Americans are dry people that can't stand us." I realized we were in fact the minority in this new city, and so far the neighbors did not care for us being here. Nevertheless, that night was spent in the same manner as the previous: dinner, loud conversation, drinking, more music, and fun.

The 23rd began in a similar way. My parents had a nanny who took care of my sister and me, and she was spending the week with us helping with all the food, and in particular, the pig. Well, she is a fairly large lady, and as I would soon find out, perfectly capable of carrying a pig on her back. The men had gone out to pick up some supplies that were needed for the grill, and all the rental chairs and tables my mom had ordered for the following night. The elders like my grandfather were in the backyard reminiscing about Cuba, and as always, discussing how much more enjoyable life in Cuba was compared to the US. This nostalgia always made me laugh, but I guess at their age, the memories were all they had left to hang on to and they embraced them. The women were all in the kitchen preparing enough food to feed a small army; the kids were spread out around the house, fighting, yelling, and making a mess, and I was with my cousin, Danny, playing catch in the front yard. As we were playing catch, an old lady walked her white poodle down the sidewalk. I remember her staring at us as if we were from another planet, which was understandable to some extent since it seemed only retired people lived in the neighborhood. Suddenly, our garage door opened, my nanny walked out looking like the bad guy from "Texas Chainsaw Massacre" with the pig on her back and her raggedy tee shirt covered in its blood. The old lady, of course, began to scream and ran inside her house. This was a different lady than the one who screamed at the first pig sighting, but it appeared a theme was developing. Time for our second brush with the law.

Again, the police came to our house. Apparently, the old lady had made up a story about us having some brutal animal ritual in our driveway, when it was just my nanny taking the pig to the backyard to begin basting it. The police again understood our situation and let us be. I remember being upset, yet at the same time finding humor in all of this; it was funny how ignorant our neighbors were and how we seemed like pig-slaughtering barbarians to them, but, oh well, we continued in good spirits. That night there was more food, more drinking, smoking, talking, yelling, and music, and I loved every minute of it: listening to the old men tell stories, smelling the Cuban coffee and cigars, watching my parents, aunts and uncles dance, the old women gossiping in the corner, the smaller kids playing on the swings, while my older cousins and I messed around causing trouble—just being there and being a part of it made me feel happy.

The happiness, though, quickly faded later that day when the police came to our house once again—not really the police, just Wackenhut security men that one of our neighbors had called because we had been making excessive noise. I could really feel the love. "Welcome to the neighborhood, you loud, annoying Cuban family!" Oh well, we were who we were and I actually began to embrace the fact that we were different in spite of how much disdain our neighbors had for us. These few experiences had strengthened my love for my ethnicity and my family as I realized just how boring some people are and what poor family bonds these people have. All I could do was pity them. I remember how angry many members of my family were about this new neighborhood we had moved into and how much they resented everyone around us. For me, it was different; I found it funny. Our type of Christmas was a form of shock therapy for all these old, stuffy people who had nothing better to do than call the police on us for enjoying ourselves.

December 24th! Ah, my favorite day of the year. Today was when I got to help the men set up the grill my grandfather had built, squirt the lighter fluid on the coals, which was my lame, little-kid job, and help keep track of the pig as it slowly cooked over the next six hours. I remember it smelling of my grandmother's homemade "mojo." If you do not know what that smells like, imagine lime juice, orange juice, fresh garlic and oregano mixed together; this was spread all over the pig. The smell never gets old and it always brings back great memories. Inside the house the women were preparing all the food to accompany the main course. The younger women who were not doing the cooking were outside serving all the appetizers for the men and children, since nothing prepares you for eating like eating. Well, the beer and wine were flowing, the women were slowly coming out of the kitchen to enjoy the weather and pre-dinner socializing. Once again, on came the Cuban music, loud as always, and once again who should arrive at our door but one of our friendly old neighbors. This time another old lady. I'll never forget her, though I now forget her name. She thought she should inform us that, not only were there too many cars parked around my house, but she was having a small get-together at her home and would like us to reduce our noise.

It was upsetting to me, being treated in that manner. Everything we did was a problem, the cars, the music, the pig, talking too loud, and it was getting to the point where we all wanted to pack up and move back to Miami, but the afternoon continued in the same way regardless of what our neighbors thought. The men were beginning to change their clothes to get ready for the dinner. My grandfather put on his usual long sleeve, white Guayabera with his "Panama Hat" which I loved and it was one of those images that will always stick with me: My dad, and all the uncles, sitting around in a circle smoking their cigars, reminiscing, and dispensing wisdom about life. As the loud music, talking, dancing and drinking continued, our neighbors were not taking kindly to it. The police came to our home again to tell us to lower the music and calm the festivities. We agreed, reluctantly, to do so. However, since it was, of course, a holiday of togetherness, my father decided to go to our neighbors' homes on either side of ours and invite them to partake in the celebration with us.

This joining of the party, which four neighbors grudgingly agreed to, turned out to be enjoyable for them and proved to me as a young boy that, through some goodwill and friendliness, we can overcome anything. As the neighbors socialized with my grandparents and the rest of the family, they eventually warmed up to us and understood that we were just a large family of people who loved each other very much and wanted to have a good time. The old neighbors even took part in picking off the toasted skin of the pig, the best part by the way, and of course, after jokingly calling us cannibals, they actually enjoyed our way of eating and celebrating. We made friends that night with the very people who had made us feel like barbarians and a very unwanted minority in their neighborhood. It was a good feeling that I will never forget.

That was my first Christmas in a larger world and our neighbors' first "Cuban Christmas." ∎

From Reflection to Response   Responding to "A Cuban Christmas"

1. The United States often is described as a "melting pot," but as Steven Fernandez's profile shows, the melting process can be difficult at times. What insights does Fernandez's profile convey about cultural conflicts, what triggers them, and how they can be moderated or overcome?

2. If you were to write a profile about your family celebrating Christmas, or another holiday that is culturally important to you, what would be distinctive, instructive, and meaningful about it? What might people from other cultures misunderstand or even dislike? Would you put yourself into the profile, as Steven Fernandez does, or write from a more objective, third-person perspective?

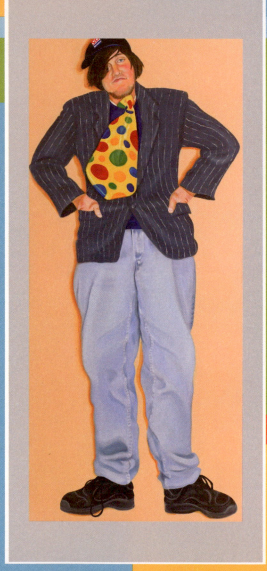

Courtesy of Sara K. Yeater

SARA K. YEATER

What Will You Be?

In this piece I was trying to portray the ambivalence
we feel regarding the potential paths we could take
at the college age.

CHAPTER SIX

Evaluations and Reviews

" GIL PENDER (aspiring novelist)
I would like you to read my novel and get your opinion.
ERNEST HEMINGWAY
My opinion is, I hate it.
GIL PENDER
I mean, you haven't even read it.
ERNEST HEMINGWAY
*If it's bad, I'll hate it because I hate bad writing. If it's good, I'll be
envious and hate it all the more.* "

—Dialogue from Woody Allen's *Midnight in Paris*

CHAPTER LEARNING OBJECTIVES

In this chapter, you will learn to:

► Apply communication principles to writing an evaluation essay
  for general readers.
► Support views that transcend opinions and taste.
► Base your evaluation and judgments on clear and thoughtful
  criteria.
► Develop descriptive information for your readers.
► Use relevant visuals to enhance your presentation.

COMMUNICATING MEANINGFUL JUDGMENTS

In our day-to-day lives, we evaluate just about everything from our pets to the food we eat, to programs on TV and the people we interact with. Because evaluation is such a pervasive human activity, evaluation essays are a popular genre of writing. These kinds of essays, in more concise forms, are called reviews.

TABLE 6.1 Common subjects of evaluations and reviews

General Categories	Examples
Consumer products and services	• Electronics (computers, TVs, video games, printers, phones, tablets, etc.) • Cars • Home and garden products and equipment • Retail stores and fashion lines • Software, web services, social networks
Wellness, health, and beauty	• Diets, exercise regimens, gyms • Cosmetics • Vitamins and supplements • Pharmaceutical drugs and treatments
Entertainment and travel	• Music/CDs • Concerts, shows, performances • Movies • Books • Restaurants, nightclubs, bars • Tourist destinations (countries, cities, regions, national parks) • Airlines, cruises, and cruise ships
Workplace, finance, and education	• Employee performance evaluations • Progress reports • Investment-product reviews (mutual funds, annuities, reverse mortgages) • Company and management reviews • College surveys and rankings • College course reviews and evaluations of professors

They make an assumption that the writer's judgment about a subject will be useful to readers: it will help them solve the problem of making informed, practical decisions.

Compelling evaluations and reviews, however, serve more than this practical purpose. They also can enlighten readers about issues that touch on every facet of life. People often read reviews just for knowledge and pleasure—reviews of cars they can't afford to buy, or books they don't have time to read—because perceptive reviews serve our aspirations to better understand and function in the complex world we inhabit. A review of Linux, an open-source, computer operating system, can raise relevant issues and support views about our reliance on commercial operating systems like Windows or Mac OS. A review of a photography exhibition in Moscow, or a socially conscious stock-market fund, can have the same kind of overriding significance: tell us what cultural interests are trending halfway around the world, or if investing in the stock market has to be a rapacious activity. Table 6.1 shows some common subjects of evaluations and reviews. Use it to generate ideas for your own evaluation or review.

A STUDENT'S ESSAY PROPOSAL

As you consider ideas for this project, read the proposal that student Thais Torquez wrote for an evaluation essay about Japanese street fashions. Note how, from the outset, Thais envisioned an essay that would intrigue readers about a fashion style they might not know about or understand. Thais wrote her proposal based on the following assignment instructions:

For this project, write an essay that evaluates a subject you know well and feel strongly about. The subject can be almost anything—a product, performance, hobby, lifestyle, art form, or form of entertainment.

The key to choosing a subject is to have a conviction that your knowledge and passion will make your essay interesting and illuminating for general readers, including your classmates and instructor.

Plan your essay with communication goals in mind. In other words, focus on an issue or problem that the subject raises and a central view or argument that your evaluation will support.

Evaluation Essay Proposal: Japanese Street Fashions

Thais Torquez

1. The Subject

Japanese street fashion has a distinctive and recognizable look that combines traditional styles with "cutting edge" fashion trends. Street fashion comes in a variety of sub-styles that appeal to different people's tastes and interests. My personal interest in Japanese street fashion grew out of my fascination for Japanese culture in Middle School, when I was introduced to anime and manga comics. Japanese street fashion immediately caught my eye, because I have always enjoyed dressing up in alternative ways.

2. The Main Issue or Problem

Some sub-styles of Japanese street fashion border on the "extreme," and evoke negative reactions. The outfits are sometimes dismissed as outrageous or abnormal. In my essay, I will explore these reactions and show that they are based on misconceptions.

3. Central View, Argument, Thesis, or Solution

The main view or argument I intend to support is that street fashions are attractive and creative, as opposed to being "weird." The criteria that apply to this argument are questions about what makes fashions attractive, how and why fashions are relevant to culture, and how social norms and creative, alternative fashions tend to clash. I will argue that negative reactions to street fashion don't take into account the creativity and the meaning of the different styles.

4. Reason for Choosing the Subject

Fashion in general is something that I have always been passionate about. I enjoy putting thought and effort into my clothing choices, hair, and accessories. I view fashion as a means of self-expression. The creativity involved in wearing alternative fashions is especially appealing to me, because I love to dress in all sorts of different ways.

5. Reader Relevance

I think the distinctive and creative styles of Japanese street fashion will intrigue both male and female readers. The styles will appeal to some readers who have never heard about them. In addition, readers will notice Western influences in certain street fashion styles, and realize that street fashions are not completely foreign. I think these Western influences will encourage readers to make comparisons and reevaluate some of their assumptions about fashion.

Interview with the Student Writer

● **Tell us a little about your background, interests, college major, and career goals.**

Courtesy of Thais Torquez

● I was born in Brazil but I've lived in the United States for about 18 years now. I'm still very much in touch with my Brazilian heritage and able to speak Portuguese fluently. Currently, I'm a sophomore at Florida International University, majoring in art history. I would like to pursue a career in curating for museums or art preservation. I'm also interested in exploring art as a means of therapy for those who suffer from anxiety, depression, and other disorders. In my free time, I love to study languages such as Korean and Japanese. I also love fashion, gaming, and trying out different restaurants and kinds of food.

● **Coming into college, how did you see yourself as a writer?**

● In high school, I had to do a lot of writing for my classes, which I definitely think gave me the necessary skill set coming into college. I thought of myself as a decent writer, being able to hit the key points and clearly convey my ideas. However, in high school, I never had a real chance to write about what was personally interesting to me. As a result, my style and tone could be pretty boring and plain.

Working Together

THINKING ABOUT CONSUMER PRODUCTS AND SERVICES

The most common evaluations that people read and write are customer reviews of products and services. With this in mind, think of a product you recently purchased (sports equipment, electronics, and so on) or a service you used (hairdresser, restaurant, hotel), and write a one- or two-paragraph customer review for a relevant website (examples of sites are below). Describe your experience with the product or service. Did it exceed or fall short of your expectations? Offer useful advice to other customers.

SOME WEBSITES THAT FEATURE CONSUMER REVIEWS

- Amazon (books and diverse merchandise)

- Angie's List (services)

- Citysearch (general, community-based business reviews)

- Cruises.com

- Epinions.com (comparison shopping)

- Ebags.com (luggage, backpacks, briefcases, and handbags)

- Rate My Professor

- Rotten Tomatoes (movies)

- Trip Advisor (travel, hotels)

- Yelp! (restaurants, bars, businesses, and more)

After you finish writing your review, read it to a group of your classmates and ask for their response. Does the review seem convincing to them? Does it provide enough information? Could they make a confident decision about purchasing the product or using the service based on the review, or would they have some doubts?

BEYOND OPINION AND TASTE

Evaluations and reviews draw on skills that are important for all kinds of writing and communication. Evaluations require analysis—that is, breaking a subject down in order to understand it better. Evaluations inevitably are arguments. The writer has to support views and judgments with facts, reasons, and insights. For a view to be meaningful, the evaluation has to go beyond the writer's opinions, and present an objective analysis based on standards or criteria. Evaluations that merely vent or convey subjective opinions are a form of self-expression. Strictly speaking, they are not "evaluations" at all.

The customer review below, for a "productivity app," is an example of a subjective evaluation that only expresses a personal opinion:

> Absolute garbage! It might be okay for you people who want a basic utility, but if your [sic] looking for real "productivity," save your money. It's not intuitive. It completely messed up my workflow.
>
> —by Organization Man

Organization Man's comments imply that the app worked for other people. We can only *guess* why it didn't work for him.

The same kind of subjectivity drives the online comment below, about Martin Amis's acclaimed novel *Money: A Suicide Note*:

> My mom and I bought this book to read on an Alaska cruise. According to one reviewer, the book is "dazzling." Yeah, right, if you're interested in BESTIALITY! This has got to be the worst book I've ever read. YUCK!
>
> —by Sara Revolted

Sara Revolted implies the book is for degenerates. Based on her standards, most of the reviewers on Amazon.com fall into that category, because 75 percent of them give the book four or five stars. Moreover, professional reviewers writing for *Time Magazine, Vogue*, the *Wall Street Journal*, and the *Boston Globe* also praise the book highly.

The problem with customer reviews like the two above is not negativity; it is the lack of objective support and information. Below is a customer review that is positive but also too subjective to be meaningful:

> Mr. Roasters is an awesome coffee shop, and if you're a college student, a great place to study. It's been a lifesaver for me, because whenever I go to my campus library, I get sick. My best friend, who's a chemistry major, says it's radon gas. So Mr. Roasters is where I do most of my studying now. I'm there almost every day, and love it!
>
> —by Rafael D.

Although Rafael D. likes Mr. Roasters, he tells us next to nothing about the place. The review is based on one criterion—the place is "great" for studying.

We don't know why, except presumably the radon gas levels are lower than in the campus library.

Good reviews support judgments with objective information and are based on clear and relevant criteria. If you were writing a meaningful review of a coffee shop in your community, your criteria might include some or all of the following:

▶ Quality of the coffee

▶ Variety of roasts

▶ Quality of food, if any is served

▶ Atmosphere, comfort (tables, sofas, and so forth), music, amenities (Wi-Fi)

▶ Location, parking, safety

▶ Service and staff

▶ Prices

▶ Clientele

▶ Fair trade standards for the products

Your final judgment would depend on which criteria are most important to you. If the coffee is so-so, but your main criterion is a pleasant place to hang out, and the atmosphere, service, music, and amenities are to your liking, then you probably would give the place a favorable review. If you are passionate about fair trade, and this coffee shop serves good coffee but the coffee is not fair-trade certified, you would have a problem with the place and probably not recommend it. Or, if almost everything about the place is positive, but the clientele is "preppy," and you dislike preppies, you might tell your readers to drink their coffee at Long John Silver's.

Table 6.2 shows examples of common criteria that apply to different subjects.

Readers respond to a review based on how the writer's criteria matches up with their own. When you write a review, a reader might agree with your criteria but not your priorities. For example, going back to the coffee shop, a reader might care more about the prices than the atmosphere or the quality of the coffee.

Sometimes readers may agree with your criteria and priorities but not your judgment—for example, agree that the clientele is important, but actually love a clean-cut, "preppy" scene. In addition, readers can have priorities or criteria that you don't bring up at all—for example, live entertainment, or scheduled events like art nights or poetry readings.

TABLE 6.2 Subjects and common criteria

Subjects	Criteria
Cars	• Styling • Reliability • Fuel economy • Performance • Safety • Comfort • Handling • Price
Travel destinations	• Location (getting there) • Affordability • Sites and attractions • Accommodations • Safety • Food and restaurants • Events • Climate • People • Entertainment, nightlife, shopping, transportation
Employee performance evaluations	• Job knowledge and skills • Initiative and creativity • Dependability • Writing and communication skills • Leadership qualities • Ability and willingness to work with others • Honesty and integrity

From Reflection to Response   Evaluating Features of Your Campus

As you consider subjects to write about for this project, think about your college campus. What features or facilities do you like or dislike? Below are a few examples:

- Classrooms
- Architecture
- Grounds and landscaping
- Geographic location
- Demographics of the student body
- Dorms, cafeteria, fitness center, lounges
- Clubs and organizations
- Student media outlets like the newspaper or a radio station
- Services such as a writing center
- Events or traditions that are special or unique to your campus

 Choose a feature of your campus, or a facility, that you have positive or negative feelings about, and write a one- or two-paragraph review that supports your judgment. After you finish writing the review, exchange reviews with a classmate and give each other feedback. Do you agree with the judgment? How well is it supported? Are the criteria clear and meaningful?

Getting readers to agree with your criteria is not the ultimate goal of an intelligent review. When reviews are based on meaningful criteria and support judgments, they can engage us even if we disagree with the writer's views or have a minimal interest in the subject.

With this in mind, read the music review that follows. Whether you are interested in the subject or not, decide to what extent, if any, the review is engaging and meaningful to general readers.

Del F. Cowie   { REVIEW OF *good kid, m.A.A.d. city* BY KENDRICK LAMAR

Del F. Cowie is a music critic and assistant editor for the Canadian music magazine *Exclaim!* Cowie also maintains a music blog called *Vibes and Stuff*.

IN DELIVERING ONE OF the most striking hip-hop major label debuts in recent memory, Kendrick Lamar has not only put himself at the forefront of the West Coast revival, but in position to be a highly influential player in the music's future. Lamar's inimitable artistry and self-assurance have been on display for a while now, but *good kid, m.A.A.d. city* is the uncompromising documentation of that treacherous journey of self-discovery. A heavily intro-spective tour de force, Lamar has created a stubbornly parochial soundtrack to his life in Compton, CA, set to a downbeat melancholy soundscape that incorporates the likes of Pharrell, Just Blaze and Dr. Dre, who are relegated to background walk-on roles. As the specter of violence, death and paranoia hov-ers ubiquitously, we bear witness to a narrative detailing Lamar's transforma-tion from a boisterous, impressionable, girl-craving teenager to more spiritual, hard-fought adulthood, irrevocably shaped by the neighborhood and familial bonds of his precarious environment.

What makes the album stand out from a rote coming-of-age story is the intricate attention to detail. Lamar's descriptive skills are so vivid that he immerses you in the topography of his world, his street corners and, ultimately, his state of mind. Even when it initially appears he may be bowing to convention, he isn't. "Poetic Justice," featuring Lamar and Drake in

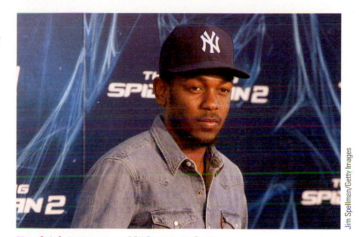

Kendrick Lamar, *good kid, m.A.A.d. city*

Jim Spellman/Getty Images

seduction mode over Janet Jackson's "Any Time, Any Place," could have gone the regular booty call route, but doesn't. This is underlined by the harrowing confrontation Lamar encounters after the song abruptly ends. Similarly, the album's T-Minus-produced lead single, "Swimming Pools (Drank)," addresses inner moral conflict, uncomfortable peer pressure and alcoholism when it could easily have been a mindless celebration of hedonism.

Skits, so often the bane of hip-hop, serve as gritty mono audio aids to Lamar's storytelling, stitched together with interference-laden voicemails and rewound cassette tapes. And in an era when style can often trump substance, Lamar takes this to the logical extreme, liberally playing with pronunciation, voice inflection and delivery, to the point where he inhabits different personas, mirroring the tumultuous emotional range and personal transformation on display. It also speaks to Lamar's latent urge to speak for those in his community who may not have been as fortunate.

On 12-minute standout "Sing About Me, I'm Dying of Thirst," he rhymes from the perspectives of a deceased friend and a woman distressed by her sister's tragic life as a prostitute, portrayed in a previous Lamar song. Lamar then rhymes as himself, responding to the people in the first two verses. At one point in this verse, a weary and sober Lamar, cognizant of communal responsibility rather than self-exaltation, rhetorically asks, "Now am I worth it? Did I put enough work in?" From this vantage point, the answer is an unequivocal yes. ■

From Reflection to Response
Responding to Del F. Cowie's "Review of *good kid, m.A.A.d. city* by Kendrick Lamar"

Working with a small group of your classmates, or on your own, respond to the following questions about Del F. Cowie's review.

1. Where in the review does Cowie first express his view of *good kid, m.A.A.d. city*? How would you sum up Cowie's view of the album?

2. Extremely positive reviews sometimes are called "rave reviews," implying that the reviewer is so enthralled that his or her judgment cannot be trusted. Do you consider Cowie's review a "rave review"? If so, indicate specific parts of the review that make you think so. If not, indicate specific parts that convince you Cowie's views are judicious.

3. On what main criteria does Cowie base his judgment of the album? Do you agree with the importance of these criteria? Can you think of other criteria that the review should address?

4. If you have not listened to *good kid, m.A.A.d. city*, does Cowie's review make you want to listen to it? If so, why? Conversely, if you have listened to the album, does Cowie's review change your opinion or perception of it in any way? Identify any observations he makes about the album that you either find enlightening or disagree with.

5. Below is a list of words that Cowie uses in his review. Go through the list and note any words you don't know. Do you think the words he uses are appropriate for the ideas he is trying to express and the audience he is writing for, or is

his vocabulary too sophisticated? Did you have any trouble understanding the review when you were reading it?

- parochial
- specter
- ubiquitously
- boisterous
- rote
- topography
- bane
- tumultuous
- cognizant
- unequivocal

Descriptive Information and Social Perspectives

Thoughtful reviews of artistic works like Kendrick Lamar's *good kid, m.A.A.d city* almost have to offer perspectives about life and living. Reviews of products—phones, TVs, vacuum cleaners—usually emphasize practical information. Below, an excerpt from a review of the BlackBerry Z10 phone in *Consumer Reports* mainly takes a "just the facts" approach to the subject:

BlackBerry Z10

Virtual keyboard. The keyboard's Flick feature essentially allows the phone to co-author memos, e-mails, and the like, through suggesting words it thinks will be next, based on what's already in the sentence. For example, begin a sentence with the word "Hurricane," and the word "Katrina" will instantly appear over the letter "K." Begin with the word "Here," and the words "we," "you," and "is," will appear over their respective first letters on the keyboard.

BlackBerry Z10 smartphone.

Oleksiy Maksymenko Photography/Alamy

Flick is a very efficient (if slightly creepy) way to enter text. The keyboard also handled more traditional predictive-text tasks with aplomb. For example, type "Thanks," and the word "Thanksgiving" will appear in the space bar. If you get tired of typing, pressing and holding the period key will engage the voice-to-text feature, which is impressively accurate. Pressing and holding the space bar presents common text formatting options, such as boldface, italics, underline, bullets, and font size.

The writer, Mike Gikas, deviates momentarily from "just the facts" when he remarks that the Flick feature is "slightly creepy." Movie lovers might recall Stanley Kubrick's classic *2001: A Space Odyssey*, in which a *very* creepy computer, HAL 9000, tells the captain of a spaceship, "This mission is too important for me to allow you to jeopardize it!"

Our electronic devices have not reached that degree of creepiness yet; however, they certainly invade our privacy and can exert a control over our lives that raises concerns. But readers of *Consumer Reports* mainly are looking for information to help them buy a product. An extended examination of social concerns about technology would be out of place. However, reviews written as essays or articles for general readers—say in a magazine like *Wired* or a newspaper like the *Wall Street Journal*—often present and explore issues of larger social interest, like Flick's "creepiness," even if the subject is just a product or a form of entertainment. The two reviews that follow present socially relevant issues and views about an Internet site and a genre of entertainment, respectively.

Clive Thompson { IN DEFENSE OF PINTEREST

Brad Barket/Getty Images

Clive Thompson is an accomplished journalist whose articles have appeared in the *New York Times Magazine*, the *Washington Post, Mother Jones, Smithsonian*, and many other publications of quality. He is known for his writing on the social impact of new technologies. "In Defense of Pinterest" originally appeared in *Wired* magazine.

THERAPISTS OFTEN RUN INTO a curious problem during treatment: Clients aren't very good at describing their emotions. How exactly do you express the nature of your depression?

So this spring, relationship counselor Crystal Rice hit upon a clever idea. She had her clients use Pinterest, the popular picture-pinning social network, to create arrays of images that map out their feelings. It's a brilliant epiphany: While emotions can be devilishly difficult to convey in words, they're often very accessible via pictures. "This way we can really identify what's going on," Rice says.

And Rice's idea, as it turns out, is a clue to a question that's been debated a lot: Why the heck is Pinterest so popular?

Critics love to hate the site, which lets you assemble collections of themed images. Because a significant majority of the first users were women—many of whom avidly set up boards to organize their weddings, fantasize about home decor, or store workout inspiration photos—numerous observers have concluded Pinterest is pure fluff. "Banal, girly crap," as one blogger posted.

Beyond that, there's also a gloomy suspicion that Pinterest, like Twitter before it, is an assault on literacy itself. Pinterest is for people who "will do anything to avoid having to read," as another critic complained.

This is almost certainly untrue (not least because women handily eclipse men in book-reading). But these critiques are, inadvertently, onto something. As Rice discovered with her clients, Pinterest's appeal is that it gives us curiously powerful visual ways to communicate, think, and remember.

Because Pinterest encourages collecting photos based on a theme, this in turn encourages categorical thinking—13 ways of looking at a blackbird. If you see one picture of a guitar, it's just a guitar; but when you see 80 of them lined up you start to see guitarness. This additive power is precisely what helps Rice's clients paint their internal worlds.

What's more, Pinterest's glanceability makes it incredibly useful as a visual memory locker. Consider the case of Josh Hirschland, a 26-year-old heading off to grad school in Chicago. He realized, as he told me, "I'm going to be broke, so I'm going to be doing more cooking." So like thousands of other folks, he began pinning recipe pictures and scanning others' food-related boards. He found that a grid of images is a better way to generate ideas—and to access what he has personally filed away.

I have used this memory function myself, by putting together a board for ebooks I've read—a virtual bookshelf for titles I don't physically possess. And I've discovered that glancing at it produces the same Proustian jolt I get from gazing at the spines of my "real" books: I suddenly remember a favorite passage.

Indeed, part of the value of Pinterest is that it brings you out of yourself and into the world of things. As the *Huffington Post* writer Bianca Bosker argued, Facebook and Twitter are inwardly focused ("Look at me!") while Pinterest is outwardly focused ("Look at this!"). It's the world as seen through not your eyes but your imagination. "In such a self-obsessed society, this is a place where people are focusing attention on something other than themselves," says Courtney Brennan, an avid Pinterest user.

Granted, Pinterest encourages plenty of dubious behavior too. It can be grindingly materialistic; all those pins of stuff to buy! Marketers are predictably adrool, and as they swarm aboard, the whole service might very well end up collapsing into a heap of product shilling.

But I suspect we'll see increasingly odd and clever ways of using Pinterest. If a picture is worth a thousand words, those collections are worth millions. ∎

From Reflection to Response
Responding to Clive Thompson's "In Defense of Pinterest"

Working with a small group of your classmates, or on your own, respond to the following questions about Clive Thompson's review.

1. What is the main issue Thompson presents at the beginning of his review? Why does Thompson think this issue is relevant to general readers?

2. What is Thompson's overall judgment, or view, of Pinterest? What are the main points he makes to support his view? Are his points convincing? Explain why.

3. In Thompson's second-to-last paragraph, he admits that Pinterest has its faults, but he immediately goes on to predict a bright future for the site. What is it about Pinterest that he criticizes, and why does he think the site has a bright future nonetheless?

Like Clive Thompson's review of Pinterest, the article below about "reality TV" supports a "contrarian" view of a subject many people "love to hate."

Grant McCracken ❴ WHY REALITY TV DOESN'T SUCK, AND MAY EVEN MAKE US SMARTER

Grant McCracken is an anthropologist, teacher, and scholar who has written extensively about cultural trends and innovations. "Why Reality TV Doesn't Suck, and May Even Make Us Smarter" appeared in *Wired* magazine.

IT'S EASY TO ASSUME reality TV is the place where bad TV went to hide when the rest of TV got a lot better. Like that old Wild West town where criminals congregate, reality TV is often perceived as the last, "vast wasteland": uncouth, desperate, lawless.

But while some shows seem irredeemably bad (*Here Comes Honey Boo Boo*, anyone?), others offer an indication of good things to come. In fact, by turning all of us into virtual anthropologists, reality TV may lead to the improvement—dare I say it—of Western civilization. Reality TV may even be the next stage in the evolution of television.

Charles Sykes/AP Images

In its early days, TV was confronted with a series of problems. It was a new medium struggling to find a place in the world. It had quality-control problems in sound and image. And it was talking to millions of Americans for whom English was a second language and American culture was still a mystery. TV solved these problems by relying on genre. Once you understood you were watching a "cop show" or a "Western," the rest was easy.

Genre was like a cheat sheet. It flattened every difficulty: technical, intellectual, cultural, linguistic.

Successive generations got better at TV, and when this happened genre TV became grueling. It bored us. These programs "jumped the shark" and we fled. Now, show runners were free and even forced to build in complexity. But then even this complexity began to bore us.

Writers were free of genre but they were still forming the narrative. They were still making a story when what we wanted was the uncontrolled, spontaneous, accident-prone, and most of all, the unpredictable. Because, by this time, it took a matter of seconds to divine what was going on and get there first. We needed to know that not even the producer knew where this baby was headed.

Reality TV is where TV has always been evolving. It just took us a century or so to get there.

Reality TV is not straight out of genre. Even when manipulated by producers, no one quite knows where things will end up. And this makes it interesting and sometimes even, as James Poniewozik has pointed out, uncomfortable. And that keeps us watching. Reality TV is where TV has always been evolving. It just took us a century or so to get there.

The anthropological question: What else is going on here?

Culture is a thing of surfaces and secrets. The anthropologist is obliged to record the first and penetrate the second.

Once we've figured out what people believe to be true about themselves, we can begin to figure out what's really going on in this culture. In this case, the surface says, "reality TV is a dumbing down." But the secret says "not always." Sometimes, reality TV contributes to a smartening up.

Case in point: My wife and I watch *Project Runway*. She's a graphic designer, so she has a clue about how decisions are being made by students and critics. Meanwhile, I get to test my grasp of this new world by predicting the picks and the pans. But right or wrong, I learn something. And I think I'm getting better (though my wife might demur). Incidentally, trial and error is the way anthropologists build up knowledge of other cultures, venturing opinions the world approves or scorns.

Reality TV makes anthropologists of us all. To be sure, there are some people so emotionally stunted or disappointed by life they treasure the humiliations inflicted by reality TV, but the rest of us are learning. Consider the show *Shark Tank*, which drew its largest audience ever and premiered recently at the top of its slot. Scores of websites analyze and dissect the sharks' every move, educating budding entrepreneurs everywhere—outside rarefied tech clusters—about the difference between a product and a plan, the difference between an idea and implementation. That's when anthropology doesn't just tell us, but shows us how to act and think and grow. Reality TV forces revelation.

A key feature of anthropology is the long, observational, "ethnographic" interview. Anthropologists believe one of the advantages of this method is that no one can manage appearances, let alone lie, successfully for a long period of time.

So while the Kardashian sisters may wish to create an impression—and the producers edit to reinforce that impression—over many episodes and seasons, the truth will out. Whether they like it or not, eventually we will see into Kardashian souls. That these souls are never as beautiful as the sisters themselves is, well, one of the truths that reality TV makes available to us, and here it performs one of the functions normally dispatched by religious or moral leaders.

Some reality TV remains, of course, appalling. Reality TV has a weakness for beautiful people who are too stupid to appreciate that their limitations are better kept from public view. But the rest of us are, I think, well served. And getting smarter because of it. ■

From Reflection to Response
Responding to Grant McCracken's "Why Reality TV Doesn't Suck, and May Even Make Us Smarter"

Working with a small group of your classmates, or on your own, respond to the following questions about Grant McCracken's article.

1. In the opening section of his article, McCracken discusses the "early days" of TV, and how programming once relied on "genres." Based on what you know about

genres, what issue is McCracken raising, and why does he think the issue is significant? What criterion for evaluating reality TV is he putting forward?

2. How would you sum up McCracken's reasons for thinking reality TV deserves more appreciation or respect? What is the significance of the statement "Reality TV makes anthropologists of us all"?

3. In the second paragraph of the article, McCracken admits that reality shows can "seem irredeemably bad." In the last paragraph, he concedes again that reality TV can be "appalling" ("[it] has a weakness for beautiful people who are too stupid to appreciate that their limitations are better kept from public view"), but he still maintains that the positives outweigh the negatives. Do you think his article deals with the "appalling" side enough? In your view, is the appalling side more negative than McCracken is willing to admit, or conversely, does he exaggerate the positive side?

CONSIDERING SUBJECTS AND COMMUNICATION GOALS

Although the evaluation essay or review that you write for this project can be about almost anything, make it your goal to write for a general audience of educated readers who may not know or care very much about your subject, but who are intelligent and curious enough to take an interest in perspectives that your essay can offer. To help you decide on a subject, ask the questions below about subjects you are considering:

▶ Do you have strong feelings or a strong opinion about the subject?

▶ Why do you feel the way you do? What criteria are your opinions based on?

▶ Do you have enough knowledge about the subject to develop a convincing evaluation?

▶ Will general readers care about this subject? If not, how can you make them care?

▶ What will be the "takeaway" for your readers—in other words, what can your readers learn that will be of value to them?

Review the subjects listed under the categories below to help you generate ideas for your essay. As you consider different subjects, choose one you feel motivated to write about—a subject you (1) know well, and (2) have convictions about.

(Note that the subjects and categories overlap. An event or travel destination can be classified as "entertainment." A college course can be considered a consumer "product." In short, the classification isn't important.)

Education, College and Campus Life

- ▶ **Your secondary schools and experiences:** your high school, your senior year; programs or activities you participated in
- ▶ **Your college campus and facilities:** for example, dorms, the cafeteria, the rec center
- ▶ **College courses and programs:** study abroad, tutoring and mentoring programs; service learning
- ▶ **Your campus organizations and clubs:** chess, debate, science, or business clubs; religious, political, and cultural organizations; honor societies, theater, dance, and athletic groups; fraternities/sororities

Media, Living, Arts and Entertainment

- ▶ Websites, services, and social networks: PolitiFact, Hubble, Second Life, Instagram, Twitter, Tumblr, Flickr
- ▶ Video games and consoles
- ▶ Restaurants, clubs, and bars
- ▶ Hobbies: sailing, paintball, motocross, crafts, biking, amateur theater, karaoke, scouting
- ▶ Civic engagement and worship: environmental work, community service, youth groups, religious institutions, missions, and outreach
- ▶ Music
- ▶ Movies and TV or radio programs
- ▶ Magazines and books

Products

- ▶ Electronics, gadgets, apps: e-books, tablets, smartphones, digital cameras, camcorders, Photoshop, GarageBand
- ▶ Cars, motorcycles, ATVs, and bicycles
- ▶ Fashion: styles, clothing lines, designers, beauty products, fragrances, body art
- ▶ Health and personal care: vitamins, supplements, diets, training regimens, aerobic dancing, yoga classes
- ▶ Food and beverages
- ▶ Sporting goods and equipment

Places and Events

▶ Travel destinations: countries, cities, regions, national parks, and nature preserves

▶ Tours and travel concepts: themed vacations (vineyards, art, fishing, "adventure"); backpacking, hostels, cruises, safaris, motorcycle and bicycle tours

▶ Live performances and exhibitions: concerts, plays, recitals, comedy shows, rodeos, circuses, art shows

▶ Festivals, fairs, and special events: Mardi Gras, Balloon Fiesta, marathons, New Year's Eve in Times Square, country and state fairs, carnivals, flea and farmers' markets

▶ Sporting events: boxing, wrestling, horse racing, Tour de France, NASCAR and Formula One races, beach volleyball

From Reflection to Response   **Planning an Evaluation**

This activity will give you practice planning an evaluation with communication goals. To get started, choose one of the following subjects:

A. A reality TV show you are familiar with—in particular, one you especially like or dislike.

B. A TV or movie family that you know well, and either identify with or find objectionable. Below are a few examples:

- *The Simpsons*
- *The Osbournes*
- *The Sopranos*
- The Bluths—*Arrested Development*
- The Whites (Walter, Skyler, and Walt Jr.)—*Breaking Bad*
- The Fishers—*Six Feet Under*
- The Griswolds—*National Lampoon's Vacation* Series
- The Conners—*Roseanne*
- The Bundys—*Married with Children*
- The Crawleys—*Downton Abbey*
- The Gallaghers—*Shameless*
- The Dreckers—*Hung*

C. A real family you know, or if you think you can be objective, your own family. (If you want, you can change the name of the family to protect its identity, but as journalists do, you should mention the name change in the writing exercise so that readers will know.)

Once you have a subject, do some freewriting, brainstorming, or clustering to generate ideas, and then follow the instructions below:

1. Write an objective description of the TV show or family (just the facts).

2. Write a brief statement expressing an issue that you or others perceive about the subject, and a view you would want to support, along with a summary of how you would support it (the reasons and examples).

3. List the criteria that your evaluation would be based on (try to arrange the criteria in order of importance).

4. To complete the activity, form a group with three or four of your classmates, summarize the evaluation you planned, and gauge their interest in the subject. What do they know about the subject? What would they like to learn? How can you make your evaluation interesting and relevant to all of them?

WRITING A PROPOSAL

Once you decide on a subject for your essay, write a proposal using the format and headings below:

1. **The Subject.** Describe the subject of the evaluation and why it is of interest to you.

2. **The Main Issue or Problem.** Describe one or more issues or problems that your subject raises and that your evaluation will address.

3. **Central View, Argument, Thesis, or Solution.** Identify the central view that you intend to support, and discuss the criteria that apply.

4. **Reason for Choosing the Subject.** Elaborate on why you chose this subject—what you know about it, and why you think it is a better subject than others you could write about.

5. **Reader Relevance.** Explain why you think your evaluation will be interesting and relevant to readers. What value will your essay have for them?

WRITING A ROUGH DRAFT

Many reviews address an implied issue that the writer does not always have to articulate: Should the reader buy a certain product, see a certain movie, visit a certain place, or go to a certain restaurant? The implied issue is sufficient to launch a review that is primarily for readers who are interested in the subject and want advice about making a decision. These kinds of practical reviews can begin with a brief description of the subject, or by simply identifying the subject, and then proceed with an analysis that states and supports the writer's main view.

Del F. Cowie's review of *good kid, m.A.A.d. city* gets right to the point: in the first sentence, Cowie calls the album "one of the most striking hip-hop major label debuts in recent memory." The rest of the review presents descriptive information, criteria, and an analysis of the album that supports his positive judgment. The review mainly targets interested or knowledgeable readers, although Cowie's criteria—deft storytelling, realism, and a delineation of "spiritual" growth—are of interest to general readers who care about music or artistic expression.

Most movie reviews that appear on popular websites or in daily newspapers also get right to the implied issue of whether a movie is "any good" or not. These reviews usually open with a view about the movie, or a combination of descriptive information and a view. Below is the opening of a review of the box-office hit *The Social Network*, about Facebook founder Mark Zuckerberg:

> It would seem a tall order to make a compelling movie about a college kid coding up a new form of social media from his dorm room, a kid so antisocial that you can't really root for him to succeed, even as you know he will.
>
> But with "The Social Network," director David Fincher has come up with a movie that, in telling the turbulent story of whiz-kid Mark Zuckerberg's creation of Facebook, isn't just compelling.
>
> It's great.

The writer of this review, Bill Goodykoontz of the *Arizona Republic*, knows that most of his readers are looking for basic information and an opinion about the entertainment value of the movie, not a probing analysis of its meaning or issues it might raise.

However, evaluation essays like the one you will write for this project reach out more explicitly to an audience of discerning, educated readers, and usually begin by presenting an issue or problem that readers perceive as relevant, regardless of how interested they happen to be in the subject of the evaluation.

Clive Thompson's review of Pinterest raises an issue about the value of pictures and visual imagery, and how visual biases affect critics' perceptions of Pinterest (an "assault on literacy itself," for people "who will do anything to avoid having to read"). Even readers who have never heard of Pinterest can take an interest in the issue Thompson presents.

Grant McCracken's evaluation of reality TV raises the issue of reality TV as an abomination, a "vast wasteland," but counters with perceptions and criteria that support a different view—reality TV as an anthropological tool, a "window" on culture and human behavior.

Student writer Thais Torquez, in her evaluation essay about Japanese street fashions, takes a similar approach. At issue are perceptions about street fashions being "weird" or "trashy," but Torquez argues that they really are about creativity and self-expression.

Movie reviews that appear in prestigious magazines and newspapers known for their quality—the *New Yorker*, the *Atlantic*, and the *Village Voice*, to name a few—have a long tradition of being written as probing essays for discerning readers, not just to support a thumbs up or a rotten tomato. These kinds of reviews raise social, aesthetic, and philosophical issues of broader significance than a movie's entertainment value.

Writer and professor Zadie Smith takes this probing approach in a critical dissection of *The Social Network* that was published in the *New York Review of Books*. *The Social Network*, upon its release, was one of the best-reviewed movies to appear in a long time. Most professional critics liked it as much as Bill Goodykoontz (quoted above), if not more, praising its "propulsive energy," "spellbinding dialogue," and "strong script." On the website *Metacritic*, features editor Jason Dietz wrote that it placed near the top of all of the movies in *Metacritic's* database. But Zadie Smith has a different view of the movie and begins her review—*Generation Why?*—remarking on issues it raises for her about generational values, groupthink, and "personhood":

> How long is a generation these days? I must be in Mark Zuckerberg's generation—there are only nine years between us—but somehow it doesn't feel that way. This despite the fact that I can say (like everyone else on Harvard's campus in the fall of 2003) that "I was there" at Facebook's inception, and remember Facemash and the fuss it caused.... Doubtless years from now I will misremember my closeness to Zuckerberg, in the same spirit that everyone in '60s Liverpool met John Lennon.
>
> At the time, though, I felt distant from Zuckerberg and all the kids at Harvard. I still feel distant from them now, ever more so, as I increasingly opt out (by choice, by default) of the things they have embraced. We have different ideas about things. Specifically we have different

ideas about what a person is, or should be. I often worry that my idea of personhood is nostalgic, irrational, inaccurate. Perhaps Generation Facebook have built their virtual mansions in good faith, in order to house the People 2.0 they genuinely are, and if I feel uncomfortable within them it is because I am stuck at Person 1.0. Then again, the more time I spend with the tail end of Generation Facebook (in the shape of my students) the more convinced I become that some of the software currently shaping their generation is unworthy of them. They are more interesting than it is. They deserve better.

Smith's review goes on to combine a probing assessment of the movie with social criticism based on the criteria she presents in her opening. Whether the movie is worth seeing or not is almost a moot point for Smith and her readers, because the review is about larger issues—who we are, our values, and where we are going. Ironically, Smith's mostly negative assessment is so discerning that readers could be motivated to go see the movie anyway.

Avoiding Long Descriptions and Summaries

Evaluations and reviews require descriptive information about the subject, but the main thing readers are looking for is the writer's analysis and assessment. Long, unbroken passages of information—for example, a detailed plot summary of a movie—bog down an evaluation and turn readers away. A reader who strictly wants that kind of information can find it on an Internet database like IMDb or a commercial website.

The most effective way to present descriptive information about the subject of an evaluation is to integrate the information with your assessments. In the passage below, from a review of Rosie Schaap's memoir, *Drinking with Men*, the reviewer, Mary Pols, seamlessly integrates information about the book with her assessments:

Schaap knows the milieu [bars and their patrons] and names it for what it is, "something both real and less than real, a kind of controlled, convivial shallowness." That flush from both liquor and the buzz of companionship practically seeps out of these easy, flowing pages.

But at the same time, as convivial as *Drinking with Men* is, it is also shallow. Whenever the deep and personal intrude, Schaap essentially picks up and relocates the narrative, in much the same way she moves on from her various bars. She treats the reader like another regular, with a regular's limited interest....

> Her biggest dodge is to only inform the reader of the illness and death of her husband, Frank, whom she meets, marries and separates from in the course of the book, in the acknowledgments. "This was a story I could not tell here," Schaap writes. Only she has, in some peculiar way, if only in the way a sad and ghostly absence of real self-examination hangs over those later chapters.
>
> It's not that Schaap doesn't acknowledge wounds, including those left by her all-too-absent sportswriter father, but that instead of examining them, she focuses on how and where she bathed these wounds.

Considering Other Opinions and Points of View

Readers can disagree with a judgment and still respect an evaluation and get something out of it, if the analysis is judicious and the views are supported. Showing an awareness and respect for opposing points of view is always a good way for a writer to gain readers' interest and trust. Del Cowie lets us know he doesn't have a blinkered view of hip-hop, and gains our trust, when he writes that one of Kendrick Lamar's songs "could have gone the regular booty call route, but doesn't." Both Clive Thompson and Grant McCracken articulate opposing views about Pinterest and reality TV, and they agree with the detractors up to a point. Even Zadie Smith, in criticizing *The Social Network*, understands the movie's charms.

Using First or Third Person

If you go back and look at the readings in this chapter, you will see that some of them use the first-person "I" and some don't. Del F. Cowie writes in the third person, keeping his focus entirely on the subject rather than himself. Cowie's approach is favored in academic writing. Sticking to the third person and avoiding "I" can help promote objective thinking.

Clive Thompson and Grant McCracken both use the first-person "I," but they do so with restraint, focusing on the subject of their reviews, except in parts where their personal experiences are relevant to the analysis. Their occasional use of the first person does not undermine the objectivity of the reviews.

Zadie Smith's review begins almost like a personal narrative, as she recalls being at Harvard at "Facebook's inception." Although she continues to use the first person as her article develops, she refers to herself more and more sparingly, shifting her focus to an analysis of the movie and the issues it raises for her.

When all is said and done, Smith's review, despite the personalized opening, is rigorously analytical, and her points are well-supported.

Using the first person or not in an evaluation is a stylistic choice. What matters most are the writing and communication principles that have been stressed throughout this chapter—that is, making the evaluation reader-relevant, and basing it on meaningful criteria, objective analysis, descriptive information, and well-supported views. A review, or any other kind of argument, can be written in the third person and still be subjective and narrow-minded, or written in the first person and still be rigorous and well-supported.

Using Visuals

Depending on the subject you evaluate, consider inserting one or more photographs or visual illustrations in your essay. A relevant visual—for example, a photograph of a place, product, or event you are evaluating—can make your essay more appealing and informative, but be selective and don't go overboard with the visuals. If you insert too many, or insert them randomly, they will be more of a distraction than an asset. Nor will visuals compensate for a superficial or poorly written essay.

YOUR ESSAY CHECKLIST

Use the checklist to guide your steps in developing your essay.

✔ Task	Description	Time Frame
☐ Choose a subject	• Take time to consider a variety of subjects. • Choose a subject you know well and have strong feelings about. • Think about your pastimes and facets of your lifestyle. • Also, think about the "reader relevance" of your subject before you make a final choice. • Don't just assume your evaluation will appeal to readers. • Ask yourself *why* it will.	At least an hour or two.
☐ Write a proposal	• Write a proposal that describes your subject, issues related to it, the judgment you want to support, the criteria behind your judgment, and your audience.	A half hour or so.

(continued)

✔ Task	Description	Time Frame
☐ **Write a rough draft**	• Draft your essay without thinking too much about the quality. • Decide whether you want to use the first person, or stick to the third, and why. • As you compose the draft, describe issues your subject raises, any misconceptions people (including your readers) might have, and why these issues or misconceptions are important. • Clarify the view you want your evaluation to support, and develop sound supporting arguments. • After you finish the draft, put it aside for at least a day before you start revising.	The time frame will vary. Compose the first draft in more than one sitting if necessary, and aim to finish the draft at least a week before the final version is due.
☐ **Revise**	As you revise, think about some of the principles covered in this chapter: • How interesting and reader-relevant is your opening? • Are your criteria clear and meaningful? • Do you consider opposing views? • Is your analysis and support detailed enough? • Do you avoid long summaries and descriptions that have no bearing on your analysis?	Plan on doing at least several revisions over the course of a week or two.
☐ **Seek peer review**	• When you have a readable draft ready, ask for feedback from classmates (see peer-review questions below). • Consider posting the draft on your course website or your Facebook page if you have one. • Visit your campus writing center to get feedback and advice from a tutor.	Varies.
☐ **Edit your essay**	Before you submit the essay, read it over carefully. Make the writing as clear and professional as you can. Consider using the text-to-speech feature on your computer to hear how the essay sounds and to help you catch mistakes, typos, and muddled phrases. Check for the following: • Helpful paragraphing and smooth transitions from one paragraph to the next • Accurate wording and word choice • Correct sentence punctuation (fix run-ons and comma splices) • Correct grammar and mechanics (check subject-verb agreement, pronoun reference, placement of commas)	Careful editing may involve a certain amount of revising, so the time frame can vary, but always plan on going over what you have written. Running a spell check is not enough.

PEER REVIEW

Your classmates are a realistic audience for this essay, and as always, a good source of feedback. Since your evaluation is for a general audience and deals with a subject you care about, consider getting feedback from other readers, too—friends, roommates, family members. See if posting your essay, or a summary of it, on Facebook or another social network site elicits any "likes" or comments. Once you have a readable draft of the essay written, ask classmates to respond to the peer review questions below:

1. Before you started reading this essay, what was your opinion of the subject of the evaluation? If your opinion was different from the writer's, did the essay change your mind or "open your eyes" in any way?

2. What are the writer's criteria for this evaluation? Are there criteria that should be added or clarified? Point out any parts of the essay that you think are too subjective and reducible to personal "taste."

3. Does the opening of the essay capture your interest? What issue or set of issues about the subject does the writer raise? If you can, offer suggestions for improving the opening.

4. Is the writer's analysis interesting and convincing? Is there enough or too much descriptive information about the subject? Point out any parts of the evaluation that you disagree with or you think should be supported more effectively.

5. Is the essay well-edited and enjoyable to read? Point out any problems you noticed with paragraphing, word choice, grammar, or punctuation, and offer suggestions for improvements. Does the writer use any visuals? Are they relevant and helpful?

STUDENT ESSAY: FINAL DRAFT

Below is the evaluation essay about Japanese street fashions that Thais Torquez wrote for this project. After the essay, Thais discusses how she came up with the idea, and offers advice about writing an evaluation.

Thais Torquez // **FROM THE STREET TO YOUR HEART**

Visualize your closet. Surely, you must own several t-shirts and pairs of jeans, perhaps nicer outfits for an evening event. Take a closer look: do you see any petticoats, any lacey, furry, leopardy things; a pair of platform boots perhaps, or ditzy beer-can patterned pants? If so, you could turn a lot of heads if you wore those items. Believe it or not, an entire fashion is based on just that kind of head-turning unconventionality. Japanese street fashion boasts some of the most creative clothing styles and designs imaginable. Street fashions, which combine Western and Japanese trends, are notable for their diverse and outlandish styles. In Tokyo, teenagers and young adults can often be seen walking around in the latest boutique brands or homemade outfits, turning normally bland urban intersections and avenues into everyday fashion shows.

My exposure to Japanese street fashions started when I was in middle school. I was interested in anime and manga comics, which led me to seeing photographs of Japanese street fashions online. The creativity of the styles made an immediate impression on me, but I didn't get into seriously wearing them until I was a senior in high school. I saw some outfits on the

Fig. 1. A stylish Japanese woman.

Internet one day, and thought, "What's not to like about that?" Soon, I started going to department stores and thrift shops to pick out pieces of clothing that I could use to create outfits. Occasionally, when I saw an outfit online that I knew I couldn't duplicate on my own, I would order it directly from Japan, which was very expensive, but the high quality of the fabrics always made those outfits worth the price!

Unfortunately, in our culture, many people are quick to judge street fashions and those of us who wear the outfits as weird or trashy. People tend to have negative attitudes about any fashions that stray too far from the norm, or aren't sanctioned by the ads and labels of mainstream designers like Dolce and Gabbana, Cavalli, or Céline. We live in a society that supposedly values freedom, free speech, individualism, creativity, and expression, yet most Americans stay inside their fashion bubbles and scoff at anything that seems off-beat. When it comes to dressing and fashion, conformity rules. But why can't fashion be an outlet for free expression? As someone who regularly wears outfits inspired by Japanese street fashions, I view my clothes as a reflection of who I am. Japanese street fashions are the opposite of department store or designer styles. The frills, ribbons, fabrics, ruffles, and all the different looks aren't safe or cliquish; they are creative and fun. In Japan, thanks to the popularity and acceptance of these fashions, real people on the street catch you by surprise, instead of just being faces in the crowd.

The aesthetics behind street fashions aren't completely foreign to people in the West. Some street fashion subcultures resemble what we call cosplay, or costume play, which usually takes place at organized events, where people dress up as characters from a movie, book, video game, or comic. But unlike street fashions, cosplay is segregated from everyday life, and for most participants, it is literally about dressing up to be a certain character (for example, Wonder Woman). In other words, it's about being something and someone you're not. Street fashion is the opposite; it's about expressing yourself and who you are.

For example, one of the more popular street fashion subcultures is known as Lolita, but it has nothing to do with the character most Westerners know by that name—the highly sexualized, twelve-year-old "nymph" whose name is the title of a famous novel and film. Lolita street fashion is innocent, demure, and sedate. Instead of being sexy or skimpy, the outfits are typically elegant and old-fashioned, characterized by frilly dresses or skirts with a petticoat underneath for volume, along with stockings and accessories. When I became interested in street fashion, Lolita was the style that intrigued me the most. It is inspired by rococo and baroque art. Wearing Lolita outfits made me feel elegant. Many of my girlfriends were drawn to it for the same reasons I was, but since we knew other people would misunderstand our fascination, we sometimes had fun hosting private tea parties at our homes, where we would show off our outfits to each other. The Lolita style contains many variations, such as Sweet Lolita, Gothic Lolita, and Classic Lolita. Each variation creates a different effect based on color, fabric, and design options that allow the individual to express herself and look her best. The significance of Lolita and other street-fashion subcultures lies in the simple idea of the person wearing the clothes being an artist and the clothes being the person's creative work. Street fashion empowers a person to make dressing creative, rather than voguish.

Visual Kei is another style that is easily misunderstood and seen as weird or trashy. This style is rooted in glam rock, popularized by Japanese musicians like Toshiki Asaki, vocalist of the band Pan-d-ra. Common features of Visual Kei are androgyny and heavy makeup for

Fig. 2. A Japanese girl dresses decoratively.

Kristen Elsby/Getty Images

Fig. 3. A Japanese youth emulates a Visual Kei style.

both men and women. This style, like Lolita, can take casual observers out of their comfort zone, and make them think street fashions are calculated to shock and get attention. But the people who wear the styles actually feel comfortable, because the styles express who they are, regardless of what an odd passersby might think. In Visual Kei, the blurring of gender lines and the deconstruction of social norms send a message about diversity and authenticity that asks observers to step out of their tried and true fashion bubbles, realize that many social norms and assumptions are misguided, and that our differences are interesting and enriching.

Although Japanese street fashions strike most Americans as bizarre, some subcultures like Gyaru ("gal" or "girly") are largely based on American styles, trends, and accessories— for example, miniskirts, hair extensions, bleached hair, tanned skin, glamorous makeup, false eyelashes, nail art, and stacked heels. The Gyaru style is reminiscent of Valley Girls and Hollywood, suggesting Japanese fascination with American culture.

Other subcultures, such as Shironuri and Dolly Kei, draw inspiration from characters in Western fairy tales but also incorporate traditional

iStockphoto.com/aluxum

Fig. 4. Some Japanese street fashions can look shocking.

Japanese clothing such as kimonos and hakamas (long, skirt-like pants worn by both men and women today). In combining a variety of cultural influences, street fashion has a truly global appeal and a unique potential for endless reinvention that can adapt to everyone's desire for novelty and expression.

Kogal (high school girls and school uniforms), Mori Girl (nature and forest themes), and Decora ("decorative") are among the many other creative street fashion subcultures. But by now, you get the general idea and have enough information to understand what street fashion is all about. Even if I have managed to pique your interest, you might think the outfits are just more trouble than they are worth, and still prefer a comfortable Ralph Lauren blouse or shirt that you can put right on, and look good in, without calling attention to yourself. But if street fashion is not your "cup of tea," I hope this essay at least has given you a better appreciation of why people wear these creative outfits.

A friend of mine once had an unpleasant experience when she was wearing a "Lolita" at a train station. A man came up to her and asked if she was going to a "clown party," and proceeded to take pictures of her without her permission. The man showed no respect for my friend, simply because she was dressed unconventionally. This type of narrow-mindedness assumes that people who choose to be different should be criticized and treated as outcasts. What this rude individual didn't understand is that street fashion is all about "thinking outside the box." Even if you don't like the outfits, you can still enjoy

Fig. 5. A sweetly dressed Japanese girl stands in a street.

seeing other people wear them. The streets of Tokyo offer party-like scenes for just this reason, and who knows, enjoyment of Japanese street fashion might tempt you to expand your clothing options. The next time you spot something out of the ordinary in your closet—those lacey, furry, leopardy things lurking behind your Forever 21s, those platform boots gathering dust behind your sandals, sneakers, and pumps, or that ditzy pair of beer-can patterned pants peeking out from behind your dependable slacks and jeans— hey, try them on and wear them with confidence! When it comes to fashion, as the Apple Inc. ads used to say, "think different" and be one of "the crazy ones." ∎

Works Consulted

Eevi, et al. *TokyoFashion.com.* N.p. 24 July 2015. Web. 26 July 2015.

Interview with the Student Writer

● **Thais, how did you come up with your idea for your essay?**

● I drew on my own exploration of Japanese street fashions. As I say in the essay, I've worn several styles of street fashion, so I had enough experience to write about the subject. I wanted to convey Japanese street fashion in an attractive and thought-provoking way to a broad audience. My biggest hesitation was trying to figure out how I was going to explain the different styles and their origins without confusing readers or overwhelming them with information. I talked to my family and friends about my concerns and basic ideas, and they encouraged me to write the essay, so I felt relieved!

● **How did you go about composing the essay?**

● I first wrote down the main points and details on a sheet of paper, as well as the gist of the opening and the conclusion. After my initial planning, I typed out the essay on a word processor and worked on it over a span of two weeks. While I was revising, my initial plan changed quite a bit, but I felt the changes made the essay more appealing.

● **Who read your drafts, and what reactions did you get?**

● My family and friends read my drafts. Because they already knew about my fascination for Japanese fashion, there were several points where they had an "Oh, I remember you wearing something like that!" moment. At the same time, they told me they learned new things from my essay and gained a deeper insight, so I felt confident!

● **What parts of the writing process were difficult for you?**

● I found the organization of the information to be the most difficult. I wasn't sure which aspect to touch upon first or last, and whether the fashions should be organized by importance or some other criteria. In the end, I decided to focus the essay on aesthetics and counterarguments about the "weirdness."

● **What parts were easy or enjoyable?**

● I really enjoyed connecting Japanese fashion to art and culture. As an art history major, I write about this type of connection all the time. I consider fashion a form of art that changes with each generation and decade.

● **What did you learn from doing this project?**

● I think I learned how to convey my passion and enthusiasm for a subject that is dear to me through writing. I wanted the essay to show how wonderful and diverse Japanese street fashion is, and possibly change a reader's viewpoint. The best way to do it was to use a mix of relevant ideas and interesting information.

● **What advice would you give to other students about this kind of writing project or writing in general?**

● I would tell students to think carefully about which topic to choose. Take advantage of your life experiences and knowledge of a certain subject. Writing can be a great tool for expressing feelings, not just ideas. Always be honest and clear in your writing, and in the end, you will have great results.

EVALUATE YOUR LEARNING

1. What subjects were you most interested in writing about for this project? Why did you end up choosing the subject you did?

2. Looking back at your essay, what are the main criteria you used in making your evaluation? Are there any relevant criteria you overlooked or could have emphasized more?

3. What strategies did you use to pique the interest of general readers?

4. What do you consider the strongest point in your essay? Do you think your overall evaluation is compelling enough to change any readers' minds about the subject?

5. Are photographs or other kinds of visuals included in your essay, and if so, what purpose do they serve? If you didn't include visuals, was it because of time constraints, or were there other reasons?

Courtesy of Matthew M. Laskowski

MATTHEW M. LASKOWSKI

Athletic Girl—Jump Study

In this piece, I was trying to develop this character to understand her better. She is supposed to be an athletic person, so I studied her in a dynamic jumping pose as seen in free-running parkour. Actions and poses can tell us just as much about a person visually as the clothes they wear or other visual markers. Combined, we have a much more immediate understanding of the nature of this character than if I'd have drawn her plainly standing, for example.

CHAPTER SEVEN

Arguments That Matter

> *Hate is not the opposite of love, apathy is.*
>
> —Rollo May, *Love and Will*

CHAPTER LEARNING OBJECTIVES

In this chapter, you will learn to:

▶ Compose arguments that focus on problem solving.

▶ Understand what makes arguments succeed or fail.

▶ Plan and compose arguments based on knowledge and sound habits of mind.

▶ Recognize rhetorical appeals and logical fallacies.

▶ Establish common ground with readers and employ "Rogerian" communication goals.

▶ Organize formal (deductive) arguments and informal (inductive) arguments.

ARGUMENTS AND COMMUNICATION

Arguments have a bad name for good reasons. Yet virtually all of the communicating we do is argumentative. When we communicate to address issues and support views in any medium, we directly or indirectly present an argument.

Paintings, operas, movies, sermons, cartoons, YouTube videos, posters, songs, bumper stickers, billboards, and TV commercials are in some ways arguments.

College and professional essays almost always present arguments in some form. Even writing that seems informational on the surface is usually argumentative. When a professor asks a student to write a summary of a chapter in a book, the summary presents an unstated argument based on the information the student chooses to include or highlight. A different student summarizing the same chapter might highlight different information, and in doing so, would be presenting a different view or argument.

ARGUMENTS AND PERSUASION

The time-honored goal of an argument is to persuade—convince people to change their minds, agree with you, or do something you think they should do. The "bad name" associated with arguments starts with the "dark side" of persuasion. Con-artists, swindlers, demagogues, and tyrants usually are masterful persuaders; they manipulate logic, rhetorical appeals, and "facts" to distort and deceive, to feed on ignorance, fear, and greed.

Persuasion also is the stock-in-trade of sales and advertising. Both are legitimate business practices but they sometimes resort to deception, if not dishonesty: for example, the diet that lets you eat all you want and shed layers of fat, the energy drink that turns you into a joyous dynamo, the infomercial-tool that will trim your trees and style your hair, or the global investment bank that exists to make your dreams come true.

Persuasion has a selfish bent. It implies that your audience or readers have the wrong view, an ignorant view, or an inadequate view, a point of departure that sometimes takes arguments in a fruitless direction. Overzealous efforts to persuade can lure even honest writers into the pitfalls of distortion.

Since arguments present and support views, all arguments involve persuasion to some degree, but arguments that matter subordinate persuasion to higher goals. They speak to a person's intelligence rather than ignorance. They persuade because they *illuminate* an issue or problem in a powerful and satisfying way. Arguments that matter are enlightened arguments. They embrace readers, but they focus on problems. Enlightened arguments look beyond agreements and disagreements: they try to find solutions.

ARGUMENTS AS A GENRE

> **❝** *If at first you don't succeed, call in an airstrike.* **❞**
>
> — BANKSY, GRAFFITI ARTIST

As a distinct genre, arguments address issues or problems that evoke diverse, divided, or adversarial *views*. Many of the essays, reports, or "papers" that students write in college are explicitly argumentative. A biology student might write a "proposal argument" that lays out a comprehensive plan for reducing childhood obesity. A psychology student might write a research paper arguing that smoking marijuana impairs cognitive development. An engineering student might write a report recommending an innovative design for an infrastructure project.

In the professional world, argumentation is at the heart of important writing and speaking tasks. An architect who composes a bid for a contract is presenting an argument. An entrepreneur who writes a business plan to attract investors is doing the same. A business report, memo, or client letter that recommends some form of action is an argument.

However, the *most* recognizable arguments deal with issues people get worked up about—sensitive, emotional issues that relate to moral values, principles, and deeply held beliefs. These kinds of issues compel people to express their views, but sometimes the arguments that arise are like wars or shouting matches. Instead of solving problems, they are all about fighting and blaming. Instead of communicating, they signal a breakdown in communication. Many of the political arguments presented on TV and radio shows, on the Internet, even in newspapers and at public meetings, are like this. The views are one-sided, the arguments distorted. This argumentation amounts to more noise than enlightenment. The bad name associated with arguments is perpetuated here, a babble of voices disguising hatreds and fears as principles.

RECOGNIZING ENLIGHTENED ARGUMENTS

To be enlightening, an argument has to aspire to solve problems and convey knowledge. Failed arguments, on the contrary, aspire to "win," and they often are based on opinions and beliefs. In other words, they present views that have little or no basis in knowledge or fact. Knowledge is a product of opinions and beliefs that are tested, examined, and supported by evidence. Unfounded and unexamined opinions and beliefs are incompatible with enlightened arguments.

Here are a few examples of arguments that are based on opinions and beliefs:

- ► New Yorkers are rude.
- ► Nirvana is the greatest rock band of all time.
- ► Illegal immigrants are taking jobs away from American citizens.
- ► College costs too much.
- ► Welfare systems make people lazy and shiftless.

None of these opinions or beliefs is inherently true or false. None of them is enlightening either. They all need to be examined and tested. Why is the statement true? What support can be offered? What objections or opposing views can be presented?

Some of these opinions or beliefs are more conducive to examination and support than others. The overgeneralization about New Yorkers (sometimes called a "hasty" or "gross" generalization) is impossible to prove. Intelligent people will recognize it for what it is and dismiss it. But if the opinion is *qualified*, changed to *some* or *many* New Yorkers, people will find it more rational or realistic and might be interested in learning what is behind the opinion.

The judgment about Nirvana cannot be proven, because it involves vague terms (what does "greatest" mean?) and criteria. In general, matters of taste (Rembrandt is better than Van Gogh, or ice cream is better than cake) are subjective and cannot be proven, but with a thoughtful definition of the criteria and reasons in support, a sensible or interesting argument can be made.

The opinions about illegal immigrants, college costs, and welfare are the most accessible to an enlightened argument, because, at least in theory, these opinions can be examined and supported with knowledge (facts, statistics, and so forth). Writers often use a number of common types of evidence to support their arguments, including:

▶ Facts

▶ Firsthand observations and real events

▶ Statistics (numerical as well as graphic)

▶ Expert or authoritative testimony

▶ Examples based on *convincing* analogies and hypothetical propositions

Moral Opinions and Moral Judgments

> **❝** *One drowning man cannot save another.* **❞**
> —GANDHI, *HIND SWARAJ AND OTHER WRITINGS*

The most widespread source of failed arguments is opinion based on moral judgments. Most of the hot-button issues behind the culture wars in American society—abortion, capital punishment, euthanasia, birth control, immigration, same-sex marriage, and so on—are approached with rigid judgments about right and wrong, and angry assumptions about people who hold an opposing view. When moral arguments dominate the discourse, progress is seldom made and solutions are seldom found. The bad name associated with arguments is epitomized here.

Moral issues *can* be approached with problem solving, rather than moralizing, in mind. For example, instead of focusing on whether capital punishment is right or wrong, a person can ask, "Does it deter crime?" or "Does it provide 'closure' for a victim's loved ones?" But rational and empirical inquiry requires research, thoughtful analysis, an open mind, and above all, an interest in solving a problem. Moralizing is much easier. As a result, it often is the way people approach problems that are not moral in nature. For example, poverty is a social, political, and economic problem that can be addressed empirically, but for many people, it is reducible to a simple, unsolvable, moral issue: human laziness.

A STUDENT'S ESSAY PROPOSAL

As you think about the information presented in this chapter so far and consider issues to write about, take a look at the proposal first-year student Brian Lawrence wrote for this project, based on the following instructions:

Write an essay that supports a position on an issue or problem that is important and relevant to you—ideally, an issue you have some firsthand exposure to or experience dealing with.

The Truth about Atheists

Brian Lawrence

1. The Main Problem or Issue

Atheists are considered to be the most unpopular social group in the United States. There are many people who believe atheists are immoral, more likely to commit crimes and less likely to contribute to society. A recent study by the University of Minnesota found that 40 percent of the people in the United States do not think atheists share their views of American Society, while 50 percent of the same respondents would not allow their children to marry an atheist.

More importantly, the study found that, except for atheists, every demographic group in America is being shown greater tolerance and acceptance than they were fifty years ago. Statistics have shown that most Americans would vote for a person from any demographic group before they would vote an atheist into public office.

2.   The Central Viewpoint, Thesis, or Solution, and an Overview of Supporting Arguments

I plan to present a case in support of atheists in the United States. I will tackle numerous misconceptions and research relevant facts and statistics to demonstrate that many common assumptions about atheists are unwarranted. Among other things, I want to find out what percentage of people in prison are atheists and how much representation atheists have in public offices across the nation.

3.   Reasons for Writing about This Issue

Right now, a number of state constitutions (including Arkansas, Tennessee, and North Carolina) have clauses that seek to prohibit atheists from holding public office. It can be argued that the mentality behind these clauses is prevalent. Many people think it is justified to treat atheists as second-class citizens. There are numerous organizations that prohibit atheist members (e.g., the Boy Scouts of America). In addition, the likelihood of an atheist holding any form of public office is quite slim.

I am selecting this issue because many people I have known classify atheists in one of two ways: A) they are ignorant, or B), they are arrogant, and think that they know everything. I have seen firsthand the prejudices people have toward atheists. I have read articles that have called atheism a detriment to society. I am concerned about all forms of discrimination in our society and I would like to learn more about this issue through writing an essay.

4.   The Relevance to Readers

Atheism can and should be a relevant topic to my readers because, with the increase in the number of atheists in the United States, readers will benefit from knowing more about atheists and understanding misconceptions and prejudices that exist toward them. ■

Interview with the Student Writer

● **Brian, how much writing did you do before you entered college?**

Courtesy of Brian Lawrence

● Until I entered college, writing was neither a hobby, nor something I ever looked forward to doing. Perhaps it was because of how little there is to enjoy about writing in middle or high school. I have always, however, considered myself an above average writer. College writing is much less restrictive than high school writing, in terms of both structure and content.

● **How did you come up with the idea for the essay?**

● In all sincerity, I do not know what prompted me to pick the subject matter, but as a Political Science major with a strong interest in law, all forms of discrimination interest me. The assignment was supposed to be an argument about something controversial, so this subject seemed to fit, but initially I struggled mightily to decide what to write about.

Working Together

INTERVIEW A CLASSMATE

Before reading the rest of this chapter and writing a proposal of your own, sit down with a classmate and take turns interviewing each other about issues or problems that have impacted your lives and that you might be interested in writing about for this project. Use this interview as an opportunity to learn about issues your classmate has been exposed to or dealt with. You might get ideas for your own essay, as well as a better sense of the kinds of issues people are interested in reading about.

As you interview each other, take notes and then give those notes to the person you interviewed. You can use the following questions to help guide your interview:

- What are some issues or problems that have had, or are having, a direct impact on your life? Think of problems related to your family, education, gender, race, ethnicity, personal values, and aspirations or goals?

- Which of the problems that you can think of would you be most motivated to write about?

- What do you know about any of those problems that intelligent readers (for example, your classmates and professor) might not know or understand?

- Can you think of a widely held opinion, belief, or assumption that you consider wrong, misguided, or ignorant? If so, who holds this opinion? Why is it "out there"? What could be done to change it?

- What are some social issues or problems that you are tired of hearing about—that you feel are overemphasized or overhyped, and why?

APPEALS TO ETHOS, LOGOS, AND PATHOS

An effective argument builds a bridge to readers or an audience—enables access and interchange between writer and readers that was difficult, impossible, or nonexistent before. The Greek philosopher Aristotle, in his study of rhetoric and argument, identified three ways that arguments build these kinds of bridges. He called them "appeals":

1. *Ethos*, or "Ethical Appeal," is an appeal to the reader's trust in the writer's character and credibility.

2. *Logos*, or "Logical Appeal," is an appeal to the reader's intellect and rational faculties.

3. *Pathos*, or "Emotional Appeal," is an appeal to the reader's heart or emotions.

All three appeals have a role in crafting strong arguments, but of the three, *logos* is the most essential to an enlightened argument. Moral judgments rely more on *ethos* and *pathos*, and in the absence of *logos*, they tend to divide and polarize.

A person who takes an allegedly moral position against an allegedly immoral position—for example, someone who is against the death penalty, abortion, or euthanasia—is by implication a good or righteous person, a person of sterling character (or *ethos*), compared to those who hold the opposing view.

The emotions (*pathos*) raised by moral arguments polarize in the same way: By implication, the person making the moral argument is good and has a heart; the person who disagrees is bad and heartless.

Logos, which prioritizes reason and knowledge, frequently is excluded from these arguments because moral questions come down to personal beliefs and opinions. However, *logos* can be misguided, too. Mistakes or *fallacies* in a writer's or speaker's line of reasoning can undermine even the most well-intentioned arguments.

FALLACIES

You should be aware of the following examples of flawed arguments—or "logical fallacies."

Ad Hominem Argument

An ad hominem argument is a personal attack—"against the man" rather than the view or position that the "man" supports. For example, the documentary movie *An Inconvenient Truth* features former Vice President Al Gore making a case about the dangers of global warming. After the film was released, some media outlets reported that Gore's personal gas and electric bills were "more than 20 times the national average." On that basis, some critics dismissed the film.

To criticize Gore for his energy consumption seems relevant. Most of us think people should practice what they preach. However, Gore's personal energy consumption has nothing to do with whether or not the movie presents a factual picture of global warming. The argument about Gore's gas and electric bills is an ad hominem argument, because it focuses on the "man" rather than the issue and the evidence.

Appeals to Authority

Using the testimony of knowledgeable people (authorities) is a legitimate way to build support for an argument, but the "authority" has to be credible and appropriate. Even respected people—Warren Buffet, Albert Einstein, former Secretary of State Madeline Albright—are not necessarily authorities on anything outside their fields. In cogent arguments, the writer or speaker explains and substantiates the authority's credentials.

Bandwagon Appeals

These appeals assume that, because most people are doing something or believe something, you should, too (jump on the bandwagon). The implication is that popular trends and public opinion deserve respect and prove something. Often experience tells us the opposite. Bandwagon appeals always have been used to create a "buzz" in advertising—"EVERYONE IS FLOCKING TO AMERICA'S NUMBER ONE_____!" But sadly, history tells us that lurking behind this sort of mindless mania is the psychology of mass hysteria and genocide.

Intelligent people approach bandwagon appeals with the same attitude that Hall of Fame baseball player Yogi Berra once expressed about a popular restaurant: "Nobody goes there anymore. It's too crowded."

Either-Or Arguments

This fallacy, like most of those above, is a form of oversimplification. It suggests there are only two sides or positions that can be taken on an issue, when there might be many more. Here is an example from a speech by Barack Obama:

> "Either we gut education and medical research, or we've got to reform the tax code so that the most profitable corporations have to give up tax loopholes that other companies don't get. We can't afford to do both. This is not class warfare. It's math."

Though Obama's views and goals may be well-intentioned, his argument presents self-constructed choices that are palatable to him and his supporters, but they are not the only possibilities. The budget could be "gutted" in other areas and tax revenues could be raised in other ways.

False Analogy

Analogies—extended comparisons—never *prove* anything, but they can be useful for defending a position or explaining an idea. A good analogy makes a meaningful comparison between different things or situations. A *false* analogy, on the contrary, makes a misleading or inappropriate comparison.

Historical precedent—a lesson from the past applied to the present—is a common form of argument by analogy. For example, when hostility between nations exists, people in favor of military action often bring up "appeasement" of Adolf Hitler before World War II to demonstrate that aggressive action equals strength, while diplomacy equals weakness. However, the value of the analogy depends entirely on the similarity of the circumstances. The analogy can serve as a legitimate "wake-up call" to action or a false premise for unnecessary and disastrous intervention.

Hasty, "Gross," or Sweeping Generalizations

Assertions based on inadequate information or support are hasty generalizations (for example, New Yorkers are rude—see the discussion on page 249–250).

Non Sequiturs

Non sequitur is Latin for "it does not follow." This fallacy involves faulty logic. For example, to make the argument that racist theories or beliefs are valid because they are protected by the Constitution would be a non sequitur.

This billboard shows an example of a *non sequitur* and/or a red herring.

Post Hoc

Post hoc is short for *post hoc ergo propter hoc*, which in Latin means "after this therefore because of this." Post hoc fallacies assume that event A causes event B because event A happened first. For example, every time you get in the shower, the phone rings: therefore, your getting in the shower causes the phone to ring. Superstitious thinking follows a similar logic (you walk under a ladder, then catch a bad cold, and so forth).

To blame the Great Recession of 2008 to 2010 on a spike in gas prices during the summer of '08 (as one politician has done) is a post hoc fallacy and oversimplification. The way to avoid this fallacy is to analyze and explain the cause-and-effect relationship.

Red Herring

"Red herring" is a term derived from training hunting dogs to follow a scent. As a fallacy, a red herring means a *false scent*—that is, an irrelevant or outlying issue brought up to divert attention from the real problem. Trial lawyers, for example, often are brought up as red herrings in arguments about consumer rights and protections. This red herring diverts attention from consumer rights and protections to the outlying issue of the money lawyers make when they litigate these cases for clients.

Slippery Slope

The slippery slope is an ominous warning or scare tactic. It implies that one small step will start an avalanche, an irreversible catastrophe—for example, national health insurance will bring on government "death panels."

Straw Man

A "straw man" is a fabricated or nonexistent position that, like a red herring, distracts from the real issue. When some Americans accuse their fellow citizens of hating America, because their views differ, hatred of America is a straw man (and for good measure, a non sequitur, a red herring, and an ad hominem attack).

A straw man is a phony argument. Any time you read or hear a sentence that begins with, "There are those who say _____," be on the lookout for a straw man. For a good overview of expressions like the one above that introduce bias or lack precision, read the Wikipedia page titled "Manual of Style/Words to Watch."

Using the knowledge about argumentation that you have acquired so far, read and evaluate the arguments presented in the section that follows.

The newspaper article below was written by a respected columnist and mother of five to support a view about a high school student's choice for a yearbook photograph. As you read the article, see if you can identify appeals to *ethos, logos,* and *pathos.* Do you notice any logical fallacies? Decide how relevant and enlightening the writer's argument is.

Ana Veciana-Suarez { **A SENIOR'S PHOTO IS TOO SEXY FOR THE SCHOOL YEARBOOK**

Ana Veciana-Suarez is a syndicated newspaper columnist who writes about family and social issues. She is the author of several books including *Flight to Freedom* and *The Chin Kiss King.*

Courtesy of Ana Veciana-Suarez

I'VE JUST SPENT THE morning strolling memory lane. For my job, no less.

After a Colorado 18-year-old hit the airwaves to advocate for her cause—getting the high school yearbook to print a racy photograph of her in a yellow miniskirt and a barely-there top—I grabbed my own yearbook to refresh my recollection of student life.

Thru The Lens

The photo used above is Sydney Spies' rejected yearbook photo.

Two things I noticed right away: We wore our plaid Catholic school skirts a lot shorter than I remember. And, Sydney Spies' come-hither shot would've never been printed in my yearbook.

I also cracked open my 18-year-old's 2011 tome. The quality of the product was much improved—color photographs, wow!—but I doubt a sexually suggestive pic of a model wannabe would have been printed there, either. The photos in his yearbook were appropriate for teenagers in a public high school.

While Spies may not understand the definition of appropriate, she seems to recognize an opportunity for her 15 minutes of fame. And she's making the most of it. Too bad she may come to regret it one day.

Spies submitted the controversial photo, taken by a professional photographer in Durango, Colo., to the yearbook because, as her mother put it, "she has grown tired of seeing all the boring pictures submitted, and she wanted to do something different." Different, I guess, means sexual and provocative.

"I honestly think (the picture) describes who I am," Spies told NBC's *Today* show. "I'm an outgoing person and I really do think it's artistic."

Artistic for a *Playboy* primer perhaps.

Submitting their own photos to the yearbook is an acceptable practice at Durango High School and seniors there often choose pictures that tell something about them and their interests. In the spirit of editorial independence, a committee of five students approves the photographs.

Initially the students did approve Spies' photo but then decided it was unacceptable. She submitted a second photo, an image of her in a form-fitting, strapless dress that was equally racy. That, too, was rejected.

Spies blames the administration, but the staff, the principal and the yearbook advisor say adults didn't make the decision. Students did.

"We didn't want this picture to make our publication seem unprofessional and inappropriate," said editor Brian Jaramillo. The award-winning yearbook has rejected other photos, including one of a shirtless male student two years ago.

So what was Spies' reaction? She bellyached about censorship and freedom of expression. She and her mom, Miki Spies, waved placards in front of the school and now say they're considering legal action.

Oh, please. This is not a reality TV show or a photo shoot. It's a yearbook put out by students of a high school with a dress code. Spies' photo belongs in her modeling portfolio, in a publicity campaign for a nightclub, maybe even on a billboard for an escort service. But in a yearbook? No way.

Yet, I'm not blaming Spies for trying to jumpstart a career. At 18, she's allowed to confuse innovation with tastelessness. But her mother should know better. Instead of warning her child about the consequences of a stupid decision—is this really how she wants her classmates to remember her?—Mama is promoting the embarrassing fiasco. After her daughter was publicly savaged on Facebook and other Internet sites, Miki Spies told CNN she was "surprised more Americans aren't on the side of freedom of expression anymore."

But freedom of expression isn't in question here. A parent's judgment is. ∎

From Reflection to Response

Responding to "A Senior's Photo Is Too Sexy for the School Yearbook"

Working with a small group of your classmates, evaluate the effectiveness of Ana Veciana-Suarez's argument. How enlightening is it? To what extent does it rely on *logos* (knowledge, facts, and reasons), and to what extent does it rely on *ethos* and *pathos* (the writer's credibility and appeals to emotion)? Does she make moral judgments and assumptions? Are they justified in your view? Can you point to "logical fallacies" that Ana Veciana-Suarez employs in her argument? As part of your analysis, comment on the accuracy or judiciousness of the following sentences (the italics have been added):

- …Spies' *come-hither shot* would've never been printed in my yearbook.
- …I doubt a *sexually suggestive pic of a model wannabe* would have been printed there [in my son's yearbook], either.
- While Spies may not understand the definition of appropriate, she seems to recognize an opportunity for *her 15 minutes of fame*.
- Artistic for *a Playboy primer* perhaps.
- The *award-winning* yearbook has rejected other photos.
- So what was Spies' reaction? She *bellyached* about censorship and freedom of expression.
- Spies' photo belongs in her modeling portfolio, in a publicity campaign for a nightclub, maybe even *on a billboard for an escort service*.
- Yet, I'm not blaming Spies for *trying to jumpstart a career*.
- Mama is promoting the *embarrassing fiasco*. After her daughter was *publicly savaged on Facebook and other Internet sites*, Miki Spies told CNN she was "surprised more Americans aren't on the side of freedom of expression anymore."

CONSTRUCTING ENLIGHTENED ARGUMENTS

Constructing an enlightened argument requires more than the ability to appeal to the ethos, pathos, and logos of your audience, and avoiding logical fallacies. An effective argument requires a knowledge of the topic about which you are arguing, an objective point of view, and a skeptical frame of mind.

Knowledge

Enlightened arguments start with knowledge, that is, knowing what you are writing or talking about. Montaigne, the first essayist, guided his thinking and writing with a simple question: "What do I know?" The question is relevant to any writer writing an argument. No one knows everything about anything, but through experience and exposure, we all know more about some issues and problems than others. The issues and problems we know the most about are the ones we can present the most enlightened arguments about.

Through research, either field research or traditional secondary research (reading books and articles), we always can learn more than we already know (see Chapters 8 and 14 for detailed information about conducting research). Doing research to acquire knowledge often is an essential part of creating strong arguments.

Objectivity

Enlightened arguments literally illuminate problems, move them out of shadows into stronger, brighter light. Objectivity—seeing problems outside the blinders of our personal opinions and feelings—is vital to that process. Arguments that matter have to be objective, and yet no one can entirely escape subjectivity. In our world, new media and technologies give us a dazzling sense of living outside of ourselves, of having limitless access to information, people, and places, but we really live within the confines of our own minds and filter experience through consciousness. Objectivity is an ideal; subjectivity is a reality. Nevertheless, good writers and thinkers strive to be objective through sound habits of mind that include the approaches described below.

Fairness to Different Sides   The best journalists are known and respected for their objectivity, but they are keenly aware of their biases. To counteract them, they force themselves to be scrupulously accurate, and above all, to deal fairly with different positions or sides of a controversy.

Counterarguments and Opposing Views   Academic writers embrace opposing views and counterarguments for the same reasons, but also, ultimately, to strengthen their own views and positions. The idea of including opposing views in an argument may seem counterintuitive when the goal of the argument is to win or persuade, but when the goal is to enlighten and solve problems, it is easy to see how opposing views enhance the richness, validity, and scope of an argument. An argument that ignores legitimate opposing views is unlikely to engage an intelligent person.

Rogerian Argument   One of the most famous approaches to fostering objectivity and enlightened argumentation is called "Rogerian argument," based on the ideas of Carl R. Rogers, a prominent psychotherapist. Rogers observed that successful therapy was about communication more than anything else. His patients had trouble communicating with themselves and other people. As Rogers saw it, his role as a therapist was to facilitate communication with his patients. In order to do this, he needed to "listen with understanding" and withhold the "natural tendency to judge." Even for him, doing that was challenging. Therapists have to treat patients who are difficult to sympathize with: compulsive liars, criminals, sociopaths, drug addicts, and alcoholics. Rogers's ideas about communication are not theories; they are based on hard-won experience, a desire to help people and solve problems, despite deep differences and disagreements.

A Rogerian argument requires that you see yourself connected to people you disagree with, and invite them to connect to you, to be partners in solving a problem. Communication and problem solving are your central goals. The methods for achieving those goals are listening, understanding the opposing views, and withholding judgment.

In his landmark study of psychotherapy, *On Becoming a Person*, Rogers offers the following advice:

> The next time you get into an argument with your wife, or your friend, or with a small group of friends, just stop the discussion for a moment and...institute this rule. "Each person can speak up for himself only after he has first restated the ideas and feelings of the previous speaker accurately, and to that speaker's satisfaction." You see what this would mean. It would simply mean that before presenting your own point of view, it would be necessary for you to really achieve the other speaker's frame of reference—to understand his thoughts and feelings so well that you could summarize them for him. Sounds simple, doesn't it? But if you try it you will discover it is one of the most difficult things you have ever tried to do. However, once you have been able to see the other's point of view, your own comments will have to be drastically revised. You will also find the emotion going out of the discussion, the differences being reduced, and those differences which remain being of a rational and understandable sort.

Rogers suggests here that we often *think* we listen—*think* we understand another's position—better than we actually do. Expressing the other position in our own words takes us closer to understanding.

Although Rogerian arguments do not follow a format or have a fixed structure, they emphasize conflict resolution and often take an informal or inductive pattern of development that includes the elements below.

1. A presentation of the issue or problem, in which the writer describes its relevance, and demonstrates an understanding of its complexity and an awareness of the opposing position that the writer will incorporate in the argument.

2. A detailed and judicious description of the opposing position, in which the writer demonstrates understanding, and as much as possible, points of agreement.

3. A statement of the writer's own position, how it differs from the opposing position, and why it might be valid or right.

4. An attempt to reconcile the two positions or show how they complement each other, or, in conjunction with each other, move the problem closer to a solution, or failing that, how one position serves the other point of view.

The two short passages that follow take diametrically opposed positions on the issue of man's fate and survival.

The first passage is a commentary on the Holocaust, delivered near the Auschwitz death camp by Jacob Bronowski in a celebrated TV series titled *The Ascent of Man*. Bronowski argues that dogma and ignorance are the main causes of man's inhumanity to man and human suffering. Science and knowledge offer our best hope for progress and survival. (Videos of Bronowski's commentary can be found on YouTube.)

The second passage is an excerpt from *Witness*, the best-selling autobiography of Whittaker Chambers, an editor for *Time Magazine* who, in the 1930s, had been a member of the American Communist party and a Soviet spy. Chambers argues that man's best hope for progress and survival is faith in God.

As you read the commentaries, adopt a Rogerian position, putting aside your own opinions. "Listen" to the ideas and concerns of each man, and see if you can find common ground between their positions.

Jacob Bronowski { **FROM *THE ASCENT OF MAN***

... THERE ARE TWO PARTS to the human dilemma. One is the belief that the end justifies the means. That push-button philosophy, that deliberate deafness to suffering, has become the monster in the war machine.

The other is the betrayal of the human spirit: the assertion of dogma that closes the mind, and turns a nation, a civilization, into a regiment of ghosts—obedient ghosts, or tortured ghosts.

It is said that science will dehumanize people and turn them into numbers. That's false, tragically false. Look for yourself. This is the concentration camp and crematorium at Auschwitz. This is where people were turned into numbers. Into this pond were flushed the ashes of some four million people.

And that was not done by gas. It was done by arrogance, it was done by dogma, it was done by ignorance. When people believe that they have absolute knowledge, with no test in reality, this is how they behave....

Science is a very human form of knowledge. We are always at the brink of the known; we always feel forward for what is to be hoped. ■

Whittaker Chambers   { **FROM** *WITNESS*

THERE HAS NEVER BEEN a society or a nation without God. But history is cluttered with the wreckage of nations that became indifferent to God and died.…The crisis of the Western world exists to the degree in which it is indifferent to God. It exists to the degree in which the Western world actually shares Communism's materialist vision, is so dazzled by the logic of the materialist interpretation of history, politics and economics, that it fails to grasp that, for it, the only possible answer to the Communist challenge: Faith in God or Faith in Man? is the challenge: Faith in God.

…Faith is the central problem of this age. The Western world does not know it, but it already possesses the answer to this problem—but only provided that its faith in God and the freedom He enjoins is as great as Communism's faith in Man. ▪

From Reflection to Response   **Common Ground in Opposing Positions**

After reading the two excerpts, write a statement that summarizes each man's view as faithfully and objectively as you can. Then explain why you think each man holds the view he does, and what conditions or factors have influenced his view.

Based on your own knowledge and experience, consider reasons for and against each position. List examples of contributions science has made to human survival and progress. List examples of contributions religion and faith have made. Also, list examples of how the two may have failed humanity or proved inadequate. Have any scientific discoveries or applications harmed mankind, or done more harm than good? Have any beliefs or applications of religious faith and doctrines had negative consequences or been put to negative use?

When you have finished writing your statement and lists, try to identify a common ground between the positions the two men take and see if you can reconcile them. What would the two men agree about, if anything? Do their positions complement each other in any way, or, taken together, move the problem closer to a solution than either position alone?

Skepticism

Along with knowledge and objectivity, enlightened arguments require doubting and questioning—a habit of mind called *skepticism*, which helps writers and thinkers think critically and see beyond conventional wisdom. Some people confuse skepticism with cynicism, which means seeing the worst in everyone and every-thing. However, unlike cynicism, which is a view of life, skepticism is a method of thinking. A skeptic is as willing to accept an idea as reject it, but only upon exami-nation, after doubting and questioning, never on authority or blind trust.

Reading and responding to the two arguments that follow will help you understand the concepts discussed in this chapter and develop habits of mind that support effective argumentation. The first reading, by David Harsanyi, deals with the role of government in our lives.

A common slogan we hear today is "get government off our backs." Indeed, most of us can think of laws, government regulations, practices, or functions that seem unnecessary, burdensome, or intrusive—anything from daylight savings time to drug laws, speed traps, taxes, and surveillance cameras. At the same time, we know that government provides order and useful services. Without efficient government, life would be chaotic, stressful, and hazardous. How much government is too much, and how much is too little? Where do we draw the line between constructive government and oppressive government?

David Harsanyi addresses this issue in the excerpt below from his book *Nanny State: How Food Fascists, Teetotaling Do-Gooders, Priggish Moralists, and Other Boneheaded Bureaucrats Are Turning America into a Nation of Children*. As you read, decide whether or not he draws the line where you would.

David Harsanyi { **TWINKIE FASCISTS**

Cyrus McCrimmon/Getty Images

David Harsanyi is a Harvard graduate and respected journalist whose work has appeared in the *Washington Post, Weekly Standard, Wall Street Journal, National Review*, and many other publications. He is the author of several books in addition to *Nanny State*.

GUARDIANS OF YOUR GULLET

THE FASHIONABLE EASTSIDE NEIGH-BORHOOD of Oakhurst in Decatur, Geor-gia, is the last place you would imagine that an establishment like Mulligan's could survive. The area, once teeming with drug dealers and home to some of the highest crime rates in the area, has undergone an astonishing gentrification the past few years. Today, Oakhurst is home to countless upwardly mobile couples inhabiting refurbished Craftsman bungalows with luxurious baby joggers sitting unattended on front lawns.

Mulligan's, located at the end of a nondescript parking lot, is a restaurant, sports bar—and counterrevolutionary enterprise. Here, I imagine, patrons would be capable of coalescing into an armed insurgency should some squeamish busybody suggest mandating smaller food portions. Mulligan's is perhaps best known for its glorious Luther Burger—purportedly named after a favorite midnight nibble of the late R&B crooner Luther Vandross. The Luther Burger is your standard bacon cheeseburger with a Krispy Kreme doughnut substituting for the traditional bun.

What's not to like?

But there's more. A lot more. Mulligan's ratchets up the fun quotient by serving a nutritionist's nightmare known as the Hamdog. This treat begins as a hot dog, sure, but then that sucker is wrapped in a beef patty, which is then, for good measure, deep fried and covered with cheese, chili, onions, a fried egg, and a heaping portion of fries. If you want a side of deep-fried Twinkies and a large soda, go for it.

Mulligan's fame—or perhaps you could call it infamy—has spread far beyond the confines of this neighborhood. During a Tonight Show monologue, Jay Leno described the particulars of the notorious Luther Burger, eliciting big laughs. The Krispy Kreme corporation has joined the fun, teaming up with an Illinois minor league team called the Gateway Grizzlies to create "Baseball's Best Burger," a thousand-calorie cheeseburger sandwiched between a sliced glazed doughnut.

* * *

Why am I hanging out here? To make a point. A free citizen exercising my right to eat the most sinfully unwholesome foods I could find in this great nation. Because, you know, not everyone finds the Hamdog as entertaining or as tempting as I do. Which is their prerogative, of course. But there are growing numbers of officious activists who would like to deny me the self-determination and pleasure of eating a Hamdog or Luther Burger.

This group of finger-wagging activists advocate enhanced government control over choice. Many folks call this particular breed of militant nanny the food police. Legendary radio personality Paul Harvey once referred to them as "the guardians of your gullet." I like to call them Twinkie Fascists—among other less polite monikers. And though this movement is still in its infancy, the Twinkie Fascists are gaining momentum and influence at a startling pace.

As with all realms of nannyism, this attack on freedom and choice is fueled by good intentions. Nannies will do whatever they can to stop us from eating via city, state, or federal regulations. They'll use litigation to limit our choices and engage in government-sponsored scaremongering, penalizing food manufacturers, restaurants, or consumers with specialized taxes.

With that in mind, I decide to go all out. I order a Hamdog. It's perfect. Huge. Greasy. Impudently harmful to my health. Nicholas Lang, a professor of surgery at the University of Arkansas for Medical Sciences, once told the Associated Press if "you choke that [Hamdog] down, you might as well find a heart surgeon because you are going to need one." But what does he know? Nannies are always so melodramatic. And sure enough, after that first bite my heart doesn't explode.

Yet the truth is that despite the scrumptiousness of the Hamdog, I could only finish half. As a human being, it seems that I possess a certain level of self-control. I gather that if I, a dreadfully weak and easily seduced man, can control myself, most Americans can do even better. Most can still find pleasure in eating and reward in self-control. Two concepts that nannies, it seems, can't wrap their minds around.

PLUMP FICTION

THE CENTERS FOR DISEASE Control and Prevention (CDC) offices are, as luck would have it, only a short drive from Mulligan's. The offices are more like a compound. This place is busy. When the CDC began as a single-floor operation more than forty years ago, it was responsible for investigating malaria and related maladies, but these days the organization deals with virtually all facets of public health, from preventing and controlling infectious and chronic diseases, to workplace hazards, to disabilities and other environmental health threats.

The CDC has a new agenda: the peculiar job not only of discouraging folks from engaging in avoidable habits but of becoming part of a propaganda war that shocks Americans. That's what happened when the CDC held a well-publicized news conference in March of 2004 to announce a new troubling study that alleged overeating was responsible for an extraordinary death toll: 400,000 Americans in 2000—a 33 percent jump from 1990. According to the report obesity was well on its way to surpassing smoking as the nation's top preventable cause of death. "Our worst fears were confirmed," claimed Dr. Julie Gerberding, the CDC's director and an author of the study.

The significance of the study was bolstered by the presence of then-secretary of the Department of Health and Human Services Tommy Thompson. "Americans need to understand," he grimly noted, "that overweight [sic] and obesity are literally killing us." As a matter of fact, the federal government promised to lend a helping hand to stop the madness to the tune of $400 million in research.

Imagine what sort of good that $400 million might have done in research on, say, cancer. Instead, the CDC had taken the first step toward creating an environment where intrusive public policy thrives. They vowed to revise food labels and to launch a public-awareness and education campaign to stop the mess—but that was only the beginning. Food was "literally" killing us by the hundreds of thousands each year, which called for more action.

To help perpetuate an atmosphere of panic, doom-and-gloom headlines blared across newspapers nationwide. (Leave it to the histrionic New York tabloids to excel at jolting the public: "Digging Graves with Our Teeth: Obesity Rivals Smoking as Killer" read the *New York Daily News*, and "Dying to Eat—Weight Woe Nears Cigs as Top Killer" countered the *New York Post*.) Journalists detailed the catastrophe french fry by french fry. The report sparked hundreds of opinion pieces that examined various ways the government—federal, state, and city—could step in and rescue us from this eruption of fat.

The problem was that the report wasn't exactly true. And although Americans hear distraught commentary from pundits, nutritionists, and nannies, there were many scientists and statisticians who were more skeptical about the CDC's extraordinary claims. Soon enough, these intellectually honest men and women began jabbing holes in the report.

The first salvo came in May 2004, in the pages of *Science* magazine. The investigative piece claimed that some researchers, including a few at the CDC itself, dismissed the report's prediction, maintaining that the underlying data of the report were quite unconvincing. One detractor within the CDC characterized the core data in the report as "loosey-goosey." Critics largely objected to the addition to the obesity category of deaths attributed to poor nutrition. It was a stat that, considering the vagaries of life, was impossible to quantify.

Even within the walls of the CDC, a source told Science, internal discussions could get contentious. Several epidemiologists at the CDC and the National Institutes of Health also had concerns about the numbers, yet before the publication of the report, some within the agency felt that the conclusions weren't debatable because of organizational pressure. One apprehensive CDC staff member went as far as to allege that he wouldn't speak out truthfully for fear of losing his job—not exactly the dynamic and transparent environment that scientific discovery thrives in. But then again, sometimes getting the right answer trumps discerning the prickly truth.

The second blow came, and it was even more damning. The *Wall Street Journal* published a front-page story in November of 2004, running a litany of errors that swamped the dramatic death number. The paper noted that the study had "inflated the impact of obesity on the annual death toll by tens of thousands due to statistical errors." In a follow-up story, the Journal reported that due to additional troubles with methodology the actual number of obesity-related deaths might be less than half of the 400,000 originally estimated in the CDC study.

But that didn't stop many nannies from brandishing the dubious numbers until the CDC was finally forced to disclose their gross miscalculation. With a different team of CDC scientists and more recent data, they revised their numbers to 112,000 deaths a year. In April 2005, *The Journal of the American Medical Association* put the CDC out of its misery, publishing its own study on the impact of obesity, which revealed a radically revised estimation. It concluded that obesity actually was responsible for around 25,000 American deaths each year. In other words, 375,000 fewer deaths than the CDC had originally maintained.

Oops.

Most news outlets had little to say on the revised numbers. The obesity "epidemic" was a great story, a jumping-off point to a nation under siege from corporate burger peddlers. The CDC, hoping to distract from their gross over-calculation, dispatched a disease detective to states like West Virginia to get the lowdown on the epidemic.

Getting people worried was precisely the point. That's step one. The next step was to figure out how to save people from themselves. Could they close down all the fast-food restaurants? Tax them heavily enough to convince people not to enter the golden archways? Could they coerce residents into morning calisthenics? Impose dietary restrictions or portion restriction at restaurants? Ban cookies? Ban commercials? Why not?

OUR PANIC DU JOUR

CHANDLER GOFF ONCE CLAIMED that there was no practical way he could calculate the fat or caloric content of Mulligan's delectable dishes.

I believe him. And I'm thankful.

As a public service, however, Goff affixes a note at the bottom of each menu that advises diners to "have the sense to realize that although delicious, we do not recommend eating fried foods every day." Goff also urges his patrons to exercise regularly and get an annual physical. "These [dishes] are great pleasures," according to Goff. "You don't want to eat this every day." Goff's message is considerate, but unnecessary. One imagines the majority of Mulligan's customers—as well as the greater part of the nation—do not plan on persisting on a diet of Hamdogs and deep-fried Twinkies.

Unlike other spheres of nannyism—alcohol and tobacco, for instance—every one of us partakes of food. Even the healthiest among us eats insalubrious treats on occasion. Likewise, most of us have turned down that second Boston cream doughnut or pushed aside those last few curly fries.

We realize the consequences. And once we recognize that it's possible to turn away food, hit the treadmill, or eat salad instead of steak, we appreciate that it's within the capacity of the other humans to follow suit. ■

From Reflection to Response   Responding to "Twinkie Fascists"

One way to examine an issue and develop an "objective" perspective about it is to play what educator Peter Elbow calls the "believing and doubting game." This "game" involves seeing more than one side of an argument by both believing and doubting it. Practice playing the game with David Harsanyi's "Twinkie Fascists."

First, using your own experience, observations, and knowledge, write a paragraph or more under the heading *Reasons to Believe* in which you try to explain and justify Harsanyi's concerns and arguments. Whether you agree with him or not, be objective and creative. Embrace his position. Try to understand why it is "out there," why it would appeal to people. Come up with all the reasons you can for believing it and defending it.

Next, under the heading *Reasons to Doubt*, develop all the reasons you can think of to doubt or reject Harsanyi's concerns and argument. Even if you agree with him, play "devil's advocate." Be hypercritical. Look for flaws, think of counterarguments, and come up with reasons his views might offend or be harmful to people.

After you finish doubting and believing, discuss what you have written with a group of your classmates. What are the strengths and weaknesses of Harsanyi's argument? How compelling is the argument overall? What could Harsanyi do, if anything, to make the argument stronger?

> **❝***There are three kinds of lies: lies, damned lies, and statistics.***❞**
> —ATTRIBUTED TO BRITISH PRIME MINISTER BENJAMIN DISRAELI

The reading that follows, written by Patrick Buchanan in 2012, presents an argument about poverty in America. We often read or hear reports about the large number of Americans, many of them children or elderly people, who are poor. Are the reports accurate? If so, are we addressing the problem in the right ways?*

---

*In 2012, the Census Bureau reported 46 million Americans, 15 percent of the population, living below the poverty line.

Buchanan's article displays some of the virtues of skepticism. Buchanan "thinks outside the box" and challenges conventional wisdom. Even better, he offers statistics to support his position. Yet anyone who has seen rural or inner-city poverty up close might wonder about the picture he presents. Read the article with an open mind but also note reasons and facts that invite skepticism *from you.*

Patrick Buchanan { **DID "THE GREAT SOCIETY" RUIN SOCIETY?** *

Patrick Buchanan, a political writer and analyst, served as an advisor for three presidents and was once a third-party candidate for president of the United States.

Brendan Smialowsk/Getty Images

WHO ARE THE POOR?

To qualify, a family of four in 2010 needed to earn less than $22,314. [This year] some 46 million Americans, 15 percent of the population, qualified.[†]

And in what squalor were America's poor forced to live?

Well, 99 percent had a refrigerator and stove, two-thirds had a plasma TV, a DVD player and access to cable or satellite, 43 percent were on the Internet, half had a video game system like PlayStation or Xbox.

Three-fourths of the poor had a car or truck, nine in 10 a microwave, 80 percent had air conditioning. In 1970, only 36 percent of the U.S. population enjoyed air conditioning.

America's poor enjoy amenities almost no one had in the 1950s, when John K. Galbraith described us as "The Affluent Society."

What about homelessness? Are not millions of America's poor on the street at night, or shivering in shelters or crowded tenements?

---

*"The Great Society" was a set of programs and reforms proposed by President Lyndon B. Johnson in the 1960s, to eliminate poverty as well as other social problems and injustices.

†Statistics from Buchanan's column are drawn from "Understanding Poverty in the United States: Surprising Facts About America's Poor" by Robert Rector of the Heritage Foundation.

Well, actually, no. That is what we might call televised poverty. Of the real poor, fewer than 10 percent live in trailers, 40 percent live in apartments, and half live in townhouses or single-family homes.

Forty-one percent of poor families own their own home.

But are they not packed in like sardines, one on top of another?

Not exactly. The average poor person's home in America has 1,400 square feet—more living space than do Europeans in 23 of the 25 wealthiest countries on the continent.

Two-thirds of America's poor have two rooms per person, while 94 percent have at least one room per person in the family dwelling.

Only one in 25 poor persons in America uses a homeless shelter, and only briefly, sometime during the year.

What about food? Do not America's poor suffer chronically from malnutrition and hunger?

Not so. The daily consumption of proteins, vitamins and minerals of poor children is roughly the same as that of the middle class, and the poor consume more meat than the upper middle class.

Some 84 percent of America's poor say they always have enough food to eat, while 13 percent say sometimes they do not, and less than 4 percent say they often do not have enough to eat.

Only 2.6 percent of poor children report stunted growth. Poor kids in America are, on average, an inch taller and 10 pounds heavier than the youth of the Greatest Generation that won World War II.

In fiscal year 2011, the U.S. government spent $910 billion on 70 means-tested programs, which comes to an average of $9,000 per year on every lower-income person in the United States.

Among the major programs from which the poor receive benefits are Temporary Assistance to Needy Families, the Earned Income Tax Credit, Supplemental Security Income, food stamps, the Women, Infants and Children (WIC) food program, Medicaid, public housing, low-income energy assistance and the Social Service Block Grant.

Children of the poor are educated free, K-12, and eligible for preschool Head Start, and Perkins Grants, Pell Grants and student loans for college.

Lyndon Johnson told us this was the way to build a Great Society. Did we? Federal and state spending on social welfare is approaching $1 trillion a year, $17 trillion since the Great Society was launched, not to mention private charity. But we have witnessed a headlong descent into social decomposition.

Half of all children born to women under 30 now are illegitimate. Three in 10 white children are born out of wedlock, as are 53 percent of Hispanic babies and 73 percent of black babies.

Rising right along with the illegitimacy rate is the drug-use rate, the dropout rate, the crime rate and the incarceration rate.

The family, cinder block of society, is disintegrating, with society itself. Writes [Robert] Rector, "The welfare system is more like a 'safety bog' than a safety net."

Heritage [Foundation] scholars William Beach and Patrick Tyrrell put Rector's numbers in perspective:

"Today 67.3 million Americans—from college students to retirees to welfare beneficiaries—depend on the federal government for housing, food, income, student aid or other assistance. … The United States reached another milestone in 2010. For the first time in history, half the population pays no federal income taxes."

The 19th century statesman John C. Calhoun warned against allowing government to divide us into "tax-payers and tax-consumers." This, he said, "would give rise to two parties and to violent conflicts and struggles between them, to obtain the control of the government." We are there, Mr. Calhoun, we are there. ∎

From Reflection to Response

Responding to "Did 'The Great Society' Ruin Society?"

Working with a small group of your classmates, evaluate how enlightening Buchanan's argument is. Begin by examining the question he raises in the third sentence. What does "squalor" mean, and how relevant is the question to the rest of the article? Then do a point-by-point analysis of the article. Examine the validity of each point, raise any questions or objections you can think of, and offer possible rebuttals or counterarguments. When all is said and done, what do you see as Buchanan's solution to the problem? Are there any views or perspectives that he might be overlooking or minimizing?

A Sample Analysis of Buchanan's Opening Points:

Point: Well, 99 percent [of the poor] had a refrigerator and stove, two-thirds had a plasma TV, a DVD player and access to cable or satellite, 43 percent were on the Internet, half had a video game system like PlayStation or Xbox.

Objection & Rebuttal: Does having these possessions preclude living in filthy, unsanitary, or appalling conditions? What do we know about the quality or working condition of all these "luxuries"? For example, how well do the refrigerator and stove work? Is the Internet connection dial-up or DSL? If it's a dial-up connection, how useful is it today?

Point: Three-fourths of the poor had a car or truck, nine in 10 a microwave, 80 percent had air conditioning. In 1970, only 36 percent of the U. S. population enjoyed air conditioning.

Objection & Rebuttal: What kinds of cars and trucks are these? How many are junkers or rustbuckets, "parked" on cinder blocks? How much do microwaves and window-unit air conditioners cost today? Can they be bought secondhand? Relative to the cost of living, do you think air conditioning units were cheaper or more expensive in 1970?

Continue with your own point-by-point analysis and your final evaluation of Buchanan's argument. Do you agree or disagree, and why? You might want to check up on some of the sources referred to in the article: Robert Rector, William Beach, Patrick Tyrrell, John C. Calhoun, and the Heritage Foundation.

COMING UP WITH IDEAS

Since argumentation overlaps with so many genres, you might read this chapter in preparation for a different writing project, for example "Navigating a Research Project" (Chapter 8) or "Public Writing and Community Engagement" (Chapter 9). However, this chapter is designed to be a guided writing project. So, based on the information in this chapter, your instructor may ask you to compose an argumentative essay that supports a view about an issue, problem, or controversy.

Some instructors might leave the decision about the subject matter up to you. Others might assign an issue for you to write about, or give you a short list to choose from. If the decision is yours, think about issues and problems that concern you, but remember that an enlightened argument has to be based on knowledge. Unless your argument is going to rely on extensive research, a crucial question to ask is "What do I know?" What issues or problems have you experienced or been exposed to? Your firsthand knowledge will be important.

To start coming up with ideas, take a look at Table 7.1 and ask yourself, "Have I experienced this issue in my life and learned something important enough to enlighten my readers?" In writing an argument, you can share relevant information about your experience. However, your main objective is not to tell a story, but rather to draw on the knowledge, insights, and information you acquired, to enlighten your readers and move the issue in a problem-solving direction.

TABLE 7.1 Categories of experience

Categories of Experience	Examples
Education & Literacy	• Standardized testing, curriculum issues, "gifted" programs, quality of teachers, favoritism, grade inflation, class size, college access, Black English, bilingual education, affirmative action • Cheating, plagiarism, violence, bullying • Private vs. public schools, or homeschooling • Extracurricular activities, community service, high school sports, social pressures and exclusion
Family & Relationships	• Family dysfunctions, battering, sexual abuse, adoption, divorce, custody, child support, single parenting • Premarital sex, teen pregnancy, stalking, date rape • LGBT issues and rights, marriage and cohabitation, abortion, birth control
Work & Responsibilities	• Minimum wage, sex discrimination, equal pay, sexual harassment • Credit cards, credit reports, consumer debt • Men and women's domestic responsibilities • Working for your family
Identity & Lifestyle	• Social networking, music piracy, identity theft • Racism, stereotyping, the immigrant experience and immigration laws • Alcohol, obesity, video games, gambling, and various psychological or physical addictions • Popular-culture issues—music genres, fashions, pornography, legalizing or decriminalizing marijuana, cosmetic surgery, reality TV • Religion, faith, pastimes, hobbies, Peace Corps, missionary work, military service

As a college student, you know more about educational issues at both the college and secondary-school levels than most people do. So consider writing about an educational issue. You certainly are qualified to compose an enlightened argument about education.

Working Together

GENERATING IDEAS

At home or in class, spend five minutes freewriting, brainstorming, or clustering about problems and issues that you have been exposed to or experienced in your life, and know enough about to enlighten readers. These problems and issues may involve prevailing laws and practices (standardized testing), or how other people perceive a facet of your identity or lifestyle (being a male cheerleader), or both (same-sex marriage).

After you finish freewriting, take a look at the list of "Issues and Problems Many Students Are Knowledgeable About" (below). Then create your own list of issues and problems that you have been exposed to or experienced. Circle all of the issues you think you could write about and discuss them with a small group of your classmates. Ask your classmates what their views are, which issues they are most interested in, and what they would like to learn.

Issues and Problems Many Students Are Knowledgeable About

- Affirmative action
- Immigration and undocumented status
- Bigotry, racism, discrimination, racial profiling
- Standardized testing
- Marijuana use or abuse
- Distracted driving or driving under the influence
- Date rape
- Premarital sex, pregnancy, and safe sex
- Sexual orientation and choice/"coming out"
- Scholarships, student loans, and the cost of higher education
- Tattoos and piercings
- Juvenile crime/shoplifting/bullying
- Gangs and gang violence
- Owning pit bulls
- Pay for student athletes
- Campus recruitment and ROTC
- Domestic responsibilities
- Drinking age/binge drinking
- Social networking/online etiquette
- Music genres (country, hip-hop, house, metal, hardcore, jazz, and so on)

- Outlying hobbies and interests: working on cars, motocross, cheerleading, paintball, hunting, fencing, and so forth
- Outlying beliefs and associations: Wicca, reincarnation, atheism, Rastafarianism, anarchism, pacifism, veganism, and so on.

Tech Tip

Although the best way to come up with an idea for your essay is to think about your own life and problems or controversies you know about, you also can do some online browsing to generate ideas. *CQ Researcher* is an excellent resource that offers lists and in-depth coverage of current issues and problems. Some of these issues may intersect with your own experiences and interests.

"Think tanks" like the Heritage Foundation or the RAND Corporation also maintain websites with comprehensive lists and other information that can be useful.

Newspaper websites can be useful, too, especially your hometown or campus newspapers, both of which will include stories and articles about issues relevant to your community or school that you may know something about. Most newspaper websites have online discussion boards that allow readers to comment on articles. Browsing these discussions can give you a perspective on what other people think.

Once you come up with an issue, if you're on a social network, share it with your friends and ask them for their views.

EVALUATING IDEAS

Once you have an idea in mind for your essay, the following checklist will help you plan the essay and clarify what you will accomplish by writing it.

1. Why is the issue important? How does it affect people's lives? What social significance does the issue have?

2. Why is the issue controversial, and what can you add to the controversy that has not already been said, or is not generally known?

3. What is the view you intend to support, and how will you support it?

4. What personal knowledge do you have about the issue, and how will that knowledge apply to your task of supporting your view and enlightening readers?

5. Provide a summary of the supporting arguments and evidence that you will present in your essay to support your main view or position.

6. What legitimate counterarguments can your readers possibly present? List all the counterarguments and how you will respond to them.

7. Describe the audience you will mainly be writing your essay for, and why the essay will be relevant and enlightening to them. Note that merely "informing" your audience is a poor purpose. People know how to use Google and find information when they need it. How will your essay engage and enlighten your audience, and most importantly, serve a problem-solving purpose?

8. How will you appeal to *ethos* in your argument—in other words, how will you establish your credibility as the writer of the argument, and try to connect to your readers' beliefs and values.

Sometimes an issue will present certain problems that may make it challenging to write about. Table 7.2 lists some of the common problems with issues and the solutions for how to resolve those issues.

From Reflection to Response   **What Other Writers Have to Say**

Even if you know a lot about an issue, knowing what other writers have to say about it will enhance your understanding and help you compose an illuminating argument. With that in mind, read the section in Chapter 8 on doing preliminary research (pages 323–329) and then, using a specialized search engine or one of the databases available in your campus library, find two or more quality articles about an issue or problem you are considering for this project. Look for articles that express different views about the issue or problem, and then analyze the articles by answering the following questions:

- What do the writers agree about?

- What do they disagree about?

- What is each writer's main view of the problem? What solution, if any, do they propose?

- Which article do you consider more (or most) enlightening, and why?

- What specific information, facts, or perspectives from the articles could you incorporate and cite in your own argument?

TABLE 7.2 Common problems with issues and their solutions

Problem	Solution
Do you know enough about the issue or controversy you want to write about? Is your knowledge sufficient to enlighten intelligent readers?	Spend more time on invention, and come up with additional ideas, or devote time to doing preliminary research to enhance your knowledge of the issue. (See Chapter 8, pages 323–329, for information about finding quality sources and doing preliminary research.)
Is your issue a moral issue that is reducible to right versus wrong?	If so, consider what, if anything, you can accomplish by writing about the issue. Do you have any personal knowledge of the issue to share? Do you have anything to say to enlighten readers that people have not already heard? Is there a way you can approach the issue from a factual or empirical perspective, rather than moral? Are you open-minded enough about the issue to take a Rogerian, problem-solving approach, rather than moralizing?
You care about the issue and know something about it, but it is complicated and you are not sure what your central argument should be—what view or thesis you will support.	As you plan and start drafting the essay, focus on answering a key question (sometimes called a "thesis question") instead of supporting a position or traditional thesis. In your final draft of the essay, the answer to your thesis question normally will become your traditional thesis or central argument. (In formal, academic writing, a question is not considered a sufficient thesis.)
You have knowledge about an issue and want to support a position on it, but you know your position is unpopular and likely to invoke strong opposition or hostility. (For example, you support "stand your ground" laws or think the use of "predator drones" by the U.S. military is tantamount to "terrorism.")	Think carefully about your supporting arguments and how enlightening they will be. Do you have strong evidence, reasons, expert testimony, or personal experience to support your position? Does your position have problem-solving implications, or is it just an opinion? Are you capable of recognizing your own preconceptions or assumptions and anticipating objections? Do you know and understand opposing views and counterarguments readers are likely to raise? Do you have rebuttals? Can you be objective enough to concede the strength of opposing views and find common ground?

WRITING A PROPOSAL

Writing a proposal for your essay will help you plan and anticipate any problems you might encounter. In addition, readers can respond to the proposal and offer suggestions. As recommended in previous chapters, compose your proposal in *business style,* to make it easier for readers to find the key information.

The following outline lists the major section headings of a proposal, along with approximate lengths for each section.

1. **The Main Problem or Issue** that your essay will address, and why it is important (length: a detailed paragraph or more).

2. **The Central Viewpoint, Thesis, or Solution, and an Overview of Supporting Arguments**. What is the view or thesis that your essay will support (or a central question that your essay will attempt to answer)? Discuss some of the reasons and evidence you will provide to support your view or thesis. What research do you plan to do, if any (length: a detailed paragraph or more)?

3. **Reason for Writing about This Issue**. Elaborate on why this issue is important to you, and what you know about it (length: a paragraph or two).

4. **The Relevance to Readers** that you think your essay will have. Elaborate on why your argument will be relevant to readers and enlighten them (length: a brief paragraph or two).

WRITING A ROUGH DRAFT

A traditional academic argument usually follows a formal, deductive pattern of development. The central view or thesis—the writer's stand or position—is expressed early in the essay as part of the opening, usually after a concise but compelling presentation of the main issue or problem. Once the view or thesis is expressed—in other words, once the writer expresses his position on the issue to the reader—the opening is functionally complete. The rest of the essay focuses on supporting the view or thesis in a deductive pattern, with specific evidence and reasons.

Effective arguments also can be organized informally—meaning the writer will develop the issue in detail and delay presenting a view or a thesis until the middle or even the end of the essay. A Rogerian argument that emphasizes "listening" and stating the opposing position will often follow this more informal or inductive pattern.

Since readers of academic arguments expect an early presentation of the view or thesis, many instructors will want you to write your essay in the formal pattern, so that you learn the conventions of an academic argument. The formal conventions have practical origins that go back to public speaking in ancient democracies, where participation in civic debate was expected of citizens. Often these debates addressed issues that the audience was familiar with—for example, whether or not to build a public monument, finance a colony, or go to war. The focus of the argument was on the decision, or how to vote—that is, the view, the course of action, or the solution to the problem, and why.

Academic arguments follow a similar pattern because the academic audience is considered a specialized audience of people who are trained or being trained in a discipline, and understand the complexity of a given issue. Therefore, the view or solution that the writer presents, and the supporting reasons and evidence, are the desired focus.

As you plan and draft your essay, remember that all the parts have real functions and communication goals. To write a compelling argument, you have to fulfill the functions of the different parts. As you think about the different parts of the essay—your communication goals—remember that the length of the parts should be proportionate to the function of each. For example, if your opening section is longer than the section that presents your supporting arguments, something is probably wrong.

Table 7.3 lists the main parts of a formal essay, their functions, their approximate lengths, and their proportions, for an essay that runs five to seven pages. Use the table to guide you as you draft your essay.

Writing the Opening

The opening of the essay is not an *introduction* in the clichéd sense of introducing the topic as though you were introducing a friend to someone. The specific function of the opening is to present the main issue or problem you are writing about, and the view, argument, or thesis that you will support. You want both the issue and your view to engage readers, to galvanize their attention for the rest of the essay.

If you start with an introduction that presents general background information about the topic, you won't be writing an effective opening or engaging your readers. An effective opening should convey the reality of the issue or problem, its social and human consequences, and its relevance to your readers.

Your view or thesis also needs to engage your readers. An effective thesis, as you learned in Chapter 3 (see pages 90–94), should present a meaningful and compelling viewpoint or argument. Use the following questions to help draft a good thesis statement:

▶ Is the statement argumentative—that is, does it express conviction, take a stand, or make a claim? Does it need to be defended, supported, or proven?

▶ Is it interesting? Does it present an idea that is new or surprising and give an intelligent reader something to think about and a reason to continue to read?

▶ Does the thesis reflect the conclusions of your thinking or research—speak to a solution to the problem your essay addresses?

▶ Is it clear and specific enough to be supported in the essay?

TABLE 7.3 Parts, functions, and proportions of formal essays

Part	Function	Proportion
Opening—the presentation of the issue or problem + the central view or thesis statement	A good opening consists of a compelling presentation of the issue, question, or problem driving the essay and a statement of the central view, argument, or thesis. Think of the opening as a blueprint for the whole essay. The opening presents the central issue and the viewpoint (or thesis) that the rest of the essay will support in detail. Once the viewpoint or thesis is presented, the reader understands the purpose and communication goals of the essay.	Usually no more than one or two pages in total (one to four paragraphs) for an essay five to seven pages in length.
Counterarguments and opposing views (optional)	Counterarguments and opposing views are not an inherent or required part of every formal essay or every argument. However, they usually are important. They can be addressed almost anywhere in an essay. The most common place is in conjunction with the thesis support or supporting arguments. However, for clarity and convenience, some writers find it helpful to bring them up immediately after the thesis statement, at the beginning of the supporting section.	If these are dealt with separately, they may require one or two pages or more. Functionally speaking, this section is actually part of your thesis support (see below), but you are composing it as a separate section to alleviate organization problems.
Thesis support, proof, or justification of the central view or argument	This is the main part of the essay—all of the reasons, evidence, examples, statistics, and so on, that support the thesis or view.	The most important and substantial part of the essay. If the support includes your counterarguments, it will usually make up about 80 percent of the essay's total length—that is, approximately five or six pages of a seven-page essay.

TABLE 7.3 (Continued)

Part	Function	Proportion
Ending—strongest supporting point, final appeal, or "food for thought"	The ending of any essay should have a realistic function; in other words, it should contribute to your communication goals. In a relatively short essay or argument (under ten or fifteen pages), *avoid a mechanical "conclusion" that restates your main points*. End with your strongest supporting point, or develop an idea that underscores or expands your thesis support or strongest argument. In classical oratory, an effective ending (peroration) often included an appeal to emotions. One way or another, try to make a final impression on your readers. Give them something to take away from the essay.	Variable length, but proportionately short. If the ending is your last and strongest supporting point, or an extension of it, it may not require a separate paragraph. If you compose an ending that contributes something to the essay and its relevance (in other words, doesn't just restate the main points), an added paragraph or two is justified.

The opening of a good argument is crucial. If readers are not engaged from the very beginning, the best a writer can hope for is that they might skip ahead in search of something interesting. But when readers do that, they already have decided the essay is predictable or deficient. In a manner of speaking, they have gone out to the lobby to buy popcorn or make a phone call while the movie is showing, because they feel they won't miss anything.

Your goal as the writer is to prevent that from happening—to engage your readers and hold their attention from the very first sentence. To do that, you need to present the issue driving your argument in a realistic way. Your knowledge of the issue and the concerns you have, if they are genuine, will tell you how to start. If you have experienced the issue, you could write about your experience, or narrate someone else's story that you know first-hand or learned from a source. You also might present significant statistics that highlight the relevance of the issue for your readers. Whatever approach you take, the goal is the same: make the issue as real and reader-relevant as you can.

Take a look at the opening below from *The Godless Constitution* by Isaac Kramnick and R. Laurence Moore. The issue at stake, the separation of church and state, is important but also legalistic, that is, based on constitutional law. Notice how the writers connect the issue to the "real world" and people's lives.

Is America a Christian Nation?

Americans seem to fight about many silly things: whether a copy of the Ten Commandments can be posted in a city courthouse; whether a holiday display that puts an image of the baby Jesus next to one of Frosty the Snowman violates the Constitution; whether fidgeting grade-schoolers may stand for a minute in silent "spiritual" meditation before classes begin. Common sense might suggest that these are harmless practices whose actual damage is to trivialize religion. Otherwise they threaten no one. Not children, who ignore them as the incomprehensible designs of absurd grown-ups. Not atheists, who may find them hypocritical and vulgar but hardly intimidating. Not Buddhists and Muslims, who in these small areas of daily practice can demand equal access to the public landscape. So why do they raise ideological storms?

The answer lies in what history has done to us....

The opening of an essay by Richard Rodriguez about Hispanic Americans also puts a human face on the main issue, and it uses an evocative litany of images to express the central view or thesis.

Surnames Reflect the Changing Face of America

Many Americans are troubled regarding the Latinization of the United States, the ubiquitous brown faces in the crowd, Spanish everywhere. On nativist talk radio, in the speeches of politicians, a legend of illegality as old as cowboy America attaches to anyone related to Latin America, whether or not one is legally here.

It made the news recently that "Garcia" and "Rodriguez" are now among the top 10 most common American surnames. We Hispanics have become a people whose presence gets told by such numbers, our ascending numbers. Our ascending numbers frighten many Americans who see Hispanics as overwhelming this country. But Hispanics are more than numbers. We are Catholics. We are Evangelical Protestants. We come in all colors, and races, and talents, and sensibilities. We are judges. We are gang-bangers. We are U.S. Marines. We are retired. We are crowding desert high schools.

Incorporating Opposing Views

Even after an effective opening, readers will "bail" on an essay that is narrow-minded or predictable. One way to keep readers interested is to establish your "ethos," or credibility as a writer, by examining opposing views and counter-arguments. In an argumentative essay, opposing views are like good plot elements in a story: they create tension, add complexity, and lead to revelations. When opposing views are called for and a writer fails to bring them up, arguments lose credibility.

As noted in Table 7.3 on page 282, experienced writers, who are good at organizing their points and making smooth transitions, can weave opposing views into almost any part of an essay without disrupting the clarity or flow.

Less experienced writers can have trouble incorporating opposing views without disrupting the organization of an essay. Sometimes an inexperienced writer will make the mistake of floating an opposing view at the very end of an essay. This "strategy" is like a man asking a woman to marry him and then saying he is not 100 percent sure he really wants to be married. In other words, it is usually a bad "strategy," because it undermines the conviction of an argument.

You can alleviate problems with organizing opposing views by presenting them immediately after you state your thesis or main argument. In effect, you make the opposing views the first part of your thesis support.

Building to a Climax

Writing an effective argument is like making a case in court, especially a closing argument to a jury. The following guidelines by Ray Moses of the *Center for Criminal Justice Advocacy* were written to help criminal defense attorneys make strong closing arguments. Note how the guidelines are similar to many of the principles covered in this chapter.

- ▶ Open with an attention-getting hook that incorporates the theme of your case.

- ▶ Be creative. Recognize, address, and negate the obvious weaknesses in your own story of the case.

- ▶ Meet and refute the prosecution's claims. Exploit weaknesses in the prosecution's story of the case.

- ▶ Underscore the absence or paucity of prosecution evidence on elements of the offense. Challenge the prosecution's weakest claims and demonstrate their logical frailty.

- ▶ Conclude your message with strength, asking for a verdict of acquittal.

Of particular importance to a criminal defense attorney is the last guideline—"conclude your message with strength." A defendant's guilt or innocence is on the line. A good attorney is not going to develop her closing argument haphazardly. The attorney's goal is to make a lasting impression on the jury and that means building to a strong conclusion.

The reasons and evidence in support of any argument, written or spoken, always vary in significance or strength. If the strongest point comes across too early, then the rest of the argument may be anticlimactic.

Keep this in mind as you draft your essay for this assignment. Don't worry about finding the ideal sequence in your first draft, but as you shape and revise the essay, arrange your thesis support so that it builds to the strongest possible conclusion.

Incorporating Research

Your goal for this assignment is to compose an argument from a position of knowledge. Ideally, you should have *some* exposure to the issue you are writing about, something to "bring to the table" as the writer. To strengthen your argument, you may want to do some reading about the issue and maybe interview or talk to people who are knowledgeable.

If you bring research into your essay, you need to find quality sources and identify them in the essay. Chapter 8 ("Navigating a Research Project") and Chapter 14 ("A Guide to Using and Documenting Sources") cover how to find sources and document them correctly. Most college professors require formal documentation for college essays (in-text citations and a Works Cited or reference list). The documentation system usually used in first-year writing courses is MLA (Modern Language Association).

Even journalists and newspaper reporters who do not use formal documentation in their articles *always* identify all the sources of information that are not their own. The sources are cited with "tags" and "lead-ins," the same way we cite them in everyday conversations ("According to my dad…" or "My girlfriend says…" and so on).

Following are some typical tags and lead-ins:

- ▶ A blogger by the name of _____ argues that…
- ▶ Professor _____ rejected that idea in an interview on *60 Minutes*…
- ▶ Paul Krugman, writing in the *New York Times*, also believes…
- ▶ In the words of Dr. Erica _____, a clinical psychologist and author of _____…

Identifying sources is ethical, but the main reason we do it is to be professional: to provide context and a trail of information for our readers (or someone we are talking to). Assessing the validity of a source, and sharing the assessment with readers, is a related, professional practice.

Whenever you write in college, and whatever you write, if you *always* identify *all* of your sources, and in addition, *always* use quotation marks, or block centering, to identify a direct quotation when you use someone's exact words, you never will have a problem with academic honesty or plagiarism. (For more information about documenting sources, direct quotations, and avoiding plagiarism, see Chapter 8, pages 343–348.)

Use of "I"

A common question students ask college writing instructors about argumentative essays is, "Can I use 'I'?"—in other words, write in the first person? The question comes up because many high school teachers, and even college instructors, think that writing in the first person invites self-indulgence and self-centeredness, at the expense of objectivity.

Of course, certain kinds of essays—personal narratives, for example—have to be written in the first person, but regardless of the kind of essay, a good writer always is "speaking" to readers, whether he uses "I" or not. Objectivity comes from habits of mind and critical thinking, not stylistic refinements.

Nevertheless, since arguments emphasize knowledge and objectivity, an objective style that minimizes use of the first person is appropriate. Many academic writers limit their use of "I" to sections of an argument that deal with their personal experiences. They avoid the first person otherwise, and in particular, avoid subjective, filler phrases like "I believe" or "in my opinion."

YOUR ESSAY CHECKLIST

Use the essay checklist in the box to guide your steps in developing your essay and as a final check to make sure you have completed all of the necessary steps. This checklist can also be used to help you plan your time effectively.

✔ Task	Description	Time Frame
☐ **Choose a subject**	• If your instructor asks you to come up with your own idea for the essay, develop a list of issues and problems that concern you and that, preferably, you know something about. • If your instructor assigns an issue or problem for you to write about, do some thinking or brainstorming about what you know and what you need to know in order to write a meaningful essay. • In either case, discuss the assignment and your ideas with your classmates, instructor, and others.	A day or two, or more.

(continued)

✔ Task	Description	Time Frame
☐ **Write a proposal**	Consider the following questions when writing a proposal: • Why is the issue important to you? • Why is it reader-relevant? • Do you have a provisional thesis, or are you going to start with a key question (or set of questions)? • What opposing views or counterarguments do you need considered? • Have you examined your own assumptions and identified moral judgments or opinions that need to be approached objectively? • What kinds of evidence or supporting arguments can you present? • Do you need to do research, and if so, how much and what kind?	One or two hours, or more.
☐ **Do some research**	• Develop a research plan. • Outline and draft parts of an essay while researching. • In your final draft, remember to identify all your sources and use lead-ins and attributive tags to introduce source material and direct quotations. Assess the validity of sources, and whenever relevant, share your assessment with readers.	Depending on the scope of the research you have to do, this part of the timeline can take a day or two, or much longer.
☐ **Write a rough draft**	• Write a rough draft of the essay without thinking too much about the quality. • Focus on getting your ideas down and developing them as much as you can. • If your argument takes a formal pattern, think about your thesis—whether it is compelling and defensible enough. • If you are not sure what your thesis is, focus your draft on a good question or set of questions that you can convert to a thesis later. • Acknowledge and address counterarguments and opposing views. • Ask good questions. • Don't be afraid to challenge "conventional wisdom." • Consider Rogerian strategies and look for common ground. • When you finish your rough draft, put it aside for a day or two before you start revising.	The time frame will vary. For many essays, it will take more than one sitting to compose the rough draft. Finish the rough draft at least a week or more before the final essay is due, so that you have ample time to revise and polish.

✔ Task	Description	Time Frame
☐ **Revise**	• Revise the essay, until you "get it right"—make it as enlightening and "reader-relevant" as it can be. • If and when necessary, adjust or change your initial thesis to fit the final support you provide. • Address legitimate opposing views. • Include comprehensive thesis support. • Build to a strong conclusion. • If you see any problems with organization or coherence, do a revision or "reverse" outline to get an overview of the different parts of the essay. • Consider your style.	Plan on doing multiple revisions over the course of a week or more.
☐ **Get peer review**	• As you revise and improve your essay, ask for feedback from your classmates, instructor, and other people. • Consider taking a draft to your campus writing center for advice from a trained tutor.	Varies.
☐ **Edit your essay**	Before you submit the essay, make sure you edit it carefully. Check for the following: • Helpful paragraphing and smooth transitions from one paragraph to the next • Accurate wording and word choice • Correct sentence punctuation (fix run-ons and comma splices) • Correct grammar and mechanics (check subject-verb agreement, pronoun reference, placement of commas) • Conscientious documentation in MLA style—in-text citations and lead-ins that identify all of your sources; a correctly formatted Works Cited list	Varies.

PEER REVIEW

Because arguments address controversies and different perspectives, feedback from classmates will help you gauge how enlightening your argument is. Even before you start to write your essay, talk to people about it. Once you have a readable draft to share, ask classmates to respond to these questions:

1. The goal of the opening is to make the central issue real and relevant to readers. What approaches or strategies does the writer use to accomplish

this? Offer any suggestions you can for making the opening more compelling.

2. What is the essay's central argument or thesis (quote exact words if you can)? Is the argument or thesis interesting, defensible, clear, and specific enough? Does it lend itself to meaningful analysis and support? Can you offer suggestions for improvements?

3. Does the writer address counterarguments or possible objections to her view or thesis? Are the counterarguments fairly presented, with problem-solving intentions? Can you think of any relevant counterarguments that are not addressed?

4. Is the thesis support and argumentation extensive enough and edifying? What is the writer's strongest point? What is his weakest point? Does the essay ever rely on personal opinion or beliefs? Are there any ideas or arguments that could use more development or support?

5. Does the essay build to a strong conclusion, or is the conclusion anticlimactic or repetitive? Can you offer suggestions for making the conclusion stronger?

6. If the writer uses any sources, are the sources properly identified in the essay? Is a correctly formatted Works Cited list included at the end of the essay? Point out any concerns or questions you have about the documentation of sources.

7. Do a short revision outline of the essay and comment on how it is organized. Does the essay transition smoothly from one paragraph to the next? Point out any problems with wording, grammar, or mechanics that distract the reader and interfere with the clarity or "flow" of the essay. Offer suggestions for improvements.

STUDENT ESSAY: FINAL DRAFT

Below is the final version of the researched argument about atheism that first-year student Brian Lawrence wrote, based on his proposal at the beginning of the chapter. Brian's essay is formatted and documented in MLA style.

After the essay, Brian discusses his writing process and offers some advice about writing an effective argument.

Use one-inch margins on all sides, and double-spacing throughout the essay.

Lawrence 1

Insert page numbers in the upper right hand corner, starting with the first page, and create a "header" that displays your last name on every page in front of the page number.

Brian Lawrence

Professor Saba

English 1105

October 15, 2016

The first-page heading consists of your name, your instructor's name, the course, and the date, double-spaced and aligned in the upper left-hand corner.

The Truth about Atheists

Religion is regarded by the common people as true, by the wise as false, and by rulers as useful.

—SENECA, ROMAN PHILOSOPHER AND PLAYWRIGHT (A.D. 3–65)

Center your title. (Don't use quotation marks, or typographical features like underlining or bold.)

At a news conference in Chicago on August 27, 1987, then Vice President George H. W. Bush made a striking remark. He told Robert I. Sherman, a reporter for the *American Atheist* news journal, "I don't know that atheists should be considered as citizens, nor should they be considered patriots. This is one nation under God."

A relevant quotation inserted after the title is called an epigraph. (It is not common or required in college papers.)

Later, during the same news conference, Sherman asked the Vice President:

"Do you support the constitutionality of state/church separation?"

"Yes, I support the separation of church and state," Bush replied. "I'm just not very high on atheists" (Sherman).

The source of information, Sherman, is named in a signal phrase. Since the Sherman's article appeared on a website, no page numbers are needed or given in parentheses.

Author's name in parentheses to indicate the same source.

The outrage over this was minimal. In fact, most Americans are unaware that Mr. Bush, who was elected President the following year, ever said such a thing. In the United States, prejudices and misconceptions regarding atheists are common and accepted. This country has a long history of discrimination against minorities; African-Americans, women, homosexuals and many other social groups are evidence of this. However, while members of these groups are breaking barriers and being shown an increased amount of tolerance, a recent study conducted by the University of Minnesota

Lawrence 2

indicates that atheists are still widely distrusted and viewed more unfavorably than any other minority group: "below Muslims, recent immigrants, [and] gays and lesbians." According to the study, "atheists are also the minority group most Americans are least willing to allow their children to marry" ("Atheists Identified").

> Since the author is unknown, this source—an online newspaper article—is identified by its title.

What is the source of all this distrust and disfavor? Sociologists Penny Edgell, Joseph Gerteis, and Douglas Hartmann observe that "a religious identity is an important way of being American" (Edgell 216). Indeed, many Americans believe atheism is, in essence, immoral, and even associate it with criminal or antisocial behavior. Senator Joseph Lieberman... etc. Senator Joseph Lieberman, once the Democratic nominee for Vice President, exemplified this kind of thinking when he warned Americans not to "indulge the supposition that morality can be maintained without religion" (qtd. in Angier). Most surveys put the percentage of Americans who are atheists at less than 10 percent of the population, yet according to a recent Pew Research survey. "religious commitment" in the U.S. as a whole is declining. A third of U.S. adults now say they do not consider themselves "religious," and about 20 percent identify themselves as either nonbelievers or religiously unaffiliated ("Growth of the Nonreligious"). Nonetheless, the stigma against the irreligious prevails. Forty-eight percent of the people surveyed by Pew said the increasing number of people who are not religious is a "bad thing" (see Fig. 1).

> The abbreviation "qtd. in" tells readers that Lieberman's words are quoted from an indirect source—in this case, an article by (Natalie) "Angier."

> A reference to the chart included below.

Some might argue that prejudices against atheists are unimportant because constitutional rights already are in place, but in reality, these prejudices can and do translate to real discrimination, and create another barrier of ignorance that unnecessarily divides Americans and weakens our society.

> After discussing the extent of the problem, the writer presents his thesis.

Lawrence 3

The Growth of the Nonreligious in America: Good or Bad?

% of U.S. adults who say "more people who are not religious" is a good thing, bad thing, or does't make much difference for American society

■ Bad thing   ■ Good thing   ■ Doesn't matter

All Adults   48   11   39

The caption includes the figure number and the source.

FIG. 1   Source: "Growth of the Nonreligious"

Most Americans are unaware that a number of state constitutions contain articles that aim to prohibit atheists from holding public office. Matthew Bulger, writing for the American Humanist Association, offers the examples below among others:

- **Arkansas, Article 19, Section 1:**

  No person who denies the being of a God shall hold any office in the civil departments of this State, nor be competent to testify as a witness in any Court.

- **Mississippi, Article 14, Section 265:**

  No person who denies the existence of a Supreme Being shall hold any office in this state.

- **North Carolina, Article 6, Section 8:**

  The following persons shall be disqualified for office: Any person who shall deny the being of Almighty God.

- **Tennessee, Article 9, Section 2:**

  No person who denies the being of God, or a future state of rewards and punishments, shall hold any office in the civil department of this state.

Lawrence 4

A 1961 Supreme Court decision, along with the "no religious test clause" in the U.S. Constitution, legally overrules these articles, yet the articles remain on the books and still make it technically illegal and problematic for an atheist to run for office in these states and others. In 2009, when Cecil Bothwell, an atheist, was elected to the Asheville, North Carolina city council, some voters challenged his right to serve, on the ground that he did not meet the requirement of believing in "Almighty God" (Bulger; Schrader).

A more publicized dispute about atheism occurred in 2008 during the heated North Carolina senatorial race between incumbent Elizabeth Dole and challenger Kay Hagen. Dole, behind in the polls, resorted to a smear campaign. One infamous attack ad portrayed Hagen as an atheist, and in the process, makes atheism appear to be some kind of cult. A foreboding narrator tells viewers: "A leader of the Godless Americans PAC recently held a secret fundraiser in Kay Hagen's honor." The ad goes on to quote members of the Godless American Political Action Committee proclaiming, "There is no God to rely on!....There was no Jesus!..." Then the narrator continues, "Godless Americans and Kay Hagen: She hid from cameras, took Godless money. What did Kay Hagen promise in return?" At this point, the ad seems to suggest that Hagen might have made a pact with the devil. And again, we hear an eerie, God-denying voice say: "There is no God!" (Frantz; "Dole Still Keeping the Faith").

Despite what the ad says, the "Godless Americans Political Action Committee" never held a secret fundraiser for Kay Hagen. To win an election, Dole and her campaign decided that it would be a good idea to smear Kay Hagen and demonize American atheists in the

The information is drawn from two sources.

Lawrence 5

process. Criticism of the ad focused on its dishonesty, but few objected to the vilification of atheists and atheism. Hagen herself countered the accusations in the ad by affirming her "Christian faith" and assuring her supporters that she went to church every week, and at one time, had been a Sunday school teacher (Frantz). Atheism and atheists obviously are political poison. In 2008, Democrats on the atheistic blog Petty Larseny joked that the most effective way to hurt Republican Presidential candidate John McCain would be to form a group called "Atheists for McCain" (Freedman A21).

> Author, section, and page number of a print newspaper article.

At the time of this writing, Representative Pete Stark (D) of California is the only openly atheist member of Congress in history. Stark, a congressman since 1973, has never been involved in any form of scandal, and has maintained the approval of his constituents for 36 years. Many believe that there are possibly even more atheists and/or agnostics in Congress who choose not to disclose their views because of the potential backlash (Krattenmaker A15).

Former Presidential candidate Mitt Romney once told an audience of supporters, "We need to have a person of faith lead the country" (Sullivan). A statement like that is a guaranteed applause line in American politics, and resonates with too many Americans. Various studies have shown that somewhere around 53 percent of people in this country would not even consider voting for a well-qualified atheist for President (Krattenmaker A15).

Despite this prejudice, some still argue that atheism is not a civil rights issue, but Dan Newman, a Democratic strategist, is closer to the truth when he states that "anti-atheism remains the last remaining prejudice that a majority of Americans don't mind fessing up to"

(Marinucci). In the military, atheists sometimes put their lives at risk by "coming out of the closet," and they experience discrimination on a grand scale. Patrick Kucera, an atheist member of the United States Air Force, writes that, although he entered the Air Force with the intent of defending the constitution, others spent much of their time attempting to convert him to Christianity and forcing him to do things that he did not want to do (Kucera). When he began training at the U.S. Air Force Academy in Colorado Springs, after evening meals he had two options: Go to church or head back to his room to relax. Being an atheist, he chose the latter. In doing so, he subjected himself to others calling his walk to his room the "Heathen Flight." There were times when his superiors forced him to recite Christian prayers and forced their Christian beliefs on him. He decided to share his problem with the Air Force Military Equal Opportunity (MEO) Program, which is responsible for eliminating discrimination on the basis of race, gender, and religion. However, while explaining his case and mentioning that he was an atheist, the MEO officer he spoke to tried to convert him to Christianity (Kucera).

At least the military allows atheists in their ranks. The Boy Scouts of America do not. A Supreme Court decision as recently as the year 2000 allows this blatant discrimination to continue (McGroarty L03). Similarly, many veterans groups do not allow atheists to join (Krattenmaker A15). These prejudices all seem to stem from the notion that atheism is synonymous with immorality, and therefore, atheists are immoral people. The Merriam-Webster online dictionary lists the word "wickedness," along with "ungodliness," as an archaic, first definition for "atheism."

Lawrence 7

Is there *any* validity to the idea that atheism and immorality are synonymous? The 2009 Global Peace Index provides rankings of how turbulent and warlike different countries are. The rankings are based on twenty-three criteria, including war, internal conflict, homicide rates, incarceration rates, arms trade, and the degree of democracy in the country. Ironically, at the top of the list of the most peaceful countries in the world are many countries that are the least religious. Sweden, which is the sixth most peaceful country in the world, has the highest percentage of atheists. At least 46 percent of its people are nonbelievers. Norway, which is listed as the third most peaceful country in the world, has the fourth highest percentage of atheists. Japan, which finished as the seventh most peaceful country, has the fifth largest percentage of atheists. Thirty-five percent of the people of Slovenia, which finished as 10th most peaceful country, are nonbelievers. Twenty to twenty-two percent of the people of New Zealand, the most peaceful nation in the world, are atheists (Zuckerman; "Global Peace Index"). The United States in comparison, which has a relatively small population of atheists, is closer to the bottom of the Global Peace Index than it is to the top. It finished as the 83rd most peaceful country, out of 144.

Other studies have found that the countries with the highest percentages of atheists tend to be among the most stable, free, prosperous, and healthy societies. Creighton University's Center for the Study of Religion looked at the correlation between levels of "popular religiosity" and various social health indicators in eighteen of the world's most prosperous democracies, including the United States. These democracies were ranked by the percentage

Lawrence 8

of the population believing in a god, the frequency of prayer reported by citizens, and attendance at religious services. The data was then correlated with rates of homicide, abortion, and teen pregnancy. The most religious democracies had a higher degree of social dysfunction than those with higher percentages of atheists. In fact, the U.S. which had the largest percentage of people who express belief in a higher being, also had the highest percentages of homicide, abortion, teen pregnancy, and sexually transmitted diseases (Brooks).

The same study found that, in the United States in 2003, six of the seven states with the highest homicide rates were among the most religious. Louisiana, which had the highest homicide rate for any state in 2003, was also one of the most religious states in the country. Mississippi, which had the second highest homicide rate in 2003, was the most religious state. In contrast, Vermont, the least religious state in the country and the state with the highest percentage of atheists, ranked 48th in the nation for homicide rate, making it one of the safest places in the nation to live. New Hampshire, which was the second most nonreligious state, ranked 50th, and had the lowest homicide rate in the nation (Brooks; Newport; United States).

Three sources of information for the statistics presented above. "United States" indicates the source is a government agency.

It would be foolish for me to suggest that atheists are necessarily more peaceful or better than people of religion. Nation-states where atheism has been imposed by government have been some of the most violent and immoral in history. Examples include the former Soviet Union and present-day North Korea. However, there is no evidence to support a correlation between atheism and

Lawrence 9

immorality, nor any evidence to suggest that atheists are unfit to hold public office, nor that atheism promotes crime. If anything, there seems to be a correlation between high levels of religiosity and social dysfunction, including crime, but at minimum, the evidence says atheists and other nonbelievers do societies no harm (Brooks).

As Karen Frantz, policy associate at the American Humanist Association, writes:

> There is no religious prerequisite for being an American, and a seven-year-old atheist should too be able to dream that one day he or she could become president of the United States. We need to continue to make the point that what binds us as a people is not a belief in God, but our shared embrace of the ideals of life, liberty, and the pursuit of happiness.

Frantz's point is valid, but ultimately being tolerant of atheists is about something more important than what is constitutional, fair, or right, something more important than even "ideals." It is about a lesson that, as Americans, we have learned again and again. Embracing diversity and inclusiveness is about being the best we can be, about progress and growth, about drawing on all of our resources and always becoming stronger and more exceptional than we were in the past.

Block-centered quotation indented one inch from the left margin for a direct quotation of more than four lines. Quotation marks are not used.

The first line of an entry is flush against the left margin. Subsequent lines of an entry are indented 0.5 inch (called a "hanging indent"). See Chapter 14 for tips on formatting Works Cited entries.

The Works Cited list starts on a separate page. The heading is centered. The list is double-spaced throughout.

URLs for Internet sources are not required, but the author provides this one (and several others) because he thinks the source might be hard to find.

Online article with no author is listed alphabetically by the title.

Newspaper article accessed in print includes a section and page number.

Scholarly journal accessed in print. The citation includes the volume, issue, year of publication, and the page numbers.

Lawrence 10

Works Cited

Angier, Natalie. "Confessions of a Lonely Atheist." *The New York Times Magazine*. New York Times, 14 Jan. 2001. Web. 27 Oct. 2013.

"Atheism." *Merriam-Webster Online Dictionary*. Miriam-Webster Online, 2009. Web. 12 Nov. 2009.

"Atheists Identified as America's Most Distrusted Minority, According to New U of M Study." *University of Minnesota News*. Free Republic, 22 Mar. 2006. Web. 15 Oct. 2013. <http://www.freerepublic.com/focus/news/1601278/posts>.

Brooks, Rosa. "The Dark Side of Faith." *Los Angeles Times*. Los Angeles Times, 1 Oct. 2005. Web. 5 Nov. 2013.

Bulger, Matthew. "Unelectable Atheists: U.S. States That Prohibit Godless Americans from Holding Public Office." *American Humanist*. American Humanist Association, 25 May 2012. Web. 30 Nov. 2013.

"Dole Still Keeping the Faith." *Politico*. Politico, 29 Oct. 2008. Web. 5 Nov. 2013.

Edgell, Penny, Joseph Gerteis, and Douglas Hartmann. "Atheists as 'Other': Moral Boundaries and Cultural Membership in American Society." *American Sociological Review* 71.2 (2007): 211–34. Print.

Frantz, Karen. "Cry If You Want To: Cases of Mistaken Atheism Still Offensive." American Humanist. American Humanist Association, 17 Dec. 2008. Web. 19 Nov. 2013.

Freedman, Samuel G. "For Atheists, Politics Proves to Be a Lonely Endeavor." *New York Times*, 18 Oct. 2008, A21. Print.

"Global Peace Index." *Vision of Humanity*. Institute for Economics & Peace, 2009. Web. 20 Nov. 2013.

"Growth of the Nonreligious." *Pew Research Center, Religion & Public Life Project*. Pew Research Center, 2 July 2013. Web. 29 Nov. 2013. <http://www.pewresearch.org.>.

Lawrence 11

Krattenmaker, Tom. "Atheism, a Positive Pillar." Editorial. *USA Today*,

17 Nov. 2008, final ed.: A15. Print.

Kucera, Patrick. "A Cadet's Oath." *The Humanist. Free Online Library*.

Farlex, 1 Sept. 2007. Web. 7 Nov. 2013.

Marinucci, Carla. "Stark's Atheist Views Break Political Taboo."

SFGate. San Francisco Chronicle, 14 Mar. 2007. Web. 7 Nov. 2013.

McGroarty, Cynthia J. "What a Boy Scout Should Be." *Philadelphia*

Inquirer, 16 Apr. 2006, late ed.: L3.

Newport, Frank. "State of the States: Importance of Religion." *Gallup*.

Gallup, 28 Jan. 2009. Web. 29 Nov. 2013.

Schrader, Jordan. "Critics of Cecil Bothwell Cite N.C. Bar to

Atheists." *Asheville Citizen-Times*. Gannett, 7 Dec. 2009.

Web. 31 Jan. 2015.

"Seneca." *New World Encyclopedia*. New World Encyclopedia, 29 Aug.

2008. Web. 10 June 2015.

Sherman, Rob. "Documents at Bush Presidential Library Prove VP Bush

Questioned Citizenship and Patriotism of Atheists." *Rob Sherman*

Advocacy. 1 Apr. 2006. Web. 20 Oct. 2009.

Sullivan, Andrew. "Romney's Bigotry." *Daily Dish* Editorial. *The*

Atlantic. Atlantic Monthly Group, 17 Feb. 2007. Web. 13 Mar. 2015.

United States. FBI. "Crime in the United States 2003, Table 5, by

State, 2003." Federal Bureau of Investigation, 5 Mar. 2003.

Web. 21 Nov. 2013. <http://www.fbi.gov/about-us/cjis/ucr/

crime-in-the-u.s/2003>.

Zuckerman, Phil. "Is Faith Good for Us?" *On Line Opinion*. The National

Forum, 22 Apr. 2009. Web. 6 Nov. 2013.

Citation for the epigraph at the beginning of the essay.

Citation for government source with no author begins with the name of the government, followed by the name of the agency or organization. The web link provided takes readers to a portal where statistics referenced in the essay can be accessed.

Interview with the Student Writer

● **Brian, how did you go about composing your essay?**

● The only tool I use for composing essays is a word processor. I created a Microsoft Word document and jotted down my thoughts about atheism and points I found interesting. For class, we had to submit an introduction before anything else. I wrote that fairly hastily. I ended up revising my introduction a great deal, however. Overall, writing the essay turned out to be quite enjoyable.

● **Did anyone read your drafts while you were composing?**

● Although students were encouraged to provide online feedback to their peers, I never received any. Perhaps the subject matter was too controversial. When I submitted my final draft and students had the chance to read it, some of my peers told me how much they enjoyed it. I realized then that I had written a solid paper.

● **Was there anything difficult about writing the essay?**

● The most difficult part was deciding how I wanted to frame my argument. I also wanted to make sure that I did not turn the essay into a case for atheism. I wanted to be as objective and factual as possible.

● **What did you learn from writing the essay?**

● I enjoyed the revision process more than anything. I made several revisions. The final draft was much different from the initial draft. This was one of the first times that I placed considerable emphasis on revision. I was pleased to realize that even the most controversial of topics can translate to a great paper if tackled in the right way. I always knew that writing could be used as a tool to educate others, but I don't think I ever thought of writing as a way of educating myself. Also, I learned a lot through researching, obviously.

● **What advice would you give to other students about writing this kind of essay?**

● The best advice I can offer other students is that the writing process, particularly in college, can be as exciting as one makes it. If one isn't interested in what he or she writes, then the paper will show it. So choosing subjects of interest is crucial. An essay that uses research, as mine did, gives a student the opportunity to learn something about a topic. It's especially rewarding to research something that intrigues you.

EVALUATE YOUR LEARNING

1. What personal knowledge or experience did you draw on in choosing a subject for your essay or in writing it?

2. To support your view, thesis, or solution effectively, did you need to learn anything about the problem that you did not already know? If so, how did you get the additional information or knowledge?

3. What do you think is the strongest point or supporting argument you made in your essay, and why?

4. Can you give some examples of appeals to "ethos" or "pathos" that you used in the essay?

5. What opposing views or counterarguments did you think about or address in your essay?

6. Imagine the argument you wrote being presented in a medium other than writing—for example, as a video, poster, cartoon, or animation. What medium would be effective? What might be gained or lost from a communication standpoint?

7. In a paragraph or two, amplify on what you learned from completing this project.

ADDITIONAL READINGS

Arlet Montes // **THE DEBATE ABOUT MODERN SEXUALITY AND PORNOGRAPHY**

Arlet Montes is pursuing a bachelor's degree in art history, while also completing courses required for admission to a dental school upon graduation. She wants to have a career that allows her to grow personally and economically while helping others feel better and have better lives. One of her biggest dreams is to travel around the world and see great works of art that she has only known through books.

Think about a subject that, when brought up in a conversation, will cause people to fidget or cringe. If you are thinking about pornography, then you just read my mind. Most people, at some point in their lives, will be exposed to pornography. With new generations moving toward a society that is gradually becoming more and more open about sexuality, it should be reasonable for people to talk about sex, or even pornography, without feeling weird. However, pornography, which has been around forever, remains something people "hide under their mattresses" because of shame and fear.

One thing most people know about pornography, regardless of what they think about it, is that it is now more readily available than ever before. *New York Magazine* feature writer, David Amsden, calls it the "wallpaper" of our lives (qtd. in Wolf). Even the most respectable Internet users can accidentally run up against it doing innocent keyword searches that include terms like toys, boys, or nature. The creators of pornography, the so-called Adult Entertainment industry, make billions of dollars in profits every year, both in the United States and globally. Large profits mean there is a large demand for the product. As many writers suggest, the demand is not limited to people on the margins of society. Today, as Naomi Wolf writes in *The Porn Myth*, pornography has "breached the dike that separated a marginal, adult, private pursuit from the mainstream public arena." Her point raises a question that people have been trying to answer for centuries. What is the difference between the acceptable, mainstream depictions of sexuality that are admired as classical art, and the controversial sexual depictions that people label as pornography? Answers to that question can vary widely. People agree there is a distinction but not on what makes it. Is the real answer that the distinction isn't terribly important or worth worrying about? Has the time come for people to take a deep breath, and acknowledge that pornography "is what it is," and undoubtedly, is here to stay? There was a time when women who wore slacks were seen as sluts, a time when marijuana was thought to make people crazy, a time, very recently, when just the idea of a gay marriage seemed unthinkable, horrific, and absurd. Now, all those things have become much more accepted. People realize that we have bigger problems to solve and more important things to worry about.

Pornography would present less of a social problem and be less controversial if it were easier to define. Everyone, without a doubt, is able to recognize some forms of graphic, sexual depictions as pornographic when they see them. However, objectively, what exactly is pornography? Some people, like psychologist Leon F. Seltzer, make a distinction between explicit sexual representations that are degrading (pornography) versus those that are artistic and humanizing (erotica). In his article *What Distinguishes Erotica from Pornography*, Seltzer compares pornography and erotica as existing in two different planes. He argues that the main difference between them is not whether or not they are explicit, but how they are perceived by the viewer, and the primary intention of the creation itself. If a depiction of the human body or sexuality focuses on the beauty of the human form and the beauty of the sexual act itself by evoking emotion, and embraces sexuality in a human way, not for the sole purpose of arousal, but to raise interest from them, then it is erotic. In Seltzer's view, the erotic transcends carnal desires, and evokes aesthetic feelings in the viewer that promote an interest in understanding the components, nature, and function of sexuality. The erotic conveys meaning in a way the artist or creator feels is beautiful. It catches the eye and inspires curiosity.

Pornography, on the other hand, Seltzer says, is produced to "turn the largest possible profit." To do so, it leaves nothing out of the picture, and wants nothing more than to provoke "immediate, intense arousal." Seltzer admits that sometimes "the erotic might end up having the same effect," but he still insists on a recognizable distinction:

> If the subjects are portrayed in a manner that focuses on their inner and outer radiance, their fleshy vitality, and the work itself seems to manifest a passionate and powerful affirmation of life and the pleasures of this world, then I think we're talking erotic. If, however, the subjects seem reduced to so many body parts, if any beauty appears subordinate to the overriding purpose of arousal, if the sex depicted seems depersonalized, controlling, non-mutual, and devoid of fun or play ... and if the sex acts pictured contain not a hint of human caring or emotional connectedness to them—that, to me, would definitely secure the work's place in the realm of pornography.

Although Dr. Seltzer's points make sense, they still present a few problems. First, the criteria he lays out are "in the eye of the beholder." People can have different opinions about what is "depersonalized" or "devoid of fun" and what isn't. Second, Dr. Seltzer's criteria seem to pathologize "casual sex," sexuality that isn't "caring or emotional." Realistically, is that truly, always a problem? Without a doubt, the majority of people who do consider pornography a problem and are opposed to it are women. According to Val Richards in an article titled *Pornography—Safe or Sexual?* some feminist groups have made it their goal to ban pornography from being produced and consumed. Quoting feminists Catharine MacKinnon and

Andrea Dworkin, Richards defines pornography as the "graphic sexually explicit subordination of women." According to these feminists, pornography dehumanizes women as "sexual objects, things, or commodities," shows them "in postures of sexual submission," and reduces them to "body parts." The overriding theme of pornography is "utter contempt for women."

These feminist views of pornography clash in some part with Seltzer's definition because they are more one-sided. For pro-censorship feminists, pornography's only purpose is to objectify women as sex objects, but do most people watch pornography to see women objectified and debased, or because of the sex itself? To some extent, Val Richards's article provides valid information; however, some of the arguments presented make no sense. For example, in a very general way, Richards links pornography to sexual violence and sex crimes. She contends that "sex and violent crime offenders have a critical link to pornography," but common sense tells us there are more important factors affecting people who commit sex crimes than watching or reading pornography. A person within a normal range of mental and emotional balance is not likely to become a sex criminal simply because of using pornography.

At the end of the article, Richards is indecisive herself about whether or not to support censoring pornography, because the views of pro-censorship feminists collide with those of feminists who are opposed to censorship and believe "the fight against pornography is peripheral to feminist struggles." Richards ultimately seems to concede that adults should be free to make their own decisions.

Richards's views and concerns about pornography are mainly social and political. Other writers, like Naomi Wolf, see pornography as a more personal problem, and are concerned about how it affects intimacy between men and women, and the ways they interact with each other sexually. In *The Porn Myth*, Wolf rejects the idea of pornography turning men into "raving beasts." On the contrary, her concern is that it is "deadening the male libido" and making men less interested in real women. In Wolf's eyes, pornography has created a society unable to connect erotically. "Today," writes Wolf, "real naked women are just bad porn." Pornography has become the runway model of modern sexuality, presenting unrealistic standards for both sexes and distorting the way people judge their bodies, sexual performance, and the opposite sex. "Being naked is not enough; you have to be buff, be tan with no tan line, have the surgically hoisted breasts and the Brazilian bikini wax—just like porn stars" (Wolf). Now, according to Wolf, the missionary position, once "considered to be a huge turn-on," is rejected by most people, both male and female, because pornography has trivialized it. For the porn industry, it is not hot or graphic enough, so people think it's just not "cool" because imitating pornography is the way to go. Wolf embraces the value of the "mystery" that makes real sex thrilling, and thinks pornography has diluted it.

Unlike feminist views, Wolf's concerns potentially affect men as much as women. In a humorous documentary reviewed by *Variety*, actor, Patrick Moote, tells the story of being rejected by a woman he hoped to marry because, among other things, he did not meet her "size" requirements (Harvey). In reading about Moote's experience, I wondered if the girlfriend's criterion had anything to do with pornography. Everyone is aware of how most women are concerned about physical appearance and looking glamorous, not only to society, but especially to men. Even though some might disagree, men have similar concerns and insecurities. Most men worry about being attractive to women and able to please, and when it comes to sex, as male friends tell me, they look to the Internet and pornography for information and guidance. Of course, what they are seeing, in Naomi Wolf's words, is a supersized, "cybervision of perfection" that does not exist in the real world, but when people are told that something is true for so long, eventually it becomes true to them. Since males are no doubt the largest consumers of pornographic material, it possibly is affecting them even more negatively than women. What they see on the Internet or in a magazine is now what they think they want but can't have.

Nonetheless, whether we like it or not, for both women and men, there is a selfish and egotistical side to sexual feelings and desire. Sex is a biological drive. Pornography may kill eroticism by eliminating the "mystery" and opening the door to unrealistic and distorted expectations, but, when all is said and done, is sexuality in real life the complete opposite of pornography? Is every person on the planet having sex in committed relationships with stable partners they love? Of course not. Modern sex happens in varying consensual situations with varying degrees of intimacy, emotion, commitment, and even eroticism. Is this the effect pornography is having on people, or is pornography to some extent a reflection of what people actually do and sometimes even want?

I have asked my friends of different ages and genders what they find in pornography that attracts them, and have gotten many different answers in return. They say that pornography is a way of living a fantasy, of leaving the real world and entering one where they can vicariously live out their desires. Others say that you can learn from porn and become a better partner. Nevertheless, as Dr. Seltzer writes, pornography is essentially "animalistic." Do people want to make this type of sex their standard and ideal? For most people, sex is about more than just satisfying the desires of the flesh; there indeed should be a level of connection other than the physical. Pornography has no loving charm, no soulful eye contact; it doesn't have a journey of sensual discovery. It lacks the intimacy and complicity that is the essence of sexuality for most people. Therefore, it is not a good exemplification of what real and meaningful sex should be.

Naomi Wolf does not believe in a radical measure to ban pornography, but rather in creating a society that values what sex really is, not the fantasy that Adult Entertainment has created. Yet she, like every author I have cited in this essay, in one way or another, agrees that the use of pornography should be left to personal choice. Pornography may be impacting the sexual lives of those who watch it in more negative than positive ways, but it is not posing a threat to society. Its harmfulness depends on how people use the product and how often, and even on personal preferences and personality. The idea of passing a law that prohibits it, the way some feminists want, is unrealistic. The use of pornography is not criminal or immoral. It may be dehumanizing, unemotional, sometimes grotesque, and a mystery killer, but unfortunately, human sexuality isn't only about a sensual and spiritual connection, or inherently beautiful.

The real issue is that, regardless of what people think is morally correct, legal, or necessary for the betterment of society, human sexuality is not something that can be generalized into a simple definition. How can we find a reasonable solution to a problem that is so subjective and dependent on personal opinion? The answer is, we can't. Most people are capable of recognizing what is or is not good for them, what works for them and what doesn't, and what is hurtful or not hurtful to others. Therefore, I think the only solution to the problem is keep people intelligently informed about the effects pornography is having on our sexuality, and then leave it up to their judgment. ■

Works Cited

Harvey, Dennis. "Film Review: 'Unhung Hero'." *Variety*. Variety, 5 Dec. 2013. Web. 25 Feb. 2015.

Richards, Val. "Pornography—Safe or Sexual?" *Pornography—Safe or Sexual?* California State University, Northridge, 15 Apr. 1996. Web. 10 Feb. 2015. <http://www.csun.edu/~vcpsy00h/pornog.htm>.

Seltzer, Leon F. "What Distinguishes Erotica from Pornography?" *Psychology Today*. Psychology Today, 6 Apr. 2011. Web. 7 Feb. 2015.

Wolf, Naomi. "The Porn Myth." *New York Magazine*. New York Magazine, 20 Oct. 2003. Web. 5 Feb. 2015.

From Reflection to Response

Responding to "The Debate about Modern Sexuality and Pornography"

1. Throughout her essay, Arlet Montes examines different points of view, but she also expresses views of her own. What do you specifically see as the main view or argument she wants to support in the essay?

2. In analyzing articles by Naomi Wolf and Dr. Leon F. Seltzer, Montes seems to agree with many, if not all, of their views. What do you see as her main disagreement with them?

3. At one point in her essay, Montes argues that pornography may be victimizing men as much as women. How valid do you consider this argument? Why do you think she presents it?

Courtesy of Ziyue Chen

ZIYUE CHEN

The Long Leap

In this piece, I was trying to communicate that it is a long leap from college to career for fresh graduates.

CHAPTER EIGHT

Navigating Research Projects

 It's not that I'm so smart; it's just that I stay with problems longer.
—Albert Einstein

CHAPTER LEARNING OBJECTIVES

In this chapter, you will learn to:

▶ Design and plan a research project that reflects a professional process and professional research goals.

▶ Conduct preliminary research and pose significant research questions.

▶ Gather information using both primary and secondary sources.

▶ Evaluate and synthesize your sources.

▶ Compose a research narrative or other interim project to build a final paper or report.

▶ Incorporate and document sources professionally.

RESEARCH: LEARNING AND DISCOVERING TO SOLVE PROBLEMS

Research means learning and discovering to solve problems. Research and analysis ("R & A") drives progress and innovation in every field, but research is not a rarefied activity. All of us do it in our daily lives whenever we need information to solve problems that concern us. When we want to buy a car, a smartphone, or good running shoes, we talk to people and read articles and reviews in print magazines or online—in other words, we do research. As travelers, we research places to go, where to stay, and things to do. When we want to lose weight, we research diets or training regimens.

Passionate Inquiry

When the problems we address through research are important to us, research is exciting. People who engage in professional research—trying to find new treatments for cancer, understand the human brain, predict earthquakes, limit nuclear proliferation, or help combat veterans overcome trauma—are passionate about what they do. The passion behind their search for solutions is the secret to successful research and the key to completing meaningful research projects in college.

Many college professors assign research or term papers as "capstone" projects in their classes, because writing, research, and analysis require more depth of understanding and promote deeper learning than tests or exams. Research projects challenge students to engage in critical thinking and make professional contributions to solving the problems they investigate.

In upper-division classes across the disciplines, students are exposed to problems, controversies, and questions that have professional ramifications. In a psychology class, students explore theories of identity, abnormality, and behavior. In an architecture class, they delve into controversies about design, public space, construction methods, and sustainability. In an economics class, students grapple with questions about business cycles, monetary policies, public finance, deficits, free trade, and protectionism. The content of these classes steers students toward research problems of complexity and significance to their future careers.

First-year writing courses also have content that raises researchable controversies about language, writing, the literary arts, and communication. However, most writing students, although they care about writing skills and communication, do not have a *specialized* interest in the discipline. As a result, instructors in writing classes often set up interdisciplinary research projects that give students more latitude to research problems of interest to them. To make the most of the opportunity, a student needs to understand the learning objectives, and how a college research project reflects the goals and standards of professional research.

Transcending Topics

In secondary schools, research projects often focus on the procedures of research rather than the goals. Students write research papers that primarily condense information about a topic. To some extent, the research topic is irrelevant: it could be volcanoes, bronze tools, the whaling industry, buffaloes, or some shopworn controversy like subliminal messages, UFOs, or the existence of aliens in our midst. The purpose of the project is artificial. Students go through the motions of conducting research, but the main goal is to gather and condense information. The topics are too broad, trite, or moralistic to demand critical thinking or analysis.

If you have conducted artificial research like this in the past—projects that did little more than package other people's ideas and document them—do some mental spring cleaning before you start this project. As a useful first step, temporarily put aside the word "topic" from your vocabulary. Meaningful research projects are about problems more than topics—problems that ideally you feel passionate about and that have a bearing on your life or career goals. Table 8.1 illustrates the difference between projects that have vague, informational goals and projects on the same topic that are focused on problem solving.

TABLE 8.1 Transcending topics

Topic-Based Projects	Problem-Based Projects
Jefferson and Monticello Describes Jefferson's life on his famous estate and the role of slaves in its day-to-day operations.	**All men are created imperfectly** Defends Jefferson's rationalizations for owning slaves in the context of his time.
Method acting Traces the evolution of "method acting" from Stanislavski to Strasberg and the Actors Studio.	**Acting or attitudinizing: a reassessment of "method"** Argues that "method" is an overhyped school of acting that narrows the skill set of actors who practice it.
The concept that launched a thousand chains Explores the origins of fast-food franchises.	**Healthy choices or dietary disasters?** Demonstrates that the fast-food industry's new "healthy offerings" are not as healthy as advertised.
Lady Chatterley's Lover: anatomy of a banned book Revisits the checkered publication history of a controversial classic.	**Lady Chatterley's Lover: pornography disguised as art** Contends that Lawrence's homage to sexuality employs the contrivances of pornography (wooden characters, bad dialogue, and a preposterous story line).

As you think of research problems on which to base a project, consider these suggestions:

▶ Reject clichéd or moral controversies, unless you can think of a fresh, problem-solving angle for researching them.

▶ Ask yourself if you have a genuine interest in the research problem and if it has an impact on your life.

▶ Ask yourself if you can make a contribution to solving the problem and what that contribution could be.

▶ Consider whether or not you have any firsthand knowledge of the problem or exposure to it. (If you do, you have a better chance of making a meaningful contribution.)

▶ Consider whether you are willing to research the problem with an open mind—ask questions, examine opposing views, and engage in critical thinking.

From Reflection to Response   Generating Ideas

Working with two or three of your classmates, review the lists of public issues, problems, and controversies in Chapters 7 and 9 ("Arguments That Matter" and "Public Writing and Community Engagement," on pages 276–277 and 387, respectively). Choose one problem, and assume you are going to base your research project on it. Evaluate the project by addressing some of the questions below.

● How does the problem affect people's lives? Is it controversial? Why hasn't the problem been solved?

● What is the goal of your project? Keep in mind that people know how to find information when they need it, so just "informing" your audience usually is an insufficient goal. How will your project serve a problem-solving purpose? What can you contribute that has not already been said or is not already known?

● What personal knowledge do you have about the problem, and how will that knowledge apply to your research goal?

● What audience do you have in mind for your paper, essay, or report?

● Can you provide a preview of the reasons and evidence that you will present to support your main view or position?

● What legitimate opposing views or counterarguments can your readers possibly bring up? List counterarguments and how you will respond to them.

The Search Within

You have a better chance of identifying a meaningful research problem if you look within yourself and your own life before you look outside. The following are some suggestions for coming up with ideas:

▶ Think about *issues or problems you wrote about in previous assignments* for this course. For example, if you wrote a narrative essay about living with a condition like OCD or growing up as an itinerant military "brat," you could research this problem.

▶ Think about *problems related to your education*, past and present—homeschooling, standardized testing, college access, loans, and grade inflation. These are problems you know something about and that are relevant to many people.

▶ Think about *problems related to your academic major or your career interests*. If you are majoring in hospitality and want to work in the tourist industry, you could research ecotourism as a "niche market" and assess its prospects for growth.

▶ Think about *problems related to your personal life*—your family, upbringing, identity, or health. Maybe your parents were overly protective or strict, or you went through a period of delinquency, or you were "undocumented," suffer from depression, or have a learning disability. Problems like these are not just your own. Millions of people struggle with them. They merit research and analysis, to enhance understanding and move us toward solutions.

Public Issues and Controversies as Research Problems

If you cannot identify a research problem related to your life or career, think about public issues and controversies in the news. An excellent resource for coming up with ideas, as well as actually starting your research, is your library website and its listings of online databases. The library website can direct you to portals and databases, like *CQ Researcher* or *Student Resources in Context*, that provide rich information and perspectives on a range of issues and controversies.

News "aggregators" like *The Huffington Post* and *Techmeme* are excellent resources, or you can browse through traditional newspapers in print or online: the *New York Times*, your local paper, or your campus paper can be excellent sources of information.

Figure 8.1 shows a section of the *New York Times* opinion page (online). Notice the range of issues that the various editorials, commentaries, columns,

FIGURE 8.1 *New York Times* **opinion page**

Source: 2015 The New York Times Company

and blogs raise about science, health, finance, and politics. For example, the editorial "Time for TV in the Supreme Court" raises the issue of limited public access to the court's judicial proceedings. "Looking 'White' in the Face" and "A Conversation with White People on Race" both examine racism and white privilege. The article titled "Is Weed the New Almond" addresses California's water crisis and the impact that growing marijuana has on the environment. "Understanding the Incomprehensible with Music" describes the healing effects that listening to heavy metal had on a writer coping with unbearable grief.

College newspapers can be a good source of ideas, too. Figure 8.2 shows editorials posted on the website of a college newspaper. The editorials deal with a range of campus and community issues. For example, "Interdisciplinary Studies Are Important" argues that liberal arts studies are undervalued and should be accorded the same resources and respect as STEM studies (science, technology, engineering, and math). The editorial "Get a Grip: Don't Buy Pennyboards" analyzes the dangers of using cheaply made skateboards.

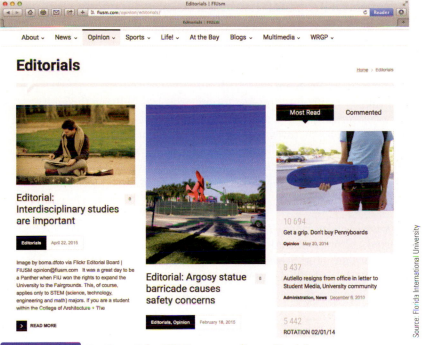

FIGURE 8.2 Section of the *FIU Beacon*, online editorials

A STUDENT'S ESSAY PROPOSAL

As you begin to design your research project, take a look at the proposal first-year student Amanda McDole wrote for her project, based on the following instructions:

This project calls for a researched essay, "paper," or report that supports a position on an issue or problem that is important to you.

The goal of your project is to investigate and try to solve the problem using factual information and objective analysis. Remember, good research incorporates the best available information and takes into consideration opposing views and perspectives that may not be aligned with your initial convictions or assumptions.

Research Proposal: Finding a Solution for Cyberbullying

Amanda McDole

1. Main Issue or Problem

The problem I will be addressing for my project is bullying through social networks. Children and teens use social networks to keep in touch with friends, post pictures, and blog, but in recent years social networks have become a tool for bullies to prey on victims. When bullying occurs online through the Internet, it is specifically known as cyberbullying. Cyberbullying is a growing problem among teens and children as young as 10 or 11 years old.

The *Journal of American Medicine* and independent research studies have reported a strong connection between bullying and adolescent suicides. In one famous incident, 14-year-old Jamey Rodemeyer committed suicide after being mercilessly bullied online by schoolmates who labeled him as being gay. According to *The Huffington Post*, Jamey's bullies were relentless, and even after his death, unrepentant. At a school dance shortly after Jamey took his own life, when a song by his favorite singer, Lady Gaga, was played, the bullies chanted, "We're glad you're dead."

Many more young people are socially humiliated and left feeling devastated because of hurtful words that are posted online and can be viewed by hundreds, or thousands, of people. Meanwhile, thanks to the Internet, bullies are more empowered than ever. They now have a way to take out their anger, get revenge, or just entertain themselves by attacking their victims, while hiding their identities behind a computer screen.

2. The Research Goal: Central Question (or Questions), the Provisional Thesis or Main Argument

Solving this problem requires finding ways to take power away from the bullies and make parents and educators more aware of the impact of the problem on young people's lives. Certainly, parents should be more involved in monitoring their children's use of social network sites. Schools can have an impact on the problem by offering mandatory bullying classes, and perhaps training teachers to recognize the problem and intervene. Among the questions I want to answer through my research is whether or not bullies are the main source of the problem or whether the main source is social networking itself, and young people's inability to use social networks responsibly.

3. Reasons for Selecting This Issue

This issue is compelling to me because I went through it. I know what it feels like to read hurtful things people write out of anger or spite. As a victim, I was not even aware I was being bullied; it was the people around me, including my true friends, who told me, and said that I needed to address what was going on and find help. Since that time in my life, I have adopted a strong stance against online bullying. While the main focus of my project will be on helping victims, I also want to find out why bullies choose to hurt others like this. Being able to hide behind a computer screen makes it easy, but I think there is more to it. Finding answers through this research project will further my understanding, and also help give me closure on the experience I had when I was younger.

4. Intended Audience and Reader-Relevance

The audience that I'm writing for may narrow as my project develops, but initially I am targeting a general audience of teachers, parents, school administrators, and mental-health professionals who have responsibilities for children's well-being. I think many adults don't realize the extent of the harm that cyberbullying can have on victims, because most of the time it goes unnoticed or is classified as harmless "drama" that everyone deals with.

5. Research Methods and Sources

For primary research, I plan to interview young people who have experienced this problem. I will also try to get firsthand perspectives on the problem from parents, teachers, and mental-health professionals who have dealt with it.

My secondary sources will include journal articles written by professionals, and stories published in magazines and newspapers. I will also look at some recent documentaries that deal with cyberbullying and ways of responding to the problem. Below are a few sources I have obtained through preliminary research:

> "Cyberbullying." *Opposing Viewpoints in Context Online Collection.* Detroit: Gale, 2015. Web. 28 Apr. 2015.
>
> Hazler, Richard J. *Breaking the Cycle of Violence: Interventions for Bullying and Victimization.* Washington, DC: Accelerated Development, 1996. Print.
>
> Michelson, Noah. "Jamey Rodemeyer Still Being Bullied After His Death Say Tim And Tracy Rodemeyer (VIDEO)." *The Huffington Post.* TheHuffingtonPost.com, 27 Sept. 2011. Web. 28 Apr. 2015.
>
> Miller, Marissa. "The RIGHT Way to Handle Social Media Harassment and Bullying." *Teenvogue.* Condé Nast, 10 Apr. 2015. Web. 28 Apr. 2015.

Neumann, Roger. "Cyberbullies Ramp Up the Taunting—Anonymously." *Social Networking*. Ed. Kenneth Partridge. New York: H. W. Wilson, 2011. 150–54. Print.

Rigby, Ken. *New Perspectives on Bullying*. Philadelphia: Jessica Kingsley, 2002. Print.

Interview with the Student Writer

● **Tell us a little about your background, interests, college major, and career goals.**

Courtesy of Amanda McDole

● I am a senior at Florida International University, majoring in health administration and minoring in sociology. I currently am a very involved student leader as a LEAD Team captain for the Greek Academy of Leaders program and student director for the Alternative Breaks program. I have a strong interest in service and leadership opportunities for students at the university. As a result, my career goals include returning to FIU to help expand programs that have helped me and other students reach their full potential.

● **Coming into college, how did you see yourself as a writer? Had you done much writing on your own or completed any major writing projects in high school? What did you see as your strengths and weaknesses as a writer?**

● Coming into college, I did not see myself as a writer. I had not completed many writing projects throughout high school except as a yearbook editor. I enjoyed writing because it has always been an area that I excelled in without much effort. I saw my strengths as being creative and genuinely enjoying writing. My biggest weakness has always been organizing my thoughts to be cohesive.

● How did you come up with your idea for your project on cyberbullying? Did you consider other ideas?

● The idea for the project came to mind when the professor mentioned some examples of past work that students had done. One of the examples was a young man who talked about a life experience he had, what he went through, and what he would do to improve the system. After hearing that, I definitely wanted to talk about my experience with cyberbullying, although I had reservations about whether I wanted my classmates to know about this experience. I considered other ideas but I decided to stay with the bullying issue, because ultimately it gave me closure to write about my experience.

Working Together

EVALUATING STUDENT TOPICS

Below are titles of research projects that students proposed to conduct in a first-year writing class. Working with two or three of your classmates, go through the list and discuss what each title suggests about the student's project and research objectives. Based on criteria covered in this chapter, rate each project on a scale of 1 to 5 (1 being the lowest rating and 5 the highest). Then share your reasons for the rating with the rest of the class—why you think a particular project sounds compelling, relevant, meaningful, *or not*?

- "Does Video Gaming Hinder Academic Success?"
- "Eating Disorders and the Effects on Brain Functions"
- "Psychedelic Drugs: Doors of Perception or Cheap Thrills?"
- "The Benefits of Virginity Before Marriage"
- "America: A Terrorist Nation?"
- "Why People Hate Cops"
- "Are Children of Divorced Parents More Prone to Depression?"
- "Bulimia: Body-Image Problem or Disease?"
- "Smoking During Pregnancy: The Effects"
- "Facebook Addiction"

DEVELOPING AND IMPLEMENTING A RESEARCH PLAN

Because a research project takes time and effort, having a clear plan and realistic timeline is crucial. Once you choose a research problem, develop a plan that includes the following steps:

▶ **Identify your audience:** Who are your readers, and what is their relationship to the problem you will address? What are they likely to know, not know, and most care about? Research writing usually is for an educated and specialized audience in a given field. Those are the readers you should keep in mind as you proceed with your research and writing. For this writing project, you don't have to worry about writing a paper or report that is of interest to *everyone*.

▶ **Define your purpose and goal:** What do you want to accomplish through your research?

▶ **Write a provisional thesis:** In the planning stage, researchers also can begin with an assumption or provisional thesis. Starting with a provisional thesis is similar to formulating a hypothesis in the sciences: the researcher has to test the thesis with evidence and answer key questions. A provisional thesis gives a project a useful direction and focus, but only to the extent that the researcher is prepared to follow the evidence and modify, or reject, the original assumption if it turns out to be flawed. Being a good researcher means being willing to adjust or change your view based on findings. Below is an example of a provisional thesis:

- Corporal punishment has a legitimate role in disciplining children.

▶ **Develop research questions:** A research project raises questions about a problem and a hypothesis like the one above. The researcher tries to answer the questions and support an argument that moves the problem toward a solution. In the planning stage, thoughtful questions give research projects a direction and goal. Below are questions a student asked in starting a project on corporal punishment of young children.

- Is corporal punishment a legitimate form of discipline? Does it do more harm than good?
- What emotional or psychological effects does it have on the child?
- What distinguishes punishment from abuse?
- What other methods of disciplining children are available? Are these methods effective? What if they don't work?

▶ **Determine your research sources:** What primary and secondary sources will you use to meet your research goal?

▶ **Create a schedule:** What is the time frame for the project? List target dates for important stages of the project, including any interim assignments (for example, an annotated bibliography) that you are given.

From Reflection to Response   From Topics to Problems

Below is a list of general topics. Working with two or three of your classmates, go through the list and identify *one general topic* that you consider interesting and worthy of research, and then narrow and shape the topic as follows:

1. Identify problems related to the topic.

2. Make a list of questions that a researcher would have to answer in order to investigate the problems and find solutions.

3. Make a list of possible arguments (provisional thesis statements) that a researcher could support in order to give the project a problem-solving direction.

After you finish the activity, discuss your narrowing process with the rest of your class.

General Topics

- Pets
- Organic fruits and vegetables
- Jobs
- Politics
- Popular music

- Space exploration
- Virtual reality
- Advertising
- Education

CONDUCTING RESEARCH

As you may recall from previous writing projects, research breaks down into two methods of collecting information: primary research and secondary. Primary research—also called "field research"—means using information you gather firsthand—that is, from interviews, surveys, observations, or original documents (letters, photographs, memoirs, and so on). Secondary research is based on work other people have done, usually work that is published in books and articles.

In many professional fields, researchers use primary methods and sources more than secondary, because primary research usually is more timely and adaptable to the specific problems driving the research. Using primary research for your project will bring your research to life, give it more of a human dimension, and get you away from your desk. Beyond that, it will give you an opportunity to make original contributions.

With that said, primary research has its drawbacks. It takes time to prepare and conduct. Interviews need to be scheduled in advance. Surveys have to be drafted thoughtfully and then disseminated. It takes time for responses to come in and more time to analyze the results. In addition, the value of the primary research you conduct can be unpredictable and sometimes disappointing. For these reasons, even though primary research can enrich your project, don't rely on it exclusively. Include secondary sources in your research plan, and in most cases, launch your project with secondary sources, to insure that it gets off to a productive start. (For more on conducting primary research, see Chapter 14 in Part III, pages 597–600.)

In planning a project, you usually need to do preliminary research to find out if enough quality sources are available to move your project forward. Preliminary research does not need to be thorough. Its purpose is to give you an overview of available sources you can start to collect and examine.

To conduct preliminary research, use previously mentioned resources like *CQ Researcher* and your library's catalogues, databases, and indexes. You also can do general Internet searches using sites like Google/Google Scholar or more specialized sites like Science.gov or the Library of Congress online index and catalogue. Figure 8.3 shows the results from a preliminary online search of a library collection for a project on cyberbullying. Online library collections like this provide a lot of information about available resources, including basic information about the resource—author, title, and publication information— but also information about the format of the resource (e-book, book, and so on) and a brief summary of the resource. This makes it easy to locate the right resources quickly.

Despite the availability of online resources, visiting the library in person is still a good option for conducting research because college libraries have research librarians who can help you get the most out of the library's resources. In addition, browsing the shelves and physically looking over books, periodicals, and bibliographies can give you more specific and useful information than you will find in electronic abstracts and indexes. Chapter 14, in Part III, offers more information about working with many common library sources. Table 8.2 lists primary and secondary sources that researchers most commonly use.

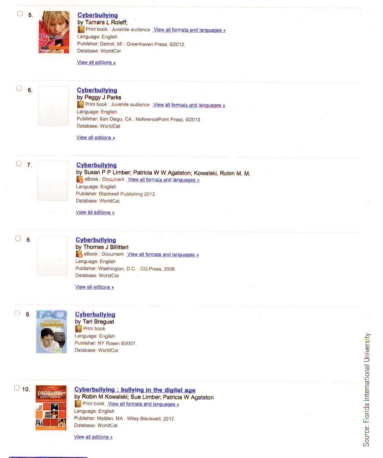

FIGURE 8.3   **Library collection: preliminary search results on cyberbullying**

Source: Florida International University

Tech Tip

As you conduct preliminary research, create a "bookmark" folder in your web browser's "favorites" menu, to help you keep track of relevant websites you visit. Bookmarking useful websites and keeping the links in one place will make it much easier to find the sites when needed.

TABLE 8.2 Primary and secondary sources

Primary Research	Secondary Research
Field Research	*Common Sources of Secondary Research*
• Personal interviews	• Scholarly books, journal articles, and critical reviews
• Surveys, questionnaires, and focus groups	• Commercial books for popular or general audiences
• Site visits and observations	• Reference books
• Case studies	• Magazine articles and reviews
• Oral histories and testimonials	• Newspaper articles (but some news stories and eyewitness accounts can be considered primary sources)
• Online discussion boards	
Primary Source Materials	• Government documents
• Speeches, performances	• Business studies
• Personal letters, diaries, memoirs, eyewitness accounts	• Newsletters
• Creative works (poems, song lyrics, novels, stories, designs, drawings, etc.)	• Blogs and sponsored websites
• Various forms of raw data—census information, market research, pilot studies, lab experiments, etc.	• Documentary films

Wikipedia: A Useful Preliminary Resource?

Professional researchers consider the Internet encyclopedia Wikipedia a questionable resource, because to some extent, the entries can be written and edited by anyone. As a result, the information may be inaccurate, oversimplified, or spotty. For that reason, many college professors ask students not to use Wikipedia as a research source.

Nevertheless, Wikipedia has some undeniable virtues that have made it a popular landmark on the Internet: it is accessible and easy to use; and the entries are timely, though they tend to be limited in scope, and they extend to almost every topic imaginable. Those virtues don't override the site's limitations, but they make Wikipedia a logical and useful place to conduct *preliminary research* for a project—a place to start collecting background information, along with dates, initial perspectives, potential references, and source material, all of which you will reevaluate, fact-check, and move beyond as your research progresses.

Today, Wikipedia articles are posted with verification warnings and status alerts that help readers judge the reliability of the information (see Figure 8.4).

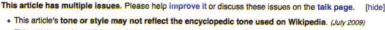

This article has multiple issues. Please help improve it or discuss these issues on the talk page.   [hide]

- This article's tone or style may not reflect the encyclopedic tone used on Wikipedia. *(July 2009)*
- This article needs additional citations for verification. *(December 2008)*
- This article is an orphan, as no other articles link to it. Please introduce links to this page from related articles; try the Find link tool for suggestions. *(December 2008)*
- The topic of this article may not meet Wikipedia's general notability guideline. *(December 2008)*

Source: wikipedia.com

FIGURE 8.4 **Wikipedia verification warnings**

Many Wikipedia articles identify sources (under "References") and provide links and cross-references to related subjects, sites, and readings (see Figure 8.5). Articles in Wikipedia tend to emphasize popular sources—sponsored websites and newspaper and magazine articles—more than scholarly articles, but many of the sources are verifiable and credible.

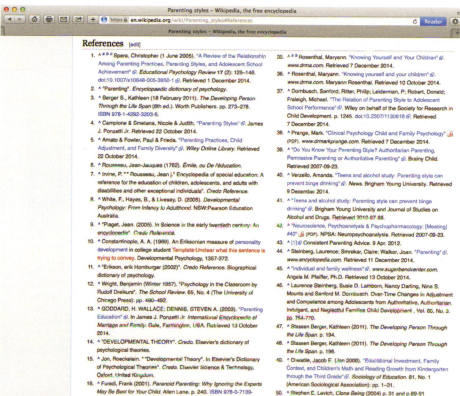

FIGURE 8.5 **Wikipedia references for an entry on parenting styles**

Wikipedia's greatest virtue is its comprehensiveness. Many subjects of recent, emerging, obscure, minor, or specialized importance, which are rarely covered in traditional encyclopedias, are included in Wikipedia. For example, Wikipedia contains an entry devoted to the video game *BioShock* (see Figure 8.6). Wikipedia provides detailed information about the game, its development, and its popularity, along with a list of references and links (see Figure 8.7), including a link to an entry about the designer of the game, Ken Levine, a former drama student and screenwriter. The Ken Levine entry, in turn, links to interviews in which Levine discusses his vision of the game and its characters. Traditional encyclopedias would not supply information as extensive as this about a specific game like *BioShock*.

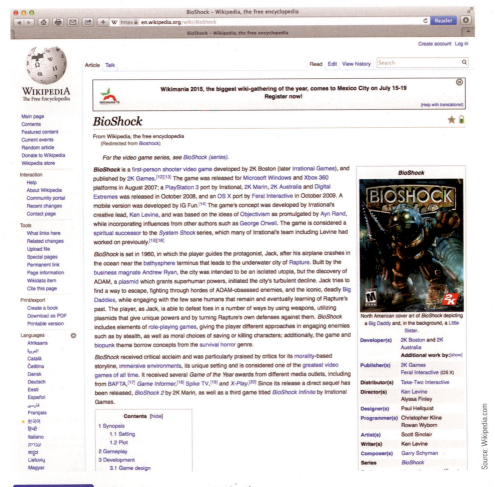

Source: Wikipedia.com

FIGURE 8.6   **Wikipedia entry for *BioShock***

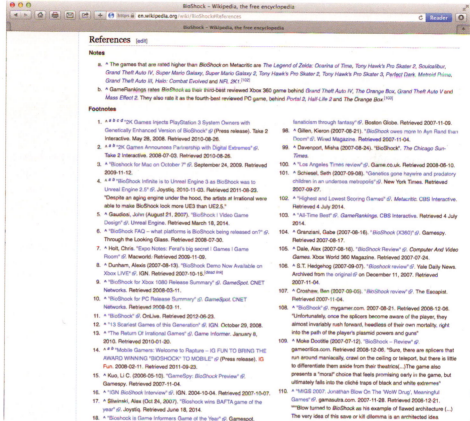

FIGURE 8.7 **Wikipedia references for *BioShock* entry**

From Reflection to Response   Finding Available Sources

Working from home or in your campus library, do some preliminary research for basic information *about one* of the general topics below. After learning more about the topic, identify at least one problem, controversy, or question that the topic raises. Then compile a list of five secondary sources that you could use to begin a research project. List the sources alphabetically in MLA style.

- The Hadron Collider (and/or Higgs Boson)
- Cell phone jammers
- Greenpeace
- Financial derivatives

- Rem Koolhaas
- The Flynn effect
- Visualization in sports
- Anomie theory

WRITING A PROPOSAL

Once you have a research plan in place and have done preliminary research, your instructor may ask you to submit a written proposal for your project. Writing a proposal will help you clarify the purpose and goals of the project. Compose your proposal in *business style*, using the section headings below (numbered or bulleted), block paragraphs, and single-spacing.

1. Main Issue or Problem. Describe the issue or problem that your research project will focus on and attempt to resolve.

2. The Research Goal: Central Question (or Questions), the Provisional Thesis or Main Argument. Present a key question or set of questions that you will attempt to answer through your research. If you have a provisional view, thesis, or argument that you intend to support, explain what it is and why you hold that view.

    Elaborate on any **counterarguments or opposing views** you will address in your project.

3. Reason for Selecting This Issue. Explain why your research problem is compelling and important to you. Is it relevant to your career interests or your academic major? Do you have a personal connection to the problem? Describe what you already know about the problem and its importance or consequences for other people.

4. Intended Audience and Reader-Relevance. Describe your intended audience and discuss the relevance of your project to this audience.

5. Research Methods and Sources. Make a preliminary list of the sources you intend to use—primary as well as secondary.

WRITING A ROUGH DRAFT

As you start drafting your paper, essay, or report, you will need to consider how you manage your time; organize your notes, findings, and source material; and convert notes, a rough outline, and annotations into a coherent document or text.

Managing Your Time

The time frame allotted for college research projects varies in different classes, but since research by nature is time-consuming, two scheduling principles invariably apply.

1. Get started right away—that is, begin gathering and analyzing information as soon as your instructor approves your project.

2. Write and research at the same time. As you conduct your research, keep detailed notes, and start planning and drafting your final paper while your research is still underway.

Taking Detailed Notes

Research and writing go together. If you take ample and detailed notes as you conduct research, you are moving your project forward. If not, you are setting yourself up for frustration and poor results. There are no rules or set procedures for note-taking. People do it in ways that suit them, but here are a few general suggestions that make sense for everyone.

1. Consolidate your notes somewhere, preferably in an electronic file that is backed up to safeguard against a time-consuming loss.

2. Create full citations for your sources as you go along. Having full citations in your notes will make it easy to compile a working bibliography, a Works Cited list (MLA), or list of References (APA) when the time comes. If you keep your notes in a word-processing file, you also can take advantage of the citation-maker tools that many word-processing programs offer. These tools will help you create citations, save them for your project, and later create an accurate Works Cited or References list for your final paper.

3. Write detailed comments about your sources. If your notes are detailed, much of the content will find its way into your final paper and contribute to your writing process. However, as you take notes, be careful to distinguish between your own comments and the words and ideas of your sources. Otherwise, you might run into citation or plagiarism problems later.

Below is a full citation, followed by a student's notes about the source.

Donnelly, Michael and Murray A. Straus. *Corporal Punishment of Children in Theoretical Perspective*. New Haven: Yale UP, 2005. 1–5. Print.
    The beginning of this book defines corporal punishment as "the use of physical force with the intention of causing a child to experience

pain, but not injury, for the purpose of correcting or controlling the child's behavior." I can use this definition of corporal punishment for my project. According to the authors, physical punishment includes spanking, slapping, or grabbing. If the punishment is administered with an object, the chances of injury come into the picture. So the use of an object might be the dividing line between punishment and abuse.

Taking thoughtful notes while you conduct research helps develop content for your final paper, but going from notes to a draft of the paper is still a big step, especially when you are under pressure to meet an assignment deadline.

You can make the transition from research to writing more seamless and efficient if you start drafting your final paper while still conducting the research. When you conduct research without drafting, it can be hard to gauge your progress. In today's "information age," conducting research on almost any subject can go on forever. There is always more information available, other angles to explore. Many scholarly projects never see the light of day because of this problem. A project lingers in a state of perpetual exploration, because the scholar does too much reading and never starts drafting the book, article, or dissertation.

Drafting as you conduct your research helps move the project forward and keeps you focused on your main goal—writing a paper that presents your findings and conclusions. Since research papers use a formal structure, composing the paper while the research is still in progress is a straightforward process.

Writing and Style

A successful research project is about the researcher as much as the research problem itself. A researcher is someone trying to make a difference by acquiring and analyzing information. Sources are a means to an end. A researcher absorbs information from sources and, using her analysis, transforms it into a unique perspective.

Researchers who fail to transform information, and merely stitch together extracts of other people's words and ideas, produce uninteresting work. Their papers and essays amount to verbal "link farms" of source material. This kind of writing is called "patchwriting." A "patch written" essay has no style, voice, or originality. It is to writing what bad karaoke is to singing. In addition, it sometimes crosses over into plagiarism (see pages 346–348 for an example), but even when it technically does not, patchwriting is a mindless way to write, and it is painful to read. Good researchers take ownership of their projects and put their own analysis and voice at the center of the papers they write.

Unfortunately, even many published, professional researchers fail to pay enough attention to their style and readers. If you read articles in academic and professional journals, sooner or later (usually sooner) you will come across one written in a "style" that borders on being incomprehensible—something along these lines:

The Impending Eschatology of Pre-Binary, Academic Discourse: A Metacontextualization of Papillion's Peripatetic Interlocutor

by Sig Lemanski

While the generation, dissemination and promotion of nascent scholarship and knowledge still constitute the benchmark objectives of post-binary academic research, the concept/models and forums of scholarly discourse and intercourse continue to include, and not preclude, traditional lecture series, symposiums, conferences, colloquia, workshops, retreats, after-hours "interfacing," and of course, the preeminent modality and repository of semiotic interlocution for academicians and practitioners alike, viz., the peer-reviewed journal.*

Journal articles are considered sources of quality for reasons already discussed. They are especially good sources for college students because the articles are research papers themselves and can serve as models for student papers. Unfortunately, however, many journal articles are written in a dense style that is hard to read. Specialized language or technical terms are necessary in scholarly articles, but often the readability problems result from careless writing, rather than the complexity of the material.

In an article titled "Do Your Job Better," Rachel Toor, a professor at Eastern Washington University, takes her fellow academics to task "for writing prose that is nearly unintelligible, not just to the general public, but also to graduate students and fellow academics." Toor goes on to say "that poor scholarly writing is the result of bad habits" and "lazy thinking."

---

*A parody.

Don't model your research writing on a dense, unfriendly style. Good writers write to communicate and always "talk" to their readers, whether writing for an academic or a general audience. With that said, research papers focus on objective analysis and evidence, rather than personal expression. An objective style that avoids the use of the first-person "I" except for references to the writer's personal experiences is appropriate for research writing. However, an objective style is a product of objective thinking, not verbiage.

Completing Interim Assignments

Since research projects take longer to complete than most essay assignments, your instructor may give you interim assignments to do before your final paper. These assignments will help keep you on schedule. They also give your instructor a chance to monitor your progress and offer guidance. Common interim assignments include the following:

- ► A research log, journal, or field notes
- ► An annotated bibliography
- ► A review of literature
- ► A documented research narrative or exploratory essay
- ► An oral presentation

The next few pages provide information about some of these assignments.

The Annotated Bibliography An annotated bibliography is a list of sources you are using, along with notes or comments about each source (also called "annotations"). The notes consist of at least a description of the source. You also can include an evaluation of the source and an analysis of its relevance to your project, as the student does in commentary on corporal punishment (see pages 331–332). In an annotated bibliography, the sources usually are listed alphabetically, using the citation style appropriate for your project (MLA in most first-year writing courses). Below are entries from student Amanda McDole's annotated bibliography on cyberbullying:

Rigby, Ken. *New Perspectives on Bullying*. Philadelphia: Jessica Kingsley, 2002. Print.
    This book has statistics on bullying in different countries, and examines the causes of bullying. The book offers insights into the prevalence of bullying, and the personalities of victims, as well as the bullies themselves. I have only read parts of the book so far. However,

the information is extensive, and will suggest useful approaches to addressing and resolving the bullying problem.

Family Safety Center. Facebook, 2011. Web. 25 Mar. 2015. <https://www.facebook.com/safety>.

In doing my research, I found that Facebook has joined in on keeping minors safe and informing parents about cyberbullying and other online dangers. I never knew this feature on Facebook existed. I think it is an excellent resource for helping to resolve the cyberbullying problem. "Safety Center" provides special safety engineers who work with the users of this site to create ways for Facebook to be a safe environment. This site offers valuable advice and tools that apply to my research problem.

Teens Against Bullying. Pacer.org, 2006. Web. 5 Mar. 2015.

This is a website that contains an abundance of information about bullying and teens, including polls, helpful tips, useful links, and personal stories from ordinary people and celebrities (teens can choose to share their stories but remain anonymous). All of this information addresses my goal of finding solutions to the problem.

A Research Narrative or Exploratory Essay

A research narrative, sometimes called an exploratory essay, is a first-person "story" about your research project and the sources you have consulted. The narrative serves as a progress report and helps you build your final research paper.

A research narrative is similar in some ways to an annotated bibliography or review of literature: it involves an analysis and evaluation of sources and *calls for formal documentation*, but it is a personal essay as well that follows the chronology of the project and your research from its inception up to the time of the writing. The writer describes and evaluates the research experience informally—that is, "thinks out loud" about findings, obstacles, different perspectives, and the progress toward a thesis or solution. See the "Additional Readings" at the end of this chapter for an example of a student's research narrative. There is no fixed template for organizing a research narrative, but if your instructor assigns one, the outline below provides useful guidelines.

▶ *Opening*: Good narratives start with a compelling presentation of an issue or problem that draws readers into the story. A good research narrative starts the same way. Make your readers care about the issue or problem driving your project. Since a research narrative is written in the first person, explain your source of interest in the problem and your connection to it. Amplify on its relevance to your readers, society, or people in general. Consider formulating your research goal in the opening and presenting a key question or questions that you will attempt to answer through your research. Doing this will give your readers a clear sense of what you want to accomplish, and it will make your narrative resemble an intriguing quest or detective story.

▶ *Middle*: The middle section of your narrative will review the research that you have done to date—in other words, analyze chronologically your most noteworthy sources and what you've learned from them. To be compelling, this part of the essay needs to be more than a summary of information. It should engage the reader in the progress of your inquiry and demonstrate you are delving into the complexities of the problem, evaluating the sources, and considering different points of view.

▶ *End*: The ending of the narrative should provide closure for the reader— not necessarily a thesis or solution to the research problem, but an indication that you have moved the project forward in a meaningful way. Typically, the ending will evaluate how close you are to a final thesis, what you expect the thesis to be, and what research remains to be done to support it. If your inquiry is still inconclusive and you cannot formulate or forecast a final thesis or solution yet, your ending can include questions that you still need to answer, along with plans for ongoing research.

Finally, remember that the narrative should identify and document all of your sources within the text in MLA style and include a Works Cited list at the end.

Oral Presentations Giving a short, oral presentation about your project to classmates and your instructor is an excellent way to gauge your progress and the value of the project to an audience. (For more about oral presentations, see Chapter 15 in MindTap online.) Your oral research presentation is a progress report about your project for your classmates and instructor. Areas to cover include the following:

1. Your source of interest in the problem you are researching.

2. Your audience and the relevance of the problem to your audience and/or the general public.

3. Your research goal and key questions that you are trying to answer.

4. Your primary and secondary sources and what you've learned from them.

5. Your progress toward a solution—in other words, a final proposal or thesis that you expect to support in your research paper.

The presentation should be an informal "talk" to your audience. However, consider distributing a handout or using visual aids—projecting a PowerPoint or photographs, for example—to enhance your talk. In professional life, these kinds of enhancements are a must.

Formal Organization and Proportions

In most disciplines, research papers use a formal pattern of organization. In other words, the central issue or problem, as well as the thesis or main argument, is presented early in the paper. The rest of the paper focuses on supporting the thesis.

Thus, research papers can be broken down into two essential parts.

1. The opening, or introduction which presents the research problem and the central thesis, argument, or solution.

2. The thesis support—in other words, the evidence and analysis that supports the central thesis, argument, or solution.

The opening or introduction, is a blueprint for the whole paper. The opening presents the research problem *and* the thesis or argument that the paper will support. The rest of the paper—the "thesis support" (sometimes called "justification")—includes your review of counterarguments, along with all of the evidence and reasons in support of your thesis (or main argument), and the conclusions of your research. This part of the paper is the more substantial of the two parts, usually 80 to 90 percent of the content.

A detailed template for organizing formal essays is provided in Chapter 7, on pages 282–283. You also might find it helpful to review the template for creating an informal outline in Chapter 3 on pages 83–85. An informal outline is a working blueprint of what will go into your paper or essay. Creating an informal outline and updating it as you go along can make your drafting and revising process more efficient and keep you from getting lost or overwhelmed.

In the academic world, most research writing is done in the form of papers, articles, or essays. In business and professional life, research findings often are delivered in the form of reports. The most challenging and in-depth professional reports serve a problem-solving purpose—that is, they address a problem that an agency, company, business, or other organization is dealing with and needs to solve. The writer or writers of the report use research and analysis to come up with solutions. In this respect, professional reports are similar to good research papers. However, reports are formatted differently for efficient reading—typically in clearly labeled sections that separate the information and make the findings more accessible. They also tend to put more emphasis on using visual enhancements.

Because reports are so common in the workplace, your instructor might ask you to write a research report for your project, instead of a traditional paper. If so, you can use the format below. It reflects qualities of professional reports but also the content and features associated with academic research papers—that is, a presentation of the research problem; a thesis statement or solution; a discussion of counterarguments and opposing views; thesis support; formal, in-text citations; and a Works Cited list in MLA style. Amanda McDole's research findings on cyberbullying are delivered in the form of a research report (see pages 357–365). For examples of more traditional academic research papers or essays, see the paper titled "A World of Possibilities" by Elizabeth Carls (in MindTap online) or Brian Lawrence's essay, "The Truth about Atheists," featured in Chapter 7 on pages 291–299.

Format for a Research Report:
Outline of Sections and Headings

Instructions

▶ *Compose the report in business style*—in other words, use single-spacing and block paragraphs.

▶ *Include appropriate visual illustrations*—photographs, charts, drawings.

▶ *Cite your sources in MLA style.* Use lead-ins and signal phrases to identify sources in the text. Include parenthetical citations when required and a correctly formatted Works Cited list at the end.

Sections and Headings

1. Letter of Transmittal or Statement of Purpose and Audience

- For this section, write a "letter of transmittal" that puts your report in the "hands" of a specific person or organization with a vested interest in your research and an ability to act on it—for example, a public official or the head of a nonprofit organization. A letter of transmittal gives your report a realistic purpose and audience. The letter should be concise but also compelling. It should be professionally written and formatted. (See a writing handbook or online resource like the Purdue OWL for more information about formatting a business letter.)

- If you cannot identify a specific person, agency, or organization for whom your report is relevant and useful, you can write a detailed overview of the purpose and audience for your report. This overview should be professionally written, realistic, and persuasive.

- Approximate section length: half a page to one page.

2. The Central Problem, Issue, or Questions
- This section of the report presents the problem, issue, and/or questions driving your research. Make the problem as interesting, compelling, real, and relevant as possible. Use examples and facts to substantiate and highlight the problem.

- This section of the report is similar to the opening or introduction of an academic research paper. You are trying to get the reader invested in reading. You also are trying to establish your credibility through clear writing and an intelligent presentation of the material.

- Approximate length: one or two pages or more.

3. Thesis, Argument, Solution, or Proposal
- This section presents the central thesis, argument, or solution that the rest of the report will support.

- Along with the thesis, include a brief preview or "map" of the supporting evidence you will develop in detail later in the report (section 5 below).

- Approximate length: half a page or more.

4. Opposing Views and Counterarguments
- In this section, examine views or arguments that run counter to your thesis or solution yet have some merit and relevance.

- By raising opposing views and counterarguments, you enrich the scope of your research and enhance your credibility as a researcher. You demonstrate to readers that you have an intelligent grasp of the problem and that you are committed to realistic problem solving rather than defending a preconceived or narrow view.

- Keep this section relatively short. If you raise an opposing view that requires lengthy examination and analysis, you can revisit it in the body of your report (in other words, section 5).

- Approximate length: one page (or slightly more).

5. Thesis Support or Justification (Body)

- This is the main and longest part of your report. It will include all the ideas, arguments, facts, examples, and statistics that support and justify your thesis, argument, or solution.

- In supporting your thesis, you are trying to present a strong case—similar to what an attorney does in court. Organize your support so that it builds to a conclusion or climax.

- If possible, use visual illustrations to enhance the support (for example, photographs, charts, drawings, and so on). Consider using subheadings within this section, to break down the supporting evidence. *Make sure that all your sources are identified and documented in correct MLA style.*

- Approximate length: five to ten pages.

6. Conclusion (Optional)

- If you have said everything you need to say in the body of your report, skip this section. In a relatively short report, summarizing your main points is not necessary. Intelligent readers will remember them.

- However, if you have final thoughts or recommendations that you have not expressed as yet, put them in this section.

- Approximate length: half a page.

7. Works Cited List

- Conclude your report with a correctly formatted Works Cited list of all your sources on a separate page.

- The list should be alphabetized in MLA format.

- See a writing handbook for details.

Writing the Opening

If you conceive your project around a problem you care about, you will know enough about the problem to draft a description of it as you begin conducting research. Eventually, you will learn more about the problem, and you can go back and add examples and statistics that will make your presentation of the problem more compelling.

As for drafting a thesis, you may not know your exact thesis until you finish your research. At an early stage of the project, a question driving your research can serve as a thesis (sometimes called a "thesis question"). For example:

> Is corporal punishment a legitimate method of disciplining children?

In your final paper, you should replace the question with a thesis statement that essentially answers the question. (In academic papers, a question is considered an inadequate thesis.)

A second option for an initial thesis is to put forth a provisional argument, as described earlier in the chapter, and as you go along, revise the argument as needed to match your research findings.

A provisional thesis might read something like this:

> When used judiciously, corporal punishment can be a beneficial method of disciplining children.

The final thesis might be more qualified:

> Some psychologists still condone corporal punishment for disciplining an obstreperous child, but the clinical evidence suggests that corporal punishment is ultimately ineffective and psychologically damaging.

Whether your thesis evolves as the answer to a question or from a provisional view, make sure your final thesis is assertive and thought-provoking. Although research papers are for specialized readers, you still have to earn your readers' trust and attention. A weak thesis that states the obvious, doesn't put forth a compelling argument, or isn't clearly worded, tells readers that you haven't done your job.

Some questions to consider in evaluating your final thesis are as follows:

▶ Does it present an argument or offer a solution to the research problem? Does the argument or solution need to be defended, proven, or supported? Are there valid counterarguments to consider? (Valid counterarguments usually are a good indicator of the relevance of a thesis.)

▶ Is the thesis interesting? Does it present an idea that is new or surprising? Does it give an intelligent reader something to think about and a reason to continue to read?

▶ Is the wording clear?

▶ Is the thesis specific enough to be supported in a paper, or is it too broad—more of a book-length topic?

As you compose a thesis for your paper, you might want to review the section on thesis statements in Chapter 3, pages 90–94.

From Reflection to Response   Evaluating a Thesis

If you have read the section titled "Thesis Statements" in Chapter 3, you know the idea of a thesis as a single, independent statement is to some extent a contrivance. In many published articles, a nuanced and thought-provoking thesis is often expressed as a sequence of related points over several sentences or more. Yet there is something to be said for conveying the essence of your thesis in a clear, self-contained sentence.

A list of single-sentence thesis statements follows. Working with two or three classmates, go through the list and decide which statements are effective and which are not. In evaluating the statements, consider whether or not they set up an interesting investigation, a paper worth reading. After you finish reviewing the statements, discuss your evaluations with the rest of your class:

- A workaholic's distorted priorities have less to do with status and success than escaping anxiety.

- This paper will consider the effects of media on "anorexia nervosa" among female adolescents.

- Due to heightened security measures, air travel is now safer than ever.

- Government funding of public radio has significant pros and cons.

- For all the outrage over *Citizens United*, the Supreme Court's unpopular ruling has strengthened our democracy.

- Although poor diet and eating habits may cause childhood obesity, the most reliable cures are physical activity and exercise.

- Claiming to support community standards, Mr. Cheever made the fourteen students who wore the T-shirt to school go home for the day.

- Most stereotypes are hasty generalizations.

- According to one source, "addiction is the inability to modify one's behavior despite the knowledge of harmful consequences."

- In today's society, being on social networks is a must if you want to have friends.

Building to a Climax

As you conduct research, you will develop arguments that apply to your working thesis. Thus, you can begin to *draft* your thesis support while you are doing the research. In your draft, the support will be incomplete and disorganized, but when you finish the research, you will have a draft to work with and can reorganize the support so that it is logical and builds to a strong climax—that is, from less consequential points and evidence to your most compelling.

Addressing Counterarguments and Opposing Views

To support a thesis that is interesting and complex, you usually have to address counterarguments and opposing views. No organizing principles govern where or when to address them. Experienced writers who understand how to transition smoothly from one point to another can address opposing views almost anywhere in an essay or paper without disrupting the clarity or flow. However, students and less experienced writers often are confused about where, or if, to address opposing views, and they sometimes make the mistake of bringing them up at the very end, which can make the ending weak or anticlimactic.

To avoid this problem, consider addressing opposing views at the beginning of your support section, immediately after presenting your thesis. At that point, readers already know what your main argument is, and they will understand and appreciate your discussion of opposing views.

Documentation

Documentation means identifying your sources of information and telling readers how to find the information. Researchers document to "give credit," but also to provide a context and trail of information for readers. In an everyday conversation, we say things like, "My mom always told me that 'if it doesn't kill you, it will make you stronger.'" Identifying someone else's thoughts or words like this is the essence of documentation. We identify the source to give a context to the point we want to make, not only or primarily to give credit.

In research writing, documentation serves this same purpose, but in addition, since research writing is specialized and readers usually have a professional interest in the research problem, we include citations (see below) to make it easy for the readers to track down the sources. In doing research yourself, you benefit from the documentation other writers do. It leads you to a variety of sources that are valuable to your work. When you write your own paper for this assignment and cite your sources accurately, you are returning the favor, doing what professional writers and scholars do.

You do not need to document the dates of historical events and other information that is common knowledge or readily available. A few examples are as follows:

▶ To the chagrin of passionate fans, Kurt Cobain's turbulent life ended on April 5, 1994, when he committed suicide.

▶ Along with the Eiffel Tower, the Champs Élysées is one of the most famous landmarks in Paris.

▶ A "New England boiled dinner" consists of corned beef, cabbage, and potatoes.

Otherwise, you always should document information, ideas, or materials that are not your own, including the following:

▶ Information that you summarize or paraphrase

▶ Direct quotations

▶ Statistics, charts, graphs, maps, drawings

▶ Audiovisual information—documentaries, videos, podcasts, photographs, and so on

▶ Information obtained firsthand from other people

Tags, Lead-Ins, and Signal Phrases

When summarizing, paraphrasing, or quoting sources, the most straightforward way to identify them is by using attributive tags, lead-ins, and signal phrases. Below are some examples.

▶ In an interview on *60 Minutes*, former President Bill Clinton admitted that _____.

▶ According to Penn Kimball, the FBI report concluded that he was "too clever" to be caught holding a Communist Party card.

▶ As Supreme Court Justice Scalia observes, _____.

▶ *Publishers Weekly* calls the book a "provocative reassessment."

When you identify a source with a tag or lead-in, you perform a key part of documentation—that is, you identify the source and the context of your information. In most magazine and newspaper articles, this kind of informal, verbalized documentation, is all that is necessary. However, in scholarly writing, it is customary to provide more specific information that leads readers directly to a source. In MLA style, you may need to include parenthetical citations within your text (for example, to provide readers with specific page numbers). You also will need to provide a comprehensive list of your sources at the end of the paper (a Works Cited list in MLA style).

Below are two examples of parenthetical, in-text citations, followed by a full citation of the source (a book) in MLA style. The full citation would be included alphabetically in the writer's Works Cited list at the end of the paper.

> ▶ In *The Shock Doctrine*, Naomi Klein suggests that the real purpose of the CIA's MKUltra program was to refine methods of torture (38–39).

This parenthetical citation provides page numbers to supplement the attributive information already provided within the writer's text.

> ▶ One respected journalist believes that MKUltra's real agenda was to refine CIA torture methods (Klein 38–39).

This parenthetical citation provides both the source (the author's last name) and page numbers, since no specific source information is provided within the text.

> ▶ Klein, Naomi. *The Shock Doctrine: The Rise of Disaster Capitalism.* New York: Metropolitan/Henry Holt, 2007. Print.

This is a full citation that gives the reader all of the information necessary for finding the source: the author's name, the title of the book, and publication details (city, publisher, and date). For an example of a complete Works Cited list in MLA style, see the list Amanda McDole created for her research report on cyberbullying (pages 365 and 366), or the annotated Works Cited list after Brian Lawrence's essay, "The Truth about Atheists," in Chapter 7 (pages 300–301). More detailed information about citations and creating a Works Cited list is presented in Chapter 14.

Summary and Paraphrase

Good writers summarize or paraphrase most of the source material they incorporate in their writing—that is, they present the information in their own words, in order to maintain a consistent style, tone, and flow. Summaries condense the original information in the writer's own words. A paraphrase translates or restates the original words, but instead of condensing them, it retains all, or most, of the content. That means paraphrases are roughly the same length as the original material but are worded differently, so that they flow smoothly into the writer's document.

Regardless of whether you are summarizing or paraphrasing, you *always* need to identify the source and cite it properly. When you paraphrase, make sure the wording is your own and that you identify the source with a lead-in.

If you retain the original wording except for minor changes, you should convert the paraphrase to a direct quotation. Changing a few words to pass off source material as your own writing is "patchwriting," and it easily slips into plagiarism.

Avoiding Plagiarism

Plagiarism means passing off someone else's thoughts or words as your own. Intentional plagiarism is dishonest and has serious consequences in college and professional life. College students sometimes plagiarize without intending to, but the consequences still can be serious. For example, summarizing information from a source without identifying the source within the text (by using a lead-in or parenthetical citation) is plagiarism, even if the source is included in a Works Cited list. Students who make this kind of mistake can receive an "F" on a college paper, fail the course, and worse, have the infraction recorded on their transcript. If that happens, the offense can militate against acceptance to law school, medical school, or other postgraduate programs.

The penalties may seem harsh for an "honest mistake," but the remedy is simple: whenever you bring source material into a paper, whether you are summarizing, paraphrasing, quoting, or reproducing examples, statistics, graphics, and so forth, *always* identify all of your sources *in your text*—either by using signal phrases or parenthetical citations. Also, be sure to enclose direct quotations in quotation marks (or block center them). Consistently and scrupulously identifying all your sources and direct quotations makes your writing virtually plagiarism-proof.

To better understand these distinctions, look at the examples below.

Source:

Seemuth, Mike. "The App Economy." *Miami Herald*. Miami Herald, 7 July 2013. Web. 8 July 2013.

Original Passage:

The worldwide number for mobile app downloads will reach 108 billion by 2017, compared to 60.1 billion last year and 29.5 billion in 2011, according to a new study by Sweden-based telecom consulting firm Berg Insight.

Summary:

Consumer demand for mobile apps has risen dramatically in just two years (Seemuth).

Paraphrase:

> A study by a Sweden-based consulting firm found that consumer demand for mobile apps doubled between 2011 and 2013 (going from 29.5 billion downloads to 60.1 billion), and is expected to double again in the next few years (Seemuth).

Plagiarized Passage:

> The worldwide number for mobile app downloads is predicted to reach 108 billion by 2017, compared to 60.1 billion last year and 29.5 billion in 2011, according to a new study by Sweden-based telecom consulting firm Berg Insight (Seemuth).

In the last example, even though the passage is documented parenthetically, most of the words are lifted straight from the source and presented without direct quotation marks. The writer's only contribution is changing "will reach" to "is predicted to reach." Most college professors would consider this passage plagiarized. A college essay or paper built on patchwritten passages is not just plagiarized but inept.

Direct Quotations

Moderate use of direct quotation adds credibility to research writing, but whenever you include direct quotations of other people's words in your writing, you interject a different voice and style. Too many direct quotations disrupt the flow of your writing and can make it hard to read. As a rule, limit your use of direct quotations to passages of importance that you think the reader should read word-for-word—passages that are controversial and/or are especially striking or memorable.

When you use direct quotations, favor short, in-text quotations (that is, quotations that are just a few lines or less), rather than longer "block-centered" quotations (normally more than four lines). Too many long, block-centered quotations are cumbersome to read and more of a distraction than an asset. Also, consider using ellipsis points (...) to shorten quotations when appropriate. Three points tell your readers that you have removed material within a sentence. Four points (....)—that is, the three points plus a period—indicate you removed material between complete sentences.

Note that, in MLA style, block-centered quotations are not presented in quotation marks. The block-centering, along with the lead-in phrase that introduces the quotation, tells the reader that the quotation is direct. Here is a block-centered quotation from Mike Seemuth's article "The App Economy."

The only quotation marks used are inside the passage, to indicate exact words someone has spoken:

> Even small improvements to existing computer applications can produce big rewards. [David] Elgena, for example, redesigned the look of the typical weather app, the user experience, rather than reinventing it. He paid almost $5,000 to a third-party software developer in Ukraine that did certain types of coding to make Weather Dial work. "As far as the very heavy, back-end coding, I haven't learned it, because I realized my time is more valuable on the front-end design, creating the user experience," Elgena said. (Seemuth)

Quotation marks and block-centered quotations present the exact words that someone has spoken or written. Sometimes quotation marks also are used for stylistic or semantic reasons—for example:

► To indicate irony (His "analysis" concludes that global warming is a scam.)

► To introduce an unfamiliar word, or a word that is used in a nonstandard or specialized way (Lancelot's "brinksmanship" sabotaged Arthurian ideals.)

► To refer to a word as a word (The word "fight" in "firefighter" has real meaning.)

► To indicate that a cliché or truism is being used intentionally (He is "Johnny on the spot" when there is money to be made.)

The following reading is an argumentative blog post from *Ms. Magazine* that illustrates different uses of quotation marks.

Martha Pitts { **HAPPY-TO-BE-NAPPY BARBIE**

THIS WEEK, A GROUP of black women in Columbus, Ga., started a campaign to donate 40 black Barbie dolls to young black girls. And here's the twist: Before gifting the Barbies, the women used boiling water and pipe cleaners to transform them into curly-haired "beauties."

In my 32 years on this earth, I've owned a total of two black Barbie dolls: Brownie (named by me) and Christie (named by her Mattel box). Brownie and Christie gave good advice, performed medical procedures on other dolls and married white Kens (since my black "Ken" came many years later and was named Steven). They had brown cottony manes close to the texture of my own hair.

After a session or two of "beauty shop," Brownie sported a puffy mullet and Christie an afro bob, which became shorter and shorter over the years.

I don't know whether owning black Barbies was one reason I had adequate self-esteem as a girl despite pervasive messages that black wasn't exactly beautiful. The self-esteem-protecting potential of natural-haired Barbies appears to be the hope underlying the Georgia toy drive. "We wanted to show the girls that basically, it's okay the way God made you," says Jennifer Henderson, a member of the natural-hair-care meetup group Fro-lific that organized the drive.

One might assume that Fro-lific's implied goal of teaching the girls self-love and self-acceptance should make me, a black mother of a black daughter, stand up and cheer like everyone else seems to be doing ... right? But here's the thing: As a feminist mom, I kinda hate Barbie, whatever her color. In fact, I would go so far as to say that Barbie represents everything I hate in the world: capitalism, sexism, racism, heteronormativity, white supremacy.

How does black Barbie reinforce white supremacy, you ask? Well, first, look at her facial features and body shape. Remind you of anyone? Down to every detail, black Barbie is standard-white-Barbie painted brown. I'm not suggesting Mattel add superficial "exotic" markers like full lips and a voluptuous butt. Rather, I'd echo a call made by scholar Ann Ducille in her 1994 essay "Dyes and Dolls: Multicultural Barbie and the Merchandising of Difference":

> Could any doll manufacturer or other image maker—advertising and film, say—attend to cultural, racial, and phenotypical differences without merely engaging the same simplistic big-lips/broad-hips stereotypes that make so many of us grit our (pearly white) teeth? What would it take to produce a line of doll that would more fully reflect the wide variety of sizes, shapes, colors, hairstyles, occupations, abilities, and disabilities that African Americans—like all people—come in?

These are all questions we and Fro-lific should think about if we're giving Barbies (nappy or not) to kids. Barbie may be too pervasive to ignore, but at least the dolls can be a starting point for important discussions about black girlhood. Hell, about girlhood, for that matter. Can we question Barbie's big breasts and tiny waist as markers of True Womanhood? Why is Ken Barbie's significant other? Why do these black Barbies have to wear Jay-Z's "Rocawear" clothing line?

If you're looking to empower girls, there are non-Barbie gifts better suited to the task. Various other dolls on the market can help kids explore racial and ethnic diversity without the toxicity. And one way I consciously empower my own curly-haired kid is to read children's books with her about self-acceptance and self-love: *Happy to Be Nappy* by bell hooks, *I Love My Hair* by Natasha Anastasia Tarpley and *The Colors of Us* by Karen Katz are three of my favorites. These books do not reduce race to skin color or other stereotypical markers, and they let me and my daughter bond by relating the plotlines and pictures to our lived experiences.

Barbie's not going anywhere—I've more or less accepted this. In fact, my kid has several Barbie dolls of varying shades and with varying hair textures (birthday presents from folks who didn't get the feminist-mom memo). My daughter knows how I feel about Barbies, and she understands that I respect and accept her decision to play with them.

What I haven't accepted is teaching empowerment to girls through Barbie dolls. Because black girls rock, and they deserve more. ■

From Reflection to Response

Understanding Direct Quotations and Quotation Marks

Go through Martha Pitts's "Happy-To-Be-Nappy Barbie," and highlight or list all of the direct quotations, as well as instances where quotation marks are used for other reasons. After you identify all of the direct quotations and uses of quotation marks, write a short explanation of each instance you identified.

Documentation Styles

Formal documentation procedures can seem mystifying and complex on the surface. There are different "styles," formats, and rules for different disciplines and kinds of writing. Eminent institutions best known by their initials—the MLA, APA, CSE, and CMS—create the styles and rules. The institutions are as follows:

▶ The Modern Language Association (MLA)

▶ The American Psychological Association (APA)

▶ The Council of Science Editors (CSE)

▶ The Chicago Manual of Style (CMS) (published by the University of Chicago Press and often called "Chicago style")

Each documentation style has guidelines for formatting documents and citing virtually every source imaginable, from a book with three authors to a public lecture, dissertation, "tweet," museum piece, or advertisement on a stadium jumbotron. But don't let this appearance of complexity intimidate you.

When you "pull back the curtain" on the elaborate methodology, documentation involves two simple procedures:

1. Identify all your sources as you present them in your paper or text.
2. Provide a comprehensive list of all your sources at the end of the paper or text.

As you already know, you can identify all the sources in your paper using direct references—that is, attributive tags, lead-ins, and signal phrases ("According to _____" and so forth). Additionally, you need to use parenthetical references in some documentation styles.

The comprehensive list of sources at the end of a paper is called a Works Cited in MLA style, or a list of References in APA. These lists are alphabetized and contain citations, in a specified format, for all of the sources used in a paper or text. The list gives readers information they need to find the sources. Here is a citation for a book in MLA style:

> Bettelheim, Bruno. *The Uses of Enchantment: The Meaning and Importance of Fairy Tales*. New York: Knopf, 1976. Print.

A citation for the same book in APA style is only slightly different:

> Bettelheim, Bruno. (1976). *The uses of enchantment: The meaning and importance of fairy tales*. New York, NY: Knopf.

These citations provide five key pieces of information.

▶ The author of the book (last name first)
▶ The title
▶ The place of publication
▶ The publisher
▶ The publication date

All formal citations are variations on this basic format, but sources are so extensive and diverse that even experienced scholars need to "look up" the correct format for many of the sources they use. As a result, a good writing handbook that is organized and indexed for quick reference is an essential resource for anyone writing academic papers that require formal documentation. Guides to documentation also can be accessed online but may be less complete and not as easy to navigate as a handbook.

The article below, about a perceived decline in the quality of college education, is presented as an interesting reading and also as material for practicing some of the approaches to research writing and documentation covered in this chapter. As you read the article, assume you are researching the value and cost-effectiveness of a college education today.

Richard Arum and Josipa Roksa { YOUR SO-CALLED EDUCATION

Andy Kropa/Getty Images Entertainment/ Getty Images

Richard Arum and Josipa Roksa are the authors of *Academically Adrift: Limited Learning on College Campuses,* published by the University of Chicago Press. Richard Arum is a professor of sociology and education at New York University. Josipa Roksa is an assistant professor of sociology at the University of Virginia.

Josipa Roksa

COMMENCEMENT IS A SPECIAL time on college campuses: an occasion for students, families, faculty and administrators to come together to celebrate a job well done. And perhaps there is reason to be pleased. In recent surveys of college seniors, more than 90 percent report gaining subject-specific knowledge and developing the ability to think critically and analytically. Almost 9 out of 10 report that overall, they were satisfied with their collegiate experiences.

We would be happy to join in the celebrations if it weren't for our recent research, which raises doubts about the quality of undergraduate learning in the United States. Over four years, we followed the progress of several thousand students in more than two dozen diverse four-year colleges and universities. We found that large numbers of the students were making their way through college with minimal exposure to rigorous coursework, only a modest investment of effort and little or no meaningful improvement in skills like writing and reasoning.

In a typical semester, for instance, 32 percent of the students did not take a single course with more than 40 pages of reading per week, and 50 percent did not take any course requiring more than 20 pages of writing over the semester. The average student spent only about 12 to 13 hours per week studying—about half the time a full-time college student in 1960 spent studying, according to the labor economists Philip S. Babcock and Mindy S. Marks.

Not surprisingly, a large number of the students showed no significant progress on tests of critical thinking, complex reasoning and writing that were administered when they began college and then again at the ends of their sophomore and senior years. If the test that we used, the Collegiate Learning Assessment, were scaled on a traditional 0-to-100 point range, 45 percent of the students would not have demonstrated gains of even one point over the first two years of college, and 36 percent would not have shown such gains over four years of college.

Why is the overall quality of undergraduate learning so poor?

While some colleges are starved for resources, for many others it's not for lack of money. Even at those colleges where for the past several decades tuition has far outpaced the rate of inflation, students are taught by fewer full-time tenured faculty members while being looked after by a greatly expanded number of counselors who serve an array of social and personal needs. At the same time, many schools are investing in deluxe dormitory rooms, elaborate student centers and expensive gyms. Simply put: academic investments are a lower priority.

The situation reflects a larger cultural change in the relationship between students and colleges. The authority of educators has diminished, and students are increasingly thought of, by themselves and their colleges, as "clients" or "consumers." When 18-year-olds are emboldened to see themselves in this manner, many look for ways to attain an educational credential effortlessly and comfortably. And they are catered to accordingly. The customer is always right.

Federal legislation has facilitated this shift. The funds from Pell Grants and subsidized loans, by being assigned to students to spend on academic institutions they have chosen rather than being packaged as institutional grants for colleges to dispense, have empowered students—for good but also for ill. And expanded privacy protections have created obstacles for colleges in providing information on student performance to parents, undercutting a traditional check on student lassitude.

Fortunately, there are some relatively simple, practical steps that colleges and universities could take to address the problem. Too many institutions, for instance, rely primarily on student course evaluations to assess teaching. This creates perverse incentives for professors to demand little and give out good grades. (Indeed, the 36 percent of students in our study who reported spending five or fewer hours per week studying alone still had an average G.P.A. of 3.16.) On those commendable occasions when professors and academic departments do maintain rigor, they risk declines in student enrollments. And since resources are typically distributed based on enrollments, rigorous classes are likely to be canceled and rigorous programs shrunk. Distributing resources and rewards based on student learning instead of student satisfaction would help stop this race to the bottom.

Others involved in education can help, too. College trustees, instead of worrying primarily about institutional rankings and fiscal concerns, could hold administrators accountable for assessing and improving learning. Alumni as well as parents and students on college tours could ignore institutional facades and focus on educational substance. And the Department of Education could make available nationally representative longitudinal data on undergraduate learning outcomes for research purposes, as it has been doing for decades for primary and secondary education.

Most of all, we hope that during this commencement season, our faculty colleagues will pause to consider the state of undergraduate learning and our collective responsibility to increase academic rigor on our campuses. ■

From Reflection to Response   Incorporating Sources

At home or in the library, review the sections of a handbook (or an online resource like the Purdue OWL) that deal with the following:

- Attributive tags, signal phrases, or lead-ins
- Summarizing and paraphrasing
- Direct quotations—short and long
- Parenthetical citations
- Ellipses

After your review, practice what you have learned by doing the following:

1. Write a paragraph or two describing and analyzing the article "Your So-Called Education." Use attributive tags and signal phrases to introduce summaries and paraphrases. Include two direct quotations, one that is under four lines and one that is longer. Use an ellipsis in one of the quotations and a parenthetical citation if needed.

2. Create a Works Cited entry for the article in MLA style. The version of the article used in this chapter appeared in the *New York Times* online on May 14, 2011.

3. Bring the finished exercise to your next class meeting, and exchange your exercise with another student's. Review each other's work for any oversights or documentation errors.

YOUR PROJECT CHECKLIST

Use the following essay checklist to guide your steps in developing your essay and as a final check to make sure you have completed all of the necessary steps. This checklist can also be used to help you plan your time effectively.

✔ Task	Description	Time Frame
☐ **Choose a research problem**	• Choose a research problem that matters to you and, ideally, that you have some exposure to, and are interested in learning more about.	A day or two, or more.
☐ **Conduct preliminary research**	• Conduct preliminary research for an overview of perspectives and available secondary sources. • Create a "Favorites" folder in your web browser to bookmark websites for your project. Also, create an electronic research file for listing and annotating sources that you consult.	A day or two.
☐ **Develop a research plan**	• Develop a research plan that includes secondary sources of quality, as well as a timetable and plan for primary research—site visits, interviews, a survey, etc.	One or two hours or more.
☐ **Write a research proposal**	• Write a research proposal; submit it to your instructor and classmates for feedback.	One hour or less.
☐ **Begin secondary research**	• Begin your secondary research and keep a record of your sources and annotations in your research file. • Begin planning and conducting your primary research as well.	Time frame varies.
☐ **Work on intermediate writing projects**	• If your instructor requires an intermediate writing project—an annotated bibliography or research narrative—begin drafting and revising the document.	A week or more.
☐ **Begin drafting**	• Begin drafting your final paper or report—starting with the opening section or introduction—as you proceed with your research. • If you completed an intermediate project like a research narrative or annotated bibliography, decide what previous material you will include in the final paper or report, and where it will go.	Time frame varies.
☐ **Revise**	• Fill in the parts until your draft is complete. When you have enough source material and insights to support a strong thesis, begin the revision and editing process.	At least a week.

✔ Task	Description	Time Frame
☐ **Seek peer review**	• Ask for feedback from your classmates, during the revision process (see peer review questions). • Consider visiting your instructor during office hours for advice and help, or take a draft to your campus writing center for advice from a trained tutor.	Time frame varies.
☐ **Edit your paper or report**	Before you submit your final paper or report, make sure you edit it carefully. Consider using the text-to-speech feature on your computer to hear how the writing sounds and help you catch mistakes or typos. Check for the following: • Helpful paragraphing (see Chapter 12 for more about this and the other elements of grammar and mechanics listed here) • Effective wording and word choice (avoid arbitrary slang or colloquialisms) • Sentence punctuation (eliminate run-ons and comma splices) • General grammar and mechanics (subject-verb agreement, pronoun reference, placement of commas) • Correct in-text documentation and a correctly formatted Works Cited list in MLA style. (See Chapter 14 for more details, and consult an up-to-date writing handbook or reliable web resource like the Purdue OWL.)	Careful editing may involve a certain amount of revising, so the time frame can vary, but always plan on going over what you have written. Running a spell check is not enough.

PEER REVIEW

Once you have a readable draft of your paper completed, show it to classmates and ask for their feedback. As you read a classmate's draft, answer the following questions:

1. What information does the writer present in the opening to make the issue compelling and relevant to readers? What more could be said, or needs to be said, about the issue? Did you learn anything new or interesting that made you want to continue reading?

2. What is the thesis (quote the exact words)? Is the thesis interesting to you, or surprising in any way? Based on the thesis, describe the goal of the paper in your own words, and whether or not you consider the goal worthwhile.

3. What opposing views or counterarguments does the writer explicitly examine? Is the writer's treatment of them fair and convincing? Point out

any legitimate counterarguments or opposing views that the writer fails to bring up but should think about.

4. List the main points (the reasons and evidence) that the writer presents to support the central thesis. Are any points underdeveloped or unconvincing? Suggest additional points that could be presented. Has the writer researched the problem extensively enough to justify her conclusions? Describe what you think an educated reader would learn from this paper.

5. Point out any issues you noticed with the documentation, in particular any plagiarism concerns. Are sources properly identified in the text? Is the Works Cited list formatted correctly?

6. On a scale of 1 to 5 (1 being lowest and 5 highest), rate the readability of this paper. Is the title effective? Evaluate the clarity of the writing. Point out any "patchwriting" concerns, or specific problems with paragraphing, punctuation, grammar, or formatting.

STUDENT ESSAY: FINAL DRAFT

Here is the final version of the research report that first-year student Amanda McDole wrote (see her proposal at the beginning of the chapter). The report is documented in MLA style. For detailed instructions on how to document sources using MLA style, refer to Chapter 14. After the report, Amanda discusses her writing process and offers some interesting advice.

Amanda McDole // **FINDING A SOLUTION FOR CYBERBULLYING**

1. Letter of Transmittal or Statement of Purpose and Audience

November 15, 2014

David Esquith, Director
Office of Safe and Healthy Students
U.S. Department of Education
400 Maryland Avenue, SW
Washington, D.C. 20202

Dear Mr. Esquith:

Enclosed is a report that I hope you will find relevant to your work as director of the Office of Safe and Healthy Students in our elementary and secondary schools.

My report deals with the dramatic rise of cyberbullying incidents involving children and teenagers who use online social networking sites. The report identifies key factors contributing to the growth of this problem, and proposes solutions.

I think the involvement of your office can have a positive impact and help reduce the number of bullying incidents that students are experiencing through social networks.

Speaking on behalf of many victims of cyberbullying, I would be grateful for any actions you might be able to take to make the online environment safer and healthier for future generations of children and adolescents.

Sincerely,

Amanda McDole

2. The Central Problem, Issue, or Questions

Bullying is a problem that has been around forever. Until recently, most bullying involved face-to-face threats and physical harm. Today, bullying has gone high-tech and frequently is done through the Internet (Neumann 151). Social networking websites in particular have found a new use in the hands of bullies, who practice what is widely known as cyberbullying, which means repeatedly attacking a person or people on the Internet. Social networking sites are a frequent bullying venue because their use has become a virtual must for children and adolescents starting in middle school and continuing through high school.

In worst-case scenarios, young people have committed suicide because of cyberbullying. Two boys, Jamey Rodemeyer and Jamie Hubley, who were bullied because of their sexuality, eventually ended their own lives because of the constant attacks and pressure. Hubley, a gay 15-year-old from Ottawa, Canada, tried to start a "rainbow club" at his high school to promote acceptance of gay teens, and as a result, was called hurtful names at school and online. His parents believe that bullying was a definite factor in his suicide ("Jamie Hubley").

Another story that has made headlines was the suicide of 13-year-old Megan Meier who was the victim of a vicious catfishing hoax involving a mother and her daughter who knew Megan suffered from body-image problems and low self-esteem. The mother-daughter team created a fake MySpace profile of a boy named Josh Evans. The fake Josh sought out Megan online, was kind to her, and then suddenly turned mean for no reason, telling her just before she took her own life that "The world would be a better place without you" ("Megan's Story").

Although these cases are extreme, there are still many young people struggling with the issue, who find themselves on the receiving end of nasty gossip, insults, threats, and social exclusion, yet feel helpless to do anything about it, and may not even completely realize they are being bullied. As Kate Harding points out in an article for *Salon*, social networking sites facilitate the bullying, but are not the cause, and in any case, they are here to stay. "Calling for kids to turn off their computers and get outside" is not the answer. A better approach is parental monitoring, teaching kids the realities of the Internet and the consequences of online behavior. However, studies have shown that children using online social networking sites are not being monitored by their parents (Neumann 152). This is understandable because in modern society most parents lead busy lives, have trouble keeping up with what their children are doing, and may even be unfamiliar with the new technologies children are using. Problems arise when no adults are teaching children the proper use of social networking websites, and the consequences of misuse. Unsupervised, some children naively expose themselves to abuse, or start using the sites as a convenient tool for bullying.

Schools have a responsibility, too, when it comes to bullying, because studies have shown that bullying is widespread in schools, and mostly happens during school hours (Sampson). This fact is worrisome because, apart from the emotional and psychological damage that bullying does, studies show that when children are bullied and feel threatened, they cannot focus on schoolwork and learning ("U.S. Education Secretary"). If schools increased their involvement with this issue, fewer students across the nation would become victims, and we could expect to see improved results in education. Given how widespread the problem is, there needs to be a new awareness and new approaches to dealing with it.

3. Thesis, Argument, Solution, or Proposal

Although some organizations, and people like Lady Gaga and Dan Savage, are bringing attention to this issue, what has been done up to this point has not been effective. Students are still being bullied every day, and in turn, living with emotional distress that affects their happiness, self-esteem, and performance in school. I propose approaching the problem in two ways: 1) in the home, through better parental awareness and involvement in what kids are doing online, and 2) in schools across the nation. I would like to introduce the idea of classes about bullying and cyberbullying that parallel sex education and anti-drug classes currently offered in many schools. These kinds of classes are cost-effective for school districts, and besides educating students, would also be informative to the most important adults in young people's lives: their parents and teachers. Offering these classes can provide the outreach that victims of bullying have been trying to find.

4. Opposing Views and Counterarguments

Some experts have argued that bullying during the school years of a young person's life is completely normal. Many young people are able to handle this "real life situation." Others need help to deal with the stress and pressure (Derbyshire), but the argument can still be made that, if children are overprotected and not given an opportunity to defend themselves from bullying, they will never learn to handle real world scenarios that involve conflict. Studies show that young people are more likely to be popular and admired by teachers if they are able to stand up and defend themselves (Derbyshire).

Although researchers know that bullying can be harmful to children, they say "mutual dislike" can help students develop healthy social and emotional skills (Derbyshire). Psychologist Melissa Witkow believes that teachers should not protect students because later those students will be unable to fend for themselves. Students should be able to just shut off the computer if they're being cyberbullied, or if they prefer, fight back.

Moreover, when kids grow up on social networking sites, they are keeping up with technology and learning useful computer skills. Social networks provide a new form of self-expression. Some researchers argue that monitoring children will inhibit self-expression. Spending time online is essential for young people to learn the technical and social skills required to be competent citizens in the digital age (Goff).

When it comes down to it, some experts also argue that educational classes in schools will not be effective. This argument is supported by the idea that sex education classes have not appeared to significantly reduce teen pregnancies or STDs. Both problems remain prevalent despite efforts to educate young people about them. Thus, introducing the same type of classes about bullying will not solve the problem.

While there is some truth to all of these counterarguments, the fact remains that cyberbullying is too widespread and too serious to just ignore. Parental monitoring and educational initiatives may not solve the problem entirely, but should still be encouraged, because they are bound to at least help some kids who are socially abused and isolated, and unable to function in school.

5. Thesis Support or Justification (Body)

Adolescents and children who are bullied have a higher risk of depression, anxiety, thoughts of suicide, health complaints, and problems with academic achievement. They are more likely to skip or drop out of school, and much more likely to engage in violence or retaliate through extreme violent measures ("Effects of Bullying"). According to *stopbullying.gov*, "in 12 of 15 school shooting cases in the 1990s, the shooters had a history of being bullied" ("Effects of Bullying").

Out of 20,000 kids polled who reported being bullied, 85% percent believed that parents, schools, the community or all three could have helped in their situation ("Popular Vote"). This left 15% who answered they felt they should have handled it themselves.

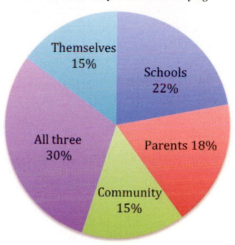

Who kids think can put an end to bullying

Themselves 15%
Schools 22%
Parents 18%
Community 15%
All three 30%

Fig. 1. Who Can Help?

Even though recent generations of kids have grown up with technology, they still need parental guidance. Bullying isn't a routine "rite of passage" that children are equipped to navigate on their own. Allowing kids to use online social networks without the proper monitoring is the same as letting kids do what they want all the time without explanations of what is right or wrong ("Internet Safety").

Internet safety companies reiterate how vital it is for parents to teach young people appropriate online behaviors and keep Internet use in common areas ("Internet Safety"). One of the most popular social networking sites in the world, Facebook, has come to realize the importance of Internet safety and created features, controls, and alerts that help parents monitor their children's activity on the site. But Facebook and other advocates of parental monitoring urge that it be done through befriending, communicating, and educating, not as a form of spying or stalking that risks alienating a child's trust. Parental involvement in what children are doing online is clearly a first step toward curbing the cyberbullying problem.

A second step, involving parents and schools at the same time, is the educational initiative mentioned earlier: anti-bullying classes that mirror sex education or drug education classes already being offered. Despite some skepticism, there is evidence that these kinds of classes can and do have positive results:

- A study of 2000 students in Houston, Texas schools revealed that middle and high school students felt they had a heightened awareness of alcohol,

Fig. 2. The idea is to get kids in the classroom involved in the issue.

Source: *A Guide to Class Management.*

drugs, weapons and theft on their campus because of D.A.R.E. (drug educational classes). D.A.R.E. also was appreciated by parents. When asked if the program should be kept, 5.85 out of 6 said yes (Santoro).

- Similarly, studies have shown that sex education programs are effective. Comprehensive sex education classes reduce pregnancy 50% more in young people than no education at all or abstinence-only programs ("Comprehensive Sex Education").

These findings show that when educational programs are done the right way, they do have an impact on informing the community, parents as well as students, and they do get results.

Introducing anti-bullying programs in schools would be the most up-to-date way of informing children and parents about the dangers of cyberbullying and how to deal with it. Teachers, many of whom need training to deal with bullying situations, or in some cases, are unaware bullying is on the rise on the Internet, would get a better understanding of the problem and be more prepared to handle situations that come to their attention (Rigby 226). This type of educational program would also enlighten victims like myself who fail to entirely realize they are being bullied online, and feel they just have to accept the mean, abusive things that are said about them.

Offering classes about an issue like cyberbullying is not costly. Classes can be funded through outside organizations that have the necessary resources. Teachers can be volunteers recruited from the community or from within the school, who understand the problem and want to share their knowledge and concerns with students. Considering the minimal costs and promising benefits, these kinds of classes are a win-win.

To be effective, however, anti-bullying classes would have to be designed around the needs of young people, and dig deep into the realities of the problem. The first thing students would need to learn is the difference between bullying and normal conflict (Snyder):

Normal Conflict	Bullying
Happens occasionally	Happens repeatedly
Accidental	Done on purpose
Not serious	Serious threat of physical harm or emotional or psychological hurt
Equal emotional reactions	Strong emotional reaction on part of the victim
Not seeking power or attention	Done to gain power or material things
Remorseful—perpetrator takes responsibility	No remorse—blames victim
Effort made to solve the problem	No effort or desire by perpetrator to solve the problem

The curriculum for the class also would include the following:

- **Teaching the effects of cyberbullying**: Since today the issue is becoming more of a problem online than in person, this first part of the program would teach students correct online behaviors and the consequences behind not following them. Putting specific rules in place and making them known to students will give them a chance to think twice before bullying.

- **Watching the movie** *Cyberbully*: This film is educational and really makes people see the consequences of cyberbullying through all the characters: the victim, the bullies, and the bystanders. It is the most recent movie to focus directly on this issue and has received many positive reviews because of how realistic it is about what goes on in schools and online.

- **Informing about the available ways to get help**: For those students who are experiencing bullying and are too embarrassed to ask for help or feel helpless altogether, this part of the program would be directed towards them. Many people aren't aware of all the resources available to them or campaigns they can join for support from other people who are experiencing the problem.

- **Getting students involved:** Have students role-play bullying scenarios, and in particular, play reversed roles. Asking students to act out being a bully and being a victim can give them new perspectives on how they are making others feel. Sometimes when people realize how much hurt they cause someone else, it makes them reflect and want to change.

Recently, because of the large number of teens seeking advice about cyberbullying, many articles on the subject have appeared in the media. *TeenVogue* magazine has addressed one widespread form of cyberbullying: social exclusion. Another popular magazine, *Seventeen*, partnered with ABC Family and its famous actors and actresses, to create a movement named "Delete Digital Drama," an effort to show young people it's okay to ask for help, regardless of who you are.

If this issue is made public in schools, students won't be afraid to ask for help anymore, and bullies won't feel so confident about hiding behind a computer screen.

Moreover, as noted before, the program would also:

- **Keep teachers informed about what kids are doing**: School psychologist Sara Vondracek has admitted she didn't know about most of the sites that are extremely popular with today's youth (Neumann 152). If teachers learned about the sites, they would be better prepared to intervene when faced with a cyberbullying situation.

- **Put anti-bullying policies in place**: Monitoring use of online social networks in school is one way schools are getting a handle on the issue. Two schools I visited in conducting my research, Monsignor Edward Pace High School and Somerset Academy, both had a policy against students' accessing social networking sites on school grounds. Authorities at both schools said this policy helped to keep kids focused on what they were in school for. Some states, such as the state of New York after the suicide of Jamey Rodemeyer, have mandated that schools implement similar policies to curb cyberbullying.

- **Make it *easy* for students to get help**: Out of about 28,000 students who responded to a survey, 90% said that bullying should be able to be reported anonymously ("Popular Vote"). We should make anonymous reporting possible for students who want to speak out against their bully, but are too afraid to make themselves known. This type of assistance might be exactly what many students are waiting for.

Lastly, the anti-bullying educational program would also be an eye-opener for parents. Placing these programs in schools will make parents more aware because young people will be able to talk about what they learned, bring home pamphlets, and take parents to school functions where information about bullying will be available to them, including the following:

- **How to help children avoid bullying situations**: There are simple ways for parents to try and avoid putting their child in the situation of bullying or being bullied online. Keeping Internet use in a communal area, or for older teens, just monitoring their Internet use, are basic, commonsense approaches (Neumann 153).

- **How to detect signs that a child is a victim or a bully**: Experts have explained that being alert and observant is critical, since victims are often reluctant to report bullying (Snyder). Teaching parents to spot warning signs that their child is a victim or a bully will allow for early interventions and address the bullying problem from both human sides.

- **How to listen to a child and be involved in what a child is doing**: Many parents don't take the time to listen and let their kids open up to them. Parents need to reassure kids that it's okay to talk about being bullied or what's happening in school because they are there to help.

6. Conclusion

Bringing parents into the picture through educational programs in schools creates a bridge between my two proposals for resolving the problem of cyberbullying. Educational programs will raise awareness about the problem, provide tools for dealing with it, and bring parents, educators, and young people together in solving the problem. These programs will ensure that cyberbullying is no longer minimized, misunderstood, or ignored.

Works Cited

"Comprehensive Sex Education: Research and Results." *Advocates for Youth.* Advocates for Youth, Sept. 2009. Web. 28 Apr. 2015. <http://www.advocatesforyouth.org/publications/1487>.

Castleman, Michael. "Sex Education in Schools Does Not Reduce Rates of Teen Pregnancy." *Teen Pregnancy and Parenting.* Detroit: Greenhaven, 2011. Print. Current Controversies.

Derbyshire, David. "Bullying Can Be Good for Children: Study Finds Those Who Fight Back Are More Popular." *Mail Online.* Associated Newspapers, 24 May 2010. Web. 19 Apr. 2015.

"Digital Drama Rally Next Week." *Just Jared Jr.* Just Jared, 9 July 2011. Web. 14 Mar. 2015. <http://www.justjaredjr.com/2011/07/09/delete-digital-drama-rally-next-week/>.

"Effects of Bullying." *Stopbullying.gov.* U. S. Department of Health and Human Services, n.d. Web. 20 Apr. 2015.

Family Safety Center. Facebook, 2011. Web. 25 Mar. 2015. <https://www.facebook.com/safety>.

Goff, Karen Goldberg. "Social Networking Benefits Validated." *Washington Times.* The Washington Times, 28 Jan. 2009. Web. 28 Apr. 2015.

MLA style rules specify that the list should begin on a separate page . For detailed information about creating a Works Cited list, see Chapter 14.

A Guide to Class Management. N.d. *Teaching.monster.com*. Web. Apr. 2015. <http://teaching.monster.com/benefits/articles/3209-a-guide-to-class-management>.

Harding, Kate. "More Teen Troubles Blamed on Social Networking." *Salon*. Salon Media Group, 23 Dec. 2009. Web. 20 Apr. 2015.

"Internet Safety." *KidsHealth*. Nemours, Jan. 2015. Web. 20 Apr. 2015.

"Jamie Hubley, Gay 15-Year-Old Ottawa, Canada Teen Commits Suicide, Cites Depression, School Troubles." *The Huffington Post*. TheHuffingtonPost.com, 17 Dec. 2011. Web. 1 Apr. 2015.

"Megan's Story." *Megan Meier Foundation*, 13 Nov. 2007. Web. 28 Apr. 2015.

Neumann, Roger. "Cyberbullies Ramp Up the Taunting—Anonymously." *Social Networking*. Ed. Kenneth Partridge. New York: H. W. Wilson, 2011. 150–54. Print.

"Popular Vote." *Teens Against Bullying*. Pacer.org, 2006. Web. 7 Apr. 2015.

Rigby, Ken. *New Perspectives on Bullying*. Philadelphia: Jessica Kingsley, 2002. Print.

Sampson, Rana. "The Problem of Bullying in Schools." *Bullying in Schools*. Center for Problem-Oriented Policing, n.d. Web. 20 Apr. 2015.

Santoro, Joseph A. "Drug Education Programs Reduce Teen Drug Use." *Teens at Risk: Opposing Viewpoints*. Ed. Auriana Ojeda. San Diego: Greenhaven, 2003. Print. Opposing Viewpoints.

Snyder, Marlene. "Understanding Bullying and Its Impact on Kids." *GreatKids*. GreatSchools, n.d. Web. 21 Apr. 2015.

"U.S. Education Secretary to Keynote Department's First-Ever Bullying Summit." *Archived Information*. U.S. Department of Education, 11 Aug. 2010. Web. 19 Apr. 2015.

Interview with the Student Writer

● **How did you go about composing your report?**

● I spent about two to three weeks at a local library composing my report. I have my favorite place in the library in a very quiet section where I use word processing to get all my ideas down and then begin putting together my research. It took me about three revisions to be satisfied with what my work looked like. I took the report to my professor and the writing center at the university for feedback before it was completed.

● **Who read your drafts, and what reactions did you get?**

● My parents and professor read my drafts. My parents were very excited to read my draft and see that I had taken a negative life experience and turned it into something positive. They were glad that I had acknowledged the situation and tried to make a change for future students. My professor was impressed by the work and commended the research and time I put into the report.

● **What parts of the writing process were difficult for you?**

● I cannot remember the exact parts of the writing process that were difficult. I can probably say that organizing all my ideas and research might have been most time consuming because there was a lot of material I wanted to include in the report.

● **What parts were easy or enjoyable?**

● I found most of the report to be easy and enjoyable. When I am able to write on a subject I am not only passionate about, but have experiences relating to it, I find writing to be simple.

● **Thinking back, what did you learn from doing the project?**

● This project was one of the biggest opportunities I had to learn from writing. Prior to the assignment, I had only written the standard five paragraph essays. This project helped me move beyond the clichéd writing assignments I had known, and helped me think outside of the box.

● **What advice would you give to other students about this kind of writing project or writing in general?**

● My advice is not to hold back or be afraid of what other people may think. When I started this project, I was afraid other students might misinterpret the problem I was working on as "pity me," but that didn't stop me.

EVALUATE YOUR LEARNING

1. How would you explain the goals of a college research project to an incoming student?

2. Describe how you came up with the idea for your project. What other ideas did you consider? What factors determined your final choice?

3. What is the most important information you learned from conducting your research?

4. What are the most interesting secondary research sources that you found in conducting your research? How did you find these sources? What advice can you offer other students about finding secondary sources of quality?

5. Describe any primary sources you used—people you interviewed, a survey you distributed, and so on. How helpful were these sources? If you did not use primary sources, would you use them if you were to continue your research?

6. If you completed any interim projects before submitting your final paper or report—for example, an annotated bibliography or an oral presentation in class—how did the interim project contribute to your final paper or report?

7. Did you have any problems documenting your sources correctly? What resources did you use to help you with documentation? (For example, did you use any kind of electronic citation tool?) What advice can you offer other students for learning how to document sources professionally?

8. Now that the project is completed, describe what you learned from your research and writing. If you had more time to work on the project, are there areas of the subject that you would like to research in more depth?

ADDITIONAL READINGS

Cristina Alonso // **THE SHOW MUST GO ON**

Cristina Alonso was born in Miami Florida, and attended Monsignor Edward Pace High School, where she was captain of her school's highly acclaimed dance team. A dance-related injury ended her dream of pursuing a professional dance career. However, she still coaches other dancers, helping them develop their talent without risking serious injuries. Cristina is currently a freshman at

Florida International University where she is majoring in business administration and pre-law. "The Show Must Go On" is a research narrative that she wrote as an interim assignment for a research project on dance injuries.

Heidi Guenther was a beautiful and talented ballerina. At the age of twelve, she received a full scholarship from the prestigious San Francisco Ballet School. After years of training and hard work, she joined the Boston Ballet and became part of the company's 25-dancer corps de ballet, but with this opportunity came many severe pressures and responsibilities. She had to please her employers to keep a job that made her feel successful and accomplished. Although she felt she had finally reached her goal, what her family and friends didn't know was that within the company she was constantly pushed and pressured to fulfill her employers' ideals of perfection. When the company's assistant artistic director told her she needed to lose weight, Heidi developed an eating disorder. She was anorexic for some time, eating very little a day, if anything at all. She later showed symptoms of bulimia, eating and then vomiting or taking laxatives to keep her weight down. At 5-foot-4, and weighing only 115 pounds, she dropped 10 pounds, though her ideal weight according to doctors should have been 120 pounds. On a fateful trip to Disneyland with her family, her body finally couldn't take it anymore. She collapsed and died from a congenital, yet rarely fatal, heart condition. The lack of nutrition from skipping meals, purging, taking herbal diet pills, and taking laxatives caught up with her. Her parents had planned a fun family vacation. Instead, they had to take a trip to the hospital and say goodbye for the last time to their 22-year-old daughter. At the time of her death, she weighed just 93 pounds (Baker; Diesenhouse).

  In essence, Heidi's tragic and untimely death was precipitated by the high standards and competitive attitudes in her profession. Young dancers, as well as young athletes around the world who participate in aesthetic sports like gymnastics and ice skating, are suffering incredible physical and mental health problems associated with training for their sports. They often acquire serious and lasting injuries that affect their everyday lives. According to Lisa Weisenberger, "High school athletes account for an estimated 2 million injuries and 500,000 doctor visits and 30,000 hospitalizations each year. More than 3.5 million kids under age 14 receive medical treatment for sports injuries each year" (Weisenberger). This injury rate is a growing concern as more and more children and teens find themselves battling lifelong injuries, or in some cases mental disorders, from their involvement in competitive sports and dancing. For young dancers, common issues that can arise from the pressures to excel include herniated discs, hip problems, and eating and mental disorders such as anorexia and bulimia. The insistence on perfection in the dance world is a direct route to these problems.

People hear about the health benefits of dancing, but often overlook the toll that competitive dancing can take on a dancer's body. Parents usually place their kids in dance thinking it is a safe sport. However, evidence is starting to show that dance can be just as dangerous as more obviously aggressive or competitive sports. According to Ronald Smith, a University of Washington psychology professor and lead author of a new study published in the current issue of the journal *Anxiety, Stress, and Coping*, "the injury rate for ballet dancers over an eight-month period was 61 percent. This is comparable to rates found in other studies for athletes in collision sports such as football and wrestling" (qtd. in Schwarz). Most of these injuries are the result of pressures coaches put on dancers, and these pressures can be more harmful than pressures coaches apply in more obviously competitive sports. For example, when a coach tells a runner she needs to work harder, this usually means running more, becoming more fit and stronger. When a dance coach tells a dancer she needs to work harder, the dancer might interpret this as needing to raise her leg higher to pass further above her head or just needing to look slimmer and more graceful in her costume—in other words, needing to lose weight. In the world of dance, perception is everything. Your foot needs to look perfect; your leg needs to be dangerously flexible; you need to look good in your costume, and you need to look good even if you are in pain. These pressures can all take a huge toll on the bodies of many dancers, but within dance companies, are seen as the norm. After Heidi Guenther's death, the corps de ballet coach who had urged Heidi to lose weight told the *Boston Globe*, "She [Heidi] was looking a little pudgy—her boobs, her hips, her thighs. You see a girl on stage, her butt is going up and down, it's not attractive. It's a visual art. Because it's a visual art, I can advise what looks good" (qtd. in Baker).

Growing up as a dancer myself, I had very competitive coaches. I know now that they were very neglectful of my health and always wanted more from me, even when my body was giving up on me. I adopted their competitive attitudes as they pushed me in that direction. Eventually, they didn't have to tell me to push myself when I knew something was wrong. They knew they had already converted me into exactly what they wanted, a girl who danced, won them trophies, pushed herself to the limit, and never complained. After all, winning was all that mattered. "The show must go on," they would always say. They would justify their demands and threatened me and my fellow dancers in subtle ways that were difficult for us as children and teens to challenge. They always insisted on the best from us and more, telling us that if our leg broke on stage we would have to keep dancing until the curtain closed. I had seen plenty of girls in competitions who dislocated their knees or shoulders and continued to dance until the show was over. This expectation obviously is very dangerous, but it was something my coaches imprinted on me as non-negotiable. I continue to feel this excessive need for perfection today, and I know it started when I began dancing.

By the time I was sixteen, I was on the school dance team with the same coaches. Over half of the dancers got injured within the first year. Torn hips, torn ACLs, and sprained ankles were common. I was among the injured when I herniated a disc severely and my doctor told me I could no longer dance. Now, I have terrible back pain and can't enjoy many of the things people my age routinely do. I feel that, if my coaches would have coached differently and been more aware and caring of my health issues, I would not have been injured. Their coaching style not only gave me a serious injury, but also stripped away my chance of ever becoming a successful dancer.

In the competitive world of ballet, the shape of your body is extremely important. "In classical ballet, there is popularly believed to be an ideal 'Balanchine' body type for women, with the jobs going to tall, slender women with long necks, long legs and short torsos" (Dunning). This physical ideal is a growing concern for doctors trying to save dancers from anorexia and other eating disorders. Competitive stress levels also contribute to binge or resistant eating. The highest level of stress falls to the dancers who are the greatest perfectionists and the most competitive because those characteristics drive them to overwork themselves. Everyone knows that eating disorders like anorexia are extremely dangerous. Many have died or lost loved ones due to these disorders. Often "the media" is singled out as a source of the problem and gets the brunt of the blame for idealizing unrealistic body types, but as Dr. Michelle Warren, a professor of obstetrics and gynecology at Columbia Presbyterian Medical Center, told the *New York Times*, dance is a huge problem area and cause: "The average incidence of eating disorders in the white middle-class population is 1 in 100. In classical ballet, it is one in five" (Dunning).

Within the community of dancers, some dancers are more susceptible than others. A study published by the *Journal of Dance Medicine & Science* shows that there is a high correlation between perfectionistic traits and dance injuries (Krasnow 52). This study tells us that, in order to solve the problems of injuries and eating disorders among dancers, perfectionism needs to be addressed. I think different coaching styles have a very big impact on dancers' attitudes, and though it may sound surprising, I believe that the most successful dancers are those who have a realistic view of "perfection" and seek it in "moderation." These are the dancers who are more likely to avoid debilitating injuries and eating disorders. But this observation, even if true, raises questions that need to be answered with further research and evidence. What exactly does moderation mean in dance? How do dancers get to a point where they can strive sensibly, yet exercise moderation and pull back from a meltdown? How do they get to the point where they realize that, if they push themselves too hard, their chances of success can actually decline since they increase the risk of incurring injuries and mental disorders that can affect their performance and health? What kinds of coaches encourage excessive perfectionism and how can this coaching philosophy be discouraged? What coaching style, on the other hand, can produce outcomes that are successful and healthy at the same time, or has dance become so competitive in nature that new coaching approaches are unrealistic and won't change anything?

My goal for my project is to discover the most positive and productive coaching style, because I think coaching is the key to the problem, but it also is possible that the source of the problem is really dance itself, and the expectations the public has. If I find there is no coaching style that can really bring about both healthy and successful dancers under present circumstances, I will look into reforms in the art or sport of dance, and people's expectations. In "Eating Disorders Haunt Ballerinas," Jennifer Dunning notes that "thinness was not always prized in ballet." Dunning quotes one ballet expert who described George Balanchine's first ballerinas as "field hockey girls." It is possible that we cannot turn back the clock on today's aesthetic standards, which means that, to produce successful dancers today, coaches have no choice but to bend and break dancers' bodies more and more to keep up with the competitive standard. However, there are successful dancers who do not "crash and burn" because of the coaching and competition. Maybe, indeed, many coaches would like to balance successful and healthy outcomes, but just do not know the right way to do it.

The research I have done so far has provided me with important data and perspectives. Using the *Journal of Dance Medicine & Science*, I was able to discover the aforementioned correlation between perfectionism and injuries. This confirmed the theory that I had developed through my analysis of my own experiences. I was striving for perfection in order to be successful. Success in dance often means being accepted into a top school like Julliard, or getting a professional job as a dancer. To be accepted into a top school or get hired professionally, dancers have to look the part, as well as be technically proficient and flexible. I pursued narrow goals of perfection with blinders on. I pushed myself too hard for my own good and got severely injured. Upon realizing this, I asked myself what made me a perfectionist to the extent that I was? I came to the conclusion that in my case having overly competitive coaches from a young age was the main reason.

In conducting my research, I found a website, *BrianMac Sports Coach,* with a page about "Coaching Styles" that provides useful definitions of different coaching styles. These definitions are important because I want to compare different styles of coaching and come up with the best style for promoting success without perfectionism and negative consequences.

As I have said before, there are successful dancers who do not suffer from the physical and psychological problems that affect so many others. As I continue my research, I hope to identify some dancers like these and interview them, or conduct a survey, to find out what they might have done differently than others, and what type of coaches they had. I will compare and contrast the stories of successful dancers with those who had to stop dancing due to injuries or eating disorders. I will also interview and survey different coaches. I want to compare their coaching styles. I already know about the correlation between perfectionism and injuries in dance, so I will try to determine what types of coaches encourage perfectionism at the expense of the health and well-being of their pupils. I hope to be able to categorize different coaching styles and identify the severity of injuries and eating disorders associated with each style.

Once I discover the best coaching style for dancers, I will describe how this style works and how it could be applied in dance schools and companies. At the same time, I want to alert dancers and their parents of the warning signs to look for, if and when a style of coaching may be counterproductive and put a dancer in harm's way. I hope my research will prove valuable to well-meaning coaches, too, so that they can help to produce wonderful, healthy, and successful dancers. Finally, I hope to offer practical advice about preventing dance injuries, and what to do if one of these common injuries occur.

As for eating disorders, I hope to make coaches, dancers, and parents more aware of the dangers and what to do. In some cases, coaches encourage weight loss with good intensions so that dancers can make it into top schools or companies. However, the standards of these schools and companies are so high that they cannot be attained by many dancers who do not have the natural body types. I want to urge good coaches to set different goals for dancers. A dancer does not have to be in a top school or company to be successful and fulfilled. I hope to prove through my research that there is a successful and fulfilling place for every talented and hardworking dancer.

Dancers who are not blessed with a tiny bone structure that is considered perfect in some companies might flourish in other companies whose choreographers and dance styles encourage other body types. I hope to prove my theory that the best forms of coaching are the ones that push a dancer to be the best dancer she can be, rather than the best dancer in the world. Coaches can push their dancers to be hardworking and dedicated, but at reasonable levels, to achieve realistic yet worthy goals.

All dancers are made differently and have different ranges of motion as well as body types. According to Dr. James Garrick, orthopedic surgeon and Director of the Sports Medicine Center at Saint Francis Hospital in San Francisco, some bodies are not meant to go into certain positions, and doing so can cause serious injuries ("Can Being Too Flexible Be Harmful?"). I want to prove that a dancer's success does not have to be determined by scoreboards that set goals that only people born with certain bone structures and body types can achieve. I also want to correlate different body types to ranges of motions so that coaches have a guide for knowing what the best plan for each dancer should be. For example, a dancer born with a certain body type may not succeed at being a prima ballerina. However, that dancer's body type might be perfect for genres of modern dance or jazz dancing. Coaches should recognize where a dancer's potential lies and encourager dancers to work for achievable goals. I want my project to show that there are opportunities for all types of healthy, yet dedicated and hardworking, dancers around the world. If I can help change the way coaches coach, so that they can maximize individual potential in each dancer, I can help save many dancers' careers, and make dancing a healthier, happier art form or sport.

Works Cited

Baker, Ken. "Heidi Guenther's Short, Tragic Life—and Death." *SfGate*. San Francisco Chronicle, 4 Apr. 1999. Web. 11 Mar. 2015.

"Coaching Styles." *BrianMac Sports Coach*. N.p., n.d. Web. 13 Mar. 2015.

Diesenhouse, Susan. "In a Darwinian World of Weight Control." *New York Times*. The New York Times, 11 Oct. 1997. Web. 13 Mar. 2015.

Dunning, Jennifer. "Eating Disorders Haunt Ballerinas." *New York Times*. The New York Times, 16 July 1997. Web. 26 Feb. 2015.

Krasnow, Donna, Lynda Mainwaring, and Gretchen Kerr. "Injury, Stress, and Perfectionism in Young Dancers and Gymnasts." *Journal of Dance Medicine & Science* 3.2 (1999): 51–58. J. Michael Ryan Publishing, Inc. Web. 13 Mar. 2015.

Kreahling, Lorraine. "Can Being Too Flexible Be Harmful?" *The Expanding Light: Ananda's Spiritual Retreat for Yoga, Meditation, and Wellness.* Ananda School of Yoga and Meditation, n.d. Web. 13 Mar. 2015.

Schwarz, Joel. "Ballet Dancer Injuries as Common, Severe as Athletic Injuries." *UW Today.* University of Washington, 11 Oct. 2000. Web. 13 Mar. 2015.

Weisenberger, Lisa. "Youth Sports Injuries Statistics." *Stop Sports Injuries, Statistics.* The American Orthopaedic Society for Sports Medicine (AOSSM), n.d. Web. 1 Mar. 2015. ∎

From Reflection to Response   **Responding to "The Show Must Go On"**

1. As noted in the chapter, a research narrative is an "interim assignment," similar to a "progress report" in the workplace, that allows a writer to assess and share research findings about a project that is still in progress. After reading Cristina Alonso's research narrative, what do you consider her key findings to date? What does she still need to do to bring her research problem closer to a specific solution, or solutions?

2. Toward the end of her narrative, Alonso discusses primary research she intends to do to move her research forward. If you were working on her project, what kinds of primary research would you do? Who would you interview, and what would you try to learn? If you conducted a survey, who would it be for, and what are some questions you would ask? Would a focus group or site observation be relevant? What about online discussion boards or social media sites?

3. Review the secondary sources in Alonso's Works Cited list. How varied and credible do they appear to be? Using your library's online portal and databases, search for some more secondary sources that are relevant to Alonso's project, and make a list of those that seem interesting or promising to you.

Will...

Going Green

Courtesy of Deanna Passarelli

DEANNA PASSARELLI

Will ... Going Green

This piece was intended to communicate the concept known as "Going Green." The figure in this piece undergoes a literal transformation of becoming one with nature. The mundane "Will" symbolizes the idea of a change. "Going Green" involves looking at things from another point of view, making a choice, and altering some aspect of one's behavior, big or small. Adding just a few leaves and varying color creates a drastic difference, inferring the idea that small changes can affect the bigger picture.

CHAPTER NINE

Public Writing and Community Engagement

> There are two basic flaws in basing a society on greed. The first is that while money motivates people to expend energy, it isn't the only thing that does so: people will work for friendship, for love, for the privilege of being part of a working group, for the enjoyment of service, for beliefs and convictions, or just to make their environment more attractive. The country is full of people working "for nothing" (an American term meaning "for no money").
>
> —Philip Slater, *The Pursuit of Loneliness*

CHAPTER LEARNING OBJECTIVES

In this chapter, you will learn to:

- ▶ Advocate for a cause, inspire action, or implement change.
- ▶ Write in a public genre or forum for a public audience.
- ▶ Strategize your writing to appeal to a public audience.
- ▶ Use thoughtful design elements to enhance your writing and strengthen your message.

WRITING TO COMMUNICATE WITH AUDIENCES BEYOND THE CLASSROOM

As we go through life, we encounter problems that concern us but seem beyond our power to resolve: we sit in our cars snarled in traffic and wonder why public transportation isn't better. We look up at the sky, see a layer of smog blotting out the sun, and wish for cleaner air. We see a homeless woman in rags and feel heartbroken. We write a monthly check to pay down a student loan and realize the interest rate is many times higher than the rate people earn for a CD or a savings account.

Our lives are so busy we cannot speak out about all the problems that matter to us, but when we do, and put our concerns in writing for a public audience, we engage in a form of communication and problem solving called "public writing." Public writing is writing people do to make an impact on issues they feel passionate about. The issues can pertain to a college campus, the surrounding community, or range far beyond, to a nation or the world. Public writing commonly addresses social and civic issues that have a bearing on the quality of our lives but also can address personal issues and experiences that are relevant to the human condition. Candy Chang conceived the "Before I Die" project as a way to "go public" about a period of confusion and grief in her life. Here is her story about the project:

Candy Chang { THE STORY

Anyone Could Pick Up a Piece of Chalk

IT'S EASY TO GET caught up in the day-to-day and forget what really matters to you. After I lost someone I loved very much, I thought about death a lot. This helped clarify my life, the people I want to be with, and the things I want to do, but I struggled to maintain perspective. I wondered if other people felt the same way. So with help from old and new friends, I painted the side of an abandoned house in my neighborhood in New Orleans with chalkboard paint and stenciled it with a grid of the sentence "Before I die I want to _____." Anyone walking by could pick up a piece of chalk, reflect on their lives, and share their personal aspirations in public space.

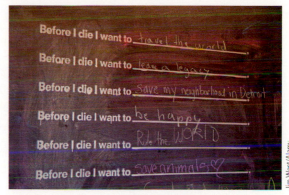

It was an experiment and I didn't know what to expect. By the next day, the wall was bursting with handwritten responses and it kept growing: Before I die I want to... sing for millions, hold her one more time, eat a salad with an alien, see my daughter graduate, abandon all insecurities, plant a tree, straddle the International Date Line, be completely myself.... People's responses made me laugh out loud and they made me tear up. They consoled me during my toughest times. I understood my neighbors in new and enlightening ways, and the wall reminded me that I'm not alone as I try to make sense of my life.

Before I Die I Want to Rule the World

After receiving many requests, my friends and I created a toolkit and project site to help people make a wall with their community. You can also download all files for free to remix or create your own stencils. Thanks to passionate people, over 250 Before I Die walls have now been created in over 15 languages and in over 40 countries, including Kazakhstan, Portugal, Japan, Denmark, Australia, Argentina, and South Africa. They have been a constant source of inspiration and therapy for me. Each wall is unique and reflects the people of that community. Each wall is a tribute to living an examined life.

Our public spaces are as profound as we allow them to be. The historian Lewis Mumford once wrote that the origins of society were not just for physical survival but for sacred things that offer "a more valuable and meaningful kind of life." At their greatest, our public spaces can nourish our well-being and help us see that we're not alone as we try to make sense of our lives. Regularly contemplating death, as Stoics and other philosophers encourage, is a powerful tool to restore perspective and remind us of the things that make our lives meaningful. Each passerby is another person full of longing, anxiety, fear, and wonder. With more ways to share in public space, the people around us can not only help us make better places, they can help us become our best selves.

Despite its personal origins, "Before I Die" draws on a basic principle of public writing: "We're in this together." Public writing makes an assumption that human interdependence is not just unavoidable, but a source of strength, comfort, progress, and happiness. (You can follow the "Before I Die" project on Twitter and Facebook, and also watch a video-talk about the project on the TED website.) ■

KINDS OF PUBLIC WRITING

Public writing can take many forms and use different media. Songs, for example, often serve as public writing, to raise awareness or advocate for change. During the 1980s when South Africa was still under a brutal system of racial segregation called "apartheid," Steven van Zandt—most famous as a guitarist for Bruce Springsteen's E Street Band—wrote a protest song titled "Sun City," to promote a boycott of a South African gambling resort that helped finance apartheid.

U2's "Sunday Bloody Sunday" condemns the shooting of innocent protestors in Northern Ireland. Country and rock legends Merle Haggard and Neil Young wrote songs criticizing the war in Iraq ("That's the News" and "Shock and Awe," respectively). Today, rappers, reggae artists, and rockers carry on the tradition of writing songs that address issues of public concern.

Below, the song "Ecocide," by the punk-metal band Earth Crisis, advocates for environmental activism. In doing so, it raises the kinds of questions about effective messages that public writers need to think about when they speak out to a public audience.

Earth Crisis ﹛ ECOCIDE

Silenced in the roar of the flames.
After the screams of the dying, nothing remains.
Desecrated, slashed, burned to the ground.
In the frenzy of greed, cries of protest are drowned.
The Earth dies—Ecocide.
The Earth's forests laid forever to waste.
Thoughts of the future trampled in their haste.
Corporations with their dollar sign focus ravage the Amazon
     like a plague of locusts.
Plumes of black smoke ascend into the sky.
A forest of beautiful creatures senselessly die.
Smoking fields of devastation left in mankind's wake.
With populations left to grow and greed, they justify this rape.
The power of the dollar can't take precedence over the inevitable
     detrimental consequence.
The time to react is long overdue from protest to confrontation by
     me and by you. ∎

From Reflection to Response | **Responding to "Ecocide" by Earth Crisis**

We can assume that "Ecocide" speaks effectively to the band's punk-metal fan base, but what about a broader audience? Working with a small group of your classmates, or on your own, analyze the song's effectiveness by addressing the points below:

1. In public writing, credibility is crucial. A problem has to be presented in a true and accurate manner or people are likely to dismiss it. With this in mind, how accurately does "Ecocide" present the problem of the earth's destruction? Can you think of factual instances that justify the images, or are the images sensationalized?

2. Who or what does the song point to as the cause of the problem? Is the blame justified and meaningful, or does it scapegoat an easy and obvious target?

3. Good public writing tries to make a difference and contribute to solutions—that is, point to what can be done, what people can do. The last line of "Ecocide" calls people to action, saying the time has come to go from "protest to confrontation." How do you respond to that appeal? What is the difference between protest and confrontation in your view? What do you think "confrontation" realistically means? Would it accomplish anything? Assuming you are someone who cares about making a difference, what could you do? Can you propose specific courses of action that could produce results?

From Reflection to Response | **Songs as Public Writing**

Think of a song in any genre of music that addresses an issue or problem of public concern—in other words, that serves as a form of public writing. Write a short description of the song. Elaborate on the main issue or problem the song deals with, and why you think the songwriter wants to address it. What is the songwriter's view?

Identify a rhetorical strategy or method that the song uses (for example, *narration* to tell a story, an *analogy* to make a comparison, or a *definition* of a concept or idea). What rhetorical appeals does the songwriter use—*ethos*, *logos*, *pathos*, or a combination of the three? (See Chapter 7, page 254, to review information about rhetorical appeals.) When you first heard the song, what impact did it have on you, and why? Did it change your view or increase your awareness? Is there any evidence that the song inspired people to act or advocate for change?

Tech Tip

To help you think of songs, review the music library on your phone or MP3 device, or visit an online music store and review albums by your favorite artists. You can also use sites like www.mldb.org, which allows you to search through over 23,000 albums by over 10,000 artists using keywords like "war" or "love."

Public Writing and Ordinary People

Songs as public writing require a special talent to produce, but public writing takes so many forms that everyone can find a genre or outlet to express their passions and concerns. When people design a T-shirt or bumper sticker (see Figure 9.1) to deliver a message—say, about animal rights, the environment, supporting teachers, or safe sex—they are engaging in a "grassroots" form of public writing. Posters and various kinds of handouts, leaflets, and flyers are also grassroots forms of public writing.

Below is a list of genres, graphic forms, and media that writers can use to "go public" about their ideals and concerns.

An Overview of Public Writing Genres and Media

▶ Blogs

▶ Brochures

▶ Fact sheets/press releases/newsletters

▶ Flyers/pamphlets

▶ Guest columns (newspapers)

FIGURE 9-1 **Bumper sticker for a local nursery**

- ▶ Letters to the editor (newspapers, magazines, journals)
- ▶ Mission statements
- ▶ Open letters and letters to public officials
- ▶ Petitions (print or online)
- ▶ Photo-essays
- ▶ Podcasts
- ▶ Posters and wall murals
- ▶ Public service ads or announcements (PSAs)
- ▶ Social media sites and pages
- ▶ Songs and lyrics
- ▶ Testimonials for an organization or agency
- ▶ Videos on YouTube and other sites
- ▶ Web pages or sites

"Letters to the editor" or "open letters" that people write for publication in newspapers and magazines, both in print and online, are a traditional form of public writing that still resonates and reaches readers. "Guest columns" that people write for college and community papers are a related form that usually goes into more depth. In the guest column below, written for a campus newspaper, Carolina Souto expresses her concerns about the quality of higher education.

Carolina Souto { COLLEGE EDUCATION NEGATIVELY AFFECTED BY CONSUMERISM

Carolina Souto has a B. A. in English and has worked professionally as a copywriter. She plans to return to college to pursue a graduate degree. Her idea for her guest column grew out of a class presentation that dealt in part with the effects of consumerism on higher education.

With higher tuition costs, constant budget cuts, teaching positions and salaries at risk, universities across the country competing for students are behaving like businesses selling a product.

At the same time, today's students, who grew up in an age of consumer culture where shopping is easy and the "customer is always right," are behaving like consumers looking for the best product. These cultural trends combined affect the foundation of higher education.

Both students and universities are responsible for this shift, feeding off the prevailing consumer culture of today.

It is important to be aware how cultural trends affect our behavior, especially when it has to do with our education.

Consequently, some of the people who are making these observations are involved in academics, like Mark Edmundson, who taught at the University of Virginia, and Rebecca Atwood, writer for the *Times Higher Education* online.

In his essay, "On the Uses of a Liberal Education: As Lite Entertainment for Bored College Students," Edmundson's frustration with the merge of consumer-based culture and university life is apparent.

"University culture, like American culture writ large, is, to put it crudely, ever more devoted to consumption and entertainment, to the using and using up of goods and images," said Edmundson.

Since, as students, we pay for education, we should have some say as to how we receive it. We should not, however, buy our education with the same attitude in which we buy our iPads and iPhones.

Part of the consumer culture is buying into commercials that make us want a product. In order to travel along the tracks of the trend, universities now have commercials, which sell fully equipped campuses, with gyms and shops, offering degrees that guarantee success—much like Edmundson's university description.

I'm sure most of us at the University have heard the "South Florida School Connection" jingle.

However, education was not built as a product, and how we treat our education is changing the way the government and universities treat students.

Even our university and Pepsi have teamed up to provide events for students, a perfect example of how universities have given in to the corporate scheme and consumer ideals.

"Students should expect to have full 'consumer rights' if universities and the Government continue to treat them as customers…growing Student Consumerism is Inevitable, says NUS," said Atwood.

Speaking at a conference on the student experience, Wes Streeting, vice president of the National Union of Students (NUS), said universities could not complain about the erosion of academic values and growing consumerism while pursuing a model that makes these trends inevitable.

As students we should be aware of our own contribution to a possible downfall in our own educational values.

We can now rate our teachers online, pick our favorites and choose an easy A. I've done it once before and cringed as I felt my education stabbing me in the back.

Universities, most importantly, should be a place to learn how to work hard, how to fail and how to climb the ladder of success. ■

Considering the cost of a college education today and the very competitive job market that college graduates are entering, Carolina Souto's column is timely, but like the song "Ecocide," its value as public writing ultimately depends on the impact it has on her audience. As a reader, how do you respond? Does the column raise concerns that you share? Does it get to the source of the problem? Is the call to action effective?

A STUDENT'S PROPOSAL

As you consider problems you might want to go public about, read a proposal first-year student Michelle Saunders wrote for a public writing project about the nutritional quality of prison food. Michelle's public writing was part of a larger research project dealing with the same issue. Her proposal addresses the assignment instructions below:

Now that you have conducted significant research for your research project, your next assignment is to convey your most significant research findings to a relevant public audience, using a medium or genre of your choice. You can consider a blog, brochure, photo essay, video, or other form. Your choice will be important. Think about the best way to deliver your research to the specific audience you want to reach.

Nutritional Meals for Prison Inmates
Michelle Saunders

1. Problem and Purpose

The goal of my public writing project is to advocate for menu changes in Florida's correctional facilities. Meals in these facilities lack nutrition and are over-abundant in soy, saturated fats, and cholesterol. I am very passionate about inmates' health, because I have a friend who is currently incarcerated, and like many others in prison, he has developed health problems due to the lack of nutritional meals.

I would like to enlighten my audience about the harmful mental, emotional, and physical effects that poor nutrition has on inmates. I feel that once my audience is aware of the issue and its consequences, a change can be made. I will argue that a nutritional diet will make inmates more productive, cooperative, and less violent.

2. Target Audience

The audience I primarily want to reach is people who have friends or loved ones in prison. I think my message will have an impact on these people and motivate them to join me in changing the status quo. Many of them already belong to advocacy groups and have experience helping inmates in other areas, such as safety and finding employment opportunities upon release.

3. Genre or Medium, and Design Elements

The genre that I will be using is a petition. I think a petition is proactive and would work best with my target audience.

I plan to organize the petition in three sections. The first section will explain why a change is needed. The second section will cover the action that needs to be taken. The third section will include a little bit of information about myself and why I started the petition.

I plan to be brief in my explanations and use a polite and respectful tone, so as not to attack the people who have created the issue. I may also include a picture on my petition that will grab the audience's attention. ■

Interview with the Student Writer

● **Tell us a little about your interests, college major, and career goals.**

● I am majoring in hospitality. It's an area I've always been interested in. I've had experience working in the service industry since I was a teenager, and currently, I am working at a hotel in South Beach [Miami Beach, Florida], while completing my college coursework. My career goal is to be the manager of a prominent hotel.

● **Coming into college, how did you see yourself as a writer?**

● I've always enjoyed reading and writing. Going back to third and fourth grades, my reading and writing skills were always above average. I especially enjoyed reading as a child. I can't say I enjoyed writing quite as much, but I definitely was better at it than I was at math!

Working Together

THINKING ABOUT SOCIAL PROBLEMS AND CAUSES

To generate ideas for your project, review the social issues listed in the table. Circle those that interest or concern you. Then create a short list of the ones you consider most important. (Note that the categories are created only for convenience. Many of the issues can fit in more than one category.)

Category	Issue
Health and well-being	Alcoholism, drug abuse, and other addictions Cycling safety Depression Suicide Eating disorders Clean air Gun safety Home birthing Obesity Safe sex
Social and political	Domestic violence Children at risk Sexual abuse, date rape, stalking Racism, anti-Semitism, Islamophobia Hate crimes, sexism, and bullying Reckless driving and vehicular homicide Police brutality Prison conditions and prisoners' rights Voting rights and registration Birth control Privacy, censorship, and free speech LGBT rights Animal rights and shelters Immigration laws, reform, and justice Littering Recycling Distracted driving Smokers' rights
Economic	College access, tuition costs, and interest rates on student loans Homelessness, poverty, hunger Jobs and joblessness Working conditions and workers' rights Disaster victims Identity theft

Select a problem from your short list that you might want to base your project on—ideally a problem you have some knowledge about and exposure to. Write a one- or two-page description of the problem, what you know about it, what you would most want to say about it, who you would say it to, what you want to see done, and what you would like to see your audience do.

After you have written your description, form a discussion group with three or four of your classmates and take turns explaining why the problem you chose is important (to you, to your classmates, to society, and so on). Address some of the following questions:

1. Do the reasons that the problem is important to you also apply to other people? All other people or just some? How do you know one way or another? Elaborate on how and why.

2. Who would be your target audience for the project? What can you say about your audience—their values, beliefs, and interests? If you were to write a brief profile or "scouting report" about them, what would it say? How can you appeal to their reason (*logos*) and emotions (*pathos*)?

3. (*Note:* Answering the following questions thoroughly may require additional research later.) What have other people *said or written* about this issue as far as you know? Have other people publicly expressed similar views to yours? Were these views effective? Is there a more effective way to state this view?

4. What *actions* have other people taken regarding this issue, and how effective have their actions been?

BECOMING A PUBLIC WRITER

Traditional, printed forms of public writing, like Carolina Souto's column, or a "letter to the editor," can be effective ways to reach an audience, but the revolution in communications offers new opportunities for people to go public and make a difference. Blogging and social networking are compelling examples. Consider the role that Twitter, Facebook, and other networks have played, and continue to play, in inciting and coordinating marches, protests, and demonstrations around the world.

With that said, access to an audience does not translate to connecting with one. A lot of writing that goes public, especially online, amounts to noise more than communication. People may take notice out of curiosity, but the ideas and positions are too emotional, extreme, shallow, or self-centered to enlighten or connect. When composing a public text, you have to make educated guesses about the makeup of your audience to grab its attention and evoke a positive response. How does the audience feel about the issue you want to address? How can you make the problem relevant to them? What genres, forms, or media will enable you to meet your goals—a flyer, brochure, blog, testimonial, web page, video, or even a speech at a public meeting?

Crazy Enough to Think You Can Change the World

Mark Shields, a resident of Washington, D.C., is a person who felt compelled to go public about an issue that concerned him. One night in early 2012, Shields, a devotee of Apple products, was "puttering around in his kitchen" listening to a radio broadcast of *This American Life* on his Apple Airbook. The broadcast was about Apple devices being manufactured in China and the working conditions there. Workers making iPhones were losing the use of their hands because of repetitive-motion injuries. Worse, suicide rates allegedly were so high at some factories that the management installed netting around the roofs to prevent workers from jumping off.

The broadcast troubled Shields. He called a friend to discuss writing a letter to Apple. His friend, like the student whose "prison food" proposal is presented on pages 385–386, thought a petition would be more useful and suggested that Shields create it on Change.org, a website that allows people "to fight for issues they care about." Shields took the friend's advice. The petition he started—an open letter to Apple on Change.org—resonated with other Apple devotees and consumers. Demonstrations took place at Apple stores around the world. Apple CEO Tim Cook responded with a promise to "not stand still or turn a blind eye" to the problem.

Later, on national TV, Shields told an interviewer, "I don't want to stop using Apple products. I love these products and what this company has done for the world. I want them to do it better. They've said, 'We're the ones that think different,' and I want them to think differently about this. I'm not alone. Consumers around the world have said, 'Hey, get on this.' I hope that Apple does."

Mark Shields $\big\{$ **PROTECT WORKERS MAKING IPHONES IN CHINESE FACTORIES**

WHY THIS IS IMPORTANT

Dear Apple,

You know what's awesome? Listening to NPR podcasts through an Apple Airport, playing through a Mac laptop, while puttering about the kitchen.

Do you know the fastest way to replace awesome with a terrible knot in your stomach? Learning that your beloved Apple products are made in factories where conditions are so bad, it's not uncommon for workers to permanently lose the use of their hands.

Last week's *This American Life* shined a spotlight on the working conditions in the Chinese factories where iPhones are made. Just one example of the hardships there: the men and women in these factories work very long days spent repeating the same motions over and over, which creates amped-up carpal tunnel syndrome in their wrists and hands. This often results in them losing the use of their hands for the rest of their lives. This condition could be easily prevented if the workers were rotated through different positions in the factory, but they are not. Why? Because there are no labor laws in China to protect these people.

Here's the thing: you're Apple. You're supposed to think different. I want to continue to use and love the products you make, because they're changing the world, and have already changed my life. But I also want to know that when I buy products from you, it's not at the cost of horrible human suffering.

Here are two simple asks (basically taken from the end of the TAL report) that could make a profound difference in the lives of the men and women in your factories and others like them:

First, in regards to the worker traumas described in the story, ranging from suicide attempts to the people losing the use of their hands from repetitive motion injuries, we ask that Apple release a worker protection strategy for new product releases, which are the instances when injuries and suicides typically spike because of the incredible pressure to meet quotas timed to releases.

Second, since the TAL story aired, Apple has announced that the Fair Labor Association will be monitoring its suppliers. Awesome step. Please publish the results of FLA's monitoring, including the NAMES of the suppliers found to have violations and WHAT those violations are, so that there is transparency around the monitoring effort.

Please make these changes immediately, so that each of us can once again hold our heads high and say, "I'm a Mac person."

Your own ads say that "the people who think they are crazy enough to think they can change the world, are the ones who do."

Please get to it. ■

Shields's petition started an ongoing controversy about labor practices in China and the responsibilities of American companies that outsource their manufacturing there. But the petition also raised questions about Shields's motives, and the accuracy of the information on the NPR broadcast he heard. If you are interested, do some research on the status of the controversy. It is an object lesson in how thorny public writing and advocacy can be.

Working Together

RESPONDING TO MARK SHIELDS'S PETITION

Working with a small group of your classmates, or on your own, respond to the following questions about Mark Shields's petition.

1. Shields addressed his petition to Apple. Do you share his views of the company? Do you think his strategy of petitioning the company directly is effective? Would the petition have been just as effective or more effective if he had addressed it to Apple customers or consumers in general?

2. What are your responses to the working conditions that Shields describes? Do you think his information is accurate and credible? Is Shields overly sensitive to the conditions? He mentions that "there are no labor laws in China to protect these people." Doesn't that suggest that the problem is China's, not ours?

3. There is a relationship between the cost of labor and the price of goods. Improving labor conditions often increases the cost of production, which in turn increases the cost of goods for consumers. Does Shields's petition take these financial factors into account? Do you think he would be willing to pay higher prices for Apple products as a way of supporting better working conditions in China? What is your own position on that issue?

4. As noted earlier in this chapter, effective public writing often does more than argue a position: it includes specific proposals for action and change. Shields makes two specific requests in his petition. What are they? Do you think they are realistic and go far enough toward solving the problem? Can you propose any other courses of action for Apple?

CHOOSING A MEANS FOR GOING PUBLIC

Online petitions, like the one Mark Shields created on Change.org, are easy to distribute and can reach many people, but petitions distributed in person have advantages, too. For example, if you solicit support from people in a public place or at a public event, you can talk to them and exchange ideas.

To make the best choice about how to go public, you need to juggle different criteria: the content of the message, the kind of audience you are targeting, and your own interests, talents, or skills—what you know how to do and like to do. Maybe you cannot write a song or sing it, but if you have a good speaking voice, a podcast might be a possibility. If you are a good writer, write a blog or guest column. If you are a good photographer, consider a photo-essay. (See Chapter 11, pages 471–473, for an example of a photo-essay about homeless people in Portland, Oregon.) If you have an eye for layout and design, you could construct a web page, brochure, or fact sheet. If you can draw, maybe you can create a cartoon, graphic story, or series of memes.

Reaching Your Audience

Once you have chosen an effective form or medium for "going public," think about how to make your message captivating. On the Internet, some texts, pictures, songs, and videos "go viral," but the vast majority of online uploads and postings languish in cyberspace and will never be seen or heard by more than a small number of people. The essence of "going viral" is delivering a message that "hits a nerve"— makes a deep impression and resonates. As you plan your public writing, think about ways that you can (1) make your voice heard and (2) make your message stand out from so much of the "ventilating" that goes on.

Above all, understanding your audience will improve your chances of delivering a message that truly resonates and makes a difference. What kind of person or group of people are you targeting? Below are some questions to consider:

▶ Who would be interested in the problem and find it relevant to their lives?

▶ Are there demographic factors to consider—for example, age, gender, religious and political beliefs, occupation, income, ethnicity, education?

▶ What does your audience already know, and what does it need to know?

▶ Does your audience have values or views that differ from yours, and if so, how can you reach out and find common ground?

▶ Can you convince this audience to act, and if so, how, and what course of action will you advocate?

From Reflection to Response

Activity One: Observing Public Discussion and Civics in Practice

Attend a meeting or event (either on or off campus) where issues are deliberated and decisions are made. Possibilities include:

• A city council meeting.

• A school board meeting.

- A district court proceeding.
- A student government meeting on campus.
- A student organization meeting or event (for an organization you do *not* belong to).
- A political rally, town-hall meeting, or political event (for example, a debate or speech).
- A public meeting or event to promote a cause you care about (or disagree with).

At the meeting or event, observe the proceedings and take notes. Afterward, write a description and analysis of your experience. Consider the following:

1. People:
   - How many people do you see here? How are they dressed? Who are they? Do they reflect the demographics of the general population where you live?
   - Is this event/meeting inclusive or exclusive—in other words, is everyone present really welcome or encouraged to be present? How do you know?
   - Talk to some people—participants, organizers, attendees. Ask them questions about the meeting or event and get their perspectives.

2. Setting and Atmosphere:
   - Where is this event or meeting taking place? Indoors or outdoors? Is the atmosphere formal or informal?
   - How are people physically situated? Is there air conditioning or central heating? Are there places to sit comfortably? How is the seating arranged? What are the acoustics of the place? Can people hear each other easily?
   - Whose participation does the physical arrangement encourage? Whose does it discourage?

3. Group Dynamic:
   - Who speaks? Who is silent? Are there officially designated speakers? What forms of nonverbal communication—attitudes, moods, responses—do you notice?
   - How is the event/meeting organized, and who determines the organization? Can the organization, format, or agenda be altered? Who can make those changes? Does the decision-making process appear to be fair and democratic? Does everyone have an opportunity to participate?
   - Are there any rituals or traditions that take place—for example, prayers or pledges?
   - What kinds of conflict, if any, occur? How are the conflicts settled? Are disagreements encouraged or discouraged?

- Are there some other, better methods of organizing and conducting the event or meeting that could be introduced?
- Do you feel encouraged to return?

Activity Two: Advocacy and Understanding

Many social views and causes that people feel passionate about are products of values most Americans hold dear—namely, freethinking and diversity. Unfortunately, freethinking and diversity produce views and causes that, by definition, are "unpopular"—that is, supported by a minority of people and generally considered outside the mainstream. As such, these views and causes tend to be misunderstood, and their adherents often are demonized: Feminists are "fem-nazis," libertarians are "cranks," pacifists are cowards, environmentalists are "tree-huggers," Christian missionaries are zealots, anarchists are bomb-throwers, and protesters of almost any kind are malcontents, misfits, or "losers." In advocating for many causes, from more funding for public parks to immigration reform or preventing rape, you will run up against indifference or resistance based on misunderstanding. Recognizing the source of the misunderstanding can be a key to connecting to more people in your audience.

With this in mind, look at the causes or movements (past and present) in the table. Most of them are viewed negatively, as outside the mainstream, or on the "lunatic fringe." What exactly do you know about them?

"Isms"	Movements
Veganism	Temperance/Prohibition (or "Straightedge")
Pacifism	LGBT
Evangelicalism	The Tea Party
Anarchism	Occupy Wall Street

Choose one that you know *very little about*, and perhaps also consider extreme or disagree with, and write a brief statement describing what the cause or movement represents to you, and your views about it. Then, go online or use your library database to find more information—read articles, watch videos, and visit relevant websites.

Is any of the information you found surprising or new—different from what you expected? To what extent is the information credible or not? Does it change your views?

> ### Tech Tip
>
> If you want to learn more about a specific issue and get differing perspectives on it, you can use CQ Researcher's browse function (http://library.cqpress.com/cqresearcher/), or try other resources mentioned in Chapters 7 and 8— "think tank" sites like *RAND* and the *Heritage Foundation*, news "aggregators" like the *Huffington Post* and *Techmeme*, and research databases like *Student Resources in Context*—that you can access through your library website. You also can try a popular social news site like buzzfeed.com.

WRITING A PROPOSAL

Once you decide on an issue to go public about, write a proposal to clarify your goals, audience, and strategies for this project. If your main goal is to *motivate people to take action*, what actions can you reasonably expect? Identify an appropriate audience, and gauge how your audience will respond.

Think of this proposal as a working document that you can refer back to and update as needed. Revising the proposal as you draft your public writing will help keep your communication goals and strategies in focus.

For reasons discussed in previous chapters, compose the proposal in *business style*, using the headings below. When you finish writing it, show it to your classmates and instructor, and ask for their suggestions.

Public Writing Proposal

1. **Problem and Purpose.** Elaborate on the problem you are addressing, and the purpose or goal of your project. Do you want to persuade, illuminate, inspire action, change, or a combination thereof? (Approximate length: one or two paragraphs.)

2. **Target Audience.** Describe the audience you primarily want to reach. Discuss why and how you think your message will have an impact on your audience. What response or action do you expect? (A detailed paragraph or more.)

3. **Genre or Medium, and Design Elements.** Describe the genre or medium that you will use to convey your message (for example, an open letter, flyer, brochure, blog, petition, fact sheet, podcast, video, and so forth). In addition, comment on materials or technology you plan to use (software such as PowerPoint, Keynote, or Audacity), as well as design

elements that you think will make your message both accessible and compelling. (A detailed paragraph or more.)

WRITING A ROUGH DRAFT

As you draft your public writing, your first concern is to present the main issue in a way that gets the attention of your audience. In other words, make the issue as relevant as you can. Your second concern is presenting the view or message you support—that is, how you want your audience to respond or take action.

Candy Chang, in her "Story" about "Before I Die," expresses the main issue driving her project in the opening sentences:

> It's easy to get caught up in the day-to-day and forget what really matters to you. After I lost someone I loved very much, I thought about death a lot.

Her view begins to emerge as she assesses her "Before I Die" experiment:

> People's responses made me laugh out loud and they made me tear up. They consoled me during my toughest times. I understood my neighbors in new and enlightening ways, and the wall reminded me that I'm not alone as I try to make sense of my life.

Chang goes on to deliver a view or message that resolves the initial problem of what people can do in their isolation to "maintain perspective":

> Our public spaces can nourish our well-being and help us see that we're not alone as we try to make sense of our lives. Regularly contemplating death, as Stoics and other philosophers encourage, is a powerful tool to restore perspective and remind us of the things that make our lives meaningful. Each passerby is another person full of longing, anxiety, fear, and wonder. With more ways to share in public space, the people around us can not only help us make better places, they can help us become our best selves.

As you compose your own public writing, draw on the communication concepts and skills you have used in previous writing projects. Above all, think about how you will engage an audience that may be unfamiliar with your issue or cause, misinformed, or unsympathetic. Public writing has to answer the "So what?" question. Why should a person reading your text care about it? How will you demonstrate that the issue is important? How will you convince or inspire people to respond in the way you want? You need to be creative and resourceful about answering these questions.

Understanding and respecting other people's perspectives on an issue, *especially* people who might disagree with you, are keys to making your message effective. In general, people who are indifferent, resistant, or opposed to your position are a more meaningful audience than people who agree with you. Rather than dismissing or ridiculing opposing views, try to treat all perspectives in a respectful, even-handed manner. The Rogerian principles covered in Chapter 7 (see pages 262–263) may help you identify common ground and reach more people. Though some may be unwilling to change their views, most at least will respect you and your arguments if they feel their own beliefs and values are respected. In composing this project, also be realistic about the demands you make on your audience. Every day, people are bombarded with requests for their time, money, and sympathies. Strive for a balance between making your message engaging and convincing on the one hand and as accessible and concise as possible on the other. People are likely to ignore a message that is too long and convoluted.

If you know something about your issue or cause through personal experience, consider sharing your experience. In addition, learn as much as you can about the issue. That means doing research to help you develop a broader perspective and strong arguments. People will see you as an authority if your writing shows that you have "done your homework." Reading secondary sources is a good way to start, but don't overlook primary research—talking to people, interviewing a professional, attending a relevant meeting or event, conducting a survey, or studying primary "texts" such as testimonials or memoirs.

Accessible Content and Design

As you draft your text, focus first on including all the facts, examples, and information that you think you need in order to be convincing. But as you revise and edit, take a "less is more" approach. Cut out nonessential information. Stress your strongest points and let them carry the message.

Tech Tip

Word processing software, like Microsoft Word, offers document templates that come with predesigned layouts for newsletters, brochures, posters, and other forms. For example, if you are going to create a flyer for a charity event, Word offers a number of templates that provide attractive layouts, stock photographs, and well-coordinated colors and fonts. These templates are designed to effectively display your content using proven design formats.

Communication...
It's what defines us

The invention of writing systems and alphabets was a breakthrough in communications, what we would call a new medium today. Until there was writing, for example, poetry, whose origins are linked to music and song, had to be heard "live." With the advent of writing, people could enjoy poetry anytime and anywhere, because the words were "recorded." In fact, before writing, all language-based communication transpired face-to-face. After the invention of writing, people could communicate outside of "real time."

Communication Yesterday
Today, visual imagery defines our communications as much as language does. Images come to us all the time and virtually everywhere. Only a few decades ago, using images to communicate required technical skills and expensive equip-

ment, but at present, computers and software programs give everyone the ability to use visuals (photographs, video, graphics), along with audio (recorded speech, sounds, songs, and music), to enhance and transform written communication, or replace printed documents.

Communication Today
In the professional world, digital and multimedia forms such as videos, podcasts, slide-show presentations (PowerPoints), and web pages are widely used to make ideas and information more accessible. With more and more people reading and writing with digital tools, being a good communicator in professional life—a good writer, in fact—means understanding multimedia forms and having some ability to use them to communicate and solve problems.

Communication and Visual Design
The communication principles that you have applied throughout this course, principles that apply to the movies you watch and songs you listen to, are relevant to this project: define the issue driving your composition, and the view you want to support. You also have to consider your audience.

H. Armstrong Roberts/Getty Images

To make your document accessible and appealing to read, consider the design elements below. (For more information about effective design, see Chapter 11, pages 467–469.)

Page Layout—Formatting, White Space, Headings, and Paragraphing
Give your text plenty of "white space," so that the writing is not too dense and cluttered. To make the information more accessible, break up the document into sections with appropriate headings. Use bullets to highlight important points. Use text boxes to separate secondary information. In general, use short paragraphs, and leave plenty of space in the margins. Make your words count and give them "room to breathe." The images below illustrate problems related to layout and formatting that you should strive to avoid.

FIGURE 9-2   Where does the first paragraph start?

Communication Defines Us
by Robert Saba

The invention of writing systems and alphabets was a breakthrough in communications, what we would call a new medium today. Until there was writing, for example, poetry, whose origins are linked to music and song, had to be heard "live." With the advent of writing, people could enjoy poetry anytime and anywhere, because the words were "recorded." In fact, before writing, all language-based communication transpired face-to-face. After the invention of writing, people could communicate outside of "real time."

Communication Yesterday

Today, visual imagery defines our communications as much as language does. Images come to us all the time and virtually everywhere. Only a few decades ago, using images to communicate required technical skills and expensive equipment, but at present, computers and software programs give everyone the ability to use visuals (photographs, video, graphics), along with audio (recorded speech, sounds, songs, and music), to enhance and transform written communication, or replace printed documents.

Communication Today In the professional world, digital and multimedia forms such as videos, podcasts, slide-show presentations (PowerPoints), and web pages are widely used to make ideas and information more accessible. With more and more people reading and writing with digital tools, being a good communicator in

professional life—a good writer, in fact—means understanding multimedia forms and having some ability to use them to communicate and solve problems.

Communication and Visual Design
The communication principles that you have applied throughout this course, principles that apply to the movies you watch and songs you listen to, are relevant to this project: You have to be clear about your purpose, define the issue driving your composition, and the view you want to support. You also have to consider your audience and the conventions of the genre you are composing in. Multimedia compositions use rhetorical appeals (ethos, logos, and pathos) and methods of development (narration, comparison and contrast, definition, etc.) that you are familiar with.

Photo essays consist of a selection of photographs that communicate visually the way traditional essays communicate through words. Photo essays have captivated and edified people since photography was invented. In the form of "photojournalism," they were the trademark of legendary magazines like *Look* and *Life* that have left a priceless legacy of images about the events, people, and social trends of previous generations.

UniversalImagesGroup/
Getty Images

Like written essays, photo essays don't conform to a fixed set of rules. The number of photographs can vary from a few to a dozen or more. The photographs can be introduced with text.

Look and Life that have left a priceless legacy of images about the events, people, and social trends of previous generations. The communication principles that you have applied throughout this course, principles that apply to the movies you watch and songs you listen to, are relevant to this project:

FIGURE 9-3   An example of cramped layout

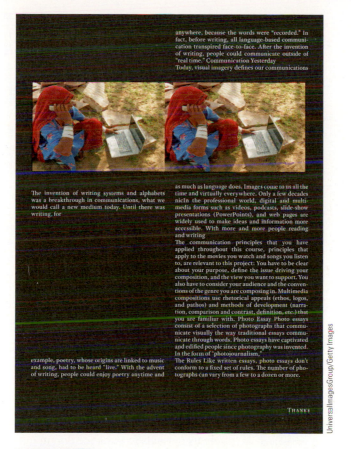

FIGURE 9-4   **An example of unbalanced formatting**

Fonts and Colors Busy, extravagant, or careless design elements can detract from your message more than help. Avoid odd fonts, typographical tricks, and loud, clashing colors. It is better to err on the side of understatement than overstatement. Figure 9.5 shows the problems that are visible when too many font styles are used. Figure 9.6 shows what can happen when white text is used on a white background.

Conversely, a creative and tasteful use of fonts and colors can enrich your message. Study print documents or web pages that you find visually appealing, and use them as models. Figure 9.7 shows the cover of a brochure that first-year student Ashley Miller created for a public writing project about the benefits of living in a multilingual and multicultural community. The vibrant, tropical green color, along with thoughtful wording and a relaxed layout, supports the positive message Ashley's brochure delivers.

Communication
Defines Us

The invention of writing systems and alphabets was a breakthrough in communications, what we would call a new medium today.

U ntil writing, poetry, gins are linked song, had to be heard "live." With the advent people could anytime and because the "recorded." In there was for example, whose ori- to music and heard "live." of writing, enjoy poetry anywhere, words were fact, before writing, all language-based communication transpired face-to-face. After the invention of writing, people could communicate outside of "real time."

Today, visual imagery defines our communications as much as language does. Images come to us all the time and virtually everywhere. Only a few decades ago, using images to communicate required technical skills and expensive equipment, but at present, computers and software programs give everyone the ability to use visuals (photographs, video, graphics), along with audio (recorded speech, sounds, songs, and music), to enhance and transform written communication, or replace printed documents.

Communication Today

In the professional world, digital and multimedia forms such as videos, podcasts, slide-show presentations (PowerPoints), and web pages are widely used to make ideas and information more accessible. With more and more people reading and writing with digital tools, being a good communicator in professional life—a good writer, in fact—means understanding multimedia forms and having some ability to use them and solve problems. Photo essays consist of a selection of photographs that communicate visually the way traditional essays communicate through words.

Photo essays have capti-vated and edified peo-ple since photography was invented. In the form of "photo-journalism," they were the trademark of legendary magazines like Look

Photo Essay Photo essays consist of a selection of photographs that commu-nicate visually the way tradi-tional essays communicate through words. Photo essays have captivated and edified people since photography was invented. In the form of "photojournal-ism," they were the trademark of legendary magazines like Look and Life that have left a priceless legacy of images about the events, people, and social trends of previous generations.

The Rules
Like written essays, photo don't conform to fixed set of rules.

UniversalImagesGroup/Getty Images

FIGURE 9-5   **An example of too many font styles**

Alo Ceballos/Getty Images

FIGURE 9-6   **An example of white text on white background**

Graphics and Visuals Word processing and desktop publishing make it easy to insert visuals into documents today. Professional writers routinely use visuals to enhance documents they create and convey important information. As with other design elements, your visuals should support communication goals, not just serve as decoration. Appropriate visuals can make your public writing more impactful as well as concise. Consider some of the following:

▶ Tables, graphs, charts, and maps

▶ Original artwork

▶ Photographs

Figure 9.9 shows a fact sheet produced by The National Campaign to Prevent Teen and Unplanned Pregnancy. Would a fact sheet be an effective form for your own project?

No Habla
Español

No problem...

Ashley, Miller, ENC 1102, March 19, 2013

FIGURE 9-7   **Cover of a student's brochure about multilingual Miami**

UNDERLYING PROBLEM:

During Miami's recent development, a clash between the city's numerous ethnic cultures has grown. While some argue that the city's native residents and their traditions have been pushed to the back of the Miami's cultural main stage, others argue that Miami's rapidly growing cultural diversity is what has turned this South Florida tourist attraction into one of the world's most unique global centers.

Benefits of a Multicultural City

Culture:
Having a city with such a diverse cultural mix creates a community like any other. Diversity in the form of more than 1,296,737 Hispanics, 427,140 African Americans, 466,772 White citizens, and 26,837 Asian's creates Miami a melting pot on par with some of the most well-known international cities in the world.

Economy:
Just like any city across the nation, Miami has experienced its share of financial troubles. However, such a unique blend of global cultures has led to Miami becoming a global center for international business, trade, tourism, and real estate.

Real estate:
Our weather, world-class attractions, and proximity to South America creates a down economy many travelers to own both commercial and residential property in Miami. The average home buyer or renter's currency background can take advantage of our current low interest. The wide range of housing prices in Miami also makes it easy to own a residence or vacation home. This provides a boost to not just the real estate economy, but also benefits all of the city's other existing businesses.

Hoberman Collection/Getty Images (top); TommL/Getty Images (middle); Visions of America/Getty Images (bottom)

FIGURE 9-8   **Foldout of *No Habla Español* brochure**

Tech Tip

If you need photographs to enhance your content and design, try the image search engine Compfight, which offers filters and options to help you locate usable images for personal, educational, and commercial projects.

Working Together

ACTIVITY ONE: TEEN PREGNANCY AND SUBSTANCE USE: EVALUATING DESIGN AND CONTENT

Working with three or four of your classmates, evaluate the design and content of the "Teen Pregnancy" fact sheet. Keep in mind that The National Campaign produces a wide variety of public-service materials for different audiences; thus, this single fact sheet has a limited role in the larger campaign. Below are some points to consider:

1. What audience is the fact sheet targeting in your opinion? Is the choice of audience appropriate for the information?

Why It
Matters

The National Campaign to Prevent Teen Pregnancy

Teen Pregnancy, Substance Use, and Other Risky Behavior

It often is the case that risky teen behavior, including drug, alcohol, and tobacco use, delinquency, and sexual activity, occur among the same groups of teens. Therefore, teens who drink or use drugs often are more sexually active and less likely to use contraception when they have sex than teens who take fewer risks. They also tend to have more sexual partners, and often start having sex at younger ages.

- Nearly four in ten high school students report having experimented with marijuana at least once, and over one-third of 12th graders report they have used some type of illicit drug.[1,2] Approximately two-thirds of 9th graders report having tried alcohol at least once and one-quarter of all high school students say they drink heavily on occasion.[1]

- Teens 15 and older who use drugs are more likely to be sexually experienced than are those teens who do not use drugs—72 percent of teens who use drugs have had sex, compared to 36 percent who have never used drugs.[3]

- Teens who have used marijuana are four times more likely to have been pregnant or to have gotten someone pregnant than teens who have never used marijuana.[4]

- More than one-third of sexually active teens and young adults age 15 to 24 report that alcohol or drug use has influenced them to do something sexual.[5]

- Nearly one-quarter of sexually active teens and young adults age 15 to 24 report that they have had sex without a condom because they were under the influence of alcohol or drugs. And 43 percent of teens and young adults say that they are concerned that they

might do more sexually than they had planned because they are drinking or using drugs.[5]

- Boys who start drinking or smoking at a young age are 40 percent more likely to start having sex at a young age when compared to boys who refrain from such activities. Girls who smoke or drink are even more susceptible—prior use of alcohol and/or cigarettes increases the risk of early sexual experience by 80 percent.[6]

> **More than one-third of sexually active teens and young adults age 15 to 24 report that alcohol or drug use has influenced them to do something sexual.**

- Many teenage girls who use alcohol when they first have sex are too drunk to use birth control successfully.[7]

- Almost one-quarter of all high school students used alcohol or drugs prior to their last sexual experience. Non-Hispanic white and Hispanic teens are more likely than non-Hispanic black teens to report having used alcohol or drugs before their last sexual experience.[1]

- Seventh graders who report being sexually experienced are more likely than their sexually inexperienced peers to report having committed a theft, damaged property, or threatened a teacher.[8]

www.teenpregnancy.org   •   202.478.8500   •   web@teenpregnancy.org

Source: ebookbrowsee

FIGURE 9-9   **The National Campaign to Prevent Teen and Unplanned Pregnancy: Fact Sheet**

2. Describe the main design elements. How effective is the layout? Does the presentation grab a reader's attention? Does the photograph at the top create an appropriate impression? Is the color scheme effective? Is the information accessible enough?

3. How compelling and persuasive are the facts and statistics? Is there too much or too little information? Would you add or take out anything? To what extent do you think the fact sheet succeeds in achieving its goals?

ACTIVITY TWO: EXISTING ORGANIZATIONS, AGENCIES, GROUPS, NONPROFITS, AND PUBLIC SERVICE CAMPAIGNS

To expand your knowledge of design, effective content, and "messaging," visit the website of an organization or agency that supports a cause of interest to you. Read the mission statement. What has the organization done, and what is it doing?

Review the content of the site. Are articles posted? Do archives, links, or testimonials offer, or point you to, useful information?

Do you see an opportunity as a college student to become involved with the organization or contribute to its mission in some way? What events could you attend?

Figure 9.10 shows the home page of an organization that has received high praise for its aggressive campaigns against hate crimes.

Source: Southern Poverty Law Center

FIGURE 9-10   **The Southern Poverty Law Center: "Dedicated to Fighting Hate and Bigotry"**

PUBLIC WRITING AND COMMUNITY ENGAGEMENT

Writing for a public audience about an issue of concern to you is the crux of this project, but if you base your public writing on volunteering in your community, you can make a contribution that is even more gratifying, as well as more valuable for your professional development. You already might be involved in some form of community work or service learning for another course. If not, consider engaging in civic work specifically for this project.

Depending on the college or university you are attending and where it is located, opportunities for community engagement will vary, but most colleges today have placement centers that help students partner with local agencies and organizations. If your college does not have a placement center, you can take the initiative to contact organizations on your own and offer to volunteer your time.

Opportunities for service learning and engagement can range from mentoring or tutoring secondary school students, to teaching English as a second language, serving food in homeless shelters, promoting AIDS awareness, or working on community farms that provide fresh produce for the poor.

Often, when you engage in service, you work with an organization or agency whose mission coincides with your personal concerns and passions. For example, if you know someone who died of AIDS, working for an AIDS-awareness organization could be a gratifying experience for you. If you have suffered through a natural disaster such as a flood, tornado, or hurricane, you might feel passionate about helping disaster victims. If you once benefited from an after-school mentoring program, you might want to "give back" as a mentor yourself. Then again, it also can be gratifying, as well as educational, to work for a project or cause you know little about—to help patients at a free medical clinic, for example, or teach children with learning disabilities, or plant trees for an environmental organization.

To locate an organization on your own, talk to people, go through your local telephone book, and do Internet keyword searches (for example, search for "community service programs" or "social services" or "environmental agencies"). Religious institutions in your area also can be a good source of information, as many of them sponsor, or are affiliated with, community-service programs.

Community service that college students perform is often called "service learning" for a realistic reason. Service is about giving your time and helping, but it also is an opportunity for you to learn and grow, expand your knowledge and experience, and contribute to improving the quality of life in your community.

Service-Based Public Writing

The practical needs of the organization you work for probably will determine any public writing you do as part of a service-learning project. For example, your supervisor or mentor might ask you to create a brochure or flyer, or contribute to a newsletter, a mission statement, or content on a website.

Doing this kind of writing for a real purpose will be an invaluable learning experience for you. Your instructor will be interested in seeing what you write, but also may ask you to write a report or reflective essay about your civic experience and any public writing you did. You might be asked to do one of the following two examples of assignments.

A Service-Learning Report

Service-Learning Report

- *Purpose:* The purpose of this report is to describe the goals and operations of the agency or organization that you worked for and the contributions you made.

- *Presentation Style:* Compose the report in business style, following the format outlined below. A binder is not necessary, but neatness and readability are paramount. Make the writing accessible and appealing to the eye by using adequate spacing and block paragraphs. Make the paragraphs as concise and unified as possible.

- *Length:* Approximately 3 to 5 pages.

Report Format

Cover Page:

Include the title of the report, who the report is for, and your name.

Sections and Headings

1. *Purpose*
To complete this section, elaborate on the first bullet point in the "Instructions" above (in other words, "The purpose of this report is to describe the goals and operations...").

2. *The "Mission" Statement of the Agency or Organization*
Summarize or reproduce the agency's "mission" statement—in other words, describe how the agency defines itself and what its goals are.

3. *Services Provided*
Describe the services that the agency provides and how the services are provided. Include an overview of the facilities that the agency owns or uses and other assets or equipment needed for delivering services—for example, vehicles, computers, software, supplies.

4. *The Management, Personnel, and Organizational Structure of the Agency*

Describe the agency's personnel and organizational structure from top to bottom, starting with the board of directors, if there is one. Conclude with related information such as the number of employees, volunteers, or interns, and affiliations with other agencies and organizations.

5. *Funding Resources and Issues*

Describe the agency's chief sources of funding—for example, federal, state, and local government contracts or grants; corporate and private foundations and trusts; private donations; fund-raising events.

Discuss funding issues that you learned about through your work, efforts being made to resolve those issues, and the prospects for new funding sources.

6. *Volunteer Experience Summary*

Describe your volunteer experience—the number of hours you worked, the task(s) performed, your assessment of the value of what you did, how well you did it, and what you learned.

7. *Final Observations and Recommendations*

Develop your final observations about the agency, its operations, and its prospects. Include any recommendations you can make about funding and services, based on your experience.

A Reflective Essay Assignment

Service Learning and Writing: Reflection and Rhetorical Analysis

- This short essay will consist of a reflection about your service-learning experience and a rhetorical analysis of the writing you did as part of the experience. It is not a formal essay in the sense that you need a thesis statement or a formal introduction and so forth. However, it should be written for a professional audience. Clarity, style, and good editing are important. The questions below will help you develop your reflections. (You also can review the report outline on pages 338–340 for more suggestions.)

- Length: Approximately 3 to 5 pages.

General Questions:

- What are the specific goals of the organization you worked for?

- Were you able to observe concrete, positive outcomes from its efforts?

- How do you feel about the work you did? Is it something you would pursue further in the future?

Rhetorical Questions about Any Writing You Did:

- Describe the writing you did. Was it collaborative or written by you alone? Were you assigned to do it, or did you come up with the idea?

- What audience did you target?

- Why did you choose this particular audience? What values do you believe this audience holds? Was the audience you actually reached the same as the audience you expected or hoped to reach?

- Describe the composing process. How did you plan and come up with ideas? Did you make significant changes as you composed? Who read your drafts, and what reactions did you get?

- What rhetorical appeals did you use to make the writing memorable and convincing (in other words, appeals to *ethos, logos, pathos*)?

- What parts of the writing process were difficult for you? What parts were easy or enjoyable?

- How satisfied are you with what you wrote? Looking back, is there anything you would do differently or think you could improve?

YOUR PROJECT CHECKLIST

Writing for a public audience draws on your passions and creativity, but as you know from reading this chapter, the project has a lot of "moving parts": you have to identify your audience; determine what genre, form, or medium you will use to reach it; clarify your communication goals; and strategize how to prevail over indifference, resistance, opposition, or ignorance. You may have

✔ Task	Description	Time Frame
☐ **Choose a subject**	• Develop ideas for the project, and discuss your ideas with your classmates, your instructor, and others. • Select an issue that you care deeply about. • Ideally, you should know something about the issue and have had some exposure that you can bring to bear on your project.	A day or two.
☐ **Write a proposal**	Plan your project by writing a proposal that describes your purpose, audience, and the form or medium you plan to use.	An hour or less.
☐ **Conduct primary and secondary research**	• Build on your knowledge of the issue by doing primary and secondary research and learning about existing organizations that advocate for awareness and change. • Go to a public meeting. • Talk to people. • Visit the offices or websites of relevant agencies or organizations. • Read secondary sources of quality. • View reputable documentaries and videos. • Listen to podcasts. • Take detailed notes.	Three days or more.
☐ **Draft and revise**	• Draft and revise your "text" or composition until you "get it right." • Make the delivery concise, without sacrificing substance and cogency. • Use graphics and features of document design to enhance your message. • Make sure you are advocating in an even-handed manner and proposing carefully thought-out solutions that strive for inclusiveness. • Have a specific outcome in mind—how you want your audience to respond, what you want your audience to do.	About a week.
☐ **Get peer review**	• When you have a working version or draft of your project ready, ask for feedback from classmates (see peer review questions on page 409). • Consider posting your draft on your course website or your Facebook page if you have one, or visit your campus writing center to get advice from a tutor.	Varies.

✔ Task	Description	Time Frame
☐ **Edit your text**	Make sure you edit your text carefully. If the text is concise, even a minor error will stand out and affect your credibility. Consider using the text-to-speech feature on your computer to help you catch mistakes or typos. Check for the following: • Helpful paragraphing • Parallel constructions in your lists (see Chapter 12, pages 533–534) • Effective wording and word choice • Sentence punctuation (fix run-ons and comma splices) • General grammar and mechanics (subject-verb agreement, pronoun reference, placement of commas, capitalization)	Varies.

to conduct research to make your content compelling. You also have to make your content as accessible and concise as possible and use effective design elements to enhance its appeal.

As always, a realistic writing process is crucial to the success of this project. Use the checklist in the table as a guide for managing your time.

Audience awareness goes to the heart of a public writing project and needs to be on your mind through all the stages of composing. Once you have a working version of your project drafted, bring it to class or post it on a course website to find out how your classmates and instructor respond. Incorporate feedback that makes sense to you.

PEER REVIEW

1. What do you know about the problem or cause being addressed? Is there background information or a perspective that the writer needs to address in more detail?

2. Do you agree with the writer's position or view? If so, or if not, explain why.

3. Describe the intended audience for your classmate's project. Imagine you are part of that audience even if you are not. How well do you think the project will connect to the audience and achieve the writer's goals? If you can, offer suggestions for improvements.

4. Is the choice of the form, genre, or medium effective? Can you think of alternatives?

5. Does the writer demonstrate knowledge of the issue and credibility (good *logos* and *ethos*)? What parts of the text are most effective? What parts need strengthening? Is more research called for, and if so, what kind of research would you recommend? Is the writing concise enough or too concise? Can you think of points, issues, or facts that are unclear, unconvincing, or missing?

6. How effective are the design elements and layout? Are engaging visuals used? Suggest improvements if you can.

7. Are there problems with wording, grammar, or mechanics that distract from the message or make the writing unclear? Point out sentences or passages that need to be revised.

REVIEW AND ASSESS YOUR COMMUNICATION GOALS

Because your public writing project is meant to make a difference—invoke action or change—you need to be especially conscious of your communication strategies. Before you go public with the project or submit a final version to your instructor, use the "Rhetorical Analysis" below to review and assess how your project communicates to your intended audience. (Your instructor may ask you to submit a written copy of the analysis with your project.)

1. **Communication Goals—Central Issue:** Where or when in the composition is the central issue presented? Why do you think the way you present the issue will have an impact on your audience?

2. **Main Message:** Where or when in the composition is the central view or message delivered? What impact do you think the main message will have on your audience, and why? How does it contribute to resolving the issue you are addressing?

3. **Target Audience:** Describe the audience you are targeting for your project. Why and how can this audience contribute to resolving the issue or problem your composition addresses? What specifically do you expect, or ask, your audience to do?

4. **Genre or Medium:** Why did you choose the genre or medium that you use for this project, and why do you think the choice is effective?

5. **Rhetorical Appeals:** Identify and evaluate rhetorical appeals you use in your composition (*ethos, logos,* or *pathos*). Why do you think the appeals you have used will have an impact on your audience?

6. **Rhetorical Methods:** Identify and evaluate a rhetorical method of development that you use in your composition—for example, *narration* (telling a story), *comparison and contrast*, an *analogy*, an *illustration or example*, a *definition* of a concept or idea, or *a cause-and-effect relationship*. Why did you opt to use this method, and what effect do you expect it to have on your audience?

7. **"Usability":** Discuss how your composition—whether it is delivered in print or digital form—would reach your intended audience. In other words, where and when do you, as the author, think a reader or viewer would encounter your public writing?

STUDENT WRITING: FINAL DRAFT

Below is the petition first-year student Michelle Saunders created to advocate for more nutritious meals to be served in Florida's prisons.

Petition Letter:

April 18, 2012

Prisontalk.com

PrisonTalk Facebook Community

Dear Prison Talk Florida,

Attached to this email is a petition I have created asking the Florida Department of Corrections for menu changes in our state's correctional facilities. The food currently being served to inmates is detrimental to their health and creates behavior issues in an already tense environment. Changing the menu from chemically processed foods and soy products to whole grains, fruits, and vegetables will promote better physical, mental and emotional equilibrium among inmates, and reduce violence and other behavior problems.

The research I have done shows that the poor quality of the foods being served to inmates is contributing to a general state of tension and discontent. Inmates are malnourished, and suffer from recurring episodes of nausea, vomiting, cramping, indigestion, and gastritis. Foods typically are served lukewarm-to-cold and contain no seasoning, so that inmates buy and consume a lot of unhealthy commissary items like potato chips and cookies that make an already bad diet worse.

The "meat" portions of prison meals consist exclusively of turkey and soy. Lizette Alvarez, writing in the *New York Times*, reports that a diet of excessive soy can lead to thyroid problems and other health issues. Twenty-five grams of soy per day is the recommended limit, yet Florida inmates are fed on average three or four times that amount.

Michael Meacher, a former British Minister of the Environment, believes there is a correlation between poor diet and behavior problems. "Quality food standards do not just ensure better nutrition," Meacher writes, "their impact on behavior is so striking that prison management programs now urgently need to incorporate them." Meacher quotes Bernard Gesch, a research scientist at Oxford University, who says, "clinical studies suggest nutrition is a humane and highly effective means of reducing antisocial behavior. It is also cheap."

On the subject of costs, Karen Weisberg argues in the *Food Service Director* that prison food can be both healthy and cost-effective. She describes a successful program launched by the Manatee County Corrections Bureau, in which inmates grow their own organic produce and raise livestock. This program not only contributes to low-cost, nutritional meals, but trains inmates for "viable work upon their release."

My petition does not ask that prisoners be overindulged or served lavish meals. The petition simply states that inmates have a right to a balanced, nutritious diet that consist of whole grains, fruits, vegetables, omega 3 fatty acids, vitamins, protein, and minerals.

I have a friend who is an inmate at the Key West Detention Facility. He and many others are adversely affected by the poor quality of the meals being served to them. I am appealing to you who are friends and family members of an inmate to join me in making a change.

I hope you will pass this petition around and ask others to sign it. I will be taking the petition to my friend's correctional facility on visitation days and asking other visitors to sign. Please consider doing the same, and also asking for support from your personal friends and neighbors.

After tabulating signatures, I will contact you again by email or regular mail with follow-up strategies for delivering the petition to state representatives and decision makers within the prison system. I plan to organize a statewide call-in day, and also ask for support from journalists around the state who have written columns and news stories about the dysfunctions and abuses within Florida's prison system.

Thank you for your consideration and participation!

Sincerely,

Michelle M. Saunders
Florida International University

Brief Bibliography

Alvarez, Lizette. "Soy Diet Is Cruel and Unusual, Florida Inmate Claims." *New York Times*. The New York Times Company, 11 Nov. 2011. Web. 5 May 2015.

Huff, Ethan A. "Feeding Prisoners Genetically Modified Soy Products May Be 'Cruel and Unusual' Punishment." *NaturalNews.com*. NaturalNews, 13 Nov. 2011. Web. 6 May 2015.

Meacher, Michael. "Diet Can Make You Nice." *New Statesman*. New Statesman, 16 Feb. 2004. Web. 6 May 2015.

"Rights of Inmates." *Findlaw*. Thomson Reuters, n.d. Web. 14 May 2015.

Weisberg, Karen. "Food Costs Drop in FLA: Cost Avoidance Gives New Meaning to Life in Prison." FoodService Director, 15 Nov. 2002, Trendsetters sec.: 24. Print.

Return Signed Petitions To:

Petition Sponsor: Michelle Saunders

Phone Number: _____

Email: _____

Address: _____

PETITION

We the undersigned respectfully petition the Florida Department of Corrections for menu changes in Florida Correctional Facilities.

Purpose: The purpose of this petition is to improve the nutritional quality of the meals being served in the state's correctional facilities. The meals currently are over-abundant in soy, saturated fats, cholesterol, and chemically processed foods. The poor quality of the meals is a form of inmate abuse that unnecessarily contributes to health and behavior issues among the inmate population.

Action: Those signing this petition recognize the existence of this problem and support menu change in the state's correctional facilities. A healthier diet that includes whole grains, fruits, vegetables, omega 3 fatty acids, vitamins, protein, and minerals will make inmates healthier, more cooperative, and more productive in completing their work details and other duties.

Information about the petition sponsor: I am a Florida International University freshman who believes everybody deserves humane treatment. I have a friend who is a member of the inmate community. I don't want my friend to suffer unnecessarily from malnutrition while serving his sentence in prison. My petition is not advocating for prisoners to have anything they want to eat. It simply says they have a right to a balanced diet and nutritious meals that will promote physical and mental health. I am asking the inmate community—that is, people like me who know and care about someone in prison—and also citizens who care about prison reform, to come together and sign this petition for change.

Interview with the Student Writer

● **How did you come up with your idea for your project?**

● I was personally involved with someone who was in prison at the time. So the issue mattered to me—it was something I learned about firsthand and wanted to try to address. Plus I had access to detailed information from my friend.

Courtesy Michelle Saunders

● **How did you go about composing the petition?**

● In general, whenever I have something I need to write, I usually write my first drafts in longhand on a writing pad, and then transfer what I've drafted to a computer. I find this approach helps me draft more efficiently. The process of transferring the draft is a first revision. Whenever I'm working on a project, and have an idea for improving it, I always make sure to write down the idea right away, so that I don't forget it. If I'm not near my desk or wherever I happen to be working, I'll e-mail the idea to myself, or leave a note on my phone.

● **Who read your drafts, and what reactions did you get?**

● The petition was part of a larger research project I conducted on the prison-food issue. My friend who was in prison at the time helped me a lot by providing information. He also arranged for me to conduct interviews with other prisoners. Since he was knowledgeable and cared about the project, I would send him my drafts for advice and suggestions.

● **What parts of the writing process were difficult for you?**

● Though I cared about the problem because of my friend, it wasn't a problem I was personally familiar with. I had no firsthand experience or knowledge to build on, so I had a lot to learn and had to rely on my primary and secondary research to get started. Usually, I prefer to write about topics or problems I'm more personally familiar with.

● **What parts of the project were easy or enjoyable?**

● Once I get started on a writing assignment or task, I usually enjoy it. If I'm contributing to a group project, more often than not, I'll get my part done first and help the others. When I enjoy the topic or task, I tend to write quickly. Although I love the hospitality field, I think professional writing could be an alternative career track for me.

● **Thinking back, what do you think you learned from the project?**

● To complete the entire project I wrote a research narrative and a professional report, along with the petition. The three documents were intended for different audiences—academic, professional, and public. The whole idea of writing in different styles and genres to reach the different audiences was a valuable learning experience.

● **What advice would you give to other students about this kind of writing project or writing in general?**

● Try to choose topics or problems you're motivated to write about, and then give yourself time to get into the project and make what you write meaningful. Even if you're very busy, find time to fit the project into your schedule. Writing becomes easier when you know you're writing something that has value.

EVALUATE YOUR LEARNING

1. In preparing this project, did you come across a current example of effective public writing (for example, a public service announcement, song, or blog), and if so, what did you find effective about it?

2. Did you come across an example of public writing that was not effective, and if so, what was wrong with it?

3. While composing your project, did your view of the main issue change in any way? If it did, what caused the change? If it didn't, what other views or perspectives did you consider, and why did you reject them?

4. Describe what you have learned from doing this project. What skills have you used, developed, or discovered that you may be able to apply to other projects in college or in your professional life?

Courtesy of Emma Rickert

EMMA RICKERT

Merry-Go-Round

For this piece, I was paying homage to classic lifestyle illustration of the 1950's and 60's, in which artists would use unexpected color schemes and compositions. The viewer gets the vague idea of a storyline—a man and a woman on a carnival ride—but the rest of the story is up for interpretation. I aim to keep my illustrations somewhat ambiguous in this way so that the viewer can take from it what they will. It is sometimes difficult to determine what details need to be added to keep the illustration interesting and what should be left out so that the storyline is up to you, but that's also the fun part.

CHAPTER TEN

Analyzing Stories

> *Now you know it's a meaningless question*
> *To ask if those stories are right,*
> *Because what matters most is the feeling*
> *You get when you're hypnotized.*
>
> —Bob Welch, "Hypnotized"

CHAPTER LEARNING OBJECTIVES

In this chapter, you will learn to:

- ► Understand the role of storytelling and the literary arts in people's lives.
- ► Analyze the key elements of stories—plot, character, and theme.
- ► Write an objective analysis based on a personal response.
- ► Illuminate the meaning and value of stories for your readers.

STORYTELLING AND THE LITERARY ARTS

Storytelling is a fundamental part of our lives. We tell stories day and night, at home, in our dorm rooms, at work, in restaurants and check-out lines, on airplanes and buses, at the gym or the hairdresser's.

Some of these stories are true, inspiring, instructive, and meaningful; some are just rumors or jokes, maybe even lies, but whatever the stories are, they go to the heart of how we communicate and connect to other people.

In college, students traditionally learn about stories and storytelling as literature or literary art, mainly in the form of fictional narratives, plays, and poems. More broadly, literary art also includes nonfictional forms of writing such as memoirs, biographies, histories, and essays that evoke human life and its problems in compelling ways. Reading and writing about literature are of value in a college writing course, because understanding how stories work and affect us is relevant to anyone who wants to be a good writer and communicator. In addition, the kind of writing students and professionals do when they write about literature is analytical. Effective analysis is the essence of critical thinking and problem solving. Exposure to literature certainly promotes a deeper understanding of life and people, but also practical skills that are valued in the professional world. Steve Strauss, a business columnist who sits on the board of the World Entrepreneurship Forum, writes that English majors are his "employees of choice," because they know how "to think for themselves, and how to analyze a problem." English majors have served as CEOs for companies like NBC, Xerox, Disney, and MTV. Bracken Darrell, an English major and CEO of Logitech, told *Business Insider*, "The older I get the more I realize the power of words and the power of words in making you think. . . . The best CEOs and leaders are extremely good writers and have this ability to articulate and verbalize what they're thinking."

Regardless of practical considerations, reading literary works is a pleasurable escape and lifeline for millions of people around the world. The eminent critic Kenneth Burke aptly has called literature "equipment for living," but some of the pleasure it provides may also come from the intimacy of the reading experience itself. Imagine, for example, that you live in Kenosha, Wisconsin, or for that matter, any place in the world—Buenos Aries, Tehran, Kiev, or Tokyo. On a stormy night, you are lying in bed with the blinds closed and see a man in pilgrim's clothes tripping through a forest, toward a fire in a clearing. The date is 1688; the forest is in Massachusetts. The fire illuminates a chanting congregation of devil worshippers who are inducting converts into their cult. The man in the forest thinks he sees his dead father beckoning him to join the ceremony. He thinks he sees his mother throwing out her hand to warn him off. Then he sees something more unbelievable: his beloved wife, pale and jittery, taking a demonic vow.

If this is happening before your eyes, you are watching a movie.

If it is happening in your mind, and you are reading words, you are experiencing what literature is. In an influential book, *Reading Without Nonsense*, Frank Smith, an esteemed educator, describes this kind of reading experience as "writing along with the author." In Smith's words, when you read in this way, "You don't *study* how the author writes, you *participate* in the author's writing."

The essence of literary art is *participation*—the intersection of a writer's imagination and a reader's, an imaginative collaboration between the two. Literary works transport you into other worlds and other lives, into the past and the future. If the experience is "literary," it has meaning: it marks you in some way. Literary works can be about anything: a Confederate saboteur with a noose around his neck; a young man who wakes up as an insect. These are situations that launch two classic stories, but if *Pet Sematary*, *Harry Potter*, or *Choke* come alive in your imagination and enlighten you, they also are works of literature. If a song by Mumford and Sons, Adele, Nas, or Axl Rose does the same, the song is literature. If a Marvel comic does it—comes alive in your imagination and enlightens you—the comic is literature.

LITERARY ANALYSIS

General readers, critics, and scholars argue about the value and quality of fictional stories and other literary works, but literary analysis does something more important: it illuminates the works and their meaning. Literary stories re-create the feeling of life being lived, the "reality of experience," in ways we can analyze and understand. Human life is too complex for anyone to comprehend. To get a handle on it, we rely on specialized perspectives—sociology, history, theology, science, psychology, and so on. No one has the intellectual capacity to assimilate and synthesize all the information. Our understanding of life is necessarily fleeting and compartmentalized. Literary art captures the flux of life and distills its complexity in a way we recognize as "real" and can contemplate for meaning.

Professional literary criticism requires a knowledge of literary genres, theories, and terms. That kind of criticism is beyond the scope of this writing course. The goal of this project is to give you exposure to analyzing literary art based on your response as a reader, your creative participation in the writer's work. To keep the project manageable, the instruction in the chapter will focus on one popular and accessible genre, the short story.

A STUDENT'S ESSAY PROPOSAL

Now that you have some understanding of this writing project, read a proposal that student Fangyu Xu (Frank) wrote for an analytical essay about James Joyce's classic short story "Araby." Fangyu Xu's essay proposal is based on the following instructions:

Write an analysis of a story you have read in the course. Your analysis should address an issue related to understanding the plot, characters, or theme of the story, and it should support a view or thesis about the story's meaning and relevance to readers.

Analysis Essay Proposal: The Romantic Ideal in James Joyce's "Araby"

Fangyu Xu (Frank)

1. The Main Issue, Question, or Problem

My essay will be a close-reading and thematic analysis of "Araby." Though the story is mainly about the boy-narrator, I want to show how the boy's environment affects his emotions and psychology, and finally, plays a role in his growth and coming of age. James Joyce uses a detailed and elaborate depiction of the environment to highlight the changes the boy undergoes in the story.

2. The Viewpoint or Thesis

The boy's environment consists of his family circumstances and the atmosphere of Dublin, Ireland, the city he lives in. The boy's secret love of Mangan's sister develops against the background of a drab city and home life. Mangan's sister inspires a romantic ideal of love and beauty in his life. In contrast to the environment surrounding him, the romantic ideal seems sacred and bright, but when the girl finally talks to him and casually mentions the Araby bazaar, an element of anxiety enters the story. The ideal that she represents becomes connected to the reality of the boy's environment, and can no longer thrive. As a result, the boy's innocence and childhood are lost. He is forced to accept that and to grow up.

3. The Relevance of the Essay to Readers

The details and description of the boy's environment are very important in understanding the story. Without the descriptions of the environment and their contrast to the boy's romantic ideal, the psychological changes the boy goes through would seem routine, but if we understand how the drab environment makes the boy long for romance and beauty, we can see that his struggles and disappointment are noble and important.

Interview with the Student Writer

● **Tell us a little about your background, interests, college major, and career goals.**

Courtesy of Fanqyu Xu

● I recently graduated from Florida International University (FIU) with a Master of Science degree in Management Information Systems. I am currently working as an IT security analyst for Herbert Wertheim College of Medicine at FIU. My career goal is to be an expert in IT security.

● **Coming into college, how did you see yourself as a writer?**

● I was a good writer when I was in high school in China, but English is not my native language, and it was not easy for me to write in English when I began my studies at Florida International University. To improve my writing skills, I started to read the news online (e.g., CNN, BBC, the *New York Times*). I would write brief comments about the news I read. That greatly helped me learn to express myself in English. I think I have strong analytical skills, but I am still working hard to expand my English vocabulary.

Working Together

THINKING ABOUT STORIES

To begin this activity, spend five minutes freewriting, brainstorming, or making a list of *stories* in different forms that have made a deep or lasting impression on you, possibly helped you better understand yourself, life, or other people. These stories can be drawn from different art forms or genres, including movies, animations, comics, novels, narrative poems, or songs.

After thinking of some stories, choose one and write a short analysis of it in three parts:

- *Briefly* summarize the story and explain what makes it interesting to you.
- Describe the main character and what you consider significant about her or him.
- Explain the meaning of the story as you see it, and its relevance to readers or viewers.

After writing your analysis, form a group with three of four of your classmates. Take turns discussing the stories you wrote about, and find out to what extent the story you picked piques the interest of your classmates. What do they relate to about the story, or possibly not relate to?

ELEMENTS OF STORIES: PLOT, CHARACTER, AND THEME

As you have learned in doing previous writing projects, analysis means breaking something down in order to understand it better. For the purposes of analysis, stories usually are broken down into three interrelated parts:

- ▶ Plot
- ▶ Character
- ▶ Theme

Understanding Plot

The words "plot" and "story" have overlapping meanings; they both refer to events that create a narrative, or what happens in a story, but writers and critics make an important distinction between "story"—the events that happen—and "plot"—the cause-and-effect relationship between events, or specifically, why events happen. In a story that has a plot, everything happens for a reason. In real life, that is not always the case. If a man walks past a construction site and a wrecking ball falls on his head and kills him, that is a story—a random incident that can be blamed on bad luck or equipment failure. However, if the man lingers by the site to gaze at a building that is about to be demolished, a building in which his father once worked, and then the wrecking ball kills him, that is a plot. The man dies for a reason: he stopped to remember his father. His death has meaning.

Good fictional stories strike us as "real" and true to life, but in fact, they are inventions that a writer constructs to express meaning. Thus, to understand a story, it helps to think about the plot—to ask why events happen as they do.

Understanding Character

When we ask questions about plot, we have to ask questions about characters, too. Characters usually make a story happen and shape the plot. They are the reason we care about stories. Centuries ago, the Greek philosopher Heraclitus said, "Character is destiny." Good stories are infused with the magnetic pull of a character's destiny.

For most people, analyzing a character is easy enough. In our day-to-day lives, we say a friend or family member is strong-willed or dishonest, sneaky, egotistical, unselfish, or brave, and we offer reasons for saying so, based on our knowledge of the person and the person's behavior. Analyzing a character in a story is the same thing. Here the director of *The Dark Knight Rises*, Christopher Nolan, analyzes Batman:

> He's someone who suffered enormous trauma as a child—his parents gunned down in front of him—and what he's carried with him all his life is an extraordinary level of rage, sadness and all kinds of angst. All these negative elements in his soul are pushing him in a certain direction, and he's desperately trying to turn that into something good. That's why his best adversaries are the ones who represent some other, darker direction he could have chosen.

Batman is a fantasy figure, but Nolan describes him as someone real, someone we could know and in some ways do know or see in ourselves. Good stories present characters that seem real to us, characters we feel we know as well as real people. Nolan's *Dark Knight* movies present an array of fascinating characters, good, bad, and in between—Bane, Blake, Harvey Dent, the Joker, Alfred Pennyworth, Catwoman, and Ra's al Ghul—but ultimately the movies are about Batman, the main character. Almost all stories, no matter how short or how long, function the same way: they are essentially about one character, a main character, more than any other. The main character, sometimes called the "protagonist," is the character the reader knows the most about. The main character usually has the greatest effect on the story and is most affected by the events of the story. As a result, the main character, or protagonist, is the key to understanding a story.

In most stories, identifying the main character is easy, but sometimes a story may seem to be about a character who is not the main character. In *The Great Gatsby* by F. Scott Fitzgerald, a popular short novel that many students read in high school, the title and the story itself invite readers to assume that Jay Gatsby, a mysterious, self-made millionaire, is the main character, but the story is told from the point of view of a first-person narrator, Nick Carraway. Nick is the main character by virtue of being the narrator, the character we know best. The story is filtered through his consciousness. He has to have the greatest effect on the story because he chooses what to tell us and interprets everything that happens. In a real sense, he is the story. We can gauge the effect the story has on him because we have access to his thoughts and feelings. We know more about him than any other character, including Gatsby. In first-person narratives, the narrator almost inevitably is the main character.

In some longer stories that are written in the third person and present an array of important characters, the main character initially may be hard to identify, but the principles of storytelling all but demand that a story have one character more essential to the story than any other, a character who most affects the story and is most affected by the story, a character we know, understand, and focus on more than others. That character is the main character for the same reasons that a narrator is.

Motivation and Change

We understand the characters in a story through their thoughts, actions, words, and the corresponding personality traits we perceive (naïve, shrewd, brave), but the most important source of our understanding is the direct effect a character has on the plot or story. Actors and actresses who portray characters in movies and plays call this direct effect "motivation." Motivation is what a character wants and why—the character's goal in a story. The main character's motivation usually launches a story and drives the plot. For the character, the story is a quest or journey from the beginning to the end. In most stories, this quest or journey affects the character in observable ways—it forces the character to change or grow.

The stories or movies that make the strongest impression on us present characters who are thematically interesting because they grow and change. Even in the best action movies—*The Dark Knight Rises* is an example—the main character changes in a meaningful way. Thus, when we analyze stories, if we identify the main character's motivation at the beginning, and assess a process of growth or change from beginning to end, we can learn a lot about the character and the meaning of the story.

At the beginning of *The Great Gatsby*, the narrator, Nick Carraway, moves to New York from his hometown in the Midwest because he is restless and wants more out of life. His motivation or goal is to find a grander, more fulfilling life. At the end of the story, he returns to his hometown. He has gone full circle, literally back to where he started. He seems changed in some significant way, a different man from what he was in the beginning, wiser and tougher, because of what he has experienced. However, if we look at what happens in the story, rather than simply Nick's interpretation, we see little evidence of real growth and change. Nick, like most of us, has blind spots when it comes to knowing himself. One significant blind spot is his assumption that he is condemned to be a passive observer of events because he is not rich or powerful enough to make a difference. In fact, he chooses that passive role. Nick could not have done anything to change Gatsby's fate, but at the end of the story, he has the opportunity to confront the people responsible and call them to account. Unfortunately, he doesn't have the courage. He makes excuses for them (tells us they are "careless" and childlike), and ultimately, for himself. In doing so, he demonstrates he has not changed in any significant way. His significance as a character lies in the gap between his self-image and the facts of the story. For him, giving up on accountability is a concession to "reality" that amounts to newfound wisdom, but by giving up without trying to make a difference, he remains what he always was, a sentimental man who has a talent for fine-tuning reality with words.

Understanding Theme

> " *It's all been said before—*
> *Make the best out of the bad, just laugh it off.*
> *You didn't have to come here anyway.* "
>
> —ROD STEWART, "EVERY PICTURE TELLS A STORY"

For many readers, analyzing themes is more difficult than analyzing characters. Most textbooks define "theme" as the main idea of a literary work. Sometimes main ideas are presented as generalized abstractions—for example, *Redemption*, *Innocence*, or *Time*—that seem to have a remote or tenuous connection to the characters and actual events in a story. These generalized themes are so much a part of human life that they apply to many or most stories. Indeed, the most general theme of all, *Illusion versus Reality*, is a quintessential theme of human life, and as such, can be put forward as the main idea or theme of every story ever written or told. Generalized themes illuminate stories when they evolve from a detailed analysis of characters and events. Unfortunately, in some critiques they evolve from fine points of minor importance in a story—symbols or images—that have little or no effect on our emotions yet are supposed to be packed with significance—a green light at the end of a dock, a faded billboard, or the mast of a ship in the shape of a crucifix. The result for students is that the story, or literary work, is transformed into a puzzle, something to study and learn about, rather than experience and enjoy.

Flannery O'Connor, a famous short story writer and novelist, complains about this "study-learn" approach to literature in an essay about her own work ("A Reasonable Use of the Unreasonable"):

In most English classes the short story has become a kind of literary specimen to be dissected. Every time a story of mine appears in a Freshman anthology, I have a vision of it, with its little organs laid open, like a frog in a bottle.

I realize that a certain amount of this what-is-the-significance has to go on, but I think something has gone wrong in the process when, for so many students, the story becomes simply a problem to be solved, something which you evaporate to get Instant Enlightenment.

A story really isn't any good unless it resists paraphrase, unless it hangs on and expands in the mind. Properly, you analyze to enjoy, but it's equally true that to analyze with any discrimination, you have to have enjoyed already.

To understand, analyze, and write about theme productively, your emotional and imaginative response to the story is crucial. Creative writers have ideas about life that they want to express, but they write stories in order to say more, to communicate in the special way that stories communicate, to create an experience of life to which readers have a visceral response.

Themes and Communication Goals

Instead of piecing together a theme from literary clues, put yourself into the story and try to experience the themes the way the main character and other characters do. From this interior perspective, themes are nothing more than views or messages a story expresses about issues and problems that the plot raises and with which characters struggle. In other words, stories communicate in much the same way that essays do: they present compelling issues or problems and support meaningful views. Since good stories re-create a rich sense of life, they usually present multiple issues and views, and by extension, multiple themes, but most stories have a central theme, that is, a large, recurring issue that dominates the story, and a view that the story expresses about that issue.

Analyzing theme according to this definition is a straightforward process that begins with *identifying the issues* that a story raises. These issues are not mysterious or mystifying. Nor are they necessarily earthshaking. But they are the main reason we read stories and find them interesting. Stories that are plotted and worth telling always start with perceivable issues that put us on the trail of a central theme or themes.

The opening of the story below, "The Sketchbook" by Fredrick Water-man, illustrates how issues—subtle as they may be—draw us into a story:

> "I don't get it."
>
> "What don't you get?"
>
> Marian Harris glanced across the airplane's aisle at the father and son sitting in Row 22, Seats A and B. The boy, about 10 years old, had his father's bright-red hair and prominent freckles, and across his lap lay a large, open book.
>
> "Clouds. I don't understand clouds."
>
> "What don't you understand about them?"
>
> "Well, look out the window. If clouds are like wisps of smoke, then how come they don't drift apart instead of sticking together? And if they stick together, how come when a plane flies through them, it doesn't come out with cloud stuck all over it?"
>
> "Aw, come on, Dad, I'm trying to read," the boy sighed.
>
> The father, in Seat A, peered out the oval window. "Just think if you could reach out, grab a piece of cloud, and take it home! You could keep it in a box in the closet, then take it out and play with it whenever you wanted."
>
> "Dad, clouds can't be pets."
>
> The father turned to his son. "Hmmm, you might be right. And if you kept it, what would you name it? And, John, what if it became tame? Would that mean you couldn't release it back into the wild? Maybe it would get so used to following you to school every day that it wouldn't want to go back to 35,000 feet. And what about the ethical and moral questions?" he wondered aloud, gazing out the window again.
>
> The boy regarded his father for a long moment then shook his head slowly and returned to his book.
>
> Marian had been careful not to give away that she was eavesdropping. She noted that the father was tall and lean, bordering on skinny, his hair was tousled, and his clothes were casual and haphazard. In odd contrast, the boy was neatly dressed with his hair combed. They both wore glasses, but the father's were wire rims while the boy's were more somber, with heavy, black frames....

Waterman's story starts with a bit of dialogue that raises a small issue: someone—we don't know who—is confused about something ("I don't get it"). We next learn that a woman, Marian Harris, is overhearing and observing a conversation between a father and son on an airplane. Readers will assume that the boy is the one who is confused about clouds. When we find out that it is the dad, a humorous issue presents itself: father and son have reversed roles. The father is curious and whimsical; the son is serious and preoccupied. "What's with this father?" we might ask, "Is he a dufus? And what about the ten-year-old boy? Is he some kind of 'brainiac'?"

The issue and the questions it raises draw us into the story and put us on the trail of two themes—views that the story expresses—about our roles in life, and the role that imagination plays. The opening also tells us that the woman, Marian Harris, who is observing, overhearing, and reporting on the conversation, is an important character, perhaps the main character (which, in fact, she turns out to be). Her significance to the story and its meaning are not clear yet, but the absorbed, nonjudgmental way she takes in the conversation tells us that something about it is relevant to her.

Issues that launch a story are thematic if they recur and evolve in importance and complexity as a story develops. The issue we see as most important in the story usually is connected to the main character's motivation—what he or she wants most and why—and this issue produces the main theme, the view the story expresses about that issue.

The Great Gatsby raises issues from the very beginning about money, ambition, social mobility, love, and fame. The story supports views (themes) about all of them; however, the central, recurring issue is connected to Nick's motivation—what he wants most out of life: something grander than the life he was living when the story begins. Gatsby's rise from humble beginnings to great wealth in the novel tells us that the American dream of financial success is alive and well, but Nick's own story, along with Gatsby's, also tells us that the larger, existential dream of reinventing ourselves without boundaries, of being whoever we want to be, transcending the past and our perceived limitations—all of that turns out to be illusory, literally a dream and nothing more. Nick goes home. When all is said and done, Gatsby makes a similar, cyclical journey back to obscurity, bearing out the aspersion of a despicable adversary who calls him "Mr. Nobody from Nowhere." The novel expresses a pessimistic view of our ability to reinvent ourselves. This view, as we have seen, is mainly based on Nick's character and choices, but at the same time, it is a view whose realism many psychiatrists would endorse.

Now that you have a better understanding of how stories work, use the following checklist as a tool to help you analyze stories that intrigue you. After reviewing the list, practice analyzing the "very short" story by Ernest Hemingway that follows (some would call it a tale, as in fairy tale). See if you can make a case for its central meaning or theme.

A Checklist for Analyzing Stories

Story Line or Plot

▶ **Create a Map of the Story:** Write a summary, or create a storyboard, reverse outline, or timeline that gives you a map of the events that form the plot.

▶ **Identify Key Scenes:** Note the most crucial, dramatic, memorable, or revealing scenes, incidents, or events in the story, and why they are so important.

▶ **Evaluate the Ending:** Describe how the story ends and consider why it ends the way it does.

Character(s)

▶ **Identify the Main Character:** Who is the main character, or "protagonist," the character whose inner life the reader knows most about, who most affects the story and is most affected by the story? Is there a narrator—a character telling the story?

▶ **Describe the Character's Motivation:** What is the main character's motivation—what does he or she most want, and why?

▶ **Evaluate Growth and Change:** How and why does the main character grow or change from the beginning of the story to the end?

▶ **Review Supporting or Secondary Characters:** Make a list of any characters, besides the main character, who have an important role in the story. What is their role and motivation? How do they change, if at all?

Theme(s)

▶ **Consider the Relevance of the Title:** A good way to begin thinking about theme is simply to note the title of a story. Sometimes a title is matter-of-fact, just a character's name ("Young Goodman Brown") or a reference to the setting ("An Occurrence at Owl Creek Bridge"). Often, however, the title points to an issue or thematic meaning that the writer wants to emphasize ("A Good Man Is Hard to Find").

▶ **Identify Key Issues:** What issues do you see at the beginning of the story? Do these issues evolve or change as the story develops? Are new issues introduced, and if so, are they related to the issues that launch the story?

▶ **Identify Views:** Ask yourself what views the story expresses about the issues it raises. These views are "themes."

▶ **Review the Ending:** How does the ending relate to the beginning of the story? What view does the ending support about any of the issues you identified in the story—especially a central or recurring issue? To develop a perspective on the ending, consider different ways the story could have ended, and how those different endings would change the view or meaning that the story conveys.

Ernest Hemingway { **A VERY SHORT STORY**

Everett Collection Historical / Alamy

Ernest Hemingway (1899–1961) was an American journalist, fiction writer, and Nobel Laureate in Literature, known for his "mastery of the art of narrative" and a style of writing that draws readers into the sensory world of his experiences and stories.

ONE HOT EVENING IN Padua they carried him up onto the roof and he could look out over the top of the town. There were chimney swifts in the sky. After a while it got dark and the searchlights came out. The others went down and took the bottles with them. He and Luz could hear them below on the balcony. Luz sat on the bed. She was cool and fresh in the hot night.

Luz stayed on night duty for three months. They were glad to let her. When they operated on him she prepared him for the operating table; and they had a joke about friend or enema. He went under the anesthetic holding tight on to himself so he would not blab about anything during the silly, talky time. After he got on crutches he used to take the temperatures so Luz would not have to get up from the bed. There were only a few patients, and they all knew about it. They all liked Luz. As he walked back along the halls he thought of Luz in his bed.

Before he went back to the front they went into the Duomo and prayed. It was dim and quiet, and there were other people praying. They wanted to get married, but there was not enough time for the banns, and neither of them had birth certificates. They felt as though they were married, but they wanted everyone to know about it, and to make it so they could not lose it.

Luz wrote him many letters that he never got until after the armistice. Fifteen came in a bunch to the front and he sorted them by the dates and read them all straight through. They were all about the hospital, and how much she loved him and how it was impossible to get along without him and how terrible it was missing him at night.

After the armistice they agreed he should go home to get a job so they might be married. Luz would not come home until he had a good job and could come to New York to meet her. It was understood he would not drink, and he did not want to see his friends or anyone in the States. Only to get a job and be married. On the train from Padua to Milan they quarreled about her not being willing to come home at once. When they had to say good-bye, in the station at Milan, they kissed good-bye, but were not finished with the quarrel. He felt sick about saying good-bye like that.

He went to America on a boat from Genoa. Luz went back to Pordenone to open a hospital. It was lonely and rainy there, and there was a battalion of arditi quartered in the town. Living in the muddy, rainy town in the winter, the major of the battalion made love to Luz, and she had never known Italians before, and finally wrote to the States that theirs had only been a boy and girl affair. She was sorry, and she knew he would probably not be able to understand, but might some day forgive her, and be grateful to her, and she expected, absolutely unexpectedly, to be married in the spring. She loved him as always, but she realized now it was only a boy and girl love. She hoped he would have a great career, and believed in him absolutely. She knew it was for the best.

The major did not marry her in the spring, or any other time. Luz never got an answer to the letter to Chicago about it. A short time after he contracted gonorrhea from a sales girl in a loop department store while riding in a taxicab through Lincoln Park. ■

From Reflection to Response   Analyzing "A Very Short Story"

Working with a small group of your classmates, or on your own, analyze "A Very Short Story." As you begin, remember that writers write stories to communicate with readers. Writers want their stories to come alive in a reader's imagination and say something meaningful about life and people. Try to experience the story and understand what the story is communicating about real life. These questions will guide your analysis:

- Does the title of the story have any thematic significance, or is it just a factual reference to the story's length?

- Where and when does the story take place, and are the time and place significant? (You might want to look up "Padua" and "the armistice.")

- Who is the main character (this is the character you know most about and whose consciousness shapes the story)?

- What is the character's motivation—what he or she wants and why?

- What is the first issue you can identify in the story?

- As the story develops, what do you see as the main issue, the issue that comes up again and again?

- What is the significance of the ending? How does it relate to the beginning of the story? What view does the ending support? (Consider other possible endings and how they would change the meaning.)

- Does the main character grow or change in the course of the story, and how is his or her growth or change relevant to the theme you identified?

CONSIDERING SUBJECTS AND COMMUNICATION GOALS

Your writing project for this chapter can be based on the reading at the end of the chapter, or those in MindTap, or your instructor may suggest additional readings from outside of class that you can write about.

An interesting analysis of a story, like any essay, has communication goals; it presents an issue relevant to understanding the story, and it supports a view that enlightens readers. Coming up with an idea for the analysis has two parts: (1) choosing a story to write about and (2) identifying a meaningful issue to explore. For this project, write about an issue that "speaks" to you, to which you have an emotional, as well as intellectual, response.

Intelligent readers can have legitimate differences of opinion about what makes a story enjoyable and edifying. Sometimes a meaningful analysis can explore and support a negative response to a work. The work of every acclaimed writer, from Shakespeare to J. K. Rowling, has been "trashed" for one reason or another by other writers and critics, but negative criticism is best done by writers who are widely read and who have thought a lot about their aesthetic principles and can defend them. Negative criticism is a risky business for inexperienced writers. A better way for you to engage and enlighten your readers is to analyze a story you enjoyed.

To prepare for this writing project, spend some time reading different stories and getting acclimated to the genre. A few stories are included at the end of this chapter; your instructor might recommend some others. Read with patience and an open mind. Some stories, like some movies, grab us right away. Others take time to settle in to, but once we do, we often find ourselves in a world that captivates us. Try to read more than one story, and jot down your impressions and responses. In particular, identify issues that are relevant to understanding the story.

USING SOURCES

The kind of essay you are writing for this project is called a "reader's response," which means the essay emanates from your perceptions about the story you analyze. Students who have been taught the study-learn approach to literature are conditioned to base an analysis on sources—published articles about a work (and/or the predigested information in "SparkNotes"). Sources can give you perspectives and insights about a work. Below, for example, is an excerpt from a source that offers insights into Hemingway's "A Very Short Story." The writer, Harold Loeb, was a friend of Hemingway's in the 1920s. The excerpt is from an article Loeb wrote titled, "The Young Writer in Paris and Pamplona," in which he describes a conversation about writing he had with Hemingway in Paris, while they were drinking wine and eating oysters on the terrace of a café:

> "What they [readers] want," I said, "is violence and women. You've got lots of violence. Why not insert some women? So far, you've given us only the shadow of a woman. That poor Marjorie...."
>
> "Women!" Hem said.
>
> "It's your good luck," I said brashly, "to be married happily. It must be wonderful. But a happily married man misses something."
>
> "Such as what?"
>
> By then I was aware of the cloud, the black ominous cloud that had spread across his features. Nevertheless, I went on blithely.
>
> "Misery," I said.
>
> "So I've not known misery! So that's what you think!"
>
> I had no desire to discuss misery. Hem had no bent for talking about abstractions, although misery was a pretty tangible abstraction. "Let's have another bottle," I said. "This one's on me. To hell with misery."
>
> Hem's anger had vanished. His eyes were intent. "So you think I haven't known misery. That I'm just a Midwestern..."
>
> "Just thought you were a little luckier than some," I interrupted.
>
> But he wasn't listening. He was talking about a girl in Italy, a trained nurse. She had taken care of him in the hospital during the war. They

had fallen in love. She had left him. Hem became quite eloquent. He described in sensual detail her head, her hair. Her body had taunted him for years, he said. I never doubted again that Hem had known misery.

And I was aware for the first time of the fury within him. Not a bad fury. Furies, like many other spirits, have more than one face. The good side of Hem's fury drove him forward, enabled him to take extraordinary pains, pushed him to writing incessantly—"putting things down," Hem called it—made him a great writer.

Loeb's article is an example of a biographical source. Biographical sources can illuminate circumstances and passions that shape a writer's life and work. Readers of "A Very Short Story" will identify the "girl in Italy" mentioned above as the nurse in Hemingway's story. Loeb's account of his conversation with Hemingway is relevant to the story because Hemingway's deep feelings for the nurse invite us to see the story as more than a cynical swipe at love, or conversely, perhaps less than a faithful picture of its human significance. Nevertheless, the article is an article and the story is a story. They have no inherent connection to each other. In general, for student writers, the problem with using, and especially relying on, sources for an analysis is that sources can suffocate a reader's response with too much information, and make an analysis dry and uninteresting.

With that said, a reader's response is not a self-centered expression of personal values and tastes ("I wish they ended up getting married"). It has to be objective. You are writing about the story, not yourself. Your goal is to illuminate an aspect of the story for your readers. Instead of drawing on observations others have made, let your own reading, the facets of the story you respond to most, guide your analysis. For example, if you are analyzing "A Very Short Story" and you once spent a long time "laid up" in a hospital, you might have special insights about the beginning of the story. If you are religious and understand the meaning of wedding banns, you might see moral ambivalence affecting the relationship between the man and Luz, and want to elaborate on that. Or if you once had a self-destructive response to rejection, you might have a different view of the end of the story than other readers.

Insofar as good stories *are* understandable, your insights may coincide with views that already have been published. As a composition student, you should not worry about that. The process of developing insights through your own response to the work will make your essay original and illuminating just the same.

CREATIVE INVENTION TECHNIQUES

When you read a story you plan to analyze, you have to read it more than once and in more than one way. The first reading should be for enjoyment. You can take brief notes and highlight passages, but your focus should be on the reading experience.

If the story intrigues you and elicits an emotional and intellectual response, then reread the story, take more detailed notes, and ask questions about plot, character, and themes.

If you have trouble understanding the story, you can play around with it to tease out more meaning. As suggested before, asking "What if?" questions can help you think about the plot as a construction that shapes meaning. Imagine a different ending or a different turn of events at an earlier stage of the story. Imagine a scene that is not included in the actual story. Or take the story beyond its boundaries and imagine a sequel: what would happen?

You can play "What if?" with characters, too. For example, you can assume a character is a real person and keeps a diary. Write an entry that deals with a significant day or event in the story. Or conduct an interview with the character. Ask questions that address your interests. The answers may help clarify parts of the story. Below is an imagined interview with the main character of "A Very Short Story":

Interviewer: What's your name?

Character: My friends call me Butch.

Interviewer: At the beginning of the story, Luz is loving and caring, but of course, she is a nurse. Considering the way things turned out, would you say you expected too much from her?

Character: The letters she wrote to me when I went back to the front answer that question. We were in love with each other, period.

Interviewer: What changed?

Character: When she decided not to go back to the States with me because I didn't have a job, that was the beginning of the end. Her priorities changed.

Interviewer: At one point in the story you and Luz go to church and pray. Are you religious, or were you doing it for her?

Character: I'm not religious, but I wasn't doing it for her. I was trying.

Interviewer: When it says in the story, "she had never known Italians," what does that mean?

Character: Italian men pursue women in a theatrical way. It means she fell for the theater.

Interviewer: Who are the "*arditi*"?

Character: Italian Special Forces.

Interviewer: What's behind the gonorrhea incident?

Character: Next question.

Interviewer: Your story is about love and war, two timeless themes. What did you learn?

Character: War teaches you everything you need to know about life. The problem is, it either kills you or damages your mind before you can use any of it.

Interviewer: And what about love?

Character: John Donne said it best—"Go and catch a falling star."*

ALTERNATIVE PROJECTS: POEMS, SONGS, AND MOVIES AS STORIES

Although short stories are the focus of this chapter, your instructor might ask you to apply the concepts you have learned to analyze other genres like poems, songs, or even movies. Writing professionally about poetry requires knowledge of poetic techniques and forms, but a meaningful analysis can be based on the information covered in this chapter. Poems, and their popular counterpart, songs, present issues and support views that the writer cares about—in other words, like stories, they distill the experience of life and convey meaning. In addition, many poems and songs are narratives—that is, they present characters and tell stories. When they do, they can be analyzed and interpreted much like stories.

Even when they lack characters or a story line, poems and songs present characters and the semblance of a story line through the voice of a writer or singer. Some poetry, for example, is "lyrical" (focused on thoughts and feelings) or, like landscape and still-life paintings, mostly descriptive of nature and inanimate objects, but behind the thoughts, feelings, and descriptions, a writer speaks to us. The writer, or speaker (sometimes called a "persona"), is the equivalent of a character. The poem suggests the writer's presence, and through the writer's presence, readers derive relevance and value from the subject matter.

For example, read the sixteen-word "imagist" poem below, by the American poet William Carlos Williams. "Imagism" is a poetic style that attempts

---

*The first line of a poem titled "Song," by the English poet and Anglican priest John Donne (1572–1613).

to express meaning and emotions through precise visual images, without explanation—in essence, "show, don't tell" taken to an extreme.

William Carlos Williams { THE RED WHEELBARROW

William Carlos Williams (1883–1963) was an influential poet and a medical doctor who practiced in his hometown of Rutherford, New Jersey. He was devoted to both of his careers. As a doctor, according to his wife, Flossie, he loved to make house calls and talk to people. He wrote poetry in the evenings, or sometimes on prescription forms between appointments with his patients.

Alfred Eisenstaedt/The LIFE Picture Collection/Getty Images

The Red Wheelbarrow

so much depends
upon

a red wheel
barrow

glazed with rain
water

beside the white
chickens. ■

Williams's poem highlights the image of the wheelbarrow and chickens. The words "red," "glazed," and "white" add color and luminescence. The first four words of the poem, however, contribute nothing visual. On the contrary, "so much depends upon" is a subjective statement, but the words infuse the image with an undercurrent of meaning because they imply that someone, a "character" (presumably the writer), is observing and commenting on the scene. We don't know what depends on the wheelbarrow and chickens, or why "so much" depends, and we can't know for sure, but the identification of the image with a human being, with human needs and desires and the human condition, gives the poem resonance, and starts a communication process between the writer and readers.

Below is a thematic selection of well-known poems and songs that, in various combinations, you could read and analyze for an alternative project:

On the Imagination

Poems

- ▶ "Kubla Khan" by Samuel Taylor Coleridge
- ▶ "A Supermarket in California" by Allen Ginsberg

Songs

- ▶ "Hypnotized" by Bob Welch (Fleetwood Mac)
- ▶ "Learning to Fly" by Pink Floyd

Love

Poems

- ▶ "Annabel Lee" by Edgar Allan Poe
- ▶ "Love Medicine" by Louise Erdrich

Songs

- ▶ "Expresso Love" by Dire Straits
- ▶ "Poem to a Horse" by Shakira

War

Poems

- ▶ "The Death of the Ball Turret Gunner" by Randall Jarrell
- ▶ *Dulce et Decorum Est* by Wilfred Owen

Songs

- ▶ "Masters of War" by Bob Dylan
- ▶ "Shock and Awe" by Neil Young

Identity

Poems

- ▶ "Daddy" by Sylvia Plath
- ▶ "Barbie Doll" by Marge Piercy

Songs

- ▶ "Behind Blue Eyes" by the Who
- ▶ "Fleshdunce" by Dead Kennedys

To write professionally about movies—the third alternative possibility—a writer needs to understand the "language" of the film medium—in other words, the effects of camera angles, lighting, tracking shots, film editing (*montage*), and transition techniques.

Nevertheless, most movies are visual stories; they are made first and foremost to tell a story and, in fact, often are based on novels, short stories, fairy tales, comic books, and other literary forms. Our initial experience of a movie is more sensual (especially visual) than imaginative, but the way a good movie stays with us—in Flannery O'Connor's words "hangs on and expands in the mind"—is very much an imaginative experience and mirrors the way we hold on to and internalize a literary work.

For these reasons, the concepts covered in this chapter about plot, character, and theme all apply to analyzing movies. Depending on your instructor's goals for this writing project, *analyzing* a movie can be an interesting alternative to writing about a short story or other literary work.

WRITING A PROPOSAL

Once you decide on a subject and an issue for your literary analysis, you are ready to write a proposal. Give your proposal a title that identifies the work you plan to write about. Compose your proposal using the section headings below (numbered or bulleted):

- ▶ **The Main Issue, Question, or Problem** that your essay will address.
- ▶ **The Viewpoint or Thesis** that you intend to support.
- ▶ **The Relevance of the Essay to Readers.** Elaborate on why you think the issue, question, or problem that you will address will interest readers. How will your essay contribute to a better understanding or enjoyment of the work?

WRITING A ROUGH DRAFT

Your proposal identifies the main issue, question, or problem your essay will explore and puts forward a preliminary thesis. As you begin actually drafting the essay, think about how you will organize it.

Organization

A literary analysis can be organized informally or formally, depending on your audience. Either way, the essay needs to begin with a compelling issue or question about the meaning or relevance of the work. The goal of your analysis is to support a view that resolves the issue or answers the question.

In newspapers and magazines, many literary essays are informally organized—that is, the writer identifies an issue about the work and proceeds to analyze or sometimes "explicate" it in an inductive pattern that supports a view (or thesis) at the end.*

An analysis written for academic readers usually is organized formally—that is, both the main issue and the main view (thesis or argument) are presented in the opening part of the essay. The rest of the essay is an analysis that supports the main view or thesis:

Formal Organization

1. Opening:

Introduce the work and the issue, question, or problem driving the analysis. Make the issue as clear, compelling, and reader-relevant as possible. In order to do that, you may need more than one paragraph. At the end of your opening, state the central view, thesis, or argument that the analysis will support.

2. Thesis Support:

This is the main part of the analysis. It includes all of the reasons, examples, direct quotations, and insights that support your main view, thesis, or argument.

Remember that formal organization does not mean the essay should be written in a dry, impersonal style. A good literary analysis is reader-friendly; it enhances your readers' enjoyment and understanding of a work. The analysis should be objective but also a conversation with your readers about the work and its significance. Let your "voice" inform the analysis with the thoughts and emotions that the work evoked for you.

Organizing a Comparative Analysis

Comparison and contrast is a common method of analysis. A comparative literary analysis addresses similarities and differences between two or more works in order to illuminate overlapping issues. If you write a comparative analysis—for example, an analysis of two stories that present similar themes, or a poem and song—make sure you plan and organize the analysis as a unified essay. That means that the issue you present in the opening—for example, a common theme—should link the two works. The view, or thesis, you intend to support also should link the two works.

---

*An "explication" is a form of literary analysis that focuses on a close reading of the "text"—a line-by-line commentary on the words and wording, and nuanced ways that the text can be understood.

After you set up a unified essay, you can take different approaches to organizing the support. In a relatively short analysis, one common approach is to analyze the relevant issue in the two works separately first, then conclude with a combined analysis. Another approach is to organize the analysis by supporting points and analyze the works in unison under each point.

Avoid Long Summaries

When you analyze a story or other work, you can expect two kinds of readers— (1) those who have read the work you are writing about and (2) those who have not. A good analysis should interest and engage both kinds of readers. Presenting a relevant issue and supporting a thoughtful view is always the key; however, since you are writing for readers who may have read the story, as well as some who have not, you need to be careful about how much summarizing you do.

A detailed summary of a story makes for tedious reading, even for readers who are unfamiliar with the story. In the opening of your essay, you can, and usually will, include a very general summary that will get your readers oriented. For example:

> James Baldwin's "Sonny's Blues," a story about a troubled relationship between two African-American brothers, was first published in 1957. At that time, rock and roll was still in its infancy, and hip-hop, as we know it, did not exist. The musical giants of the era had names like Charlie Mingus, Dizzy Gillespie, and Thelonious Monk....

As you develop your essay, you will need to refer to specific events in the story to support your observations about the plot, characters, and themes:

> ....A subtle but significant change in the brothers' relationship occurs when they witness a revival meeting that takes place in the street outside the older brother's apartment.

In contrast to long plot summaries, these specific references convey information about the story in an interesting way and are necessary for all of your readers whether they have read the story or not.

Notes, Marginal Comments, and Highlights

The notes you take about a story create a record of reactions, observations, questions, or impressions that are relevant to your analysis. If you have trouble understanding a story, a good way to start taking notes is to identify issues that the story raises. Begin with the very first sentence. The openings of good stories are designed to be meaningful, as well as interesting. Go through the story and note all the significant issues that arise. Going through a story in this way will help clarify the meaning, because issues drive the plot, shape the characters' motivation, and raise the thematic questions that stories express a view about.

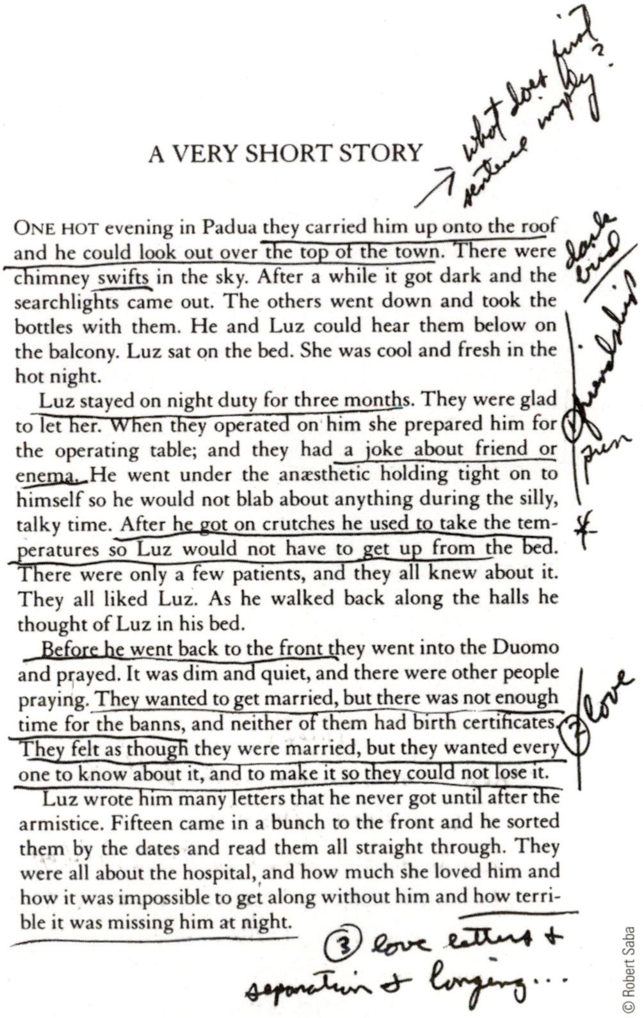

A VERY SHORT STORY

ONE HOT evening in Padua they carried him up onto the roof and he could look out over the top of the town. There were chimney swifts in the sky. After a while it got dark and the searchlights came out. The others went down and took the bottles with them. He and Luz could hear them below on the balcony. Luz sat on the bed. She was cool and fresh in the hot night.

Luz stayed on night duty for three months. They were glad to let her. When they operated on him she prepared him for the operating table; and they had a joke about friend or enema. He went under the anæsthetic holding tight on to himself so he would not blab about anything during the silly, talky time. After he got on crutches he used to take the temperatures so Luz would not have to get up from the bed. There were only a few patients, and they all knew about it. They all liked Luz. As he walked back along the halls he thought of Luz in his bed.

Before he went back to the front they went into the Duomo and prayed. It was dim and quiet, and there were other people praying. They wanted to get married, but there was not enough time for the banns, and neither of them had birth certificates. They felt as though they were married, but they wanted every one to know about it, and to make it so they could not lose it.

Luz wrote him many letters that he never got until after the armistice. Fifteen came in a bunch to the front and he sorted them by the dates and read them all straight through. They were all about the hospital, and how much she loved him and how it was impossible to get along without him and how terrible it was missing him at night.

what does final sentence imply?
dark bird
1 friendship
fun
2 love
3 love letters + separation + longing...

© Robert Saba

Annotations of "A Very Short Story"*

*The most practical way to annotate a text is directly on the page as you are reading. However, if you are annotating a text that you don't own or don't want to mark, make a photocopy and annotate the copy.

Using the Present Tense

When you write about a fictional story, or a movie for that matter, you normally use the present tense when you summarize or refer to the events in the story. The past tense is appropriate for referring to your actual reading experience—for example, "I first *read* 'The Sketchbook' by Fredrick Waterman while I *was* on an airplane" [italics added]—but the present tense is correct and logical for referring to events within a fictional story, because the story has a continuous existence outside a specific time frame:

Correct [**Italics added**]

> A subtle but significant change in the brothers' relationship *occurs* when they *witness* a revival meeting that *takes* place in the street outside the older brother's apartment.

Incorrect [**Italics added**]

> A subtle but significant change in the brothers' relationship *occurred* when they *witnessed* a revival meeting that *took* place in the street outside the older brother's apartment.

Document Any Sources That You Use

If you decide to do research and use sources to complement your analysis, remember to identify all of your sources in your essay and cite them correctly in MLA format. (See Chapter 8, "Navigating a Research Project," and Chapter 14, "A Guide to Using and Documenting Sources," for more about documentation.)

YOUR ESSAY CHECKLIST

Use the following essay checklist to guide your steps in developing your essay and as a final check to make sure you have completed all of the necessary steps. The timeline for this essay will depend on how much reading you do in preparation for writing, but the process will require the stages listed in the table.

✔ Task	Description	Time Frame
☐ **Read**	• Read a number of works—at least several stories—and decide what to write about.	Several days.
☐ **Reread**	• Reread the work or works you decide to write about. • Take detailed notes. • Analyze the plot, the main character or characters, and the themes that seem important to you. • Identify an issue or question that will drive your analysis and a provisional thesis that your analysis will support.	Several hours or more.
☐ **Write a proposal**	• Review your notes and write a proposal that expresses the communication goals of your essay and its relevance to readers.	An hour or so.
☐ **Write a rough draft**	• Think of a working title that suggests the point of your analysis. • Make sure your opening explains the significance of the issue that you are analyzing in your essay, and makes the issue relevant and interesting for readers, including those who may not have read the work. Remember you are writing an essay, not doing homework. • Avoid straight, informational summaries of the work or works you are analyzing. In other words, summarize to analyze and express ideas, not for the sake of summarizing. • Whether your analysis is formally or informally organized, make sure that the thesis or main view you are supporting is meaningful and clearly expressed. • Support your thesis with detailed analysis and examples. Use direct quotations from the work and short summaries to illustrate and support your points. However, don't overuse direct quotations. The substance of good support should be your own thoughts, in your own words. When you quote directly, remember to use appropriate lead-ins or signal phrases. Keep your quotations as brief as possible. Use block centering for direct quotations that are longer than a few lines. • Try to end with your strongest supporting point or a relevant point for readers to think about. Unless your essay is very long, you need not repeat your main points at the end. If your conclusion seems wordy or flat, delete it and see if the essay can end earlier. In rough drafts, writers often write past their best conclusions.	Several hours or more. Rough drafts often take more than one sitting.

(continued)

✔ Task	Description	Time Frame
☐ **Revise**	• Revise the draft as many times as necessary until the essay is ideally compelling and readable. • Strive to maintain a strong focus and "flow"—that is, coherent development of your points and smooth transitions from one point, or paragraph, to another. • Improve your title if you can, and review other elements covered in the drafting section above.	Plan on doing at least several drafts over the course of a week.
☐ **Get peer review and suggestions**	• As your essay begins to take shape, use feedback from classmates, your instructor, and writing-center tutors to help you revise.	Varies
☐ **Edit your essay**	Before you submit the essay, make sure you edit it. Use the text-to-speech feature on your computer to hear how the essay sounds and help you catch muddled ideas or typos. Check specifically for the following: • Reader-friendly paragraphing • Correct and consistent use of the present tense when referring to events in a work • Clear pronoun reference • Lead-ins and signal phrases to introduce direct quotations • Correct formatting of block-centered quotations. • Clear and precise wording • Correct sentence punctuation (fix run-ons and comma splices) • Subject-verb agreement and placement of commas	Careful editing may involve a certain amount of revising, so the time frame can vary, but always plan on going over what you have written. Running a spell-check is not enough.

PEER REVIEW

More than most essays, a literary analysis can be a "hard sell." General readers see this kind of essay as academic, dry, and less relevant to their lives than most essays are. However, when a literary analysis is insightful and well-written, it can be as enjoyable as any essay, but the writer has to make the relevance of the essay clear from the very beginning. With that in mind as the writer, be especially attentive to suggestions from your classmates about improving your opening.

Below are some peer-review questions to guide your classmates' feedback. You also can ask questions of your own that focus on parts of a draft that you have doubts or concerns about.

1. Describe what the writer does to make the opening interesting. What is the central issue? Does the writer do a good job of making the issue real and important to readers? Can you offer any suggestions for improving the opening?

2. Does the opening present a thesis, or does the thesis emerge later in the essay? What is the thesis (quote the writer's exact words)? Is it insightful and thought-provoking, or is it too obvious? Explain why.

3. In supporting the thesis, does the writer do a good job of using quotations and specific examples? Indicate specific parts of the analysis that you find effective, and explain why. Also, indicate parts that seem unnecessary, redundant, or off topic, and why. Are there any observations or statements that need to be clarified, or that you disagree with?

4. How well is the essay organized? Point out any problems you notice with transitions or coherence. Is the writing clear and reader-friendly? Note any problems with wording, grammar, or mechanics. Is the paragraphing helpful? Are direct quotations smoothly introduced with lead-ins or signal phrases? Conclude your review with two or three suggestions for improving the readability of the essay.

STUDENT ESSAY: FINAL DRAFT

Here is the final version of the essay that student Fangyu Xu (Frank) wrote, based on the proposal presented earlier in this chapter.

Fangyu Xu // **THE ROMANTIC IDEAL IN JAMES JOYCE'S "ARABY"**

In an essay titled "Mysticism and Logic," the English philosopher Bertrand Russell writes: "It is only in marriage with the world that our ideals can bear fruit: divorced from it, they remain barren. But marriage with the world is not to be achieved by an ideal which shrinks from fact, or demands in advance that the world shall conform to its desires."

These words are relevant to James Joyce's coming-of-age story, "Araby." Ideals sustain us, and in that sense, they are as important to us as the realities of our environment, but in order to "bear fruit" and be sustaining, ideals also have to be realizable. Without the support of reality, an ideal is an impossible dream or illusion that is bound to disappoint us.

"Araby" takes place in a dreary part of the city of Dublin, Ireland. The narrator of the story is a nameless boy who at first seems to be normal, well-adjusted, and accepting of his environment, but early in the story, the boy starts to change in a way he barely understands himself. He becomes obsessed with an attractive, apparently older girl who is the sister of a neighborhood friend of his called "Mangan."

The boy tells us, "Every morning I lay on the floor in the front parlour watching her door. The blind was pulled down to within an inch of the sash so that I could not be seen." When the girl comes out of her house, the boy grabs his schoolbooks and follows her down the street, keeping "her brown figure always in my eye." A first "love," of course, is supposed to be awkward and a little foolish, but this boy's obsession, the romantic ideal he creates in his mind, is magnified beyond reason. He thinks constantly of the girl, "even in places the most hostile to romance." He is often on the verge of tears without knowing why. She becomes a "single sensation of life" for him, a romantic ideal he transforms into something holy. Her name springs to his lips "in strange prayers," and he doubts he can ever actually tell her about his "confused adoration." Though he was grounded in reality when the story began, by this point he has lost touch with it. Yet, as obsessive and hopeless as the boy's love for this girl seems to be, he expresses it in a beautiful way. "My body" he says, "was like a harp and her words and gestures were like fingers running upon the wires." The story grabs ahold of us because the boy's feelings are powerful and real, but in Bertrand Russell's words, the romantic ideal is too divorced from reality to bear fruit. Like Icarus in Greek mythology, the boy is flying too high, too close to the sun, and has put himself in a position for a terrible fall.

James Joyce refrains from directly elaborating on the boy's background or family circumstances, but readers learn a lot through the detailed descriptions of the boy's environment. The street where he lives is "blind"—in other words, a dead-end. The houses are "somber" and arranged in rigid order with "brown imperturbable faces." Everything the boy describes gradually creates a bleak atmosphere. For example, the drawing-room in his home is a "musty" place in which a former tenant of the home, a priest, had died; the books the priest left behind are old and decayed; the wild garden behind the house is "straggling." The streets and alleys where the boy plays with his friends are silent, dark, and muddy.

The descriptions of the boy's home life and neighborhood make it clear that his family has little money and is just getting by. This dreary background helps us understand why the boy's love for Mangan's sister is so magnified and intense. In contrast to the drab environment, everything the boy sees in the "figure" of the girl is light, stirring, and sweet. She seems to cleanse the coarse surroundings. When the boy accompanies his aunt to market, and they are jostled by "drunken men and bargaining women," and they hear "the curses of laborers," the "shrill litany of shop-boys" and "the nasal chanting of street-singers," his love of the girl and her image are like a holy "chalice" he imagines carrying "safely through a throng of foes." The sacred feelings he has reach a peak on a "dark rainy evening" when he is alone in the drawing room where the priest died, and finds himself slipping out of his senses and drawn into a strange spiritual experience that ends in an ecstatic prayer: "I pressed the palms of my hands together until they trembled, murmuring: '*O love! O love!*' many times."

Immediately afterwards, as if that prayer is answered, the boy tells us the girl finally speaks to him; she casually mentions a bazaar called "Araby," which she would love to go to but cannot. Enchanted by the "white curve of her neck," her "easy" posture, and the "border of a petticoat," he promises, if he goes to the bazaar, to bring her something. Strangely, for the rest of the story, except at one point early in the evening on the night he goes to the bazaar, he seems to forget about the girl and no longer experiences the powerful emotions that consumed him before their brief conversation. The focus of his whole existence is on going to the bazaar, so much so that when he eventually is on his way there, and again, after he arrives, he has "difficulty" remembering what his mission is. What seems to be happening is that reality is pulling him back to earth, the way gravity pulls Icarus once his wings start to melt. The boy, in Bertrand Russell's words, is conforming to the desires of the world again. Instead of being consumed by love, he is consumed by his plans to get to the bazaar, and he seems to know instinctively, as a creature of his environment, that it won't be easy. Even before any real obstacles arise, we see him changing. He becomes irritable, impatient, distracted, and uninterested at school, almost as though he already knows he will be defeated.

On the evening of his trip to the bazaar, while he waits impatiently for his uncle to come home and give him some money, he watches the neighborhood children, his old companions, playing in the street. Nothing has changed for them, but it is clear the boy has changed. He is growing up, and helpless to do anything about it, but also still not in control of his own life. While waiting with more and more impatience for his uncle to come home, he has to suffer through a tedious dinner with his aunt and a gossiping old friend of hers, and after the old friend leaves, he ends up pacing around the house with his fists clenched, while his aunt tells him, "You may have to put off your bazaar for this night of Our Lord."

His uncle's last-minute arrival makes going to the bazaar still possible, but the slow ride on a deserted train that draws up to "an improvised wooden platform" is agonizing and only intensifies the process of reality pulling him back to earth, Icarus falling from the sky. Is Araby really a spectacular bazaar? It is closer to a bad dream or nightmare: "Nearly all the stalls were closed and the greater part of the hall was in darkness." A few vulgar, young merchants, two men and a woman, are counting money by a stall. The woman is having a shallow, flirtatious conversation with the men, and breaks it off to ask the boy if he wants to buy anything. Her indifferent tone is a final snub. She is a mockery of his romantic ideal. When she resumes her conversation with the two men, the boy makes a pretense of being interested in her wares but the illusions that brought him to the bazaar are gone. The lights turn off one by one. He walks out in almost total darkness, and sees himself and his romantic ideals for what they are, "driven and derided by vanity." He has fallen all the way back to earth, but unlike Icarus, who died from the fall, the boy is still alive. What he doesn't know in this moment of anger, defeat, and humiliation is that his disillusionment is for the better. He is stronger and wiser, and in the future, his ideals will be married to the world and have a better chance of bearing fruit. ∎

Works Cited

Joyce, James. "Araby." *Dubliners*. New York: Penguin, 1977. Print.

Russell, Bertrand. "Mysticism and Logic and Other Essays." *Project Gutenberg.org*. Project Gutenberg, 12 May 2008. Web. 28 Mar. 2015.

Interview with the Student Writer

How did you come up with your idea for your essay?

When I first read "Araby," I realized the whole story is about a boy's unrealistic love. The story did a great job of presenting to readers the strong contrast between the boy's environment and his inner life. I decided it would be interesting to write about this problem.

How did you go about composing the essay? How much revising did you do?

I usually study and write at night in my room. I used Microsoft Word to compose the essay. After writing a proposal that my professor accepted, I started working on the essay itself. I wrote several drafts and revised them before submitting the final version.

What parts of the writing process were difficult for you?

The hardest part was figuring out the main issue to focus on, and organizing my ideas.

What parts were easy or enjoyable?

Reading, and rereading, Joyce's story was the most enjoyable part.

> ● **Looking back, what do you think you learned from the project?**

> ● I learned from reading the story and analyzing it that words can be powerful and writing can be beautiful.

> ● **What advice would you give to other students about this kind of writing project or writing in general?**

> ● To write a literary analysis essay, you need to read carefully and try to understand why the writer writes the way he does. I read Joyce's story four times to make sure I understood his intentions. I even imagined myself as being that boy. A good understanding of the story is the first and most necessary step towards writing a literary analysis.

EVALUATE YOUR LEARNING

1. How would you explain the value and popularity of fictional stories to a younger brother or sister or an elementary school student?

2. Describe how you came up with the main idea for your essay, and why the idea interested you.

3. Looking back on the essay you wrote, what do you consider to be your most "reader-relevant" insight, and why?

4. If you used any sources in preparing your essay, how helpful were they? Did they change your view or enhance your understanding of the work you analyzed?

5. Imagine a story you read or wrote about being written from the point of view of a different character (for example, "A Very Short Story" from the point of view of the nurse). How would this different point of view change the story and affect the story's theme or your interpretation?

6. In completing this assignment, what did you learn about writing a literary analysis that might be helpful to other students who have to complete a project like this one?

7. Ernest Hemingway is known for a distinctive style of writing that readers tend to love or hate. Looking back on his very short story, how would you describe his style? How long or varied are the sentences? How sophisticated is his choice of words? Does he use crude or inappropriate language? Does he write "poetic" descriptions? What specifically do you think some readers love about his style and other readers hate?

ADDITIONAL READINGS

James Joyce { ARABY

James Joyce (1882–1941) was born in Dublin, Ireland, but lived most of his life on the European continent where he worked as a language teacher and earned a reputation as one of the preeminent writers of the 20th century. "Araby" appeared in a collection of stories titled *Dubliners*, which Joyce composed in his early twenties. Known for its blend of lyrical prose and unflinching realism, *Dubliners* is still read and admired today as one of the greatest story collections ever written.

NORTH RICHMOND STREET, BEING blind,* was a quiet street except at the hour when the Christian Brothers' School set the boys free. An uninhabited house of two storeys stood at the blind end, detached from its neighbours in a square ground. The other houses of the street, conscious of decent lives within them, gazed at one another with brown imperturbable faces.

The former tenant of our house, a priest, had died in the back drawing-room. Air, musty from having been long enclosed, hung in all the rooms, and the waste room behind the kitchen was littered with old useless papers. Among these I found a few paper-covered books, the pages of which were curled and damp: *The Abbot*, by Walter Scott, *The Devout Communicant*, and *The Memoirs of Vidocq*. I liked the last best because its leaves were yellow. The wild garden behind the house contained a central apple-tree and a few straggling bushes, under one of which I found the late tenant's rusty bicycle-pump. He had been a very charitable priest; in his will he had left all his money to institutions and the furniture of his house to his sister. When the short days of winter came, dusk fell before we had well eaten our dinners. When we met in the street the houses had grown sombre. The space of sky above us was the colour of ever-changing violet and towards it the lamps of the street lifted their feeble lanterns. The cold air stung us and we played till our bodies glowed. Our shouts echoed in the silent street. The career of our play brought us through the dark muddy lanes behind the houses, where we ran the gauntlet of the rough tribes from the cottages, to the back doors of the dark dripping gardens where odours arose from the ashpits, to the dark odorous stables where a coachman smoothed and combed the horse or shook music from the buckled harness. When we returned to the street, light from the kitchen windows had filled the areas. If my uncle was seen

---

*"Blind" refers to a dead-end street.

turning the corner, we hid in the shadow until we had seen him safely housed. Or if Mangan's sister came out on the doorstep to call her brother in to his tea, we watched her from our shadow peer up and down the street. We waited to see whether she would remain or go in and, if she remained, we left our shadow and walked up to Mangan's steps resignedly. She was waiting for us, her figure defined by the light from the half-opened door. Her brother always teased her before he obeyed, and I stood by the railings looking at her. Her dress swung as she moved her body, and the soft rope of her hair tossed from side to side.

Every morning I lay on the floor in the front parlour watching her door. The blind was pulled down to within an inch of the sash so that I could not be seen. When she came out on the doorstep my heart leaped. I ran to the hall, seized my books and followed her. I kept her brown figure always in my eye and, when we came near the point at which our ways diverged, I quickened my pace and passed her. This happened morning after morning. I had never spoken to her, except for a few casual words, and yet her name was like a summons to all my foolish blood.

Her image accompanied me even in places the most hostile to romance. On Saturday evenings when my aunt went marketing I had to go to carry some of the parcels. We walked through the flaring streets, jostled by drunken men and bargaining women, amid the curses of labourers, the shrill litanies of shop-boys who stood on guard by the barrels of pigs' cheeks, the nasal chanting of street-singers, who sang a *come-all-you* about O'Donovan Rossa, or a ballad about the troubles in our native land. These noises converged in a single sensation of life for me: I imagined that I bore my chalice safely through a throng of foes. Her name sprang to my lips at moments in strange prayers and praises which I myself did not understand. My eyes were often full of tears (I could not tell why) and at times a flood from my heart seemed to pour itself out into my bosom. I thought little of the future. I did not know whether I would ever speak to her or not or, if I spoke to her, how I could tell her of my confused adoration. But my body was like a harp and her words and gestures were like fingers running upon the wires. One evening I went into the back drawing-room in which the priest had died. It was a dark rainy evening and there was no sound in the house. Through one of the broken panes I heard the rain impinge upon the earth, the fine incessant needles of water playing in the sodden beds. Some distant lamp or lighted window gleamed below me. I was thankful that I could see so little. All my senses seemed to desire to veil themselves and, feeling that I was about to slip from them, I pressed the palms of my hands together until they trembled, murmuring: *"O love! O love!"* many times. At last she spoke to me. When she addressed the first words to me I was so confused that I did not know what to answer. She asked me was I going to *Araby.*

I forgot whether I answered yes or no. It would be a splendid bazaar; she said she would love to go.

"And why can't you?" I asked.

While she spoke she turned a silver bracelet round and round her wrist. She could not go, she said, because there would be a retreat that week in her convent. Her brother and two other boys were fighting for their caps, and I was alone at the railings. She held one of the spikes, bowing her head towards me. The light from the lamp opposite our door caught the white curve of her neck, lit up her hair that rested there and, falling, lit up the hand upon the railing. It fell over one side of her dress and caught the white border of a petticoat, just visible as she stood at ease.

"It's well for you," she said.

"If I go," I said, "I will bring you something."

What innumerable follies laid waste my waking and sleeping thoughts after that evening! I wished to annihilate the tedious intervening days. I chafed against the work of school. At night in my bedroom and by day in the classroom her image came between me and the page I strove to read. The syllables of the word *Araby* were called to me through the silence in which my soul luxuriated and cast an Eastern enchantment over me. I asked for leave to go to the bazaar on Saturday night. My aunt was surprised, and hoped it was not some Freemason affair. I answered few questions in class. I watched my master's face pass from amiability to sternness; he hoped I was not beginning to idle. I could not call my wandering thoughts together. I had hardly any patience with the serious work of life which, now that it stood between me and my desire, seemed to me child's play, ugly monotonous child's play.

On Saturday morning I reminded my uncle that I wished to go to the bazaar in the evening. He was fussing at the hallstand, looking for the hat-brush, and answered me curtly:

"Yes, boy, I know."

As he was in the hall I could not go into the front parlour and lie at the window. I felt the house in bad humour and walked slowly towards the school. The air was pitilessly raw and already my heart misgave me.

When I came home to dinner my uncle had not yet been home. Still it was early. I sat staring at the clock for some time and, when its ticking began to irritate me, I left the room. I mounted the staircase and gained the upper part of the house. The high, cold, empty, gloomy rooms liberated me and I went from room to room singing. From the front window I saw my companions playing below in the street. Their cries reached me weakened and indistinct and, leaning my forehead against the cool glass, I looked over at the dark house where she lived. I may have stood there for an hour, seeing nothing but the brown-clad figure cast by my imagination, touched discreetly by the lamplight at the curved neck, at the hand upon the railings and at the border below the dress.

When I came downstairs again I found Mrs Mercer sitting at the fire. She was an old, garrulous woman, a pawnbroker's widow, who collected used stamps for some pious purpose. I had to endure the gossip of the tea-table. The meal was prolonged beyond an hour and still my uncle did not come. Mrs Mercer stood up to go: she was sorry she couldn't wait any longer, but it was after eight o'clock and she did not like to be out late, as the night air was bad for her. When she had gone I began to walk up and down the room, clenching my fists. My aunt said:

"I'm afraid you may put off your bazaar for this night of Our Lord."

At nine o'clock I heard my uncle's latchkey in the hall door. I heard him talking to himself and heard the hallstand rocking when it had received the weight of his overcoat. I could interpret these signs. When he was midway through his dinner I asked him to give me the money to go to the bazaar. He had forgotten.

"The people are in bed and after their first sleep now," he said.

I did not smile. My aunt said to him energetically:

"Can't you give him the money and let him go? You've kept him late enough as it is."

My uncle said he was very sorry he had forgotten. He said he believed in the old saying: "All work and no play makes Jack a dull boy." He asked me where I was going and, when I told him a second time, he asked me did I know *The Arab's Farewell to his Steed*. When I left the kitchen he was about to recite the opening lines of the piece to my aunt.

I held a florin tightly in my hand as I strode down Buckingham Street towards the station. The sight of the streets thronged with buyers and glaring with gas recalled to me the purpose of my journey. I took my seat in a third-class carriage of a deserted train. After an intolerable delay the train moved out of the station slowly. It crept onward among ruinous houses and over the twinkling river. At Westland Row Station a crowd of people pressed to the carriage doors; but the porters moved them back, saying that it was a special train for the bazaar. I remained alone in the bare carriage. In a few minutes the train drew up beside an improvised wooden platform. I passed out on to the road and saw by the lighted dial of a clock that it was ten minutes to ten. In front of me was a large building which displayed the magical name.

I could not find any sixpenny entrance and, fearing that the bazaar would be closed, I passed in quickly through a turnstile, handing a shilling to a weary-looking man. I found myself in a big hall girded at half its height by a gallery. Nearly all the stalls were closed and the greater part of the hall was in darkness. I recognized a silence like that which pervades a church after a service. I walked into the centre of the bazaar timidly. A few people were gathered about the stalls which were still open. Before a curtain, over which the words *Café Chantant* were written in coloured lamps, two men were counting money on a salver. I listened to the fall of the coins.

Remembering with difficulty why I had come, I went over to one of the stalls and examined porcelain vases and flowered tea-sets. At the door of the stall a young lady was talking and laughing with two young gentlemen. I remarked their English accents and listened vaguely to their conversation.

"O, I never said such a thing!"

"O, but you did!"

"O, but I didn't!"

"Didn't she say that?"

"Yes. I heard her."

"O, there's a...fib!"

Observing me, the young lady came over and asked me did I wish to buy anything. The tone of her voice was not encouraging; she seemed to have spoken to me out of a sense of duty. I looked humbly at the great jars that stood like eastern guards at either side of the dark entrance to the stall and murmured:

"No, thank you."

The young lady changed the position of one of the vases and went back to the two young men. They began to talk of the same subject. Once or twice the young lady glanced at me over her shoulder.

I lingered before her stall, though I knew my stay was useless, to make my interest in her wares seem the more real. Then I turned away slowly and walked down the middle of the bazaar. I allowed the two pennies to fall against the sixpence in my pocket. I heard a voice call from one end of the gallery that the light was out. The upper part of the hall was now completely dark.

Gazing up into the darkness I saw myself as a creature driven and derided by vanity; and my eyes burned with anguish and anger. ∎

From Reflection to Response Responding to "Araby"

1. At the beginning of the story, the boy uses the plural pronoun "we" to describe himself playing in the street with his friends, as though they have a shared identity, but based on how the story develops, what would you say makes the boy different from his friends?

2. Why do you think Mangan's sister approaches the boy and speaks to him about the bazaar? Would the story have been any different if the boy had initiated the conversation instead?

3. As student Fangyu Xu points out in his essay, the boy idealizes the girl, and he uses a lot of religious, or devotional, terminology to describe his feelings for her. Is there any evidence in the story that he has physical feelings for her as well?

Courtesy of Esther Hong

ESTHER HONG

Friendlies

In this illustration, I wanted to showcase a playful encounter between friendly acquaintances, hence the title, "Friendlies." As for the technical side of things, I was interested in experimenting with a limited, bright color palette to organize elements of the scene and to imbue the interaction between the characters with energy.

CHAPTER ELEVEN

Writing Beyond the Page: Shifting Genres and Using New Media

> *Most people find it difficult to understand purely verbal concepts..... In general, we feel more secure when things are visible, when we can "see for ourselves."*
>
> —Marshall McLuhan, *The Medium Is the Message*

CHAPTER LEARNING OBJECTIVES

In this chapter, you will learn to:

- ▶ Convert written documents to multimedia genres and forms.
- ▶ Create original multimedia "texts" or compositions.
- ▶ Apply communication concepts and rhetorical modes to multimedia projects.
- ▶ Manage principles of visual rhetoric and design.
- ▶ Apply a design plan and production process to a multimedia project.
- ▶ Analyze the "usability" of a multimedia "text" or composition.

COMMUNICATIONS YESTERDAY AND TODAY

The use of language to communicate all but defines us as human beings, yet writing, as opposed to speaking, is a recent development, only a few thousand years old.

The invention of writing systems and alphabets was a breakthrough in communications, what we would call a "new medium" today. Until there was writing, for example, poetry, whose origins are linked to music and song, had to be heard "live." With the advent of writing, people could enjoy poetry anytime and anywhere, because the words were "recorded." In fact, before writing, all language-based communication transpired face to face. After the invention of writing, people could communicate outside of "real time."

Even before people developed writing systems, they created visual images—cave paintings, pictures on rocks—as a way of recording experience and communicating (see Figure 11.1).

Today, visual imagery defines our communications as much as language does. Images come to us all the time and virtually everywhere. Only a few decades ago, using images to communicate required technical skills and expensive equipment, but at present, computers and software programs give everyone the ability to use visuals (photographs, video, graphics) along with audio (recorded speech, sounds, songs, and music) to enhance and transform written communication, or replace printed documents.

In the professional world, digital and multimedia forms such as videos, podcasts, slide-show presentations (PowerPoints), and web pages are widely used to make ideas and information more accessible. With more and more people reading and writing with digital tools, being a good communicator in professional life—a good writer, in fact—means understanding multimedia forms and having some ability to use them to communicate and solve problems.

Sisse Brimberg/National Geographic/Getty Images

FIGURE 11.1   **Lascaux Cave Paintings, circa 15,000 BC**

This writing project is designed to help you apply the writing and communication skills you have learned so far in the course to multimedia forms and audiences. Some popular multimedia forms that you might use include:

- A web page
- A video
- A podcast
- A slide show or multimedia presentation (PowerPoint, Keynote, PechaKucha 20×20, Prezi, Impress.js)
- A photo-essay
- An illustrated blog or a vlog (video blog)
- A meme or series of memes (images and verbal messages that are shared and often personalized electronically)
- A poster, illustrated flyer, or brochure

UNDERSTANDING THE PROJECT

Some students, as well as instructors, might have legitimate concerns about technical aspects of a project like this. Some colleges offer specialized courses that teach students to compose in video and other multimedia forms. These courses usually start with technical training. However, this project is not designed to require proficiency with any hardware or software. The focus is on transferring communication principles and strategies that you already know to multimedia forms. The goal of your final composition is to use effective concepts and design elements, rather than achieve technical polish.

Your instructor may give you one of these two options for the project:

1. A "genre-shift" project
2. A new multimedia project

Genre-Shift Project

Professional writers are asked to shift genres in order to better address the needs and expectations of their audience. In the workplace, a written report often will be revised into a video, podcast, or multimedia presentation to make the information more accessible to coworkers and clients. This kind of conversion is called a *genre shift*. The message of the original document or "text" essentially stays the same, but the medium changes. An effective conversion requires an ability to understand how different media present ideas to audiences.

To complete a genre-shift project, choose an essay or research paper you already have written for the course and re-create the most essential insights and messages in a digital or multimedia form—in other words, as a video, podcast, web page, PowerPoint presentation, photo-essay, and so on. Note that your audience can change as you shift genres, so make sure the medium you choose is well-suited for the audience you want to reach.

If your genre shift, for example, is based on a research paper you wrote about divorce rates in America, your original paper may have been intended for a specialized audience of marriage counselors, psychologists, or sociologists. In planning a genre shift, you might want to convey your findings to a more public audience—maybe married couples with children, or young adults who are single, or a demographic group, such as African-Americans. Depending on your choice, you will need to choose your medium and shape your message to address the interests and needs of the people you are targeting.

As to what previous project to choose, many of them might translate well for this assignment, but especially the "argument" (Chapter 7) or the research project (Chapter 8). The public writing project (Chapter 9) and this one have objectives in common. For that project, you may have used a multimedia form or genre to reach a public audience, but if you composed a traditional written document like a letter to the editor, or a guest column, then you could distill and deliver the ideas and message in multimedia form for this project. If you are creative and thoughtful about your communication goals and the value your ideas have for a real audience, almost any previous writing project could serve as a basis for this one, even a meaningful narrative essay or a profile. Consider all of the writing you have done in the course and how the ideas and messages could be adapted to a different genre and different audiences.

The student comments below are a good illustration of the kind of thinking and planning that a genre shift requires. This student wants to convert a traditional written argument to a photo-essay or other multimedia form. Notice how the student focuses on the audience and the "usability" of the conversion:

> My topic, texting while driving, can easily be glossed over in a couple pages so I tried to think of ways to make it more real for the audience. I started reworking my proposal by adding pictures, but I realized I wanted my audience to interact with my text in a way that provided instant response. The only way to do that was by creating a website the audience could click through, so I moved away from the written page and shifted the genre more than I originally planned. I created a website totally devoted to texting while driving and what the average person could do to be safer on the road. I chose the website also because I could promote to other people online just by sending the link out,

> and I thought people would be more likely to look at a website than a written proposal with images.

Creating a website makes the most sense for this student because he wants the message to have a real and immediate impact. When shifting genres, consider how the new medium will affect the delivery of your ideas. The social philosopher Marshall McLuhan often is quoted as saying, "the medium is the message." McLuhan meant that a medium in and of itself (for example, television or even Facebook) has more of an impact on society than the content that it delivers.* However, the narrower and more popular understanding of McLuhan's point also is meaningful: the medium directly affects how we design a message and what the message can say.

For example, a video can use audio, but a podcast normally is an audio file that does not use video. So, if you are converting a document that would be enhanced by the use of visuals, then it makes sense to try a video, website, or photo-essay. On the other hand, if you are converting a document that is compelling and impacting as it is, but you mainly want it to be more easily or widely accessible, then perhaps a podcast makes sense. Every genre or medium offers new possibilities for expressing ideas. The key to choosing the medium is to think about how you want your audience to experience your ideas and whether or not the medium can help make your ideas more compelling.

From Reflection to Response   Practice Podcast

As an invention activity or way of testing an idea for this project, use the memo feature on your smartphone or free software like Audacity to create a sixty-second podcast that summarizes the content of a subject you are considering—the issue you want to address and the view or message you want to support. When you finish creating the podcast, play it for some classmates and friends and see how they respond to it. The podcast can serve as an initial draft, script, or outline for your project.

New Multimedia Project

For the second assignment option, a *new multimedia* project, you will build your project from the ground up, starting with an issue you want to address and a multimedia genre or form you want to use. For instance, you could create an original photo-essay, a combination of words and pictures that explores

---

*"Societies have always been shaped more by the nature of the media by which men communicate than by the content of the communication."

an issue, tells a story, or records an event. Your photo-essay might profile a place—let's say, your hometown—in a way that is different from what people usually see or imagine.

Or if you know and care about issues such as cyberbullying, obesity, child abuse, or domestic violence, you could compose a public service announcement (PSA) in any of a number of forms, from a meme, or series of memes, to a Facebook page, video, podcast, website, or multimedia slide show (PowerPoint).

Multimedia genres have the potential to make information more impacting or usable. One simple presentation can include sound, images, video, text, and color. A video presentation can be prerecorded and accessed at any time from any computer connected to the Internet. A podcast can be uploaded to a server and distributed to subscribers' inboxes in an instant, then listened to by subscribers in their cars, on a bike ride, or during a workout at the gym. When effectively created, these kinds of compositions offer your audience unique and memorable visual and audio messages that, for many, are more accessible than a traditional document.

A STUDENT'S PROPOSAL AND DESIGN PLAN

As you begin to consider ideas for this project, read the proposal first-year student Aaron Cervantes wrote for a genre-shift project based on the following instructions.

Choose a finished writing project that you have completed for this course, and present it in a different form or medium. For example, you might create a slide show for a talk, a brochure, video, photo-essay, or a website that distills the view and findings you presented in an argumentative essay, profile, or research paper you wrote. Design your composition for a targeted audience, and as much as possible, use the new medium to enhance the potency of your message.

How to Interact with the Police and Prevent Police Misconduct

Aaron Cervantes

1. The Main Problem and Purpose
The goal of my project is to help people, in particular young people, understand how to interact with the police in a way that protects their legal rights but does not provoke police misconduct, abuse, or violence.

While instances of police misconduct have been widely documented and appear to be on the rise, I am hoping to show that there are two sides to this problem, and that a resolution can only come through mutual understanding and cooperation.

2. Target Audience

I am mainly targeting young people, but I want to propose approaches and solutions that appeal to police officers, as well as my primary audience. I hope to change minds on both sides by educating people about the negative effects this issue is having on everyone. I want to show that the majority of decent, brave, and hardworking police officers are victims themselves, who suffer from psychological stress and are socially ostracized and unappreciated because of the misconduct and violent behavior of just a few "bad apples."

3. Genre or Medium, and Design Elements

I want to create a video that presents statistics and shows examples of the problem, but I don't want to show anything too controversial, like shootings that have been in the national news, because I'm afraid the controversies, which everyone knows about anyway, would distract from finding solutions. I will focus more on the fears and other harmful effects the problem has on both regular citizens and police officers, and I will offer information about how citizens can insure proper treatment and protect their civil rights without provoking confrontations or violent behavior.

I plan to use video-editing software like Movie Maker or some other program to create the video, and incorporate footage of interactions between people and police. I'll also include highlights from an interview I conducted with two police officers. I think the right mix of images and narration will make this video interesting and deliver my message effectively. ∎

Interview with the Student Writer

● **Tell us a little about your background, college major, interests, and career goals.**

● I was born and raised in Miami, Florida, where I attended both private and public secondary schools. At present, I'm a criminal justice major at Florida International University. I want to pursue a career in law enforcement, law, or the military. My family is originally from Nicaragua, and as far as my interests

© Robert Saba

go, though I love Nicaraguan food, I'm not a big fan of Latin music, or for that matter, contemporary American music. My tastes run more toward R & B and classic rock, Chuck Berry, early Led Zeppelin, and Jimi Hendrix.

● **Coming into college, how did you see yourself as a writer?**

● I wasn't very confident in my writing. I went to a private school for 10th and 11th grades. The teachers didn't assign much writing or give very helpful feedback. In 12th grade, I transferred to public school, and the writing instruction was better. We did a lot of reading, which helped me appreciate good writing and develop my writing skills. But when I started college, there was a big difference in demands of the assignments. In my first year of college, my writing improved tenfold.

Working Together

ASSESS YOUR USE AND KNOWLEDGE OF TECHNOLOGY

Spend ten or fifteen minutes drafting a "technology narrative" that explores the role technology has played in your life from childhood to the present. Start by remembering and reflecting on your first electronic toys, games, or devices. When did you begin going online? How often? What sites did you visit? What did you do? Continue through your teen years to the present, describing games, devices, software, social networks, and websites that were, and perhaps still are, important to you, and why. End your narrative with a "summing up" of your experience with technology, how it has impacted your life in positive and negative ways, and in particular, note specific skills you have acquired through your use of technology—for example, word processing, document design, photography, photo editing, web development, or creating videos or audio recordings.

When your draft is finished, form a group with three or four classmates and take turns discussing what you wrote. (1) Summarize your experience with technology. (2) Describe the skills you have acquired. (3) Assume you were going to do a genre shift of a writing project you have already completed in the course. Describe what you wrote to your classmates and what multimedia form or genre you might use to transform it.

COMMUNICATION AND VISUAL DESIGN

Whether you compose a genre-shift or a multimedia project from scratch, remember that communicating through multimedia does not mean you have to "reinvent the wheel." The communication principles that you have applied throughout this course, principles that apply to the movies you watch and songs you listen to, are relevant to this project: You have to be clear about your purpose, define the issue driving your composition, and identify the view you want to support. You also have to consider your audience and the conventions of the genre you are composing in. Multimedia compositions use rhetorical appeals (*ethos*, *logos*, and *pathos*) and methods of development (narration, comparison and contrast, definition, and so on) that you are familiar with. Mainly, what will change is that, along with words, you will use images and design elements to achieve your communication goals (see Figure 11.2). That means you have to apply a "visual rhetoric" to your composition, in addition to the principles of rhetoric you already know.

In a multimedia composition, if you use colors, you have to consider the effects the colors will have on viewers. Different colors—red, blue, green, or black—evoke different moods and emotional responses (see Figure 11.3). In videos or photographs, camera angle and depth of focus can express different moods or feelings. The same applies to design elements for a web page or a PowerPoint slide—the

SMOKING IS POISON.

DON'T SMOKE. QUIT. NOW.

Education Images/UIG/Getty Images

Bob Thomas/Popperfoto/Getty Images

FIGURE 11.2   **Using words, images, and design elements to communicate**

Carol Guzy/The Washington Post/Getty Images

MediaForMedical/UIG/Getty Images

STOP ANIMAL ABUSE BEFORE IT LEADS TO DOMESTIC ABUSE.

SHE'S NEXT.

FIGURE 11.3   **Using color to command empathy and attention**

spatial arrangement of visuals and text can affect emphasis, mood, and feelings. Or, if sound is a feature of your design—say, music for a web page, video, or podcast—should the music be upbeat, relaxing, spiritual, or sad?

Good design makes content compelling without calling attention to itself. Vincent Flanders, author of the book *Web Pages That Suck*, hosts a website (WebPagesThatSuck.com) that helps people "learn good web design by looking at bad web design."

Flanders's site offers useful, refreshing, and entertaining information about poor design elements. Some of the most common web-design problems—elusive purpose, clutter, and what Flanders calls "mystery meat navigation"—are mainly a result of designers ignoring the needs of the audience.

Some common problems with website design include:

▶ Text that is too small

▶ Poor contrast between elements (text, background, and images)

▶ Disorganized page layout

▶ Lack of clarity regarding the intent of the site

Contrast, Repetition, Alignment, and Proximity

The home page of San Francisco–based app designer Kerem Suer (see Figure 11.4) exemplifies effective design. Suer makes use of four well-known design principles described by Robin Williams (not the actor) in *The Non-Designer's Design Book*. These principles, which you should apply to your own multi-media compositions, are:

▶ Contrast

▶ Repetition

▶ Alignment

▶ Proximity

Source: Kerem

FIGURE 11.4   **The home page of San Francisco-based app designer Kerem Suer**

Together they form an acronym, CRAP, which is easy to remember, but if you prefer a more polite term, you can also call them PRAC (for practical) because the principles operate separately and in no fixed order. Here is a brief overview of how Kerem Suer applies the principles on his web page:

Kerem's name, top left—in bold, dark letters but a modest-sized font—**contrasts** with the gray theme that dominates the page. The French word "Bonjour" says "welcome" in a larger font than "Kerem" but in an understated gray color that blends with the theme. Conversely, the image of Kerem and his dog looms out of the central frame because of the **contrast** between the color photograph and the gray background.

Under "Bonjour," Kerem uses a **repetition** of aquamarine font colors to highlight five keywords in hypertext ("Dribble," "my blog," "Twitter," "Facebook," and "blog"). The two pillows in the photograph (one under the dog's muzzle, the other under Kerem's laptop) are a thematic use of **repetition** that underscores the bond between Kerem and his dog.

Alignment means how things line up. The page displays **alignment** features in the arrangement of the primary text along the left border. Kerem's face and upper body, in addition, are **aligned** to the right of "Bonjour" to balance the use of space on the left and right sides of the frame.

> **Proximity** means closeness. The page uses **proximity** to join functional elements. For example, the four rollover buttons above Kerem's head are in **proximity**. In addition, **proximity** is the main organizing principle of the photograph: Kerem and his dog—buddies "doing their own thing."

From Reflection to Response　**Analyze a Multimedia Composition**

To expand your knowledge for this project, find an effective multimedia composition in a genre or medium you are interested in using—for example, a web page, video, photo-essay, graphic story, blog, or series of memes, and analyze how the composition communicates.

Start by creating a "revision outline" or storyboard that maps out the content of the composition, and then analyze the communication strategies and the use of contrast, repetition, alignment, and proximity. Describe what you consider to be the most effective design elements.

After you finish, post the composition, or a link to it, on your course website if you have one, or print out a sample. Bring the sample to class, along with your analysis, for a group discussion.

CONSIDERING GENRES, FORMS, AND MEDIA

Depending on your skills and your target audience, your project can take many forms. Keep in mind that "multimedia" does not only refer to digital or electronic genres or forms. Print magazines and newspapers use both words and images, and therefore are "multimodal" forms of communication. The same is true of other printed genres and forms such as posters, brochures, and flyers. The following are various genres and forms you might consider for this project:

▶ Animations and videos (on YouTube and other sites)

▶ Blogs

▶ Documents in multimedia (brochures, flyers, posters, fact sheets)

- ► Memes
- ► Photo-essays
- ► Podcasts
- ► Presentations and slide shows
- ► Websites and web pages

COMPOSING A PHOTO-ESSAY

Because there are too many genres and media to cover in detail for this project, the specific instruction will focus on photo-essays, one of many possible forms you can use for a genre-shift or multimedia writing project. Even if you end up using a different medium or genre, the principles that apply to composing a photo-essay will help you with other compositions.

Photo-essays consist of a selection of photographs that communicate visually the way traditional essays communicate through words. Photo-essays have captivated and edified people since photography was invented. In the form of "photojournalism," they were the trademark of legendary magazines like *Look* and *Life* that have left a priceless legacy of images about the events, people, and social trends of previous generations.

Like written essays, photo-essays don't conform to a fixed set of rules. The number of photographs can vary from a few to a dozen or more. The photographs can be introduced with text, and include captions, but generally the point is to let the images tell the story with a minimum of words. Below is an excerpt of a contemporary photo-essay published on the Portland *Oregonian* website. Note that some of the captions are repeated. The photographs, much more than the text, drive the narrative.

Benjamin Brink { **PORTLAND CITY HALL CAMPERS FORCED TO MOVE**

RESPONDING TO NEWLY ENFORCED sidewalk regulations, homeless Portlanders packed up before city workers power-washed the sidewalk on Tuesday. 15 total photos:

1. Folks from Portland Habilitation Center replaced marked up signs around City Hall.

2. By Tuesday afternoon, only a few [homeless Portlanders] remained and no one had been arrested.

3. Police gently asked everyone to move before washing the sidewalks.

7. Responding to newly enforced sidewalk regulations, homeless Portlanders packed up before city workers power-washed the sidewalk around 10 a.m. By Tuesday afternoon, only a few remained and no one had been arrested.

9. Responding to newly enforced sidewalk regulations...

10. Folks from Portland Habilitation Center tried three different power washers before they found one that would work to clean the sidewalks in front of City Hall where the protesters had been. ■

15. Responding to newly enforced sidewalk regulations...

Because Brink's photo-essay is also a news story, the author has an obligation to make it informational and avoid "editorializing." Still, the images and captions elicited emotional reactions and different views from the audience. Here are some comments that were posted online:

► Good for the police, but the homeless just moved a block or two away in front of other businesses or moved across the street to the park. Time to cut off the benefits these sponges get.

► One of the ironies I see in all this is that those who typically shout "bum" are also those who say we're a nation founded on Christian principles.

► "Sleep is a human right." No... sleep is a body function... like excreting waste... and should be done in an appropriate place. Sorry, but on this one I gladly go "NIMBY [Not In My Back Yard]."

► The City can scrub the sidewalks till they shine but they can't erase the reality that thousands of people experience on a daily basis.

► Yep, living on the street is a full time job, which is why they need to be bused to a work camp so they can learn what society expects from them.

The fact that these comments focus on the issue itself, rather than Brink's photo-essay, tells us that the author did his job as a journalist and evoked the event objectively. But assume you were creating Brink's photo-essay, not as a news story, but as a public service announcement advocating for the homeless and more shelters. How would you change the presentation in order to reach out to people who are indifferent to the homeless—in particular, those who posted negative comments?

Basic Guidelines

If you decide to create a photo-essay, here are some guidelines that will help you.

▶ Keep the length manageable. Six to twelve pictures is a practical range.

▶ The essay will need a title and some kind of introductory "text," but as noted earlier, the focus should be on the photographs.

▶ Photos can be captioned, but they don't have to be. Either way, the pictures should "speak" for themselves.

▶ Choose photos thoughtfully, and arrange them so that they create a coherent "flow" that impels your audience from one photograph to the next.

▶ Apply the same communication principles you would for a written essay: present an issue and support a view, making sure that the issue and its relevance to your audience are clear and compelling from the beginning.

▶ As you arrange the photographs, ask yourself how each image adds to the whole. It might be helpful to think of each photograph as a single paragraph in a written essay, performing a clear function—either presenting or probing the complexity of the issue, or supporting the view you want to get across.

▶ To enhance coherence and "flow," think about how the pictures transition visually from one to the next. Are there visual redundancies or gaps in the story or information?

▶ Ideally, a photo-essay would be best if composed entirely of your own original images, but that may not be possible for every subject. Because this project is not commercial, you can consider using images from the web, but make sure you keep track of where you found them, and include a list of "credits" at the end of your essay.

Taking Pictures

When taking pictures, think about basic photographic principles (many apply to video as well). Your distance from the subject and the camera angles you use, whether from below or above the subject, send messages to the viewer. If you are close to the subject, that means the background and setting are of less importance to the meaning of the photograph. If the subject is far away, that tells the audience the background and setting are important. Photos taken from below a subject tend to make it look larger, or if the subject is a person, often strong, powerful, or dangerous. Photographs taken from above tend to make the subject look smaller, a person more vulnerable or weak.

Uncropped

Cropped

Courtesy of Robert Saba

Courtesy of Robert Saba

FIGURE 11.5   **Barcelona guitar player—uncropped and cropped**

Take more pictures than you plan to use so that you have choices. Once you have taken pictures, you may want to use photo-editing software to improve the composition. Photo-editing programs are preloaded on most computers. Among the tools, cropping can help to improve or change the effect of an image. For example, the original, uncropped version of the photograph shown in Figure 11.5—a guitar player in Barcelona—emphasizes the symmetry of the columns and the isolation of the man. The cropped and enlarged version of the image puts more focus on the man as a musician and the pastel wall in the background.

You also might want to experiment with exposure and different effects, enhancing colors, using sepia, or trying black-and-white versions of pictures (see Figure 11.6). Color photography is realistic, but black and white can have a different feel, highlight a person's expression and state of mind, or create a more dramatic or retro mood. (Table 11.1 on page 483 includes a list of resources that can help you organize and edit photographs and other kinds of images.)

As you consider whether a photo-essay is a good choice for your project, take a look at a photo-essay about graffiti by first-year student Okeko Donaldson. Donaldson's photo-essay is a genre shift based on a traditional essay she previously wrote about graffiti and the Wynwood Art District in Miami. Donaldson condensed and revised some of the text from her original essay and used it to introduce the photo-essay. She chose to present the photographs without captions, and let the images speak to a theme that a graffiti artist expresses in the introduction: "Getting emotions out."

Color

Antique/sepia

Black and white

FIGURE 11.6   **Leipzig train station—color, antique/sepia, and black and white**

Okeko
Donaldson // **GRAFFITI IN THE WYNWOOD ART DISTRICT**

Introduction

I discovered the Wynwood Art District by taking a wrong turn in my car; my heart stopped because here I was in the "hood" of downtown Miami, surrounded by homeless people, but then I came upon a street in which the walls were lined with graffiti paintings, and my impression started to change. Niel de la Flor, in an article for *Frivole Travel*, gives a perfect description of the district:

> The Wynwood Art District... is home to over 70 art galleries, funky
> thrift stores, antique shops, eclectic bars, and amazing outdoor
> graffiti....
>
> Drive around Wynwood (yes, it's not pedestrian friendly)
> and you'll notice a mix of overgrown lots and crumbling
> buildings abutting newly constructed and virtually empty
> ultramodern high-rise apartment buildings....But what lies
> beneath or behind this odd façade is a fabulous district, thriving
> and ebbing, young and hip. Proof exists on the streets, on the
> graffitied walls of the neighborhood and inside the world-class art
> galleries, such as the fabulous Rubell Family and Margulies art
> collections....

I didn't know when I made the wrong turn that Wynwood has one of
the most extensive collections of legal street art in the world. Most areas
of Miami have laws that prohibit graffiti, but in order to help eliminate
the violations of public property by graffiti artists, some cities, such as
Wynwood, allow graffiti artists to display their art without being charged
for vandalism. Wynwood has introduced "free walls" that provide legal
opportunities for urban youths to express their creativity ("Miami Using
High Tech Way to Battle Graffiti").

After my accidental introduction to Wynwood, I became interested in
graffiti art and started reading about it.

Recently I spoke to a graffiti artist by the name of Roberto, and asked
him what graffiti means to him. He said:

> Graffiti to me is memories. It's whatever I feel. It's an expression, and
> getting my emotions out. When people think of graffiti they think
> of vandalism, criminals and troublemakers, but graffiti is more than
> that. It's an art and people seem to look past that just because it's
> painted on a wall. That wall is my canvas.

Of course, people continue to have mixed feelings about the art of
graffiti, but the Wynwood Art District is definitely a place that can change a
person's view.

Photo-Essay

Okeko Donaldson

Okeko Donaldson

Okeko Donaldson

Okeko Donaldson

Okeko Donaldson

Okeko Donaldson

CREATING A PHOTO-ESSAY FOR A NEW MULTIMEDIA PROJECT

As noted, Okeko Donaldson's photo-essay was composed as a genre-shift project. If your instructor asks you to compose a multimedia project from scratch, here are some suggestions for the project (these suggestions can be adapted to projects using other genres and forms as well):

Option One: Illuminate a Place or Event

Create a photo-essay that illuminates something misunderstood or inadequately understood about an event or place you care about and know well. For example, events like rock concerts, raves, roller derbies, arena football games, beauty pageants, carnivals, protest marches, performance art exhibitions, and religious feasts may be misunderstood or scorned by some people. If you feel passionate and are knowledgeable about an event like any of these, create a photo-essay or other multimedia composition to edify your audience.

Like events, many places, or regions, around the world are misunderstood. Small towns are seen as boring and backward. The same is true of countries that are little known and seldom visited because they are remote, poor, or culturally different. What is special about life in Papua or Kazakhstan? What is special about living in cities like Homer, Alaska, or Tijuana, Mexico? Outsiders know most major cities around the world by a few landmarks and oversimplified ideas. New York City conjures images of Times Square, the Empire State Building, and Rockefeller Center. But what about Riverside Park, the Chelsea Hotel, the Flatiron Building, P. J. Clarke's, and the old Fulton Fish Market? New Yorkers are stereotyped as affluent or dangerous—standoffish and disdainful on the one hand, pushy and predatory on the other. Is that true? Not if you have lived there. The city is much more than the sum of its oft-photographed landmarks and stereotypes.

The same is true of Paris, Miami, Berlin, and Hong Kong, as well as cities of less renown like Pittsburgh, Cartagena, Fresno, or Weimar. If you know and love a place or region that is misunderstood or inadequately understood, you can create a photo-essay or other multimedia composition to edify your audience.

Option Two: Illuminate a Cultural Tradition or a Subculture

Most people identify with a culture—the values, beliefs, and customs associated with a nationality, religion, and family origins. Every culture has traditions that are cherished by those within it, but may be misunderstood or even repellent to outsiders. Think about the culture you belong to, and create a photo-essay (or other multimedia composition) that illuminates a tradition you cherish but that may be misunderstood.

Within larger cultures, many people identify with a subculture—that is, a lifestyle, pastime, or set of beliefs they feel passionate about. Subcultures can be as innocuous as bird watching ("birding"), or as unsavory as soccer hooliganism, but either way, because they are outside the mainstream culture and their members by definition are a minority group, subcultures are almost by definition misunderstood. If you belong to a subculture, consider creating a photo-essay (or other multimedia composition) that illuminates its meaning and value. Below are a few examples of people, activities, and beliefs seen as subcultures:

- ▶ Bikers
- ▶ Bodybuilders
- ▶ Bow hunters
- ▶ Cyclists
- ▶ Deadheads
- ▶ Gamers

- ▶ Goths and cybergoths
- ▶ Magicians
- ▶ Ravers

- ▶ Skaters
- ▶ Wiccans

Tech Tip

For more help conceiving and composing a photo-essay, visit websites known for their photojournalism. Three excellent sites are *Time Photography*, *Mother Jones* ("Photo Essays"), and *National Geographic*. Along with compelling photo stories, *National Geographic* offers useful tips for taking memorable photographs.

WRITING A PROPOSAL AND DESIGN PLAN

Writing a proposal for this project will help you think through the communication principles and design elements that you will use. In addition, your classmates and instructor can review your proposal and offer useful suggestions.

Projects of all kinds evolve and change after the proposals are written, but this project is especially likely to, because the medium you plan to use may be new to you. With that in mind, in addition to using the proposal to share your ideas with others, use it yourself as a "living document" or blueprint and make revisions as your project evolves.

Compose your proposal using the section headings below (numbered or bulleted):

- ▶ **Problem and purpose.** In this section, identify the problem you want to address and explain its importance, then elaborate on what you want your project to accomplish (persuade, enlighten, prove, explain, and so on, or a combination thereof).

- ▶ **Target audience.** Describe the audience you primarily want to reach. Discuss why and how you think your composition and message will have an impact on your audience. What response or action do you expect from them?

- ▶ **Genre or medium, and design elements.** Describe the genre or medium—video, web page, photo-essay, podcast, multimedia presentation, and so forth—that you will use to convey your message. In addition, comment on the materials you will use (for example, software like Audacity, iMovie, PowerPoint, or Keynote) and the design elements that you think will make your message accessible and compelling.

DRAFTING YOUR PROJECT

If you are converting a previous essay project to multimedia, your overriding goal is to address an issue and support a view. Making the issue clear and compelling from the outset is the key to connecting to your audience and holding its attention. Your composition also needs to present and support a view or message. Whether you express the view early, in the manner of a formal argument, or delay the view, is another decision you will need to make, based on the genre, medium, and audience you have in mind.

If you are designing a new multimedia project "from the ground up," be clear about your purpose and communication goals. You might want to try a photojournalism approach and present an issue "objectively" without taking sides or supporting a view but then again, as a college writer, you are not bound by the rules of journalism. Your composition might be more compelling if you express and support a view you feel strongly about.

Choosing a Genre or Medium

Although technical proficiency is not the goal of this project, as you consider multimedia forms to use, favor those that are most compatible with your interests and skills. If you have never made a video, you could still create one by reaching out for help from a knowledgeable friend or a studio on campus. You also could draw on the resources provided by websites like GoAnimate. But you might be better off choosing a medium that requires less of a "learning curve." For example, presentation software like PowerPoint and Keynote can incorporate multimedia including video and music, and these programs provide templates and instructional material that may make the presentations easier to create than a video from scratch. Similarly, creating a website using software and services like *iWeb*, *Wix*, or *Webs* may be easier than composing a video.

Also keep in mind that you do not have to go "high tech" at all. A poster, illustrated blog, brochure, or a Facebook page—all can serve to convey issues and views in fresh and creative ways to different audiences.

TABLE 11.1 Technology and resources

Genres and Forms	Resources
Animation and video	Animoto (video), Avid, GoAnimate, Blender (3D animation), ComicLife, iMovie, Vimeo, Windows Movie Maker, Xtranormal
Audio	Audacity, GarageBand, Logic Pro, Narrable (audiovisual stories), The Moth (audio stories)
Blogging (words and multimedia)	Blogger, Edublogs, Facebook, Storify, Tumblr, Twitter, Typepad, WordPress
Documents in multimedia (brochures, flyers, posters)	Desktop publishers, word-processing programs
Images and photographs	Adobe Photoshop, BeFunky, Blurb (photo book), Corel Painter, Exposure.co/, Flickr, Fotor (photo editing), Gimp (photo editing), Glogster (multimedia collages/glogs), Inkscape, Memloom, Narrable (audiovisual stories), Padlet (multimedia bulletin boards), PhotoScape (photo editor), Pixlr (photo editor), Pinterest, Storybird (visual storytelling)
Memes	Meme Generator (app), Quickmeme (share and caption memes)
Presentations and slide shows	Keynote, PowerPoint, PechaKucha 20×20, Prezi, Impress.js
Web pages and website creators	Google Sites, KompoZer, Moonfruit, Virb, Weebly, Webs, Wix

Table 11.1 presents a list of various genres and forms and current resources you might draw on.

Editing and Proofreading

Multimedia projects usually involve a lot of writing, especially in the planning and drafting stages. Even projects that are mainly visual develop from written scripts, design plans, storyboards, or "shot lists." The final products—for example, a multimedia slide show, poster, or photo-essay—are likely to include writing as well. The number of words may be fewer than a traditional essay, but the writing can be proportionately more important. Every word and every sentence has to count and will be conspicuous by its presence. As a result, careful editing and proofreading are crucial.

If you go through a popular magazine, say, *Men's Health, Sports Illustrated,* or *Redbook,* and look at all the ads, you will have a hard time finding a spelling error or obvious grammatical mistake. In fact, you could go through the ads in many issues without finding one. Ads in popular magazines cost millions of dollars to produce. One spelling or grammatical mistake would call attention to the ad for the wrong reason, undermine its credibility, and detract from the message. As a result, ads are very carefully edited. Your multimedia project needs to be well edited for the same reasons. Poor editing can invalidate messages that deserve attention.

In a multimedia composition that includes written words, elements of document design—font selection, headings, and bulleting—are part of your visual design. In other words, the written content needs to be both readable and visually appealing. To review information about accessibly formatting your written words, see Chapter 9, pages 397–402.

Research and Documentation

If you base your project on a previous essay, you may have researched the subject before and be able to shift genres without developing more information, content, or perspectives. However, depending on the genre or form you choose, doing more research, especially field research, may be helpful or necessary—for example, making a site visit, taking photographs, taping or filming an interview, or finding testimonials or oral histories online. If you are designing a new multimedia project from the ground up, doing both primary and secondary research probably will be indispensable.

As suggested earlier in the chapter, even working in multimedia, you should identify all your sources. Mention sources in your text or audio, and include a comprehensive list of credits at the end.

Storyboarding Your Project

Because this project in most cases will contain visual elements, creating a storyboard (sometimes called a mock-up or a "shot list" for photo-essays) will help you plan and visualize the composition. Below is a sample storyboard that you can use as a model:

STORYBOARD OR "SHOT LIST" FOR: (WORKING TITLE)

Image/Shot etc. # 1 Description and Details: (Duration, Audio, Narration, Captions, etc.)	Image/Shot etc. # 2 Description and Details: (Duration, Audio, Narration, Captions, etc.)
Image/Shot etc. # 3 Description and Details: (Duration, Audio, Narration, Captions, etc.)	Image/Shot etc. # 4 Description and Details: (Duration, Audio, Narration, Captions, etc.)
Image/Shot etc. # 5 Description and Details: (Duration, Audio, Narration, Captions, etc.)	Image/Shot etc. # 6 Description and Details: (Duration, Audio, Narration, Captions, etc.)

> **Tech Tip**
>
> To create your storyboard online, and make it easy to share, try using Mindmup, a free resource for planning, brainstorming, and storyboarding multimedia projects.

YOUR PROJECT CHECKLIST

A realistic process and timeline for completing this project will vary depending on the kind of project you are doing and the medium you compose in. At this stage in the course, you should be familiar with the process that an effective composition requires. The process that movie production requires can serve as a useful model.

✔ Task	Description	Time Frame
☐ **Preproduction (invention and planning)**	• Script or story synopsis and treatment; screenplay; storyboard; production and shooting schedules.	Will vary from a few days to many.
☐ **Production (drafting)**	• Filming all the scenes (in other words, producing a "rough cut" of the final product).	Will vary from a few days to many.
☐ **Postproduction (revision and final editing)**	• Cutting and editing the film footage (sometimes called "montage") to give the movie a good flow, pace, and optimum clarity. • Adding visual and sound effects, and music. • Screening for feedback.	Will vary from a few days to many.

PEER REVIEW

Once you have a working version of your project, your instructor may ask you to bring it to class or post it on a course website for peer review. Here are some review questions for feedback:

1. Describe the genre or medium the writer is using, and the writer's purpose or goal. Does the genre or medium seem appropriate and effective? Are the purpose and goal realistic and worthwhile to you?

2. Comment on the target audience as you see it. Is it a realistic and relevant audience for the writer's purpose and goals? Is the medium or genre

the writer is using a good vehicle for reaching this audience? Can you imagine an audience the writer has not thought of or should consider? Role play the audience if you can, and suggest additional content or strategies that might appeal to it.

3. Comment on the opening, or beginning, of the composition (or the layout and design if it is a graphic). Does it present a clear issue? What strategies does the author use to make the central issue relevant to the audience?

4. How do you respond to the writer's main view or message? How does the composition support the message?

5. Discuss the "production qualities" of the composition. What improvements can you suggest that might add polish or professionalism? Offer any final suggestions or thoughts that might help the writer make the composition more effective.

Sometimes the technicalities of working in "multimedia" can distract writers from their communication goals. Before you submit a final version of the project to your instructor, use the "Rhetorical Analysis" below to assess how well your project communicates to your intended audience. (As in Chapter 9, "Public Writing and Community Engagement," your instructor may ask you to submit a written copy of the analysis with your project.)

Multimedia Project: Rhetorical Analysis

1. **Project Description:** Describe what you have composed or produced for your project and why you chose the genre or medium that you used. Why do you think the choice is effective?

2. **Communication Goals—Central Issue:** What is the central issue your project addresses? Where or when in the composition is the central issue presented? Why do you think the way you present the issue will have an impact on your audience?

3. **Main View or Message:** What is the main view or message your composition supports, and where is the view or message delivered? What impact do you think it will have on your audience, and why?

4. **Target Audience:** Describe the audience you are targeting for your project. Why and how can this audience contribute to resolving the

issue or problem your composition addresses? What specifically do you expect, or ask, your audience to think or do?

5. **Rhetorical Appeals:** Identify the rhetorical appeals you use in your composition (*ethos, logos*, or *pathos*). Why do you think the appeals you have used will have an impact on your audience?

6. **Rhetorical Methods:** Identify and evaluate a rhetorical method of development that you use in your composition—for example, *narration* (telling a story), *comparison and contrast*, an *analogy*, an *illustration or example*, a *definition* of a concept or idea, or *a cause-and-effect relationship*. Why did you opt to use this method, and what effect do you expect it to have on your audience?

7. **"Usability":** Discuss how your composition—whether it is delivered in print or digital form—would reach your intended audience. In other words, where and when do you, as the author, think a reader or viewer would encounter your project?

STUDENT PROJECT: FINAL VERSION

Below is the outline of a talk and excerpts from a slide show that first-year student Aaron Cervantes composed for his project about public interactions with the police. After writing his proposal and design plan, Cervantes decided to specifically target an audience of students in middle school or high school, rather than just "young people" in general. He felt middle school and high school students were the least informed about how to deal with the police and the most at risk to suffer the consequences. He saw himself going back to his middle school or high school as a school alumnus, mentor, and current criminal justice major who understood where his audience was "coming from" and could offer useful advice.

His original idea was to create a video for the project, but he had seen an excellent film online that he preferred to use in some way—*10 Rules for Dealing with the Police*—narrated by Baltimore trial attorney Billy Murphy (from HBO's *The Wire*). The film was too long to screen for his talk, so he decided he would create a slide show (in PowerPoint or Keynote) that would present information from the film, along with other source material and images, to support his talk and stimulate a productive discussion. Following is his informal outline of his oral presentation and slide show.

HOW TO INTERACT WITH THE POLICE AND PREVENT MISCONDUCT

Students attending the talk will receive a handout listing tips and helpful resources including the website flexyourrights.org.

Informal Outline of Aaron Cervantes's Talk

1. Problem:

a. How many people in the audience have been stopped, questioned, or ticketed by the police? How many were scared or felt they were treated rudely, unfairly, or improperly?

- Ask for a show of hands.

b. Proceed with discussion of the problem, and some names and places:

- Michael Brown, Freddie Gray, Tamir Rice. Ferguson, Baltimore, Cleveland.
- Briefly review details of the incidents.
- General statistics and trends (*Indianapolis Star*).
- FBI director's speech at Georgetown University (Comey).

c. Time for change:

- Describe my personal views, aspirations, and respect for police.
- Unfortunate animosity and distrust between public, especially teens, and police.

d. Story of my neighbor "Maria":

- Routine traffic stop. Afraid. Refused to lower window all the way. Ordered out of car. Grabbed by the wrist. Pulled onto the pavement. Searched without cause or charge. Eventually let go, but felt abused, violated, and powerless to defend herself.

e. Results from survey of 30 other neighbors:

- Policies that govern police conduct are too lenient and encourage bad or illegal behavior. Police officers abuse their power. Officers have too much liberty and discretion in enforcing the law.

f. Cases in point:

- Police can legally lie to you—make false threats or promises (Murphy).

- Rule 1.4, Florida code of ethics for police conduct, says:

  "Police officers, whether on or off duty, shall not *knowingly* commit any criminal offense...*except where permitted in the performance of duty under proper authority*" (emphasis added).

- Citizens need to know and exercise their rights.

2. Solutions:

a. *"The Talk"*:

- What it is?
- Why incidents happen?
- What can be done, and what you can do to ensure your safety and protect your rights, without antagonizing or disrespecting the police.

b. Understand the problem:

- Police officers have a difficult and dangerous job.
- The majority of officers are dedicated and serve communities with honor.

c. Interviews with officers "Gonzalez" and "Hernandez":

- Gonzalez = official line and lecture. Apologist.
- Hernandez = candid concerns.
- Elaborate on Hernandez's views about the problem and solutions: what police departments need to do.

d. Solutions from the other side:

- Angry online comment about the police: "Problem with these motherf_____s...."
- What's wrong with comment? Is it true or untrue? Is it productive or counterproductive? Why?

e. Rules to follow when dealing with police (using Maria's traffic stop as a default situation):

- Be calm, cool, and polite. Turn off the engine. Keep hands on the wheel. Don't reach for paperwork until requested, etc.
- Right to refuse searches. Why you should refuse a request to search. What to say and how to say it.
- Exit the vehicle, if ordered to do so.
- Determine if you are being detained or free to go. How to say it.
- Right to remain silent. Billy Murphy (*Wired*): "If arrest appears to be a possibility, the smartest way to take the Fifth is to keep your mouth

shut. You always have the right to remain silent. Asking for a lawyer is a good way to exercise the right."
- Things that might happen if these rules aren't followed.

f. Stopped on the street ("Stop and Frisk" scenario): Same general rules apply.
- Don't get tricked into waiving your rights. (Again, police can legally lie to you.)
- Identify yourself. ID not required unless you're driving.
- Verbally and politely refuse search, as above. Don't empty pockets—same as consenting to a search.
- But never resist search. Don't touch officers. *Never* run.
- Determine if you are being detained or free to go.
- Right to remain silent. Ask for a lawyer.

g. Report misconduct:
- Complaints *are* read by law enforcement agencies. Murphy: "Lots of bad cops are off the streets because they received too many complaints." Also, police departments can be sued.

h. Tips for reporting misconduct:
- Never threaten or say you are going to file a complaint.
- Remember details: order of events, what officers looked like, exact words they said.
- Record details in writing or voice memo immediately after the incident. Don't wait.
- Talk to witnesses.
- Photograph any injuries. Keep medical or hospital records.
- Visit flexyourrights.org.

3. Conclusion:

a. The way forward:
- Upgrade the talk.
- A better, safer, and more respectful society.

"You don't have to boast and brag and automatically think it's us against the police."

—LeBron James

Selected Slides from Aaron Cervantes's Presentation:

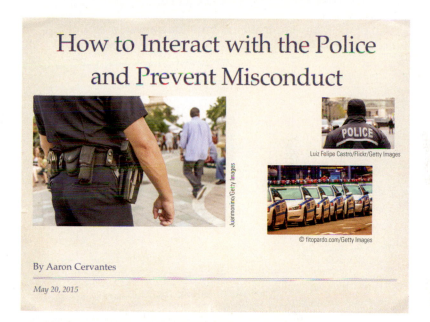

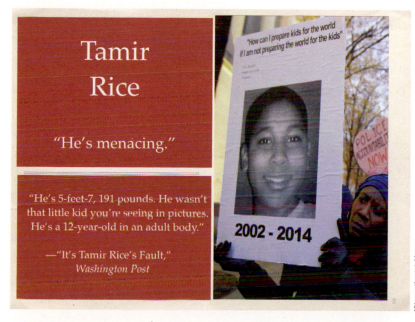

Time for Change

"All of us in law enforcement must be honest enough to acknowledge that much of our history is not pretty."

—FBI Director James Comey

Jordan Gonzalez/Getty Images

JORDON GONZALEZ/Getty Images

Maria

"When she refused to lower her window more than half way, he ordered her out of her car."

Spencer Grant/Getty Images

Luka TDB/Getty Images

The Talk

✦ "You be respectful. You do what's asked and you let them do their job, and we'll take care of the rest after."

—LeBron James

Officer Hernandez

Hill Street Studios/Getty Images

Police departments have to do a better job of:

✦ Screening the men and women they hire.

✦ Hiring qualified minorities.

✦ Training and supervising new officers.

8

Westend61/Getty Images

"Problem is these motherf_____s feel threatened by anything and they can't wait to kill someone. You think these monsters feel bad about killing all these people in the last year?"

Dieter Spears/Getty Images

What's wrong with this comment?

Rules You Need to Know and Follow

Juan Estey/Getty Images

Helen H. Richardson/Getty Images

Doug Menuez/Getty Images

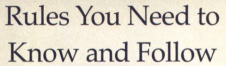

Steve Debenport/Getty Images

Shane Hansen/Getty Images

Be Calm, Cool, and Polite

✤ "Check your ego at the door"—Police work is dangerous.

✤ Turn off the engine.
✤ Keep your hands on the wheel.
✤ Don't reach for paperwork until it is requested.

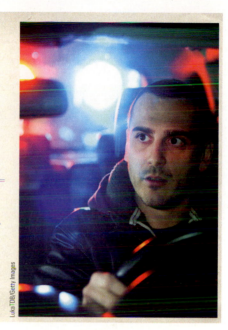

LukaTDB/Getty Images

You Have a Right to Refuse Searches

Do it politely:

✤ "I know you're only doing your job, but I don't consent to searches."

Andy Cross/Getty Images

Police *can* order you out of your car, and you should comply.

Helen H. Richardson/Getty Images

Determine If You Are Being Detained or Are Free to Go

bikeriderlondon/Shutterstock

❖ "Officer, are you detaining me, or am I free to go?"

❖ If you are being detained, you have a right to remain silent.

❖ Asking for a lawyer is a good way to exercise the right to remain silent.

Report Misconduct:
<u>Complaints Are Read, and They Matter</u>

❖   Never threaten or say you are going to file a complaint.

❖   Record details immediately after an incident.

❖   Talk to witnesses.

❖   Photograph any injuries you incurred, and keep medical records.

❖   Visit <u>flexyourrights.org</u> to learn more.

Time to Upgrade the Talk

❖   "The talk we inherited from the 20th century was based upon fear."

❖   "The talk of the 21st century should include vision, encouragement, enlightenment and awareness."

—Mike Green, writing in the *Huffington Post*

digitalskillet/Getty Images

Credits

10 Rules for Dealing with Police. Dir. Tim Lynch. Perf. Narrated by William "Billy" Murphy and Neill Franklin. Flex Your Rights, n.d. QuickTime. Cato Institute, 24 Mar. 2010. Web. 22 May 2015.

Capehart, Jonathan. "It's Tamir Rice's Fault." *Washington Post*. The Washington Post, 3 Mar. 2015. Web. 23 May 2015.

Comey, James B. "Speeches." *FBI*. FBI, 12 Feb. 2015. Web. 25 May 2015.

Green, Mike. "Time for Black Parents to Update 'The Talk.'" *The Huffington Post*. TheHuffingtonPost.com, 28 Feb. 2014. Web. 24 May 2015.

Johnson, Kevin. "Police Killings Highest in Two Decades." *Indianapolis Star*. Gannett, 11 Nov. 2014. Web. 22 May 2015.

Williams, Brennan. "LeBron James Explains the Precautions He Takes to Protect His Sons from Police Misconduct." *The Huffington Post*. TheHuffingtonPost.com, 12 Feb. 2015. Web. 25 May 2015.

Interview with the Student Writer

● **How did you come up with your idea for your project?**

● The professor asked us to do a genre shift that was part of a larger research project. My idea for the larger project—relations between police and young people—came to me pretty easily because it was relevant to my criminal justice major and career goals. Also, as a young person myself, I know from my friends, and from being on social media, that 80 percent of people my age or younger have a negative view of police officers. So I saw a real problem that was worth addressing and had potential to be solved.

I originally intended to create a video for this project but I switched to the idea of a slide show that would support a face-to-face talk to an audience of middle school or high school students. Overall, I think the idea of speaking face-to-face to the students and using the slide show as a visual aid was the best way to get my message across to this audience.

● **How did you go about composing the project?**

● I started with some general goals. I wanted the content of both my talk and the slide show to be interesting—not too inflammatory or controversial, but not bland or clichéd either. For example, I didn't want to use an image like the flower in the gun barrel that you see sometimes. That's too easy and could make people groan. I wanted to focus on realities—the realities of police work and also the realities behind the negative feelings about police that many young people have. I wanted the talk and slide show to say (1) here is how it is, and (2) here is how it should be.

● **Who read your drafts, and what reactions did you get?**

● I showed a draft to my family, and they thought it was pretty good, but my mother and sister suggested removing some "realistic" profanity that I had included in the slide show. They said that even though the profanity was realistic, it took away from the professionalism. I thought about it and finally decided they were right.

● **What parts of the writing process were difficult for you?**

● The thing about writing projects is that they are always difficult for me, but once I'm done, the difficulty fades away. That said, what I struggled with most was presenting a balanced view of both sides, the police and young people. I wanted to create a presentation that police officers would agree with, but that young people would, too. I definitely wanted to avoid talking down to the teenagers, with a lot of "don't do this and that."

● **What parts of the project were easy or enjoyable?**

● I enjoyed presenting the project in class, but I also enjoyed the challenge of designing the project to reach out to a younger, teenage audience. That forced me to be creative.

● **Thinking back, what did you learn from the project?**

● It goes back to the audience again. The teenage audience I had in mind was very real and specific to me—young people who mostly just think of the police as "pigs." The project gave me an opportunity to be creative about tailoring a message to a specific audience, and it also forced me to review my own opinions and assumptions.

● **What advice would you give to other students about this kind of project or writing in general?**

● Whenever possible, choose a subject that is close to your heart and that you feel passionate about. Once you have a subject, don't be afraid to talk to people and ask them questions. Find out what people think, and air out your own thoughts and opinions. Try to be as open-minded as you possibly can, and then think realistically about your audience. Put yourself in their position, and be creative about reaching out to them.

EVALUATE YOUR LEARNING

1. How was doing this project different from a more traditional writing assignment? Was anything more enjoyable about it? Was anything harder than you expected?

2. If you had more time to work on the project, what changes or improvements would you make?

3. What advice would you give to other students who were assigned a project like this one? In particular, what advice would you give about working in the specific medium that you used?

4. Imagine a stranger coming across your project on the Internet. What kind of response would you want that person to have?

PART THREE

Clear Writing and Professional Presentations

> *By the reckoning of three Israeli researchers, nothing imprisons the mind more thoroughly, nothing stifles inventiveness and artistry more brutally, than too much freedom, too much wiggle room for the imagination. Instead, they argue, the real source of productive creativity may lie in art's supposed bugaboos: rules, structure, even the occasional editor or two.*
>
> —Natalie Angier, "Route to Creativity: Following Bliss or Dots?"

The four chapters presented in Part 3 of the book offer detailed, practical advice that complements the writing instruction and projects presented in Parts 1 and 2.

MindTap

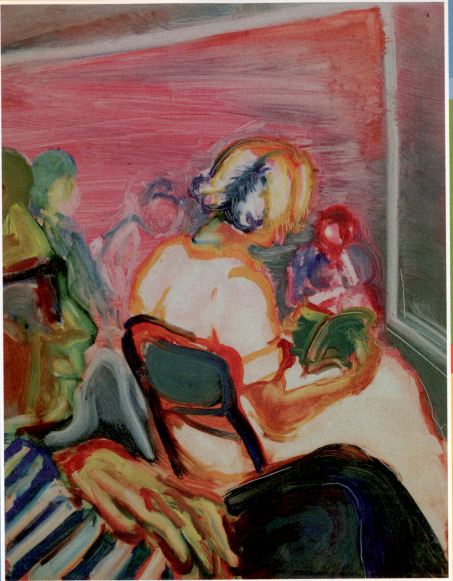

Courtesy of Chloé Dorgan

CHLOÉ DORGAN
Scalp

It came from a quick sketch I had made in class. I was trying to evoke the space yet at the same time retain an element of strangeness. From my simple drawing, I found that I was able to construct a more ambiguous and uneasy tension within the painting. Relationships were forming between figures, through the color and their treatment. What originally was a drawing that focused on a scalp showing through the hair on the woman evolved into an entirely different narrative in paint.

CHAPTER TWELVE

Developing an Effective Style

> *Great painters are often less skillful than mediocre painters; it is their concept of painting—not their skills—that defines their activity.*
> —Francis-Noel Thomas and Mark Turner, *Clear and Simple as the Truth*

CHAPTER LEARNING OBJECTIVES

In this chapter, you will learn to:

▶ Understand the role and meaning of style.
▶ Use specific, precise, and common words.
▶ Understand usage.
▶ Navigate "rules" of writing.
▶ Overcome common mistakes.

STYLE IS THE WRITER

Most people associate style with language skills and the mechanics of writing—a good vocabulary and rules of grammar and punctuation. In fact, style is the complete impression a writer makes on readers, a fusion of words and ideas. Nevertheless, language skills and mechanics play an important role in shaping an effective style, because they help make writing clear and accessible. Clarity is a precondition of good writing and the essence of an effective style. Writing that is unclear blocks the communication process and readers' access to our ideas. Unclear ideas, strictly speaking, are not ideas at all; they are notions until we find words to express them. Finding the words makes ideas real, not only for our readers but also for ourselves as writers.

If you already have completed writing projects in this course, you have made progress toward developing an effective style. You understand communication goals and the value of basing your writing on your own voice. This chapter will focus on the mechanics of style, and offer advice about using language to convey your ideas clearly. The goal is to enhance your awareness of style. As you proceed, take the words "advice" and "awareness" literally, and try not to confuse them with rules. Writing is more of an art than a science. In regard to style, rules may apply, but they are always conditional, because the essence of an effective style is adapting language to a purpose. The purpose dictates the choices we make, not rules. Writers who make good choices are good stylists.

WORD CHOICE

Words are a writer's basic tools, so it stands to reason that using words effectively is the foundation of a good style. Conversely, poor wording—wrong words, too many words, vague or confusing words—makes writing unclear and works against a good style. Sometimes students think a large vocabulary solves wording problems. It is true that a large vocabulary gives a writer more tools to work with, but the tools don't produce good writing any more than a carpenter's tools produce a beautiful table or cabinet. The end product comes from a whole set of skills and a professional attitude toward the craft. Good writers, whether they have a large vocabulary or not, take pains and often struggle to find words to express their ideas clearly. The opposite is true of bad writers: they settle for words as they come to mind, words that are in the ballpark of what they are trying to say, that offer a glimpse but not the exact meaning.

Finding the right words to express your ideas doesn't mean you should labor over every word you choose or sentence you write. Effective wording is part of a revision process. When you are drafting, you should let the words fly. If they miss the mark and don't express your ideas clearly, don't worry. Your goal in the early stages of writing is to get words down. But as you move from an early draft through revisions, you need to examine your words, and change them when necessary. To make the changes effective, you should have some criteria in mind, as well as an understanding of the "tools" you are using.

Using Abstract Words

Words are powerful. We respond to them emotionally and viscerally, not just intellectually. But we respond to what they represent. In and of themselves, they are just sounds and labels for things, ideas, and situations that exist outside of language. In order for written words to communicate effectively, a writer's understanding of words has to be the same as a reader's. If a writer thinks a word means one thing and a reader understands the word differently, the communication process breaks down. This problem occurs when (1) the writer uses words incorrectly or (2) the reader understands the words imperfectly (even though the writer uses them correctly).

As economist Stuart Chase points out in his classic study of language, *The Tyranny of Words*, when we use words that have concrete and specific meanings, that refer to things we can touch or see—a dog, a tree, a waterfall—we communicate without much difficulty. But as we move from the concrete to the more abstract and use words that refer to "clusters and collections of things"—Hispanics, investors, workers—we start to run into problems. Is someone from Barcelona "Hispanic"? Are investors rich? Do workers carry lunch pails and wear hard hats?

At the highest level of abstraction, when we use words that refer to concepts, "essences," or "qualities"—freedom, justice, love, dignity, individualism—communication becomes problematic because the words have different meanings for different people. When abstract words are used carelessly or manipulatively, we enter what Chase calls a "fantastic wonderland" of vague or failed communication. "Freedom" and "liberty" have different meanings to progressives, conservatives, evangelicals, financiers, and neo-Nazis. Those categories of people are just labels that have different meanings to different people, too. The people who fall under the labels see themselves differently from the way they are seen by people who apply the labels.

We cannot simply avoid using abstract words. We need them. They refer to areas of experience that are as real to us as things we can touch and see. But good writers are aware of the inherent limitations of words, especially abstract words, and make it a point to keep their word choice and writing as concrete and specific as possible. If they use abstractions, they define them or give examples that make the intended meaning clear. To write that a man "conducts himself with dignity" or "looks dignified" means little. "Dignity" is an abstraction. But to elaborate on the dignity of a man who once was rich and influential but has fallen on hard times and lives in a small apartment with no regrets, enjoying a life of reading, gardening, and playing dominos with neighbors and friends—the elaboration gives the word "dignity" a meaning.

Even when using more concrete words that refer to things we can see and touch, good writers try to use the most specific and meaningful word possible. Instead of just *dog*, writing *Rottweiler, beagle,* or *Dalmatian* tells the reader more. Instead of *tree*, specific trees, a *date palm* or *elm*, are less abstract. Instead of *restaurant*, kinds of restaurants, a *steak house, truck stop, family restaurant, diner*, or more specific still, *Arby's, Red Lobster, The Cheesecake Factory,* or *P. F. Chang's.* Choosing the least abstract words we can, words that are specific and concrete, enables the most effective communication.

In our everyday lives, we function with the assurance that ideas, principles, institutions, and issues we talk about are real and understandable, but in Stuart Chase's view, they often are minimally so—"noises without meaning, personified abstractions, and semantic blanks." Many of our political debates revolve around the "founding fathers" and their intentions for this country, but seldom is a "founding father" mentioned by name, or much less, quoted. For many politicians, media pundits, and ordinary citizens, the founding fathers are what Chase calls a "personified abstraction," a monolithic pantheon of secular saints hovering in the stratosphere to guide our national destiny. It hardly matters that historians disagree about who they exactly are, or that among the core group—Jefferson, Adams, Franklin, and so on—they had different views about religion, slavery, class, and government. As a personified abstraction, they stand united for just about anything anyone believes in, from Christianity (endowed by a "Creator") to the legalization of marijuana ("the pursuit of Happiness").

Many politicians, pundits, and ordinary citizens who laud the founders' wisdom and vision, think the country is a "mess" today. A Fox News poll conducted in December 2014 found that nearly two-thirds of registered voters believed the government was "broken." But what does "the government is broken" actually mean? Is it a meaningful expression or just what Chase calls "semantic noise"?

From Reflection to Response   **What Does "The Government" Mean?**

With Stuart Chase's concerns about language in mind, form a group with three or four of your classmates and spend a few minutes deciding what the term "the government" means. To what does it factually refer? Since it is the source of the problem, the problem cannot be solved without knowing what it is. Create a list of specific institutions and offices that constitute "the government."

Once you reach some conclusions about what the government is, discuss what specifically is "broken" about it. What does "broken" actually refer to? Create a list of broken pieces and parts.

Conclude the discussion by asking some of the following questions:

1. Why is whatever is "broken" broken?

2. Who is responsible?

3. Can it be "fixed" or repaired? If so, how? If not, should we consider replacing it, and with what?

4. Would fixing it help everyone equally?

5. What do you think the founding fathers would do?

6. Is it possible the problem is something other than "the government"?

7. Is there a way to describe the problem more accurately and perhaps improve the prospects for solving it?

When you are done, share your conclusions with the class.

Using Familiar or Common Words

Whenever a writer uses a word that isn't in a reader's vocabulary, a communication problem occurs. Readers' vocabularies vary depending on age, education, and other factors. Writers have to make educated guesses about words readers will or won't understand. Using a word here and there that is unfamiliar to a reader is not a problem. The context can suggest the meaning, or the reader can look up the word in a dictionary. But if too many of the writer's words are unknown to the reader, the communication process breaks down.

Virtually all good writing guides recommend using familiar or common words as the foundation of your writing—that is, base your writing on the same words you use when you talk. Familiar words are familiar because "they get the job done." They are tested and useful, and at our disposal. We don't need to search for them in a thesaurus or look them up in a dictionary. They work in writing, too.

Writers who see style as mainly "window dressing" often go out of their way to use "big" words to impress readers, but good writers don't do that, and don't need to do so. The passage below, about war and the human condition, by the Spanish philosopher George Santayana is an example:

Certainly war is hell, as you, my fair friends, are fond of repeating; but so is rebellion against war. To live well you must be victorious. It is with war as with the passion of love....Often love, too, is a torment and shameful; but it has its laughing triumphs, and the attempt to eliminate it is a worse torture, and more degrading. When was a coward at peace? Homer, who was a poet of war, did not disguise its horrors nor its havoc, but he knew it was the shield of such happiness as is possible on earth.

Except for a word or two, Santayana uses an everyday vocabulary to express a profound paradox about war and peace.

The passage below, from Charles Bukowski's fictionalized autobiography, *Ham on Rye*, is another example of simple, familiar words doing the writer's "heavy lifting":

I made practice runs down to skid row to get ready for my future. I didn't like what I saw down there. Those men and women had no special daring or brilliance. They wanted what everybody else wanted. There were also some obvious mental cases down there who were allowed to walk the streets undisturbed. I had noticed that both in the very poor and very rich extremes of society the mad were often allowed to mingle freely. I knew that I wasn't entirely sane. I still knew, as I had as a child, that there was something strange about myself. I felt as if I were destined to be a murderer, a bank robber, a saint, a rapist, a monk, a hermit. I needed an isolated place to hide. Skid row was disgusting. The life of the sane, average man was dull, worse than death. There seemed to be no possible alternative. Education also seemed to be a trap. The little education I had allowed myself had made me more suspicious. What were doctors, lawyers, scientists? They were just men who allowed themselves to be deprived of their freedom to think and act as individuals. I went back to my shack and drank.

Bukowski writes in a vocabulary that a ten-year-old child can understand, but the words are a perfect expression of his ideas and experiences. To dress up this passage with fancy words would destroy it, as the following rendition demonstrates:

I ventured into the ghetto to make preparations for my future. I abhorred what I saw. The indigent possessed no special intrepidity or acumen....I was keenly aware of the fact that I wasn't one-hundred percent of sound mind myself. Since early childhood, I had been cognizant of feelings of alienation and anomalousness, as though I was preordained to pursue a marginalized existence....I actively yearned for a sanctuary removed from society....I returned to my pestiferous hovel and promptly indulged in alcohol.

The big words—"abhorred" for "didn't like," "acumen" for "brilliance," "cognizant" for "knew," "sanctuary" for "isolated place to hide," and "pestiferous hovel" for "shack"—bleed the life out of the passage and offer nothing in return.

This kind of arbitrary dressing up usually occurs when the writer is more concerned about impressing readers than saying something meaningful.

COMMUNICATING TO SOLVE PROBLEMS

●●● Neil Rogers, "Shock Jock" (1942–2010): Clear and Simple as the Truth

Like most people in South Florida, radio legend Neil Rogers came from somewhere else—Rochester, New York, in his case—but he didn't identify with his hometown or any particular group. Jewish by birth, he was an atheist who ridiculed "organized religions" as the equivalent of organized crime. He was gay, and in 1977, at the height of an antihomosexual campaign led by singer Anita Bryant, he risked his broadcasting career by "coming out" live on the radio. "While it's not really anybody's business," he told his listeners, "I am, myself, a member of the gay community." True to form, though, whenever members of his "community" behaved in ways he considered dumb or irresponsible, he called them out using words usually associated with female monarchs and meteors.

So it went with every group, institution, and lifestyle. In his thesaurus, flatulence was a synonym for old people; he loved to describe mobs of the "living dead" descending on a luckless restaurant, to devour the "early bird special" and plunder packages of Sweet'n Low. Cubans, also known as the "Cuban mafia" for their political dominance and self-styled status as "Exiles," rather than immigrants, were "idiots screaming like banshees on Spanish radio stations." Rogers had a sensitive ear for language; the Ebonics pronunciation of "ask" as "ax" annoyed him, so

Patrick Farrell/Miami Herald/ZUMAPRESS/Newscom

"Uncle" Neil

he adopted it, along with a smattering of Yiddish interjections, Spanglish, and youth-culture slang to annoy people back. He called the mainstream "Moral Majority" (a precursor of today's Tea Party) a "dangerous, warped pack of fanatics." And though he grew up following sports, and was especially fond of hockey, he excoriated the cult of sports in America.

Below is an example of a classic Neil Rogers harangue, triggered by a male sports fan who called Rogers's show to discuss an incident involving former Golden State Warriors basketball player Latrell Sprewell, who attacked and choked his coach, P. J. Carlesimo, during a practice.

Caller: Do you know what the circumstances were when he [Sprewell] choked the coach?

continued

Neil: What difference does it make?

Caller: You're saying about how he's a high paid athlete, but isn't it the truth that they play under tremendous pressure?

Neil: Oh, get out of here. Call one of those sports shows, you jackass. We work under tremendous pressure here, too. If I went into the hallway and started choking my boss, I'd be behind bars for assault! [Click] You see [people like this caller] will apologize for anybody, anything they do. They never met a scumbag they didn't like. Yeah, [these athletes] play under tremendous pressure, getting paid 10 or 15 million dollars a year to play a game! Poor babies. And you know something; if they lose, they still get paid. If they stink the joint out, they get paid. Here's another guy who takes it seriously, who thinks that it's important. That's what's wrong with sports talk radio; it appeals to [bleeps] like this guy—playing under tremendous pressure; therefore if they happen to try to choke the coach, well, you got to understand the circumstances. Yeah, right, like when Lawrence Phillips [a former NFL running back] stashed his girlfriend in that stand-up mailbox and tried to kill her after he beat her. He was under a lot of pressure. Don't you understand? And the fact that some [bleep] like you would call and apologize, and try to rationalize—all you're trying to do is make yourself feel better about you, not about Latrine [sic] Sprewell, not about anybody else but you. And they're talking about the kids in Colorado [the Columbine shooters] and people can't figure out why the kids don't know right from wrong. It's because they're learning from parents like this guy, who I pray is not reproducing.

The sports talk phenomenon is terrifying to me because it brings them into a concentration. They're all like in one spot; it's like all the ants if there's a thing of sugar on the counter—all the ants are running around that one spot. *"Do you know the circumstances?"* Yeah, uh-uh. I'm almost speechless. Of course, he sounded like a New Yorker to me. And since Latrine just happens to play on the Knicks now—there you go! And by the way, let's go Spurs! Not that I give a [bleep], but in this case I'll make an exception, just for guys like him. I can't complain about your values, sir, because you don't have any.

Rogers falls into a general category of radio broadcasters known as "shock jocks," but though he was brash and outspoken, the term never quite fit him. He didn't say things to be outlandish or shocking; he said them because he thought they were true, and was willing to pay the price for speaking his mind. Ironically, the price in his case was to become someone he never set out to be, "Uncle Neil" to his listeners, a unifying and much-beloved presence in a divided community.

Rogers's success in radio illustrates the idea that "style" in speaking or writing is not just about using words; it's also about the content of a person's character. Most of us routinely suppress saying things we believe in and would like to say, because we're afraid of upsetting people or losing friends. Have you ever thought that you could express those ideas and a person would respect them, if you presented the ideas in a way that was as much about being honest and truthful—about the content of your character—as about the ideas themselves? ●●●

Bureaucratese

An especially bad tactic for impressing readers is to use bureaucratic or official-sounding language (also known as "bureaucratese"). Writers who do this imitate the "style" of a collection notice or lease agreement, and use words like *endeavor* and *terminate*, or puffed up phrases like "afford the opportunity," in the hope of impressing readers with the big words. Nobody likes to read this kind of writing, and nobody with any brains is impressed. Below are examples of words that lend themselves to bureaucratese, followed by their familiar meanings. The words are not inherently bad or useless, but when they are overused, or always preferred to simpler alternatives, they deaden a writer's style:

- ▶ accompany—go with
- ▶ apprise—inform
- ▶ concur—agree
- ▶ desist—stop
- ▶ determine—find out
- ▶ domicile—address/home
- ▶ furnish—give
- ▶ implement—carry out
- ▶ initiate—start

- ▶ locate—find
- ▶ permit—let
- ▶ possess—have
- ▶ provide—give
- ▶ subsequent to—after
- ▶ sufficient—enough
- ▶ transmit—send
- ▶ utilize—use

From Reflection to Response   **Translating Bureaucratese**

Read the job description below for a "Senior Project Officer," reprinted from William Lutz's *Doublespeak*. As you read, try to determine what the job is and what the actual responsibilities are, and then completely rewrite the announcement in "plain English," removing unnecessary words and translating bureaucratic jargon ("functional coordinator," "horizontal issues"). Your goal is to make the ad appeal to a competent professional, a human being rather than a droid. When you are finished, form a group with three or four of your classmates. Compare your revisions and compose a final version that is both professional and clear. Share your final version with the rest of your class.

> Leads project teams to implement Branch Plans; co-ordinates selective horizontal administrative activities and acts as a functional co-ordinator for cross sectoral development initiatives; assists in Branch policy formulation in response to horizontal issues impacting on sector industries;

identifies strategic issues impacting on the sector development process and then formulates and recommends strategies and initiatives to address these issues; develops, delivers, administers, and monitors projects under Branch programs to foster development of the sector; participates in investment, marketing, trade missions, fairs, and promotional activities to encourage sector investment and trade development.

Finding the Right Word

Word hunting with a thesaurus or synonym finder sometimes is done just for "dressing up" purposes, but thoughtful writers do it for a good reason: to try to find the right word, and make their writing more accurate, compelling, and clear.

Official-sounding synonyms like *terminate* for *end*, or *utilize* for *use*, add nothing to our ideas, but the English language offers many synonyms and alternative expressions for words that can add important shades of meaning. *Anger*, for example, is similar in meaning to the following words:

- ▶ fury
- ▶ indignation
- ▶ ire
- ▶ outrage
- ▶ rage
- ▶ wrath

Depending on the context, if you were using the word "anger," any of these other words could be a better choice to express your meaning. Let's say you wrote the following sentence about a teacher: "For some reason, he always directed his anger at me."

To change *anger* in that sentence to *fury* or *rage* or *wrath* would suggest that the anger was intense and out of control. *Wrath*, in addition, would add a hint of vindictiveness or a righteous response on the teacher's part. *Indignation* and *outrage* suggest a strong reaction, or overreaction, to a grievance or slight. *Ire* of all the synonyms probably is the least usable in this context, because it sounds outdated. But in a different context, if you were writing about anger that has primeval or patriarchal connotations—let's say the anger of a clergyman—*ire* could be a perfect choice.

Figure 12.1 shows an illustration from the *New Oxford American Dictionary*, depicting the rich range of English words and phrases that express different shades of meaning between contrasting emotional states, from "angry" to "pleased."

In choosing the right word, a writer has to consider readers, not just the meaning of a word. For example, in an essay in the *Atlantic Monthly*,

WORD SPECTRUM: angry/pleased

angry		indifferent
livid		dispassionate
choleric		detached
wrathful		unemotional
ranting and raving		phlegmatic
foaming at the mouth		insouciant
seething		equable
enraged		even-tempered
furious		nonchalant
irate		cool as a cucumber
raging		unruffled
incandescent		unperturbed
outraged		undisturbed
in high dudgeon		unfazed
hopping mad		unmoved
seeing red		aloof
boiling		cool
hot under the collar	impassive	together
doing a slow burn		collected
fuming		laid-back
fit to be tied		content
mad		contented
vexed		satisfied
cross		complacent
riled		smug
provoked		gratified
galled		pleased as Punch
irritated		tickled pink
pissed off		on cloud nine
annoyed		over the moon
irked		thrilled
piqued		elated
displeased		delighted
sour		glad
unfriendly		**pleased**
cold		

Word spectrums show shades of meaning between two polar opposites.

FIGURE 12.1 **Word spectrum from *angry* to *pleased***

Christopher Hitchens, a respected author and journalist, uses the word "rebarbative" to describe a repulsive dessert (a "rebarbative lobster ice cream"). The word means unattractive, objectionable, or repellant. It comes from the French word for beard (*barbe*). Most people don't know what "rebarbative" means. Hitchens could have written *repulsive, repellant,* or *disgusting.* But readers of the *Atlantic Monthly* tend to be highly educated. Many are writers themselves. Writing for that kind of audience gives Hitchens leeway to use an unusual word. Is it a word you can use yourself? Certainly, it is worth storing away, but an opportunity to use it sensibly might never come up.

Writers have to make similar decisions when using slang and colloquialisms. Slang is an enriching feature of language, and as noted in Chapter 4 (see page 147), has a legitimate role in writing, but most slang terms are less precise than other words at a writer's disposal. Moreover, a lot of slang comes from youth culture—kids in secondary school—and tends to sound immature or trite in an adult context like college writing. If slang slips into your drafts—words and expressions like *psyched, jacked, slamming, pissed off, legit, tight, totally tight*, and so on—try to find more precise and original words to say what you mean. When you are writing for college students, professors, and other kinds of professionals who are attuned to the meaning and value of words, the negatives of using slang (sounding immature or trite) usually far outweigh the positives (an added touch of color or realism).

In addition to being careful about using slang, good writers are aware that words have "connotations," not just literal meanings. The connotations of a word—the associations and feelings that the word evokes—can work for or against a writer. The style manual of a respected American newspaper tells its reporters not to use the word "gutted" to describe a building that has burned in a fire. *Gutted* has connotations of *guts*, intestines and internal organs—*gutting* an animal or fish. According to the newspaper's manual, *"gutted* is an ugly word." Perhaps true, but a building that a fire has gutted is an ugly sight! Apparently, the editors of this newspaper did not want to offend the sensibilities of its fine readers.

Finally, good writers are aware that words are pronounced and have sounds. A thoughtful writer takes the sounds of words into consideration and makes sure they don't grate on readers. For example, a sentence that includes a string of words ending in "tion"—"The informa*tion* about his demo*tion* caused quite a commo*tion* and consterna*tion*"—would be worth changing. Maybe to: "The news about his demotion caused quite a stir and a lot of hand-wringing."

From Reflection to Response   Word Awareness

Go through the list of words below and put each word in one of the following three categories:

1. Words you have used in speaking and writing.

2. Words you recognize and understand but don't use.

3. Words you don't recognize or understand.

   After categorizing the words, look up the definitions of the ones you don't recognize. Decide which of those might be useful to you. Write a short explanation of why. In what context, writing or speaking, could you use the word(s)? Then, working with a small group of your classmates, decide on five words you consider most useful and share them with the rest of the class.

adamant	caustic	holistic	prim	sedate
adept	consensual	jaded	prodigious	truncate
arrogant	cryptic	lugubrious	remiss	turgid
banter	feign	meld	rift	undermine
bemused	foment	nascent	salacious	vie

GOOD SENTENCES

When you know a language well enough to speak it fluently, you have a natural ability to produce varied, complex, and well-formed sentences. What we call fluency in speech helps create "flow" in writing, a pleasing variation of sentence patterns that makes the writing easy to follow and contributes to a good style. Writing that lacks this "flow" strikes us as *unnatural* and unpleasant to read. When a writer's sentences are all simple and short, the effect is choppy and monotonous. If the sentences are all long and complex, the effect is ponderous. But some writers have the same misconception about sentences that they have about words—that is, bigger is better; longer sentences create an impressive style. Take a look at the sentence below, from a customer-service announcement quoted by William Lutz in *Doublespeak*:

> One item of expense included in the rate increase recently granted to P G & E [Pacific Gas & Electric] by the Public Utilities Commission, amounting to $177.4 million, was attributable to President Reagan's Economic Recovery Tax Act of 1981, which requires the Public Utilities Commission to charge ratepayers for the expense of taxes which are not now being paid to the Federal Government and which may never be.

The sixty-six-word sentence suffers from long-windedness, as well as elusive wording. Who knows what it means? Not all long sentences are like that. Here is Vladimir Nabokov, an admired stylist, defending his novel *Lolita* against charges of obscenity:

> While it is true that in ancient Europe, and well into the eighteenth century (obvious examples come from France), deliberate lewdness was not inconsistent with flashes of comedy, or vigorous satire, or even the verve of a fine poet in a wanton mood, it is also true that in modern times the term "pornography" connotes mediocrity, commercialism, and certain strict rules of narration.

Nabokov's sixty-three-word sentence is clear and graceful, yet an unbroken sequence of long sentences, even when well-written, can be hard to read. Good writers strive for a natural variety of sentences that reflect speech patterns, and they are not afraid to rely on short sentences. If you go back and look at the passages written by Santayana and Bukowski (on pages 7–8), you will see that both are built on short sentences, in which the subjects and verbs are easy to identify, not embedded between wordy clauses and phrases. Readers rely on the subjects and verbs at the core of sentences in order to determine meaning. Short sentences make the subjects and verbs easy to find. For that reason, they have impact, and usually are the best way to make a strong point or emphasize an idea. In the passage by Santayana, the short sentence "To live well you must be victorious" expresses the essence of his thoughts on war and peace. In the passage by Bukowski, "Skid row was disgusting" drives home the writer's dilemma about having no place to go.

Thinking about sentences and how they flow should be part of your revision process. As you revise, keep in mind that writing good sentences requires punctuation. Nothing disrupts the flow of writing more than run-on sentences, comma splices, and unintended sentence fragments. They make readers stop, scratch their heads (mentally), and reorient themselves—in effect, waste their time cleaning up the writer's mess. (For more details on sentence punctuation, see pages 44–46 at the end of this chapter.)

A sentence generally is defined as a sequence of words that contains a subject (commonly a noun or pronoun) and a predicate (or main verb). Below is a basic overview of sentence structures from simple to complex:

- ► *A Simple Sentence (subject-predicate):* He ate.

- ► *A Simple Sentence (subject-predicate-object):* He ate cereal.

- ► *A Simple Sentence (with a participle and prepositional phrases):* Raising the spoon from the bowl to his lips, he ate for the first time in days.

- ► *A Complex Sentence (simple sentence preceded by a subordinate clause):* When his appetite returned, he ate light meals.

- ► *A Compound Sentence (simple sentences linked by a coordinating conjunction):* His appetite returned, and he ate light meals.

- ► *A Compound-Complex Sentence (compound sentence with a subordinate clause):* When his appetite returned, he ate light meals, but [he] avoided starches.

- ► *A Compound-Complex Sentence (compound sentence with a subordinate clause and a participle):* When his appetite returned, he ate light meals, but still suffering from indigestion, [he] avoided starches.

Parts of Speech

A sentence can be as short as one word—"Go!"—or as long as hundreds of words, but not just any word or combination of words can form a sentence. As shown in the "snapshot" above, sentences have a basic, grammatical structure consisting of a subject and predicate (or a predicate with an implied subject). To create sentences, words perform grammatical functions that categorize them beyond their meaning. These word categories are called "parts of speech." Arranging words according to their parts of speech allows us to form sentences that convey meaning. (Table 12.1 lists the traditional parts of speech and their functions.)

If we take a random sentence and randomly redistribute the words with no regard for their grammatical functions, most, or all, of the meaning will be lost. Compare the sentence below to the random rearrangement of the same words that follows it:

▶ *Sentence:* The angry protestors chanted outside the building.

▶ *Random words:* Building the protestors outside angry the chanted.

TABLE 12.1   Traditional parts of speech and their functions

Parts of Speech	Functions
Nouns	Nouns identify a person, place, thing, concept, etc. (*friend, gym, rock, integrity*), and often, but not always, need to be preceded by an article (*the, a/an*).
Verbs	Verbs report action (*eat, destroy, evade*) or a state of being (*is*).
Pronouns	Pronouns take the place of a noun (*I, you, she, it, this, these*).
Adjectives	Adjectives modify or describe nouns (*large, blue, priceless*).
Adverbs	Adverbs modify verbs, adjectives, and other adverbs (often, quite, extremely, softly).
Prepositions	Prepositions appear as part of a prepositional phrase before a noun or pronoun to indicate place, position, or time (*on, under, against, to, within, since, beyond, until*).
Conjunctions	Conjunctions connect words, phrases, and clauses (*and, or, but, yet, if*).
Interjections	Interjections usually indicate spontaneous emotion, surprise, etc. (*ouch, oh, Mmmm, dear me!*).

The opening stanza of Lewis Carroll's famous "nonsense" poem "Jabberwocky" (from *Through the Looking Glass*) is an illustration of how grammatical structure and parts of speech help create meaning:

> 'Twas brillig, and the slithy toves
> Did gyre and gimble in the wabe:
> All mimsy were the borogoves,
> And the mome raths outgrabe.

Most readers will recognize '*Twas* as an archaic contraction for "It was" ("'Twas the night before Christmas..."). Other words in the stanza—*and, the, did, were*—also are recognizable; however, the words that *seem* to carry the most meaning—*toves, gimble, borogoves*, and so on—are made up, and in fact, have no meaning. Nevertheless, the stanza seems to say something, because the words sound similar to real words, and more importantly, are arranged to suggest parts of speech and familiar word patterns. We can ask and answer grammatical questions that construct meaning: What are the *toves* doing, and where are they doing it? What kind of *toves* are they? Who or what is *gimbling*? What is notable about the *borogoves*?

From Reflection to Response   Identifying Sentences and Parts of Speech

To practice recognizing sentence patterns and parts of speech, analyze the "Jabberwocky" stanza by doing the following:

1. Identify how many sentences are in the stanza.

2. Try to identify the parts of speech of the words that are italicized. *Hint:* Most of the words probably will be nouns, verbs, adjectives, or adverbs. (If you're not sure, take a guess and don't worry. This is a learning activity, not a quiz.)

> 'Twas *brillig*, and the *slithy toves*
> Did *gyre* and *gimble* in the *wabe*:
> All *mimsy* were the *borogoves*,
> And the *mome raths outgrabe*.

3. Translate the stanza into words that mean something. You can start by converting '*Twas* to "It was," and then go through the stanza, sticking to the original word order and sentence structure as much as possible, but replacing the nonsense words with real words. After you finish translating, go through your translation and try to identify the parts of speech for the words you changed. If you

have trouble doing your own translation, you can use the one below; however, doing your own will be more interesting.

> It was *dawn*, and the *happy campers*
>
> Did *walk* and *trot* in the *woods*:
>
> All *colorful* were the *leaves*,
>
> And the *birds were chirping*.

After you finish this activity, form a group with three or four of your classmates, and compare the sentences and parts of speech you identified. Then decide whose translation is the most "faithful" to the structure and spirit of the poem.

RULES AND USAGE

To speak a language with any fluency, we have to know the definitions of common words, as well as grammatical rules for putting words together, so that others can comprehend what we say. Most people think of definitions and rules of grammar as linguistic commandments that a "higher authority" hands down. In fact, we ourselves create the definitions and rules, those of us who use the language every day. What we see as commandments are descriptive of the way we use language, the tacit agreements we make that allow us to "talk to each other." The specialized term for these agreements is *usage*. Usage is the way language is actually used, and as such, the source of definitions and rules.

A "living language" is always evolving, as people adapt the language to a changing world and changing needs. The English of six or seven hundred years ago was much different from today's. Most of us can no longer read it. The English of two hundred years ago also is different, not unreadable, but it takes getting used to. Even in our lifetimes we see dramatic changes in the way language is used. Words and phrases like *blogs, apps, social networks*, and *data processing* are products of the computer age. If they existed twenty-five years ago, they sounded futuristic and strange.

A few decades ago, the word "relate" primarily meant to tell or narrate—"relate a story." Today *relate* primarily means to identify with, as in "I can relate to your problem." Not so long ago, the word "fun" only functioned as a noun, as in "The fun started when Jon arrived." Today "fun" also is widely used as an adjective—"It was a fun wedding." The word "democrat" is a noun, not an adjective, but decades ago members of the Republican Party began referring to the "Democratic Party" as the "Democrat Party," presumably to prevent Democrats from implying they are "democratic"! This linguistic tic used to anger some Democrats, but today it has lost its power because many Democrats themselves now refer to their party as the "Democrat Party," unaware that they have relinquished claims to being democratic.

In some countries, France, for example, an appointed body of intellectuals makes decisions about language and usage that everyone is supposed to follow. The idea is to codify rules and enhance the integrity of the language. The French institution—it is called the *Académie Française*, or French Academy—has been concerned for decades about the invasion of English words into the French language. The Academy has ruled that English words never should be used when French equivalents are available, but French people notoriously ignore the rules; like most people, they care more about the functionality of the language than its integrity and have no reservations about uttering "Anglicisms" like *bon weekend, top chef, podcasté,* or *c'est hard*.

English rules of usage are codified more democratically. An unofficial consensus about what constitutes "acceptable" usage finds its way from spoken language and published writing into our dictionaries and handbooks. But consensus means that there really is no final authority, and writers and speakers ultimately have to rely on their own judgment (as, in fact, the French do). Most dictionaries make distinctions between informal usage, which is established in speech, and formal, or standard, usage, which is generally acceptable in writing (and for "educated" readers). The word "fun" used as an adjective ("a fun wedding") is well established in informal usage now but not in standard usage. It's up to a writer to decide if and when using *fun* as an adjective is appropriate.

With this in mind, let's look at some rules and areas of usage that raise questions for writers at all levels.

Never Split Infinitives

Many teachers and writers once argued that splitting an infinitive is a grammatical mistake and a sign of sloppy writing. In case you are unaware of the rule, splitting an infinitive means inserting a word, usually an adverb, into a basic verb form (called an "infinitive").

These are basic verb forms, or infinitives:

► to eat
► to know
► to love

These are split infinitives (basic verb forms with an adverb inserted between *to* and the verb):

▶ to barely eat

▶ to really know

▶ to deeply love

Strictly following the rule can lead to sentences like this one:

> They rearranged the furniture in order to create eventually space for their mother's bed.

Breaking the rule makes the sentence sound much better:

> They rearranged the furniture in order to eventually create space for their mother's bed.

Today writers routinely break the rule, but some teachers and writers still subscribe to it. In *The Practical Stylist*, Sheridan Baker, a respected authority on style and usage, advises against splitting infinities:

> They are cliché traps: *to really know, to really like, to better understand*. They are misleaders....*To better know* is to make *know* better; *to even like* is to make *like* even, all of which is nonsense.

Baker's point about "to really know" is hard to dispute. *Know* means *know*. You either know or you don't. But is "to never love" nonsense or a cliché? A great poet, though not splitting the infinitive, wrote, "...Better to have loved and lost than never to have loved at all." The famous *Star Trek* motto—"to boldly go where no man has gone before"—still resonates in our culture.

The real problem is not the split infinitive; it's whether or not the adverb is meaningful or just filler. Good writers always double-check adverbs, regardless of where they put them. William Zinsser, who like Baker is an authority on style, offers this advice in his book *On Writing Well*:

> Most adverbs are unnecessary. You will clutter your sentence and annoy the reader if you choose a verb that has a specific meaning and then add an adverb that carries the same meaning.

Of course, adverbs often are necessary (I just used one), but whenever you use an adverb, ask yourself if it is necessary or redundant. The phrases below are split infinitives, but the adverbs are the real problem, because the verbs carry the meaning by themselves:

▶ to tightly squeeze

▶ to loudly scream

▶ to strongly chastise

Beginning a Sentence with *And* or *But*

The rule against beginning a sentence with *and* or *but* has some basis in grammar, because both words are conjunctions that often function as "coordinating conjunctions" to create compound sentences. Purists argue that it is incorrect to break up a compound sentence in the manner that follows:

> I love the campus. But the dorms need to be remodeled.

Instead, those two sentences should be connected by the conjunction:

> I love the campus, but the dorms need to be remodeled.

However, precedents for beginning sentences with *and* or *but* go back to the King James Bible and before. Based on usage, no rule applies. Sometimes writers begin sentences with *and* or *but* for emphasis. More often, the reason is to give readers a break, when the first part of a compound sentence is long or complex. But if you begin a sentence with *and* or *but*, remember that they are conjunctions and should be punctuated as such. Don't confuse them with transitional words and expressions like *however, furthermore,* or *in consequence,* which are set off with commas from sentences they begin:

▶ *Incorrect:* But, the dorms need to be remodeled.

▶ *Correct:* But the dorms need to be remodeled.

Ending a Sentence with a Preposition

"Never end a sentence with a preposition" is another arbitrary rule. Winston Churchill, the famous British statesman and orator, debunked the rule with humorous indignation:

> This is the sort of English up with which I will not put.

To follow the rule slavishly is to torture the English language, and self-censor good sentences like "Where do you come from?" or "That's an approach we can agree on." The real rule is this: if you write a sentence that ends in a preposition, and it sounds unnatural, change the wording. If it sounds fine, leave it alone.

Of course, advice like this only applies when you are free to make your own decisions as a writer. If you are writing for an organization or publication that has style rules, you have to observe those rules, even if you think they are arbitrary. If your instructor has style rules, you have to observe them, too.

Contractions: Dos and Don'ts

You probably use contractions in most of the writing you do, and you should. They are well-established in English usage, and in all kinds of modern writing, from blogs, to newspaper stories, business reports, magazine articles, and critically acclaimed books on virtually any subject. Most professional writers use contractions without any misgivings. Contractions reflect the way we talk. They bring a natural tone to writing and promote a reader-friendly and conversational style.

Contractions also are acceptable in academic writing, but if you look at articles in most scholarly journals, you will find fewer contractions than in newspapers and magazines. Most academic writers seem to believe that avoiding contractions establishes a more serious tone. In other words, to write "Patients do not always respond to empathy" is a better choice than "Patients don't always respond to empathy." At a glance, the difference between the two sentences seems insignificant, but most writers, academic or not, probably would agree that an essay or article replete with contractions—*won't, isn't, haven't, doesn't, there's*—will sound "breezier" than the same article using the full words—*will not, is not.*

The breeziness comes from reflecting speech, which most of the time is breezier than writing, but the breeziness has another source. Contractions incorporate simple verbs—*have, do, will, be*—whose functions are mainly grammatical, as opposed to strong verbs with specific meanings like *argue, infer, dismiss, portray, ignore.* Writing that favors strong verbs is likely to be more substantial and less breezy than writing that is replete with contractions. For academic writers, the avoidance of contractions is a self-imposed discipline, not just a cosmetic enhancement. It helps them improve their writing.

You should use contractions when appropriate for the freshness they bring to your writing, but think about your audience and genre. For general purposes, it might be a good idea to stick to common, widely used contractions like *don't, aren't, I'll,* and except in writing dialogue, avoid more colloquial contractions like *should've, would've, they'd, it's been,* which may call too much attention to mimicking speech, and move your style in the direction of "eye dialect" (contractions like *gonna* and *wanna*) and the lingo of text messaging and chat.

If you use contractions only to shorten words and reduce syllables, you may not need them at all. Ernest Hemingway, admired as a great stylist, begins one of his stories with this sentence:

> In the fall the war was always there, but we did not go to it any more.

Hemingway chose to write "*did not* go to it any more" instead of *didn't*. In many of his stories, Hemingway uses contractions freely, but in this particular story and others he avoids them. From a reader's perspective, the difference between reading *did not* and *didn't* is slight. But for Hemingway, writing *did not* allows him to present his ideas without the echo of colloquialism that contractions create. The clean, depersonalized detachment of *did not* actually lightens the weight of the sentence.

Finally, keep in mind that when you use contractions, you have to be careful about spelling. Contractions are easy to confuse with other words that sound the same but have different meanings (called "homonyms"). Here are some common mistakes that spell-checkers won't catch:

▶ you're / your

   I love you're house. Your a special person.

▶ they're / their

   They're game is tomorrow. Their nice people.

▶ who's / whose

   The man who's wife died last year. The girl whose a fashion model.

If you write out your contractions in their original, unabridged form, you can avoid most of these mistakes, but be especially careful with *it's* and *its*. *It's* is always a contraction for *it is*, but the apostrophe makes it look like a possessive. *Its* without an apostrophe always is the correct possessive form of *it*.

Incorrect

▶ The dog wagged it's tail.
▶ Its a nice day.

Correct

▶ The dog wagged its tail.
▶ It's a nice day.

The First-Person "I" and the Passive Voice

> **"***It was recommended to avoid using a passive voice.***"**
>
> —A FIRST-YEAR WRITING STUDENT

If you have completed writing projects for this course, you know that "never use I" is a false rule. Personal narratives have to be written in the first person and use "I." Other genres—formal arguments or research papers—call for using "I" with restraint in order to curb subjectivity, but avoiding "I" altogether, even in formal writing, can create stylistic problems—cumbersome sentences, a stilted tone, and overuse of the passive voice.

Many languages have an indefinite pronoun that can be used in place of "I" to mean anyone. In German, the word is *man*, in French, *on*. In English, the word is *one*, as in "One has to wonder about LeBron's motives," but the English *one*, used in this sense, sounds stiff to many readers, especially when repeated ("One has to wonder about LeBron's motives, but one still has to admit...."). In conversation, *you* is an acceptable alternative ("You have to wonder about LeBron's motives"), but in writing, using *you* in this sense comes across as lax or too colloquial. *We* is a third option many writers use ("We have to wonder about LeBron's motives"), but some readers think using *we* to mean the writer and people in general sounds pretentious.

Journalist William Zinsser urges writers to use the first person as much as possible, but understands that "there are vast regions of writing where 'I' isn't allowed."

> Newspapers don't want "I" in their news stories; many magazines don't want it in their articles; businesses and institutions don't want it in the reports they send so profusely into the American home; colleges don't want "I" in their term papers or dissertations.

Zinsser concedes that there are legitimate reasons for not using "I" but also thinks the source of the problems we have with using "I" is cultural:

> We have become a society fearful of revealing who we are. We have bred a language of impersonality. The institutions that seek our support by sending us their brochures sound remarkably alike, though surely all of them—hospitals, schools, libraries, museums, zoos—were founded and are still sustained by men and women with different dreams and visions. Where are these people? It's hard to glimpse them among all the passive sentences that say "initiatives were taken" and "priorities have been identified."

Of course, the existence of the Kardashians, reality TV, Facebook, and Twitter tells us that Americans are not "fearful of revealing" themselves. Americans *love* self-revelation.* Yet it also is true that we hear and read a "language of impersonality" that advises us about initiatives all the time. The real problem seems to be that we swing between extremes, an egocentric use of the first person that is grating, or a disembodied use of passive voice and bureaucratese that is equally grating.

Neither style is suitable for college writing, but students often find themselves in a dilemma. Professors say, "Don't use the first person," because it leads to subjectivity, but also say, "Don't use the passive voice," because it is wordy and ponderous. Unfortunately, avoiding the first person makes it hard to avoid passive constructions and their corollary, general wordiness, but the alarms that purists sound about passive voice can be as exaggerated as alarms about using "I." In *A Sense of Style*, author and professor Steven Pinker attests to this point:

> We now know that telling writers to avoid the passive is bad advice. Linguistic research has shown that the passive construction has a number of indispensable functions because of the way it engages a reader's attention and memory. A skilled writer should know what those functions are and push back against copy editors who, under the influence of grammatically naïve style guides, blue-pencil every passive construction they spot into an active one.

Some examples used to illustrate the atrocities of the passive voice are minimally realistic. Why would anyone choose the passive alternatives below unless the context required it?

▶ *Active*: Every Saturday, Jean cleaned the house.

▶ *Passive*: Every Saturday, the house was cleaned by Jean.

Or an odder alternative still:

▶ *Active*: In his last at bat, Bonds drove a curve ball into the gap.

▶ *Passive*: In his last at bat, a curve ball was driven into the gap by Bonds.

Persistent strings of passive constructions create a bureaucratic tone and colorless writing that leaves out information, muffles strong verbs, and

---

*Zinsser was writing in 1995, before the Kardashians and so on, but he was acquainted with self-revelatory zeal in the form of "Queen for a Day," the "Me Generation," *The Happy Hooker*, and Janis Joplin.

subordinates important subjects. In fact, no one likes to read even one sentence that sounds like mindless droning:

▶ In view of the evidence that has been presented, it is possible to conclude that solutions to the problem can begin to be implemented by the forging of dedicated alliances between government, the private sector, philanthropic organizations, and altruistic individuals from every walk of life.

But a moderate use of passive constructions is harmless and even helps to preserve the coherence or flow of a paragraph, vary sentence patterns, or express some ideas. To write "the announcement infuriated shareholders" (active) might have more punch than "shareholders were infuriated by the announcement" (passive), but in an actual paragraph focused on the shareholders, the passive construction could be a better choice.

Here is the opening of an article titled "Boomerangs and Duds," by A. J. Liebling, an admired journalist, writing about an experience as a correspondent during World War II:

The first half of the summer produced two fine illustrations of the working principle that...I denominated Liebling's Law. This is that if a man is smart enough, he can kick himself in the seat of the pants, grab himself by the collar, and throw himself out on the sidewalk. My formulation of the law was prompted by the sad case of the newspaper correspondents who so effectively ingratiated themselves with the Army public-relations authorities that when the Armistice with Germany was signed at Reims not a single representative of an American daily [newspaper] was allowed in the room where the ceremony took place. To paraphrase a great man's *mot* [saying], they had ingratiated themselves out. The Army press agents had decided that such a subservient bunch could not possibly count for anything, and, although they had no trouble finding space for the pretty fiancée of the naval aide of a general, they excluded the newspapermen.

Liebling's paragraph contains 156 words. The third sentence, a long, passive construction ("My formulation of the law was prompted by...."), takes up almost half of the paragraph. Converting the sentence to active voice makes it harder to read and follow by comparison:

The sad case of the newspaper correspondents who so effectively ingratiated themselves with the Army public-relations authorities that when the Armistice with Germany was signed at Reims not a single representative of an American daily [newspaper] was allowed in the room where the ceremony took place prompted my formulation of the law.

Avoiding passive constructions generally is a good idea but not a rule that you need to follow religiously. Don't worry about passive voice at all when you are drafting. Don't worry about using "I" either. When you are revising, look for passive constructions, especially droning strings of them, and convert them to active voice when you can. Usually doing that will give your writing more punch.

From Reflection to Response   **Analyzing the Style of "Baby Shoes"**

Now that you have a better understanding of style and how it is created, spend a few minutes analyzing the stylistic choices that apply to the six words quoted below. According to legend, an unknown writer wrote those words to show that she or he could compose a short story only six words long:

For sale. Baby shoes. Never worn.

To guide your analysis, remember that "style" essentially means to adapt language to a purpose. The writer's main purpose here is to create a story. When we analyze writing and other forms of communication, we routinely separate form and content—that is, *how* something is said, the manner or "form," from *what* is said, the meaning or "content." However, in our experience of communication, form and content are inseparable. Keeping that in mind, address the following questions about the unknown writer's six-word story:

1. What story might the six words be telling? What is the plot? Who are the characters? What is the theme?

2. How does the arrangement of words—the "style" of writing—create the impression of a story, instead of just an advertisement? To answer the question, try changing the punctuation and rearranging the words in different ways that preserve the literal meaning. You also can try changing the words slightly while still preserving the literal meaning. What happens to the verbal rhythms and connotations that suggest a story? Review the examples below, and analyze how and why they change or destroy the original effect of the words.

   • Never worn baby shoes for sale.

   • For sale. Never worn. Baby shoes.

- Never worn. For sale. Baby shoes!
- For sale: A pair of brand new baby shoes.
- I'm selling a pair of baby shoes that have never been worn.
- Last pair of baby shoes for sale. Never worn!
- For sale. Baby shoes. Original packaging.
- For sale. Baby shoes. Hardly worn.
- For sale. Burberry baby shoes. Never worn.

A FEW GOOD RULES

> "*Everything written with vitality expresses that vitality: there are no dull subjects.*"
>
> —RAYMOND CHANDLER, *THE SIMPLE ART OF MURDER*

The previous section reviewed some rules that are arbitrary or misunderstood. The section that follows covers rules, conventions, and elements of style that good writers pay attention to.

Watch Your Paragraphs

Many students wish there was an easy way to improve their writing. There *is* an easy way, not a cure-all, but a big help: pay attention to your paragraphing. Readers (including your professors) appreciate thoughtful paragraphing. It helps them move through your writing and assimilate your ideas. When paragraphs are too long, readers have to scale a wall of words that makes reading difficult and unpleasant. If you look at newspaper articles, you will see short paragraphs designed to make the writing easy to read and absorb. The paragraphing in magazines of quality, like *Smithsonian* or the *New Yorker*, is not as short but still short enough to be easy on the eyes and give readers frequent breaks. Magazine-length paragraphs—paragraphs that run from seventy-five words to less than two hundred—generally are suitable for academic essays.

Some style manuals describe paragraphs as "units of thought" that develop an idea expressed in a "topic sentence." Although this structural description may be helpful to some beginning writers, it doesn't stand up to analysis. Paragraphing isn't a science. Good writers don't need a formula for creating paragraphs. They use common sense and create breaks to show distinctions in the ideas they present (a lesser, new, divergent, or contrasting point), indicate chronology (then, next, afterward, meanwhile), and show shifts of location (here, there, nearby, on the other side). As a rule of thumb, if a page of an essay you write is all one paragraph, you should create a break somewhere.

From Reflection to Response Creating Paragraphs and Readable Sentences

Working with one or two of your classmates, read the newspaper story that follows, and edit it as needed. Insert necessary punctuation, capitalizations, and paragraph breaks where you think they should be [¶]. The story originally contained eleven paragraphs; however, you don't have to end up with the same number (short paragraphs are the norm for newspaper stories), but you should have an explanation for the breaks you choose. If you notice mistakes or editing problems other than punctuation, capitalizations, or paragraphing, make a note of them, and discuss them with your classmates. (To do this activity, you might want to make a photocopy of the text and work on the photocopy, or download a digital version on this book's companion website and edit the text digitally.)

Newspaper Story

December 25, 2012

high-speed chase means christmas in jail

laura rager 46 who lives in boynton beach [florida] remained in the monroe county detention center on stock island in lieu of $20500 for allegedly taking police on a us 1 chase in which she hit 120 mph in her toyota while driving drunk and while flipping off a deputy becky herrin from the monroe county sheriff's office said that around 2:20 am sunday deputy juan martin-reyes clocked rager doing 73 mph southbound while martin-reyes was working a drunk-driving patrol the speed zone where she was driving is 45 mph so martin-reyes turned around and attempted to pull her over backed up by deputy jon huff rager pulled over but just as martin-reyes was getting out of his car she took off he followed and she hit 120 mph while crossing both the white and yellow lines of us1 herrin said forcing several vehicles off the road with her dangerous behavior at that point deputies realized they had a major problem and got more backup and deputy scott ward was traveling toward her with his lights and siren activated in an attempt to slow her down she crossed the center line and drove directly at him forcing him off the road at mile marker 16 herrin said rager reportedly drove 11 more miles to mile marker 5 saw the red and blue lights of deputies setting up a stinger spike strip in an attempt to puncture her tires then did a u-turn that's when martin-reyes said she rolled her window down and stuck her hand out extending her middle finger at him he headed back north behind her and at mile marker 10 five miles away she again crossed the center line forcing a tractor-trailer truck off the road herrin said finally at mile marker 205 while she was still heading north more deputies were stationed with a stinger spike system punctured her tires and the car slowly came to a stop herrin said rager jumped out of the car and fled running toward a wooded area the deputies chased her when they caught up with her they ordered her to show her hands so they could be sure she did not have a weapon she refused to comply and a taser was used to subdue her she kept yelling why don't you just shoot me get it over with herrin said and was arrested once at the jail she refused to submit to a breath test or sign her traffic tickets which where numerous turns out she has two prior dui herrin said rager is charged with fleeing and eluding police reckless driving driving under the influence of alcohol and/or drugs (third violation) aggravated assault with a deadly weapon speeding in excess of 50 mph over the posted speed limit failing to maintain a single lane refusal to submit to a breath test and five counts of resisting arrest

Pay Attention to Formatting and Layout

Like paragraphing, a good format and layout can enhance your writing without costing you much time and effort. Whether you are writing an essay, report, or just a memo, make sure your pages look inviting to read. Here are some tips:

▶ **Always have ample margins**. When words crowd the edges of a page, they make a document look uninviting.

▶ **Use page numbers** if a document is more than one page.

▶ **Know the difference between essay-style formatting and business style**. In essay style, lines are double-spaced and the first word of every paragraph is indented (MLA style specifies one half-inch from the left margin). In business style, lines are single-spaced and the first word of a paragraph is not indented. Paragraphs are separated by an extra space and called "block paragraphs." Use the appropriate style, and don't mix the two.

▶ **Use bullets and numbering**. These formatting devices are easy to incorporate and help readers grasp important points. They also create more white space on a page, which makes the text easier to follow and more inviting. In shorter, business-related documents, you can use bulleted paragraphs.

▶ **Use internal headings** to break up the text and label sections of longer essays and documents. For example, if you were writing a research paper on voter suppression, you might use internal headings like these:

History of voter suppression

Electronic voting machines

Absentee and early voting

Incidents of posthumous voting

Internal headings normally are written in bold type, with the first letter of the first word capitalized. The headings are positioned flush to the left margin above the paragraph that begins the relevant section.

Use Parallel Constructions in Your Sentences

> **"***No matter who you are, resist the urge to wear colored pants.***"**
> —*GQ MAGAZINE*, "FASHIONS FADE, STYLE IS ETERNAL"

Think of how you coordinate colors when you dress. Parallel constructions coordinate the parts of your sentences in much the same way, and make your writing "flow." Mixed constructions are like wearing colors that don't match. Here are some simple examples of *parallel* constructions:

▶ The police officer was rude, obnoxious, and dishonest.

▶ Pamela spent the summer swimming, hiking, riding horses, baking cookies, working part-time at the mall, and devouring romance novels.

Here are the same sentences written with faulty or broken parallelism:

▶ The police officer was rude, had an obnoxious attitude, and dishonest.

▶ Pamela spent the summer swimming, liked to hike, horseback riding, baking cookies, working at the mall, and devoured romance novels.

Even accomplished writers sometimes struggle with parallelism, as they try to balance the flow of their sentences with the meaning they want to express. For example, in the parallel sentence about the rude police officer, the writer might feel the word "dishonest" is not strong enough, and prefer the word "liar." But substituting *liar* for *dishonest* would break the parallel structure, because liar is a noun and the other words are adjectives:

▶ The police officer was rude, obnoxious, and a liar.

That sentence is not hard to read in isolation, and in most cases, would be an acceptable choice, but broken parallelism has a cumulative effect on the flow of a writer's sentences. Thoughtful writers are aware of that, and though they might "fudge" on parallelism now and then, they keep broken constructions to a minimum.

Parallel Constructions in Lists

When you use bulleted or numbered lists, keep the items in a parallel form. The purpose of a list is to make your points easy to grasp. Parallel structure helps readers move through the list. A jumbled structure has the opposite effect. Compare the two lists below.

Not parallel

Reasons to consider seeking help from a therapist:

▶ Loss of trust in friends and family members

▶ You are hypercritical of yourself and others

▶ Behaving in self-destructive ways

> ▶ Self-victimization
> ▶ Blaming your problems and deficiencies on your parents

Parallel

Reasons to consider seeking help from a therapist:

> ▶ You have lost trust in friends and family members.
> ▶ You are hypercritical of yourself and others.
> ▶ You behave in self-destructive ways.
> ▶ You see yourself as a victim.
> ▶ You blame your parents for your problems and deficiencies.

Also Parallel

Consider seeking help from a therapist, if you:

> ▶ Have lost trust in friends and family members
> ▶ Are hypercritical of yourself and others
> ▶ Engage in self-destructive behavior
> ▶ See yourself as a victim
> ▶ Blame your parents for your problems and deficiencies

Use Clichés Sparingly

Clichés are worn-out expressions that jump to mind because we hear them all the time. Most of us use them in casual conversations because they are handy and keep conversations moving. In writing, they can be useful on occasion—they add a touch of color or convey the right combination of meaning and tone:

> ▶ Mrs. Hudson is a savvy teacher. No one pulls the wool over her eyes.

"Pull the wool over her eyes" is a cliché; it means Mrs. Hudson can't be fooled. In this instance, maybe the cliché livens up what would otherwise be an abstract statement ("no one fools her"). The important thing is for writers to be aware they are using a cliché.

In most cases, clichés are weak substitutes for original thinking and fresh language. For example, in any context except humor, a sentence like "I was trapped like a rat" is a dud. If the writer is serious about being trapped, simply writing "I was trapped" resonates much more. "Like a rat" weakens *trapped* because it shifts the attention from (presumably) a real person in a real bind to a metaphorical rat that (with due respect to Remy in the movie *Ratatouille*) no one cares about.

Clichés that flourish in the media, advertisements, and greeting cards, and therefore seem to have legitimate status, can be seductive but just as vapid as the trapped rat. The boundless caring of a person who is "always there" for someone has become a sappy cliché. Being specific about that person's traits and supportive deeds is a better tribute than the "always there" label.

Skillful writers are good at detecting clichés and replacing them with more original words or expressions, but clichés are so deeply ingrained in the language that they slip into everyone's writing now and then. The mock interview below, which appeared in the *New Yorker* magazine in 1935, is a humorous reminder of just how ingrained some clichés are:

Q—Now then, Mr. Arbuthnot, what kind of existence do you, as a cliché expert, lead?

A—A precarious existence.

Q— And what do you do to a precarious existence?

A— I eke it out.

Q—How do you cliché experts reveal yourselves, Mr. Arbuthnot?

A— In our true colors, of course.

Q— Now, Mr. Arbuthnot, when you are naked, you are...

A— Stark naked.

Q— In what kind of daylight?

A— Broad daylight.

Q— What kind of outsider are you?

A— I'm a rank outsider.

Q— You are as sober as...

A— A judge.

Q— And when you are drunk?

A— I have lots of leeway here. I can be drunk as a _____ [fill in the blank].

Table 12.2 shows a list of words and trendy expressions (also called "neologisms") that have been submitted to Lake Superior State University's annual "Banished Words" competition. Included are comments by the people who nominated the words and expressions for banishment.

> **From Reflection to Response**   **Banning Clichés and Trendy Expressions**

Working with two or three of your classmates, go through the list shown in Table 12.2 and decide if you agree with the nominations and supporting comments. After discussing the list, create your own short list of words and expressions that you think deserve banishment, and explain why. Share your list with the rest of the class.

Eliminate Unnecessary Words

Virtually all handbooks and style manuals urge writers to be concise and cut out unnecessary words. The advice sounds reasonable, yet writers often resist it. After working hard to organize and express ideas clearly, writers have a tendency to leave well enough alone. A few extra words here and there seem like no big deal. But wordiness accumulates. Even in a short essay, extra words and phrases quickly add up to an extra paragraph or page of verbiage. The cumulative effect isn't lost on readers.

Good writers go through their writing with an eye on making it as concise as possible. Once you develop the habit of doing this, you will take a big step toward improving your style. To decide what to cut, read over what you write from a reader's perspective. Here are a few general guidelines:

- ▶ **Check your adverbs and adjectives**, and make sure you need them. As noted earlier in the chapter, adverbs often are filler words (*really, very, basically*) or redundant (*loudly* scream). Adjectives can be unnecessary, too—for example, "a *difficult* ordeal" (*ordeal* denotes difficulty). Sometimes we use adjectives in pairs when one is enough—for example, "She is a witty and amusing woman."

- ▶ **Check long sentences** and make sure every word counts. Take out filler words and phrases, unnecessary details, or obvious information that readers don't need.

- ▶ **Check for passive voice.** Passive sentences usually are wordier than active sentences.

TABLE 12.2 Lake Superior State University's "Banished Words"

TO BE PERFECTLY HONEST WITH YOU

"When someone says that to me, it shows me he has already considered the possibility of lying to me and, for some reason, has discarded it. It also makes me wonder if he's lied to me before, and now is trying to lead a more moral life."

–Dianne Linden, Edmonton, Alberta, Canada.

STATE OF THE ART

Applied to everything from plastic garbage to the Mona Lisa. Denny MacGougan, Tacoma, Wash., points out "latest design" or "modern" would suffice.

LEVEL PLAYING FIELD

"Is there any other kind?"

–Margaret DeChant, Newberry, Mich.

CAUTIOUSLY OPTIMISTIC

"Can you be cautiously reckless, or recklessly cautious? Let's find a less bombastic phrase." (Ed.: We're cautiously cynical that banishment will be effective.)

–David McFarlane, Haslett, Mich.

COMMUNITY

Should be banished for overuse. "The original meaning of this word has been lost in the media, which blithely gives us such nonsense as the ballet-dancing community; the stock-broking community; the international community (whatever it is) and, my all-time favorite, the intravenous drug-using community."

–Eli Levine, Santa Barbara, California.

JOB CREATORS/JOB CREATION

"It implies supernatural powers—such as the ability to change the weather or levitate. Most new jobs pay less than the lost jobs to ensure stratospheric CEO compensation and nice returns on investments. I respectfully propose a replacement term that is more accurate—job depleters."

–Mark Dobias, Sault Ste. Marie, Mich.

CARBON FOOTPRINT

"It is now considered fashionable for everyone, tree hugger or lumberjack alike, to pay money to questionable companies to 'offset' their own 'carbon footprint.' What a scam! Get rid of it immediately!"

–Ginger Hunt, London, England.

YOLO

"Stands for 'You Only Live Once' and is used by wannabe Twitter philosophers who think they've uncovered a deep secret of life. Also used as an excuse to do really stupid things, such as streaking at a baseball game with YOLO printed on one's chest. I only live once, so I'd prefer to be able to do it without ever seeing YOLO again."

–Brendan Cotter, Grosse Pte. Park, Mich.

▶ **Check for negative statements that use the word "not" (or a negative contraction).** The sentence "He did not pay attention to the instructions" can be shortened to "He ignored the instructions." (The number of words is reduced from eight to four.) "She could not remember where she put her keys," can be shortened to "She forgot where she put her keys," or "She misplaced her keys." (The number of words is reduced from nine to seven to four.)

In a memoir titled *The Summing Up*, English author William Somerset Maugham discusses the weaknesses he had to overcome to become a writer, and the strengths he was able to build on. His weaknesses included a small vocabulary and a colorless style. His strengths were his powers of observation and his ability to describe what he saw "in clear terms." To cultivate those strengths, he developed a no-frills style of writing that emphasized clarity and accessibility. As an experiment, he wrote for a time without using any adjectives at all.

With Maugham's experiment in mind, read the passage below by David Foster Wallace from "Authority and American Usage," an essay that examines controversies about "correct English." Within Wallace's passage, you will notice that certain adjectives and adverbs have been highlighted. As you read, consider how significant the highlighted words are to the meaning of the passage.

As a practical matter, I **strongly** doubt whether a guy who has four **small** kids and makes $12,000 a year feels more empowered or less ill-used by a society that **carefully** refers to him as "economically disadvantaged" rather than "poor." Were I he, in fact, I'd **probably** find the PCE [Politically Correct English] term insulting—not just because it's patronizing (which it is) but because it's hypocritical and self-serving in a way that oft-patronized people tend to have **really** good **subliminal** antennae for. The **basic** hypocrisy about usages like "economically disadvantaged" and "differently abled" is that PCE advocates believe the beneficiaries of these terms' compassion and generosity to be poor people and people in wheelchairs, which again omits something that everyone knows but nobody except the **scary** vocabulary-tape ads' announcer ever mentions—that part of any speaker's motive for using a certain vocabulary is **always** the desire to communicate stuff about himself. Like many forms of Vogue Usage, 65 PCE functions primarily to signal and congratulate **certain** virtues in the speaker—**scrupulous** egalitarianism, concern for the dignity of all people, sophistication about the political implications of language— and so serves the **self-regarding** interests of the PC far more [than] groups renamed....

The **unpleasant** truth is that the same **self-serving** hypocrisy that informs PCE tends to infect and undermine the US Left's rhetoric in almost every debate over social policy. Take the **ideological** battle over wealth—redistribution via taxes, quotas, Welfare, enterprise zones, AFDC/ TANF [Aid to Families with Dependent Children/Temporary Assistance to Needy Families], you name it. As long as redistribution is conceived as a form of charity or compassion (and the **Bleeding** Left appears to buy this conception every bit as much as the **Heartless** Right), then the whole debate centers on utility—"Does Welfare help poor people get on their feet or does it foster **passive** dependence?" "Is government's **bloated** social-services bureaucracy an effective way to dispense charity?" and so on—and both camps have their arguments and preferred statistics, and the whole thing goes around and around....

From Reflection to Response   **Spotting Unnecessary Adverbs and Adjectives**

Go back and read the passage by David Foster Wallace again, but this time, place each highlighted word in one of the two categories below:

Category 1	*Category 2*
Words that add nothing significant to the meaning of the passage and can be removed:	Words you consider meaningful and necessary:

After you finish, compare the choices you made with those of two or three of your classmates and discuss the reasons for your choices.

OVERCOMING TEN COMMON ERRORS

At the very beginning of this course, you learned that mistake-free writing is not good writing; all writers make mistakes now and then. However, effective writers care about mistakes because they create distractions and interfere with communication goals. Reading an essay littered with mistakes is like trying to watch a movie on a defective DVD.

Always approach your writing with a focus on communication goals, but pay attention to mistakes for the right reasons. The pages that follow cover ten common and distracting mistakes students make in their writing. A writing course presents a perfect opportunity to work on these mistakes. If your instructor or a classmate points out a mistake in your writing, consult a writing handbook or a web-based resource like the Purdue OWL to learn more about the mistake. Once you have knowledge of a certain kind of mistake, you'll be on your way to overcoming it for good.

1. Wrong Word

Proofreading symbols: ww or wc (for "wrong word" or "word choice")

In *The Everyday Writer* handbook (4th edition, 2009), Andrea Lunsford writes that "wrong-word errors are by far the most common errors among first-year student writers today." Sometimes these errors are obvious and occur because a writer uses an unfamiliar word without looking it up. For example:

▶ Tennyson never wallows in disparity.

Most readers would flinch at that sentence because *disparity* means "a great difference," not hopelessness.

Usually, wrong-word errors are subtler and might get past some readers but distract others. See if you notice errors in the sentences below (one paraphrases a sentence by a famous writer):

▶ She was completely disinterested in the course.

▶ Based on the tone of her report, I could only imply that she was out to get me.

▶ He lay prone, gazing at the sky and thinking of new possibilities.

▶ Some analysts are predicting double-dip inflation next year.

▶ This and many other images of him are deeply engraved in my heart.

Using, learning, and working with words is an ongoing process for every writer. To minimize wording errors, look up words in a dictionary when you have *any* questions or doubts about their meaning or how they are used. When you get in the habit of using a dictionary, every writing task will contribute to building your vocabulary and knowledge of words.

2. No Comma after Introductory Elements

Proofreading symbols: p or , ("punctuation" or "comma needed")

Sentences that begin with clauses, phrases, transitional words, and parenthetical expressions usually need a comma to set off the introductory part from the main part of the sentence. The comma helps readers identify the structure of

> ### *Tech Tip*
>
> You can refine your knowledge and awareness of words by trying some of the online resources listed below:
>
> - *Lexipedia.com*: Provides useful, instant information about words you input, including the definition, part of speech, and pronunciation (in audio). *Lexipedia* also generates an interactive mind map that displays related words and their definitions.
> - *COCA Corpus* (Corpus of Contemporary American English): Offers extensive information about words, including many examples of their use in context (but the site takes a little patience to navigate).
> - *TagCrowd:* Creates word clouds that show the frequency of words used in a text.
> - *Voyant:* Creates word clouds and other visuals that can help you visualize and analyze texts.
> - *Rewordify.com:* Analyzes and clarifies words in a text.

the sentence and read it without stumbling. Below are examples of introductory elements correctly set off by a comma:

- ► After she sent in her résumé, she realized the graduation date was wrong.
- ► Failing to grasp the point of the tirade, Harvey finally interrupted.
- ► Consequently, he canceled the reservation.
- ► Well, grooming and hygiene should matter to everyone.

A short, prepositional phrase at the beginning of sentence does not need to be set off with a comma:

- ► In the fall the war was always there...

But longer or linked prepositional phrases need to be set off:

- ► In the alley behind the supermarket, crates of produce festered in the heat.

3. General Comma Mistakes and Unnecessary Commas

Proofreading symbols: , or p ("comma needed" or "punctuation")

Commas help steer readers through sentences. Single commas set off single introductory elements as illustrated above. Single commas also set off each item in a series:

- ► He bought milk, bread, eggs, cereal, and flowers.

A single comma should be used to separate the independent clauses in a compound sentence:

▶ A server poured the water, and the wine was placed in an ice bucket.

Without the comma, readers might at first think the server "poured the water and the wine" and then have to reread the sentence.

To steer us through sentences, commas also need to be used in pairs. Paired commas usually set off parenthetical information that is added to sentences but could be left out. Leaving out one or both of the commas in these instances can confuse readers. Here are examples of commas used correctly in pairs:

▶ The big jet, a Boeing 747, landed gracefully in the storm.

▶ I, too, love to swim.

▶ His position on immigration, however, is unclear.

▶ She remarked, changing the subject, that he had lost weight.

▶ I promise you, if I accomplish anything this year, I will finish building the shed.

In all of these sentences, the word or words set off by commas could be left out. However, when added words are not parenthetical but essential to the meaning of a sentence, commas are not used. For example:

▶ A climate that is warm all year long attracts many tourists.

Not:

▶ A climate, that is warm all year long, attracts many tourists.

The words "that is warm all year long" are essential to the meaning of the sentence and create what is called a "restrictive clause." Restrictive clauses should begin with *that* and are not set off with commas.

But a similar sentence, with added words that are not essential to the meaning, would take commas:

▶ The climate, which is warm all year long, attracts many tourists.

Not:

▶ The climate which is warm all year long attracts many tourists.

The words "which is warm all year long" insert nonessential information and create what is called a "nonrestrictive clause." Nonrestrictive clauses usually begin with *which* (sometimes *who*) and are set off by commas.

4. Vague Pronoun Reference

Proofreading symbol: ref ("reference")

Pronouns—*I, you, she, it, this*, and so on—refer to nouns and take their place. Pronouns help make writing more economical, but when we use them, we have to make sure the noun they refer to is clear. Here is an example of a vague reference drawn from an actual newspaper story (the names have been changed):

> ► Joe Lannon, whose truck collided with a fireman's car in an accident that killed his girlfriend, says police are improperly pinning the blame on him.

Whose girlfriend was killed—Joe Lannon's or the fireman's? It is supposed to be Lannon's, but the reference in the sentence could be to a girlfriend of the fireman. To clear up the reference, the sentence should be rewritten:

> ► Joe Lannon, whose girlfriend was killed when his truck collided with a fireman's car, says police are improperly pinning the blame on him.

5. Incorrect Pronoun Agreement

Proofreading symbol: agr ("agreement")

Along with clear reference, pronouns need to agree in number and gender. In other words, if the noun that a pronoun refers to is singular or plural in number, the pronoun needs to agree: the singular noun *woman* takes the singular pronoun *she*; the plural *women* takes the plural *they*.

Problems mainly occur with pronouns that are considered singular in standard English grammar but have collective connotations—for example, *none, everybody*, and *someone*. Each of the sentences below is considered incorrect:

> ► None of them *were* willing to step up.

> ► Everybody brought *their* own lunch.

> ► When someone makes a contribution, *they* get a free poster.

If you understand that *none* means *no one*, then giving *none* a singular verb—"None of them *was* willing to step up"—makes sense and sounds fine.

But using singular pronouns to agree with antecedents like *everybody* and *somebody* can sound awkward:

> ► Everybody brought *his or her* own lunch.

The grammar is correct but "his or her" is wordy. (To write, *his/her* would be worse: it sounds like bureaucratese.)

An accepted alternative, which also is grammatically correct, is to use a singular pronoun to stand for both genders:

▶ Everybody brought *his* own lunch.

Or:

▶ Everybody brought *her* own lunch.

Since those sentences say "everybody," readers would understand that the singular pronoun refers to both genders. At one time, the masculine pronoun was the preferred generic; now, using the masculine is consider sexist, so the feminine pronoun often is used. But either way, one gender gets left out.

The best solution is to reword the sentence if possible. A plural noun often can be substituted for the indefinite pronoun:

▶ The *volunteers* brought their own lunch.

Or:

▶ When *people* make a contribution, they get a free poster.

The truth is, "everybody brought their lunch" is acceptable to most readers in most contexts, but dictionaries and handbooks still consider it ungrammatical, so for the time being, it is unacceptable in academic and professional writing.

6. Random Shift in Verb Tenses

Proofreading symbol: vt ("verb tense")

Appropriate verb tenses help make writing coherent and easy for readers to follow. Random tense shifts, like the shift from past to present in the sentence below, are distracting and confusing:

▶ I was sitting in the living room playing solitaire, when I hear something outside and decided to investigate.

Keep your verb tenses logical and consistent, unless you have a reason to shift.

7. Fused Sentences (Run-Ons) and Comma Splices

Proofreading symbols: fs and cs ("fused sentences" and "comma splice")

These mistakes all pertain to sentence punctuation. Fused sentences (also called "run-ons") are independent sentences joined together without any punctuation between them:

▶ Talleyrand never bothered to pose the question Napoleon's ridicule deterred him for once.

Comma splices link independent sentences together with a comma, instead of separating them with a period or other appropriate punctuation mark:

▶ A good first step is to promote internships, statistics show that internships lead to permanent jobs.

▶ What in the world was she thinking, about every recommendation was way over budget.

▶ It was a tough loss, however, we learned something from it.

Incorrect sentence punctuation, especially when it recurs, disrupts the flow of a piece of writing and distorts meaning. Punctuating sentences correctly should be a priority when you revise and edit your writing.

8. Sentence Fragment

Proofreading symbol: frag ("fragment")

A sentence fragment is an incomplete sentence presented and punctuated as if it were a complete sentence. For example (the fragments are italicized):

▶ She lied to him about the watch. *A white-gold Piaget. Then tried to make a joke about it.*

Even in this short passage, the fragments have a choppy effect. Combining the fragments into one complete sentence creates a better flow:

▶ She lied to him about the watch, a white-gold Piaget, and then tried to make a joke about it.

An accumulation of fragments disrupts the "flow" of writing in much the same way that fused sentences and comma splices do. But sometimes writers use fragments intentionally for emphasis, or to simulate the rhythm of their thoughts. An intentional use of fragments can add a dash of style now and then (the fragments are italicized):

▶ Should we care about the poor? *Of course.* But should taxpayers pay higher taxes to fund a broken welfare system? I don't think so.

▶ The cabin was clean. That was good. *And nicely furnished*. But what the ad failed to say was that there was no electronic equipment at all. *No radio. No television. No computer, modem, router, or Wi-Fi. Not even a telephone.*

These passages could be reworked into complete sentences but would lose some emphasis or rhythm:

▶ Should we care about the poor? Of course, we should. But should taxpayers pay higher taxes to fund a broken welfare system? I don't think so.

▶ The cabin was clean, and nicely furnished, which was good, but what the ad failed to say was that there was no electronic equipment at all, no radio, television, computer, modem, router, or Wi-Fi. There was not even a telephone.

9. Dangling Modifier

Proofreading symbol: dm ("dangling modifier")

Dangling modifiers usually are introductory phrases that don't modify the grammatical subject of a sentence, and therefore, sound illogical. For example:

▶ Driving to New York, the engine died.

▶ Wondering why Tom hadn't called, the doorbell rang.

▶ Known for his integrity, they appointed him treasurer.

In the first sentence, the modifying phrase "Driving to New York," refers to the *engine* of the car. The sentence suggests that the engine is driving to New York.

The problem in the second sentence is the same: the doorbell is wondering why Tom hadn't called.

In the third sentence, the man known for integrity modifies *they*, the people who appointed him treasurer.

Dangling modifiers slip into everyone's drafts, but they are easy to fix. One way is to make the modifying phrase the main clause of the sentence or turn it into a clause with its own subject:

▶ I was driving to New York when the engine died.

▶ While I was driving to New York, the engine died.

Another way is to change the subject of the sentence, so that it refers to the modifying phrase:

▶ Known for his integrity, he was appointed treasurer.

10. Missing or Incorrect Apostrophes

Proofreading symbol: sp ("spelling")

Missing or incorrect apostrophes cause disruptive spelling mistakes. Some of these mistakes are covered in the section on contractions (for example, *it's* and *its*). Other common mistakes include using an apostrophe to form a plural noun:

▶ He tried several store's but they were completely sold out.

Store's should be *stores*, a plural, not a possessive. The opposite mistake, leaving out the apostrophe when it is needed, also confuses readers:

▶ The soldiers uniform was spotless.

Soldiers should be *soldier's*, a singular possessive noun. The plural possessive form would be *soldiers'* with the apostrophe after the *s*, as in:

▶ The soldiers' uniforms were spotless.

Possessive pronouns like *yours, hers*, and *its* never take apostrophes. The same is true of the plural forms of proper names; they should be spelled without apostrophes:

▶ The *Roosevelts, Joneses*, or *Fernandezes* (not the *Roosevelt's, Jones's*, or *Fernandez's*).

Plural nouns that don't end in *s* take an apostrophe followed by an *s* to form the possessive—for example:

▶ A *children's* TV show, or the *men's* room.

Most current handbooks and dictionaries recommend forming plural numbers without an apostrophe:

▶ 1980s is preferable to *1980's*

▶ Three *9s rather* than *9's*

The same apples to abbreviations:

▶ *CDs* rather than *CD's*

However, if the plural form looks confusing without an apostrophe—as is the case with letters—an apostrophe should be used:

▶ Two b's rather than bs; the three *R*'s rather than *Rs*

To form the possessive of singular nouns that end in *s*—a name like *Alexis* or the word *mistress*—most current handbooks recommend adding an apostrophe followed by the letter *s*:

▶ *Alexis's* house, rather than *Alexis'* house

▶ "My *mistress's* eyes" (from Shakespeare's sonnet 130), rather than "My *mistress'* eyes"*

For more information about these fine points, refer to your handbook, or ask your instructor for guidance.

Tech Tip

There are many interesting apps and websites that can help you improve your knowledge of grammar and mechanics. Below are a few you might want to try:

- Grammar Express: Parts of Speech
- Grammar Girl
- Dr. Grammar
- Lousy Writer
- Road to Grammar
- Grammarly Handbook
- Grammar Bytes

From Reflection to Response

A Panel Discussion or Presentation on Elements of Style

Working with a small group of classmates, spend a few minutes discussing information presented in this chapter that is new or helpful to you and problems with style, wording, usage, grammar, or punctuation that have affected your writing.

Choose a problem you think many students need help with (some examples are listed below), and plan a five-minute panel discussion or presentation for the next class meeting. Each member of your group should be responsible for a specific task or covering a specific aspect of the problem. The goal is to provide your classmates with useful information that will help them understand and correct the problem.

To prepare for the discussion or presentation, learn more about the problem by doing research online or reading about the problem in your writing handbook. Develop your own examples for the presentation. If time permits, and you have

---

*"My *mistress's* eyes are nothing like the sun." Following the conventions of his time, Shakespeare actually did not use an apostrophe to form the possessive.

the resources, create a handout to distribute, or a short PowerPoint presentation. Some suggested topics include:

1. Problems with words and their meanings—abstractions, bureaucratese, wordiness, commonly misused or misunderstood words (*effect* and *affect*), and clichés.

2. Sentence punctuation—fused sentences, comma splices, and fragments.

3. General punctuation—the function of commas and other punctuation marks like semicolons, colons, dashes, parentheses, and so on.

4. Pesky possessives and common spelling mistakes.

5. Common grammatical mistakes—dangling and misplaced modifiers, subject-verb agreement, pronoun-antecedent agreement.

6. Principles of paragraphing—where to find breaks—and general advice for formatting a document (bullet points, internal headings, and so forth).

EVALUATE YOUR LEARNING

1. Looking back at the ten common errors covered in this chapter on pages 39 to 48, which of those errors gives you the most trouble and why?

2. After reading this chapter, if you wanted to give a friend some good advice for improving his or her writing, what would it be?

3. Look over a finished page of an essay you wrote earlier in this course (or for another course). How would you describe the "style"? Is it what you were aiming for when you wrote the essay? What changes, if any, would you make that might improve the style?

4. How would you explain the difference between correct writing and an effective style to a friend or younger sibling?

5. Can you think of something you have read for this course, or for your own purposes, that is written in a style you dislike? What is it you dislike? Can you think of something you have read that is written in a style you like or admire? What is it that appeals to you about the style?

Melissa McGill

MELISSA McGILL

The Office

In this piece, I was trying to capture the personalities and visual likeness of characters Dwight and Jim from the television show "The Office." The tension between the characters is an essential and hilarious part of the show. I placed them next to each other on a clean white background so the viewer may clearly observe and appreciate their relationship as an isolated unit. Constructing the portraits out of cut paper added an exciting challenge to the overall process.

CHAPTER THIRTEEN

Writing in the Workplace: How College Writing Skills Transfer

> *When Frank Carey was Chairman of IBM, he stated that the four qualities required of the truly successful top executive were intelligence, integrity, empathy, and the ability to communicate. Of the four, only the last, communication, is a learnable skill.*
>
> —John S. Fielden and Ronald E. Dulek,
> "What Is Effective Business Writing?"

CHAPTER LEARNING OBJECTIVES

In this chapter, you will learn to:

▶ Understand the importance and demands of writing in the workplace.

▶ Understand the principles of "transactional" writing for professional purposes.

▶ Transfer your college writing skills to important workplace tasks.

▶ Use workplace forms and genres.

COLLEGE AND THE WORKPLACE

If you are planning a career in law, journalism, or marketing, you know strong writing skills are crucial. If you are planning a career in nanotechnology, cancer research, software development, engineering, nursing, accounting, or business management, you may think writing is tangential to your aspirations, but professionals in those fields know better. A scientist who cannot record and analyze experiments in writing, who cannot describe, share, and publish discoveries, is a scientist who lacks a crucial career skill. The same is true of an engineer who cannot compose effective proposals or reports that describe design concepts and production processes. Nurses, accountants, business executives, and entrepreneurs who cannot write compelling reports, proposals, client letters, and business plans are deficient in an important professional skill.

Writing in the workplace is diverse and specialized. To prepare for your career, you should consider taking courses in business and technical writing, along with writing-intensive courses in your major concentration. However, the concepts you learn in a first-year writing course provide a solid foundation for writing in the workplace, because communication goals, strategies, and elements of style carry over. This chapter will introduce you to writing in the workplace, and explain how writing concepts learned in college transfer to the kinds of writing people do in their jobs and careers.

PURPOSE AND AUDIENCE

All of the writing projects in this course are presented in a framework of "reader relevance" and communication. A compelling narrative is written to enlighten readers, not for self-expression or reflection. The same applies to a review, formal argument, story analysis, or a research paper. The ultimate goal of good writing in any genre is effective communication. In college, the context is "academic," and so is the audience. Academic readers are intellectually curious and discriminating. As a rule, they expect academic writing to be detailed and comprehensive. Therefore, they like a probing analysis that may re-create aspects of a writer's discovery process. In academic writing, as in all categories of writing, the readers' needs and expectations shape the conventions that writers follow, as well as the style.

Readers also shape the conventions of writing in the workplace, but the readers are different. The "audience" often is just one person or a small number of people, and the purpose usually is more practical than intellectual. As Bill Baker observes in "The Business Side of Academic Writing,"

writing in the workplace is "primarily transactional"—that is, the goal is to get results:

> [Writing in the workplace] must be clear, complete, coherent, concise and compelling. Further, it must be well organized and visually effective so the reading process will be quick and easy.

Although the conventions of "transactional" writing are different from academic writing, the concepts and approaches you learn as a student still apply. If a business document—for example, a long report or proposal—is important and substantial in content, the writing requires a series of "steps"—in other words, a *process* that includes planning, drafting, conscientious revision, and editing. A writer in the workplace often will incorporate feedback from others, or very often, write in collaboration with others. The style and tone should emphasize clarity and come across as "real"—qualities you have learned and practiced in this course. Organizational concepts that you have used also transfer. In the workplace, people are busy and want to know your main point up front. The *formal* pattern of organization that is used to construct academic arguments translates to what Bill Baker calls a "direct approach" in the workplace: "Put the main point at or near the beginning of the message, and then follow with supporting details."

All of these concepts and conventions emanate from readers' needs and expectations. Notice how the advice below, from Kevin J. Harty's introduction to *Strategies for Business and Technical Writing*, focuses on an assessment of audience, that is, readers:

THREE KEY QUESTIONS

Business and technical writing situations present us with a variety of challenges. One of the ways to meet these various writing challenges is to begin by asking ourselves these three key questions:

1. Exactly who is my audience?

2. What is the most important thing I want to tell my audience?

3. What is the best way of making sure my audience understands what I have to say?

Exactly Who Is My Audience?

Whatever we write on the job, somebody—across the hall, across the city, across the country, or even across the world—will eventually read what we have written. Most likely, our readers will receive our message in their own offices or homes. Since we won't be on hand to explain anything that is unclear or that doesn't make sense, our message will have to speak for itself.

Whenever we sit down to write, we become experts, which in large part is why we are the writers and not the readers. Our readers depend on us for clear, effective writing, so that they may share in our expertise. Although this point seems obvious, business, industrial, and technical practice shows that the single most common cause of bad writing is ignoring the reader. There are any number of ways to ignore our audiences: we can talk over their heads; we can talk down to them; we can beat around the bush; we can leave out important details—and, as a result, we can undermine our credibility.

When you next sit down to write, therefore, it is important to ask yourself what you know about your audience—you must determine your audience's situation and anticipate your audience's potential reaction to your message. To cite just one example of potential confusion between the reader and the writer: Will an audience for a major sales proposal, which could include some international clients or customers, read 02/03/10 as a date in February (by U.S. standards) or in March (by European standards)? To paraphrase the golden rule, make sure you are prepared to write unto others the way you would have them write onto you.

COMMUNICATING TO SOLVE PROBLEMS

●●● GoldieBlox™: Engineering Toys for Girls

The image most people have of an engineer is a man in a hard hat on a construction site. That image is changing. Encouraged by a high school math teacher, Debbie Sterling took an engineering course during her freshman year at Stanford. She liked inventing and designing things, and ended up pursuing an engineering degree, but she had some humiliating experiences along the way. Most of her classmates and professors were men, and they were not always supportive of her efforts. She discovered that, like most women, she had underdeveloped spatial skills. Kids with well-developed spatial skills, she later found out, usually grow up playing with construction toys—in other words, they are not your average girl!

After earning her degree, Sterling dreamed of creating an engineering toy to help girls develop their spatial skills much earlier than she had. Working out of her apartment, she built a prototype of the toy, but when she let some real girls play with it, they got bored, and told her they preferred reading. Sterling had an "aha" moment: why not combine a construction toy with a reading experience about the adventures of a girl engineer who solves problems by building simple machines? Sterling named her toy GoldieBlox, and built a prototype. Her initial efforts to raise business capital were unsuccessful, but when she launched a funding campaign on Kickstarter, she hit her target goal in just four days. Soon, orders for GoldieBlox were pouring in from around the world. Today, Sterling is CEO of her own company. "Some girls like princesses and tiaras," Sterling says, "and I like that stuff too, but there's so much more to us than that. There's so much potential."

A dream scenario for many college students is to achieve financial success while also helping to promote positive change in the world. In theory, all businesses are based on the idea of "service," but thanks to misleading ads, deceptive sales practices, hidden fees, recalls, and consumer alerts, many people feel businesses mainly focus on serving themselves. GoldieBlox, the company Debbie Sterling founded to sell her toys, is an exception. According to Kristen Nicole, senior editor at *SiliconANGLE*, the combination of language and science skills that GoldieBlox toys help to develop does more than

Debbie Sterling, Founder and CEO of GoldieBlox

promote engineering for girls; it addresses a growing need in the sciences for people who "have a handle on analytics and language." In designing GoldieBlox, Debbie Sterling says, "I was showing people why we need female engineers. I don't know if a guy would be able to build this toy."

As a college student preparing for a career, what do you see yourself doing four or five years from now? What are some of the obstacles you and others might face in entering a field or starting a business of your choice? What could be done to create more opportunity and remove unnecessary obstacles? What could you do in your field or business to promote positive change in the world? ● ● ●

LOW- AND HIGH-STAKES WRITING IN THE WORKPLACE

In every workplace, people perform routine writing tasks every day at all levels of an organization—for example, writing a memo or e-mail to schedule a meeting or report a maintenance problem. Tasks like these are what author and entrepreneur Craig Wortmann calls "low-stakes communications" (*What's Your Story?*). They can be important, but the content is primarily informational. The main challenge for the writer is to be clear and concise. Problems that occur with this kind of writing usually result from carelessness or haste, as in the example below:

> To: All Production Unit Employees
>
> From: Brad Knoll, Senior Production Supervisor
>
> Just FYI before I leave for Dallas, if you've been to the website, you know that we're expecting to run a deficite in the fourth quarter (after six strait quarters of profitably). Management will be announcing austerity measures deigned to streamline operations, but I've been assured that these measures are going to effect our unit. Back on Thursday.
>
> Brad

In contrast to low-stakes writing, a "high-stakes" task, as defined by Wortmann, addresses situations or problems that "demand a unique solution." An important category of writing in the workplace that bridges low- and high-stakes territory is writing for the record.

Writing for the Record

Professionals write for the record to formalize agreements, plans, and ideas that originate in oral discussions or conversations. Spoken communications are indispensable to conducting business but are always susceptible to misunderstandings. The details of a handshake agreement with a client or a plan discussed at a meeting have to find their way into writing to become "official" and be implemented reliably. As Philip C. Kolin notes in *Successful Writing at Work,* "If it isn't written, it didn't happen."

Writing for the record sounds informational, but it also solves problems in all kinds of situations. An accountant, for example, may have a face-to-face consultation with a prospective client, say the owner of a chain of restaurants, and in response to the client's needs, propose a range of services from basic tax preparation to bookkeeping, sales tax filings, and cash-flow projections. This kind of consultation covers complex details and corresponding fees.

If the accountant and client reach a verbal agreement, the accountant has to follow up with a written proposal that summarizes the consultation and puts the agreement on record. The proposal has to reflect "transactional" qualities mentioned earlier in this chapter—that is, be clear, complete, coherent, concise, and compelling. If it is incomplete, inaccurate, or confusing, and raises concerns in the client's mind, the relationship might not go forward. In short, a thoughtfully written proposal "seals the deal"; a poorly written proposal can make the client look for another accountant.

ADDRESSING ISSUES AND SOLVING PROBLEMS

The most important and challenging writing in the workplace addresses issues and supports views to solve problems. These are high-stakes communication tasks. Craig Wortmann offers the following examples:

> If you are asking for an action or behavior that involves a significant change or shift in how something currently gets done, consider it high stakes. If you are trying to enhance a performance skill, support a project that a company has spent significant money on, or ask for something that impacts clients or customers, you definitely are in high-stakes territory.

Documents like business plans, long reports, internal proposals, and grants usually are written to address high-stakes problems, especially to resolve "bottom line" issues like funding, revenues, and personnel needs. Entrepreneurs often have to compose compelling business plans to secure loans or raise capital to start a new business. Educators and people who work for public agencies or nonprofits have to submit compelling grant proposals to secure funding for their missions and achieve their goals.

High-stakes writing isn't limited to longer documents. A memo announcing changes in policies, procedures, or responsibilities within a workplace can be a high-stakes document, too. This kind of announcement has the potential to demoralize or threaten good employees who think their roles, status, or responsibilities are being undercut or disrespected. To alleviate legitimate concerns, the memo has to be thoughtfully composed.

A short letter or e-mail responding to a customer's complaint also can have high-stakes implications. Because workplace problems are so common and varied, many courses in business and technical writing use hypothetical "scenarios" to prepare students for writing tasks they may have to face. Here is an example:

> ### The problem:
>
> You supervise the product-development department of a large company. Your current output is satisfactory, but you have experienced a frustrating pattern of production delays because of turnover in personnel. At a recent meeting, you presented a detailed plan for moving to "flex-time" scheduling to increase productivity and workers' job satisfaction. Your plan was well-received at the meeting. Your manager, in particular, *seemed* receptive, but now weeks have passed, and there has been no

> follow-up whatsoever. You suspect the manager has conveniently for-
> gotten your plan, because she is stuck in her ways and doesn't want the
> "headache" of changing entrenched procedures. You decide to write her
> a memo that addresses her inaction and your frustrations. What do you
> say and how do you say it?

In this situation, the employee has to be persuasive but also professional. Whining or ranting won't be effective. Conversely, the manager receiving the memo also will find herself in high-stakes communication territory. If she thinks the idea is ill-conceived or premature and needs to reject it, she has to decide how to "frame" the reply. She can always be blunt and dismissive, but as communications professors John S. Fielden and Ronald E. Dulek point out, a harsh, tactless reply can have consequences ("What Is Effective Business Writing?"):

> While it is true that senior people can, in the short run, write to those
> beneath them in just about any fashion they like, effective business
> writers do not choose to do so. They know that life is long and that
> in large corporations, today's subordinate or equal may be tomorrow's
> boss.

More importantly, a good manager values devoted employees who are engaged and enterprising. This kind of manager will go to the trouble of composing a constructive response, even if she thinks "flex time" is a terrible idea.

The article that follows offers an excellent illustration of a manager trying to resolve a problem in the workplace through thoughtful writing.

Marvin H. Swift { CLEAR WRITING MEANS CLEAR THINKING MEANS...

Marvin H. Swift (1923–2007) was a World War II veteran, a graduate of the University of Michigan, and a distinguished professor of business and technical communications at the General Motors Institute.

IF YOU ARE A manager, you constantly face the problem of putting words on paper. If you are like most managers, this is not the sort of problem you enjoy. It is hard to do, and time consuming; and the task is doubly difficult when, as is usually the case, your words must be designed to change the behavior of others in the organization.

But the chore is there and must be done. How? Let's take a specific case.

Let's suppose that everyone at X Corporation, from the janitor on up to the chairman of the board, is using the office copiers for personal matters; income tax forms, church programs, children's term papers, and God knows what else are being duplicated by the gross. This minor piracy costs the company a pretty penny, both directly and in employee time, and the general manager—let's call him Sam Edwards—decides the time has come to lower the boom.

Sam lets fly by dictating the following memo to his secretary:

To: All Employees

From: Samuel Edwards, General Manager

Subject: Abuse of Copiers

It has recently been brought to my attention that many of the people who are employed by this company have taken advantage of their positions by availing themselves of the copiers. More specifically, these machines are being used for other than company business.

Obviously, such practice is contrary to company policy and must cease and desist immediately. I wish therefore to inform all concerned—those who have abused policy or will be abusing it—that their behavior cannot and will not be tolerated. Accordingly, anyone in the future who is unable to control himself will have his employment terminated.

IF there are any questions about company policy, please feel free to contact this office.

Now the memo is on his desk for his signature. He looks it over and the more he looks, the worse it reads. In fact, it's lousy. So he revises it three times, until it finally is in the form that follows:

To: All Employees

From: Samuel Edwards, General Manager

Subject: Use of Copiers

We are revamping our policy on the use of copiers for personal matters. In the past we have not encouraged personnel to use them for such purposes because of the costs involved. But we also recognize, perhaps belatedly, that we can solve the problem if each of us pays for what he takes.

   We are therefore putting these copiers on a pay-as-you-go basis. The details are simple enough…

Samuel Edwards

This time Sam thinks the memo looks good, and it is good. Not only is the writing much improved, but the problem should now be solved. He therefore signs the memo, turns it over to his secretary for distribution, and goes back to other things.

From verbiage to intent

I can only speculate on what occurs in a writer's mind as he moves from a poor draft to a good revision, but it is clear that Sam went through several specific steps, mentally as well as physically, before he created his end product:

- He eliminated wordiness.
- He modulated the tone of the memo.
- He revised the policy it stated.

   Let's retrace his thinking through each of these processes.

Eliminating wordiness

Sam's basic message is that employees are not to use the copiers for their own affairs at company expense. As he looks over his first draft, however, it seems so long that this simple message has become diffused. With the idea of trimming the memo down, he takes another look at his first paragraph:

> It has recently been brought to my attention that many of the people who are employed by this company have taken advantage of their positions by availing themselves of the copiers. More specifically, these machines are being used for other than company business.

He edits like this:

Item: "recently"
Comment to himself: Of course, else why write about the problem! So delete the word.

Item: "It has been brought to my attention"
Comment: Naturally. Delete it.

Item: "the people who are employed by this company"
Comment: Assumed. Why not just "employees"!

Item: "by availing themselves" and "for other than company business"
Comment: Since the second sentence repeats the first, why not coalesce!

And he comes up with this:

Employees have been using the copiers for personal matters.

He proceeds to the second paragraph. More confident of himself, he moves in broader swoops, so that the deletion process looks like this:

> Obviously, such practice is contrary to company policy and ~~must cease and desist immediately. I wish therefore to inform all concerned – those who have abused policy or will be abusing it — that their behavior cannot and will not be tolerated. Accordingly, anyone in the future who is unable to control himself will have his emoployment terminated.~~ (will result in dismissal.)

The final paragraph, apart from "company policy" and "feel free," looks all right, so the total memo now reads as follows:

> To: All Employees
>
> From: Samuel Edwards, General Manager
>
> Subject: Abuse of Copiers
>
>
> Employees have been using the copiers for personal matters.
>
> Obviously, such practice is contrary to company policy and will result
>
> in dismissal.
>
> If there are any questions, please feel free to contact this office.

Sam now examines his efforts by putting these questions to himself:

Question: Is the memo free of deadwood?
Answer: Very much so. In fact, It's good, tight prose.
Question: Is the policy stated?
Answer: Yes—sharp and clear.
Question: Will the memo achieve its intended purpose?
Answer: Yes. But it sounds foolish.
Question: Why?
Answer: The wording is too harsh; I'm not going to fire anybody over this.
Question: How should I tone the thing down?

To answer this last question, Sam takes another look at the memo.

Correcting the tone

What strikes his eye as he looks it over? Perhaps these three words:

- Abuse…
- Obviously…
- …dismissal…

The first one is easy enough to correct: he substitutes "use" for "abuse." But "obviously" poses a problem and calls for reflection. If the policy is obvious, why are the copiers being used? Is it that people are outright dishonest? Probably not. But that implies the policy isn't obvious; and whose fault is this? Who neglected to clarify policy? And why "dismissal" for something never publicized?

These questions impel him to revise the memo once again:

To: All Employees

From: Samuel Edwards, General Manager

Subject: Use of Copiers

Copiers are not to be used for personal matters. If there are any question, please contact this office.

Revising the policy itself

The memo now seems courteous enough—at least it is not discourteous—but it is just a blank, perhaps overly simple, statement of policy. Has he really thought through the policy itself?

Reflecting on this, Sam realizes that some people will continue to use the copiers for personal business anyhow. If he seriously intends to enforce the basic policy (first sentence), he will have to police the equipment, and that raises the question of costs all over again.

Also, the memo states that he will maintain an open-door policy (second sentence)—and surely there will be some, probably a good many, who will stroll in and offer to pay for what they use. His secretary has enough to do without keeping track of affairs of that kind.

Finally, the first and second sentences are at odds with each other. The first says that personal copying is out, and the second implies that it can be arranged.

The facts of organizational life thus force Sam to clarify in his own mind exactly what his position on the use of copiers is going to be. As he sees the problem now, what he really wants to do is put the copiers on a pay-as-you-go basis. After making that decision, he begins anew:

To: All Employees

From: Samuel Edwards, General Manager

Subject: Use of Copiers

We are revamping our policy on the use of copiers. ...

This is the draft that goes into distribution and now allows him to turn his attention to other problems.

The chicken or the egg?

What are we to make of all this? It seems a rather lengthy and tedious report of what, after all, is a routine writing task created by a problem of minor importance. In making this kind of analysis, have I simply labored the obvious?

To answer this question, let's drop back to the original draft. If you read it over, you will see that Sam began with this kind of thinking:

- "The employees are taking advantage of the company."
- "I'm a nice guy, but now I'm going to play Dutch uncle."
- "I'll write them a memo that tells them to shape up or ship out."

In his final version, however, his thinking is quite different:

- "Actually, the employees are pretty mature, responsible people. They're capable of understanding a problem."
- "Company policy itself has never been crystallized. In fact, this is the first memo on the subject."
- "I don't want to overdo this thing—any employee can make an error in judgment."
- "I'll set a reasonable policy and write a memo that explains how it ought to operate."

Sam obviously gained a lot of ground between the first draft and the final version, and this implies two things. First, if a manager is to write effectively, he needs to isolate and define, as fully as possible, all the critical variables in the writing process and scrutinize what he writes for its clarity, simplicity, tone, and the rest. Second, after he has clarified his thoughts on paper, he may find that what he has written is not what has to be said. In this sense, writing is feedback and a way for the manager to discover himself. What are his real attitudes toward that amorphous, undifferentiated gray mass of employees "out there"? Writing is a way of finding out. By objectifying his thoughts in the medium of language, he gets a chance to see what is going on in his mind.

In other words, *if the manager writes well, he will think well.* Equally, the more clearly he has thought out his message before he starts to dictate, the more likely he is to get it right on paper the first time round. In other words, *if he thinks well, he will write well.*

Hence, we have a chicken-and-the-egg situation: writing and thinking go hand in hand; and when one is good, the other is likely to be good.

Revision sharpens thinking

More particularly, rewriting is the key to improved thinking. It demands a real openmindedness and objectivity. It demands a willingness to cull verbiage so that ideas stand out clearly. And it demands a willingness to meet logical contradictions head on and trace them to the premises that have created them. In short, it forces a writer to get up his courage and expose his thinking process to his own intelligence.

Obviously, revising is hard work. It demands that you put yourself through the wringer, intellectually and emotionally, to squeeze out the best you can offer. Is it worth the effort? Yes, it is—if you believe you have a responsibility to think and communicate effectively. ■

From Reflection to Response   **Revising a Memo**

Read the memo shown in Figure 13.1 and make a list of problems you notice and improvements that could be made. Then, working on your own, or with a class-mate, and applying advice from Marvin H. Swift's article above, rewrite the memo to improve its professionalism.

As you consider revision strategies, pay attention to the tone of the writing. Tone, as defined in Chapter 1, is a writer's attitude toward the subject matter and readers. Tone in writing is largely created by the choice of words. So think about words or wording that you can change to ensure a positive response from the readers.

Interoffice Memo

To: Claims Department Abstractors

From: Harris W. Randellson, Executive Manager, NPI Group, Inc.

Subject: Coffee Pot Procedures

Date: December 23, 2011

It has come to my attention that the coffee pot in the brake room is not being turned off before you people leave for the day. Yesterday, I had to turn it off myself. The decanter was burnt, and there was a fowl odor in the room. Further-more, it doesn't take a rocket science to figure out this could be a fire hazard!

I know I have my coffee right after lunch, but I know more pots are being made later in the day. I don't have time to patrol the room to find out who's making coffee when so I can turn off the pot for you! So here's what I'm requesting: turn off the pot after 3:00 PM or else it will be taken away from you! If you have any questions or problems with this, come see me. We'll work it out!

Thanks for your cooperation.

Randellson

FIGURE 13.1   **An interoffice memo**

COMMON WORKPLACE GENRES, FORMS, AND TASKS

The most important thing you learn in a college writing course is that communication goals guide your writing. Most college writing courses today use genre or aims-based projects to expose students to different conventions (patterns of organization) and methods of writing (narration, description, analysis, argumentation). But as you know, genres of writing and aims are not rigidly distinct and disconnected. Basic communication goals—addressing issues and supporting views—as well as methods and conventions, cross over to different kinds of writing tasks. Formal arguments sometimes incorporate narration to support a point. Narrative essays can segue into analysis and argumentation. Writers make intuitive "judgment calls" about the methods based on their communication goals, the audience, and the conventions of the genre.

Below is a list of forms or genres that are common in the workplace. Each has conventions that a writer needs to be aware of, but as in academic writing, communication goals guide the writing. The conventions don't translate to formulas or templates a writer can rely on.

- ▶ Booklets and brochures
- ▶ Business and trade blogs
- ▶ Business letters (for external communications, including job applications and inquiries)
- ▶ Business plans
- ▶ E-mails
- ▶ Feasibility studies
- ▶ Meeting agendas and handouts
- ▶ Memos (mainly internal or "in-house")
- ▶ Newsletters
- ▶ Performance evaluations
- ▶ Proposals
- ▶ Social media posts (Facebook, Twitter, LinkedIn, and so on)
- ▶ Reports (related to sales, progress, incidents, travel)
- ▶ Résumés

The following sections review some important conventions that apply to e-mails, memos, business letters, résumés, and cover letters.

E-mails

In the workplace, e-mails convey routine information quickly and efficiently, but also can address high-stakes problems. E-mails tend to be more relaxed in style and tone than business letters, but they still need to conform to professional standards.

Problems occur when people don't make a distinction between the e-mails they write for social purposes and those they write professionally. In a business setting, e-mails are public and potentially legal documents. Idiosyncrasies and "personal touches" that may seem charming or funny in personal e-mails are likely to be inappropriate and distracting in the workplace.

Below are some things to consider when you write e-mails for professional purposes:

▶ **Use an appropriate e-mail account**. If you have an e-mail account that consists of a "handle" to impress your friends—for example, paintballwizard@ or reggaetonchick@—don't use it for business purposes. Create a different account that consists of your last name and initials.

▶ **Subject line**. In personal e-mails, people sometimes don't bother to write anything in the subject line, or they write enigmatic teasers like "Killing Me Softly" or "HELP!!!!" In the workplace, an e-mail that arrives with "no subject" is annoying. The recipient can't judge its importance. The same is true of an e-mail with an enigmatic subject line. Always put something in the subject line, preferably words that convey the purpose of the message. Instead of "Killing Me Softly," identify what is "killing" you ("Another Complaint about the Website"). Instead of "HELP!!!!" write "Printer Misfiring Again!"

▶ **Salutation**. The accepted salutation for e-mails, including those written for business purposes, is *Hi* _____, or *Hello* _____. Also widely used and accepted is *Dear* _____. E-mail salutations, unlike those in business letters, usually end with a comma, rather than a colon:

> Hi Diane,
>
> Hello Mr. Jimenez,
>
> Dear Olivia, or Dear Board Members,

In general, unless a recipient is a personal friend of yours, avoid slangy shout-outs like *Hey* _____. *Hey* sounds immature or rude in a professional context. Similarly, avoid the IM convention of skipping the salutation altogether and just writing the message. On occasion, when e-mails are going back and forth on the same subject, you can dispense with a salutation. Otherwise, leaving out a salutation can make you come across as gruff or rude.

▶ **Complimentary close**. Business e-mails usually close like business letters, using traditional courtesies like *Cordially*, or *Sincerely*, followed by the writer's name. When a request is being made, simply writing *Thanks*, is a widely used and accepted alternative. Think twice about dispensing with courtesies altogether and simply writing your name, unless you know the recipient well. Someone who doesn't know you may find that approach cold or rude.

In addition to observing the conventions above, keep your e-mails concise and focused. Below are some "noisy" adornments you should avoid:

- **Emoticons or emojis.** Some people think these are cute or funny, but some don't. Save them for your friends and loved ones.

- **High-priority, red exclamation marks.** More often than not, they don't serve the intended purpose. They are associated with junk mail. Pertinent information in the subject line is more effective.

- **IM shorthand** (OMG, ANFSCD, BRB, LOL, 4COL, IMHO). Not everyone needs to GAL.

- **Too many acronyms and abbreviations** (FHA, CAS, IRB, CMMS, SBAR). Acronyms and abbreviations are fine when the reader knows what the letters stand for. Otherwise, they are irritating. If you are unsure, write out the words—for example, Federal Housing Authority—the first time the term comes up. After that, you can use the abbreviation.

- **ALL-CAP WORDS AND PHRASES.** For adding emphasis, use italics. Using all-caps looks childish.

- **No capitalizations when capital letters are called for** ("meanwhile i'll tell herb you're going to rochester and we need to reschedule for wednesday…"). Disregarding conventional capitalization gives an impression of laziness. If you do it to emulate the poetry of e. e. cummings, chances are your readers won't know who cummings is, or won't see the connection between your e-mail and his poetry.

- **Animated objects, cartoon figures, or furries that scurry across your message.** Some recipients may cackle. Others will go home with a migraine.

- **A photograph of your dog, cat, snake, ferret, child, grandchild, or prize-winning heirloom tomato.** (See the notation for emoticons and emojis.)

- **Inspirational quotations** ("Dream big and dare to fail"). Inflicting random "pearls of wisdom" on your readers is usually more of an annoyance than an inspiration.

College students frequently write e-mails to their professors and campus administrators. Those e-mails, unlike the ones students write for social purposes, have professional implications and should conform to professional standards. Today, many students and their professors maintain friendly relationships. So writing to a professor in a friendly tone is appropriate, but sending a sloppy, semiliterate message is not. Professors, no matter how friendly and approachable, are in the business of preparing students for success in professional life. A poorly written e-mail says the student is out of touch with the realities of the "real world." College is a place for students to start developing a professional identity. You are doing just that when you write e-mails to your professors that are friendly and professional at the same time.

From Reflection to Response   **Revising and Editing an E-mail**

Read the e-mail shown in Figure 13.2, from a student to his professor. Make a list of problems you notice and corrections you would make. Then, working alone, or with a classmate, rewrite the e-mail to improve its professionalism.

From: dents@ait.edu

Sent: Monday, March 29, _____ 1:46 AM

To: Neil L. Cassidy

Subject: [empty]

[no attachments]

Hey proffesor,

This is Steve Denton, who was in your EC – 101 class two years ago. I'm the one who wrote the papers on marijuana and steroids. While I actually didn't do very good in the class, I'm an International Relations major now, and I definitely think your one of the best proffesors I've had at AIT. So I'm wondering if you could write me a recommendation for a Knight-Horizon grant that I'm applying for.

My parents got divorced last thanksgiving, and neither one of them want to pay my tuition anymore. They also stopped payment on my car, which was reposses, and right after that, my girlfriend broke up with me.

I really do appreciate you writting this letter. If I can get the grant, it will really me out. Your letter needs to be on offical stationary of the school, and should be sent with the from I'm attached to this email. Also, it needs to be received by, April first. So if you can please mail it tomorrow. My AIT student number is 991483.

I definitely think you're one of the best proffesors I've ever had! Thanks for your time. :)

[no signature]

FIGURE 13.2   **E-mail from a student to his professor**

Memos

"Memo," short for "memorandum," means "something that needs to be remembered." Memos sometimes are printed and distributed as "hard-copy" messages within an office or organization, or are sent electronically via e-mail. Either way, memos are for people working inside an organization. The "something that needs to be remembered" can range from low-stakes information to high-stakes problems that require immediate attention and action.

Memos usually are received by many different people. Even when a memo is addressed to a single person, the writer usually has an expectation that others will read it. As a result, memos are formal documents that should be written in a professional style and tone and carefully edited. The reason or issue prompting the memo should be clear right away. Figure 13.3 illustrates the components and qualities of a professional memo.

From Reflection to Response   **Composing a Memo**

Working alone, or with one or two of your classmates, compose a memo that will help future students have a successful experience taking this first-year writing course. Describe the course, class activities, key assignments, workload, expectations, required skills, and learning objectives in such a way that future students know what to expect and what it will take to do well. Keep the following points in mind as you draft your memo:

- Write the memo for students who will be taking the course with your specific instructor. Or if you prefer, you can write the memo for a general audience of students who will be taking the course, but not necessarily with your instructor.

- Make the memo clear and helpful for readers. Avoid abbreviations, acronyms, and specialized terms that readers might not know. (For example, don't refer to the course website as "Moodle" or "Blackboard," or use rhetorical terms like "ethos" that an incoming student might not know.)

- Offer examples and advice based on your experience, but be selective about the information you include—not so detailed that the memo becomes too long and a chore to read.

- Limit the length to two pages maximum.

- Pay attention to the layout and design elements. Depending on whether the memo will circulate in print or electronically, choose an effective font, and use design features such as block paragraphing in business style, internal headings, and bullet points or bulleted paragraphs.

- Block paragraphing in business style
- Internal headings
- Bullet points or bulleted paragraphs
- If visuals or graphics will enhance the memo, consider including them.

R & G Media Group and Marketing

Memo

To: Posner Public Relations Team

From: Jill Ducharme, Vice President

Subject: Dryer Health Services Account

Date: September 12, 2015

As you all know, we were unsuccessful in winning the Dryer account, but certainly not for lack of creative ideas and effort from your team.

The presentation you put together was outstanding! One senior manager at Dryer's told me it was the most original and visually stunning he has ever seen (*far superior*, in fact, to Remington's).

Unfortunately, a fabulous presentation isn't the only factor that goes into winning an account. Remington sweetened the pot with perks and services that we are not in a position to offer at this time.

No matter. Everyone is proud of the work you guys did. There will be bigger and more prestigious accounts to win going forward, and now we know we have the talent and determination to win them. So on to GenTech and Greenbrier!

With sincere appreciation,

Jill Ducharme
Vice President

FIGURE 13.3 **A professional memo**

Business Letters

Business letters sent out via postal services still have an important role in the workplace. In general, letters are more confidential, secure, and personal than e-mails. Business letters normally are formatted in "business style" (single-spaced with block paragraphs), and include the basic components shown in Figure 13.4.

14 Wacholla Lane
Pemberton, CA 95199

Writer's Address (or Letterhead)

December 8, 2015

Date

Jack Sinclair
Managing Editor
The Valley Times
8991 Modesto Boulevard
Orland, CA 95424

Recipient's Name and Address (also called "inside address")

Re: Features Reporter Position

Subject Line or Reference Line

Salutation

Dear Mr. Sinclair:

Text of Letter

Of course, I'm disappointed that you chose another applicant, but I enjoyed meeting with you, and deeply appreciate your interest in my background and career.

I took the suggestion you made in your letter, and called Ellen Wortenbaker in Whittier. She doesn't have a full-time opening right now, but expressed an interest in having me write a story about app startups. Even though I'll be freelancing, it's an opportunity to get my "foot in the door" and start putting together a professional portfolio. I can't thank you enough for this generous lead.

Meanwhile, if I can be of any assistance to you, please let me know. I always keep my profile and contact information up to date on LinkedIn.

Very best,

Complimentary Close

Jeff Gomez

Signed Name

Jeff Gomez

Typed Name

FIGURE 13.4 **Business letter in "full-block" format**

Keep in mind these formatting variations:

▶ **Full-block and modified formats**. Jeff Gomez's letter uses a "full-block" format. That means all the parts of the letter are flush against the left margin. Full-block is popular, easy to manage, and looks professional, but business letters can use "modified" formats as well; the most common variation aligns the date and complimentary close on the right side of the letter rather than the left.

▶ **Date format**. The month/day/year format that Jeff uses is common in the United States, but day/month year (12 September 2015) is common in many other countries and also used in the United States.

▶ **Reference or subject line**. A reference or subject line is not always necessary in a business letter. Jeff Gomez uses "Re" (meaning "in the matter of" or "regarding") to indicate the subject of his letter. The word "Subject" (followed by a colon) also is widely used.

▶ **Salutation**. The traditional salutation for a business letter is *Dear*, followed by the recipient's name and a colon (not a comma—*Dear Mr. Collins:*).

   If the recipient is a woman, and you are unsure of her marital status, *Ms.* is an accepted substitute for *Miss* or *Mrs.* (Dear Ms. Johnson). Some names like Kim and Robin are used for both genders. So if you are unsure of the person's gender, write out the full name (Dear Kim Johnson), rather than *Mr.* or *Ms.*

   If your letter is directed to an organization rather than a specific person, you can skip the salutation and simply use a reference or subject line to indicate why you are writing. Skipping the salutation is preferable to using a generic salutation like *To Whom It May Concern*, which sounds stiff and bureaucratic. *Dear Sir* won't go over well if the recipient is a woman. *Dear Sir/Madame* is now mainly used by scammers and identity thieves.

▶ **Complimentary close and signature**. For most business letters, stick to a standard, traditional close such as *Sincerely* or *Sincerely yours*. Other options, especially when writing to a person you know, are *Warmest regards, Best regards, Best, Respectfully,* or *Cordially*. Skip four lines after the close, type your full name, and sign the letter in ink above your typed signature:

Sincerely,

Edith Muncasey

Edith Muncasey
Clinical Director

If you are writing about a business matter but are on a first-name basis with the recipient, you should still type your full name but can sign your first name only:

Sincerely,

Edith

Edith Muncasey
Clinical Director

▶ **Enclosure (enc.) and copy (cc) notations.** These are abbreviations that go directly under the typed signature, to provide relevant information when necessary. The notation *enc.* (sometimes *encl.*) is short for *enclosure* and tells the reader you have included additional materials with your letter—for example, a résumé, an application form, a brochure, sales report, invoice, and so forth. If you have mentioned these materials in the text of your letter, the enclosure line is unnecessary. Sometimes, if there are multiple enclosures, writers just indicate the number in parentheses after the notation, instead of identifying each by name—Enc.: (2).

A copy notation—abbreviated *cc*—tells the reader that the letter has been sent to one or more other people, and who those people are. Below is an example of a complimentary close followed by an enclosure and copy notation:

Sincerely,

Edith Muncasey

Edith Muncasey
Clinical Director
Enc. Memorial Grant Report
cc: Darrel Allegro and Jessica Bernstein

Note that the mechanics for capitalizing and punctuating these notations can vary. You can model your notations on the example above, or consult a writing handbook for acceptable alternatives.

From Reflection to Response

Writing a Business Letter to Request an Interview

Review the section above about the components and format of a business letter, and then compose a letter to a person you would like to interview for a hypothetical writing project you are working on—an essay, profile, research paper, or article for your campus newspaper. Before composing the letter, decide what your project will be, and then choose someone you would like to interview for the project. Consider these people:

- Your college president
- The athletic director
- A prominent professor
- The community police chief
- The mayor or other public official
- A business leader or media personality

Your goal is to make the letter professional and courteous, but also to make a case for the interview. Try to align your interests with those of the person whose time you are requesting. For convenience, propose to follow up your letter with a phone call, and indicate that you can conduct the interview by phone or e-mail if the person prefers.

After composing the letter, bring it to class and exchange letters with a classmate. Give each other feedback on how effective the request is, and its chances of receiving a positive response.

Résumés

A résumé is a document that contains your work history, relevant experience, education, and training. When you prepare a résumé, you are essentially making an argument about your qualifications for a job. In order to effectively argue your case, your résumé should:

- ▶ Be concise—ideally no more than a page in length.
- ▶ Be free of spelling, punctuation, and grammatical errors.
- ▶ Be easily readable, with headings that stand out.
- ▶ Include your contact information, objective, education, work experience, and other relevant accomplishments (see Figure 13.5).

Compose your résumé with communication goals in mind. Think about what prospective employers are looking for, and shape the information to respond to their needs. The following list presents common parts of a résumé, along with details about information each part should contain. Figure 13.5 shows a sample résumé.

- ▶ **Contact Information:** Include your full name, your mailing address with the zip code, your telephone number, and your e-mail. If you maintain a website for professional purposes, include the web address as well.

Contact
information

Jeffery P. Gomez

108 Seton Avenue • Fresno, CA 93726 • Phone: 559.442.____ • email: gomezj@webnet.com

List a specific
position that
matches your
qualifications

Career Objective

Reporter/features writer position utilizing excellent skills in writing, research, and covering news stories

Starts with most
recent degree
earned

Education

Fresno State University, Bachelor of Arts in Journalism   June 2014

Related Experience and Accomplishments:

Assistant News Editor and Staff Reporter, *Fresno State Collegian*   Sept. 2012 to June 2014
- Contributed news stories and columns on campus life,
  and performed editorial duties including fact-checking and headline writing

Teaching Assistant, Dr. Ellen Harmon, "Journalism and the Constitution"   Spring 2014
Teaching Assistant, Dr. Ellen Harmon, "Public Affairs Reporting"   Fall 2013

List the most
recent position
first and work
backwards.
Include job title,
the name of
the company or
business, and
location (city and
state).

Experience

Design Creations Custom Greeting Cards, Inc., Fresno, CA   June 2014 to Present
- Copywriting for custom cards and marketing materials (contract employment)

Central Valley Life & Times (Weekly), Bakersfield, CA   2014
- Freelance features on "Fitness Apps" and "Millenial Lifestyles"

O'Brian's Bar and Gastro Pub, Fresno, CA   2011 to Present
- Bus-person, server, bartender (part-time)

Internship, San Jose Mercury News Summer   2013
- Contributed research and topic exploration for business and technlology features

Emphasize skills
that are relevant
to the job
objective.

Skills

- Fully bilingual English-Spanish; intermediate to advanced competency in Adobe
  Photoshop, InDesign, Audacity, and Wordpress

Only list
people whose
permission you
have obtained.

References

- Maurice Krulak, Managing Editor, Central Valley Life & Times, 661.392.____
  (x-4141)
- Sasha Shen, Owner, Design Creations Greeting Cards, 559.894.____
- Dr. Ellen Harmon, Fresno State University, Dept. of Mass Communication and
  Journalism, 559.872.____

FIGURE 13.5   **A sample résumé**

▶ **Objective:** Make this section reflect a realistic view of the job market and your qualifications. Be as specific as possible about the exact kind of job or position you are looking for. Avoid vague generalities like "looking for creative challenges." If you are willing to travel or relocate, you can say that in this section. If you are submitting the résumé with a detailed cover letter, you can consider omitting the "objective" section.

▶ **Education:** Begin with you most recent degree. Leave out high school if you have earned a college degree. Include honors, achievements, special certificates, and relevant experiences such as service learning or study abroad. You can list your overall GPA, or your GPA in your major, if either or both are above 3.0.

▶ **Experience:** Begin with your most recent job and work backward. Include the name of the company or business, the location (city and state), your job title and/or a brief description of your responsibilities, and the dates you were employed (the year is sufficient). People who have extensive work experience often place this "experience" section ahead of "education" in their résumé.

▶ **Skills:** Include subheadings and corresponding information that is most relevant to the job you are seeking—for example, "Honors and Awards," "Trainings," "Professional Memberships," or "Personal Interests." Your overriding goal is to provide the most relevant information about your abilities, interests, and achievements.

▶ **References:** Listing two or three people, with their business addresses and/or phone numbers may be more helpful than simply noting "available upon request." But always be sure to ask permission from your references first.

Résumés can be formatted in different ways depending on the objective and a person's work experience. Useful models and templates are widely available, and in some cases, employers provide and require a specific format.

Résumés created to be accessed and read digitally, rather than in print, are a relatively new phenomenon called "infographic" résumés. They are not appropriate for every job, but submitting a good one for the right job can make you stand out. Although you can find web services and articles that will help you create one, no standard models or templates exist, so you have to be both creative as well as smart about meeting the expectations of prospective employers. Figure 13.6 shows an example of an infographic résumé

FIGURE 13.6   Hagan Blount's infographic résumé

that uses a mix of bold fonts, colors, and images to highlight the person's accomplishments.

The article that follows describes a resourceful job seeker who created an infographic résumé to highlight her experience and skills.

Sheryl Jean {

GOODBYE PAPER, HELLO SOCIAL RÉSUMÉ

Sheryl Jean

Sheryl Jean joined *Dallas Morning News* in 2008, and she writes about the economy, business, and airlines. When she is not writing, she enjoys long-distance running, cycling, and yoga.

WHEN MELISSA MIHELICH RECENTLY found herself out of work, she decided to try a new strategy in her job search.

Using a free website, she created cool color graphics to showcase her skills, experience and even a recommendation. Then, instead of mailing a traditional résumé to potential employers, she emailed an infographic résumé.

"I'm one of those people who's always looking for something new and different," said Mihelich, who was laid off Jan. 25 from her marketing director job. "It was a nice snapshot of who Melissa Mihelich is as director of marketing."

More job seekers like her are trying alternative ways to share their résumés and portfolios as hiring and job searching shifts more and more to the Internet. They've shelved the linen paper and manila envelopes in favor of Twitter, blogs and LinkedIn.

Local recruiters and career center managers say they began seeing "social résumés" in 2009, but the trend has really taken off in the last two years.

"It's a numbers game," said Guy Davis, assistant director of Southern Methodist University's Hegi Family Career Development Center. "Just sending application after application to job listings doesn't give you great results."

A survey by the National Association of Colleges and Employers found that 41 percent of new college graduates in 2012 used social media to look for work, up from 7 percent in 2008. They also used social résumés online instead of mailing traditional résumés to prospective employers.

Not one printed résumé

Dan McMillan, 23, a recent graduate of Southern Methodist University, has not printed or mailed one traditional résumé as part of his job search, which began last summer in Dallas and continues from his hometown of Chicago.

He posted his résumé and looks for work mainly on the professional network site LinkedIn.

The use of—and response to—social résumés depends more on the job level and type of industry than a job candidate's age, said Ashley Waggoner, regional vice president of Robert Half International's technology and creative group in North Texas. Social résumés are more likely to be used in the Web development world than in the private equity or banking industries, she said.

Job seeker Mihelich said the feedback has been positive and her infographic résumé has led to three interviews.

Employers also are adapting to social résumés. Wells Fargo doesn't "really take paper résumés anymore" for the roughly 8,000 job openings it posts each month—ranging from a bank teller job to people who lease farmland to jobs in the gaming industry, said Aaron Kraljev, employment branding manager for the San Francisco-based bank.

"The ways people choose to make themselves stand out is amazing," he said. "We've seen some pretty amazing infographics and video résumés via YouTube. We've even had people copy and paste a résumé into a comment on a Facebook page, which raises privacy issues. We'll take that down, but we like their excitement."

Innovative Southwest Airlines Co. prefers people to apply for jobs through its career site and not send résumés through social media, spokesman Brooks Thomas said. That's partly because the Dallas-based airlines is a federal contractor and must follow certain protocol, he said.

Last month, 30-year-old Antwane Davis of Keller landed a job as a Wells Fargo mortgage underwriter after being laid off from a similar job two weeks earlier. He posted his résumé on LinkedIn and looked for work on Craigslist, Facebook and Google.

"It saves time and money, and the results are better," Davis said of social media. ▪

From Reflection to Response   Creating an Infographic Résumé

Review your own print résumé (or create a basic one, if necessary), and convert it to an infographic that you can keep as a model or draft for future use. After you create your infographic, bring a copy to class, and ask your instructor and classmates to give you feedback about the design elements.

Note: If you have concerns about displaying personal information, you can use fictitious information and a fictitious name. The content of the résumé is secondary. The goal is to practice effective layout and graphic design.

Cover Letters

The first business letter many students write is a cover letter—or job-application letter—that accompanies a résumé. Cover letters have a lot riding on them. They have to be professionally written. Most are relatively short. Employers often receive dozens, if not hundreds, of them, and won't devote time to reading detailed information about an applicant's personal qualities unless the information is compelling and germane.

On the other hand, if the letter says little more than "Here is my résumé," it won't stand out or help your cause. The reader might infer that you don't care about the job. Planning and writing a good cover letter starts with remembering that your reader is a real person. Try to address what the reader is looking for.

From Reflection to Response   **Writing a Complaint Letter**

Think of a service or product you recently used or purchased and were dissatisfied with. Some examples follow:

- You were served a poor meal in a restaurant.
- You were treated in a discourteous manner by an employee or public official.
- You experienced an extended interruption of your Internet, phone, electric, or other service.
- You have been receiving unsolicited "courtesy" calls, junk mail, or spam.
- You were overcharged for a car repair, or charged for unsatisfactory work.
- You were misled by a salesperson or a deceptive ad.
- You purchased a product that is defective or was damaged during delivery.
- You were unable to get through to a helpful customer-service agent on the phone, or spoke to one whose English was unintelligible.

As a result of your frustrating experience, write a complaint letter to an appropriate individual or customer relations department. Even if the experience infuriated you, your letter should be businesslike. Avoid ranting, insults, name calling, or threats. Clarify your communication goals. State the facts accurately, and do more than just complain: Explain what you want done. Do you want a refund, credit, or replacement? Do you want some other form of compensation? Do you want an apology from the company or persons responsible, or assurances that you and others will receive better service in the future?

EFFECTIVE DESIGN ELEMENTS AND USING NEW MEDIA

Given the "transactional" goals of writing in the workplace, good layout and visual design—subjects covered in Chapters 9 and 11—are critical. Documents that contain ample white space, helpful headings, bullet points, and graphics tell readers that the author is capable and the document deserves attention. For transactional purposes, visual aids like graphs, charts, and photographs enhance the appeal and usefulness of written document, and should be included when they are relevant.

Thinking "outside the box" and using new media to reinvent traditional documents and deliver content—the subject of Chapter 11—is increasingly part of the "job description" of a writer. Videos, podcasts, web pages, blogs, and slide shows provide opportunities for writers to reach an audience in creative, new ways. Instead of composing a conventional brochure, memo, or report, a writer can design new kinds of "texts" in multimedia that make content more accessible and impacting.

WRITING AND YOUR CAREER

In today's job market, employers talk about applicants having "hard" and "soft" skills. Hard skills refer to job-specific knowledge and training—for instance, training as an engineer or a nurse. Soft skills include qualities like creativity, determination, leadership, and the ability to communicate effectively as a speaker and writer. Both hard and soft skills are important. They tend to be seen and assessed distinctly, but in many essential ways, they are inseparable.

Some careers don't require writing, but in a world where businesses, employers' needs, and job descriptions are evolving all the time, it is unwise to assume that writing is a skill you can do without. The smart strategy is to leave college with abilities that will create maximum opportunities for you, and help you seize those that come your way. Writing may not turn out to be central to your job or career, but writing ability, and the range of soft skills it encompasses, will never be a detriment to your aspirations.

Over many years, communications professors John S. Fielden and Ronald E. Dulek researched the role of writing in some of the nation's best-managed companies and found that "people in the highest managerial positions write the most effectively." Indeed, the ability to write well "influenced their advancement to the top of their organizational ladders" ("What Is Effective Business Writing?"). Warren Buffet, Jack Welch, Martha Stewart, Bill Gates, and many other successful executives are very good writers. Nevertheless, many students believe, or want to believe, that successful managers, executives, and CEOs don't need to know how to write well; they can delegate writing to low-level employees. No doubt, executives and senior managers sometimes delegate writing tasks, but the people they delegate to are not low-level employees; they are highly paid managers and executive-level employees themselves.

EVALUATE YOUR LEARNING

1. Think about some professional fields you would like to work in. Based on what you know about the work, what are some situations that might require high-stakes writing tasks?

2. Go to your e-mail inbox and search for e-mails that you have written for professional purposes—perhaps to an employer or prospective employer; or a teacher, college administrator, or professor. Did you follow the professional conventions discussed in this chapter (see pages 18–21)? Could anything about the e-mail be improved to make a more professional impression or elicit the response you wanted?

3. In the opening of the film *Gladiator,* the Roman general, Maximus (Russell Crowe), tells his troops, "What we do in life, echoes in eternity." Assuming you live by that precept, is there any reason you *shouldn't* quote it as part of your regular, e-mail signature?

4. If you were reserving a rental in the south of France through a service like Airbnb, and sent the owner an e-mail saying you would be arriving on 6/8/20___, what mistake would you be making?

Courtesy of Emma Rickert

EMMA RICKERT

Geo Street Art

In this piece, I was trying to communicate the relationship between graffiti and the ever growing presence of social media and publicity. As public art is created, it is often immediately put online to be seen by as many people as possible. This illustration uses drop pins, as seen in online map applications, to show where different pieces of street art can be seen throughout a city via a map.

CHAPTER FOURTEEN

Using and Documenting Sources

> " The remarkable thing about dinosaurs is not that they become
> extinct, but that they dominated the earth for so long. Dinosaurs
> held sway for 100 million years while mammals, all the while, lived
> as small animals in the interstices of their world. After 70 million
> years on top, we mammals have an excellent track record and good
> prospects for the future, but we have yet to display the staying power
> of dinosaurs. "
>
> —Stephen Jay Gould, "Were Dinosaurs Dumb?"

CHAPTER LEARNING OBJECTIVES

In this chapter, you will learn to:

- ▶ Evaluate and use secondary sources—books, journal articles, magazines, and newspapers.
- ▶ Evaluate and use Internet resources.
- ▶ Conduct primary or field research.
- ▶ Format research papers in MLA style.
- ▶ Document your sources in MLA style.
- ▶ Understand basic rules of APA style.

INTRODUCTION TO THIS GUIDE

Chapter 8, "Navigating a Research Project," provides detailed instruction about conducting a research project. Chapter 8 also provides an overview of different documentation styles (MLA, APA, *Chicago*) and how to document sources.

This chapter will provide more specific information about (1) how to evaluate and use sources efficiently, especially secondary research sources (books, journal articles, and so on) and (2) how to format papers and cite sources in MLA style (Modern Language Association).

Keep in mind that documentation systems like MLA specify how to cite dozens of different kinds of primary and secondary sources ranging from surveys and personal interviews, to variously authored kinds of books and articles, and to growing varieties of unconventional or emerging sources that can include anything from advertisements to lectures, live performances, police reports, posters, leaflets, electronic billboards, Internet videos, and information on a blog site or a Facebook page.

Different citation systems have different rules, and sources themselves are so varied that entire reference books—writing handbooks, like the *MLA Handbook*, and dedicated websites, like the Purdue OWL—are devoted to providing the information writers need to cite sources professionally. This chapter offers basic instruction that will enhance your understanding of sources and citations, but it is not a substitute for the comprehensive coverage provided by an up-to-date handbook or a reliable online resource. Using a comprehensive reference guide to documentation is a must for students and scholars who write academic research papers, reports, and researched essays.

UNPACKING SECONDARY SOURCES

When researchers do "primary" or "field" research, that is, interview people, conduct surveys, run a focus group, examine correspondence, or visit a relevant place to record their observations, they get their hands on a project and have a chance to make original discoveries. Rather than just absorbing and analyzing information passively, they enter the "arena" of their project, so to speak.

Nevertheless, most academic research projects rely heavily on secondary research, because it yields the most comprehensive and incisive findings. Compared to primary research, however, secondary research—delving into other people's writing and observations—can seem dull and lifeless, especially to students. When students work with secondary sources, they tend to see the medium as the source—a book, an article, and so on—rather than the person or people who produced it. The truth is, secondary sources have a living presence behind them. The people who produce the sources are not as real to us as people we interact with when we do field research, but they still *are* real people and in many ways just as interesting and knowable. Keeping that in mind—thinking about the person or people behind the source—will put you in a more active relationship with your secondary sources and also make you a more perceptive researcher.

Evaluating sources always comes down to evaluating the person or persons who produce the source or are the source. If you read a book or article that you consider narrow-minded, you can blame the person who wrote it. If you read an article that you find inspirational or illuminating, you can praise the writer and feel grateful that you "met" her. As a starting point for evaluating secondary sources, evaluate authors in the same way you evaluate real people: What credentials do they have? What kind of "track record"—professional experience, awards, publications—do they have? How objective are they? What are their assumptions, values, and beliefs? Do they have an unstated or biased agenda? Also, consider whether a person's reputation or professional credentials apply to the problem you are researching.

Making these kinds of assessments and sharing them with your readers is an essential part of secondary research. If you can get in the habit of evaluating your sources and sharing your evaluations in the papers you write, you will become a more effective researcher and write better papers. The pages that follow cover some common secondary sources and offer advice about assessing them.

Books

Books are substantial and comprehensive sources, but because they take so much time to read, they are not always practical for college research projects. You may be able to read one or two books for a research project, but usually you won't have time to read all of the books that might be worth reading.

An alternative to reading books from cover to cover is to selectively review the content, identify parts that are significant to your research, and read those parts only.

You can "review" many books in a short period of time at the library. Locate promising titles in the catalogue. Find the books in the stacks. Take them to a table and look them over one by one, "skimming" for useful material. "Skim reading" is a research skill. It is not being lazy. It means reading quickly to assess a source and locate important material that you will read carefully later on.

> ### Tech Tip
>
> If you would like to practice efficient skim reading, consider visiting spreeder.com. This site is a free service that provides exercises, tips, web links, and blog posts that can help you improve your reading speed and comprehension.

As you review books, you will find that some are especially valuable to your project. You may want to read them in their entirety. Some books with promising titles may disappoint you when you look at the contents. Others may not be worth reading in their entirety but contain chapters, sections, or pages that are worth reading carefully.

In reviewing books, the most important parts to look at are the following:

▶ Copyright page

▶ Table of contents

▶ Foreword (if there is one) by a notable person who is not the author

▶ Bibliography (if there is one)

▶ Index (if there is one)

▶ Author's bio (if there is one)

▶ Excerpts from reviews (if provided)

Copyright Page and Table of Contents: Front Matter Everything in a book that comes before the first chapter is called "front matter." Two parts of the front matter are always worth looking at—the copyright page and the table of contents (sometimes just "contents").

The copyright page usually is at the beginning of the book, inside the front cover after the title page, and offers two important pieces of information, the date of publication (and/or the copyright), and the name of the publisher—that is, the company, person, or institution publishing the book.

The copyright page of *Heat Wave: A Social Autopsy of Disaster in Chicago*, by Eric Klinenberg (see Figure 14.1), includes the date of publication as well as the copyright date, both 2002. In general, the copyright date is sufficient to tell a researcher what he needs to know—approximately when a book was written, and by extension, how current it is. A book does not have to be current to be useful, but knowing when it was written is important for assessing the information and understanding its value and relevance to your research.

Eric Klinenberg is assistant professor of sociology at Northwestern University and a faculty fellow at the Institute for Policy Research. He is coeditor of *The Making and Unmaking of Whiteness* and a regular contributor to *Le Monde Diplomatique*. Klinenberg was awarded an Individual Projects Fellowship by the Open Society Institute in 2000.

The University of Chicago Press, Chicago 60637
The University of Chicago Press, Ltd., London
©2002 by The University of Chicago
All rights reserved. Published 2002
Printed in the United States of America

11 10 09 08 07 06   5
ISBN: 0-226-44321-3 (cloth)
ISBN: 0-226-44322-1 (paperback)

Library of Congress Cataloging-in-Publication Data

Klinenberg, Eric.
    Heat wave : a social autopsy of disaster in Chicago / Eric Klinenberg.
        p. cm.
    Includes bibliographical references and index.
    ISBN 0-226-44321-3 (cloth : alk. paper)
    I. Sociology—Urban.   2. Chicago (III.)—Social conditions.   3. Disasters—Social aspects—Illinois—Chicago.   4. Heat waves (Meteorology)—Illinois—Chicago.   5. Social problems.   6. Social science.   7. Aged—Services for—Illinois—Chicago.   8. Aged—Services for.   9. Aged—Illinois—Chicago—Social conditions. I. Title.
    HV1471.C38 K585 2002
    363.34'921—dc21
                                                    2001043724

⊗ The paper used in this publication meets the minimum requirements of the American National Standard for Information Sciences—Permanence of Paper for Printed Library Materials, ANSI Z39.48-1992.

FIGURE 14.1 Copyright page of *Heat Wave: A Social Autopsy of Disaster in Chicago*

Publishing Company or Imprint: University Presses, Commercial Publishers, and Specialty Presses

The second important piece of information on a copyright page is the publisher of the book. The reputation of the publisher is an *indication* of quality and credibility. *Heat Wave* is published by The University of Chicago Press. This publisher's "mission statement" includes the following objectives:

▶ Publish important scholarly books that do not recover their costs.

▶ Fund the development of ambitious large-scale projects.

▶ Support especially costly works such as translations and illustrated books.

In general, university presses strive to publish books for the advancement of knowledge rather than for sales and profit. These are books of quality that are carefully researched, "peer-reviewed" prior to publication, and well documented, but usually written for a specialized audience.

Commercial publishers—HarperCollins, Random House, Holt, and many others in the industry—are familiar names to readers. These publishers are in business to turn profits. They publish a variety of books, including fiction and nonfiction "trade" books that target general audiences. Unlike books published by academic presses, trade books are not peer-reviewed prior to publication. Nevertheless, commercial publishers often publish books of quality, by professional writers and scholars.

"Small presses," or specialty presses, publish books that, for one reason or another, do not meet the scholarly criteria of university presses or the commercial criteria of large publishers. Small presses sometimes publish books of quality by unknown or upcoming authors, or by authors who *are* known and respected, but whose views on certain subjects may be unpopular—too radical or politically incorrect for mainstream readers. The quality of small presses and the books they publish vary. Be suspicious of imprints that brandish words like "freedom" and "liberty." Those words stand for noble ideals, and precisely for that reason, often are appropriated by purveyors of bigotry, paranoia, and hate. When you come across a book by a small or specialty press, go to the website for information about the company's mission and the books it publishes. If you see werewolves, or a fossilized Martian, or photographs of men in black emerging from the rubble of the World Trade Center, you probably are not dealing with a credible publisher.

Contents or Table of Contents
The contents, or table of contents, gives you a list of chapters and a general overview of what the book covers. By checking the "contents," you can determine if parts of a book are pertinent to your project. For example, if you were conducting research on fear mongering in the news media and came across Eric Klinenberg's *Heat Wave* in your library, you might not have time to read the book from cover to cover, but by reviewing the contents page (see Figure 14.2), you would see that Chapter 5, "The Spectacular City: News Organizations and the Representation of Catastrophe," deals with your research problem and would be worth your time to read.

Notes and Bibliography: Back Matter
Everything that comes after the main text of a book is called "back matter." If a book is scholarly, it will include endnotes and a bibliography. These appear at the back, before the index.

The endnotes provide citations along with other information that complements the content of a book. If parts of a book are relevant to research you

Contents

FIGURE 14.2 Contents of *Heat Wave: A Social Autopsy of Disaster in Chicago*

are doing, review the endnotes for additional information and sources. For example, the "Introduction" to *Heat Wave* contains a note—number 4—that addresses how the media sensationalizes natural disasters even when the "human toll is slight" (see Figure 14.3). The note also includes references to sources ("Gans" and so on) whom you will find listed alphabetically in the bibliography that the author provides. These sources may offer valuable information for your project and be worth tracking down.

Notes

PROLOGUE
1. Official city reports list two different heat-related mortality totals for the month of July; 514 and 521. I use the latter figure throughout this hook. The excess death measure, however, is the more accurate count.
2. National Weather Service 1995, x.
3. Whitman, et al. 1997, 1517.
4. Bachelard [1934] 1984, 104.
5. Farmer 1995, 5.
6. Park [1916] 1969, 126.

INTRODUCTION
1. Laczko's story was initially reported by journalist Michael Lev (1995), and I extended the inquiry into his case by examining files at the Office of the Cook Country Public Administrator. According to public investigators, the practice of collecting junk is common among people who live and die alone.
2. City of Chicago 1995, 2.
3. This will not to know about U.S. social problems was the subject of Philip Slater's "toilet assumption" in his best-selling book. *The Pursuit of Loneliness* (1990). Slater's provocative claim is that Americans live with the hope that ignoring the noxious social byproducts of the world they have created is a means of making them go away.
4. Weather systems such as hurricanes, tornadoes, earthquakes, and floods not only make a direct and recognizable physical impact on the people and property in their paths, they also provide graphic and spectacular images for the news media to display. Television, newspaper, and magazine reports feature such disasters prominently, making them the focus of local and often national attention even when their human toll is slight (Gans 1979; Singer 1987; Sood, Stockdale, and Rogers 1987).

There is a long line of epidemiological and public health research that establishes an association between heat wave mortality and poverty, old age, sex, and ethnoracial status, with poor and elderly black men being most vulnerable (Applegate, et al. 1981; Jones, et al. 1982; Martinez, et al. 1989; Oechsli and Buechley 1970; U.S. Centers for Disease Control and Prevention 1995a). In addition to the nearly annual review article on heat-related mortality published in the *Morbidity and Mortality Weekly Report*, medical and public health scholars

243 • • •

FIGURE 14.3 Notes from *Heat Wave*

The bibliography is an alphabetical listing of all the sources used in the book—similar to a Works Cited list that comes at the end of an academic essay or journal article. However, in some books and citation styles, a bibliography may include sources ("works consulted") that are not used in the book but that the author considers useful and important.

In reviewing a book that deals with your research problem, always check and see if there is a bibliography or list of references at the end. The bibliography can lead you to relevant books and articles, or primary documents like government reports.

Index The index, which comes at or near the very end of a book, is an alphabetical listing of people and topics that the book covers, and the specific page numbers to go to. You can examine an index to find out if a book has content of interest to you. Thus, for a project about fear mongering in the news media, the index of *Heat Wave* (see Figure 14.4) would point you to relevant sections

FIGURE 14.4 An Index Page from *Heat Wave*

of the book dealing with "media" and "news" (in particular, pages 190 to 234). Indexes are an indispensable tool for reviewing books, although unfortunately, not all books have them.

Reviews and "Blurbs": Front Matter, Dust Jacket, or Cover

Many editions of hardcover books, as well as paperbacks, include excerpts from professional reviews that appeared in magazines, newspapers, journals, and other media outlets. These excerpts—sometimes called "blurbs"—may be included in the front matter or on the "dust jackets" of hardcover books, or on the front and back covers of paperbacks. If the sources of the excerpts are reputable, then you can consider them an indication of a book's quality. The blurbs printed on the back cover of *Heat Wave* come from reviews that appeared in the *New Yorker* magazine, the *Nation*, the *Boston Globe*, and *Salon*, among others. These are reputable sources of quality, though not necessarily without political or cultural biases.

Periodicals: Journals, Magazines, and Newspapers

Because of time limitations, students rely on articles from periodicals—that is, journals, magazines, and newspapers—more than books for their research, but as with books, the quality of articles from these sources needs to be evaluated.

Professional journals exist for just about every field, from education to law to international relations, to medicine, veterinary medicine, environmental sciences, physics, math, business, engineering, and so on. Articles in journals are considered excellent sources because they are peer-reviewed before publication and written by recognized scholars or specialists in a given field. Still, journal articles have to be assessed on their merits. As noted in Chapter 8, the writing can be ponderous and hard to read. In addition, because the readers mainly are specialists in the field, many journal articles are freighted with pages of material that may seem peripheral to the main thesis or point. Authors sometimes spend more time reviewing current scholarship than presenting their own ideas. If you start reading a journal article and find that the review of scholarship is not giving you information you need, you can skim ahead. Often, the crux of what the writer has to say is reserved for the last three or four pages.

Popular and Commercial Magazines

As research sources, popular magazines are similar to commercial books. They can be excellent sources, but they vary in quality. Magazines like the *New Yorker, Smithsonian,* and the *Atlantic Monthly* target well-educated readers and have a reputation for outstanding quality. Magazines like *National Geographic, Vanity Fair, Psychology Today,* and *Time* target a broader readership, but still publish articles of quality. The same generally is true of many magazines that are geared toward narrower categories of readers (*Men's Health, Vogue, Esquire, Wired, Rolling Stone*) or specialized audiences (*Car and Driver, Condé Nast Traveler, Popular Mechanics*).

Although articles in popular magazines are not formally documented, the writers for the most part identify their sources within the articles (using lead-ins and signal phrases). The editors of reputable magazines have a stake in making sure that the articles they publish are fact-checked and contain reliable information.

Newspapers Newspapers publish timely stories and reports about current events. For a researcher, newspapers are a compelling source of information about the world at large and events as they happen. Some major newspapers like the *New York Times* and the *Wall Street Journal* have a reputation for outstanding quality, but overall, because newspaper articles usually are written on short notice to meet deadlines, they are not as comprehensive or reliable as articles in other kinds of periodicals. However, what newspaper articles lack in depth, they often make up for in the immediacy of the details, the realism of the context, and the scope of the coverage.

For example, if you were conducting research on educating autistic children, books and journal articles would be your most valuable sources. However, a news story from a news website could provide you with a real-life perspective and useful information.

Internet Sources

The Internet is an indispensable tool for all kinds of researchers, in all kinds of ways. The "information highway" makes traditional print sources—articles, dissertations, government reports, encyclopedia entries—more readily available than ever before. Using your campus library website and its online databases is the best way to obtain digital versions of print sources. College libraries have subscriptions that allow students to access these sources without a charge. (If you find them on your own, you may have to pay an access or subscription fee.)

Accessing print sources online is a convenient way to conduct traditional secondary research, but be careful about using source material that *originates* online. Most reputable businesses, corporations, nonprofits, health services, educational institutions, advocacy groups, and government agencies (even the CIA) have websites that offer researchers unprecedented access to useful information; however, in the realm of blogs, social networks, and independent or unsponsored websites, much of the information you access will be anecdotal at best.

Internet-based research is not necessarily efficient either. The hit-and-miss method of using general search engines like Google or Bing to conduct research can turn up very few sources of value and quality. A better alternative is to use specialized databases, directories, and deep-search engines. You can find listings and access information about these resources on your library website. As a rule, an hour or less spent on your library website, using the search tools and databases that you can link to from there, will be much more productive than hit-and-miss searches on Google or Bing.

Audiovisual Sources: Videos, Documentaries, and Podcasts

Audiovisual sources can make meaningful contributions to your research. Documentary films that used to be hard to find are now readily available from companies like Netflix or on websites like YouTube. Thoughtful documentaries like *Roger and Me, Harlan County USA, Hoop Dreams*, or *Point of Order* can be credible and illuminating research sources, although they may reflect biases that you need to identify and evaluate.

Podcasts also can be excellent sources. They are available on a wide range of serious subjects. Some are produced by respected broadcasters like NPR or the BBC, some even by the world's greatest universities (see "iTunes U"). Podcasts offer convenience and flexibility for a researcher. You can deepen your knowledge of your research problem while driving your car, working out at the gym, or walking to class.

From Reflection to Response   **Evaluating a Secondary Source**

Go to the library or use your library's online database to find a print source that deals with the problem you are researching—a book, or a journal or magazine article. Review the source and then compose a citation for it in MLA style, and write a summary or annotation that evaluates it, addressing all the points that follow:

- Consider whether the source is relevant to your project, and why.
- Consider the reputation of the publisher or sponsor of the source. Is there a hidden or biased agenda?
- Consider the credentials of the author.
- Consider the audience or readership for the source. Does the audience have a bearing on the credibility of the source?
- Consider the timeliness of the source—when the information was written or published—and how that affects its usefulness.

- Consider the reliability of the information. How verifiable is it? Is it formally documented with notes, citations, and references? If not, are sources identified and traceable?

PRIMARY OR "FIELD RESEARCH": METHODS AND PROCEDURES

Though conducting secondary research is usually the best way to *start* a research project, primary research (or "field research") helps you take ownership of your project and make original contributions. Below is a list of the most common primary research methods or sources:

- ▶ Personal interviews (including interviews via telephone or e-mail)
- ▶ Surveys/questionnaires
- ▶ Focus groups
- ▶ Site visits and observations
- ▶ Oral histories, testimonials
- ▶ Online discussion boards
- ▶ Lectures and speeches
- ▶ Government documents (for example, census information, statistical reports, and congressional hearing transcripts)

Personal Interviews

Interviews are one of the most common and compelling forms of primary research. You may have conducted personal interviews for projects in this course—for example, to gather information for a profile (Chapter 5) or an argumentative essay (Chapter 7). If so, you already know that personal interviews can provide valuable information and perspectives. On your campus, professors, administrators, coaches, trainers, and support staff, including those responsible for campus security, housing, and student life and events, can provide professional expertise on a wide range of issues. Your community, even if it is small, has many knowledgeable people and professionals who could contribute insights for your project—doctors, police officers, farmers, business owners, social workers, union members, attorneys, and so on.

You can find a list of tips for conducting effective interviews in Chapter 5, on pages 178–180. As a rule, before conducting an interview, be clear about what you want to learn and what the person can contribute to your research goals. In most cases, you should be looking for people with professional credentials who can give you professional perspectives, but sometimes it can be useful to interview someone who simply has experience with the problem you a researching—for example, on the problem of marine pollutants, a commercial fisherman (as opposed to a marine biologist or oceanographer) might be able to give you firsthand insights.

Prepare questions in advance but don't overprepare or be afraid to deviate from the questions. Good interviewers are good listeners. Listening carefully to what someone has to say and being responsive to the person's words will reward you with a productive interview. Observe the work of an accomplished interviewer like Anderson Cooper (*60 Minutes* and CNN news). You will notice that, first and foremost, he is an attentive listener.

Surveys

Conducting a survey can infuse your research with meaningful information. Creating and distributing a printed survey is always an option, but today, user-friendly websites like SurveyMonkey.com (see Figure 14.5) provide software and tools (with limited, free use) for creating surveys and distributing them electronically (via e-mail, discussion boards, or social media pages).

These sites also provide excellent tutorials for composing survey questions and getting good results. If you conduct a survey, keep in mind these basic pointers:

▶ Be clear about the goals of the survey. Write down what you want to learn.

▶ Begin the survey with a short letter or note to respondents that explains the purpose of your research and what you expect to gain from the survey.

▶ Make the survey as brief and easy to complete as possible (less than five minutes is a realistic time frame).

▶ Make sure to include questions that give you demographic information that you need for evaluating responses—age, level of education, gender, or marital status, and so forth.

▶ Avoid open-ended questions that require lengthy, essay-type answers (for example, "What were your expectations when you entered college?"). People are busy and likely to skip open-ended questions or provide curt, unhelpful responses.

▶ Use fixed-choice and scaled questions that respondents can answer more easily (for example, "check all that apply," or "on a scale of one to five"). Thoughtful fixed-choice and scaled questions are the key to an effective

7. In your work-related writing, how important are the following qualities? (Rate any that apply.)

	Very important	Somewhat important	Not important
Creativity and originality	○	○	○
Document design (page layout and/or visual aides)	○	○	○
Good organization	○	○	○
Persuasiveness	○	○	○
Clarity	○	○	○
Good word choice and vocabulary	○	○	○
Good grammar, punctuation and spelling	○	○	○
Concision (keeping it short and to the point)	○	○	○

FIGURE 14.5 Sample Fixed-Choice Survey Question about Writing in the Workplace

survey. They can give you meaningful information without demanding much time or effort from your respondents. If you want to solicit more detailed information, you always can add an "additional comments" box after the question.

Focus Groups

Businesses use focus groups to find out what customers think about a new product or service. As a general research tool, focus groups bring together a small number of people who have something to contribute to a research problem. The researcher asks questions and moderates a "focused" discussion. For example, if you were researching whether or not college athletes should be paid, you could organize a focus group of student athletes to learn about their views and needs.

Other Primary Sources and Methods: Lectures, Site Visits, Discussion Boards, and Oral Histories

Depending on what you are researching, many other kinds of primary research can contribute to your project. Attending public lectures, political meetings, or various kinds of rallies can provide useful information. If you were researching voting rights or voter suppression, a visit to a polling place might be useful. You might consider observing a trial if you were researching a criminal-justice issue.

The Internet also offers access to useful primary sources like discussion boards, testimonials, and oral histories. The discussion boards on medical or newspaper websites can offer revealing (albeit anecdotal) information about all kinds of controversies, products, treatments, and so on.

Testimonials and oral histories (people remembering and talking about their own experiences) are a form of primary research that you can conduct yourself—for example, if you have a grandparent who witnessed a historical event related to your research. Testimonials and oral histories also can be accessed online, in written or audiovisual forms, on many sponsored or dedicated websites. Here are a few:

▶ Alexandriava.gov (Oral History Summaries)

▶ NPR.org (StoryCorps)

▶ Tellingstories.org (Oral History Archive Project presented by the Urban School of San Francisco)

Testimonials and oral histories can be an excellent source of historical information or insights into the lives of people dealing with problems, hardships, and injustices.

From Reflection to Response

Conducting Primary Research about College Education and Students' Attitudes

Read or review the article in Chapter 8 titled "Your So-Called Education" (on pages 352). Form a group with two or three classmates. Assume your group is going to conduct research about the problem of inadequate student learning in college. Part of your research will involve gathering firsthand information from students about their learning experiences and attitudes. To gather the information, decide to use *one* of the following primary research methods:

• An interview

• A survey

• A focus group

Discuss what you want to find out from students to enhance your knowledge of the problem, and then compose a list of five or more questions you would ask to elicit the information you need. After the list is finished, discuss your group's chosen method and questions with the rest of the class.

DOCUMENTING SOURCES IN MLA STYLE

A writer documents sources in a paper for a simple and straightforward reason: to share source information with readers so that they can access the sources themselves. Formal documentation systems created by the Modern Language Association (MLA), the American Psychological Association (APA), and the *Chicago Manual of Style* (*Chicago*) standardize documentation procedures in order to make sharing efficient. Without standardized rules, documentation would be unreliable, confusing, and chaotic. Unfortunately, because systems like MLA and others are comprehensive, they present a "learning curve" for writers. Even most professional researchers and scholars don't know all the details and fine points of documentation by heart. They consult an up-to-date handbook or website for instructions they need. As a college writer, whenever you compose an essay or a paper that requires formal documentation, you should do the same.

Keep in mind, however, that your overriding goal as a research writer is to *be a writer,* not simply to present source information, but to write a paper or essay that is interesting and illuminating for your readers. All too often, when students write research papers, they focus so much on sources and documentation that the actual writing becomes dull and lifeless. Indeed, many papers amount to bibliographies stitched together with words. Don't allow that to happen to your research papers and essays. Do your "due diligence" to provide all of the necessary information about your sources, and cite them correctly, but don't forget to be a real writer and write a compelling essay in a real voice that conveys the value of your findings and your engagement with the subject.

The documentation system usually used in first-year writing courses is MLA (Modern Language Association). The MLA system covers guidelines for formatting and documenting research papers and essays. Below are basic formatting guidelines you should apply:

MLA Document Format

- ▶ Use *one-inch margins* on all sides.
- ▶ *Double-space your text.*
- ▶ Use a common and legible *12-point font like Times New Roman.*
- ▶ Insert *your name and page numbers in the upper right-hand corner of each page,* starting with the first page. (Create a "header" so that your last name is displayed on every page before the page number.)

MLA First-Page Formatting Guidelines

▶ On the first page, *type your name, your instructor's name, the course, and the date, in the upper left-hand corner.* (No title page is required unless your instructor asks for one.)

▶ *The title of your essay.* Center your title and capitalize the first word and most of the other words except articles (*a, the*), prepositions (*of, on*, and so on), and conjunctions (*and, but*). Don't put your title in quotation marks, or use italics, underlining, bold, or all uppercase letters. *Double-space between your title and the first line of your regular text.* Make sure your title says something meaningful ("Research Paper" is not a meaningful title).

▶ *Indent the first word of your first paragraph and all subsequent paragraphs five spaces* (using the tab key).

Below is the first page of a student's researched essay, formatted according to MLA guidelines (to read the complete essay, see Chapter 7, pages 291–301):

Use one-inch margins on all sides, and double-spacing throughout the essay.

The first-page heading consists of your name, your instructor's name, the course, and the date, double-spaced and aligned in the upper left-hand corner.

A relevant quotation inserted after the title is called an "epigraph." (It is not common or required in college papers.)

Author's name in parentheses to indicate the same source.

Insert page numbers in the upper right-hand corner, starting with the first page, and create a "header" that displays your last name on every page in front of the page number.

Center your title. (Don't use quotation marks, or typographical features like underlining or bold.)

The source of information, Sherman, is named in a signal phrase. Since the Sherman article appeared on a website, no page numbers are needed or given in parentheses.

Lawrence 1

Brian Lawrence

Professor Saba

English 1105

October 15, 2016

The Truth about Atheists

Religion is regarded by the common people as true, by the wise as false, and by rulers as useful.

—SENECA, ROMAN PHILOSOPHER AND PLAYWRIGHT (A.D. 3–65)

At a news conference in Chicago on August 27, 1987, then Vice President George H. W. Bush made a striking remark. He told Robert I. Sherman, a reporter for the *American Atheist* news journal, "I don't know that atheists should be considered as citizens, nor should they be considered patriots. This is one nation under God."

Later, during the same news conference, Sherman asked the Vice President:

"Do you support the constitutionality of state/church separation?"

"I support the separation of church and state," Bush replied. "I'm just not very high on atheists" (Sherman).

The outrage over this was minimal. In fact, most Americans are unaware that Mr. Bush, who was elected President the following year, ever said such a thing. In the United States, prejudices and misconceptions regarding atheists are common and accepted. This country has a long history of discrimination against minorities; African-Americans, women, homosexuals and many other social groups are evidence of this. However, while members of these groups are breaking barriers and being shown an increased amount of

Lawrence 2

Since the author is unknown, this source—an online newspaper article—is identified by its title.

tolerance, a recent study conducted by the University of Minnesota indicates that atheists are still widely distrusted and viewed more unfavorably than any other minority group: "below Muslims, recent immigrants, [and] gays and lesbians." According to the study, "atheists are also the minority group most Americans are least willing to allow their children to marry" ("Atheists Identified").

MLA General Formatting Guidelines

▶ *Italicize the titles of longer works*—books, movies, plays, websites, magazines, newspapers, and journals. *Put the titles of shorter works in quotation marks*—articles, essays, songs, poems, short stories, or the episodes of a TV show (for example, "The Bug" episode from *Breaking Bad*).

▶ *Direct quotations*. Present direct quotations that are up to four lines long using traditional *quotation marks*. Present direct quotations longer than four lines in a *block-centered format*. That means indent one extra inch or ten spaces from the left margin and present the quotation *without quotation marks*.

Toward the end of his speech, Wallace waxes grandiloquent:

> If you worship money and things, if they are where you tap real meaning in life, then you will never have enough, never feel you have enough. It's the truth. Worship your body and beauty and sexual allure and you will always feel ugly. And when time and age start showing, you will die a million deaths before they finally grieve you.

▶ *Parenthetical citations—how to punctuate* (the content of parentheticals is covered in the next section). Enclose parenthetical, in-text citations inside the punctuation mark at the end of sentences in which they appear (in other words, inside the period, question mark, or exclamation point that ends the sentence).

> ...Louise appeared well-adjusted socially and academically (Kuehnle 179).

If the sentence concludes with a quoted passage that ends in a period, insert the parenthetical citation after the closing quotation mark and put the period after the parenthetical.

> ...According to Kuehnle, Louise engaged in "dance lessons, roller skating, and bike riding with her peers in the neighborhood" (179).

If the quoted passage concludes with a question mark or exclamation point, the end punctuation remains inside the quotation mark, but a period is added after the parenthetical.

> ... Parks's retort to the policeman was, "Why do you push us around?" (Halberstam 542).

When presenting a block-centered quotation that requires a parenthetical citation, the parenthetical goes outside the closing punctuation mark.

> He denied that he ever tried to convert anybody into anything, insisting that as a therapist he merely attempted to assist his patients to gain insights into their problems and the strength to deal with them. And he denied ever violating the therapist-patient rule of confidentiality and said he never turned over the "life stories" of his patients...to the FBI. (Navasky 139–140)

▶ *Footnotes*. In MLA style, footnotes are only used for brief explanations or comments that are too tangential to include in your text. Don't use footnotes to cite sources.

Understanding In-Text MLA Citations

All of the source material you present in a research paper or an essay—that is, all of the sources you quote directly, or draw information from—must be identified and cited. Within your paper or essay, MLA style requires that you provide basic, "in-text" source information that does two things: (1) takes the reader to a full citation in a "Works Cited" list at the end of the paper and (2) when applicable, helps the reader find the exact location of the source material—for example, by providing a page number or page range.

The in-text information that takes readers to your Works Cited list usually is an author's name. For a source whose author is not known, sometimes the title is provided, or the name of a government institution or sponsoring organization that produced the source. This basic source information can be woven into a signal phrase in your written text, or if not woven in, presented parenthetically (in parentheses) after a relevant summary, paraphrase, or direct quotation.

In-text information about the location of material within a source—for example, a page number or page range—always goes in parentheses. The example below is an in-text citation for an article by columnist Paul Krugman that appeared in the *New York Times* online:

> As Paul Krugman observes in the *New York Times*, the average American taxpayer suffered the most from the financial crisis, yet ended up bailing out the very banks that caused it.

No parenthetical citation is needed, because Krugman is mentioned in a signal phrase, and typically, online articles do not have stable page numbers that need to be provided. Krugman's name will efficiently take the reader to a full citation presented alphabetically in the research writer's Works Cited list under "K." This citation tells the reader that Krugman's article was published online ("Web") on October 9, 2011, and accessed by the writer of the research paper on June 9, 2015:

> Krugman, Paul. "Panic of the Plutocrats." *New York Times*. The New York Times Company, 9 Oct. 2011. Web. 9 June 2015.

However, if the writer did not mention Krugman in her text, a parenthetical citation would be needed:

> The average American taxpayer suffered the most from the financial crisis, yet ended up bailing out the very banks that caused it (Krugman).

As is often the case with online sources, Krugman's article also appeared in print—the printed New York edition of the *New York Times*. An in-text citation referring to the printed version of the article would need to include the location of the article within the newspaper—that is, the section and page number in parentheses:

> As Paul Krugman observes in the *New York Times*, the average American taxpayer suffered the most from the financial crisis, yet ended up bailing out the very banks that caused it (A23).

Or:

> The average American taxpayer suffered the most from the financial crisis, yet ended up bailing out the very banks that caused it (Krugman A23).

The full citation in the Works Cited list for a print version of the source would be different from the citation for the web version. The print version tells the reader that the article appeared in "print" and also provides the print publication date and the location of the article in the newspaper (Section "A," page 23):

> Krugman, Paul. "Panic of the Plutocrats." *New York Times* 10 Oct. 2011: A23. Print.

Identifying Sources in Your Writing

As the examples above illustrate, when you cite a source in an essay or a paper, you can choose to mention the source in a signal phrase or use a parenthetical citation. Often, the best choice for in-text citation in any essay, whether you are following MLA guidelines or not, is to use a signal phrase to identify the source in your writing ("As Paul Krugman observes..." or "Krugman argues that..." and so on).

As discussed in Chapter 8, using signal phrases to identify sources helps you avoid inadvertent plagiarism and the consequences it can have. If you mention the source in a sentence, you don't have to worry about forgetting to include a parenthetical citation: Your source is cited. In addition, weaving source information into your writing helps make your writing more interesting and professional. Sometimes student writers become so stuck on using parenthetical citations that their writing becomes monotonous. Consider the difference between the two sentences below:

▶ One doctor states that most of his patients prefer pharmaceutical treatments to traditional psychotherapy (Cohen).

▶ Dr. Stanley Cohen, my GP since 2013, told me in a personal interview that most of his patients prefer pharmaceutical treatments to traditional psychotherapy.

The first sentence has the virtue of being shorter, but it offers no information about the doctor, who, for all the reader knows, could be an orthopedic surgeon, an oncologist, or a podiatrist. Nor does the sentence say how the information was received. In addition, the sentence *requires* a parenthetical citation, which, if omitted, would undermine any credibility the information has.

The second sentence, though slightly longer, does not require a parenthetical citation (only a citation for a personal interview in the writer's Works Cited list). In addition, the sentence informs readers about the doctor's specialty (general practitioner), the writer's relationship to him, and how the information was received (though a personal interview).

Of course, whenever you identify sources in your writing, you have to strike a balance between being ideally informative and concise. If your only criterion is being informative and you jam too much information into your text, your writing can become wordy and hard to read, but if your only criterion is being concise, and you rely so much on parenthetical citations that you say nothing about your sources in your text, your writing will tend to be monotonous and uninteresting. Thoughtful writers decide what source information is most important and interesting for readers to know and try to strike the best balance between information and being concise. Below is a passage that summarizes information from an article by journalist Seth Borenstein titled "Private Industry Responding to Hurricanes":

> In 2006, the Red Cross signed a disaster-response partnership with Wal-Mart, which prompted one attendee at the National Hurricane Conference in Orlando, Florida, to express concerns about private enterprise taking over disaster relief for profits (Borenstein).

The passage tells us nothing about who the "attendee" is or the extent of the concerns. In contrast, read the passage below from *The Shock Doctrine*, in which the author, Naomi Klein, presents similar information about the same article:

> In 2006, the Red Cross signed a new disaster-response partnership with Wal-Mart. "It's all going to be private enterprise before it's over," said Billy Wagner, chief of emergency management for the Florida Keys. "They've got the expertise. They've got the resources...."

Although both passages provide the same basic information, Klein's presents a real person with a real name, tells us his qualifications ("chief of emergency management"), and clarifies his concerns by quoting him. Her passage is a few words longer than the summarized example, but more interesting to read.

MLA Parenthetical Citations

In MLA style, even if you weave source information into your writing, you will still need to include parenthetical citations at times—for example, when you provide page numbers for a print source, or when you already have provided information about a source in a previous signal phrase and simply need to cite it again. Table 14.1 lists examples of what some common parenthetical citations look like.

TABLE 14.1 Types of common parenthetical citations and examples

Type of Citation	Example
Author and page number. *No comma is inserted between the name and page number within the parentheses. The citation goes inside the period that ends the sentence.*	The recovery has been much slower than in previous recessions (Kent 19).
Page number or page range (when the author or title already has been named).	All four attended Harvard University (211). He received a lot of "flak" for expressing those views (312–313).
Location information for sources without page numbers (for example, online). *Provide other content identifiers if possible— for example, paragraph or section numbers. (If the author's name is also included, use a comma within this type of parenthetical.)*	What few readers realize is that he was raised in foster homes (Vaughn, par. 17). Vaughn tells us a little known fact: he was raised in foster homes (par. 17).
An organization is the author, or the author is unknown. *Put the name of the organization in the parenthetical, or the title of a work whose author is unknown (use a shortened version of the title if the title is long). Note that the lack of an author is not necessarily a credibility issue. Most newspaper editorials and reference works do not identify the author or authors.*	The agency defines a flood as a "general and temporary condition of partial or complete inundation…" (National Flood Insurance Program 1). Without exactly saying so, the editors suggest that Snowden deserves a pardon ("Traitor or Patriot?").
A combination of two or more sources cited together. *If the information you are citing is drawn from two or more sources, put the sources in the same parentheses separated by a semicolon or semicolons.*	Phone messages on "voicemail" are disappearing from corporate communications but several observers think the alternatives, texting and email, are not adequate replacements (Schrader; Fauvre B4).
A work by two or three authors. *Provide the authors' last names in parentheses and any relevant page number(s), if applicable.*	American F-86 pilots in Korea respected the enemy MiGs, but say the F-86 had better maneuverability (Foss and Brennan xii).
A work by more than three authors. *Provide the last name of the first author, followed by "et al."(Latin for "and others").*	Tison's affidavit contains several inconsistencies (Izzy et al. 3).

(continued)

TABLE 14.1 Types of common parenthetical citations and examples *(continued)*

Type of Citation	Example
Two different sources by the same author. *If you use and refer to more than one source by the same author—for example, an article and a book—include the author's last name and a shortened version of the title of the work in your parenthetical citation.*	New water polices have been on the state's agenda for years, but nothing ever seems to really get done (Urrutia, "Desalination Isn't the Answer"). It is virtually meaningless to talk about "average" rainfall, because the averages encompass extremes from severe droughts to torrential floods (Urrutia, *Not Just California* 211).
A source quoted from within another source. *If you present a quotation that you found in a source that is not the original source, then use the words "qtd. in" ("quoted in") in your parenthetical.*	One prominent dismissal of the word came from former governor of Michigan George Romney, who announced that "Americans buried capitalism long ago, and moved on to consumerism" (qtd. in Gross 93).

Creating an MLA Works Cited List

MLA style requires a formal, alphabetized list of references, called a "Works Cited" list, at the end of researched essays or papers.

Unlike a bibliography, which is a general list of sources a researcher has read, consulted, or reviewed, a Works Cited list literally refers to sources cited in a writer's paper or essay. No other sources should be included in a Works Cited list.

This section will present general guidelines for creating a Works Cited list, along with examples of common entries. As suggested earlier in the chapter, you should always consult an up-to-date handbook or library-recommended website for guidelines and instructions about documenting a formal researched essay or paper. In addition, there are websites and digital tools that can help you create a Works Cited list. Below are a few you might want to try:

- ▶ EasyBib
- ▶ KnightCite
- ▶ Son of Citation Machine
- ▶ Writinghouse.org

Keep in mind that the citations generated by websites or digital tools are not always 100 percent correct or up to date. Often, you will need to do some revising. Nevertheless, these tools can help you draft your citations and put them in correct alphabetical order.

General Guidelines for Formatting an MLA Works Cited List

As you create your list, follow these basic guidelines (see pages 616–617 for an example of a student writer's Works Cited list):

▶ Start your list *on a separate page* after the end of your paper or essay.

▶ *Center* the title of the list—*Works Cited*—without underlining, using italics or quotation marks.

▶ *Align each entry along the left margin* but *indent subsequent lines* (called a "hanging" indent).

▶ Double-space the entire list.

▶ *Alphabetize* the list *by entry*. Many, or most, entries will begin with an *author's or editor's last name*. Some will begin with a *title* (if the author is unknown) or the name of a *sponsoring institution or organization*.

▶ Include the *medium of the source* in your entries—for example, *Print, Web, Radio, Lecture.*

▶ *Exclude URLs* (that is, web addresses) for most online sources. Because URLs often change or can be long and unwieldy, writers no longer need to include them in MLA citations. Most citations for Internet sources now simply include the word *Web* followed by a period, and then the date the source was accessed online, followed by another period. However, if you cite an Internet source that you think may be hard for readers to find, you have the option of including the URL in angle brackets followed by a period at the end of your citation. For example: <https://www.onlineopinion.com.au/view.asp?article=8813>.

Sample Citations in MLA Style

Although the content of citations varies depending on the medium and available information, most citations follow a pattern of basic, sequential information that is separated by periods.

This basic information includes (1) the name of the author, authors, or editor, when available; (2) the title of whatever it is that you are citing, and then (3), depending on the kind of source, selective information about the publisher, database, location, relevant dates, and medium. Reviewing the examples below will help you grasp the content of citations.

Common Sources

A book with one author:

> Hitchens, Christopher. *Hitch-22: A Memoir*. New York: Twelve, 2010.
> Print.

E-book edition of a print book (italicize the e-book format, file, or database, and in lieu of "Print," write "Web" and the access date):

> Gladwell, Malcolm. *Outliers: The Story of Success*. New York: Little,
> Brown and Company, 2008. *Kindle Book*. Web. 20 June 2013.

A book with two or three authors (cite the authors in the order they are listed on the title page, and use last name first for the first author only):

> Albright, Joseph, and Marcia Kunstel. *Bombshell: The Secret Story of
> America's Unknown Atomic Spy Conspiracy*. New York: Times Books,
> 1997. Print.

A book whose author is unknown:

> *Michelin Red Guide 2008 France: Restaurants & Hotels*. Michelin Travel
> Pubns, 2008. Print.

Two or more books listed by the same author (use three hyphens followed by a period instead of the author's name for additional sources by the same author, and list the entries alphabetically by the titles):

> Palahniuk, Chuck. *Choke: A Novel*. New York: Anchor, 2002. Print.
>
> ---. *Stranger Than Fiction: True Stories*. New York: Doubleday, 2005.
> Print.

A book with an editor and an author (list according to the name you cited in your text, and use the abbreviations U and P when referring to a university press, as below):

> Smoller, Sanford J., ed. *The Nightinghouls of Paris*. By Robert McAlmon.
> Urbana: U of Illinois P, 2007. Print.

Or:

> McAlmon, Robert. *The Nightinghouls of Paris*. Ed. Sanford J. Smoller.
> Urbana: U of Illinois P, 2007. Print.

Sacred book (the full title, and because there are many different versions, publication information):

> *Holy Bible: New International Version*. Grand Rapids: Zondervan, 2011.
> Print.

Article in a reference book (include author, if noted, and/or the title of the article, the name of the book, and publication information if the book is not well known):

"Gold Rush Country." *Historic Places.* Pleasantville: Reader's Digest Association, 1993. Print.

Article in a well-known reference book (online version):

"Daedalus." *Encyclopedia Britannica Online.* Encyclopedia Britannica. 2015. Web. 12 June 2015. <http://www.britannica.com/topic/ Daedalus-Greek-mythology>.

A chapter in an edited book or anthology (begin with the author and title of the chapter, and then continue with the title of the book, the names of the editors, publication information, and the page numbers of the chapter):

Goudsmit, Samuel. "The Gestapo in Science." *Great Essays in Science.* Ed. Martin Gardner. New York: Washington Square Press, 1970. 341–357. Print.

A preface, introduction, foreword, or afterword (begins with the author and the section you are citing, and then continues with the title of the book, the author referenced with "By" and first name first, followed by publication information and the page numbers of the section cited):

Gitlin, Todd. Introduction. *The Pursuit of Loneliness.* By Philip Slater. Boston: Beacon Press, 1990. x–xviii. Print.

Magazine article in print:

Brown, Joe. "Save Them All, Don't Delete: Never Trash a Photo." *Wired* May 2015: 72. Print.

Magazine article accessed online:

Ratliff, Evan. "The Mark." *The New Yorker.* Condé Nast, 2 May 2011. Web. 11 June 2015.

Journal article in print (the numbers after the journal's title refer to the volume and issue, the year of publication, and the page numbers):

Newark, Patricia, and Rolf-Dieter Stieglitz. "Therapy-Relevant Factors in Adult ADHD from a Cognitive Behavioral Perspective." *ADHD Attention Deficit and Hyperactivity Disorders.* 2.2 (2010): 59–72. Print.

Journal article from a website (note that a work with four or more authors like the one below can be listed by the first author's last name followed by a comma and *et al.* ("and others"):

Compton, William M., Bridget F. Grant, James D. Colliver, Meyer D. Glantz, and Frederick S. Stinson. "Prevalence of Marijuana Use Disorders in the United States 1991–1992 and 2001–2002." *Journal of the American Medical Association.* 291.17 (2004): 2114–2121. Web. 19 Mar. 2011.

Newspaper article (print):

Turkel, Bruce. "Growing Your Business: Here's How to Make Big Money from a Little Blog." *Miami Herald.* 8 June 2015. G7. Print.

Newspaper article (online):

Plaschke, Bill. "Frustrated Dodgers' Organist Signals Last Notes, Until Team's Overture." *Los Angeles Times.* Los Angeles Times. 11 June 2015. Web. 12 June 2015.

Letter to the editor in a newspaper or magazine:

Rose, B. "Gangster Wrap." Letter. *Vanity Fair.* June 2012. 74. Print.

A review in a newspaper or magazine (start with the author and the title of the review, if provided):

Schama, Chloe. Rev. of *The End of Men and the Rise of Women*, by Hanna Rosin. *Smithsonian* Oct. 2012. 80. Print.

Common Media and Field Sources

Entire website:

FactCheck.org. Annenberg Public Policy Center, 10 June 2015. Web. 12 June 2015.

Entire personal website (use "N.p." for no sponsor):

Saulter, Carla. *Bus Chick.* N.p. 3 May 2015. Web. 12 June 2015.

Personal interview (the name of the person interviewed, followed by the method, and the date:

Bach, Janet. Personal interview. 2 May 2015.

Or:

Fernandez, Natalie. Telephone interview. 5 June 2015.

Lecture or speech live:

Claus, Kenneth. "Last Lecture." What Would You Say? Lecture Series. Florida International University, Graham Center, Miami. 26 Jan. 2011. Lecture.

Lecture or speech online:

Claus, Kenneth. "Last Lecture." What Would You Say? Lecture Series. *YouTube*. YouTube. 11 Feb. 2011. Web. 12 June 2015.

A blog post:

Clarke, Erin. "A {big} Bite of the Big Apple: What to See and Eat in New York." *Well Plated by Erin: Recipes for a Wholesome Life*. N.p., 3 June 2015. Web. 12 June 2015.

A discussion board post:

Nina46. "Worried My Dad May Have Alzheimer's." *Health Boards*. Oct. 2014. Web. 2 May 2015.

Online video ("N.d." means "no date" of posting is provided):

McMillian, Don. "A PowerPoint Proposal." *Vimeo*. Vimeo. N.d. Web. 5 June 2015.

Movie or documentary (theater version, "Dir." refers to director):

The Fog of War. Dir. Errol Morris. Sony Pictures Classics, 2004. Film.

Movie or documentary (DVD version, "Perf." refers to performer):

Citizenfour. Dir. Laura Poitras. Perf. Edward Snowden. Praxis Films, 2015. DVD.

Television program:

"Iraq's Christians." *60 Minutes*. CBS. 22 Mar. 2015. Television.

Radio program:

"Cops See It Differently, Part One." *This American Life*. Host Ira Glass. Chicago Public Media. WLRN, Miami, 6 Feb. 2015. Radio.

Podcast:

"Predicting Terrorism." *SpyCast*. Host Peter Earnest. International Spy Museum, 1 June 2008. Web. 24 Apr. 2015.

Below is the Works Cited list for Brian Lawrence's researched essay "The Truth about Atheists." As mentioned earlier, the list starts on a separate page at the end of the essay. The entire list is alphabetized and double-spaced.

The first line of an entry is flush against the left margin. Subsequent lines of an entry are indented 0.5 inch (called a "hanging indent").

The Works Cited list starts on a separate page. The heading is centered. The list is double-spaced throughout.

Works Cited

Angier, Natalie. "Confessions of a Lonely Atheist." *The New York Times Magazine.* New York Times, 14 Jan. 2001. Web. 27 Oct. 2013.

"Atheism." *Miriam-Webster Online.* Web. 12 Nov. 2009.

"Atheists Identified as America's Most Distrusted Minority, According to New U of M Study." *University of Minnesota News.* Free Republic, 22 Mar. 2006. Web. 15 Oct. 2013. <http://www.freerepublic.com/focus/news/1601278/posts>.

Brooks, Rosa. "The Dark Side of Faith." *Los Angeles Times.* Los Angeles Times, 1 Oct. 2005. Web. 5 Nov. 2013.

Bulger, Matthew. "Unelectable Atheists: U.S. States That Prohibit Godless Americans from Holding Public Office." *American Humanist.* American Humanist Association. 25 May 2012. Web. 30 Nov. 2013.

"Dole Still Keeping the Faith." *Politico.* Politico, 29 Oct. 2008. Web. 5 Nov. 2013.

Edgell, Penny, Joseph Gerteis, and Douglas Hartmann. "Atheists as 'Other': Moral Boundaries and Cultural Membership in American Society." *American Sociological Review* 71.2 (2006): 211–34. Print.

Frantz, Karen. "Cry If You Want To: Cases of Mistaken Atheism Still Offensive." *American Humanist.* American Humanist Association, 17 Dec. 2008. Web. 19 Nov. 2013.

Freedman, Samuel G. "For Atheists, Politics Proves to Be a Lonely Endeavor." *New York Times.* 18 Oct. 2008, A21. Print.

Global Peace Index. "*Vision of Humanity.*" Institute for Economics & Peace, 2009. Web. 20 Nov. 2013.

"Growth of the Nonreligious." *Pew Research Center, Religion & Public Life Project.* Pew Research Center, 2 July 2013. Web. 29 Nov. 2013. <http://www.pewresearch.org>.

URLs for Internet sources are not required, but the author provides this one (and several others) because he thinks the source might be hard to find.

Online article with no author is listed alphabetically by the title.

Scholarly journal accessed in print. The citation includes the volume, issue, year of publication, and the page numbers.

Newspaper article accessed in print includes a section and page number.

Krattenmaker, Tom. "Atheism, a Positive Pillar." Editorial. *USA Today* 17
    Nov. 2008, final ed.: A15. Print.

Kucera, Patrick. "A Cadet's Oath." *The Humanist. Free Online Library.*
    Farlex, 1 Sept. 2007. Web. 7 Nov. 2013.

Marinucci, Carla. "Stark's Atheist Views Break Political Taboo."
    SFGate. San Francisco Chronicle, 14 Mar. 2007. Web. 7 Nov. 2013.

McGroarty, Cynthia J. "What a Boy Scout Should Be." *Philadelphia
    Inquirer.* 16 Apr. 2006, late ed.: L3. Print.

Newport, Frank. "State of the States: Importance of Religion." *Gallup.*
    Gallup, 28 Jan. 2009. Web. 29 Nov. 2013.

Schrader, Jordan. "Critics of Cecil Bothwell Cite N.C. Bar to Atheists."
    Asheville Citizen-Times. Gannett, 7 Dec. 2009. Web. 31 Jan. 2015.

"Seneca." *New World Encyclopedia.* New World Encyclopedia, 29 Aug.
    2008. Web. 10 June 2015.

Sherman, Rob. "Documents at Bush Presidential Library Prove VP Bush
    Questioned Citizenship and Patriotism of Atheists." *Rob Sherman
    Advocacy.* N.p., 1 Apr. 2006. Web. 20 Oct. 2009.

Sullivan, Andrew. "Romney's Bigotry." *Daily Dish* Editorial. *The
    Atlantic.* Atlantic Monthly Group, 17 Feb. 2007. Web. 13 Mar. 2015.

United States. FBI. "Crime in the United States 2003, Table 5, by State,
    2003." Federal Bureau of Investigation, 5 Mar. 2003. Web. 21 Nov.
    2013. <http://www.fbi.gov/about-us/cjis/ucr/crime-in-the-u.s/2003>.

Zuckerman, Phil. "Is Faith Good for Us?" *On Line Opinion.* The National
    Forum, 22 Apr. 2009. Web. 6 Nov. 2013.

Citation for the epigraph at the beginning of the essay.

Citation for government source with no author begins with the name of the government, followed by the name of the agency or organization. The web link provided takes readers to a portal where statistics referenced in the essay can be accessed.

Tips for Formatting the MLA Works Cited List

Manually formatting a Works Cited list can be difficult. Citation tools mentioned earlier in the chapter—EasyBib, Writinghouse.org—can help you organize and format your list. You also can use word processing resources to help you create hanging indents and alphabetize the entries in your list.

If you have created all your individual citations properly but the list is not correctly formatted, do the following (in Microsoft Word):

1. Highlight all the entries in the list.
2. Click "Format" on your menu bar.
3. Click "Paragraph" on the drop-down menu.
4. Set "Line Spacing" to double-spaced, if your list is not already double-spaced.
5. Set "Special" to "hanging."
6. Set "By" to 0.5 (if it is a different figure).
7. Select "OK."

Your list will now be double-spaced with hanging indents.

To sort the entries alphabetically, do the following (in Microsoft Word):

1. Highlight all the entries in the list.
2. Click "Table" on your menu bar.
3. Click "Sort" on the drop-down menu.
4. Set the sort options in the first row to "Paragraphs," "Text," and "Ascending."
5. Select "OK."

Your list will now be in alphabetical order, *provided that* all of your entries start with authors' last names or other words. However, if you have any entries that begin with a quotation mark (for a title) or other symbol, they will be at the beginning of the list, and you will need to move them to the right place manually.

A BRIEF INTRODUCTION TO APA STYLE

The American Psychological Association style system, APA, is widely used in the social sciences and also sometimes used in the applied sciences (nursing) and professions (business). This final section of the chapter will review some general features of APA Style. For detailed information, the best resource is the *Publication Manual of the American Psychological Association*. Most writing handbooks also cover details of APA Style, as do some online resources like the Purdue OWL.

The basic approach to documentation in APA Style is similar to MLA: briefly and accurately identify sources in your text, and then provide the complete source information in an alphabetized list of citations at the end of your paper. However, APA has different guidelines for organizing papers, as well as for presenting source material and creating citations.

APA *Title Page* Formatting Guidelines

▶ APA Style requires a *title page* (see Figure 14.6).

▶ *Page numbers*, starting on the title page, appear in the upper right-hand corner and are included throughout the document.

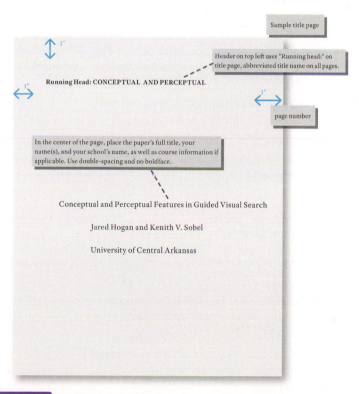

Sample title page

Header on top left uses "Running head:" on title page, abbreviated title name on all pages.

Running Head: CONCEPTUAL AND PERCEPTUAL

page number

In the center of the page, place the paper's full title, your name(s), and your school's name, as well as course information if applicable. Use double-spacing and no boldface.

Conceptual and Perceptual Features in Guided Visual Search

Jared Hogan and Kenith V. Sobel

University of Central Arkansas

FIGURE 14.6 Title Page in APA Style

- A header aligned to the top left margin opposite the page number on the title page includes the *title of the paper in full caps*. (Use an abbreviated title if the title is long.) The full-cap title on the title page is introduced by the words "Running head" and followed by a colon. (On subsequent pages, the full-cap title in the header appears without those introductory words.)

- In the middle of the title page, the paper's full title is centered in conventional title case, along with the writer's name and school (and/or any other information requested by your instructor).

APA *Abstract Page* Guidelines

- APA papers often include an "abstract" on the second page (see Figure 14.7). An abstract is a brief summary or overview of the paper (approximately 150 words).

- The abstract page, like all subsequent pages of the document, includes the page number (2) in the upper right-hand corner, and the paper's title in full caps aligned to the left margin of the header (but without the words "Running head").

- The word "Abstract" is centered at the top of the page. The abstract itself—that is, the brief summary or overview—is written in one block paragraph, double-spaced (without indenting the first word).

- An effective abstract summarizes the central research problem, research questions, methods, and key points presented in the paper.

APA First-Page Guidelines

- The first page of the article or essay includes the full title centered at the top of the page under the header (see Figure 14.8).

- The first word of the first paragraph is indented five spaces (use the tab key).

- The entire document is double-spaced and paragraphed in conventional essay style (first word of every paragraph is indented five spaces).

Abstract: If your instructor requires an abstract (a 150–250 word summary of your paper), place it just after the title page, on a page of its own.

CONCEPTUAL AND PERCEPTUAL   2

Abstract

Visual search experiments have long concluded perceptual features such as color and shape can guide visual search to efficiently locate a target object. Krueger (1984) argued manipulating conceptual features (i.e., "6" is a number and "G" is a letter) entails manipulating perceptual features ("6" and "G" have different shapes) so there is no way to disentangle the influence of conceptual and perceptual features on visual search. Nevertheless, Lupyan (2008) carefully controlled for shape while manipulating letter categories, and showed conceptual features such as one letter's identity can be used to guide search. We expanded on this by looking at numbers. Our results were largely consistent with Lupyan's, but also revealed a surprise: participants were faster to find targets based on numerical magnitude than numerical parity (even vs. odd). This could be due to the way numbers were arranged on the number line or to the fact judgments of numerical magnitude were more familiar than judgments of numerical parity. Future experiments are described to explore the role of the mental number line and familiarity in visual search for conceptual features.

FIGURE 14.7 Abstract in APA Style

APA In-Text Citations

All of the sources of information in the paper have to be identified and cited, using signal phrases and/or parenthetical citations that correspond to full citations in a reference list at the end (see Figure 14.9).

CONCEPTUAL AND PERCEPTUAL   3

On the first page of
the paper, center the
full title at the top of
the page, below the
header.

Conceptual and Perceptual Features in Guided Visual Search

Double-space the title
from the paper's text,
but do not use any
additional formatting
or spacing.

Visual search may seem like an abstract idea but is a surprisingly common activity, for example when trying to locate one car from among all the others in a crowded parking lot. For this kind of search, features such as color and shape can typically distinguish a target car from all the others. For example, if the target is a yellow sedan, there might be cars with the right color but wrong shape (e.g., yellow coupe) and other cars with the wrong color but right shape (e.g., blue sedan), but hopefully there is just one car with the right combination of color and shape. If the yellow sedan target is parked in a lot owned by a taxi company then it doesn't have a unique combination of color and shape so search must rely on the alphanumeric characters on the license plate, which are unique. When searching for a number such as 15 does vision need to use perceptual features such as a straight shape next to a curvy shape, or can conceptual features such as the number's parity (oddness or evenness), or magnitude (bigger than 10 but smaller than 20) be used to guide search?

FIGURE 14.8 First Page in APA Style

APA in-text citations include the last name of an author, a year of publication, and a page number for direct quotations and specific references.

An important feature of APA Style is that the publication year of a work is included in parentheses within a paper when an author's name is mentioned in a signal phrase. When a parenthetical citation is used, the year is included in the parenthetical:

A direct quotation from a work that is introduced with the author's name and the year of publication (in parentheses) also should include a parenthetical citation for a page number (preceded by "p.") at the end of the sentence:

CONCEPTUAL AND PERCEPTUAL 5

(Wolfe, 1994) explain the disparity between conjunction and feature search results by appealing to neurophysiological research showing simple visual features such as color, orientation, and motion are represented in different locations in the visual cortex (De Valois, Yund, & Hepler, 1982). In this context, a feature target pops out from distractors because it can be located by examining the features registered in a single area of visual cortex, whereas conjunction search requires comparisons of features across different regions of visual cortex. If the Guided Search model describes visual search behavior, can other, non-perceptual features guide search as well?

Krueger (1984) carried out visual searches in which the distinction between target and distractor was conceptual, such as a single digit target among letter distractors or a letter target among digit distractors. Krueger argued there was no way to tell if participants used conceptual categories to guide visual search because digits are distinct from letters perceptually as well as conceptually. Wolfe and Horowitz (2004) extended Krueger's argument by noting although the difference between uppercase and lowercase letters

FIGURE 14.9 Authors' Names and Year of Publication in APA In-Text Citations

Kuehnle (1996) cautioned about therapeutic interventions that become "blurred with investigation" (p. 47).

Signal phrases in APA Style, as in the example above, use the *past tense to report conclusions*—in other words, Kuehnle (1996) *cautioned* (not *cautions*). The *present tense is used to report results*.

The titles of any sources named in the text are presented in APA title case (the main words are capitalized). In addition, the titles are either italicized (for longer works like books, websites, newspapers, journals, and movies) or enclosed in quotation marks (for shorter works like essays, articles, and songs). Below is the title of a book italicized in title case:

Young Children and Trauma: Intervention and Treatment

CONCEPTUAL AND PERCEPTUAL   19

References

Center the word "References" and double-space it from the entries that follow. Do not use any additional formatting.

Begin a new page for the References list Maintain the header and continue page numbering from the paper.

De Valois, R. L., Yund, E. W., & Hepler, N. (1982). The orientation and direction selectivity of cells in macaque visual cortex. *Vision Research, 22,* 531–544. doi:10.1016 /0042–6989(82)90112–2

List sources in alphabetical order by the lead author's last name.

D'Zmura, M. (1991). Color in visual search. *Vision Research, 31,* 951–966. doi:10.1016/0042–6989(91)90203–H

Krueger, L. E. (1984). The category effect in visual search depends on physical rather than conceptual differences. *Perception & Psychophysics,* 35, 558–564. doi: 10.3758/ BF03205953

Double-space within and among entries.

Lupyan, G. (2008). The conceptual grouping effect: Categories matter (and named categories matter more). *Cognition, 108,* 566–577. doi:10.1016/j.cognition.2008.03.009

Indent all lines but the first by 0.5 inch.

Pinhas, M., Pothos, E. M., & Tzelgov, J. (2013). Zooming in and out from the mental number line: Evidence for a number range effect *Journal of Experimental Psychology: Learning, Memory, & Cognition, 39,* 972–976. doi:10.1037/a0029527

FIGURE 14.10 Formatting Guidelines for "References" in APA Style

However, in APA style, titles named in the References list at the end of the paper are presented in lowercase, except for the first letter of the first word, the first word after a colon, and any proper nouns or proper adjectives (Freud, Freudian):

Young children and trauma: Intervention and treatment

EVALUATE YOUR LEARNING

1. In just a few sentences, how would you explain the basic concepts and procedures of documentation to a fellow student?

2. If you were advising a fellow student about a research project, what would you say about the benefits, as well as the drawbacks, of using primary sources?

3. Why is identifying sources in signal phrases often a better idea than relying on parenthetical citations?

4. Based on the information provided in this chapter, what are some widely available resources that can help writers document sources correctly and create a professionally formatted reference or Works Cited list?

CREDITS

Chapter 1: pages 34–36, "Unconditional Love" by Tupac; pages 36–39, "Fifth Grade Was a Little Better," from *Ham on Rye* by Charles Bukowski, 80–84.

Chapter 2: page 62, Quentin Deakin, "Virtual Living—the Impact of Electronic Technology," *Contemporary Review* 292.1698 (2010): 348+. Global Issues in Context. Web. 1 Oct. 2015. Contemporary Review Company Ltd.; pages 68–69, From "The War on Drugs: Opposing Viewpoints," by Stephen P. Thompson, Greenhaven Press, 1998; pages 71–74, *Putting Humans First: Why We Are Nature's Favorite* by Machan. Reproduced with permission of Rowman & Littlefield in the format Republish in a book via Copyright Clearance Center.

Chapter 3: pages 100–104, "Simplicity" from *On Writing Well*, Seventh (30th Anniversary) Edition by William K. Zinsser. Copyright © 1976, 1980, 1985, 1988, 1990, 1994, 1998, 2001, 2006 by William K. Zinsser. Reprinted by permission of the author; pages 104–109, "The Maker's Eye: Revising Your Own Manuscripts." *The Writer*, 1973. Copyright © 1973 by Donald M. Murray. Reprinted by permission of The Rosenberg Group on behalf of author's estate; pages 109–112, "Black Men in Public Spaces" by Brent Staples. *Harper's Magazine*, Dec. 1986; pages 112–116, "My Life as a Dog" from *Stranger Than Fiction: True Stories* by Chuck Palahniuk, copyright © 2004 by Chuck Palahniuk. Used by permission of Doubleday, an imprint of the Knopf Doubleday Publishing Group, a division of Penguin Random House LLC. All rights reserved.

Chapter 5: pages 171–172, "Old Dameron" from "Second World War" in *One Man's Meat* © 1942 by E. B. White and Tilbury House Publishers. Used by permission. All rights reserved; pages 192–193, Christopher Goffard, "Former Black Panther Patches Together Purpose in Africa Exile." Reprinted with permission from *Los Angeles Times;* pages 203–209, Reprinted with permission from Steven Fernandez; MindTap edition, "Under the Influence" by Scott Russell Sanders, pp. 68–75. Copyright © 1989 *Harper's Magazine*. All rights reserved. Reproduced from the November issue by special permission.

Chapter 6: MindTap edition, Gerard Jones, "Violent Media Is Good for Kids." *Mother Jones*. Foundation for National Progress, 28 June 2000. Web. 17 Apr. 2015; "Generation Why?" by Zadie Smith. Copyright © Zadie Smith 2010. First published in the *New York Review of Books*, 2010. Reproduced by permission of the author c/o Rogers, Coleridge & White Ltd., 20 Powis Mews, London W11 1JN.

Chapter 7: pages 258–259, From *The Miami Herald*, September 27, © 2013 McClatchy. All rights reserved. Used by permission and protected by the Copyright Laws of the United States; page 304, *New York Magazine*, Oct. 20, 2003.

Chapter 8: pages 352–354, From *The New York Times*, May 14 © 2011. *The New York Times*. All rights reserved. Used by permission and protected by the Copyright Laws of the United States; MindTap edition, Elizabeth Carls, "A World of Possibilities: An Examination of the Human Impact on the Earth as Portrayed in Environmentalist Rhetoric." Young Scholars in Writing. University of Missouri-Kansas City, Fall 2012. Web. 06 Mar. 2015. Reprinted with permission from Elizabeth Carls.

Chapter 9*:* page 380: From the album, *All Out War,* by Earth Crisis, Victory Records; MindTap edition, Instagram opinion piece in *Wired*. Reprinted with permission from Conde Nast Publications, Inc.; *The Gazette* (Montreal), "Life after Rape: A Victim's Tale," September 2, 2006.

Chapter 10: pages 453–457; "Araby" by James Joyce, from *Dubliners;* MindTap edition, "Row 22, Seats A & B" by Frederick Waterman, p. 99. Canfield & Mackenzie Publishers, 2002; "The Summer of Vintage Clothing" from *Plan B for the Middle Class* by Ron Carlson. Copyright © 1992 by Ron Carlson. Used by permission of Brandt & Hochman Literary Agents & W.W. Norton & company, Inc. All rights reserved.

Chapter 12: MindTap edition, Rachel Toor, "What Writing and Running Have in Common."

Chapter 13: pages 579–580, *The Dallas Morning News*, 16 February 2013, http://www.dallasnews.com/business/headlines/20130216-goodbye-paper-hello-social-resume.ece. Reprinted with permission from *The Dallas Morning News*.

Chapter 15 (MindTap edition only): Defying "Fragilitis" by Kenneth Claus. © Kenneth Claus.

INDEX